THE STORY OF THE NEGRO

BOOKER T. WASHINGTON

The Story of the Negro

The Rise of the Race from Slavery

BOOKER T. WASHINGTON

VOLUMES I AND II

PENN

University of Pennsylvania Press
Philadelphia

Originally published 1909 by Doubleday, Page & Company
Printed in the United States of America on acid-free paper

10 9 8 7 6 5 4 3 2 1

Paperback edition first published 2005 by
University of Pennsylvania Press
Philadelphia, Pennsylvania 19104-4112

ISBN-10: 0-8122-1936-8
ISBN-13: 978-0-8122-1936-4

A U.S. Library of Congress Cataloging-in-Publication record
is available from the Library of Congress

PREFACE

IN WRITING this volume it has been my object to show what the Negro himself has accomplished in constructive directions. I have not undertaken to discuss the many problems which have arisen through the contact of the Negro with other races, but to tell a simple, straight story of what the Negro himself has accomplished in the way of attaining to a higher civilisation.

It ought to be explained, too, that I have not undertaken to write any formal or detailed history of the entire Negro race. In many cases names of worthy and successful individuals have been omitted for want of space. In other cases I have used names merely as illustrations of what the race has been able to accomplish.

I want to make grateful mention, also, of the service which Dr. Robert E. Park has rendered in the preparation of this volume. Without his constant and painstaking assistance I could not have accomplished the object which I have had in view. I am deeply grateful, also, to Mr. Monroe N. Work for valuable assistance.

If the reading of these chapters shall in any degree inspire any Negro to make himself useful and successful in the world, and if in any degree what I have written will cause any individuals, not members of my own race, to take a more generous and hopeful view of the condition and prospects of the Negro, I shall feel that I have accomplished what I started out to do in the writing of these pages.

BOOKER T. WASHINGTON.

Tuskegee Institute, Alabama.

CONTENTS—Volume I

PART I

THE NEGRO IN AFRICA

Chapter		Page
I.	First Notions of Africa	3
II.	The American Negro and the Native African	18
III.	The African at Home	36
IV.	The West Coast Background of the American Negro	57

PART II

THE NEGRO AS A SLAVE

		Page
V.	The First and Last Slave Ship	85
VI.	The First Slaves	107
VII.	The Indian and the Negro	125
VIII.	The Negro's Life in Slavery	144
IX.	Slave Insurrections and the Negro "Peril"	171
X.	The Free Negro in Slavery Days	192
XI.	Fugitive Slaves	215
XII.	Negro Settlements in Ohio and the Northwest Territory	233
XIII.	The Negro Preacher and the Negro Church	251
XIV.	The Negro Abolitionists	279
XV.	The Negro Soldier's Fight for Freedom	310

CONTENTS — Volume II

PART III

THE NEGRO AS A FREEMAN

Chapter		Page
I.	The Early Days of Freedom	3
II.	The Rise of the Negro Land-owner	30
III.	The Negro Labourer and the Mechanic in Slavery and Freedom	57
IV.	Negro Crime and Racial Self-help	85
V.	The Negro Teacher and the Negro School	114
VI.	The Negro Secret Societies	148
VII.	The Negro Doctor and the Negro Professional Man	171
VIII.	The Negro Disfranchisement and the Negro in Business	190
IX.	The Negro Bank and the Moral Uplift	211
X.	Negro Communities and Negro Homes	234
XI.	Negro Poetry, Music and Art	259
XII.	Negro Women and Their Work	297
XIII.	The Social and Mission Work of the Negro Church	332
XIV.	Law and Order and the Negro	356
XV.	The Negro's Place in American Life	383
	Index	403

THE STORY OF THE NEGRO

VOLUME I

PART I

THE NEGRO IN AFRICA

The Story of the Negro

CHAPTER I

FIRST NOTIONS OF AFRICA

SOME years ago, in a book called "Up From Slavery," I tried to tell the story of my own life. While I was at work upon that book the thought frequently occurred to me that nearly all that I was writing about myself might just as well have been written of hundreds of others, who began their life, as I did mine, in slavery. The difficulties I had experienced and the opportunities I had discovered, all that I had learned, felt and done, others likewise had experienced and others had done. In short, it seemed to me, that what I had put into the book, "Up From Slavery," was, in a very definite way, an epitome of the history of my race, at least in the early stages of its awakening and in the evolution through which it is now passing.

This thought suggested another, and I asked myself why it would not be possible to sketch the history of the Negro people in America in much the same way that I had tried to write the story of my own life, telling mostly the things that I knew of my own personal knowledge or through my acquaintance with persons and events, and adding to that what I have been able to learn from tradition and from books. In a certain way the second book, if I were able to carry out my design, might be regarded as the sequel of the first, telling the story of a struggle through two and one-half centuries of slavery, and during a period of something more than forty years of freedom, which had elsewhere been condensed into the limits of a single lifetime. This is, then, the task which I have set myself in the pages which follow.

There comes a time, I imagine, in the life of every boy and every girl, no matter to what race they belong, when they feel a desire to learn something about their ancestors; to know where and how they lived, what they suffered and what they achieved, how they dressed, what religion they professed and what position they occupied in the larger world about them. The girl who grows up in the slums of a large city, the Indian out in the wide prairie, the "poor white" boy in the mountains of the Southern states, and the ignorant Negro boy on a Southern plantation, no matter how obscure their origin, each will feel a special interest in the people whose fortunes he or she has shared, and a special sympathy with all that people have lived, and suffered and achieved.

The desire to know something of the country from which my race sprang and of the history of my mother and her people came to me when I was still a child. I can remember, as a slave, hearing snatches of conversation from the people at the "Big House" from which I learned that the great white race in America had come from a distant country, from which the white people and their forefathers had travelled in ships across a great water, called the ocean. As I grew older I used to hear them talk with pride about the history of their people, of the discovery of America, and of the struggles and heroism of the early days when they, or their ancestors, were fighting the Indians and settling up the country. All this helped to increase, as time went on, my desire to know what was back of me, where I came from, and what, if anything, there was in the life of my people in Africa and America to which I might point with pride and think about with satisfaction.

My curiosity in regard to the origin and history of the dark-skinned people to which I belong, led me at first to listen and observe and then, later, as I got some schooling and a wider knowledge of the world, to inquire and read. What I learned in this way only served, however, to increase my desire to go farther and deeper into the life of my people, and to find out for myself what they had been in Africa as well as in America.

What I was first able to hear and to learn did not,

I confess, take me very far or give me very much satisfaction. In the part of the country in which I lived there were very few of my people who pretended to know very much about Africa. I learned, however, that my mother's people had come, like the white people, from across the water, but from a more distant and more mysterious land, where people lived a different life from ours, had different customs and spoke a different language from that I had learned to speak. Of the long and terrible journey by which my ancestors came from their native home in Africa to take up their life again beside the white man and Indian in the New World, I used to hear many and sinister references, but not until I was a man did I meet any one, among my people who knew anything definite, either through personal knowledge or through tradition, of the country or the people from whom my people sprang. To most of the slaves the "middle passage," as the journey from the shore of Africa to the shore of America was called, was merely a tradition of a confused and bewildering experience, concerning whose horrors they had never heard any definite details. Nothing but the vaguest notions remained, at the time I was a boy, even among the older people in regard to the mother country of my race.

In slavery days the traditions of the people who lived in the cabins centred almost entirely about the lives and fortunes of the people who lived in the

"Big House." The favourite stories around the cabin fireside related to what this or that one had seen on some distant journey with "old master," or perhaps to the adventures they had when master and they were boys together.

It has often occurred to me that people who talk of removing the Negro from the Southern states and colonising him in some distant part of the world do not reflect how deeply he is rooted in the soil. In most that the white man has done on this continent, from the time Columbus landed at San Salvador until Peary penetrated farthest North, the Negro has been his constant companion and helper. Any one who considers what the Negro has done, for example, in the Southern states alone, in cutting down the forests, clearing the land, tilling the soil and building up the farms and the cities, will recognise that, directly and indirectly, his labour has been an enormous contribution to the civilisation of the Western world. Any one, on the other hand, who will listen to the songs that we sing, and the anecdotes that are told by the Negro and concerning him; any one who will read the literature and the history of the Southern states, will see that the Negro has contributed, not merely his labour, but something also of his inner life and temperament to the character and quality of the South.

Until freedom came the life of the Negro was so intimately interwoven with that of the white man that it is almost true to say that he had no separate history. To the slave on the plantation the "Big House," where the master lived, was the centre of the only world he knew. It was after freedom came that the masses of the Negro people began to think of themselves as having a past or a future in any way separate and distinct from the white race. There were always some among them, like Frederick Douglass, who were different in this respect from the masses. They became the fugitive slaves.

After I began to go to school I had my first opportunity to learn from books something further and more definite about my race in Africa. I cannot say that I received very much encouragement or inspiration from what I learned in this way while I was in school. The books I read told me of a people who roamed naked through the forest like wild beasts, of a people without houses or laws, without chastity or morality, with no family life and fixed habits of industry.

It seems to me now, as I recall my first definite impressions of my race in Africa, that the books I read when I was a boy always put the pictures of Africa and African life in an unnecessarily cruel contrast with the pictures of the civilised and highly cultured Europeans and Americans. One picture I recall vividly was in the first geography I studied. It was the picture of George Washington placed side by side with a naked African, having a ring in his nose and a dagger in his hand. Here, as elsewhere, in order to put the lofty position to which the white race has attained in sharper contrast with the lowly condition of a more primitive people, the best among the white people was contrasted with the worst among the black.

Naturally all this made a deep and painful impression upon me. At this time I had the feeling, which most of us are likely to have when we are young and inexperienced, that there must be something wrong with any person who was in any way, whether in dress or manners, markedly different from the persons and things to which I was accustomed. It seemed to me at that time a mark of degradation that people should go about with almost no clothes upon their backs. It did not occur to me that, possibly, the difference in the customs of wearing clothes in Africa and in America, and the difference in the feeling that people in Europe and in Africa have about clothes, was largely a matter of climate. It seemed to me that a human creature who would willingly go about with a ring in his nose must be a very fierce and terrible sort of human animal, but it never occurred to me to have any such feelings in regard to the persons whom I had seen wearing ornaments in their ears. In spite of all this, I still held fast to the notion that a race which could produce as good and gentle and loving a woman as my mother must have some good in it that the geographers had failed to discover.

It is hard for one who is a member of another race and who has not had a like experience to appreciate the impression that has often been made upon me, and upon other members of my race as they have listened, as inexperienced boys and girls, to public speeches in which the whole Negro race was denounced in a reckless and wholesale manner, or as they have read newspapers and books in which the Negro race has been described as the lowest and most hopeless of God's creation. Sometimes, when I was a young man, I was driven almost to despair by the hard and bitter, and frequently, as it seemed to me, unjust statements about my race. It was difficult for me to reconcile the ruthless denunciations which men, with whom I was acquainted, would make in their public speeches, with the uniform courtesy and kindness which they had shown to me and others of my race in all their private relations. Even now it is difficult for me to understand why so many Southern white men will allow themselves, for the purpose of enforcing an argument or in the heat of a political discussion, to go so far in the denunciation of the Negro as to do injustice to their own better natures and to their actual feelings toward coloured people whom they meet, perhaps, in business, or toward the servants employed in their own household, the woman who cooks their food, looks after

their house and cares for their children. I mention
these facts because they serve to illustrate the singular relations of interdependence and opposition in
which the white and black people of the South stand
to each other to-day, all of which has had and is having a very definite influence upon the development of
my people in the South.

The hard and discouraging statements which I
was compelled to hear in regard to my race when I
was a boy, had, at different times, two very different
effects upon me. At first they sometimes made me
feel as if I wanted to go away to some distant part of
the earth and bury myself where I might be a stranger
to all my people, or at least where the thing that we
call race prejudice did not exist in the way it does in
the Southern states. Sometimes I thought of doing
something desperate which would compel the world,
in some way or other, to recognise what seemed to
me the wrongs of my race. But afterward, and on
second thought, the effect was to drive me closer to
my own people, to make me sympathise with them
more intimately and more deeply, to feel toward
them as I did toward my own dear mother who had
brought me into the world when she and they were
slaves.

In the end there grew up within me, as a result of
both these feelings, a determination to spend my life
in helping and strengthening the people of my race,
in order to prove to the world that whatever had

been its feelings for them in the past it should learn to respect them in the future, both for what they were and what they should be able to do. I made up my mind, also, that in the end the world must come to respect the Negro for just those virtues for which some people say he is despised, namely because of his patience, his kindliness, and his lack of resentment toward those who do him wrong and injustice.

The feelings that divided my mind and confused my purposes when I was a young man, have also divided the members of my race. The continual adverse criticism has led some of us to disavow our racial identity, to seek rest and try our successes as members of another race than that to which we were born. It has led others of us to seek to get away as far as possible from association with our own race, and to keep as far away from Africa, from its history and from its traditions as it was possible for us to do.

My attention was first called to this disposition of members of certain section of my race to get away from themselves, so to speak; to be ashamed, in other words, of their history and traditions, when I found them bashful or lukewarm in regard to singing the old songs which are the peculiar and unique product of Negro life and civilisation in this country. I have heard musical critics, whose judgment the world respects, say that the old plantation hymns and songs were among the most original contributions that

America has made, not only to music but to any one of the so-called fine arts, and this not merely for their intrinsic charm and beauty but for their qualities, which make it possible for the trained musician to develop out of them more elaborate and refined musical forms, such as have been given to them recently by the Negro composer, Coleridge-Taylor. For myself, though it has been my privilege to hear some of the best music both in Europe and America, I would rather hear the jubilee or plantation songs of my race than the finest chorus from the works of Handel or any other of the great composers that I have heard. Besides, this music is the form in which the sorrows and aspirations of the Negro people, all that they suffered, loved, and hoped for, in short their whole spiritual life, found its first adequate and satisfying expression. For that reason, if for no other, it should be preserved.

What I have said here of my own feelings in regard to my race is representative of the feelings of thousands of others of the black people of this country. Adverse criticism has driven them to think deeper than they otherwise would about the problems which confront them as a race, to cling closer than they otherwise would have done to their own people, to value more highly than they once did, the songs and the records of their past life in slavery. The effect has been to give them, in short, that sort of race pride and race consciousness which, it seems to me, they need to bring out and develop the best that is in them.

So it was that, thinking and studying about the origin and the destiny of my people, and of all of the forces that were working for and against them in my own country and elsewhere, the desire to know more about the history of my own people steadily increased and I tried, as well as I was able, to understand the Negro thoroughly, intimately, in those qualities in which, as a race, he is weak, as well as in those qualities in which he is strong.

This habit of observation and study of my own race, in the way I have described, led me to inquire into the personal histories of the men and women of my own race whom I have met in all parts of the United States. I sought to make myself acquainted with their difficulties and their successes, to understand their feelings and their habits of thought, to discover the inner drift and deeper currents of their lives; for any one who knows to any extent the character of the Negro people, knows that they have, just as other people, an outside and inside, and one cannot always tell what is going on deep down in their hearts merely from looking in their faces. Sometimes the Negro laughs when he is angry and cries when he is happy. Very often, has it seemed to me, the Negro himself does not know or fully understand what is going on in the depth of his own mind and heart.

Perhaps it will not be out of place for me to say here, at the beginning of this book, that the more I have studied the masses of the race to which I belong, the more I have learned not only to sympathise but to respect them. I am proud and happy to be identified with their struggle for a higher and better life.

Now and then I have read or heard it said that, in consequence of the inconveniences, the hardships and the injustices that members of my race frequently suffer, because of the colour of their skins, there was something exceptional and tragic about the situation of the Negro in America, "the tragedy of colour," as one writer has called it. No doubt there is much that is exceptional in the situation of the Negro, not only in America, but in Africa. No one is more willing than I to admit this to be true. But hardships and even injustice, when they concern the relations of people who are divided by creed, by class, or by race, are not exceptional. On the contrary, they are common, and every race that has struggled up from a lower to a higher civilisation has had to face these things. They have been part of its education. Neither is there, as far as my experience goes, anything peculiarly tragic connected with the life of the Negro, except in the situation of those members of my race who, for one reason or another, have yielded to the temptation to make a secret of their lowly birth and appear before the world as

something other than they are.   Every coloured
man knows, or has heard, of such cases, and in the
whole history of the Negro race there are few sadder
stories than some of these lives.   I should say it was
only when an individual suffers from his own folly,
rather than the mistakes of others, that he is likely
to become the hero of a tragedy.   This is just as true
of a race.   The Negro race has suffered much
because of conditions for which others were responsible.   As a rule Negroes have had very little chance
thus far, to make mistakes of their own.   We have
not been free long enough.   While the world hears
a great deal about "the tragedy of colour" and
other phrases of the so-called Negro problem, I have
observed that the world hears little, and knows,
perhaps, less about the Negro himself.   This is true
of white people but it is also true of coloured people.

Some time ago, I had the privilege of meeting at
Cambridge, Mass., a group of about twenty-five
young coloured men who were studying at Harvard
University.   I found that most of these young men
had a high standing in the University, were respected
by their professors and, upon inquiring in regard to
the subjects of their studies, I learned that several of
them had taken extended courses in history.   They
seemed to know in detail, the story of Greek and
Roman and English civilisations, and prided themselves upon their knowledge of the languages and
history of the French and German peoples.   They

knew a great deal about the local history of New England and were perfectly familiar with the story of Plymouth Rock and the settlement of Jamestown, and of all that concerned the white man's civilisation both in America and out of America. But I found that through their entire course of training, neither in the public schools, nor in the fitting schools, nor in Harvard, had any of them had an opportunity to study the history of their own race. In regard to the people with which they themselves were most closely identified, they were more ignorant than they were in regard to the history of the Germans, the French, or the English. It occurred to me that this should not be so. The Negro boy and girl should have an opportunity to learn something in school about his own race. The Negro boy should study Negro history just as the Japanese boy studies Japanese history and the German boy studies German history.

Let me add that my knowledge of the Negro has led me to believe that there is much in the story of his struggle, if one were able to tell it as it deserves to be told, that it is likely to be both instructive and helpful, not merely to the black man but also to the white man with whom he is now almost everywhere, in Africa as well as America, so closely associated. In the last analysis I suppose this is the best excuse I can give for undertaking to tell "The Story of the Negro."

CHAPTER II

THE AMERICAN NEGRO AND THE NATIVE AFRICAN

THE stories which I heard as a child were what the average American Negro boy is likely to hear in regard to his African ancestors, and my chief reasons for repeating them is that they were very largely mistaken and need to be corrected.

I had always heard Africa referred to as the "Dark Continent"; I pictured it to myself as a black, sunless region, with muddy rivers and gloomy forests, inhabited by a people, who, like everything else about them, were black. I supposed that the nearer I got to the original African, the blacker I would find him, and that all lighter coloured Negroes I had seen were a spurious sort, whose blood had been adulterated by mixture with some of the lighter races. I was much surprised, therefore, to learn, when I came to study the native races of Africa, that the man, whom scientists believed to be the original African, namely, the Bushman — and with him I include his near relatives, the Dwarfs of Central Africa — was not black but yellow; that the Negro, the real black man, is after all merely one of the

earliest settlers of the continent, coming from somewhere else, probably Asia, no one knows exactly
where or how.

In a recent volume upon "The Native Races of
South Africa," George W. Stow says in regard to
relations of the Bushmen and the other Negro people
of South Africa:

> It seems somewhat surprising that so many writers have con-
> tinued to class these people [Bushmen] with the Negroes and other
> dark-skinned species of men; whereas, if we are to judge from
> the physical appearance, with a solitary exception of the hair, no
> two sections of the human race could be more divergent. Their
> closest affinities in this respect are certainly more frequently to be
> found among those inhabiting the Northern Hemisphere than any
> other portion of the world.*

On the other hand it appears from native traditions
that, with the exception of the Bushmen, all the native
peoples emigrated from the North to the South.
Other traditions state that, "when their forefathers
migrated to the South, they found the land without
inhabitants, and that only the game and the Bushmen
were living in it."

It is an indication of the low estimate which the
other South African tribes put upon the Bushmen
that they did not count them as "inhabitants."

One who studies the books about Africa will read
a great deal about the true Negro who lives, as the
books tell us, in the Soudan, a part of Africa that is

---

* "The Native Races of South Africa," George W. Stow, p. 6.

often referred to as Negroland.   After I had learned
that the original African was not a black man and
not a Negro, in the strict scientific sense of the word,
I was led to explore, as well as I was able by the aid
of books and maps, that part of Africa where the
Negro is supposed to be at home.   I wanted to find
more about the real black man.

The true Negro, I learned, is only one section of
what is ordinarily known as the Negro race; the
other is the Bantu, a mixed people, generally brown
in colour, who were the first invaders of South Africa,
driving out the original Bushmen, and gradually
extending themselves over most of that part of the
continent below the equator.

Negroland, stretching clear across the country,
or at least from the Atlantic to the Nile, as
far north as the Desert of Sahara and as far
south as the equator, is a wide region, and there
are many different tribes and many different
types of people inhabiting it.   From the North
Arab invaders and merchantmen have entered the
country and mingled with the earlier and darker
races.   Wave after wave of conquest has poured
itself out over the rich lands between the desert
and the mountains that divide these inland regions
from the coast and hundreds of years of slave-
raiding have so broken up and intermingled the
different racial stocks that it is as hard for one, not
an expert, to find the "true Negro" in Africa — that

is without any mixture of foreign blood — as it is to find the colour line in the United States.

How difficult this sometimes is I may, perhaps, illustrate by an experience of my own a few years ago in Alabama. I was travelling at this time with one of our students at Tuskegee, who was very light in colour, when we had some distance to go in a carriage. At the end of our journey, the owner of the carriage, who was a white man, collected fifty cents from me but called upon the student who was with me for a dollar. After considerable argument and some inquiry, we discovered that it was the rule to charge white men a dollar for the same service for which Negroes paid only fifty cents, and my companion had been taken for a white man. But even after this the student was not inclined to pay the extra price. He seemed to think fifty cents was too much pay for being a white man, at least for so short a time.

Upon another occasion, when an important exposition was being held in one of our Southern states, I recall that, in order to encourage Negroes to attend, the exposition authorities decided that on certain days of the week coloured people could be admitted at half price. The white people were to pay the regular price, fifty cents. The notion of the managers was that many coloured people were staying away from the exposition because they were too poor to pay the regular entrance fee, and that if the price were lowered on certain days large numbers, who could not otherwise afford it, would go. The event proved that the calculations of the managers were correct. Large numbers of coloured people crowded into the exposition on Negro day, but at the end of two weeks the doorkeepers had become desperate. They wanted to throw up their jobs because, as they said, it was too embarrassing work to pick out, by their colour, the black people from the white.

As an illustration of the way in which the intermingling of the racial stocks has come about in Africa, I may mention the fact that, when Dr. Barth, in 1850, first visited the Negro city of Kano, which is the most important trading centre of Western Soudan, he found it, a place of thirty to forty thousand inhabitants, which at certain seasons of the year was increased to sixty thousand, divided into numerous quarters, each of which was inhabited by a different type of people. One quarter was devoted almost exclusively to Arab merchants; a second was inhabited by Fellani, the ruling class; still other quarters were taken up by different tribes of the subject people, among them the merchant and manufacturing people, the Hausas. In addition to these, there were the slaves — gathered from all portions of the country but principally from the tribes living near the coast — who made up nearly half the population.*

* "Discoveries in North and Central Africa," Henry Barth, P.H.D., Vol.I, p. 507.

I cannot now remember where I first got the idea
that a man who was dark in colour was necessarily
more ignorant and in a lower stage of civilisation
than one who was lighter.   At any rate there seemed
to be a general understanding to that effect, when I
was a boy — at least among most people.   Perhaps
it was due to the fact that on the plantations, as a
rule, lighter coloured slaves were more often employed
as house servants, and, because of their more
intimate association with their masters, were held
in higher esteem and had more opportunities for
advancement than the field hands.   Perhaps it was
merely a reflection of the general opinion, which
slaves somehow imbibed, that everything white was
good and everything black was bad.   I recall that
in the matter of religion, although, it may never have
been directly referred to, we, always understood that
God was white and the Devil was black.

In any case I grew up with the idea that in Africa
the lowest and most degraded type of man was black,
and the blacker he was the further down in the scale
of civilisation I expected him to be.   The fact seems
to be that this is nowhere true in Africa.   For
instance, the Hausas, the great trading people of the
Soudan, who live in walled cities and carry on a trade
extending over the whole region between the West
Coast and the Nile, are, according to Dr. Charles
Henry Robinson, "as black as any people in the
world."   The Bushmen, on the other hand, who,

as I have already said, are yellow, have nowhere risen above the hunting stage of civilisation.

No one question, I may say right here, is more frequently asked me than this: "What is the relative ability of the Negro of mixed and unmixed blood?" I usually answer that my experience and observation convince me that, where the environment has been equally favourable, there is no difference in ability.

As an illustration I may say that at Tuskegee it has been customary to award the honour of delivering the valedictory address to the student making the highest average in scholarship, industrial work and deportment, and during a period of about twenty years, ten of those who gained this honour were Negroes of pure blood. I understand that at Hampton Institute, in Virginia, where they have had an experience covering a considerably longer period, the same thing has been found to be true. I might add that the late J. C. Price, during his lifetime by all odds the leading and most prominent man of his race in North Carolina and one of the most eloquent men in the country, was pure black. The two leading and most progressive men, in commercial and business directions, in the State of Mississippi, Isaiah T. Montgomery and Charles Banks, have no mixture of blood. W. W. Brown, who founded the largest and most successful fraternal organisation that has ever existed among the black people in America, was a pure black. It would not be difficult to multiply examples of this kind, but there is one other name that should not be omitted — Major R. R. Moten, Commandant at the Hampton Institute, Hampton, Va., who is one of the few Negroes in this country who can trace his ancestry, in an unbroken chain, back to his people in Africa. The most conspicuous example of a success in literature is, perhaps, Paul Lawrence Dunbar, the poet, who was a man of unmixed blood.

Let me add that, as my observation and experience of human life have widened, I have learned to doubt the wisdom of laying down any general rules that fix for all times the status of any people, or determine in advance the progress they are able or likely to make under conditions different from those in which they happened, at the present time, to be found.

I had a lesson in this respect a few years ago at Tuskegee. It happened that in one of the geography classes, which at that time were studying Africa, the students came one day upon a passage in which the Bushmen were described as the lowest type of human being to be found in Africa. The writer went on to describe this people in a way which made our students feel that the Bushmen were about as low, degraded and hopeless a type of human nature as could well be imagined.

While the class was discussing this passage, a boy in the back of the room raised his hand and indicated that he had something to say. It turned out that he had recently come from South Africa and knew something of the natives, and he did not agree with the statements in the geography. He went on to say that his mother was a Bushwoman and that his father was a Hottentot, a tribe which is generally supposed to be closely related to the Bushmen. He had been born in the bush. Afterward, while he was still a small boy, his father and mother had moved into town and he had been enabled in this way to get something of an education. As the young Bushman happened to stand near the head of his class and spoke with personal knowledge of both his father's and mother's people, as well as of the other tribes of South Africa, what he had to say was listened to with the greatest interest and attention. When he followed it up by going to his room and bringing back photographs with which to illustrate his statement, both the class and the teachers were convinced that, however much truth there might be in the general description given in geographies, the Bushmen who, for a hundred years or more, had been hunted like wild beasts by the other stronger tribes of South Africa, were to a very large extent, the victims of circumstances.*

*" Every race of man, savage or civilised, that came in contact with them [the Bushmen] appropriated their land without a single pretext of justification, and waged a war of extermination against them as soon as they resisted or resented the wrong that was done them. The pastoral tribes of natives and colonial flock-owners could not appreciate the feelings of attachment which those who lived by the chase alone had to their hunting-grounds, while the constant encroachments which were made upon them impressed the untutored minds of the hunter race with the idea

This incident helped to confirm me in the belief that in our efforts to help the weaker peoples of the earth, we should not despair even in the case of the most humble and backward of the human family. In mathematics and in physical sciences it is possible to make exact statements and lay down laws that are universal and unchanging, but in what concerns human life and history we cannot be so precise and definite. Human beings are constantly doing unprecedented things and it is usually, I suspect, the unexpected and unprecedented things that men do that are the most important.

As a boy I had been accustomed to hear Africa referred to as one hears of Mexico, as if it were a place where a comparatively homogeneous people lives, having much the same customs, language, and civilisation; in short, as if it were a country instead of a continent. It was some time before I was able to realise the vast extent and variety of the territory over which the dark races of Africa are spread. Africa is larger and considerably more varied in its geographical structure than North America. The territory occupied by the dark races of Africa, for example is more than two times that occupied by the United States.

that the whole world was arrayed against them. Their almost fierce love of independence, their almost equally unalterable determination to maintain and die in their primitive modes of life, utter contempt — at least of the majority of them — for all pastoral or agricultural pursuits, made them to be looked upon by all the larger and more robust of the African races as a species of wild animal, which it was praiseworthy to exterminate whenever an opportunity offered."—"Discoveries in North and Central Africa," Henry Barth, Ph. D., Vol. I, p. 215.

I found also that I had only the vaguest notion of the multitude of different peoples that inhabit Africa and the variety of civilisations represented among its inhabitants, not only among the more advanced races along the Mediterranean but also among the Negro peoples who still hold possession of nearly seven-eighths of the continent. For instance, Sir Harry H. Johnston says of the people inhabiting the English protectorate of Uganda, where a careful study has been made of the native peoples:

Within the limits of the Protectorate are to be found specimens of nearly all the more marked types of African man — Congo Pygmies, and the low types of the Elgon and Semliki forests, the handsome Bahima, who are negroids and are as much related to the ancient Egyptians as to the average Negro, the gigantic Turkana and the wiry and stunted Andorobo, the Apollo-like Masai, the naked Nile tribes, and the scrupulous clothed Baganda. These last again are enthusiastic, casuistic Christians, while other tribes of the Nile provinces are fanatical Mohammedans. The Bahima are burdened with a multiplicity of minor deities, while the Masai and kindred races have practically no religion at all. Cannibalism lingers in the western corners of the protectorate; while natives of the other provinces are importing tinned apricots or are printing and publishing in their own language summaries of their history.*

Speaking of the popular notion of the African people to which I have referred, Professor Jerome Dowd, a Southern white man who resides in Charlotte, N. C., author of a recent sociological study of the African races, says:

---

* " The Uganda Protectorate," Sir Harry H. Johnston, Vol. I, preface.

When the average European or American white man thinks or writes of the Negroes he considers them as one race and attributes to them certain traits which are supposed to be equally common to all groups and to all localities.   This is a mistaken view and may be likened to an attempt to class all of the Aryan peoples as a homogeneous race, having common features and traits.   In fact the Negroes of the world, just as the Aryans, are scattered over a great area, live in different environments and have varied and opposite mental and physical peculiarities.   Indeed, the Negro races of the world differ from each other even more widely than the different branches of the Aryan stock.   In Africa, for example, the Negroes are distributed over the territory of much greater extent and of greater physical diversity than is true of the Aryan races of Europe.   They also differ more than the Aryan races in general appearance, in stature, physiognomy, and mental and moral constitution.   Hence, to speak of all Negroes in Africa as one race, having common characteristics, is as misleading and is as unscientific as if we should consider all Europeans and Americans as of one race, and attribute to all of them the same traits.*

Another statement which one frequently hears, made indiscriminately of the dark races of Africa, is that they are constitutionally lazy and cannot be induced to work. I shall have something to say about the Negro as a labourer later in this work; here it is, perhaps, sufficient to recall the fact that in the greater portion of Africa the black man is still almost the only labourer. It is he who builds the railways and the bridges, digs the gold in the South African mines, and collects the rubber in the Congo forests. Miss Mary Kingsley, in her volume, "Travels in West Africa," says of the Kruboys,

* *Southern Workman*, May, 1908.

"that they are the most important people of West Africa; for without their help the working of the Coast would cost more lives than it already does, and would be in fact practically impossible." In his book on Tropical Africa, Henry Drummond, describing the way in which the natives come from far and near to try the sensation of methodical work on the building of the Cape to Cairo railway, says:

The severest test to which the Native of Central Africa has yet been put is in the construction of the Stevenson Road between Lakes Nyassa and Tanganyika. Forty-six miles of this road have already been made, entirely by native labour, and the work could not have been better done had it been executed by English navvies. I have watched by the day a party of seventy Natives working upon the road. Till three or four years ago, none had ever looked upon a white man, nor till a few months previously had one of them ever seen a spade, a pick-axe or a crow-bar. Yet these savages handle these tools to such purpose that with only a single European superintendent they have made a road full of difficult cuttings and gradients, which would not disgrace a railway contractor at home. The workmen keep regular hours, six in the morning till five at night, with a rest at midday — work steadily, continuously, willingly and, above all, merrily. This goes on in the heart of the tropics, almost under the equator itself, where the white man's energy evaporates and leaves him so limp that he cannot be an example to his men.*

The fact is, very little comes out of Africa, from an elephant's tusk to a diamond, that is not the result of the labour of the African. This does not mean that the native labourer is always as persistent and intelligent as he should be, nor that native labour is,

* "Tropical Africa," Henry Drummond, p. 64.

everywhere and for all purposes, of the same value. Experience has shown that one tribe is more useful in one form of labour and another tribe in some other form. What the African has needed most to make him a better labourer has been the same incentive to work which the white man had. Where one stick sharpened forms a spear, two sticks make a fire, and fifty sticks a place to live, there is little incentive to systematic and persistent work. This completeness and modesty of wants is, in my opinion, at the bottom of the difficulty in Africa. The truth is that the Negro in Africa or out of it develops in industrial efficiency, as other human beings do, in response to his needs and his opportunities.

I had this fact impressed upon me in a very striking way during a recent visit to Cleveland, Ohio, when I went to see a little brass foundry run by a coloured man who is engaged in the manufacture of those little brass wheels that run along the trolley wires of our electric railways and, by means of the trolley pole connect the cars with the electric current.

The operation of casting these wheels, as I was informed, requires unusual skill and experience, because it is necessary to secure just the right degree of hardness and toughness in the metal, and I was the more interested in noticing the way in which this man and his assistants did their work because I recall that the art of working in iron was one of the crafts that had been the special property, from time immemorial, of the people of my race.

Dr. Franz Boas, Professor of Anthropology at Columbia University, says that, "while much of the history of early invention is shrouded in darkness, it seems likely that at the time when the European was still satisfied with rude stone tools, the African had invented or adapted the art of smelting ore."

I had been reading a few days before a description of the rude methods by which, with little more than a simple bellows and a charcoal fire, native Africans reduced the ores and forged the implements, many of them of great beauty as well as usefulness, which one may still meet with in many parts of Africa.

I am not sufficiently familiar with the detailed methods of smelting ores and casting metals to be able to even suggest the vast distance between the primitive methods of the Native African and the infinitely more intricate and complicated technique of the modern industry. The thought, the study and the invention of thousands, perhaps of millions of minds, have contributed to create the very conditions of the modern iron industry. The contrast between the Native African, working laboriously in the solitude of the African forests, with his primitive tools, after a traditional method, and the American Negro, in his own foundry, with the advantage of all the machinery, knowledge, and the skill that modern science and modern invention have contributed to the improvement of iron industry, is impressive enough. But this contrast does not represent the difference in innate qualities in the men themselves, but rather the difference in the civilisations that surround them.

It probably requires just as much skill and just as much patience to make one of those long and graceful spearheads you may see on the end of an African lance as it does to make the trolley wheel; but it takes all our civilisation to make the trolley wheel possible.

In what I have written thus far in regard to Africa and African peoples I have sought to emphasise the vastness of the territories which they inhabit; the distances which divide them from one another; the variety of physical types in which they are represented; the complicated social relations that sometimes exist among them, and the difficulty of making general statements, laying down general laws that hold good at all times and all places for all of the African peoples.

There is, however, a tie which few white men can understand, which binds the American Negro to the African Negro; which unites the black man of Brazil and the black man of Liberia; which is constantly drawing into closer relations all the scattered African peoples whether they are in the old world or the new.

There is not only the tie of race, which is strong in

any case, but there is the bond of colour, which is specially important in the case of the black man. It is this common badge of colour, for instance, which is responsible for the fact that whatever contributes, in any degree to the progress of the American Negro, contributes to the progress of the African Negro, and to the Negro in South America and the West Indies.   When the African Negro succeeds, it helps the American Negro.   When the African Negro fails, it hurts the reputation and the standing of the Negro in every other part of the world.

I have rarely met in America any one of my race who did not, in one way or another, show a deep interest in everything connected with Africa.   The millions of Negroes in America are almost as much interested, for example, in the future of Liberia and Abyssinia, as they are in their own country.   There is always a peculiar and scarcely definable bond that binds one black man to another black man, whether in Africa, Jamaica, Haiti, or the United States. One evidence of this interest of the Negro in America in the Negro in Africa is the work that the American Negro churches are doing in Africa to help civilise and Christianise their brethren there.   There is scarcely any branch of the Negro church in America that does not have an organisation through which it is sending men and women and money into some portion of Africa.   The readiness with which some of the strongest and brightest men and women in

America, who have had superior opportunities, are ready to return to Africa and give their lives in an effort to uplift their fellows, indicates the strong racial tie that binds the black people of the world together.

On the other hand, it is true that Negroes in other parts of the world are beginning to interest themselves more and more in the fortunes of the Negro in America. In a very marked degree the one hundred and thirty millions of black people outside of America are looking to the ten millions of Negroes in the United States for guidance and for inspiration. They are watching closely the progress of these American Negroes. They are beginning to realise that if it is possible for the ten million black men in America, surrounded by modern machinery and all the other forces of civilisation, to get into line and march with the procession, that it is also possible for them, in time, to follow, somewhat more slowly, perhaps, but in the same direction.

CHAPTER III

THE AFRICAN AT HOME

SOME time during the latter part of 1899, or the early part of 1900, I received through the German Embassy, in Washington, a letter saying that the German Colonial Society wanted a number of students from Tuskegee to go out to German West Africa to teach the natives how to produce cotton by American methods.

While I had been a student at Hampton Institute, Virginia, it was one of my ambitions, as it has been the ambition of a great many other Negro students before and since, to go out some day to Africa as a missionary. I believed that I had got hold at Hampton of a kind of knowledge that would be peculiarly helpful to the Native Africans and I felt that my interest in the people out there, vague and indefinite as it was, would in some way or other help and inspire me in the task of lifting them to a higher plane of civilisation.

After I went to Tuskegee I gave up my ambition of going to Africa. I had not been long there, however, before I was convinced that I could, perhaps, be of larger usefulness through the work I was able to do in this country, by fitting, for the same service I wanted to perform, Africans who came as students to America, and by sending from Tuskegee men and women trained in our methods, as teachers and workers among the native peoples. The request I received through the German Embassy was, therefore, particularly welcome to me, for it gave me an opportunity to realise, in a direct way, the ambition I had never wholly lost sight of.

A group of our best students was selected for this African mission. They went out to Togoland, West Africa, and began to establish stations in different points in that colony, and then started in to grow cotton, using the native labour as far as they were able, but necessarily, at first, doing a large part of the work themselves.

They met all sorts of difficulties. They found the American cotton was not suited to African soil, and were compelled to cross it with native varieties in order to produce an hybrid type that possessed the valuable qualities of both. They had considerable difficulty, at first, with the native labourers. I remember that John Robinson, one of the party who remained to carry out the work after the others had returned home, told me of an incident, which made me see, in a way in which I had not been able to see before, that the education of the native African in the white man's civilisation must begin much farther back and with much simpler matters than most of us are likely to imagine.

Among the other things this party had taken out to Africa was a wagon, which had been manufactured by the students at Tuskegee. While this wagon was being unloaded and put together, the native porters looked on with interest, never having seen anything that went on wheels before. After the wagon had been loaded ready to start the attention of members of the party was turned for a time in another direction. When they came back to the wagon they were greatly surprised to see that the natives had unloaded and taken it apart, and were busily engaged in fastening its wheels and other parts on their heads, preparatory to carrying them, along with the other goods, to their destination in the interior. Mr. Robinson explained to them, through an interpreter, the use of the wagon, and tried to show them the advantage of it. They were interested in seeing this curious machine of the white man work, but they were quite positive in their conviction that the good old-fashioned way of carrying everything on their heads was the better. Now that roads have been opened up and the natives have actually seen a wagon worked, Mr. Robinson tells me they take it as a hardship if they are asked to carry anything.

During the time this experiment in educating the Native African was going on, I followed its progress, through the accounts I received from students on the ground and from the reports of the German Colonial Society, with close attention and intense interest. It was the nearest I had come, up to that time, to anything like a practical and intimate acquaintance with the African at home.

Among the first thing the Tuskegee students did in Africa was to build for themselves comfortable houses, to supply them with well made but simple furniture, to put in these houses not only the necessities, but some of the comforts of life. I was interested to note that, within a few months the Natives and, especially the women, had gotten the notion that they wanted the same kind of houses and some of the same kind of furniture. The women naturally made their wants known to the men, and before these students had been in Africa half a dozen years the Natives in their vicinity had reached the point where, with the training they had received and with the desire they had gained for better homes to live in, better tools to work with, and for all the other advantages which the black man in America seemed to possess over the black man in Africa, they were performing about as satisfactory service as the same class of human beings would have performed in any other part of the world.

Native Africans have been sent from Africa to Tuskegee. Our Tuskegee students have returned from time to time and made their reports of successes. Thus in a very vital and practical manner has our institution become connected with the progress and civilisation of our brethren in the darker continent.

Some time ago in looking through the pages of some magazine or book of science, I ran across a statement that, when men first began to study the stars systematically and with telescopes, they discovered a certain class of errors in their calculations which were due to the personality of the observers. One man's brain, acting quicker, would record the stars as moving more rapidly; another would record them as moving more slowly than their actual movements. It became necessary, therefore, in order to make the calculations correct, to study and take account of these personal aberrations.

It has occurred to me, in the course of my reading about the African peoples, that it would contribute much to the accuracy of our knowledge, if some study were made of the sort of errors that creep into our observations of human beings. Important as it is that we should have a correct knowledge of the stars, it is more important that we should have an accurate knowledge of men. For instance, I have noticed that a man born and reared in the Southern states invariably looks upon the Negro with different eyes from the man born and reared in the Northern states. In their reports and interpretations of the simplest facts they are often widely divergent in their views. Even when they agree with each other about

the Negro, for instance, it has often seemed to me
that their agreement was due to a misunderstanding.

Frequently amusing situations occur in the discussion of the Negro.   Many of these have occurred
in my presence.   It seldom occurs, for instance, when
I am travelling on a train that the discussion
does not turn on the question as to what is the
physical, moral, and mental effect on the individual
when he is of mixed blood.   One man will argue
very seriously that there should be no mixture of
blood, for the reason that he is quite sure that wherever there is a mixture it results in a weakened
individual, bodily, mentally, morally.   Within ten
or fifteen minutes another man will begin, in the
absence of the first, to discuss the same subject and
will, in an equally serious and positive manner,
state that wherever in all history the Negro has been
able to accomplish anything of value to the world
it had been because he had some tincture of white
blood in his veins.

During these discussions I am sometimes reminded
of an incident that occurred during my early boyhood,
which, because it illustrates a phase in the development of the Negro in America, I may be permitted
to mention it here.   Very soon after the days of
slavery and even before the public school system had
been organised, there arose in the community a
discussion among our people as to whether the world
was round or flat.   It lasted for several days, and

divided the community into two pretty stubborn factions. During the discussion a coloured man came along, a school teacher, who had very little actual learning, and made application to open a school. The question as to whether the world was flat or round was submitted to him, or rather he was asked how he would treat the question in the school-room, and he replied that he was prepared to teach either "flat," "round," or just as the individual family requested.

The continual discussion of the Negro often reminds me, as I have stated, of this story. The Negro question or the Negro himself seems able to be accommodated to almost any and every shade of opinion. That explains how two men with diametrically opposite views sometimes come to an agreement about the Negro; one thinks he should be flat and not round, the other thinks he should be round and not flat; but both agree that there is something wrong with him.

If it is difficult for people of the same race to understand one another when they are talking about things in regard to which their experience has been different, it is still more difficult for one race to pass judgment upon another, particularly when these races differ so widely from one another as the white man and the Negro. Dr. Franz Boas has called attention to this difficulty in a paper before the American Association of Science. "As the white race is the civilised race," he says, "every deviation from the white type is considered as the characteristic feature of a lower type; . . . the greater the difference between the intellectual, emotional and moral processes and those found in our civilisation, the harsher the judgment of the people."*

Under these circumstances it is natural enough that the black man, who is furthest removed physically from the white man, should suffer more than others from the sort of prejudice Professor Boas describes. With the possible exception of the Jew, no race has ever been subjected to criticisms so searching and candid, to state it mildly, as the Negro. And yet I have found that those who have known and understood the Negro best, have usually been kindest in their judgment of him and most hopeful of his future.

For instance, the late Miss Kingsley, an Englishwoman, who seems to have entered deeper into the mind of the West African than most others, says of the West Coast Negro:

The true Negro is, I believe, by far the better man than the Asiatic; he is physically superior, and he is more like an Englishman than the Asiatic; he is a logical, practical man, with feelings that are a credit to him, and are particularly strong in the direction of property. He has a way of thinking he has rights whether he likes to use them or no, and he will fight for them when he is driven to it. Fight you for a religious idea the African will not; he is not the stuff you make martyrs out of, nor does he desire to shake off the shackels of the flesh and swoon into Nirvana. . . .

* "Proceedings of the American Association for the Advancement of Science," Vol. XLIII., 1894.

His make of mind is exceedingly like the make of mind that thousands of Englishmen of the stand-no-nonsense, Englishman's-house-is-his-castle type. Yet, withal, a law-abiding man, loving a live Lord, holding loudly that women should be kept in their place, yet often grievously henpecked by his wives, and little better than a slave to his mother whom he loves with the love he gives to none other.*

Concerning the affection which the African has for his mother, Miss Kingsley quotes the Rev. Leighton Wilson.

Mr. Wilson was born and educated in South Carolina. In 1834 he went to Africa as a missionary and remained there for eighteen years, in close contact with the civilisation of the forefathers of the present American Negroes. He was among the first missionaries to Africa. He remained in the active service of the Southern Presbyterian Church until his death in 1886. While in Africa he studied the languages and reduced the native tongue of some of the tribes to writing. He says:

Whatever other estimate we may form of the African, we may not doubt his love for his mother. Her name, whether dead or alive, is always on his lips and in his heart. She is the first thing he thinks of when awakening from his slumbers and the last thing he remembers when closing his eyes in sleep; to her he confides secrets which he would reveal to no other human being on the face of the earth. He cares for no one else in time of sickness, she alone must prepare his food, administer his medicine, perform his ablutions, and spread his mat for him. He flies to her in the hour of his distress, for he well knows if all the rest of the world turn against him, she will be steadfast in her love, whether he be right or wrong.

* "West African Studies," p. 373.

If there be any cause which justifies a man using violence towards one of his fellowmen it would be to resent an insult offered to his mother. More fights are occasioned among boys by hearing something said in disparagement of their mothers than all other causes put together. It is a common saying among them, if a man's mother and his wife are both on the point of being drowned, and he can save only one of them, he must save his mother, for the avowed reason if the wife is lost he may marry another, but he will never find a second mother. . . .*

Mr. Wilson points out that the Africans of the Grain Coast have long since risen above the hunting life; they have fixed habitations, cultivate the soil for means of subsistence, have herds of domestic animals, construct for themselves houses which are sufficient to protect them alike from the scorching heat of the sun and the chilly damps of the night; they show a turn for the mechanical arts, and in the fabrication of implements of warfare and articles of ornament they display surprising skill.

"As we see them in their native country," he continues, "they show none of that improvidence or want of foresight for which they have almost become proverbial in this country, which shows that circumstances have made them what they are in this respect. They plant their crops with particular reference to the seasons of the year, and they store away provisions for their future wants with as much regularity as any people in the world, so that times of scarcity and want are less frequent among them

*"Western Africa," pp. 116, 117.

than among others who pretend to a much higher degree of civilisation."

Referring to the farms of the Kru people, the tribes from which the seamen of the West Coast are drawn, Mr. Wilson says:

The Natives of the Kru country cultivate the soil to some considerable extent. Their farms are generally two or three miles distant from the villages, and are made at this distance to keep them out of the reach of their cattle. Nearer to the villages they have inclosed gardens in which they raise small quantities of plantains, corn, bananas, peas, beans, and a few other vegetables.

Of the mechanical skill of the neighbouring Ashanti people, whose territory is in the English Gold Coast colony, Mr. Wilson tells us, "that they manufacture gold ornaments of various kinds and many of them of much real taste. They fabricate swords, agricultural implements, wooden stools, and cotton cloths of beautiful figures and very substantial texture."*

From time to time, as Tuskegee graduates have returned from the various stations in Africa in which they have been at work, they have brought back with them specimens of native workmanship in iron, wood and leather. I have frequently been impressed with the beauty of some of the designs that native craftsmen have worked out upon their spears and in their homespun cotton cloth. The leather tanned by some of these native tanners is often surprisingly

* " Western Africa," p. 187.

beautiful in colour, design and finish. Some of
the specimens of the native handicrafts have been
placed on exhibition in the museum at Tuskegee, and
in one or two cases we have been able to reproduce
in our classes in basketry the shapes and designs of
some of these native articles.

"Nothing, perhaps," says Professor Franz Boas,
"is more encouraging than a glimpse of the artistic
industries of the native African. A walk through
the African museums of Paris and London and
Berlin is a revelation. I wish you could see the
sceptres of African kings, carved of hardwood and
representing artistic form; or the dainty basketry
made by the people of the Kongo River and of the
region of the Great Lakes of the Nile, or the grass
mats of their beautiful patterns.

"Even more worthy of our admiration," he
continues, "is the work of the blacksmith who
manufactures symmetrical lance heads, almost a
yard long, or axes inlaid with copper and decorated
with filligree. Let me also mention in passing the
bronze castings of Benin and the West Coast of
Africa, which, although perhaps due to Portuguese
influences, have so far excelled in technique any
European work, that they are even now almost
inimitable."*

The blacksmith seems to occupy a very important
place in the social life of Africa. Travellers have

---

* Atlanta University Leaflet, No. 19.

found these smiths at work in the most remote and inaccessible parts of the continent, where they may be seen collecting the native iron and copper ores; smelting and reducing them, and then working them in their primitive forges, into hoes, knives, spear and arrow heads, battle-axes, wood-working tools, rings and hatchets.

Just as everywhere in the Southern states to-day, especially in the country districts, at the crossroads, or near the country store, one finds the Negro black-smith, so, in some of the remote regions in Africa, every village has, according to its size, from one to three blacksmiths. Each smith has an apprentice and his art is a craft secret most zealously guarded.

Samuel P. Verner, like the Rev. Leighton Wilson, a Southern white man and missionary of the Southern Presbyterian church, says in his book, "Pioneering in Central Africa," of these African blacksmiths:

The proficiency of some of these men is astonishing. I frequently have my work done by them and their skill amazed me. They have the art of tempering copper as well as of making soft steel. Some of the objects of their craft which I placed in the National Museum at Washington are revelations to the uninitiated in their remarkable complexity and variety.

Mr. Verner's mission station was in the Kongo Free State, on the upper courses of the Kasai, in the heart of savage Africa where the people have never been touched by the influences of either the European or Mohammedan civilisations. Speaking of the carving and wood working of some of these tribes, Mr. Verner says:

Some of these Africans are wonderfully adept. They can produce a geometrical figure whose perfection is amazing. Their tools are of the simplest, yet they can carve figures of men and animals, pipes, bowls, cups, platters, tables, and fantastic images. I saw a chair carved out of a solid block of ebony. Their work in ivory is also rare and valuable and I believe their talent in those lines ought to be developed.

Throughout West Africa, wherever the European has not established his trading factory, the native market is an institution which is a constant source of surprise to travellers. These markets are the native clearing houses for the produce of the soil and the fabricated articles of the land. They are generally the centre of the trading operations of a district ranging from ten to thirty miles. Here will be seen vegetables and fruit, poultry, eggs, live pigs, goats, salt of their manufacture, pottery of their own make, strips of cloth, grass-woven mats, baskets and specimens of embroidery and art work, besides numberless other articles of various sorts and kinds which are essential to African comfort and well being. From the small group of native merchants who travel with their wares within a radius of thirty or fifty miles, to the large caravans of the Hausa traders who cross the Desert of Sahara, and at times reach the Eastern and Western confines of the continent, everywhere in Africa the black man is a trader.

Among the more primitive tribes the village markets are confined to two or three hundred buyers or sellers, but in the greater markets like that of Kano and Upper Nigeria, twenty or thirty thousand traders will be gathered together at certain seasons of the year. It is an interesting fact, as indicating the African's interest in trade, that in many tribes the market place is considered sacred ground, and, in order that trade may be carried on there without interruption, no strife is permitted within its precincts.

Professor Boas, writing in 1904, said:

The Negro all over the African continent is either a tiller of the soil or the owner of large herds; only the Bushmen and a few of the dwarf tribes of Central Africa are hunters. Owing to the high development of agriculture, the density of population of Africa is much greater than that of primitive America and consequently the economic conditions of life are more stable.

It may be safely said that the primitive Negro community with its fields that are tilled with iron and wooden implements, with its domestic animals, with its smithies, with its expert wood-carvers, is a model of thrift and industry, and compares favourably with the conditions of life among our own ancestors.*

It is just as true in America, as it is in Africa, that those who know the Negro intimately and best have been, as a rule, kindest and most hopeful in their judgments of him. This may seem strange to those who get their notion of the Southern white man's opinion of the Negro, from what they see in the press and hear from the platform, during the heat of a

* *Ethnical Record*, March 1904.

political campaign, or from the utterances of men who, for one reason or another, have allowed themselves to become embittered. Southern opinion of the Negro, particularly as it finds expression in the press and on the platform, is largely controversial. It has been influenced by the fact that for nearly a hundred years the Negro has been the football in a bitter political contest, and there are a good many Southern politicians who have acquired the habit of berating him. The Negro, in the South, has had very little part in this controversy, either before or since the war, but he has had a chance to hear it all, and it has often seemed to me, if, after all that has taken place, the Negro is still able to discuss his situation calmly, the white man should be able to do so also. But that is another matter.

Nineteen times out of twenty, I suppose, a stranger coming South, who inquires concerning the Negro from people he meets on the train or on the highways, will get from these men pretty nearly the same opinion he has read in the newspapers or heard in political speeches. These criticisms of the Negro have been repeated so often that people have come to accept and repeat them again without reflection. The thing that shows this to be true is, that the very men who denounced all Negroes will very likely before the conversation is ended tell of one, and perhaps, half a dozen individual Negroes in whom they have the greatest confidence.

A Southern white man may tell you, with the utmost positiveness, that he never knew a single Negro who would not steal — except one. Every white man knows one Negro who is all right — a model of honesty, industry, and thrift — and if he tries to remember, he will think of other Negroes in whom he has the greatest confidence, and for whom he has a very genuine respect. Considering that there are a good many more white people in the South than there are Negroes, it seems to follow, logically, that in spite of what one hears about the Negro in general, there are a good many individual Negroes who are pretty well thought of by their white neighbours.

It is well to take into consideration, also, that when Southern people express their confidence and their respect for an individual black man, they are speaking of one whom they know: on the contrary, when they denounce in general terms the weakness and the failure of the Negro race, they have in mind a large number of whom they know a great deal less.

I do not mean to suggest that there is no justification for the criticism of the Negro that one often hears in the South. I have never thought or said that the Negro in America was all that he should be. It does seem to me, however, that the Negro in the United States has done, on the whole, as well as he was able, and as well as, under all the circumstances, could be reasonably expected.

It was not unusual, particularly in the early part of the last century, to find among the slaves men who could read and write Arabic and were learned in the lore of the Koran. W. B. Hodgson, a Southern slave holder, published in 1857 a paper in which he gave an account of a Negro slave who had translated the gospel of John into Negro dialect, using "the letters of the Koran, the book of his first religious instruction, in transcribing the gospel, the book of his second instruction and conversion, and in the adopted dialect of his land of captivity." Most of the slaves came from what were known as the pagan tribes of the coast. In spite of the fact that so large a proportion of the slaves came from these interior tribes it was not until Mungo Park made his famous first journey to the interior of the Soudan in 1795 that the Western world knew anything definite about that region. The eminent German traveller and scholar, Dr. Henry Barth, first reached the famous commercial city of Kano in 1850, and until 1900 it was said not more than five Europeans had ever visited that city. The accounts that travellers give of the region and the people present a picture of African life so different from that of the coast cities that I am tempted to quote at some length from these descriptions.

Several peoples, of strikingly different characteristics, contributed to form the several loosely connected states which now form the British Colony of Northern Nigeria, of which Kano is the principal city. The most important and interesting of these are the Hausas and the Fulahs or Fellani, as they are sometimes called. The Fulahs are noted for their military spirit; the Hausas for their commercial enterprise. One has a light complexion and the other is dark.

The Fulahs are an equestrian people, with a cavalry armed with lances and swords. They are zealous Mohammedans with a knowledge how to "divide and govern." Their independent character is described by the proverbial saying that "a Fulah man slave will escape or kill his master, and that a Fulah girl slave will rule the harem or die." The Hausas are superior to the Fulahs in the arts of peace. They are possessed of unusual industry, judgment and intelligence and have a considerable degree of literary taste. The Hausas carry on the internal trade of the North and Central Soudan. They are well clothed and have many well built cities with population sometimes of from twenty to sixty thousand. Barth, in describing Kano, which is, perhaps, to West Africa, what Chicago is to the United States, tells us that he mounted on horseback, "rode for several hours round all the inhabited quarters, enjoying at his leisure from the saddle the manifold scenes of public and private life, of comfort and happiness, of luxury and misery, of industry and indolence, which were exhibited in the streets, the market places, and in the interior of the courtyards." Here he saw "a row of shops filled with articles of native and foreign produce with buyers and sellers in every variety of figure, complexion, and dress." Now an "open terrace of clay with a number of dye-pots and people busily employed in various processes of their handicraft; here a man stirring the juice and mixing with indigo some colouring wood in order to give it the desired tint, there another drawing a shirt from the dye-pot, there two men beating a well-dyed shirt"; further on, "a blacksmith busy with his tools in making a dagger, a spear or the more useful ornaments of husbandry," and, in another place, "men and women hanging up their cotton thread for weaving."

The market of Kano, said to be the largest in Africa, is celebrated for its cotton cloth and leather goods. Traditions of Kano go back over a thousand years. It is surrounded by walls of sun-dried clay from twenty to thirty feet high and fifteen miles in circumference.

The greatest chieftain that ever ruled in West Africa, Mohammed Askia, lived in Kano. He became ruler in 1492 and held sway over a region probably as large as the German Empire. Barth tells us that Mohammed Askia was an example of the highest degree to which Negroes have attained in the way of political administration and control. His dynasty, which was entirely of native descent, is the more remarkable if we consider that this Negro

king was held in the highest esteem and veneration
by the most learned and rigid Mohammedans.   Not
only did he consolidate and even extend his empire,
but went in 1495 on a pilgrimage to Mecca accompanied by 1,500 armed men, 1,000 on foot and 500 on
horseback, and founded there a charitable institution.
He extended his conquests far and wide from what
is now the centre of Nigeria, westward almost to
the borders of the Atlantic Ocean and northward to
the south of Morocco.   Askia governed the subjected tribes with justice and equity.   Everywhere
within the borders of his extensive dominions his
rule spread well-being and comfort.*

The career of Mohammed Askia is possibly the
best example of the influence of Mohammedanism
on that portion of Africa from which our American
slaves were taken.

---

* "Discoveries in North and Central Africa," Henry Barth. See also, "A
Tropical Dependency" : an outline of the ancient history of the Western Soudan
with an account of the modern settlement of northern Nigeria," Thora L. Shaw,
(Lady Lugard.)

CHAPTER IV

THE WEST COAST BACKGROUND OF THE AMERICAN
NEGRO

SLAVES were probably brought to America from every part of Africa, for the slave trade seems to have penetrated, before it ended, to every corner of the continent. But the larger number of them came, undoubtedly, from the West Coast. It is said that, at one time, 200,000 slaves sailed annually from the West Coast of Africa, and during a period of two hundred years, it is estimated that 3,200,000 slaves were shipped to America from a single point in the Niger Delta.* These people of the West Coast were, for the most part, the broken fragments of races that had been driven to the sea by the stronger races of the interior. They did not represent the highest to which the black man had attained in Africa, and their contact with the white man of the slave-trading class during the four hundred years or more that the foreign slave trade was in existence, did not improve them.

The African slave trade was not the source of all that was evil in the native life of the West Coast,

* " West African Studies," Mary H. Kingsley, p. 510.

but it is responsible for a great deal of it.   The slave trade did not, for instance, cause the destructive tribal wars among the Natives, but it incensed them. It added the motive of gain and gave the savage warfare the character of a commercial enterprise. The evils of the traffic did not end, however, with the immediate and tangible destruction that it wrought.   It corrupted the native customs and destroyed the native industries.   It substituted the cheap machine-made European goods for the more artistic native manufactures, which take a great deal more time and energy to produce.

"At the present time," says Professor Boas, "the distribution of Negro culture in Africa is such that in all the regions where the whites have come in contact with the Negro, his own industries have disappeared or have been degraded.   As a consequence, all the tribes that live near the coast of Africa are, comparatively speaking, on a low level of industrial culture.   It is but natural that the blacksmith, who can exchange a small lump of rubber picked up in the woods for a steel knife, prefers this method of obtaining a fine implement to the more laborious one of making a rather inefficient knife of soft iron with his primitive tools.   It is not surprising that the cheap cotton goods replace the fine grass-cloth and the bark-cloth which the African women prepare.   The European trader carries to the coast of Africa only the cheap products of European factories, but nothing that would give to the Negro the white man's method of work."*

Of course the degradation of the native industries, in the way Professor Boas has described it, is not confined to Africa nor to the slave trade; it goes on wherever machine-made goods come in contact with native and home-made products. Much the same thing may be seen among the Negro farmers in the Southern states where they have yielded to the temptation to raise nothing but cotton — what is called the "money crop." For example, the Tuskegee Institute is located in the midst of one of the finest sweet potato growing soils in the world. Notwithstanding this, canned sweet potatoes used to be shipped into this part of Alabama. It requires less work to use the canned sweet potatoes which have been dug, cleaned, and cooked, than it does to prepare the land, produce the sweet potato crop, clean them, and cook them. But it makes the farmer dependent upon the store-keeper or more frequently on the money-lender.

One of my favourite ways of emphasising this mistake, in my talks to the Negro farmers, is to get a basket of canned vegetables from the store, show them what they are buying, calculate what they are paying for them, and make clear to them how much they could save and how much more independent they would be if they raised these things at home.

* *Ethnical Record*, March, 1904, p. 107.

It may be interesting to note here exactly what it was the white man gave the black man for those cargoes of human beings that were shipped from Africa to America. The list of trade goods was somewhat different at different periods of the slave traffic and for different parts of the coast. The following is a list of trade goods as used in the latter part of the seventeenth century for the region about Sierra Leone:

French brandy or rum
Iron bars
White calicoes
Sleysiger linen
Brass kettles
Earthen cans
All sorts of glass buttons
Brass rings or bracelets
Bangles and glass beads of sundry colours
Brass medals
Gunpowder
Musket balls and shot
Old sheets
Paper
Red caps
Men's shirts
Earrings
Dutch knives
Hedging bills and axes
Coarse laces
Crystal beads
Painted calicoes (red), called chintz
Oil of olive
Small duffels
Ordinary guns
Muskets and fuzils
All sorts of counterfeit pearls
Red cotton
Narrow bands of silk stuffs or worsted, about half a yard broad for women, used about their waists

In those early days it was customary to reckon the value of slaves in hides and in bars or iron. A slave was worth at Gambia from twelve to fourteen bars of iron, which is equal in value to about one-half a hogshead of brandy.

The slave trade brought to the surface the worst in

both the white and the black races.   In the slave
marts of the coast towns it was usually the worst
elements of both races that met, but it was here that
the African got his first notion of the white man's
civilisation, and it was here also that the white man
gained his first and most intimate acquaintance with
the African.

There is, I understand, a very natural and a very
widespread distrust among the Natives of the coast
towns and of the civilisation they represent.

One hears so little from the Natives themselves in
regard to this subject, or any other for that matter,
that I am tempted to quote here a statement of Miss
Kingsley which gives an insight into the way the
African mother looks upon these matters:

It is to the mass of African women, untouched by white culture,
but with an enormous influence over their sons and brothers, that
I am now referring as a factor in the dislike to the advance of
white civilisation; and I have said they do not like it because,
for one thing, they do not know it; that is to say, they do not know
it from the inside and at its best, but only from the outside.
Viewed from the outside in West Africa white civilisation, to a
shrewd mind like hers, is an evil thing for her boys and girls.   She
sees it taking away from them the restraints of their native culture,
and in all too many cases leading them into a life of dissipation,
disgrace, and decay; or, if it does not do this, yet separating the
men from their people.   .   .   .   Then again both the native
and his mother see the fearful effects of white culture on the young
women, who cannot be prevented in districts under white control from going down to the coast towns and to the devil.   It is
this that causes your West African bush chief to listen to the old
woman whom you may see crouching behind him, or you may not

see at all, but who is with him all the same, when he says, "Do not listen to the white man, it is bad for you."*

The Negro people of the country districts in the Southern states are, I suspect, much more like the masses of the Africans, who live beyond the influences of the coast towns, than any other portion of any race in the United States. As often as I can find the time to do so, I get out into the country among this class of people. I like to sleep in their houses, eat their food, attend their churches, talk with them as they plant and harvest their crops. In this way I have gotten the inspiration and material for much that I have written and much that I have had to say from time to time about the Negro in America.

In recent years I have noticed among the people, in what I have called "the country districts," a growing distrust for the city, not unlike that distrust of the Africans in the bush for the coast towns. Among the debating societies that are frequently formed among the country people, and in the churches and in the school houses, wherever the people get together, as they are fond of doing, to talk over their local affairs or discuss some abstract question, one of the favourite topics of discussion is the relative merits of the town and country. In the absence of other forms of excitement it frequently happens that a whole community will divide on some purely abstract question of this kind, and the debate

---
* "West African Studies," p. 376 et seq.

will continue for months at a time. Usually the younger people are for the city and its opportunities, but the older people are for the country and its independence.

The most self-reliant and substantial characters among my race that I know in the South are those who have been so surrounded as not to get hold of the vices and superficialities of towns and cities, but remained in the country where they lead an independent life. I have seen many of these characters who have come to our Tuskegee Negro conferences. I have in mind one man in particular, J. M. Sanifer, a farmer from Pickins County, Alabama, who comes to our Negro conference every year. The first thing that he usually exhibits when he begins to speak is a new suit of clothes. The history of this suit of clothes is interesting. The wool out of which it has been made has been grown upon the backs of sheep owned by himself and pastured on his land. The wool has been woven into cloth by his wife. The garments have been made entirely by his wife and daughters. This man takes great pride in explaining to his fellow members of the conference how he produces his own clothes, his own food, and I remember on one occasion he mentioned that during the previous twelve months he had had, except coffee, nothing in his home in the way of food that had not been produced on his farm. Mr. Sanifer has had very little of what we sometimes call "book learn-

ing," but there are some things that one learns from
the study of things as well as from the study of books.
There were some things that the African learned in
American slavery; there are some other and quite
different things the American Negro is now beginning
to learn in freedom. None of these more fundamental matters are ordinarily taught from books;
but if they are to be counted as part of what we
call education, then Mr. Sanifer is educated.

I have suggested in what I have already written
some of the reasons why the white man has not found
the black man at his best on the West Coast and
particularly in the West Coast towns. To judge
the African by what one may see in these coast towns
or by what one may see in South Africa, or in the
Nile regions of the Soudan, or wherever the native
African has come in close contact with white civilisation, is much the same as if one were to judge the
civilisation of America by what one can see in the
slums of great cities. The people who live in these
slums are, for the most part, uneducated, and have
lost many of the habits and customs that make life
decent and dignified. But few people, I dare say,
would wish to pass judgment, either on the future
of America or of the people who live in the city slums
merely from what they were able to see there during
a hurried or casual visit.

The descriptions of travellers often give one the
impression that the moral, religious, and intellectual

life of the African is a mere jumble of cruel and fantastic superstitions.   But the African religion is not a mere superstition.

"After more than forty years' residence among these tribes," says Rev. R. H. Nassau, "fluently using their language, conversant with their customs, dwelling intimately in their huts, associating with them in the varied relations of teacher, pastor, friend, master, fellow-traveller and guest, and in my special office as missionary, searching after their religious thought (and therefore being allowed a deeper entrance into their soul life than would be accorded to a passing explorer) I am able unhesitatingly to say that among all the multitude with whom I have met, I have seen or heard of none whose religious thought was only a superstition."*

In reading Dr. Nassau's book, I was impressed with the fact that Fetishism, as he defines it, is not merely a West African religion, but a West African system of thought, a general point of view and way of looking at things which enters into all the Native's ideas, and gives its colour to most of the affairs of his daily life.

This way of looking at and interpreting things so thoroughly pervades everything West African, is so different from our way of looking at things and is, as it seems to me, so important to any one who wants to get at the back of the African's mind, and find

---

* " Fetishism in West Africa," R. H. Nassau, p. 36.

something consistent in his institutions and behaviour that I am tempted to quote again here at some length from Miss Kingsley on this subject.   She says:

> One of the fundamental doctrines of Fetish is that the connection, of a certain spirit with a certain mass of matter, a material object, is not permanent; the African will point out to you a lightning-stricken tree and tell you that its spirit has been killed; he will tell you when the cooking pot has gone to bits that it has lost its spirit; if his weapon fails it is because some one has stolen or made sick its spirit by means of witchcraft.   In every action of his daily life he shows you how he lives with a great, powerful spirit-world around him.   You will see him before starting out to hunt or fight rubbing medicine into his weapons to strengthen the spirits within them, talking to them the while; telling them what care he has taken of them, reminding them of the gifts he has given them, though those gifts were hard for him to give, and begging them in the hour of his dire necessity not to fail him.   You will see him bending over the face of a river talking to its spirit with proper incantations, asking it when it meets a man who is an enemy of his to upset his canoe or drown him, or asking it to carry down with it some curse to the village below which has angered him, and in a thousand other ways he shows you what he believes if you will watch him patiently.*

The fundamental difference between the African and the European way of thinking seems to be that for the African there is no such thing as dead matter in the world.   Everything is alive, and for that reason there is no such thing as a machine, at least in the sense that we think of it.   We are inclined to look at the physical world about us as if everything that happened was turned out relentlessly by some

* "West African Studies," p. 130.

great passionless machine.   But the African thinks
that the world is alive in every part; it is a world of
spirits and persons like ourselves.

Miss Kingsley continues:

The more you know the African the more you study his laws
and institutions, the more you must recognise that the main
characteristic of his intellect is logical, and you see how in
all things he uses this absolutely sound but narrow thought-form.
He is not a dreamer or a doubter; everything is real, very
real, horridly real to him.   It is impossible for me to describe
it clearly, but the quality of the African mind is strangely
uniform.   This may seem strange to those who read accounts of
wild and awful ceremonials, or of the African's terror at the white
man's things; but I believe you will find all people experienced in
dealing with uncultured Africans will tell you that this alarm and
brief wave of curiosity is merely external, for the African knows,
the moment he has time to think it over, what the white man's thing
really is, namely, either a white man's Juju or a devil.

It is this power of being able logically to account for everything
that is, I believe, at the back of the tremendous permanency
of Fetish in Africa, and the cause of many of the relapses into it
by Africans converted to other religions; it is also the explanation
of the fact that white men living in districts where death and danger
are every-day affairs, under a grim pall of boredom, are liable to
believe in Fetish, though ashamed of so doing.[*]

African medicine, so far as it has any system at all,
is based on Fetish.   The African believes that
diseases are caused by an evil spirit, and the efficacy
of drugs depends on the benevolent spirits, which,
being put into the body, drive away the malevolent
disease-causing spirits.

"There is," says Miss Kingsley, "as in all things

---

[*] *Ibid.*, p. 124.

West African, a great deal of Fetish ceremonial mixed up with West African medical methods. Underlying them throughout there is the Fetish form of thought, but it is erroneous to believe that all West African native doctors are witch doctors, because they are not. One of my Efik friends, for example, would no more think of calling in a witch doctor for a simple case of rheumatism than you would think of calling in a curate or a barrister; he would just call in the equivalent to our consulting physician, the country doctor, the *Abiadiong*. But if he started being ill with something exhibiting cerebral symptoms he would have in the witch doctor at once."

What Miss Kingsley calls the *Abiabok* is really the village apothecary, who is also a sort of country doctor whose practice extends over a fair-sized district, wherein he travels from village to village. Big towns have resident apothecaries, and these apothecaries are learned in the properties of herbs, and they are surgeons as far as surgery is ventured upon. "A witch doctor," says Miss Kingsley, "would not dream of performing an operation."

Ex-President G. W. Gibson of Liberia, with whom I have talked, who went out to Africa as a boy, shortly after the colony was founded, speaks the native language fluently and has a long and intimate acquaintance with the native peoples, says that certain of the African methods of dealing with disease are very effective. For instance, the people in Liberia are frequently troubled with rheumatism and dropsy. For these diseases, he says, no medicines have been found equal to those of the Native doctor.

Like all the other crafts in Africa the use of drugs is a trade secret, and the native doctor has to go through a long apprenticeship before he is allowed to practise. It is not unusual, Mr. Gibson says, for some one living in the settlements, white men as well as black, to go out to those Bush doctors to obtain relief from certain kinds of disease.

Sometimes the coloured people in America, particularly those of the older generation, have had very quaint notions about medicine, but many of them, even those most ignorant of books, seem to be natural doctors or nurses. Frequently at Tuskegee a boy or girl having after been given the best care by our resident physician has remained sick for several months with few signs of recovery. Then the mother of this student would come to the institution and ask permission to take her child home for a few weeks. Notwithstanding the fact that the mother lived a long way in the country, miles from any doctor, the student would return within a few weeks in an apparently sound and healthy condition.

The methods of the witch doctor, as distinguished from the methods of the ordinary village doctor, seem to me, to a certain extent, like those of the Christian Scientist, at least in so far as he seeks to work directly on the soul and to drive out the disease by driving the idea of it out of the patient's mind. The witch doctor has to do with malevolent spirits, but as some of these malevolent spirits are human beings, his methods often take the form of a criminal proceeding, he being called in to assist in the conviction of the persons who are responsible for the disease. It is these criminal proceedings that have given the witch doctor his present bad reputation. And yet it is admitted that the witch doctors, as a rule, are very skilful in ferreting out crime.

One of the most interesting books in regard to Africa which I have been able to lay my hands on is Sarbah's "Fanti Customary Laws," a collection made by a native lawyer and member of the English bar, from cases tried under English jurisdiction in native courts. This customary law corresponds, in the life of the Fanti people, a tribe inhabiting what is known as the Gold Coast, to the common law of England, and Mr. Sarbah, in collecting it in a permanent form has performed a service for his people not unlike that of Blackstone for the English common law. Everywhere in Africa where the life of the people has not been disturbed by outside influences, the people are governed by law. There is law relating to property, to morality, to the protection of life, in fact, in many portions of Africa law is more strictly regarded than in many civilised countries.*

"No other race on a similar level of culture," says Professor Boas, "has developed as strict methods of legal procedure as the Negro has. Many of his legal forms remind us strongly of those of mediæval Europe. For instance, it is hardly a coincidence that the ordeal as a means of deciding legal cases when all other evidence fails, has been used in Europe as well as throughout Africa, while it seems to be entirely unknown in ancient America."

In looking at the social institutions of the African we must not ignore his popular assemblies that are generally held in the palaver house or in the open air. Here matters legislative as well as judicial are settled. Though there are no written laws, certain ancient customs and usages form the precedent for discussion and settlement. When a law has been agreed upon, it is customary in some of the coast tribes for a public crier to proclaim it through the town. This is repeated at dusk when all the people are supposed to be at home so that no one can plead ignorance in case the law is violated. In

---

*"Fanti Customary Laws, a brief introduction to Principles of the Native Laws and Customs of the Fanti and Akan Sections of the Gold Coast, with a Selection of Cases thereon Decided in the Law Courts," John Mensah Sarbah.

trial cases the witness takes an oath of which the following is an example:

> O God! come down, thou givest me food.
> In this case I come as a witness and I will speak.
> If I tell lies, I will go in the bush and serpent bite me;
> If I go in a canoe, the canoe will sink and I drown;
> If I climb a palm-tree I must fall and die.
> You (God) let the thunder fall and kill me.
> If I tell the truth, then I am safe in Thee.

The native African tribes, which have never been touched by the Mohammedan civilisation have, as is generally known, no written literature. Only one tribe, the Vei people who live in the hinterland of Sierra Leone and Liberia, have invented an alphabet.* But Africans are great story-tellers and, according to Leighton Wilson, they have almost any amount of "unwritten lore, in the form of fables, allegories, traditionary stories and proverbial sayings, in which is displayed no small share of close observation, lively imagination and extraordinary shrewdness of character." He describes one famous African story-teller, Toko, by name, who might have been an ancestor of Joel Chandler Harris's "Uncle Remus."

"Toko," he says, "has a very remarkable and intelligent countenance, strongly marked with the

---

* It [the Vei language] possesses a syllabic alphabet of over two hundred characters, invented in 1834 by Doalu Bukerè, a powerful member of the tribe. This writing system is even still used in correspondence and for recording family events, and in it the inventor wrote a history of his nation and a treatise on ethics.—*Africa, Élisée Reclus, Vol. III, p.* 218.

deep vein of natural humour which pervades his whole composition. He is careless in dress, unpretending in his manners, but his shrewdness and unbounded humour, almost in spite of himself, peer out at every turn in conversation. When he sets out to rehearse one of his favourite fables, all his humour is at once stirred up, and he yields himself to the spirit of the story. He is all glee himself, the hearer cannot for his life avoid being carried along with him. The wild animals of the woods are summoned before his audience, they are endowed with all the cunning and shrewdness of man and before you are aware of it, you have before your imagination a perfect drama."

Heli Chatelain, who has collected some of this unwritten literature in a volume entitled "Folk Tales of Angola," says that those who "think the Negro is deficient in philosophical faculties ignore their proverbs which both in direction and depth of meaning, equal those of any other race."

"At the bottom of patience," says one of these proverbs, "there is heaven." "Hold a true friend with both hands," says another. "Hope is the pillar of the world," and, "He is a heathen who bears malice," are others.

Perhaps the Native African, except under Mohammedan influences, has been less successful in building up and maintaining permanent and lasting governments than in other directions, but he has been more successful in this respect than is generally supposed.

Professor Boas, speaking of some Negro Central African tribes that have never come under Mohammedan influence, says:

The power of organisation that manifests itself in Negro communities is quite striking. Travellers who have visited Central Africa tell of extended kingdoms, ruled by monarchs, whose power, however, is restricted by a number of advisers. The constitution of all such states is, of course, based on the general characteristics of the social organisations of the Negro tribes, which, however, have become exceedingly complex with the extension of the domain of a single tribe over neighbouring peoples.

The Lunda empire, for instance, is a feudal state governed by a monarch. It includes a number of subordinate states, the chiefs of which are independent in all internal affairs, but who pay tribute to the emperor. The chiefs of the more distant parts of the country send caravans carrying tribute once a year, while those near by have to pay more frequently. The tribute depends upon the character of the produce of the country. It consists of ivory, salt, copper, slaves, and even, to a certain extent, of European manufactures. In case of war the subordinate chiefs have to send contingents to the army of the emperor. The succession in each of the subordinate states is regulated by local usage. Sons and other relatives of the subordinate chiefs are kept at the court of the emperor as a means of preventing disintegrations of the empire.

A female dignitary occupies an important position in the government of the state. She is considered the mother of the emperor. She has a separate court, and certain districts pay tribute to her. Both the emperor and female dignitary must be children of one of the two head wives of the preceding emperor. The emperor is elected by the four highest counsellors of the state, and his election must be confirmed by the female dignitary; while her election takes place in the same way, and she must be confirmed by the emperor. The office of counsellors of the state is hereditary. Their power is important, because four among them have the privilege of electing the emperor and the female dignitary, as described before. Besides this, there is a nobility, consisting, as it would seem, of the wealthy inhabitants, who have the privilege of expressing their opinion in regard to the affairs of the state. This empire is known to have existed since the end of the sixteenth century, although its extent and importance have probably undergone many changes. It would seem that sometimes the boundaries of the state were limited, and that at other times many tribes were subject to it. In 1880 the state was about as large as the Middle Atlantic states.

One reason for the instability of the kingdoms that have grown up and flourished from time to time on the Western Coast is, as Mr. Dowd has pointed out, that the forests and rivers cut the population into fragments and prevent coöperation.

It is interesting to note that Negro freedmen have not only established governments in Haiti in America, Liberia in Africa, but from 1630 to 1700 fugitive slaves maintained the Negro State of Palmares in what is now Brazil, against all the other slave-holding provinces of that colony. Negro slaves, imported from East Africa to become guards of palaces and fighting seamen for the Indian princes, became so powerful that they carved out states for themselves, one or more of which are still ruled by Negro princes, as dependencies of the government of India.*

Of the native states of Central Africa none have been more studied, or better known than the

* "The Colonisation of Africa," Sir Harry H. Johnston.

Kingdom of Uganda. In a recent article Mr. Winston Churchill, M. P., writes concerning the country and the people:

The Kingdom of Uganda is a fairy tale. You climb up a railway instead of a bean stalk, and at the end there is a wonderful new world. The scenery is different, the vegetation is different, and, most of all the people are different from anything elsewhere to be seen in the whole range of Africa. Instead of the breezy uplands we enter a tropical garden: in place of naked painted savages clashing their spears and gibbering in chorus to their tribal chiefs, a complete and elaborate policy is presented. Under a dynastic King, a parliament, and a powerful feudal system, an amiable, clothed, polite, and intelligent race dwell together in an organised monarchy upon the rich domain between the Victoria and Albert Lakes. More than two hundred thousand natives are able to read and write. More than one hundred thousand have embraced the Christian faith. There is a court, there are regents and ministers and nobles, there is a regular system of native law and tribunals; there is discipline, there is industry, there is culture, there is peace.

This description of conditions in Uganda strikes me as the more interesting because this progress has been made in a land where the white man cannot live. "Every white man," says Mr. Churchill, "seems to feel a sense of indefinable depression. A cut will not heal, a scratch festers. In the third year of residence even a small wound becomes a running sore. One day a man feels perfectly well; the next, for no apparent cause, he is prostrated with malaria, and with malaria of a peculiarly persistent kind, turning often in the third or fourth attack to blackwater fever. In the small European community at Entebbe there have been quite recently two suicides. Whether, as I have suggested in East Africa, it be the altitude, or the downward ray of the Equatorial sun, or the insects, or some more subtle cause there seems to be a solemn veto placed upon the white man's permanent residence in these beautiful abodes."

It has often seemed to me that, in estimating the possibilities of the Negro race, one should not overlook the extraordinary capacity of the Negro for adapting himself, whether in Africa or in America, to the conditions in which he finds himself. It is this power of fitting himself into, and adapting himself to, new conditions, which has enabled him to survive under conditions in which other peoples have perished. The Indian in the West Indies, in South America and North America, the Sandwich Islanders, the Australians and the New Zealanders have steadily receded before the advance of the white civilisation. The Negro is the only primitive people, as I have said elsewhere, which has looked the white man in the face and lived.

The Natives of South Africa are an illustration of the quality I refer to. The changes which the white man has made, during the last fifty years in South Africa, have brought enormous hardship to the native peoples. Against these changes they have frequently rebelled, but in the end, as they saw they were facing the inevitable, they have sought to adapt themselves to it. And they have not become discouraged; and they have not died out. On the contrary, they have steadily increased in numbers as the inter-tribal wars died out.

I remember some years ago meeting a young African who had come to Tuskegee as a student from the region around Johannesburg, South Africa. He had managed to save a considerable sum of money at the time of the late Boer war in South Africa, and he had made use of that money to come to America to get an education. He had not learned, at this time, to speak our language fluently, and it was with some difficulty that he expressed himself in English. I managed to get from him, however, a vivid impression of the change that had come over him and his people since the white men first invaded their country. He had grown up, he said, in the kraal, with no thought and no ambition to do otherwise, than his father had done before him — to till a little strip of land, to tend the cattle, and, as he said, "to play." In the simplicity of this life there was no thought and no care for the future, no notion that life could ever be other than it was. Looking back upon it, this seemed one long, unbroken holiday. He very well understood how crude and how aimless this savage life was likely to seem to people who lived in a higher stage of civilisation, but he made no apologies for it. He said it was "glorious"; that was his word.

But the white man came, and soon all was changed.

At first his people welcomed the strangers, for they had long been acquainted with the missionaries and liked them.   But after the discovery of gold and diamonds the white man came in ever increasing numbers, bringing with him strange customs and wonderful machinery.

At the same time came the drought and pestilence and a great war.   For the first time within his memory people began to die of hunger.   Many of the young men left their villages and went into the mines and then wandered away into the cities and never came back.   The old men were much troubled and began to sit long in council considering what was to be the future of the people and what was the best thing to do.

Out of all this unrest there has grown up among the Natives an ardent desire for education.   It is pathetic to note the earnestness with which, at the present time, these people are seeking the white man's education in order that they may fit themselves and their people for the white man's civilisation. And this desire for education, so far as I can learn, is not confined to those who live in the settlements but it has taken hold, also, of the people living in the remote regions, wherever a Christian missionary has penetrated.

Some of the African chiefs have sent their sons as students to Tuskegee and I have frequently been touched by the appeals for assistance in the way of teachers that have come to us through these students and from other sources.*

An incident quoted by Archibald Colquhoun in a recent book on South African affairs, gives some idea of the earnestness of this desire of the Natives for education.

A Native family, squatting on a Dutch Africander farm, earned between them a small sum weekly for rooting up prickly pear, the farmer's pest. Not being near any school, they paid the whole sum,

---

* As showing the widespread desire for education among these people a report of an educational meeting, which I ran across some time ago, struck me as significant. As a result of a general invitation 160 natives of note assembled December 28, 1905, at Lovedale, the seat of the first important industrial school for Natives in Africa. They came from the most populous districts of Cape Colony, from Bechuanaland, from the Orange Free State and from Basutoland. There were pastors of all denominations, chiefs of tribes sent by their headchiefs, men of influence representing no special part of the country, among them two editors of native newspapers.

This meeting was called at the instance of Dr. James Stewart, who for forty years had been the director of the Lovedale school. The commission appointed after the Boer war to investigate the condition of the natives had recommended, after two years investigation, the establishment of a university for blacks. The purpose of this meeting was to secure the carrying out of this project. Unfortunately, five days before the assembly convened Dr. Stewart died. He did not live to see the realisation of his plan, but the meeting was a success. It was announced at this meeting that if the Natives would raise $200,000 among their own people the Government would give the school an annual grant of $50,000. After two days of discussion the proposition was unanimously endorsed by the convention.

The report of this meeting makes the following comment upon the proceedings:

"A remarkable fact in regard to the action of this convention was the spirit of union that reigned. The Natives who had come together from all points of the compass, laid wholly aside their tribal jealousies and their bloody quarrels of former times. More than that the ordinary barriers which divide the sects seemed no longer to exist; the Lutherans voted with the Presbyterians, the Anglicans with the Wesleyans and the Congregationalists. Finally the Native chiefs put off their dignities and surrendered for the time being their prerogatives in order to discuss and to vote in the ranks with their subjects. The blacks who had never been able to unite for war, when the whites were killing and robbing them of their lands, were all now of one mind and purpose for establishing a great center of higher education for all the natives of South Africa."

their entire income, to a Native teacher (a half educated man from the nearest kraal) to act as tutor to their children, and they subsisted on what they could glean, or (it is to be feared) steal. When they were questioned on the subject these people were perfectly clear as to their motive, which was to give their children a better chance in the world. "In the face of such a strong demand," says Mr. Colquhoun, "it is useless to make any attempt to stop the tide of progress. If Natives cannot get the education they demand in South Africa, they can and will go to America for it."*

* "Africander Land," p. 51.

PART II

THE NEGRO AS A SLAVE

CHAPTER V

THE FIRST AND LAST SLAVE-SHIP

SOME time in August of the year 1619 a strange vessel entered the mouth of the James River, in what is now the State of Virginia, and, coming in with the tide, dropped anchor opposite the little settlement at Jamestown. This ship, which carried the Dutch flag, had the appearance of a man-of-war, but its mission, as it turned out, was peaceful enough, for its purpose was trade, and among other merchandise it carried twenty Negro slaves.

This Dutch man-of-war, which brought the first slaves to the first permanent English settlement in the new world, is, so far as the United States is concerned, the first slave-ship, for it was probably the first slave-trader to visit the North American continent.

But the twenty Africans were not the first slaves to reach what is now the territory of the United States, and the oversea African slave-trade had been in existence for a century before this time. In fact, Negro slaves were known in ancient Greece and Rome and regular accounts of the African slave trade with Europe are in existence since 990 A. D. In 1442 Portuguese ships brought back Moorish prisoners from a voyage to the Coast of Africa. As ransom the Portuguese accepted a certain amount of gold and a number of "black Moors," with curled hair. About this same time the Spanish merchants of Seville began to import gold and slaves from Western Africa. As witness to the extent of this traffic, there is still preserved an interesting letter, written in 1474 to the celebrated Negro, Juan de Valladolid, also called the "Negro Count," which not only shows that the number of these dark-skinned aliens in Spain was at that time considerable, but gives some idea, also, of the manner in which they were treated.

"For the many good, loyal, and signal services which you have done us, and do each day," the letter begins, "and because we know your sufficiency, ability, and good disposition, we constitute you mayoral and judge of all the Negroes and mulattoes, free or slaves, which are in the very loyal and noble city of Seville, and throughout the whole archbishopric thereof, and that the said Negroes and mulattoes may not hold any festivals, nor pleadings among themselves except before you, Juan de Valladolid, Negro, our judge and mayoral of the said Negroes and mulattoes.

"And we command," the letter continues, "that you, and you only, take cognisance of the disputes, pleadings, marriages, and other things which may

take place among them, for as much as you are a
person sufficient for that office and deserving of your
power, and you know the laws and ordinances which
ought to be kept, and we are informed that you are
of noble lineage among the said Negroes."* The
letter is signed Ferdinand and Isabella, King and
Queen of Spain.

When the Spanish explorers and adventurers came
to America they brought many of these Spanish
Negroes with them as servants and as slaves. It is
probable that a few Negroes were sent out to the
West Indies as early as 1501. Soon after this date,
as shown by a letter of King Ferdinand, dated September 15, 1505, a considerable number of slaves
were introduced into Santo Domingo. In this letter
the following sentence occurs: "I will send you
more Negro slaves as you request. I think there
may be a hundred." Here we have the beginning
of African slavery in America, over a century before
its introduction into Jamestown, Va.

The records show that Negroes in 1516 worked
with Balboa on the Isthmus of Panama; that Pizarro,

---

*The organization of a quasi-independent Negro state within the limits of
a larger controlling white state, the existence of which is suggested in this letter,
has a parallel, I may say in passing, in Connecticut, where a state organisation
with governor, judge and other officers formerly existed with jurisdiction over
the minor offences of slaves. In this way the slaves of Connecticut, long before
emancipation was seriously considered in the United States, were given a form of
self-government. The plan seems to have been conceived by some of the older
Negroes who exercised their office, with the consent of their masters, but also
with the authority which their age and experience exercised over the younger
members of the community.—" Economic Co-operation Among Negro Americans," Atlanta University Publications, No. 12, p. 19.

the conqueror of Peru, and Las Casas, the Dominican Bishop and missionary, had Negro bodyguards.

Negroes also accompanied the expeditions of Vasquez de Ayllon, Narvaez, Coronado and De Soto. With the ill-fated expedition of Narvaez was the Negro Estevan, in English, Stephen. For eleven years, from 1528 to the year of his death, 1539, this Negro Stephen was with the Spanish explorers on the mainland of North America. He wandered hundreds of miles across what is now the southwestern part of the United States, two centuries or more before our western frontier touched that section of the country. He was a slave of one of the survivors of the Narvaez expedition and must have been a man far above the average type. In one of the folk-tales of the Zuni Indians he lives to-day, after a lapse of more than three and a half centuries, and one well-known writer of American history has called him the discoverer of Arizona.

According to the Spanish historian, Oviedo, Negroes were among the settlers of the Spanish colony of Chicora, in 1526, on what is now the coast of South Carolina, and this, so far as known, was the earliest appearance of the black man on the soil of the United States. In 1526, when, under Vasques de Ayllon, eighty-one years before the English, the Spaniards tried to found a settlement on the James River near the present sight of Jamestown, Virginia. Negro slaves were employed in the work. An insurrection of the Negro labourer and the death of Ayllon were among the causes for the failure of the venture. African slaves accompanied the expedition of De Soto to Florida in 1539. Negro slaves were settled at St. Augustine, Florida, by Pedro Menendez, in 1565. These, however, were Spanish slaves who had been trained as artisans and cultivators of the soil and were of a different character from those fresh levies of labourers who were brought direct to America from Africa.*

Almost nothing is known of the history of the ship that brought the first slaves, in 1619, to the settlement of Jamestown; not even its name is remembered. The coincidence has often been noted, however, that the *Mayflower*, which is said to have brought to America the first seeds of civil and religious liberty, reached Plymouth a year later, 1620, so that Negro slavery is older than Anglo-Saxon liberty on the soil of the United States.

In reading the early history of the United States, I have been impressed with the fact that religious animosities among European people were largely responsible for the settlement of America.

The original thirteen states of the Union were very generally settled by refugees from the religious wars and religious persecutions of Europe, and three of them at least, Massachusetts, Pennsylvania, and Maryland, were settled by religious sects who

---

* Magazine of American History, Vol. 26, pp. 349-366.

had crossed the ocean in order to secure freedom of religious worship.

The Scotch-Irish, who so widely settled the southern colonies, left their homes in Ireland to a large degree because of the oppression that they suffered in consequence of their religious faith.

North Carolina, which was one of the first of the English colonies to grant religious liberty to the persecuted sects of Europe, was frequently referred to as a "Quaker Colony," because of the number of those persecuted people who settled there.

South Carolina was also a refuge for a large number of Huguenots, who were the Calvinists of France. As an illustration of some of the milder forms of persecution to which these people were subjected in their homes, in France, because of their religious opinions, I may quote the following paragraph, from Bancroft's History of the United States:

Huguenots were, therefore, to be employed no longer in public office; they were, as far as possible, excluded from the guilds of tradesmen and mechanics; and a Calvinist might not marry a Roman Catholic wife.*

It is a very curious fact that, at the very same time ships were leaving Europe with people who were seeking in America a solution and an escape from the religious controversies that had for centuries torn Europe asunder, other ships were leaving

* Bancroft's History of the United States, Vol. 11, p. 176.

Africa bearing to this continent other people who
were to be the seeds of new conflicts and leave, as
a heritage, a new problem; a problem in many ways
as difficult and perplexing as that which faced
Europe at the beginning of the Protestant
Reformation.

Religious prejudice, transplanted to American
soil, did not at once die out. A study of some of
the older colonial codes will show that Quakers,
who were nonconformists, and Catholics, who were
not always counted as Christians, were subjected to
restrictions which were frequently quite as severe
as those imposed upon the free Negroes before
the war. Under the law of Virginia in existence in
1705, for instance, Catholics, Indians and Negro
slaves were denied the right to appear "as witnesses
in any case whatsoever, not being Christians," but
this was modified somewhat in 1732, when Negroes,
Indians, and mulattoes were admitted as witnesses
in the trial of slaves.*

In one particular instance religious prejudice
against the Catholics was curiously associated
with prejudice, on account of race, against the Negro.
I refer to what is known in the history of New York
as the "Negro Plot of 1741."

In this year the city of New York was thrown
into convulsions of excitement by the rumours of a
conspiracy among some of the lower class of Negroes,

---

* History of the Negro Race, Williams, Vol. I., p. 129.

supposed to have been instigated by Spanish
Catholics, to burn the city and destroy the inhabitants.   These rumours were confirmed by a letter,
received about this time from General Oglethorpe
of Georgia, which reported that Spain had employed
a number of Catholic priests, who were to go through
the country pretending to be physicians, dancing
masters, "and other such kinds of occupations,"
who were to get the confidence of families and so
further the plans "to burn all the considerable
cities in English North America."

Shortly before this time a Spanish vessel, manned
in part by Spanish Negroes, had been captured
and the Negroes, although they claimed to be free,
sold into slavery in the colony.   Suspicion directed
to one of these slaves added to the excitement.
Among other persons arrested was a man supposed
to be a Catholic priest.   Circumstances seemed to
connect certain other Catholics in the colony with
the supposed conspiracy.   As usual, in such instances
of intense social commotion, fresh rumours and
fresh suspicions added fuel to the excitement and
before it had died away one hundred and seventy-
eight persons were arrested, thirty-six were executed
and seventy-one transported.   Among those executed
was the supposed Catholic priest to whom I have
referred.   Eighteen Negroes were hanged and
fourteen were burned.   They were executed in
sight of the spot where the United States Custom

House now stands in the square that still has the name of Bowling Green. It occurs to me, as I am writing this, as an illustration of the progress of the Negro, that Charles W. Anderson, the United States Collector of Internal Revenue, who occupies a suite of offices in this building is a Negro.

In spite of the numerous "confessions" of white people and black, arrested during the period that the excitement lasted, there does not seem to have been any sufficient evidence that any conspiracy to burn the city existed. The explanation seems to be that the community was for the time labouring under one of those strange social delusions, like that which seized upon the people of New England during the period of the Salem witchcraft panic. The situation, as it existed at the height of the excitement, as well as the circumstances that finally brought the prosecutions to an end, are summed up in the following paragraph from Smith's "History of New York":

The whole summer was spent in the prosecutions; every new trial led to further prosecutions: a coincidence of slight circumstances was magnified by the general terror into violent presumptions; tales collected without doors, mingling with the proofs given at the bar poisoned the minds of the jurors; and the sanguinary spirit of the day suffered no check till Mary, the capital informer, bewildered by frequent examinations and suggestions, lost her first impressions, and began to touch characters which malice itself did not dare to suspect.*

* Quoted in Williams, "History of the Negro Race," Vol. I., p. 169.

I have referred here at some length to these circumstances because they show that in times past religious prejudice, like racial prejudice, has often been the source of those wild fears and vague suspicions by which one class of people in the community is sometimes incited to violence against another and weaker class.

In spite, however, of the bitter animosities that once divided them, the people of the different religious creeds have since learned to live side by side in peace. Is there any sound reason why the white man and the black man, who, after all, understand one another here in America pretty well, should not do as much? I do not believe there is.

In 1741, at the time of the "Negro Plot," the population of New York City numbered 10,000, of which 2,000 were Negroes. At this time the number of slaves in the whole colony of Massachusetts did not amount to more than 3,000. The number in Pennsylvania had reached 11,000 in 1754, but in some of the more southerly colonies the number of slaves, particularly in proportion to the number of inhabitants was considerably larger. In South Carolina, for instance, the Negroes were at one time in the proportion of 22 to 12 of the white population.* In 1740 this state had 40,000 slaves.

---

* Bancroft's "History of the United States," Vol. II., p. 171.

In spite of restrictions that were put upon it from time to time the slave-trade continued to flourish down to the time of the American Revolution, when for a time it ceased, only to leap into more vigorous life at the close of the war. At the beginning of the nineteenth century England held in all her colonies in the new world 800,000 slaves. France had 250,000; Denmark 27,000; Spain and Portugal 600,000; Holland 50,000; Sweden 600. There were about 900,000 slaves in the United States and about 2,000,000 in Brazil.*

I was much impressed in reading some years ago Mungo Park's travels with his account of slavery as he found it in those parts of Africa which he visited. His description enabled me, as I thought, to see how easily and naturally the milder form of domestic slavery, which seems to have existed in those countries from the earliest times, had grown, under the influence of contact and commerce with European people, into foreign slave-trade. In other ways, also, it seems to me I have learned something about African slavery in America, from what I read of African slavery in Africa.

At the time of Park's famous journey he estimated that the proportion of slaves to the free population, in the regions through which he travelled, was about three to one. These slaves were of two descriptions: those who were born slaves and those

* "Suppression of the Slave Trade," DuBois, p. 131.

who had become slaves either through capture in war, insolvency, or as punishment for crime.

There existed at that time in Africa regular markets for the purchase and sale of slaves, just as they afterward existed at Alexandria, at Natchez, and New Orleans in America. Mungo Park noted, also, the interesting fact that in the eye of an African purchaser the value of a slave increased in proportion to his distance from his native kingdom, for the reason that when slaves were only a few days' journey from their homes they frequently succeeded in making their escape. On the other hand, when several kingdoms intervened, making escape more difficult, they were more easily reconciled to their situation.

The same thing was true, and for the same reason, during the existence of slavery in America. For instance, from 1820 to 1830, slaves were selling at from $150 to $300 each in Virginia, while during the same time the same slaves in New Orleans would be worth from $800 to $1,200. The difference was due, in large part, to the agricultural conditions, since at that time an able-bodied Negro could earn $200 a year for his master on a sugar plantation in Louisiana, over and above the cost of his keep. But the difference was due in a considerable degree, also, to the fact that in Louisiana the slave was, under ordinary conditions, beyond all hope of freedom.*

---

* "The Domestic Slave Trade of the Southern States," Winfield N. Collins, pp. 28 and 29.

"The slaves which are purchased by Europeans on the coast," Mungo Park continues, "are chiefly of this description" (i.e., from the interior). "A few of them are collected in petty wars, which take place near the coast, but by far the greater number are brought down in large caravans from the inland countries, of which many are unknown, even by name, to Europeans."

It was true in Africa, as it was afterward in America, that slaves of mild disposition and such as were not disposed to run away were retained by their masters, while others who showed signs of discontent or appeared in other ways intractable, were disposed of in some distant state. Thus the domestic slave-trade merged easily and naturally nto the foreign slave-trade and the intractable slaves from the interior were sent to America.

On his way back to the coast, after his long journey to the interior, Mungo Park joined company with a party of merchants on their way to the coast, having among other merchandise a coffle of slaves, which they exchanged later for European rum and tobacco.

These long marches of the slave-caravans and the methods of caring for and confining the slaves in the part of the country through which Mungo Park travelled were not unlike those which one might have seen fifty years ago on one of the old slave-roads, from Alexandria, Virginia, to Natchez, Mississippi, although the African journey was in many respects more difficult.*

In the course of this long and tedious journey from the interior of Africa to the coast, Mungo Park had an opportunity to become thoroughly acquainted with all phases of the slave-traffic, as it then existed, and he has given many intimate and interesting glimpses into the life, thoughts, and feelings of the unfortunate captives, whom he seemed to have an unusual ability to understand and sympathise with. Of one party of captives which, at one point in his journey, were added to the caravan, he said:

Eleven of them confessed to me that they had been slaves from their infancy, but the other two refused to give any account of their former condition. They were all very inquisitive, but they viewed me at first with looks of horror, and repeatedly asked if my countrymen were cannibals. They were very desirous to know what became of the slaves after they had crossed the salt water. I told them they were employed in cultivating the land; but they would not believe me, and one of them, putting his hand upon the ground, said, with great simplicity: "Have you really got

* In his history, " The Domestic Slave Trade of the Southern States," pp. 52, 101, Prof. Winfield N. Collins, of Claremont College, N. C., says:

"The number of slaves currently estimated to have been transported to the South and Southwest during 1835 and 1836 almost staggers belief. The Maryville, Tenn., *Intelligencer* made the statement in 1836 that, in 1835, 60,000 slaves passed through a Western town on their way to the Southern market. Also, in 1836 the Virginia (Wheeling) *Times* says, intelligent men estimated the number of slaves exported from Virginia during the preceding twelve months as 120,000, of whom about two-thirds were carried there by their masters, leaving 40,000 to have been sold. . . . In the transportation of slaves the utmost precautions were necessary to prevent revolt or escape. When a 'coffle' or 'drove' was formed to undertake its march of seven or eight weeks to the South the men would be chained — two by two, and a chain passing through the double file and fastening from the right and left hands of those on either side of the chain."

such ground as this to set your feet upon?" A deeply rooted idea that the whites purchase slaves for the purpose of eating them, or of selling them to others that they may be devoured hereafter, naturally makes the slave contemplate a journey toward the coast with great terror, insomuch that the 'slatees' are forced to keep them constantly in irons and watch them very closely to prevent their escape.

At another part of the journey one of the slaves belonging to the coffle, who had travelled for several days with great difficulty, was unable to travel farther and his master therefore determined to exchange him for a young girl belonging to the townspeople with whom they were stopping. "The poor girl," Park continues, "was ignorant of her fate until the bundles were all tied up in the morning, and the coffle ready to depart, when, coming with some other young women to see the coffle set out, her master took her by the hand and delivered her to the singing man. Never was a face of serenity more suddenly changed into deepest distress; the terror she manifested on having the load put upon her head and the rope fastened round her neck, and the sorrow with which she bade adieu to her companions were truly affecting."

This dread of the African slave of being sent down to the slave-markets of the coast towns is like the fear that constantly haunted the slaves in Maryland, Virginia, and the other border states, that some day they might be sold into the Far South. The most heartrending scenes of slave-life in the South

occurred when owners, on account of debt or some
other misfortune, were compelled to separate families
and sell them to the traders.   It was not alone the
parting of children from parents, husbands from
wives, that made these scenes sad and memorable, but
frequently it was just as hard for the slaves to part
from their owners and members of his family, to
which, through years of association, they had become
deeply attached.   This feeling of sorrow has found
expression in the words of an old plantation song
that originated in Virginia, the words of which
are in part as follows:

Mother is Massa goi'n to sell, sell us to-morrow?
Yes, my child! Yes, my child! Yes, my child!
Going to sell us down in Georgia?
  Yes, yes, yes,
Going to sell us way down in Georgia.
     Yes, yes, yes!
    Oh! Watch and pray!
      Fare you well mother,
      I must leave you.
      Fare you well,
      Fare you well, Mother,
      I must leave you.
      Fare you well.
      Oh! Watch and pray!

The slave-caravan, to which Mungo Park was
attached, finally reached the river Gambia, where
the slaves were set on board a ship and brought down
to the coast.   At Goree one hundred and thirty, of
whom about twenty-five had been of free condition

and were able to read and write Arabic, were shipped to America. There being no other vessel at hand, Park took passage on the slaver and followed the slaves, whom he had accompanied from the interior to their destination in America.

"My conversation with the slaves," he said, "gave them great comfort and, in truth they had need of every consolation in my power to bestow; not that I observed any wanton acts of cruelty practised either by the master or seamen toward them, but the mode of confining and securing Negroes in the American slave-ships made these poor creatures suffer greatly and a general sickness prevailed among them. Besides the three who died at Gambia, and six or eight while we remained at Goree, eleven perished at sea, and many of the survivors were reduced to a very weak and emaciated condition."

After 1808, when it became a crime to bring slaves from Africa to the United States, the conditions under which the trade was carried on grew worse. In the course of the next forty years, before the trade with the United States finally ended in 1862, it seems that every possibility of cruelty and of suffering, inherent in the traffic, was exhausted by the experience of those who were merchants and those who were merchandise in this iniquitous traffic. Of the slaves imported from the region at the mouth of the Niger it was estimated that one-third and often more perished before they reached the coast, 15

to 20 per cent. more were lost in the voyage on the
middle passage or while they were going under the
process of seasoning, so that the number of slaves
that finally found their way to the plantations did
not, in many cases, represent more than one-third
of those who were originally torn from their homes
by slave-raiders in order to meet the demand for
labour in America.*

Sometimes people, enticed down to the coast
by showing them strips of bright coloured calico,
were seized and put on board the slave-ships. In
other cases, after the slave-traders had successfully
got on board a party of slaves, they seized the
native slave-merchants themselves and carried them
off, in turn, into slavery. I have often heard Major
R. R. Moton, of Hampton, relate the story, which
was told him by his grandmother, of the manner in

---

*A writer quoted by Miss Kingsley (West African Studies, p. 511), says that a
moderate allowance for loss of life between the interior and the slave-ship would
be at least 40 per cent. This was in the region of the lower Niger, whence, according to Mr. Clarkson, the historian of the abolition of the slave trade, more slaves
were taken than from all the other slave-dealing centres of the West and
Southwest Coast of Africa.

"Death hovered always over the slave-ship," says the historian Bancroft. "The
Negroes, as they came from the higher level to the seaside — poorly fed on the
sad pilgrimage, sleeping at night on the damp earth without covering, and often
reaching the coast at unfavourable seasons — imbibed the seeds of disease, which
confinement on board ship quickened into feverish activity. There have been
examples where one-half of them — it has been said, even, where two-thirds of
them — perished on the passage. The total loss of life on the voyage is com-
puted to have been, on the average, fifteen, certainly full twelve and one-half, in
the hundred: the harbors of the West Indies proved fatal to four and one-half more
out of every hundred. No scene of wretchedness could surpass a crowded slave-
ship during a storm at sea, unless it were the same ship dismasted or suffering from
a protracted voyage and want of food, its miserable inmates tossed helplessly to
and fro under the rays of a vertical sun, vainly gasping for a drop of water.—
"History of the United States," Vol. III, p. 405.

which his great-grandfather, at that time a young African chief, was enticed on board a slave-ship and brought to America.   He had successfully brought down to the coast and sold a party of slaves which he had taken as captives in one of the tribal wars. The trade concluded he was himself invited to dinner on board the slave-ship.   He was given something to drink which put him to sleep.   When he awoke he found himself far out at sea, no longer a prince but merely one among the number of slaves he himself the day before had sold.

Some few years ago during a stay of a few days at Mobile, Alabama, I visited a little colony of Africans, who local tradition says are the remnants of the last cargo of the last slave-ship which was landed in the United States.

Mobile Bay during the latter days of the slave-trade was a favourite entrance for slave-smugglers to the United States.   At the upper entrance of the bay, where the Alabama and Tombigbee rivers pour their waters into it through a number of different channels, there are many places in which it was possible to hide a slave-ship.   It was in one of these ships, smuggled in through these channels, by which the majority of the people in the "African Colony" were brought to America.

In this community I met native Africans who still speak the old tribal language and still retain to some extent, I was told, their ancient tribal customs. I talked with one of these men who still passes by his African name. He is called Ossie Keebe. He told me his were a hill people. They lived in the uplands of Dahomey, seven days from the sea. There had been a war — there was always war in those slave-raiding days, he said — and one night their village had been captured and all who were not killed were marched down to the sea and sold.

When I asked this old man if he ever thought of returning to Africa, he replied: "Yes, I goes back to Africa every night, in my dreams." Meeting this old man whose dreams carry him back to Africa, I felt as if I had discovered the link by which the old life in Africa was connected with the new life in America.

The people I met in the African colony were not, however, the last slaves brought to the United States. The famous yacht, Wanderer, which carried 500 slaves into Georgia in 1858, is supposed to have brought 420 slaves more in 1860. But as late as 1862 a ship ran the blockade of Federal ships and landed slaves in Mobile. Far up the river in some remote part of that wilderness of swamp and water there still may be seen, I have been told, above the surface of the water portions of the iron work of the *Lawrence*, which was possibly the last ship to bring slaves into the United States. The ship was burned to keep it from falling into the hands of the

"Yankees" during the war, but there are young men in the African colony who still remember to have played about the hull when they were boys. There are still people living in Mobile who were brought over as slaves upon it in 1862.

No one will ever know how many thousands of Africans, during the progress of the slave-trade, were carried from their homes in Africa to be used as labourers in the opening up of the new and wild country in North and South America. It has been estimated that 270,000 slaves were brought into the United States between the years 1808 and 1860, from the time that the slave-trade was legally abolished to the time when it practically ceased. In view of the fact that other estimates indicate that fifteen thousand slaves were smuggled into the United States in 1858; that at another time fifteen thousand slaves were brought into Texas alone in one year, this may be taken as a low estimate.

Even this is no indication of the number of slaves that were imported during this time and before into the West Indies and into South America. South America and the West Indies, like some of the states of the Far South, were slave-consuming countries, and it was necessary to constantly bring in new levies to keep up the supply.

I have taken some pains to examine the different estimates made by different writers at different periods of the slave-trade and for different portions of North and South America, and I have reached the conclusion that the total number of slaves landed in the western world from the beginning to the end of the slave-trade cannot have been less than twelve millions, and was probably much more.

Perhaps twelve millions more were taken in the slave-raids, perished on the way to the coast or in the "middle passage," or in the process of seasoning, so that no less than twenty-four million human beings were either brought to America as slaves or perished on the way hither. I have not examined carefully the figures of European emigration, but I venture to say that from the time America was discovered down to 1860, the number of white people that have immigrated from Europe to North and South America is less than the number of black people who were brought over in slave-ships during the same period.

CHAPTER VI

THE FIRST SLAVES

URING a recent visit to Baltimore, Maryland, chance threw in my way a facsimile
copy of an old Baltimore newspaper, the
Maryland Journal, the first number of which was
published August 20, 1773. This paper contained
one or two items of news, and several advertisements
that were peculiarly interesting to me. One of these
advertisements, which attracted my attention, was
about as follows:

TEN POUNDS REWARD

RAN away, on the 6th of July laſt, from the ſubscriber, living in Bond's
forest, within eight miles of Joppa, in Baltimore County, an Irish
Servant Man, named OWEN M'CARTY, about 45 years old, 5 feet 8 inches
high, of a swarthy complexion, has long black hair, which is growing a
little grey, and a remarkable ſcar under the right eye.   He had on and
took with him when he went away, a ſhort brown coat, made of country
manufactured cloth, lined with red flannel, with metal buttons, oznabrigs
trowſers patched on both knees, a white ſhirt, an old pair of ſhoes, and an
old felt hat.   He was a ſoldier in ſome part of America about the time of
Braddock's defeat, and can give a good deſcription of the country.   Whoever takes up the ſaid Servant and brings him to Alexander Cowan, or
John Clayton, Merchants, in Joppa, or to the ſubſcriber, if he is taken in
the County, ſhall receive FIVE POUNDS, and if out of the County, the above-
mentioned TEN POUNDS, as a reward and conſideration for his trouble
and expenſe. BARNARD REILLY.

Until a short time ago the condition of bondage
had always been associated in my mind, as in the
minds of most coloured people in this country, with a
black skin. I had heard, as most schoolboys have
heard, that centuries ago there had been white slaves
in England and that in other parts of Europe slavery
and serfdom had lasted to a much later period than
in England. I remember reading somewhere the
story of Pope Gregory who, seeing some beautiful
English slaves exposed for sale in the Forum at Rome,
was so impressed by their sad condition that he determined to undertake the conversion of Britain.
These events, however, all belong to a remote past.
I never had the least idea until I began to investigate
the subject that any human being except the Indian
and the Negro had ever been bought and sold, and
in other respects treated as property in America.
The fact is, however, that, although Negro slaves were
brought to Jamestown, only twelve years after the
first settlement there, the system of white servitude
had preceded black slavery in both the Plymouth
and Virginia colony. Most of the work on the
plantations and elsewhere was performed at first by
white servants who were imported from England and
sold like other merchandise in the markets of the
colony. The historian, Bancroft, says of this matter:

Conditional servitude, under indentures or covenants, had
from the first existed in Virginia. The servant stood to his master
in the relation of a debtor, bound to discharge the cost of emigra-

tion by the entire employment of his powers for the benefit of his creditors. Oppression early ensued: men who had been transported into Virginia at the expense of eight or ten pounds, were sometimes sold for forty, fifty, or even threescore pounds. The supply of white servants became a regular business, and a class of men, nicknamed "spirits," used to delude young persons, servants, and idlers, into embarking for America, as to a land of spontaneous plenty. White servants came to be an article of traffic. They were sold in England to be transported, and in Virginia were sold to the highest bidder; like Negroes they were to be purchased on shipboard, as men buy horses at a fair. In 1672 the average price in colonies where five years of service were due, was ten pounds while a Negro was worth twenty or twenty-five pounds.*

It has often been said that the almshouses and the prisons were emptied to furnish labourers for the colonies of Virginia, South Carolina, and Georgia. But it was not merely the destitute and the outcast that were sold into servitude in the English colonies in America. Many of these persons were political prisoners and persons of quality.

"So usual," according to the same historian, "was this manner of dealing in Englishmen that not the Scots only, who were taken in the field of Dunbar, were sent into involuntary servitude in New England, but the Royalist prisoners of the battle of Worcester; the leaders in the insurrection of Penruddock were shipped to America."

At other times large numbers of Irishmen were sold into servitude in different parts of America. Because the number of slaves brought to America

---

* Bancroft's "History of the United States," Vol. I, p. 175.

was so immense, the sufferings which they under-
went has made a profound impression upon the
world, but from all that I have been able to learn, the
sufferings endured by these unfortunate Irish bond-
servants during the course of the long voyages to
America were frequently as hard as those of the
slaves. "The crowded exportation of Irish Catholics," Bancroft remarks, "was a frequent event, and
was attended by aggravations hardly inferior to the
usual atrocities of the African slave-trade."

In 1685, when nearly a thousand prisoners were
condemned to transportation for taking part in the
insurrection of Monmouth, "men of influence at
court scrambled for the convicted insurgents as a
merchantable commodity."

Bond-servitude as it existed in the English colonies
was in many respects peculiar and unlike any form
of servitude which had existed among English people.

The first bond-servants were sent out by the London
company, the company by which the Virginia colony
was founded.   It was not intended that servants
should be transferred from one master to another.
But the depressed condition of agriculture following the massacre of 1622, according to James Ballagh,
compelled planters to sell their servants and thereafter
"made the sale of servants a very common practice
among both officers and planters."

For instance, in 1623, George Sandys, the treasurer
of Virginia, was forced to sell the only remaining

servants of the company, the seven men on his plantation, for one hundred and fifty pounds of tobacco.

"Gradually," says Mr. Ballagh, "the legal personality of the servant was lost sight of in the disposition to regard him as a chattel and a part of the personal estate of the master, which might be treated and disposed of very much in the same way as the rest of the estate. He became thus rated in inventories of estates, and was disposed of both by will and deed along with the rest of the property."*

At the same time there grew up a systematic speculation in servants both in England and in Virginia. A servant could be transported to America for from six to eight pounds and sold for from forty to sixty pounds. London and Bristol were the chief markets for young men and women who were sold to shipowners who transported them to America and sold them.† The number of servants imported who were obtained in this and other ways was, from 1650 to 1675, when the trade began to decline, considerable. The number

---

* "White Servitude in the Colony of Virginia," Johns Hopkins University Studies, p. 44.

† Bristol, which was the last to give up the practice of selling bond-servants to the English colonies in America, had been six hundred years before, at the time of the Norman Conquest, the chief stronghold of the slave-trade. At that time any one who had more children or more servants than he could keep, took them to the market-place at Bristol. A historian of that time, William of Malmesbury, says that it was no uncommon thing to behold young girls exposed for sale in the Bristol market, in the days when Ireland was the greatest mart for English slaves.— Greene's "Short History of the English People," Vol. I., p. 110. "History for Ready Reference," Larned, Vol. I., p. 317.

of such white servants imported into Virginia alone from 1664 amounted to 1,500 a year. And it is said that the number sent from England to the colonies and the West Indies amounted to 15,000 a year.

It was surprising to me to learn that a little more than two hundred years ago Englishmen sold the prisoners taken in their civil wars in much the same way that the African people captured and sold people of their own race. But the knowledge of these facts has helped me to understand that when Negro slavery began in this country the condition of the African slaves was not so exceptional as it afterward became and as it now seems.

Under the conditions I have referred to, the gradual transition from white servitude to Negro slavery, which took place during the seventeenth and eighteenth centuries, came about naturally and easily. At first the condition of the Negro slave was in most respects like that of the white servant, except that one was a servant for a fixed period of years and the other was a servant for life. As time went on, however, the two things, black slavery and white servitude, began to grow apart. The condition of the white servant was continually improved, and the condition of the black slave grew steadily worse. The same thing which took place in Virginia took place in other Southern colonies. Finally, at the close of the eighteenth century Negro slavery had almost entirely replaced white servitude in all the Southern colonies.*

Speaking of the causes which brought white servitude to an end in North Carolina, Dr. John Spencer Bassett, formerly Professor of History and Political Science in Trinity College, N. C., says:

The incoming of Negro slaves, who, when the experimental stage was passed, were seen to be cheaper than the white servants, was probably the most powerful of all the causes of the decreased importation of bond-servants. The rivalry was between the whites and the blacks. The blacks won. It is impossible not to see in this an analogous process to that by which Negro slavery supplanted Indian slavery in the West Indies. The abuses connected with Indian slavery touched the conscience of the people, and the Negroes who could better stand slavery were introduced to replace it. The abuses connected with white slavery touched the hearts of the British people, and again the Negro was called in to bear the burden of the necessary labour. In each case it was a survival of the fittest. Both Indian slavery and white servitude were to go down before the black man's superior endurance, docility, and labour capacity.†

I have referred at some length to conditions of white servitude in the English colonies before the introduction of the Negro slaves in order to illustrate how easily and naturally the transition was

---

* The condition of the apprenticed servants in Virginia differed from that of slaves chiefly in the duration of their bondage, and the laws of the colony favoured their early enfranchisement. . . . Had no other form of servitude been known in Virginia than such as had been tolerated in Europe, every difficulty would have been promptly obviated by the benevolent spirit of colonial legislation. But a new problem in the history was now to be solved. For the first time the Ethiopian and the Caucasian races were to meet together in nearly equal numbers beneath a temperate zone.— Bancroft, "History of the United States," Vol. I., pp. 176, 177.

† "Slavery and Servitude in the Colony of North Carolina," Johns Hopkins University Studies, p. 77.

made from slavery in Africa to slavery in America. But I confess these facts have for me another and a different interest. It is important that the people of my race should not gain the idea that, because they were once in slavery, their situation is wholly exceptional. It is important that we should bear in mind, when we are disposed to become discouraged, that other races have had to face, at some time in their history, difficulties quite as great as ours. In America Negro slavery succeeded white servitude and it seems probable if the Negro had not been discovered and brought to this country as a labourer the system of white servitude would have lasted in this country a great deal longer than it actually did.

I was interested in noting in what I have read concerning the relations of the races at this early period that the first distinctions made between the black man and the white man were not on the ground of race and colour, but on that of religion. That is no doubt characteristic of a time when people were divided by religion rather than by race. The Negroes were "heathen," and the law distinguished between those who were Christians and those who were not. For instance, the law declared that no Christian could be made a slave for life. The white bondmen were usually referred to as "servants," or "Christian servants," and were in this way distinguished from slaves. "The right to enslave a Negro," says Professor Bassett, "seems to have been based on the fact that he was a pagan." There was a general notion throughout all Christendom that it was wrong for one Christian to enslave another, and that as soon as a pagan was baptised he could be no longer held as a slave. This prevented, for many years, the work of Christianising the Negroes. So strong was this feeling that it was necessary in several of the colonies to pass laws expressly stating that the condition of the slave was not changed when he was taken into church.*

On the other hand, as the white servant was a Christian, the principle was gradually established that he could only be held in servitude by Christians, or those "who were sure to give him Christian usage!" "Thus free Negroes, mulattoes, or Indians," says Mr. Ballagh, "although Christians, were incapacitated from holding white servants, as also were infidels, 'such as Jews, Moors, and Mohammedans.' Where a white servant was sold to them, or his owner had intermarried with them, the servant became *ipso facto* free."†

It is a curious fact that one of the first laws passed discriminating against the Negro because of his race took away from him the right to hold a white man in bondage.

In Virginia and Maryland it was one hundred and

---

* "Slavery and Servitude in the Colony of North Carolina," Johns Hopkins University Studies, p. 45 *et seq.*

† "White Servitude in the Colony of Virginia," Johns Hopkins University Studies, p. 63.

fifty years before white servitude finally gave way to Negro slavery.   In other Southern colonies, Negro slavery, introduced from the West Indies, was almost from the first the only form of labour known on the plantations.

In South Carolina an effort was made to re-estab- lish serfdom, as it had existed one hundred years before in England, and as it still existed in Europe. In Georgia it was hoped, by prohibiting slavery, to establish a system of free labour.   But in both cases the effort failed.

General Oglethorpe, the founder of Georgia, declared that slavery was "contrary to the teachings of the gospel and opposed to the fundamental law of England," and when it was proposed to introduce slavery into the colony he declared that "he declined to permit so horrid a crime."   But within fifteen years from the founding of the colony slavery was fully established there and the law against it had been repealed.

The fact seems to be that the white "servants," such as the company was able to obtain from Eng- land, were not fitted to withstand the climate.   Rev. William B. Stevens, formerly Professor of History in the University of Georgia, says that strenuous efforts were made to import white servants but "many escaped to Carolina. . . . Even the German servants so often pointed to as patterns of industry and sobriety were complained of as being 'refractory, filled with ideas of liberty and clandestinely quitting their masters', who 'were compelled to resort to corporal punishment or other summary means to bring them to obedience.'"

In one of the several documents prepared at that time, setting forth "the true state of the colony," it is said that so general was the sickness during the summer months that "hardly one-half of the servants or working people were even able to do their masters or themselves the least service; and the yearly sickness of each servant, generally speaking, cost his master as much as would have maintained a Negro for four years."

With the introduction of the rice planting the necessity of employing Africans was doubled. So difficult did the first settlers find the task of clearing the land and planting and harvesting the rice that one writer declares the "white servants would have exhausted their strength in clearing a spot for their own graves, and every plantation would have served no other purpose than a burying ground to its European cultivators."*

No doubt the black man withstood the climate, particularly in the states of the Lower South and the West Indies, and did the rough pioneer work that was required at that time better than the white man did or could. Even to-day in most of the West Indies, in many parts of South America, and in some

---

* "A True and Historical Narrative of the Colony of Georgia," p. 120.

parts of the United States, as for instance in the rich lands of the Yazoo Delta, the Negro is almost the only man who labours with his hands. But even with Negro labour the work of clearing the forests and planting the crops was carried on in those early days with great loss of life. During the whole period of slavery plantations in the West Indies, in South America, and in some parts of the United States the plantations had to be constantly recruited with fresh levies from Africa to carry on the cultivation of the soil.

After doing all this pioneer work, making it possible for other human beings to live and prosper there, one cannot wonder that the Negro thinks it a little strange that Italians and people from other parts of Europe and even Asia are invited into the South and granted privileges that even the Negro himself does not enjoy. Having performed a service so necessary and so important for the white man at a time and under circumstances such as other persons could not or would not have performed it, it is not strange if the Negro feels that, at least, the Southern people ought to deal more kindly with him than with any foreign race which, after nearly three hundred years of occupation by the white man and the black man, has just begun to enter this country.

Among the early colonists of the Carolinas were the Moravians and the Salzburgers, who were opposed to slavery upon religious grounds. These people withstood for some time the temptation to employ Negro slaves. At length, however, they received a message from the head of the church of Europe to the effect that if they took slaves with the purpose of receiving them into the church and leading them to Christ, not only was this not a sin, but it might prove a blessing.*

It is an interesting fact which I learned when I visited their community a few years ago, that the first person baptised among the Moravians of Salem, N. C., was a Negro. The Moravians of Salem are still among the black man's warmest friends. I might add that, so far as I know, the Moravian is the only religious sect whose missionaries ever voluntarily sold themselves into bondage, as did Leonard Dober and Tobias Leupoldt at San Crux in the West Indies, that they might evangelise their fellow slaves.

This desire to Christianise the African and give him the benefit of a higher civilisation was frequently, during slavery, offered as an excuse for importing African labourers to this country and holding them in slavery.

People differ, and will always differ no doubt, as to whether the desire to civilise the African was a sufficient excuse for bringing him to America, at the cost of so much suffering and expense. For my own part, I am disposed to believe that it was worth all

* "History of Georgia," Stevens, p. 312. Bancroft, Vol. III., p. 448.

that it had cost. At any rate, now that the black man is here and permanently settled in the midst of the white man's civilisation, there can be no good reason for depriving him of the benefits of being here. If any race other than the Anglo-Saxon has earned a right to live in this country and to enjoy the opportunities of American civilisation, it seems to me the Negro has earned that right.

One who has not studied the economic conditions under which the first slaves lived and laboured cannot understand the enormous service that the Negro performed for the civilisation of America during these early and pioneer days.

The Indian, both in North and South America, was pressed into the service of the white man, but he was not equal to the task and perished under the hard conditions in which he was compelled to labour.

Concerning the value of the Negro in Brazil, Heinrich Handlemann, the German historian of that country, says: "The service of the African under conditions as they then existed was, in fact, indispensable. On the other hand, the Indians, either as slaves or as free labourers, were always poor labourers, without industry and without persistence."

In Brazil, in Cuba, and in other portions of the West Indies, one Negro as a labourer was counted equal to four Indians.*

---

* " History of Slavery in Cuba, 1511–1868," Herbert H. S. Aimes.

It seems to be equally true that no part of the white race was equal to the task which the Negro performed in the forests and in the sugar, rice, and cotton fields of the far South. Repeated attempts were made to bring in white labourers to perform the work of the Negro, but without success.

In his history of Louisiana, Gayarré mentions the fact that about 1718 John Law, the author of the great speculation in Louisiana lands, agreed to bring 1,600 Germans to Louisiana and settle them on a concession of twelve miles square granted to him on the Arkansas River. Other grants were made upon the same terms. In accordance with the terms of the grant the Mississippi Company, of which Law was the head, sent out a number of German peasants, but they were soon swept away by the climate. Several different attempts of this kind were made and when they failed it was determined to bring Negroes direct from Africa. Vessels were accordingly sent out and brought back cargoes of Negro slaves, who were distributed among the inhabitants. By 1728 there were 2,600 Negroes in the colony and lands were rising in value.

Early attempts were made to introduce German labourers into some of the more tropical states of Brazil, but they "perished wholesale of famine and hardships of all kinds." In 1764, 400 exiled Acadians were settled in the region known as St. Nicholas, Haiti, but they were unable to stand the climate and were transferred to Louisiana. About the same time 2,400 Germans founded there the state of Bombardopolis, but they met the same fate. Some of them accompanied the Acadians to Louisiana, where traces of them still remain. The others who survived were soon absorbed by the black population about them and it is said that some of their descendants of mixed blood may still be found inhabiting the district.*

The history of the first attempt to settle German peasants in Louisiana reminds me of an interesting story told by George W. Cable in his book of "Strange True Stories of Louisiana." The incidents to which I refer occurred in connection with another and later German immigration, when some poor people were sent over, not as settlers, but as labourers, to Louisiana.

Some time early in the last century a shipload of these Germans arrived in New Orleans. Many of them were respectable people who had paid their own way to America. Others had been sent over with the understanding that they were to work out their passage after they reached this country. The journey was a hard one; there had been a great deal of sickness, and, as was often the case among those early immigrants, many of them had died. When they arrived in port they were sold, much after the fashion of the bond-servants of Virginia, for a period

---

* "North America," Reclus, Vol. II, p. 411.

of service. In the confusion, it is said, many of those who had paid their way and were entitled to their freedom were sold with the rest. Among these was a little girl, who had lost both her father and mother on the journey to America. She was sold as a servant, upon the landing of the ship, and years passed before her friends again got any trace of her. She was at this time a slave. She had no memory of her parents, nor of a time when she had been free. She believed herself to be a Negro and called herself a "yellow gal." Her resemblance to her mother was, however, so great that her friends began proceedings to secure her freedom, and after a long trial, lasting years, her identity was finally established and she was freed.

One thing that made it difficult to prove that she was free was the fact that at this time so many others of the slaves in Louisiana were as white as she. It was testified that the man who owned her had several other slaves upon his plantation who were white.

I mention this story here because it is one of the curious facts that have happened in connection with African slavery and because it illustrates how close the servitude of the white man brought him to the condition of the Negro slave. To a very large extent the curse of slavery rested not merely upon the African but upon every man who worked with his hands.

In the same way and to the same extent the uplifting of the Negro in the South means the uplifting of labour there; for the cause of the Negro is the cause of the man who is farthest down everywhere in the world. Educate him, give him character, and make him efficient as a labourer, and every other portion of the community will be lifted higher. Degrade the Negro, hold him in peonage, ignorance, or any other form of slavery and the great mass of the people in the community will be held down with him. It is not possible for one man to hold another man down in the ditch without staying down there with him.

VII

THE INDIAN AND THE NEGRO

SHORTLY after I went back to Hampton Institute, in 1879, to take a further course of
study, General Armstrong, the head of that
institution, decided to try the experiment of bringing
some Indian boys from the Western states and giving
them an opportunity, along with the Negro, to get
the benefits of the kind of education that Hampton
Institute was giving. He secured from the reservations something over one hundred wild, and for
the most part entirely unlettered, Indians, and then
he appointed me to take charge of these young men.
I was to live in the same building with them, look
after the discipline, take charge of their rooms, and
in general act as a sort of "house father" to them.

This was my first acquaintance with the Indians.
I do not know that I had ever seen an Indian previous
to this time, although I had read something of them
and had become greatly interested in their history.
During the few years that I was in charge of these
Indian boys I had an opportunity to study them close
at hand, and to get an insight into their characters.
At the same time I had an opportunity to compare

them, in their studies, in their deportment, and in their conduct generally, with the Negro boys by whom they were surrounded. Within a short time I noticed that, in spite of the great differences between them, each race seemed to have acquired a genuine regard and respect for the other. This is the more remarkable from the fact that the Indian, as he comes from the reservations, is very proud; feels himself superior to the white man, and is very doubtful about the value of the white man's civilisation that he has been sent to study. Of course, he naturally feels very much superior to the Negro, for one reason because he knows that the Negro has been at one time held in slavery by the white man.

At this time I had no idea of the close and intimate relations into which the Indian and the Negro had been brought at various times and in various places during the history of their life together in the Western world. The association of the Negro with the Indian has been so intimate and varied on this continent, and the similarities as well as the differences of their fortunes and character are so striking, that I am tempted to enter at some length into a discussion of the relations of each to the other, and to the white man in this country.

Recently I heard a story which illustrates to a certain extent what these relations of the three races are at the present time. The story was told me by a teacher who had in his class a certain number of Indians and an equal number of Negroes. They had been together for some time, and had managed to get pretty well acquainted with one another. One day, while the teacher was discussing with them some facts in their history in which he referred to the contribution that each of the races had made to the civilisation in this country, he called upon one of the Indians to tell the class what seemed to him the good qualities of the Negroes, as he understood them. This young Indian seemed to have discovered a number of valuable qualities in the Negro. He referred to his patience, to his aptitude for music, to his desire to learn, etc. Then the teacher called upon one of the Negro students to tell what qualities he had discovered in the Indian that he regarded as admirable and worth cultivating. He referred to his courage, to his high sense of honour, and to his pride of race. After this, the teacher called upon any one in the class to stand up and tell them in what respects he thought the white man was superior. The teacher waited for a few moments, but no member of the class rose. Then he spoke again to the class, asking them if there was no one there who was willing and able to say a word for the white race. But, to his surprise, not one of the class had a word to say.

This comparatively trivial incident illustrates, I suspect, pretty well the relations that now exist in this country between the three races — the Indian, the Negro, and the white man. One of the first things that a student of another race learns, when he begins to study the history, the literature, and the traditions of the Anglo-Saxon, is the superiority which that race has, or feels it has, over all others. No doubt these boys, both the Indian and the Negro, had been made to feel this superiority. It had led them, perhaps, to have a special interest in one another, and given each a desire to discover and note the qualities that were rare and valuable in the other. They had never learned to note the valuable qualities in the white race, because they had been made to feel that the white race did not need, and perhaps did not deserve, their sympathy. It was to me an interesting illustration of the way in which all the dark-coloured people of this country, no matter how different in disposition or in temperament they may be, are being drawn together in sympathy and interest in the presence of the prejudice of the white man against all other people of a different colour from his own.

As a matter of fact, the Negro and the Indian have been in very close and very intimate association in America from the first. The Negro was introduced as a labourer in the West Indies, in the first instance, to take the place of the native Indian, who was the first slave in America. But Indian slavery in the West Indies, South America and in North America did not by any means cease upon the first appearance of Negro slavery.   After the Spaniards had used up nearly all the native population of the islands of Cuba and Haiti, in working the mines, they sent out slave-raiders to the coasts of Florida, to the other West Indies, and to the coast of South America to get Indian slaves, particularly from the stronger Carib tribes.   During the long wars between the Spanish in Florida and the English in the Carolinas, in which Indians took part on both sides, many hundreds of Indian prisoners were shipped as slaves to the West Indies.

For a long time a price was fixed on every Indian prisoner that should be brought into Charleston and the enslavement of the Indians, according to an early historian of the colony, "was made a profitable branch of trade."   Not only were Indian slaves shipped to the West Indies but large numbers of them were sold into the New England colonies from South Carolina.   For instance, in 1708 an Indian boy brought thirty five pounds, and an Indian girl brought fifteen pounds at Salem, Massachusetts, in 1710. So large, in fact, was, at one time, this traffic in Indian slaves between the southern and the northern provinces that in 1712 a law was passed in Massachusetts prohibiting the importation of Indian servants or slaves; the reason given for this measure in the preamble to the law is the bad character of the Indian: "being of malicious, surley, and very ungovernable."   This law was directed especially against the Southern Indians, the Tuscaroras and others, of whom 800 were made prisoners as a result of a war which expelled that tribe from the Carolinas. Similar laws were passed by Pennsylvania in 1712, New Hampshire in 1714, and Connecticut and Rhode Island in 1715.*

When the French troops fought and destroyed the Natchez Indians, under Governor Perier, in 1731, forty male Indians and four hundred and fifty women and children were sent to San Domingo, where they were sold as slaves. At the close of the Pequot War in New England something like two hundred of the Indians that remained were sent to the Bermuda Islands and exchanged for Negro slaves. An extensive trade in Indian slaves was carried on for many years with the coast of Venezuela.

During all this time, for a hundred years or more, the Indian and the Negro worked side by side as slaves. In all the laws and regulations of the Colonial days the same rule which was applied to the Indian was also applied to the Negro slaves. For instance, in Bishop Spangenberg's "Journal of Travel in North Carolina," written in 1752, it is stated that the law declared "whoever marries a Negro, Indian, mulatto, or any other person of mixed blood, must pay a fine of fifty pounds." In all other regulations that were made in the earlier days for the control of the slaves, mention

* History of Slavery in Massachusetts, G. H. Moore, pp. 61, 62.

is invariably made of the Indian as well as the
Negro.

Gradually, however, as the number of Negro slaves
increased the Indians and their descendants who were
held in slavery were absorbed into and counted with
the body of the Negro slaves. I venture to say that
the amount of Indian blood in the American Negro
is very much larger than anyone who has not investigated the subject would be inclined to believe.
Very frequently I have noticed Indian features very
distinctly marked in the students who have come to
us, not only from the Southern states, but also from
Cuba, Porto Rico, and the other West Indian islands.
In some parts of South America this amalgamation
of the two dark-skinned races has gone very much
further than it has elsewhere. The Negro maroons
of Dutch and British Guiana, who have established
little republics of their own back in the mountainous
parts of those two states are very largely mixed with
Indians. Most of the inhabitants of Panama, I
understand, like some of their Central American
neighbours, are of mixed blood, the various
elements being the Spanish, Indian, and the Negro.
In some of the villages of the Atlantic coast side of the
Isthmus of Panama Negroes largely outnumber the
natives with whom they have intermingled to form
the present population. In several of the other
islands of the West Indies, where Negroes make up
nearly the whole population, there are still distinct

traces among them, of remnants of the Indian race that formerly inhabited these islands, as, for instance, in the islands of St. Vincent and Dominica.

A number of the Negroes of the United States, I might add, who have become prominent in one direction or another, are known to have Indian blood in their veins.   I have heard it said, for instance, though I do not know it to be true, that Frederick Douglass had some Indian blood.   It is pretty well known that Crispus Attucks, the leader of the Boston Massacre, was a runaway slave with considerable Indian blood in his veins.   Paul Cuffe, the noted Negro skipper, who took the first shipload of Africans back to Africa, and who therefore deserves the honour of being the first actual coloniser of Africa by American Negroes, was a man of Indian ancestry. Among the Negroes in our day who are of Indian ancestry I might mention T. Thomas Fortune, who always speaks with pride of the fact that he has in his veins the fighting blood of his Seminole ancestors.

I remember hearing Mr. Fortune say that he had in his veins Negro, Indian, and Irish blood, and that sometimes these antagonistic strains fell to warring with each other, with very interesting results.

In many other ways besides their connection with slavery, the Indian and the Negro have been brought together in this country.   In Louisiana, at different times, the Negroes fought with the white man against the Indians.   At other times, the Indians conspired

with the Negro slaves against the white man in an
effort to throw off the yoke of slavery.   In 1730 the
Chickasaw Indians conspired with some of the slaves
of New Orleans to destroy the whole white population.
The conspiracy was discovered, however, and the
leader, Samba, and seven other Negro leaders were
broken on the wheel to pay the penalty for their
crime.   In Alabama the Negroes fought with the
whites against the Indians.

One of the most interesting and picturesque chapters in the history of the warfare of the white man and
the Indian is that which relates the long struggle of
the Seminoles, who were mixed with and supported
by runaway Negroes from the plantations of Georgia
and the Carolinas, to maintain their independence
and preserve their territory.   There is a pretty well
established tradition that the famous Seminole chief
Osceola, who, for a long time, had been their faithful
friend, finally turned against the whites, because his
Negro wife, who was the daughter of a fugitive slave,
was captured and sold across the border into slavery.

In a recent account of the last of the unconquered
Seminoles, who are still living in the Everglades
of Florida, I noticed reference to an Afro-Indian,
who apparently holds a position among these people
corresponding to that of a sheriff, since he is
described as executioner of the tribe.

The Cherokee Indians of Georgia were large slave-
owners, as were also the Creek Indians of Alabama.

When, in 1838, these Indians were compelled to move westward to the Indian Territory they took a great many of their Negro slaves with them. During the Civil War the Indians of the Territory along with the white people of the South, defended their right to hold slave property, but the terms of peace freed these slaves of the Indians as they did those of the other Southern slave-holders, and since that time the freedmen have been incorporated in the different Indian nations of Indian Territory to which they belonged as slaves.

So thoroughly have the Negroes and the Indians intermingled in some of the Indian nations that in travelling through the country nearly every Indian you meet seems to be, if I may judge by my own experience, either a Negro, or a white man.

A few years ago I visited that part of Oklahoma that was formerly known as Indian Territory, and I recall my feeling of disappointment and surprise when I saw almost no Indians either at the railway stations or in the towns that I visited, whereas I had expected to see the streets thronged with them. When I asked a man I met quite casually on the street where the Indians had all gone, he replied that they "were back in the hills."

"You know," he continued, "as soon as the Indian sees a whitewashed fence he thinks it is time for him to get out. He is afraid if he stays he will get civilised."

Now this is one respect in which the Negro, largely,

I believe, because he has passed through the condition of slavery, differs from the Indian.   The Negro has learned, during his contact with the white man in slavery, not to be afraid of civilisation.   The result is that as soon as he sees a whitewashed fence he tries to get next to it.

The two races, the Indian and the Negro, have often been compared to the disadvantage of the Negro. I have frequently heard it stated that the Indian proved himself the superior race by not submitting to slavery.   As I have already pointed out, it is not exactly true that the Indian never submitted to slavery.   What is nearer the truth is that no race which has not at some time or other submitted to slavery of some kind never succeeded in reaching a higher form of civilisation.   It is just as true of the Bushmen of South Africa, as it is of the Indian, that they never submitted to slavery.   The Bushmen, like the Indian, were a hunter race that obstinately refused to adapt themselves to new conditions, and the result was that when they met a stronger people in the Kaffir, of South Africa, they were hunted off the face of the earth.   The same thing, or something like the same thing, happened in America.   At the time that the white people of New England and of the Southern states were offering a bounty for every Indian scalp they could obtain, they were sending ships across the ocean to get Negro slaves to furnish the necessary labour for opening up the country and tilling the farm.   At the time that the Indians were fighting the white man in the Ohio valley they relentlessly killed the white men they captured, and, it is said, sometimes ate them, but spared the lives of the Negro prisoners, in order to sell them to the French settlers in Canada and the Mississippi valley.*

The fact is that, so far as the Indian refused to become a slave of the white man, he deprived himself of the only method that existed at that time for getting possession of the white man's learning and the white man's civilisation.   To me it seems that the patience of the Negro, which enabled him to endure the hardships of slavery, and the natural human sympathy of the Negro, which taught him, finally, to love the white man and to gain his affection in return, was wiser, if you can speak of it in such terms, than the courage and independence of the Indian which prevented him from doing the same.

In the long run it is not those qualities which make a race picturesque and interesting, but rather those qualities which make that race useful, that fit it to survive and profit from contact with a civilisation higher than its own.   So far as I have been able to learn, the white man, as yet, has never been able to

---

* It adds something to our notion of the condition of life in the early days in this country when slavery was first established, if we recall that many of the Indians of the United States were cannibals when the white man first met them.   "For the purpose of terrifying their Indian enemies, the French commanders used to threaten to turn them over to the friendly Indians to be eaten, and they did not hesitate to carry out their threats when they wished to please their anthropophagous allies."—"Indiana: A Redemption from Slavery," J. P. Dunn, Jr., pp. 23, 24.

make the Indian of value, in any large way, in the great task of civilisation. While the Negro, in this country, at least, has steadily increased in numbers, the Indian has steadily decreased, until at the present time there are nearly ten million Negroes and less than three hundred thousand Indians in the United States. Not only has the Indian decreased in numbers, but he has been an annual tax upon the Government for food and clothing to the extent of something like $10,000,000 a year, to say nothing of the large amount spent in policing him. It has been estimated that the entire amount expended by the people of the United States is something more than a billion dollars.*

The Negro, on the contrary, for two hundred and fifty years, was brought to this country at an enormous expense, and during that time, judging, at any rate, by the prices which were paid for him, the value of

---

*The expenditure of the United States for these wards of the nation, in the fiscal year ending June 30, 1902, aggregated $10,049,584.86. From July 4, 1776, to June 30, 1890, the civil expenditures of the Government on account of the Indians aggregated a little more than $250,000,000.

The Indian wars of the United States have been more than forty in number. It is estimated that they have cost the lives of some 19,000 white men, women, and children, and of more than 30,000 Indians. The military expenditures have exceeded the civil expenditures doubtless more than four to one. It is impossible to get at thoroughly trustworty statistics, but it is estimated that something like two-thirds of the total expense of the army of the United States from 1789 to 1890, save during periods of foreign and civil wars, is directly or indirectly chargeable to the Indian account. Upon this basis, the total is more than $800,000,000. Add thereto the civil list, and we have more than a billion dollars expended on account of the Indians within a century and a quarter of our national existence. . . . A comparison of the military and the civil expenditures as above stated would indicate that it was much cheaper to support the Indian than to fight him. . . . History of the United States, Avery. Appendix, p. 361.

his services was constantly increasing. I venture to
predict that when the economic history of the Negro
comes to be written it will be found that, both in this
country and in Africa, the black man has proved himself superior as a labourer to any other people in the
same stage of civilisation.

In seeking to draw here a comparison between the
red man and my own race I do not believe it is
necessary for me to say that I am not influenced in
any way by racial prejudices against the Indian. I
think that when the first Indians were brought to
Hampton I was disposed to feel, as most of the students did at that time, that since Hampton was
established for the benefit of the Negro, the Indian
should not have been permitted to come in. But it
did not take me long, after getting in personal contact with individual Indians, to outgrow that prejudice. During the time that I had these young men
under my charge, living in intimate daily contact
with them as I did, I learned to admire the Indian.

Perhaps all of us were more kindly disposed toward
the Indians as we learned that they, like ourselves, felt
that they had suffered wrongs and had been oppressed.
In this respect the presence of the Indians at Hampton has been, I believe, a valuable experience to the
mass of the Negro students of the school. It taught
me, at any rate, that other races than the Negro had
had a hard time in this country, and that was, and is, a
valuable thing for the young men of my race to know

and understand.   Just so far as we, as a race, learn
that our trials and our difficulties are not wholly
exceptional and peculiar to ourselves; that, on the
contrary, other peoples have passed through the same
period of trials and have had to stand the same tests,
we shall cease to feel discouraged and embittered.
On the contrary, we shall learn to feel that in our
struggles to rise we are carrying the common burden
of humanity, and that only in helping others can we
really help ourselves.   It was from my contact with
the Indian, as I remember, that I first learned the
important lesson that if I permitted myself to hate
a man because of his race I was doing a greater
wrong to myself than I could possibly do to him.

What is true of the Negro in comparison with the
Indian is equally true in his comparison with any
other primitive race.   The fact seems to be, as I
have said elsewhere, that the Negro is the only race
that has been able to look the white man in the face
during any long period of years and not only live but
multiply.

So much has been said about Negro labour in
this country, and so much has been said about
Negro labour in Africa, that I feel disposed to
quote at some length here a statement of the late
Professor N. S. Shaler, formerly Dean of the
Lawrence Scientific School, of Harvard University.
Professor Shaler was not only a scientific man
of broad and deep culture, but he was also a

Southern man, and had abundant opportunity to get the facts.

Professor Shaler says:

The Negroes who came to North America had to undergo as complete a transition as ever fell to the lot of man, without the least chance to undergo an acclimatising process. They were brought from the hottest part of the earth to the region where the winter's cold is of almost arctic severity; from an exceedingly humid to a very dry air. They came to service under alien taskmasters, strange to them in speech and purpose. They had to betake themselves to unaccustomed food and to clothing such as they had never worn before. Rarely could one of the creatures find about him a familiar face or friend, parent or child, or any object that recalled his past life to him. It was an appalling change. Only those who know how the Negro cleaves to all the dear, familiar things of life, how fond he is of warmth and friendliness, can conceive the physical and mental shock that this introduction to new things meant to him. To people of our own race it would have meant death. But these wonderful folk appear to have withstood the trials of their deportation in a marvellous way. They showed no peculiar liability for disease. Their longevity or period of usefulness was not diminished, or their fecundity obviously impaired. So far as I have been able to learn, nostalgia was not a source of mortality, as it would have been with any Aryan population. The price they brought in the market, and the satisfaction of their purchasers with their qualities, show that they were from the first almost ideal labourers.

A little further on Professor Shaler compares the Indian as a labourer with the Negro, pointing out the superiority of the black over the red man in this respect. It should be remembered in this connection, however, that almost everywhere, in Africa, the Negro before coming to America had reached a higher stage of civilisation than the Indian. He already had possession of some of the fundamental industries, like agriculture and the smelting of ores, while the system of slavery existing everywhere in Africa had long accustomed large portions of the population to the habit of systematic labour.

The Indians who first met the white man on this continent do not seem to have held slaves until they first learned to do so from him. It is interesting to note also that Indian slavery, as practised by both the white man and the Indian, seems to have maintained itself among the French population in the Mississippi valley and in Canada for a considerable time after it had begun to die out in the English seaboard colonies. Speaking of the Indian, as compared with the Negro slave, Professor Shaler says:

If we compare the Algonquin Indian, in appearance a sturdy fellow, with these Negroes, we see of what stuff the blacks are made. A touch of housework and of honest toil took the breath of the aborigines away, but these tropical exotics fell to their tasks and trials far better than the men of our own kind could have done. .   .   .   Moreover, the production of good tobacco requires much care, which extends over about a year from the time the seed is planted. Some parts of the work demand a measure of judgment such as intelligent Negroes readily acquire. They are, indeed, better fitted for the task than white men, for they are commonly more interested in their tasks than whites of the labouring class. The result was that before the period of the Revolutionary War slavery was firmly established in the tobacco-planting colonies of Maryland, Virginia, and North Carolina; it was already the foundation of their only considerable industry.   .   .   .   This industry (cotton), even more than that of raising tobacco, called for abundant labour, which could be absolutely commanded and severely tasked in the season of extreme heat. For this work the Negro proved to be the only fit man, for while the whites can do this work, they prefer other employment. Thus it came about that the power of slavery in this country became rooted in its soil. The facts show that, based on an ample foundation of experience, the judgment of the Southern people was to the effect that this creature of the tropics was a better labourer in their fields than the men of their own race.

Referring to what he calls "the failure of the white man to take a larger share in the agriculture of the South," Professor Shaler says of the Negro as a farm labourer:

Much has been said about the dislike of the white man for work in association with Negroes. The failure of the white to have a larger share in the agriculture of the South has been attributed to this cause. This seems to be clearly an error. The dislike to the association of races in labour is, in the slaveholding states, less than in the North. There can be no question that if the Southern folk could have made white labourers profitable they would have preferred to employ them, for the reason that they would have required less fixed capital for their operation. The fact was and is, that the Negro is there a better labouring man in the field than the white. Under the conditions he is more enduring, more contented, and more trustworthy than the men of our own race.*

I have written at some length of the relations of the Negro and the Indian in this country because these relations are interesting in themselves and because they show how thoroughly the Negro, by uniting himself with the indigenous population of the country, has knitted himself into the life and rooted himself in the soil of America. I think I am perfectly safe in

*"Translation of our Race." Popular Science Monthly, Vol. 56, pp. 513, 524.

saying that the Negro in America has a great deal more of the blood of the original American in him than any other race on this continent, other than the native Indian himself. In fact, if we confine ourselves to certain parts of the West Indies and South America, the Negro is the only man who can still be said to represent, by inheritance of blood, the original American.

I have taken some pains to find out, as near as I was able, from the imperfect statistics at hand, the actual number of people of African descent in the Western world. Including the ten million persons of Negro blood in the United States, I believe I am safe in saying that there are in North and South America and the West Indies no less than twenty-one million descendants of the original slaves who were brought from Africa during the period of two hundred and fifty years in which the slave-trade existed.

CHAPTER VIII

THE NEGRO'S LIFE IN SLAVERY

SOME years ago one of the frequent subjects of discussion among the white people and the coloured people was the question: Who was responsible for slavery in America? Some people said the English government was the guilty party, because England would not let the colonies abolish the slave-trade when they wanted to. Others said the New England colonies were just as deep in the mire as England or the Southern states, because for many years a very large share of the trade was carried on in New England ships.

As a matter of fact there were, as near as I have been able to learn, three parties who were directly responsible for the slavery of the Negro in the United States. First of all there was the Negro himself. It should not be forgotten that it was the African who, for the most part, carried on the slave-raids by means of which his fellow African was captured and brought down to the coast for sale. When, some months ago, the Liberian embassy visited the United States, Vice-President Dossen explained to me that one reason why Liberia had made no more progress during the eighty-six years of its existence was the fact that for many years the little state had been engaged in a life-and-death struggle with native slave-traders who had been accustomed for centuries to ship their slaves from Liberian ports and were unwilling to give up the practice. It was only after the slave-trade had entirely ceased, he said, that Liberia had begun to exercise an influence upon the masses of the native peoples within its jurisdiction.

The second party to slavery was the slave-trader who, at first, as a rule, was an Englishman or a Northern white man. During the Colonial period, for instance, Newport, Rhode Island, was the principal headquarters of the slave-trade in this country. At one time Rhode Island had one hundred and fifty vessels engaged in the traffic. Down to 1860 Northern capital was very largely invested in the slave-trade, and New York was the port from which most of the American slave-smugglers fitted out.

Finally there was the Southern white man who owned and worked the bulk of the slaves, and was responsible for what we now ordinarily understand as the slave-system. It would be just as much a mistake, however, to assume that the South was ever solidly in favour of slavery as it is to assume that the North was always solidly against it. Thousands of persons in the Southern states were opposed to slavery, and numbers of them, like James G. Birney, of Alabama, took their slaves North in order to free them, and afterward became leaders in the anti-slavery struggle.

Like every other human thing, there is more than one side to slavery and more than one way of looking at it. For instance, as defined in the slave-laws in what was known as the Slave Code, slavery was pretty much the same at all times all over the South. The regulations imposed upon master and upon slave were, in several particulars, different for the different states. On the whole, however, as a legal institution, slavery was the same everywhere.

On the other hand, actual conditions were not only different in every part of the country, but they were likely to be different on every separate plantation. Every plantation was, to a certain extent, a little kingdom by itself, and life there was what the people who were bound together in the plantation community made it. The law and the custom of the neighbourhood regulated, to a certain extent, the treatment which the master gave his slave. For instance, in the part of Virginia where I lived both white people and coloured people looked with contempt upon the man who had the reputation of not giving his slaves enough to eat. If a slave went to an adjoining plantation for something to eat, the reputation of his master was damned in that

community. On the whole, however, each plantation was a little independent state, and one master
was very little disposed to interfere with the affairs
of another.

The account that one gets of slavery from the
laws that were passed for the government of slaves
show that institution up on its worst side. No
harsher judgment was ever passed on slavery, so
far as I know, than that which will be found in the
decision of a justice of the Supreme Court of
North Carolina in summing up the law in a case
in which the relations of master and slave were
defined.

The case I refer to, which was tried in 1829, was
one in which the master, who was the defendant,
was indicted for beating his slave. The decision,
which acquitted him, affirmed the master's right
to inflict any kind of punishment upon his slave
short of death. The grounds upon which this
judgment was based were that in the whole history
of slavery there had been no such prosecution of a
master for punishing a slave, and, in the words of
the decision, "against this general opinion in the
community the court could not hold."

It was a mistake, the decision continued, to say
that the relations of the master and slave were
like that of a parent and child. The object of
the parent in training his son was to render him fit
to live the life of a free man, and, as a means to

that end, he gave him moral and intellectual instruction. With the case of the slave it was different. There could be no sense in addressing moral considerations to a slave. Chief-Justice Ruffin, of North Carolina, summed up his opinion upon this point in these words:

The end is the profit of the master, his security, and the public safety; the subject, one doomed in his own person and his posterity to live without knowledge and without the capacity to make anything his own, and to toil that another may reap the fruits. What moral consideration shall be addressed to such a being to convince him, what it is impossible but that the most stupid must feel and know can never be true — that he is thus to labour upon a principle of natural duty, or for the sake of his own personal happiness. Such services can only be expected from one who has no will of his own, who surrenders his will in implicit obedience to that of another. Such obedience is the consequence only of uncontrolled authority over the body. There is nothing else which can operate to produce the effect. The power of the master must be absolute to render the submission of the slave perfect.

In making this decision Justice Ruffin did not attempt to justify the rule he had laid down on moral grounds. "As a principle of right," he said, "every person in his retirement must repudiate it. But in the actual condition of things it must be so; there is no remedy. This discipline belongs to the state of slavery. It constitutes the curse of slavery both to the bond and free portion of our population."*

This decision brings out into plain view an idea that

* "Slavery in the State of North Carolina," John Spencer Bassett.

was always somewhere at the bottom of slavery —
the idea, namely, that one man's evil is another
man's good. The history of slavery, if it proves anything, proves that just the opposite is true, namely,
that evil breeds evil, just as disease breeds disease,
and that a wrong committed upon one portion of a
community will, in the long run, surely react upon
the other portion of that community.

There was a very great difference between the
life of the slave on the small plantations in the
uplands and upon the big plantations along the
coasts. To illustrate, the plantation upon which I
was born, in Franklin County, Va., had, as I remember, only six slaves. My master and his sons all
worked together side by side with his slaves. In
this way we all grew up together, very much
like members of one big family. There was no
overseer, and we got to know our master and he
to know us. The big plantations along the
coasts were usually carried on under the direction of an overseer. The master and his
family were away for a large part of the year.
Personal relation between them could hardly be
said to exist.

John C. Calhoun, South Carolina's greatest
statesman, was brought up on a plantation not very
much different from the one upon which I was
raised. One of his biographers relates how Patrick
Calhoun, John C. Calhoun's father, returning from

his legislative duties in Charleston, brought home on horseback behind him a young African freshly imported in some English or New England vessel. The children in the neighbourhood and, no doubt, some of the older people, had never before seen a black man.   He was the first one brought into that part of the country.   Patrick Calhoun gave him the name of Adam.   Some time later he got for him a wife.   One of the children of the black man, Adam, was named Swaney.   He grew up on the planta-tion with John C. Calhoun, and was for many years his playmate.   Swaney lived to a great age, and in after years used to be fond of talking about the early years that he and John Calhoun had spent together. They hunted and fished together, and worked together in the fields.

"We worked in the field," Swaney is reported to have said, "and many a time in the hot brilin' sun me and Marse John has ploughed together."

I have taken these facts from an account of Cal-houn's early life by Colonel W. Pinkney Stark, who has given, besides, a very excellent account of the institution of slavery as it existed in the early days in that part of the country in which he lived.   At that time and in that part of the country the planter worked his own plantation.   The overseer did not come in until later, and Colonel Stark believes that "whatever was most harsh in the institution of

slavery was due to the rise of this middleman."
He says:

Not far from the Calhoun settlement lived a man who had
ridden with Sumter in the old war for liberty. During a long
and active life he managed the business of the plantation himself.
Toward the close of his life he consented to try an overseer, but
in every case some difficulty soon arose between the middleman
and the Negroes, in which the old planter invariably took sides
with the latter and rid himself of the proxy. On rainy days
the Negro women spun raw cotton into yarn, which was woven
by his own weaver into summer goods, to be cut by a seamstress,
and made by the other women, assisted by her, into clothing for
the "people." The sheep were shorn and the wool treated in
the same fashion for winter clothing. The hides of cattle eaten on
the place were tanned into leather and made into shoes by his own
shoemaker. He had his own carpenters, wheelwrights, and blacksmiths, and besides cattle and sheep the old planter raised his own
stock of horses and mules. He grew his own wheat for flour,
besides raising other small grain, corn, and cotton. He distilled
his own brandy from peaches and sweetened it with honey manufactured by his home bees. His Negroes were well fed and clothed,
carefully attended to in sickness, virtually free in old age, and
supported in comfort till their death. The moral law against
adultery was sternly enforced, and no divorce allowed. His
people were encouraged to enjoy themselves in all reasonable
ways. They went to a Methodist church in the neighbourhood
on Sunday, and had besides a preacher of their own, raised on the
place. The young people were supplied with necessary fiddling
and dancing. I was present when he died, and heard him say
to his son that he would leave him a property honestly made and not
burdened with a dollar indebtedness. His family and friends
gathered about his bedside when the time had come for him to
go. Having taken leave of his friends, he ordered his Negro
labourers to be summoned from the field to take farewell of him.
When they arrived he was speechless and motionless, but sensible
of all that was occurring, as could be seen from his look of intelli-

gence. One by one the Negroes entered the apartment, and filing by him in succession took each in turn the limp hand of their dying master, and affectionately pressing it for a moment, thanked him for his goodness, commended him to God, and bade him farewell.

The faithful discharge of the duties of the proprietor of a plantation in former times demanded administrative as well as moral qualities of a high order. There was never a better school for the education of statesmen than the administration of a Southern plantation under the former régime. A well-governed plantation was a well-ordered little independent state. Surrounded with such environments, Calhoun grew at this school.*

The conditions of the Negro slave were harder on some of the big plantations in the Far South than they were elsewhere. That region was peopled by an enterprising class of persons, of whom many came from Virginia, bringing their slaves with them. The soil was rich, the planters were making money fast, the country was rough and unsettled, and there was undoubtedly a disposition to treat the slaves as mere factors in the production of corn, cotton, and sugar.†

---

*American Historical Assn. Report, Vol. II., 1899, p. 74 et seq.

† That the Negroes were overtasked to the extent of being often permanently injured, was evident from the complaints made by the Southern agricultural journals against the bad policy of thus wasting human property. An Alabama tradesman told Olmsted that if the overseers make "plenty of cotton, the owners never ask how many niggers they kill"; and he gave the further information that a determined and perfectly relentless overseer could get almost any wages he demanded, for when it became known that such a man had so many bales to the hand, everybody would try to get him.   .   .   .

Louisiana sugar-planters did not hesitate to avow openly that, on the whole, they found it the best economy to work off their stock of Negroes about once in seven years, and then buy an entire set of new hands.—"History of the United States," James Ford Rhodes, Vol. I., p. 308.

And yet there were plantations in this region where the relations between master and slave seem to have been as happy as one could ask or expect under the circumstances. On some of the large estates in Alabama and Mississippi which were far removed from the influence of the city, and sometimes in the midst of a wilderness, master and slaves frequently lived together under conditions that were genuinely patriarchal. But on such plantations there was, as a rule, no overseer.

As an example of the large plantations on which the relations between master and slave were normal and happy I might mention those of the former President of the Confederacy, Jefferson Davis, and his brother, Joseph Davis, in Warren County, Mississippi.

The history of the Davis family and of the way in which their plantations, the "Hurricane" and "Brierfield," came into existence is typical. The ancestors of the President of the Confederacy came originally from Wales. They settled first in Georgia, emigrated thence to Kentucky, and finally settled in the rich lands of Mississippi. In 1818 Joseph Davis, who was at that time a lawyer in Vicksburg, attracted by the rich bottom-lands along the Mississippi, took his father's slaves and went down the river, thirty-six miles below Vicksburg, to the place which is now called "Davis's Bend."

There he began clearing the land and preparing it for cultivation.

At that time there were no steamboats on the Mississippi River, and the country was so wild that people travelled through the lonely forests mostly on horseback. In the course of a few years Mr. Davis, with the aid of his slaves, succeeded in building up a plantation of about five thousand acres, and became, before his death, a very wealthy man. One day he went down to Natchez and purchased in the market there a young Negro who afterward became known as Ben Montgomery. This young man had been sold South from North Carolina, and because, perhaps, he had heard, as most of the slaves had, of the hard treatment that was to be expected on the big, lonesome plantations, had made up his mind to remain in the city. The first thing he did, therefore, when Mr. Davis brought him home, was to run away. Mr. Davis succeeded in getting hold of him again, brought him back to the plantation, and then, as Isaiah, Benjamin Montgomery's son, has told me, Mr. Davis "came to an understanding" with his young slave.

Just what that understanding was no one seems now to know exactly, but in any case, as a result of it, Benjamin Montgomery received a pretty fair education, sufficient, at any rate, to enable him in after years, when he came to have entire charge, as he soon did, of Mr. Davis's plantation, to survey the line of the levee which was erected to protect the plantation from the waters of the Mississippi, to draw out plans, and to compute the size of buildings, a number of which were erected at different times under his direction.

Mrs. Jefferson Davis, in her memoir of her husband, referring to Benjamin Montgomery and to the manner in which Joseph Davis conducted his plantation, says:

A maxim of Joseph E. Davis was: "The less people are governed, the more submissive they will be to control." This idea he carried out with his family and with his slaves. He instituted trial by jury of their peers, and taught them the legal form of holding it. His only share in the jurisdiction was the pardoning power. When his slave could do better for himself than by daily labour he was at liberty to do so, giving either in money or other equivalent the worth of ordinary field service. One of his slaves kept a variety shop, and on many occasions the family bought of him at his own prices. He shipped, and indeed sometimes purchased, the fruit crops of the Davis families, and also of other people in "The Bend," and in one instance credited one of us with $2,000 on his account. The bills were presented by him with promptitude and paid, as were those of others on an independent footing, without delay. He many times borrowed from his master, but was equally as exact in his dealings with his creditors. His sons, Thornton and Isaiah, first learned to work, and then were carefully taught by their father to read, write, and cipher, and now Ben Montgomery's sons are both responsible men of property; one is in business in Vicksburg, and the other is a thriving farmer in the West.

Some years after the settlement on the bottomlands at Davis's Bend had been made, Mr. Jefferson Davis joined his brother and lived for several years upon an adjoining plantation. The two brothers had much the same ideas about the management of their slaves. Both of them took personal supervision of their estates, and Jefferson Davis, like his brother, had a coloured man to whom he refers as his "friend and servant, James Pemberton," who, until he died, seems to have had practically the whole charge of the Brierfield plantation in the same way that Benjamin Montgomery had charge of the Hurricane. After the war both of these plantations were sold for the sum of $300,000 to Benjamin Montgomery and his sons, who conducted them for a number of years until, as a result of floods and the low price of cotton, they were compelled to give them up.

Thornton Montgomery afterward moved to North Dakota, where for a number of years he owned and conducted a large wheat farm of 640 acres near Fargo. His brother Isaiah afterward founded the Negro town of Mound Bayou, Miss., of which I shall have more to say hereafter.

As illustrating the kindly relations and good will which continued to exist between the ex-President of the Confederacy, Jefferson Davis, and his former slaves, both during the years that they lived together on the plantation and afterward, Mrs. Davis has printed several letters written to her by them after Mr. Davis's death. The following letter was written by Thornton Montgomery, who is at present associated with his brother, Isaiah, in business at Mound Bayou.

CHRISTINE, NORTH DAKOTA, December 7, 1889.

MISS VARINA: I have watched with deep interest and solicitude the illness of Mr. Davis at Brierfield, his trip down on the steamer *Leathers*, and your meeting and returning with him to the residence of Mr. Payne, in New Orleans; and I had hoped with good nursing and superior medical skill, together with his great will-power to sustain him, he will recover. But, alas! for human endeavour, an over-ruling Providence has willed it otherwise. I appreciate your great loss, and my heart goes out to you in this hour of your deepest affliction.

Would that I could help you bear the burden that is yours to-day. Since I am powerless to do so, I beg that you accept my tenderest sympathy and condolence.

Your very obedient servant,

THORNTON.

To Mrs. Jefferson Davis, Beauvoir, Mississippi.*

From all that I have been able to learn, the early slaves, and by these I mean the first generation which were brought to America fresh from Africa, seem to have remained more or less alien in customs and sympathy to their white masters. This was more particularly the case on the large plantations along the Carolina coast, where the slaves came very little in contact with their masters, and remained to a very large degree and for a considerable time merely an African colony on American soil.

But the later generations, those who knew Africa only by tradition, were different. Each succeeding

---

* "Jefferson Davis, Ex-President of the Confederate States," A memoir by his wife, Vol. II., p. 934.

generation of the Creole Negroes — to use the expression in its original meaning — managed to pick up more and more, as it had the opportunity, the language, the ideas, the habits, the crafts, and the religious conceptions of the white man, until the life of the black man was wholly absorbed into that of the plantation upon which he lived.

The Negro in exile from his native land neither pined away nor grew bitter. On the contrary, as soon as he was able to adjust himself to the conditions of his new life, his naturally cheerful and affectionate disposition began to assert itself. Gradually the natural human sympathies of the African began to take root in the soil of the New World and, growing up spontaneously, twine about the life of the white man by whose side the black man now found himself. The slave soon learned to love the children of his master, and they loved him in return. The quaint humour of the Negro helped to turn many a hard corner. It helped to excuse his mistakes and, by turning a reproof into a jest, to soften the resentment of his master for his faults.

Quaint and homely tales that were told around the fireside made the Negro cabin a place of romantic interest to the master's children. The simple, natural joy of the Negro in little things converted every change in the dull routine of his life into an event. Hog-killing time was an annual festival, and the corn shucking was a joyous event which the whites and blacks, in their respective ways, took part in and enjoyed. These corn-shucking bees, or whatever they may be called, took place during the last of November or the first half of December. They were a sort of a prelude to the festivities of the Christmas season. Usually they were held upon one of the larger and wealthier plantations.

After all the corn had been gathered, thousands of bushels, sometimes, it would be piled up in the shape of a mound, often to the height of fifty or sixty feet. Invitations would be sent around by the master himself to the neighbouring planters, inviting their slaves on a certain night to attend. In response to these invitations as many as one or two hundred men, women, and children would come together.

When all were assembled around the pile of corn, some one individual, who had already gained a reputation as a leader in singing, would climb on top of the mound and begin at once, in clear, loud tones, a solo — a song of the corn-shucking season — a kind of singing which I am sorry to say has very largely passed from memory and practice. After leading off in this way, in clear, distinct tones, the chorus at the base of the mound would join in, some hundred voices strong. The words, which were largely improvised, were very simple and suited to the occasion, and more often than not they had the flavour of the camp-meeting rather than any more secular proceeding. Such singing I have never heard on any other occasion. There was something wild and weird about that music, such as I suspect will never again be heard in America.

One of these songs, as I remember, ran about as follows:

I.

Massa's niggers am slick and fat,
  Oh! Oh! Oh!
Shine just like a new beaver hat,
  Oh! Oh! Oh!

REFRAIN:

Turn out here and shuck dis corn,
  Oh! Oh! Oh!
Biggest pile o' corn seen since I was born,
  Oh! Oh! Oh!

II.

Jones's niggers am lean an' po';
  Oh! Oh! Oh!
Don't know whether dey get 'nough to eat or no,
  Oh! Oh! Oh!

REFRAIN:

Turn out here and shuck dis corn,
  Oh! Oh! Oh!
Biggest pile o' corn seen since I was born,
  Oh! Oh! Oh!

Little by little the slave songs, the quaint stories, sayings, and anecdotes of the slave's life began to give their quality to the life of the plantation. Half the homely charm of Southern life was made by the presence of a Negro. The homes that had no Negro servants were dreary by contrast, and that was not due to the fact that, ordinarily, the man who had slaves was rich and the man who had no slaves was poor.

The four great crops of the South — tobacco, rice, sugar, and cotton — were all raised by slave labour. In the early days it was thought that no labour except that of the Negro was suited to cultivate these great staples of Southern industry, and that opinion prevails pretty widely still. But it was not merely his quality as a labourer that made the Negro seem so necessary to the white man in the South; it was also these other qualities to which I have referred — his cheerfulness and sympathy, his humour and his fidelity. No one can honestly say that there was anything in the nature of the institution of slavery that would develop these qualities in a people who did not possess them. On the contrary, what we know about slavery elsewhere leads us to believe that the system would have developed qualities quite different, so that I think I am justified in saying that most of the things that made slavery tolerable, both to the white man and to the black man, were due to the native qualities of the African.

Southern writers, looking back and seeking to reproduce the genial warmth and gracious charm of that old ante-bellum Southern life, have not failed to do full justice to the part that the Negro played in it. The late Joel Chandler Harris, for instance, has given us in the character of "Uncle Remus" the type of the Negro story-teller who delights and instructs the young children of the "big house" with his quaint animal stories that have been handed down to the Negro by his African ancestors. The "Br'er Rabbit" stories of Uncle Remus are now a lasting element in the literature, not only of the South, but of America, and they are recognised as the peculiar contribution of the American Negro slave to the folk-lore stories of the world.

In my own state of Virginia, Mr. Thomas Nelson Page has given us, in "Uncle Billy" and "Uncle Sam," two typical characters worthy of study by those who wish to understand the human side of the Negro slave on the aristocratic plantations of that state.   In Mr. Page's story, "Meh Lady," Uncle Billy was guide, philosopher and friend to his mistress and her daughter in the trying times of war and in their days of poverty.   He hid their silver, refused to give information to the Union soldiers, prayed the last prayer with his dying mistress, comforted her lonely daughter, and at last gave her away in marriage.   At the close of the wedding, the old man sits in front of his cabin door and thinks again of the old days.   The musings of Uncle Billy Mr. Page tells in the following quaint dialect:

An' dat night when de preacher was gone wid he wife, and Hannah done drapt off to sleep, I wuz settin' in de do' wid meh pipe, an' I heah 'em setting dyah on de front steps, dee voices soun'in' low like bees, an' moon sort o' meltin' over de yard, an' I sort o' got to studyin', an' hit 'pear like de plantation 'live once mo', an' de ain' no mo' scufflin', an' de ole times done come back ag'in, an' I heah meh kerridge-horses stompin' in de stall, an' de place all cleared up again, an' fence all roun' de pahsture, an' I smell de wet clover blossoms right good, and Marse Phil and Meh Lady done come back, an' running all roun' me, climbing up on meh knees, calling me Unc Billy, an' pestering me to go fishing while somehow Meh Lady and de Cun'l, setting dyah on de steps wid de voices hummin' low like water runnin' in the dark.

In the story of "Marse Chan" Mr. Page lets Uncle Sam, the slave bodyguard, tell in the following language what happened to his young master during the Civil War on the field of battle:

Marse Chan he calls me, an he sez, "Sam, we 'se goin to win in dis battle, an den we 'll go home an' git married; an' I 'm goin' home wid a star on my collar." An' den he sez, "Ef I'm wounded, kyah me, yo' hear?" An' I sez, "Yes, Marse Chan." Well, jes' den dey blowed boots an' saddles an' we mounted — an' dey said, "Charge 'em," an' my King ef ever yo' see bullets fly, dey did dat day. . . . We wen' down de slope, I 'long wid de res' an' up de hill right to de cannons, an' de fire wuz so strong dyah our lines sort o' broke an' stop; an' de cun'l was kilt, an' I b'lieve dey wuz jes' 'bout to break all to pieces wen Marse Chan rid up an' cotch holt de flag and hollers, "Follow me." . . . Yo' ain' never heah thunder. Fust thing I knowed de Roan roll head over heels an' flung me up 'gainst de bank like yo' chuck a nubbin over g'inst de foot o' de corn pile.

An' dat what kep me from being kilt I 'spects. When I look 'roun' de Roan was lying dyah stone dead. 'Twan' mo'n a minit, de sorrel come gallupin' back wid his mane flying and de rein hangin' down on one side to his knee. I jumped up an' run over de bank an' dyah, wid a whole lot ob dead mens and some not dead yit, on de one side o' de guns wid de flag still in he han' an' a bullet right thru' he body, lay Marse Chan. I tu'n 'im over an' call 'im, "Marse Chan," but twan' no use. He wuz done gone home. I pick him up in my arms wid de flag still in he han' and toted 'im back jes' like I did dat day when he wuz a baby an' ole master gin 'im to me in my arms, an' say he could trus' me, an' tell me to tek keer on 'im long as he lived. I kyah'd 'im way off de battle-fiel' out de way o' de balls an' I laid 'im down under a big tree till I could git somebody to ketch de sorrel for me. He was kotched arter a while an' I hed some money, so I got some pine plank an' made a coffin dat evenin' an' wrap Marse Chan's body up in de flag an' put 'im in de coffin, but I did n't nail de top on strong, 'cause I knowed de old missus wan' to see 'im; an' I got a' ambulance an' set out fo' home dat night. We reached dyah de nex' evenin' arter travellin' all dat night an' all nex' day.

In the Palace of Fine Arts in St. Louis during the Exposition of 1904, there was a picture which made a deep impression on every Southern white man and black man who saw it, who knew enough of the old life to understand what it meant. Rev. A. B. Curry, of Memphis, Tenn., referring to this picture in a sermon in his home city on November 27, 1904, said:

When I was in the Palace of Fine Arts in St. Louis this summer, I saw a picture before which I stood and wept. In the distance was a battle scene; the dust of trampling men and horses, the smoke of cannon and rifles filled the air; broken carriages and dead and dying men strewed the ground. In the foreground was the figure of a stalwart Negro man, bearing in his strong arms the form of a fair-haired Anglo-Saxon youth. It was the devoted body-servant of a young Southerner, bearing the dead body of his young master from the field of carnage, not to pause or rest till he had delivered it to those whose love for it only surpassed his own; and underneath the picture were these words: "Faithful Unto Death"; and there are men before me who have seen the spirit of that picture on more than one field of battle.

The slaves in Virginia and the border states were, as a rule, far superior, or at least they considered themselves so, to the slaves of the lower South. Even in freedom this feeling of superiority remains. Furthermore, the mansion house-servants, of whom Mr. Page writes, having had an opportunity to share to a large extent the daily life of their masters, were very proud of their superior position and advantages, and had little contact with the field-hands. It is perhaps not generally understood that in slavery days lines were drawn among the slaves just as they were among the white people. The servants owned by a rich and aristocratic family considered that the servants of "a poor white man," one who was not able to own more than half a dozen slaves, were not in the same social class with themselves. And yet the life of these more despised slaves had its vicissitudes, its obscure heroisms, and its tragedies just like the rest of the world. In fact, it was from the plantation hands, as a rule, that the most precious records of slave-life came — the plantation hymns. The field-hands sung these songs and they expressed their lives.

I have frequently met and talked with old men of my race who have grown up in slavery. It is difficult for these old men to express all that they feel. Occasionally, however, they will utter some quaint humorous turn of expression in which there is a serious thought underneath.

One old farmer, who owns a thousand acres of land not far from Tuskegee, said: "We's jes' so ign't out heah, we don' see no diff'rence 'twe'n freedom an' slav'ry, 'cept den we's workin' fer someone else, and now we's workin' fer oursel's."

Some time ago an old coloured man who has lived for a number of years near the Tuskegee Institute, in talking about his experience since freedom, remarked that the greatest difference he had found between slavery and freedom was that in the days of slavery his master had to think for him, but since he had been free he had to think and plan for himself.

At another time out in Kansas I met an old coloured woman who had left her home in Tennessee, directly after the war, and settled with a large number of other coloured people in what is called "Tennessee Town," now a suburb of Topeka, Kansas. In talking with her about her experiences in freedom and in slavery, I asked her if she did not sometimes feel as if she would like to go back to the old days and live as she had lived on the plantation.

"Sometimes," she replied, "I feel as I'd like to go back and see my old massa and missus"—she hesitated a moment and then added, "but they sold my baby down South."

Aside from the slave-songs very little has come down to us from slavery days that shows how slavery looked to the masses of the people.

There are a considerable number of slave narratives, written by fugitive slaves with the assistance of abolitionist friends, but as these were composed for the most part under the excitement of the anti-slavery agitation they show things, as a rule, somewhat out of proportion. There is one of these stories, however, that gives a picture of the changing fortunes and vicissitudes of slave-life which makes it especially interesting. I refer to the story of Charity Bower, who was born in 1779 near Edenton, North Carolina, and lived to a considerable age after she obtained her freedom. She described her master as very kind to his slaves. He used to whip them, sometimes, with a hickory switch, she said, but never let his overseer do so. Continuing, she said:

My mother nursed all his children. She was reckoned a very good servant, and our mistress made it a point to give one of my mother's children to each one of her own. I fell to the lot of Elizabeth, the second daughter. Oh, my mistress was a kind woman. She was all the same as a mother to poor Charity. If Charity wanted to learn to spin, she let her learn; if Charity wanted to learn to knit, she let her learn; if Charity wanted to learn to weave, she let her learn. I had a wedding when I was married, for mistress did n't like to have her people take up with one another without any minister to marry them. . . . My husband was a nice, good man, and mistress knew we set stores by one another. Her children promised they never would separate me from my husband and children. Indeed, they used to tell me they would never sell me at all, and I am sure they meant what they said. But my young master got into trouble. He used to come home and sit leaning his head on his hands by the hour together, without speaking to anybody. I see something was the matter, and begged him to tell me what made him look so worried. He told me he owed seventeen hundred dollars that he could not pay, and he was afraid he should have to go to prison. I begged him to sell me and my children, rather than to go to jail. I see the tears come into his eyes. "I don't know, Charity," he said; "I 'll see what can be done. One thing you may feel easy about: I will never separate you from your husband and children, let what will come."

Two or three days after he come to me, and says he: "Charity, how should you like to be sold to Mr. Kinmore?" I told him I would rather be sold to him than to anybody else, because my husband belonged to him. Mr. Kinmore agreed to buy us, and so I and my children went there to live.

Shortly after this her new master died and her new mistress was not so kind to her as he had been. Thereupon she set to work to buy the freedom of her children.

"Sixteen children I 've had, first and last," she said, "and twelve I 've nursed for my mistress. From the time my first baby was born, I always set my heart upon buying freedom for some of my children. I thought it was more consequence to them than to me, for I was old and used to being a slave."

In order to save up money enough for this purpose she set up a little oyster board just outside her cabin which adjoined the open road. When anyone came along who wanted a few oysters and crackers she would leave her washing and wait upon them. In this way she saved up $200, but for some reason or other she never succeeded in getting her mistress's consent to buy one of the children. It was not always easy for a master to emancipate his slave in those days, even if he wanted to do so. On the contrary, as she says, "One after another — one after another — she sold 'em from me."

It was to a "thin, peaked-looking man who used to come and buy of me," she says, that she finally owed her freedom. "Sometimes," she continued, "he would say, 'Aunt Charity, you must fix me up a nice little mess, for I am poorly to-day.' I always made something good for him; and if he did n't happen to have any change I always trusted him."

It was this man, a Negro "speculator," who, according to her story, finally purchased her with her five children and, giving her the youngest child, set her free.

"Well," she ended, "after that I concluded I 'd come to the free states. Here I am takin' in washing; my daughter is smart at her needle; and we get a very comfortable living."

There was much in slavery besides its hardship

and its cruelties; much that was tender, human and beautiful. The heroic efforts that many of the slaves made to buy their own and their children's freedom deserve to be honoured equally with the devotion that they frequently showed in the service of their masters. And after all, considering the qualities which the Negro slave developed under trying conditions, it does not seem to me there is any real reason why any one who wishes him well should despair of the future of the Negro, either in this country or elsewhere.

CHAPTER IX

SOMETHING like twenty-five insurrections of the slaves took place in the United States, according to Professor Albert Bushnell Hart, previous to the American Revolution. This is taking no account of the outbreaks that took place before that time in Louisiana, nor of those that took place in the other Spanish, French, and English colonies in the West Indies.*

After the English invasion of Jamaica in 1655, for instance, the Negro slaves who had fought with their Spanish masters against the English, betook themselves to the mountains and maintained a number of little insurgent governments for nearly a hundred years until, in 1738, these independent governments were formally constituted and their right of existence recognised. They continued until 1796, when their attempt to build roads and improve the condition of their villages opened the way for attacks by the English and resulted in their downfall. It is said, however, that even to this day some of the wild descendants

---

* "Slavery and Anti-Slavery," p. 51.

of those maroons are still living in the mountainous passes of Jamaica.

The insurrection of the slaves which finally resulted in the establishment, in 1804, of the little Black Republic of Haiti was a part of the revolutionary movement that began in France in 1789. Much has been said and written about the frightful cruelties which characterised the revolution in this island, but any one who will compare what took place in Haiti and Santo Domingo with the events which took place during this period in France will not find, I believe, much to say, considering all of the circumstances, in disparagement of these revolting slaves and their heroic leader, Toussaint L'Overture.

The most important, because the most far-reaching in their effects, of these efforts of Negro slaves to gain their freedom by force, were the attempted insurrection of Denmark Vesey in 1822 and the outbreak under Nat Turner in 1831. These two events, following closely upon the bloody revolution in Haiti and the disturbances in other parts of the West Indies, made a profound impression upon the people of the Southern States.

But even before the memorable insurrection of Nat Turner, two Negroes, Gabriel and Jack Bowler, were the leaders, in 1800, of an attempted revolt in Virginia. These two slaves got together and organised something like a thousand Negroes in

Henrico County, and with this force marched on the city of Richmond. A swollen stream, impassable owing to a recent storm, forced them to halt. They disbanded, expecting to renew the attempt the following night, but the plot was discovered and the citizens of Richmond were aroused before the attack could be made. A reward was offered for Gabriel and Jack Bowler. They were caught and executed.

Twenty-two years later, in Charleston, S. C., an extensive conspiracy was organised by a free Negro, Denmark Vesey. Vesey was known among his people as a deep student of the Bible and exerted a marked influence over them, particularly through their religious meetings which, then as now, were of the nature of popular assemblies for the discussion of all questions relating to the welfare of the race. Vesey's plot failed of its purpose, and he was caught, duly tried and, with thirty-four others, put to death.

When a boy in Virginia I recall the stories that were told around the cabins by the older slave men and women of the "Prophet" Nat Turner, as he was called, and of the dreadful incidents that took place during the insurrection of 1831. Nat Turner was a slave preacher in Southampton County, Virginia. During his boyhood days, as I have heard, his mother, who was known to be a very religious woman, taught him that, like Moses, he was to be the deliverer of his race. She took great pains to give him the advantage of what lore and learning she possessed, and taught him verses and parts of chapters from the Bible, particularly from the Prophets of the Old Testament. He was nursed in the quaint and primitive theology of the plantation hymns, which helped to stimulate the belief in his mission to free his people.

He grew up to be a silent, dreamy kind of man, going, whenever he could, to the caves of the mountains to brood over the condition of the slaves.

It appears to have been Turner's plan to collect a large number of slaves and take refuge in the Dismal Swamp, in the extreme southeastern section of Virginia. On August 21, 1831, with the belief that he was executing the will of God, Nat Turner started forth with six companions who were soon joined by others, making a force of sixty men. Their plan was to exterminate, as far as they were able, the white race about them. In a short time sixty white people on different plantations had been killed. The local militia and United States troops were called out. The insurgents resisted, but the resistance proved useless, and after more than a hundred of them had been killed the uprising was crushed. Forty-three Negroes in all were put on trial, of whom twenty-one were acquitted, twelve were convicted and sold out of the state, while twenty others, including Nat Turner and one woman, were convicted and hanged.

When the John Brown raid took place at Harper's Ferry in 1859, five coloured men were a part of his little band. Of the five men, three were free-born Negroes and two were fugitive slaves. Two of them, Dangerfield Newby and Lewis Leary, were killed during the fighting; John A. Copeland and Shields Green were captured, tried, and executed; Osborne Anderson was the only one to escape from the scene of the disaster.

Newby was tall, well-built, and about thirty years of age, with a pleasing face. Leary came originally from North Carolina and was a member of the colony of Southern coloured people at Oberlin, Ohio. He was twenty-four years of age and quite well educated.

Copeland, who was related to Leary, was twenty-two years of age and came from Oberlin. His letters, written from the jail to relatives, show him to have been a young man of intelligence and courage. In a letter to his brother, written shortly before his execution, were these words, which can be read with profit to-day after a lapse of nearly fifty years:

My jailer, Captain John Avis, is a gentleman who has a heart in his bosom as brave as any other. He met us at Harper's Ferry and fought us as a brave man would do. And since we have been in his power he has protected us from insult and abuse which cowards would have heaped upon us. He has done as a brave man and gentleman would do. Also one of his aids,

Mr. John Sheats, has been very kind to us and has done all he could to serve us. And now, Henry, if fortune should ever throw either of them in your way, and you can confer the least favour on them, do it for my sake.

On the morning of his execution Copeland wrote a long letter to his family in Oberlin from which the following extract is taken:

Let me tell you that it is not the mere fact of hanging to meet death, if I should express regret, but that such an unjust institution should exist as the one which demands my life, and not my life only, but the lives of those to whom my life bears but the relative value of zero to the infinite.

Shields Green was a fugitive slave from South Carolina, twenty-four years of age, with no knowledge of letters, but he is said to have possessed considerable natural ability and a courage which showed that, if better trained, he might have become a man of some importance. He had come to Chambersburg, Pa., the meeting-place of those who were to aid Brown, with Frederick Douglass. Douglass tells how, when he turned to leave the Chambersburg quarry, where his interview with John Brown was had, that, on telling Green he could return with him to Rochester, N. Y., the Negro turned and looked at the bowed figure of John Brown, then asked, "Is he going to stay?"

"Yes," was the answer.

Green looked again at Brown, then at Douglass, and slowly said: "Well, I guess I goes wid de ole man."

When the fight had begun at Harper's Ferry some of the men soon saw that resistance was useless and decided to try to make their escape. Green came under fire while on his way to the arsenal. One of the men told Green he had better go with them. He turned and looked toward the engine-house, before the door of which stood its few defenders and asked: "You think der 's no chance ?"

"Not one," was the reply.

"And de ole captain can't get away ?"

"No," said the men.

"Well," he replied, slowly, with a long, lingering look, "I guess I 'll go back to de ole man."

In prison Green was constantly sending expressions of consolation and of devotion to Brown and, on the morning of John Brown's execution, Green sent him word that he was glad he came, and that he waited willingly for his own death.

Anderson, born free in Pennsylvania, was twenty-four years of age. He was well-educated and by trade a printer. He was a man of natural ability, simple in manner and address. He wrote a very interesting pamphlet of the raid after his escape entitled, "A Voice from Harper's Ferry." He served during the latter part of the Civil War in one of the Negro regiments, and died in Washington in 1871.

The great slave insurrection which, during the whole period of slavery, was frequently expected and always feared, never actually took place; but the fear of such a general outbreak always haunted the South and helped to harden the hearts of the Southern people against the Negro race. This fear was responsible, for instance, for the passage of laws which made it difficult, if not impossible, in many of the Southern states, for a master to emancipate his slaves; made it a crime for him to teach his slaves to read and write; and imposed such limitations and burdens on the free Negroes as reduced that unfortunate class to a condition often counted worse than that of slavery.

In the relations which existed between the white man and the black man in slavery, just as in the relations which exist to-day between the races in the South, there was much that was strange and contradictory, much that was and is hard to understand. For instance, it seems to me that in Virginia, at any rate, the relations between master and slave were usually kindly. The master frequently trusted his slave, usually cared for and protected him, and had for him, in many instances, a feeling of genuine affection. And yet the slaveholder was never able to shake off his sense of danger of an uprising of the slaves. "The night-bell is never heard to toll in the city of Richmond," said John Randolph of Roanoke, referring to this fear, "but the anxious mother presses her infant more closely to her bosom."

As a result of his experience in slavery the Southern white man seems to have learned to make a
pretty complete distinction between the individual
Negro, whom he knows and protects, and the Negro
as a race, whom he denounces in the political campaign and sometimes flaunts in the faces of strangers
who do not understand the situation in the South.
These two ways of looking upon and dealing with
the Negro are well represented in the cases of ex-
Governor Vardaman, of Mississippi, and Senator
Tillman, of South Carolina, both of whom, ordinarily so violent in all their public utterances in
regard to the Negro, are frequently spoken of by
coloured men who know them as unusually kind in
all their personal relations with the Negro.   Mr.
Vardaman and Mr. Tillman, it would seem, hate
the Negro in the abstract, but they get along
very well with the actual black man who is their
neighbour.

It is sometimes said that the vague, impersonal
sort of fear which the master felt for the Negro during
slavery was due to his knowledge of the savage
instincts of the black man which, unless proper
precautions were taken, might at any moment break
out and overwhelm the country.   I am more inclined to the opinion, however, that the majority
of the Negroes who were brought to this country,
either because of their previous training in Africa
or because of their natural disposition, were more

submissive, more disposed to attach themselves and remain faithful to their masters, than any other race or class of people would have been under similar circumstances.

I am disposed to believe that the real reason why the white man feared the black man was because he felt the injustice of the condition of slavery, and realised that it was but human nature that, when the slave began to understand his position, he should seek to become free.

When I hear of a certain type of public man of the present day, either in the press or on the political platform, talking about the danger in which the white race is placed by reason of the presence of the Negro in this country I cannot but feel that these men, in their efforts to stir up prejudice against the Negro, are moved by a bad conscience. If they really believe there is danger from the Negro it must be because they do not intend to give him justice. Injustice always breeds fear.

When I hear people talking about the savage instincts of the Negro and about the danger with which they are threatened in consequence, I wish these people could know and talk, as I have, with some of the men and women who have gone as missionaries to Africa and have spent years of their life alone in the midst of the wildest and most uncivilised peoples of that continent, with never so much as a thought of fear. There are scores of

cases in all the Southern States where a few white
people live surrounded by coloured people without
fear of insurrection or murder, because they have
convinced the coloured people that they want to do
the fair thing by them, that they are anxious to
help them, and to see them make progress.   I
know personally of a case where for ten years
a half-dozen white women have lived in a
community surrounded by thousands of coloured
people and with no white man near to protect
them, but they have never had the least fear
of violence because they went there to help the
coloured people.

In looking into the history of these insurrections
and conspiracies I have been impressed with the
fact that, so far as concerns the leaders of them,
none of these outbreaks seems to have been inspired
by revenge or to have been due to the ill-treatment
which the slaves had received.

Denmark Vesey was not a slave.   In 1822 he
drew a fifteen-hundred-dollar prize in a lottery and
bought his freedom for $600.   His real reason for
organising the conspiracy of which he was the
author seems to be revealed in the explanations he
made to some of his fellow-conspirators in inducing
them to join him.

"He said," according to the confession of one
of these men, "he did not go with Creighton
to Africa because he had not a will; he wanted

to stay and see what he could do for his fellow-creatures."

To another witness he stated that "he was satisfied with his own condition, being free, but, as all his children were slaves, he wished to see what could be done for them."

Denmark Vesey was a man of some education. He had travelled all over the world with his master, who was a ship captain. In his talks with the slaves he not only quoted the Bible, citing the passage about the deliverance of the children of Israel, but he read the speeches in Congress, particularly one speech of a certain Mr. King who, he said, was "the black man's friend," adding that "he, Mr. King, had declared he would continue to speak, write, and publish pamphlets against slavery the longest day he lived, until the Southern States consented to emancipate their slaves, for that slavery was a great disgrace to the country."

Nat Turner was a very different type of man. He was a dreamer, as I have said, and a fanatic. So deeply was he himself imbued with the belief that he was inspired, that his presence impressed with a sense of awe, not merely the Negro slaves, but many of the white people who came in contact with him after his arrest and before his execution.

He is described as a man of ordinary stature, having "the true Negro face, every feature of which is strongly marked."

Mr. Gray, the gentleman who took his confession, says of him:

It has been said that he was ignorant and cowardly, and that his object was to murder and rob for the purpose of obtaining money to make his escape. It is notorious that he was never known to have a dollar in his life, to swear an oath, or drink a drop of spirits. As to his ignorance, he certainly never had the advantages of education; but he can read and write, and for natural intelligence and quickness of apprehension is surpassed by few men I ever have seen. As to his being a coward, his reason, as given, for not resisting Mr. Phipps, shows the decision of his character. When he saw Mr. Phipps present his gun, he said he knew it was impossible for him to escape, as the woods were full of men; he therefore thought it was better for him to surrender, and trust to fortune for his escape.

He is a complete fanatic, or plays his part admirably. On other subjects he possesses an uncommon share of intelligence, with a mind capable of attaining anything, but warped and perverted by the influence of early impressions. I shall not attempt to describe the effect of his narrative, as told and commented on by himself, in the condemned hole of the prison: the calm, deliberate composure with which he spoke of his late deeds and intentions; the expression of his fiend-like face when excited by enthusiasm; still bearing the stains of the blood of helpless innocence about him, clothed with rags, and covered with chains, yet daring to raise his manacled hands to Heaven, with a spirit soaring above the attributes of man. I looked on him, and the blood curdled in my veins.

The history of these conspiracies proves that the very contact of the slave with his master tended to breed a desire for freedom. Every slave who became educated sufficiently to read the Bible or to read the ordinary school books came into contact with the sentiments and traditions of a people that was proud of its independence, and the slave learned from his master the desire to be free. Frederick Douglass got his first notions of freedom from reading the great orations of William Pitt, Lord Chatham, Fox, and Sheridan in a book called "The Columbian Orator," which he picked up by chance.

Once this notion of freedom got into the mind of a slave with a vigorous intellect it never left him. In Frederick Douglass's "Narrative," published in 1845, he tells us that when he was a slave in Maryland on the shores of Chesapeake Bay he often watched the ships as they sailed by, and as they passed he would express himself in this way:

You are loosed from your moorings, and are free, I am fast in my chains and am a slave! You move merrily before the gentle gale, and I sadly before the bloody whip! You are freedom's swift-winged angels that fly round the world, I am confined in bands of irons! O that I were free! O that I were one of your gallant decks, and under your protecting wing!

It is as true to-day as it was before the war that, while the personal relations of the white man and the black man in the South are frequently all that could be desired, the natural development of these good relations is hindered and held back by the impersonal fear which the white man seems to have of the Negro race as a whole. The success of the Negro as well as that of the white man is, for that reason, hindered by the efforts to force upon the South a system which does not fit the

desires or the needs of either race. Ever since
the war, for instance, the normal political development of the South has been stunted by the fear, or
the ghost of the fear, that the Negro would some
time or other again secure the upper hand in the
South as he was supposed to have done directly
after the war. As a matter of fact, the Negro was
never in control in the South. The people who
were in control were representatives of the Republican party in the North who came South and used
their influence with the Negro and with the Government at Washington to control the course of
events. Just such a condition never will and
never can arise again. Even if it were possible, the
Negro does not desire it any more than the white
man. What he desires most is the good will of his
white neighbours and the opportunity for the peaceful development of those fundamental interests
which are the same for both races.

The Negro gained just as little from the temporary power which he held during the Reconstruction
time as he did from the successful and unsuccessful
insurrections by which he sought to gain his freedom before the war. He has no desire to try that
experiment again.

Scarcely a month or a week has passed since the
Negro became free that some newspaper has not
expressed a fear or made a prediction that there
was going to be an uprising or insurrection of the

Negroes at some time in some part of the country. That uprising has never taken place. The nearest to anything like an uprising of the Negroes in the South since emancipation took place at the end of the seventies, when, as a result of real or fancied oppression in some of the Southern states, delegates from fourteen states and territories met in Nashville, Tenn., May 7, 1879, and advised the coloured people of the South to "emigrate to those states and territories where they can enjoy all the rights which are guaranteed by the laws and Constitution of the United States." As a result of this advice 40,000 emigrants, within the period of a few months, poured into Kansas, largely from the "Black Belt" of Mississippi and Louisiana. This movement created such embarrassment among the planters in the region from which the emigration took place, and such distress among the immigrants themselves, because of their helplessness when they reached their destination, that the movement became an object of national concern, and it required the most energetic efforts upon the part of Frederick Douglass and other leaders of the race to prevent the movement assuming larger and more dangerous proportions.

The chances for another such movement, or for an uprising of any kind, grow less every year, just in proportion as the Negro himself gains in property and in intelligence; in proportion as he enters into the business of the community in which he lives, and becomes a permanent and definite factor in its industrial life. The only possible chance for such an uprising at the present time would be in a community where the Negro has little or no interest at stake, and such communities are now few in the Southern states.

I can best illustrate what I have in mind by referring to a specific instance which I came across during a trip of observation through Mississippi in the fall of 1908. During that visit I spent a day in Marshall County where, although the Negro population outnumbers the white more than two to one, there has not been, with one exception, an outbreak of any character between the races since the Civil War. I inquired of the coloured and the white people there how it was that peace and harmony prevailed in their community. I received practically the same answer from both races, which was in substance this: In that community the coloured people are large owners of farm land; they are successful farmers; they own in the principal town of the county, Holly Springs, valuable business blocks; they are not only engaged in farming, but they are engaged in business, selling groceries, dry-goods, buying and selling cotton. Besides the coloured people of Mississippi own several important schools and colleges in Holly Springs. A racial outbreak would cost the Negroes of the county quite as much as the white people, and this fact has helped to bring about racial peace. What is true in that community is equally true in others where the Negro is making real progress.

In these places the people of both races have discovered that their material and moral interests are so interlaced that if one race suffers the other must suffer too.

One Negro in Marshall County, Mr. E. H. McKissack, is the Treasurer of the State Odd Fellows organisation, which handles practically $200,000 each year. This money, which is distributed among the different banks in Holly Springs, is a visible evidence of the way in which the material interests of the races are bound together. I was told during my visit that, whenever the least danger of racial conflict arose in Marshall County, the leading coloured men and the leading white men were in the habit of taking counsel together, in order to form plans that would result in the maintenance of peace and friendly relations. On one occasion, for instance, when the son of a poor white woman was murdered by a coloured man, the coloured people were the first to get together and hold a mass meeting, in which a considerable sum of money was collected and presented to the mother of the murdered boy.

In recent years we have had several outbreaks of mobs, sometimes in the North, sometimes in the

South, but I have noticed this difference between
a mob in the North and a mob in the South: A mob
in the South is more short-lived than the one in
the North, and with few exceptions, does not
seek to visit its punishment upon the innocent as
well as upon the guilty. There is a reason for
this. In the South every Negro, no matter how
worthless he may be as an individual, knows one
white man in the town whose friendship and
protection he can always count upon; perhaps he
has gained the friendship of this white man by
reason of the fact that some member of the white
man's family owned him or some of his relatives,
or it may be that he has lived upon this white man's
plantation, or that some member of his family
works for him, or that he has performed some act
of kindness for this white man which has brought
them into sympathetic relations with each other. It
is generally true, as I have said before, that in the
South every white man, no matter how bitter he
may seem to be toward the Negro as a race, knows
some one Negro in whom he has complete confidence, whom he will trust with all that he has. It
is the individual touch which holds the two races
together in the South, and it is this individual
touch between the races which is lacking, in a large
degree, in the North.

In bringing to a close what I have written on
the subject of Negro insurrections I am tempted

to say a word on the subject of Negro courage.
While certain people have fallen into the habit of
denouncing the Negro because he is unduly ambitious, and because he refuses to remain, as they
say, "in the place for which God made him,"
there are others who claim that the Negro is too
submissive. These latter insist that, if he had the
courage to stand up and denounce his detractors in
the same harsh and bitter terms that these persons
use toward him, in a short time he would win the
respect of the world, and the only obstacle to his
progress would be removed.

It is interesting, sometimes amusing, and sometimes even pathetic, to note the conception of
"bravery" and "courage" which some coloured
men, who put their faith in this solution of the
Negro problem, occasionally apply to other members of their race. For a long time after freedom
came, and the same is not infrequently true at the
present time, any black man who was willing,
either in print or in public speech, to curse and
abuse the white man, easily gained for himself a
reputation for great courage. He might spend but
thirty minutes or an hour once a year in that kind
of "vindication" of his race, but he got the reputation of being an exceedingly brave man. Another
man, who worked patiently and persistently for
years in a Negro school, depriving himself of many
of the comforts and necessities of life, in order to

perform a service which would uplift his race, gained no reputation for courage. On the contrary, he was likely to be denounced as a coward by these "heroes," because he chose to do his work without cursing, without abuse, and without complaint.

There is an element of white people which has gained a reputation for courage by abusing the Negro in the same way that certain of the Negroes have gained a reputation by abusing the white man. No account is taken by these people of the kind of courage shown by the white man in the South who, in an unostentatious way, is helping to lift the Negro to a higher plane of usefulness. It requires no real courage for a man to stand up before a sympathetic audience and denounce wrongs that had been committed by people thousands of miles away. Neither does it require any real courage for five hundred armed men to march out and kill one helpless individual.

The encouraging thing about the relations of the races in the United States is that an increasing number of white men and black men are learning that the highest courage is that of the man or the woman who is helping some one else to be more useful or more happy; that, in the last analysis, it is not the courage that hurts some one and destroys something, but the courage that helps some one and builds something up which the world needs most.

CHAPTER X

THE FREE NEGRO IN SLAVERY DAYS

SOME time in the fall of 1828, Benjamin
Lundy, the Quaker abolitionist, met by
accident, in a Boston boarding house, a young
man by the name of William Lloyd Garrison, who
was then publishing a total abstinence newspaper,
the *National Philanthropist*. The next year, after
returning from a visit to a colony of emancipated
slaves which he had succeeded in settling in the
island of Haiti, Lundy announced in his paper
that William Lloyd Garrison had joined him
at Baltimore, Maryland, and would henceforth
be associated with him in the publication at
that city of *The Genius of Universal Emancipation*, the first abolition newspaper in the
United States.

This meeting of Benjamin Lundy and William
Lloyd Garrison and their subsequent association in
Baltimore marks the point in time when the agitation
for the emancipation of the Negro was transferred
from the Southern to the Northern States, and
slavery became for the first time a National issue.
After the Southampton uprising in 1831, the abolition

societies, which up to that time had existed in different parts of the South, almost wholly disappeared.
With the exception of a few individuals like Cassius
M. Clay who, as late as 1845, published an anti-
slavery weekly, the *True American*, at Lexington,
Kentucky, there was no public opposition to slavery
in any of the Southern States.

Opposition to slavery, though silenced in the South,
never wholly ceased there, and the evidence of its
existence was the Free Negro.   In spite of the efforts
that were made to limit and check emancipation of
the slaves, the number of free Negroes continued to
increase in the Southern as well as the Northern
States, and the existence of this class of persons was
the silent protest of the Southern slaveholder
against the system which he publicly defended
and upheld.

Under the conditions of slavery, the position of
the free Negro was a very uncomfortable one.   He
was, in a certain sense, an anomaly, since he did not
belong to either class.   He was distrusted by the
white people, and looked down upon by the slaves.
In spite of this fact, individual slaveholders — sometimes by providing in their wills for the emancipation
and transportation of their slaves to a free state or
to Liberia, sometimes by permitting individual
slaves to buy their own freedom — were constantly
adding to the number of "free persons of colour."
Among the most illustrious of those who freed their

slaves were George Washington, John Randolph, and Chief-Justice Roger B. Taney, author of the famous Dred Scott decision.

When a master liberated his slaves by will, it was frequently with the explanation, expressed or understood, that he believed slavery was morally wrong. When he allowed them to buy their own freedom, it was a practical recognition that the system was economically a mistake, since the slave who could purchase his own freedom was one whom it did not pay to hold as a slave.   This fact was clearly recognised by a planter in Mississippi who declared that he had found it paid to allow the slaves to buy their freedom.   In order to encourage them to do this he devised a method by which they might purchase their freedom in instalments.   After they had saved a certain amount of money, by extra labour, he permitted them to buy one day's freedom a week.   With this much capital invested in themselves they were then able to purchase, in a much shorter time, a second, a third, and a fourth day's freedom, until they were entirely free.

A somewhat similar method was sometimes adopted by certain ambitious freedmen for purchasing the freedom of their families.   In such a case the father would purchase, for instance, a son or a daughter.   The children would then join with their father in purchasing the other members of the family. It was in this way, I have been informed by Mr.

Monroe Work, who is at present a teacher at Tuskegee, that his grandfather purchased his wife and ten
of his children, including Mr. Work's father. The
grandfather, Henry Work, after securing his own
freedom, went first to Cincinnati, and then to
Decatur, Michigan, where he owned a farm, and on
this farm he and his children earned the money to
purchase one by one the other members of the family.
How much it cost the family to free itself in this way
Mr. Work says he was unable to learn. He knows,
however, that his father sold at one time for $1,400.
When Henry Work died there were still three of his
children in slavery whom he had not been able to
redeem. Ex-President Gibson, of the Negro State of
Liberia, told me that his father purchased himself
and most of the other members of the family in instalments and transported them to Liberia. Two sons,
who did not care to go back to Africa, were left in
slavery in this country, but with the understanding
that after a certain time they were to become free.

In this and other ways, in spite of the fact that there
were at this time something like 30,000 fugitives in
Canada and 20,000 colonists in Africa and elsewhere,
the number of free Negroes in the United States
increased from 59,466 in 1790 to 434,495 in 1860.
This was about 10 per cent. of the whole Negro
population at that time. Of these free Negroes
considerably more than half — 262,000 — were in the
Southern States. In the South, the three states of

Maryland, Virginia, and North Carolina contained by far the largest number of the "free citizens of colour," as they were sometimes called. At the census of 1860, the slave population of Maryland was something like 87,000 and the number of free Negroes was 83,942. From 1830 to 1860 the slave population of Maryland decreased nearly 16,000 while the population of free Negroes increased something over 31,000.

In estimating the number of slaves who were, in one way or another, given their freedom by their masters, some account should be taken of those who were, for one reason or another, re-enslaved. A free Negro might be sold into slavery to pay taxes or to pay fines, and in Maryland free Negroes might be sold into perpetual slavery for the crime of entering the state. In 1829 the practice of selling any free Negro, who could not account for himself, in order to pay the jail fines, had become such a scandal as to attract public attention.

There were other means by which a considerable number of free Negroes were re-enslaved. The practice of kidnapping, in spite of severe laws against it in all the Southern states, was carried on to a very great extent. In his book on the domestic slave-trade, Professor Collins, of Claremont College, Hickory, N. C., estimates that the number of free Negroes kidnapped and sold into slavery "must have ranged from a few hundred to two or three thousand,"

and he adds, "it appears quite certain that as many
were kidnapped as escaped from bondage, if not
more."*

A disposition to free slaves for personal considerations of one kind or another began at a very early
period.   In York and Henrico counties, Virginia,
as far back as the middle of the seventeenth century,
we find records of the emancipation of Negro slaves.
For example, Thomas Whitehead, of York, emancipated his slave John, and bequeathed to him, among
other things, two cows and the use of a house and
as much ground as he could cultivate.   He further
showed his confidence in the discretion and the
integrity of this Negro slave by appointing him guardian of Mary Rogers, a ward of Mr. Whitehead.   He
also made him trustee of her property, but the court
refused to allow him to fill either one or the other of
these positions.†   Another instance recorded about
this time was that of John Carter, of Lancaster,
Virginia, who was one of the largest slaveholders in
the colony.   He gave freedom to two of his Negro
slaves who were married to each other.   To each he
gave a cow and a calf and three barrels of Indian
corn.   He also instructed his heirs to allow them
the use of convenient firewood, timber, and as much
land as they could cultivate.   He provided that the

---

* "The Domestic Slave-Trade of the Southern States," Winfield H. Collins
M. A., p. 94.
† " Economic History of Virginia in the Seventeenth Century," Bruce, Vol.
II., p. 123.

two daughters of this couple should receive their liberty when they reached their eighteenth year, and, as a provision for them when they reached that age, he gave each a yearling with its increase, which was to be permitted to run with the cattle of his wife after his death.*

In the interval between 1635 and 1700, although the Negro slaves were few in number, and most of the labour was performed by white servants, there were a number of persons of African blood in the colony of Virginia who raised themselves to positions of some importance. Several of them were able to write at a time when there were very few schools and education was a decided luxury. Several had obtained patents to land. For instance, in 1654, one hundred acres of land in Northampton County were granted to Richard Johnson, a Negro, and in the description of this tract reference was made to the contiguous estates of John Johnston and Anthony Johnson, both Negroes. There are in the records of Northampton County, also, evidences that a suit was begun by Anthony Johnson for the purpose of recovering his Negro servant.

During the early years of slavery, the free Negroes seem to have had about the same rights under the law that other free persons had, except, as I have already stated, they were not allowed to hold persons of white blood as bond-servants. It appears that,

* "Economic History of Virginia in the Seventeenth Century," Bruce, Vol. II., p. 124.

until after the Revolution, Negro freemen were
allowed to vote in every state, except Georgia and
South Carolina.   Between 1792 and 1834 the four
bordering states, Delaware, Maryland, Virginia,
and Kentucky, denied suffrage to the Negro.   In
North Carolina, Negroes who paid a public tax
took part in the election until 1835, when a new
constitution excluded them from the suffrage.   New
Jersey took away the suffrage of the Negro in 1807,
Connecticut in 1814, and Pennsylvania in 1838.
New York, in 1821, required from them an unusually
high property qualification.*

These changes were all evidences of the steady
growth in the United States, both North and South,
of a caste system which excluded the Negro from
the ordinary privileges of citizenship exclusively upon
the ground of his colour.   In 1803 Ohio demanded
a bond of five hundred dollars for Negroes who came
into the state.   A Negro, even though a free man,
could not at that time testify in a case in which a
white man was a party, and Negroes were not
admitted to the public schools.   Similar provisions
were made by Illinois, Indiana, and Iowa when they
became states.   Illinois prohibited the entrance of
Negroes to the state at any time.   In 1833 Judge
Dagget, of Connecticut, twenty-four years before the
Dred Scott decision, held that a free Negro was a
person and not a citizen.   This was in the trial of the

---

* " Slavery and Abolition," Hart, pp. 53, 83.

case against Prudence Crandall, the young Quakeress who had established a school for Negroes in Canterbury, Connecticut, contrary to a law which provided that no school could be established for coloured people who were not inhabitants of Connecticut.

The effect of the agitation for abolition seems to have made the condition of the free Negroes steadily worse, particularly in the Southern states. In some of these states, they were forbidden to sell drugs, in others they might not sell wheat and tobacco, and in still others to peddle market produce or own a boat was against the law. In several states it was against the law for a free Negro to cross the state line; in others, a slave who was emancipated was compelled to immediately leave the state.

Notwithstanding the hardships and difficulties under which the free Negro population laboured, both in the North and in the South, those who have had occasion to study the local history of the Southern States have found that the number of Negroes who had succeeded in making some impression upon their community, either by their native qualities or by their success in business, was more considerable than is usually imagined. Solomon Humphreys, for instance, after purchasing his freedom, became a well-known business man in Georgia. Benjamin Lundy found at San Antonio a Negro who, after purchasing his own freedom and that of his wife and family, had become the owner of several houses and lots.*

The number of free Negroes in North Carolina was considerable because, in spite of the rigorous laws against the free coloured people, conditions were more lenient than those of any other Southern state. The result was that many free Negroes crossed into North Carolina and settled, undisturbed, in the northern or southern counties. Speaking of this class of people, Professor John Spencer Bassett says:

They were well-diggers, shoemakers, blacksmiths, fiddlers, hucksters, peddlers, and so forth. Besides, they were easily called in to help the whites on occasions of need. There were a very few who accumulated money and some of these became slave-owners. Although it was against the law for them to come into the state, their arrival was tolerated both because the law was recognised as severe and because their services were wanted in the community. Many of them had Indian blood in their veins, and when such was the case they were a little distant toward the slaves. . . . I have been speaking of free Negroes who lived in the country districts. In towns they fared better and accumulated wealth.†

Professor Bassett gives an account of several free Negroes, of whom he had been able to obtain records, who were citizens of Newbern, Craven County, North Carolina. One of the men to whom he refers was John C. Stanley, the son of an African-born slave woman, who was liberated by the General

---

* *Cf.* Hart's " Slavery and Anti-slavery," p. 90.
† Johns Hopkins University Studies: " Slavery in the State of North Carolina," by John Spencer Bassett, p. 43.

Assembly under the petition of Mrs. Lydia Stewart, his mistress. Because he got his start in the barber business, he was generally known as "Barber Jack." He became the owner of several plantations on which he employed sixty-four slaves, of which he was the owner, and as many more bound free Negroes. He had three sons, John, Alexander, and Charles. John became an expert book-keeper, and was employed in that capacity by a prominent firm. John C. Stanley amassed a fortune, or what was supposed to be a fortune in those days, of something like $40,000. Speaking of some of the other successful Negroes of whom he was able to obtain the records, Professor Bassett says:

Many of the free Negroes were in circumstances of independent thrift, and from many parts of the state I have had evidence that some Negroes were slaveholders. In Newbern especially there were a number of such thrifty coloured men. Notable among these was John Good. He was a son of his master, and for a long time a slave. When the master died, his two surviving children, who were daughters, had but little property besides this boy, John, who was a barber. John took up the task of supporting them. He boarded them in good houses and otherwise provided for them well. His faithfulness won him many friends among the best citizens, and when both of his mistresses were married these friends united to persuade the owners to liberate him as a reward for his services. . . . There were other thrifty and notable free Negroes in the same place, as, for example, John Y. Green, a carpenter and contractor; Richard Hazel, a blacksmith of means; Albert and Freeman Morris, described as "two nice young men," and thoroughly respected, tailors by trade; and Scipio, slave of Dr. Hughes, who was a blacksmith and owner of a livery stable. Another was Fellow Bragg, a tailor who was

thoroughly conscientious and so good a workman that prominent
people were known to move their custom to the shops at which
he was employed in order that he might work on it.   Most of
these men moved to Cincinnati sooner or later.   What became
of them I do not know.   The conditions here recorded for Newbern were not unusual for North Carolina towns in general.
Everywhere there were usually a number of prosperous free
Negroes.   Most of them were mulattoes, not a few of them were
set free by their fathers and thus they fell easily into the life around
them.*

Among the descendants of the free coloured people
of Newbern, North Carolina, with whom I am
personally acquainted is the Hon. John P. Green,
who was for twelve years a justice of the peace
in Cleveland, Ohio, four years a member of the Ohio
House of Representatives, two years a member of the
State Senate, and for nine years at the head of the
Postage-stamp Distribution Bureau of Washington,
filling in the intervals of his public service with practice at the Cleveland bar.   His father was a master
tailor in Newbern, and a member of a family of
free coloured people whose traditions go back something more than one hundred years.

Charles W. Chesnutt, author of "The Conjure
Woman" and other popular stories of Southern life,
was descended from free coloured people in Fayetteville, North Carolina.   Mr. Chesnutt informs me that
a coloured man by the name of Matthew Leary is
still remembered in Fayetteville who, before the war,
was the owner of considerable land, a number of

* Johns Hopkins University Studies: "Slavery in the State of North Carolina,"
by John Spencer Bassett, p. 45.

slaves, a brick store in the business part of the town, and a handsome residence in a good neighbourhood. His sons gained some prominence in North Carolina during the Reconstruction era. Matthew Leary, Jr., went into politics and afterward became a clerk in one of the Government offices in Washington. A younger brother, Hon. John S. Leary, was the first coloured man in North Carolina to be admitted to the bar, of which he remained a respected member until he died at Charlotte, N. C. He was, I understand, at one time a member of the North Carolina Legislature.

Another of the successful free coloured people of North Carolina was James D. Sampson, who began life as a house carpenter and became in the course of time a man of considerable wealth and some local distinction. I have been informed that one time the Legislature passed a bill granting his family special privileges which were not permitted to other free people of colour. His children, John, Benjamin, and Joseph, were all educated in the North. Benjamin graduated from Oberlin College and afterward became a teacher at Wilberforce, Ohio. John P. Sampson published at Cincinnati, during the war, the *Coloured Citizen*. After the war he was commissioned by General Howard to look after the coloured schools established by the Freedmen's Bureau in the Third District of North Carolina. He was elected treasurer and assessor of Wilmington,

and was candidate for Congress, but was defeated
because of the fact, it is said, that his father had been
the owner of slaves before the war.   While it was true
that James D. Sampson owned a number of slaves, it
is said that many, if not all, of them were held in trust
in order to secure them practical freedom.   Recently,
George M. Sampson, a grandson of James D. Sampson, visited Tuskegee.   He is now a teacher in the
State Normal School at Tallahassee, Florida.

There is no reason to believe that the coloured
people of North Carolina made more progress in a
material way than they did in some of the other
states in the South.   For instance, in the city of
Charleston, South Carolina, there was a colony of
"free persons of colour" who were proud of the fact
that they sprang from a generation of free ancestors
going back to before the Revolutionary War.   In the
list of taxpayers in the city of Charleston for 1860
the names of three hundred and sixty "persons of
colour," whose property was assessed in that year,
are given.   They owned real estate which was valued
for taxation at $724,570.   Of these three hundred
and sixty taxpayers, one hundred and thirty owned
slaves, aggregating three hundred and ninety in
number.   The largest number of slaves held by a
coloured person was fourteen.   In this list of "persons of colour" thirteen are classed as Indians, but
it is quite certain that these so-called Indians were
largely mixed with Negro blood.   Like so many other

communities, there were Indians in Charleston who had been but partially absorbed by coloured people with whom they had been associated.

In 1860 the population of Charleston was 48,409, of whom 26,969 were white, 17,655 slaves, and 3,785 were "free persons of colour." It would appear from the figures given that these free coloured people probably owned, including slaves, a million dollars' worth of property. Among the slaves held by coloured people of Charleston were a number who were actually free men, and only nominally slaves. For instance, Richard Holloway, who was a prominent man among the free coloured people in Charleston, owned Charles Benford, who was his friend, and with him one of the leaders in the Methodist Church, at that time. The circumstances were these: Charles Benford had arranged with his white master to purchase his freedom, but at that time the laws were such that it was difficult for a master to free his slaves, particularly if the slave purchased his own freedom. In order to get around this law Charles Benford asked his friend, Richard Holloway, to purchase him, Benford himself furnishing the money for the purchase.

There were a number of other slaves held in trust by the free coloured people of Charleston. The wealthiest family in Charleston, among the free coloured people, were the Westons. They had among the various members of the family taxable property to the amount of $80,000. They also owned thirty-six slaves, nine of whom they held as trustees. It is said that the number of slaves held by St. Philip's Church, which was the aristocratic church of the city, amounted to something over one hundred. These consisted for the most part of slaves who had actually bought their freedom and whom the church held in trust.

Of the free coloured people of Louisiana, of whom there were a very considerable number before the war, many were slaveholders and large owners of land. There were a number of settlements of Creole Negroes, as they were called, in various parts of Louisiana. When Frederick Law Olmsted visited that state in 1853, he visited one of these settlements in the neighbourhood of Natchitoches. The information which he obtained in regard to these people was to the effect that they were "honest and industrious and paid their debts quite as promptly as the white planters, and were, as far as anyone could judge, good citizens in all respects!" One of them, he learned, had lately spent $40,000 in a law suit, and it is believed that they were increasing in wealth. Several of these coloured planters were worth four or five hundred thousand dollars. The little town of Washington, near Opelousas, in St. Landry Parish, was formerly called Negroville from the number of free Negroes living in that village. A number of them, according to Olmsted, were wealthy and thriving. They owned some of the best cotton and sugar plantations.

"An intelligent man whom I met at Washington," he said, "who had been travelling most of the time for two years in the plantation districts, told me that the free Negroes in the state in general, so far as he had observed, were equal in all respects to the white Creoles. Much the larger part of them were poor, thriftless, unambitious, and lived wretchedly, but there were many opulent, intelligent, and educated. The best house and most tasteful grounds that he had visited in the state had belonged to a nearly full-blooded Negro — a very dark man. He and his family were well educated and, though French in their habitual tongue, they spoke English with a liberal tongue and one much more eloquent than most of the liberally educated whites. They had a private tutor in their family, and owned, he thought, a hundred and fifty slaves.

It is near here, in the adjoining parish of St. Martin, that my friend Paul Chretien lived. His father was a free coloured man who made his money in the neighbourhood of Calcasieu, but afterward returned to St. Martin and built himself a beautiful home there in which his son, whose name I have mentioned, is now living.

A considerable portion of the Negro population of Mobile, Alabama, at the present day are the descendants of these Creole Negroes whose freedom was guaranteed to them by the France treaty which transferred Louisiana to the United States in 1803. There is an island in Mobile Bay, about twenty miles below the city, Mon Louis Island, which is owned by the descendants of two families. The lower end of the island was settled by the veterans of the Revolutionary War, who lived to a great age; the upper part of the island was settled by a man known as Captain Jack Collins, but his real name was Maximilian Collins, who settled on this island in 1808. He left a large tract of land to his descendants with the injunction that they should sell none of it; it has remained in their hands up to the present time, and there has grown up there, as a result, a little patriarchal colony made up of the descendants of the free Negro, Captain Jack, and the descendants of his slaves. The oldest living descendant of this patriarch is the widow of the late Belthair Durette, who had seventy-two grandchildren, fifty-two great-grandchildren, ninety-seven of whom are living in this community of Mon Louis.

I have mentioned here several cases which indicate that, even in the South and before the Civil War, the Negro had made some progress along material lines. It is impossible to tell, of course, how much property these people possessed. But the aggregate value of the property of the 262,000 Negroes in the South in 1860 has been estimated at something like twenty-five millions of dollars. I should judge, from what I have been able to learn, that that was a low estimate.

The question might very well be asked, considering the success that individuals were able to make before the war, why it was that the great mass of the Negro people who were free did not do better? In reply to that I might say that there were the same reasons and others why the Negro should not get on or succeed that there were why the class known as the "poor whites" in the South did not succeed. If the conditions of slavery operated to keep the poor white man in a low stage of civilisation, they certainly operated to keep the free Negro in a still lower stage.

Not only did the free people of colour have to meet all the difficulties to which I have referred, but it was against the law for them to meet together in any large number in order to coöperate to improve their condition. The great benefits of coöperation which go so far to extend to the mass of individuals the benefits which are obtained by a few were denied them.

In spite of this fact, in Charleston, Baltimore, Washington, New York, and in other places where there were large numbers of free Negroes, little societies for mutual helpfulness were established. For instance, in 1790 there was formed in Charleston what was known as the "Brown Fellowship Society." This society was started at the suggestion of the director of St. Philip's, of which a number of free Negroes

were members. Besides cultivating a spirit of fellowship among its members, it sought to provide school
privileges for their children and to provide relief
and extend aid to worthy persons of their colour.
One of the first things they did was to purchase
a burial lot for their dead. This organisation
befriended helpless orphans; one of these orphans
was the well-known Bishop Daniel A. Payne, the
founder of Wilberforce University. This organisation still maintains its existence, and celebrated a few
years ago its centennial. The records have all been
preserved, and one of the most interesting of these is
one which commemorates, in a formal way, the
expulsion of one of its members on suspicion of
having assisted in kidnapping and selling into slavery
a free coloured man. The success of this first organisation led to the establishment of other similar
organisations. "The Humane and Friendly Society"
was established in 1802; "The Friendly Union,"
in 1813; and later still, "The Friendly Moralist,"
and the "Brotherly Association," and the "Unity
and Friendship." Each of these had its own burial
plot and system of mutual benefit.

After the attempted conspiracy of Denmark Vesey,
in 1822, all these organisations came under suspicion,
and there was a time when they were kept up under
the greatest difficulties, but they never ceased to
exist. There were similar organisations, as I have
said, in several of the larger cities of the South.

Frederick Douglass, while living in Baltimore, attended one of these societies, known as the "East Baltimore Mental Improvement Society." This society was formed by a number of free coloured young men who, like Frederick Douglass, were engaged, as ship caulkers. In this organisation he frequently took prominent part, although, being a slave, he would naturally have been excluded. He has said that the society of the young men he met there aided him considerably in completing the education that he had already begun in secret. As Baltimore probably had more free coloured people at the time than any other city, with the exception of Washington, it was natural that there should be a large number of these societies of a literary and mutual-benefit and benevolent character. Baltimore, in fact, seems to have been the home of the Negro mutual benefit societies, many of which now in existence date back to 1820.

The New York African Society, for mutual relief, which has been in existence for over a hundred years in New York City, held its first meeting in a coloured school-house in Rose Street in 1808, nearly twenty years before the final emancipation of the slaves in New York State. Although it has not increased its membership in recent years, this society has become, I understand, comparatively wealthy as a result of its earlier investments. The first property owned by this society was on Baxter Street not far from the spot that afterward became notorious under the name of Five Points. It was purchased in 1820 for $1,800, and when it was sold later the funds were used to purchase a five-story flat at No. 43 West Sixty-sixth Street and another building at No. 27 Greenwich Avenue, both of which the society still owns.

In Maryland these beneficial organisations were especially exempt from the general prohibition against public meetings of free coloured people   In other places in the Southern States there was no such exemption and, although the law was usually got around in some way or other, not infrequently members of these organisations were arrested, fined, and sometimes sent to prison. Frederick Law Olmsted records one such instance in Washington, D. C., in the first chapter of his journals of "In the Seaboard Slave States."

He says:

The coloured population voluntarily sustain several churches, schools, and mutual assistance and improvement societies, and there are evidently persons among them of no inconsiderable cultivation of mind. Among the police reports of the city newspapers, there was lately (April, 1855) an account of the apprehension of twenty-four "genteel coloured men" (so they were described), who had been found by a watchman assembling privately in the evening, and been lodged in the watch-house. The object of their meeting appears to have been purely benevolent, and, when they were examined before a magistrate in the morning, no evidence was offered, nor does there seem to have been any suspicion, that they had any criminal purpose. On searching their persons there were found a Bible, a volume of Seneca's "Morals"; "Life in Earnest;" the printed constitution of a society, the object of which was said to be "to relieve the sick, and bury the dead"; and a subscription paper "to purchase the freedom of Eliza Howard," a young woman, whom her owner was willing to sell at $650. I can think of nothing that would speak higher for the character of a body of poor men, servants and labourers, than to find, by chance, in their pockets, just such things as these.*

Nothing contributed more to keep the free Negroes from making the great advancement that they did during the period of slavery than the fact that they were not allowed to organise and unite their efforts for their own improvement in any large way. On the other hand, nothing has more prevented and held back the progress of the coloured people since slavery than the fact that they have had to learn how to unite their efforts in order to improve their condition.

---

* " Seaboard Slave States," by Frederick Law Olmsted, pp. 14, 15.

CHAPTER XI

FUGITIVE SLAVES

IN THE latter part of the year 1852 was organised or rather re-organised, in the rooms of the Anti-slavery Society, at 107 North Fifth Street, Philadelphia, what was known as the "Vigilance Committee." The chairman of this committee was a coloured man, Robert Purvis. He was descended from a free coloured woman of Charleston, whose mother was said to have been a Moor. His father, Robert Purvis, was an Englishman. He was brought to Pennsylvania by his parents in 1819; was a member of the Anti-slavery Convention in 1833, and was one of the signers of its declaration of sentiments. When the fiftieth anniversary of the Anti-slavery Society was held in Philadelphia, December 4, 1883, he was one of the three original signers who were present. The other two were John G. Whittier, the poet, and Elizur Wright, the anti-slavery editor. The Secretary of the Philadelphia Vigilance Committee was William Still.

This Vigilance Committee, which was the successor of an earlier organisation of the same name that dates at least as far back as 1838, soon became the principal directing body for all the numerous lines of the Underground Railroad which centred in Philadelphia at that time. As secretary of this organisation, William Still kept a record of all the fugitive slaves who passed through the hands of this committee from the time of its organisation until the breaking out of the Civil War. During the period of the Civil War he kept this record hidden, but in 1872 it was published in the form of a book called "The Underground Railroad."

This book is one of the most remarkable records in existence, concerning the history of slavery. It is made up in large part of the letters that were written by the different agents of the Underground Railroad to the secretary of the Vigilance Committee, and of letters written by fugitive slaves, sometimes while they were en route to Canada, and sometimes after they had reached their destination. They tell, in words of the fugitives themselves, of the difficulties, sufferings, fears of runaway slaves, and of all the various devices which they used to escape from bondage to freedom.

Of his own motives for keeping this record, Mr. Still says:

Thousands of escapes, harrowing separations, dreadful longings, dark gropings after lost parents, brothers, sisters, and identities, seemed ever to be pressing on my mind. While I knew the danger of keeping strict records, and while I did not then dream that in my day slavery would be blotted out, or that the time would come when I could publish these records, it used to afford me great satisfaction to take them down, fresh from the lips of fugitives on the way to freedom, and to preserve them as they had given them. *

Sometimes these fugitives reached free soil packed in boxes, shipped as merchandise by rail or by steamship, from some of the nearby Southern ports. This was the case of Henry Box Brown, who was shipped from Richmond, Va., by James A. Smith, a shoe dealer, to William H. Johnson, Arch Street, Philadelphia. He was twenty-six hours on the road from Richmond to Philadelphia. Though the box was marked "This side up," in the course of his journey, Mr. Brown was compelled to ride many miles standing on his head. When the box arrived at the anti-slavery office, there was the greatest apprehension lest, in the course of the journey, the fugitive had perished and the society would find itself with a corpse upon its hands. Mr. Still described, in the following words, the scene when this box was opened in the presence of a number of prominent members of the Anti-slavery Society:

All was quiet. The door had been safely locked. The proceedings commenced. Mr. J. Miller McKim, Secretary of the Pennsylvania Anti-slavery Society, rapped quietly on the lid of the box and called out, "All right!" Instantly came the answer from within, "All right, sir!"

The witnesses will never forget that moment. Saw and hatchet quickly had the five hickory hoops cut and the lid off, and the marvellous resurrection of Brown ensued. Rising up in his box,

* Quoted in Siebert's "The Underground Railroad," pp. 7, 8.

he reached out his hand, saying, "How do you do, gentlemen?"
The little assemblage hardly knew what to think or do at the
moment.   He was about as wet as if he had come up out of the
Delaware.   Very soon he remarked that, before leaving Richmond,
he had selected for his arrival-hymn (if he lived) the psalm beginning with these words: "I waited patiently for the Lord, and He
heard my prayer."   And most touchingly did he sing the psalm,
much to his own relief, as well as to the delight of his small audience.
He was then christened Henry Box Brown, and soon afterward
was sent to the hospitable residence of James Mott and E. M.
Davis, on Ninth Street, where, it is needless to say, he met a cordial
reception from Mrs. Lucretia Mott and her household.*

Other attempts were made after that time to
ship fugitive slaves out of the South as express
packages. In 1857, a young woman was shipped
from Baltimore to Philadelphia in a box of freight.
After reaching Philadelphia, this box with its living
freight, after having been turned upside down
several times, was left standing nearly all of one
night at the freight shed, and it was not secured
by the persons to whom it was consigned until
ten o'clock the next day. When the box was
opened the young woman inside was unconscious
and could not speak for some time. She recovered,
however, and eventually escaped to Canada.

Samuel A. Smith, who shipped Henry Box
Brown from Richmond to Philadelphia, attempted,
shortly after this successful venture, to send
two other slaves by express to the anti-slavery
office. The deceit, however, was discovered and

---

*" The Underground Railroad," William Still, pp. 83, 84.

Smith was arrested, convicted, and sentenced to eight years in prison, and served out his time in the penitentiary.

Frequently fugitives were secreted upon steamships and sailing vessels. There was usually a coloured steward on these vessels who was willing to run the risk of assisting a fugitive to escape. Men dressed themselves as women, and women dressed themselves as men in order to escape from slavery. Sometimes fugitives travelled hundreds of miles in skiffs in order to reach free soil.

William Still, the author of the book on "The Underground Railroad," had a singular experience. One summer day in 1850, as he was engaged in mailing the weekly issue of the *Pennsylvania Freeman*, two coloured men entered the office. One of these was a stranger, a man who had purchased his freedom and gone to Philadelphia in the hope of finding his relatives.

"I am from Alabama," he said, speaking slowly and deliberately. "I have come in search of my people. My little brother and I were kidnapped about forty years ago, and I thought by coming to Philadelphia and having notices published and read old people would remember about it, and I could find my mother and people."

"Where were you kidnapped from?" asked Mr. Still.

"I don't know," was the reply.

"Don't you know the name of the place?"

"No."

"Don't you know the name of any town, river, neighbourhood or state?"

"No."

"What was your name?"

"Peter."

"What was your brother's name?"

"Levin."

"What were the names of your father and mother?"

"Levin and Sidney."

By the time the dialogue had reached this point William Still was so fully convinced that the stranger was one of his long-lost brothers that he scarcely knew what to do.

"I allowed a full hour to pass," he says, in relating the circumstance, "meanwhile plying him with questions before intimating to my brother the discovery I had made. Then seating myself by his side, I said, 'I think I can tell you about all your kinsfolk — mother, father, and all,' and then I went on to say, 'You are an own brother of mine.'"

Such proved to be the case. It seems that Peter Still had been stolen from his parents when they were living on a farm in New Jersey, in an obscure little settlement of Free Negroes and fugitive slaves called "Springtown," in Cumberland County.*

* Springtown is one of the several little Negro communities still existing in New Jersey.

The father of William Still and his brother, Peter, had purchased his own freedom from his master, about 1800. The mother was a fugitive slave. Peter had been carried from his mother when he was six years old and taken to Alabama. After he had grown to be a young man he made up his mind to save money by performing extra labour, to buy his freedom. Fearing that his master would be unwilling to sell him his freedom, he secured the friendly offices of a Jew named Friedman who made the purchase and set him free.

After reaching Philadelphia and finding his brother William, as has been described, Peter Still made several attempts to secure the freedom of his wife and children, whom he left in slavery in Alabama. It was in an attempt to secure the freedom of Peter Still's wife and children that Seth Concklin, the Shaker Abolitionist, lost his life. Seth Concklin was one of the few white men who, in their efforts to rescue the slaves, penetrated the slave country. He succeeded in bringing the fugitives by boat down the Tennessee and up the Mississippi and the Wabash rivers, as far as Vincennes, when he and they were captured and taken back. Concklin was killed in an attempt to escape.*

---

* Among the other Northern white men who went into the South to abduct slaves were the Reverend Calvin Fairbank, the Reverend Charles T. Torrey, and Dr. Alexander M. Ross, of Canada. Mr. Fairbank carried off from the neighbourhood of Covington, Ky., the Stanton family, father, mother, and six children, by packing them in a load of straw. The Reverend Charles T. Torrey went to Mary-

One of the most singular and interesting figures among the people who were engaged in the work of the "Underground Railroad" was Harriet Tubman. She escaped from slavery some time about 1849, when she was between twenty and twenty-five years of age. It was the fear that she and her brothers were to be "sold South" that finally led her to make the attempt to escape. She started, with her brothers, from her home in Maryland, guided, as she said, only by the North Star. But after the fugitives had made some distance, the brothers, who feared that they would not succeed, turned back and Harriet went on alone. After making her own escape, she went back repeatedly to different parts of the South and aided in the escape of other fugitives. Many of the slaves who had escaped to Canada, and who had learned to have complete faith in "Moses," as they called her, employed her to secure the freedom of their friends. The fugitives in Canada believed that she had a charmed life. As a matter of fact, Harriet Tubman succeeded, in the course of nineteen different trips into the South, in bringing more than three hundred slaves from the South into the

land and from there sent some four hundred slaves over different routes to Canada. Dr. Alexander M. Ross made extensive tours through various slave states for the purpose of spreading information about Canada and the routes by which that country could be reached. He made trips into Maryland, Kentucky, Virginia, and Tennessee. He went to New Orleans, and from that point set out upon a journey, in the course of which he visited Vicksburg, Selma, and Columbus, Mississippi, Augusta, Georgia, and Charleston, South Carolina. — "The Underground Railroad," Siebert, p. 28.

Northern states and Canada, and in no case was a fugitive under her care ever captured. During the Civil War, she was employed in the secret service of the Federal Army, and, in the last year of the war, carried papers which admitted her through the lines of the Union Army in any part of the country, wherever she cared to go. She was still living, in 1908, in retirement at Auburn, New York.

The most distinguished fugitive who escaped from slavery was Frederick Douglass, who secured a "sailor's protection," which certified that he was a free American sailor. Armed with this on Monday, September 3, 1838, he boarded the train at Baltimore and rode directly to New York City. From there he went into New Bedford, where he found refuge in the home of a coloured man by the name of Nathan Johnson. After Frederick Douglass went to live in Rochester, New York, his home there became one of the principal stations of the "Underground Railroad," which ran from New York City through Albany to the Great Lakes and Canada.

He has told, in his autobiography, the manner in which fugitives were brought to his home, concealed there, and then hurried on to the little town of Charlotte, seven miles from Rochester, and there placed on board a little lake steamer en route for Canada.

"On one occasion," he said, "I had eleven

fugitives at the same time under my roof. And it was necessary for them to remain with me until I could collect sufficient money to get them on to Canada.

"But," he added, "it is due to the truth to state that we seldom called in vain upon a Whig or a Democrat for help. Men were better than their theology and truer to humanity than to their politics or their offices."

He refers here to the fact that at one time, when a master was in the office of a United States Commissioner, getting the papers necessary for the arrest of three young men who had escaped from slavery in Maryland, the law-partner of the commissioner, a distinguished Democrat, sought him out, told him what was going on in his office, and urged him by all means to get these young men out of the way of pursuit.

In Syracuse, New York, there was another station of the "Underground Railroad," conducted by another fugitive slave. This was the Rev. J. W. Loguen, afterward a bishop of the A. M. E. Zion Church. "Jarm" Loguen, as he was called, was born a slave in Kentucky. His mother came of free parents in Ohio, but was kidnapped and sold in Kentucky when she was a child. She seems to have been a woman of great sense and character, and after her son grew up he inherited from her, apparently, a determination to be free.

He and another young man made their escape on horseback. They reached the Ohio River, crossed the ice, and finally, after a long series of adventures, during which they spent some time with the Indians, and passed several weeks in a settlement of fugitive slaves in Indiana, crossed the river at Detroit into Canada. They remained for some time on British soil, but Loguen finally returned to the United States and settled in Northern New York.

Although he had no education when he left Kentucky, young Loguen was industrious, thrifty, and succeeded in making money. He used the first money he accumulated to secure for himself an education at the Oneida Institute, Whitesboro, New York, a school started for coloured children by the noted Abolitionist, Beriah Green. Afterward, he went to Syracuse to live and interested himself, as a minister and anti-slavery leader, in the welfare of the coloured people of that city. It was while he was there that the famous "Jerry Rescue" took place, in which some of the citizens stormed the United States Commissioner's Office and forcibly carried off a fugitive named Jerry, who had been arrested under the recently enacted Fugitive Slave Law. At this time, Syracuse was the home of Samuel J. May and Gerrit Smith, and this first case under the Fugitive Slave Law was at once a defiance and a test of the abolitionist temper of the people of that city.

Though thousands of fugitive slaves succeeded in making their escape by routes that led from the South through Pennsylvania and New York, and also through New England, by far the larger number of the fugitives passed through the State of Ohio. In all the little coloured settlements in Ohio, Indiana, and Illinois, and in the larger cities like Cincinnati, there were men who were known to be fugitive slaves. Some of these men were slowly paying for their freedom from their earnings in the free states. In his life of Salmon P. Chase, Prof. Albert Bushnell Hart, of Harvard University, refers to a theological student who was known to have provided for his education "from the instalments thus paid by a man for his own flesh, and to have charged the poor Negro twelve per cent. on deferred payment." As further illustration of the number and variety of these cases, he mentions a Negro child in a charitable school who excused her absence with the explanation, "I am staying at home to help buy father."

After the passage of the Fugitive Slave Law, September 26, 1850, large numbers of these fugitive slaves living in Ohio became frightened for fear that they were to be sent back into slavery and fled into Canada. At that time, J. C. Brown, a free man who had paid $1,800 for his freedom, organised a colonisation society for the purpose of inducing coloured people to leave the State of Ohio and settle in Canada.

"At this time," says Mr. Brown, "Cincinnati was full of women, without husbands, and their children. These were sent by planters from Louisiana, Mississippi, and some from Tennessee, who had got fortunes and had found that white women could live in those states, and in consequence, they had sent their slave wives and children to Cincinnati and set them free."

These people were now, of course, in a state of terror and their former masters were of course anxious to get them upon free soil where there would be no doubt of their security. It was at this time that a number of refugees in different parts of Canada, sprang up. Under Mr. Brown's direction, four hundred and sixty people were settled in the township of Biddulph, near Little York. These were joined afterward by fifteen families from Boston, Mass. They purchased twelve hundred and twenty acres which were divided into tracts of from twenty-five to fifty acres to a family.

One of the most romantic of the fugitive slave stories is that of William and Ellen Craft. William Craft was a slave on a plantation near Macon, Georgia. He had learned the trade of cabinet-maker and had become so proficient in that craft that, in addition to his daily work for his master, he had been able to earn a considerable sum of money for himself by work performed in his leisure moments. William Craft was a black man, but on this same plantation there was another slave, a young woman, who was almost white. They became acquainted with each other and after a time they were married. They had not lived together very long before the fear that they might at some time be sold and thus parted from one another, made them think about the possibilities of escape from slavery. After studying over the matter for some time, William Craft hit upon a plan.

There were always white people in the slavery times who were willing for the sake of a little money to carry on a secret traffic with the slaves. From one of these white men he secured a suit of men's clothing that would fit his wife. He had the suit made in the latest fashion in order to make the disguise as complete as possible. He secured shoes, hat, neckties, all the other pieces of wearing apparel necessary to complete the wardrobe of a wealthy young planter. In this disguise, Ellen Craft, having secured a permit from her mistress for a visit of a few days to a neighbouring plantation, took the train at Macon for Savannah. The husband, William, having secured a similar permit for himself, boarded the same train and, passing himself off as the Negro servant of his wife, they made the journey out of slavery into freedom together.

At Savannah they took the boat for Charleston.

From Charleston they went to Wilmington, North
Carolina, and from there took the train to Philadelphia. They had a great many curious and
exciting adventures on the way. The young
"planter" who, in order to more fully disguise
herself, had tied a bandage around her head, as
if she had a toothache, seemed to arouse the interest
and sympathy of a number of people, who gave
her advice how to keep her Negro servant from
running away from her when she reached free
soil. Both at Savannah, when they were boarding
the boat, and at Wilmington, when they were
taking the train to the North, they found it was
the rule to require passengers to register their names.
As neither of them could read and write, Ellen
Craft had put her right hand in a poultice and
supported it with a sling about her neck, pretending
that she was suffering from rheumatism. Even
then, it was with the greatest difficulty that she
was able to persuade the agents of the steamship
and railway companies to sign her name for her.
At length, however, they reached Philadelphia in
safety and for several days found refuge in the
home of philanthropic Quakers in that city. From
there, they went to Boston, where William Craft
secured employment at his trade as cabinet-maker.

They had left their home in Macon in 1848.
Two years later the Fugitive Slave Law was passed
and a determined effort was made by many Southern

slave-holders to get possession of their runaway slaves, who were living in freedom in many parts of the North. It was not long before such an effort was made to get possession of the two fugitives from Macon. For some months they lived in daily apprehension of being seized and carried away. Finally, upon learning that a warrant had been issued for their arrest, some of their anti-slavery friends smuggled them aboard one of the ships leaving Boston for England. Arriving in Liverpool they went directly to friends in London. Shortly after their arrival there they went to live in the town of Hammersmith, not far from London, which was their home for a number of years. William Craft secured employment in the African trade, and took several ship-loads of merchandise out to Africa where he was able to dispose of them with special advantage because he was of the same colour and race as the people with whom he sought to trade.

After emancipation and the Civil War had made it possible for them to return to the country of their birth, William and Ellen Craft came back to Boston and lived for several years in Cambridge, Massachusetts, where their children were educated. While they were in England several children were born to them, one of them, William, is still living there. Another has since become the wife of Dr. W. D. Crum, who was collector of customs at

Charleston, South Carolina, under President Roosevelt. A grandson of William and Ellen Craft, Henry K. Craft, who was graduated from Harvard University in 1908, is, at the time this is written, in charge of the electrical plant and the teaching of Electrical Engineering at Tuskegee Institute. William and Ellen Craft finally returned to Georgia and passed their last days in a comfortable home not far from Savannah.

Directly and indirectly, the fugitive slaves probably did more to bring about the abolition of slavery than any other one agency. The Northern people learned from the lips of these fugitives — from the strange, romantic, pathetic, and tragic stories they told — that the slaves, no matter how ignorant or how different in colour or condition they might seem, were very much the same kind of human beings as themselves. They learned from the sufferings of these fugitives, from the desperate efforts which they made to escape, that no matter what might be said to the contrary the slaves wanted to be free.

At the same time, the fugitive slaves learned in the United States, in their very efforts to be free, something about the nature of freedom that they could not have learned in Africa. Slavery, however hard or cruel it might be, appeared to the native African, as it did to the Greek and Roman, to be the natural condition of the majority of men. It was only after the African slaves learned the language of their masters and possessed themselves to some extent of their masters' ideas that they began to conceive that the natural condition of man was not slavery but freedom.

When the fugitive slaves came in contact with the anti-slavery people of the North they made the acquaintance for the first time of a people who hated slavery in a way and with an intensity which few of them had ever felt or known. They learned from these anti-slavery people to believe in freedom for its own sake, not only for themselves but for every one. They were transformed in this way from fugitive slaves to abolitionists. They became, as a result, the most determined of anti-slavery people, and many of them devoted their lives most unselfishly to securing the freedom of other members of their race.

In 1860 it was estimated that the number of Negroes that journeyed annually from Canada to the slave states to rescue their fellows from bondage was about five hundred. These persons carried the Underground Railroad and the Underground Telegraph into nearly every Southern state. *

* "The Underground Railroad," Siebert, p. 28.

CHAPTER XII

A FEW miles west of Xenia, Ohio, is a quiet little community of which one occasionally sees the name in the newspapers, but in regard to which very little is known by the outside world, even among its immediate neighbours. This is the Negro town of Wilberforce, which is, however, not a town in the ordinary sense of the word, but rather a suburb of Xenia, from which it is distant an hour's walk and with which it is connected only by stage.

What distinguishes Wilberforce from other communities in the North is the fact that it is the home of what is, so far as I know, the first permanent Negro institution of learning established for Negroes and by Negroes in the United States. A few years ago, I visited this community in order to take part in the semi-centennial celebration of the founding of the University there. During my visit I was especially impressed with the quiet charm of the surroundings, the comfort and simplicity of the homes I visited, and the general air of culture and refinement which pervaded the whole community. I doubt if there is any Negro community in the United States in which, in proportion to the population, there is so large a number of beautiful and well-conducted homes. Besides that, there was an air of permanence and stability about this community which one does not meet elsewhere, even in the quiet and orderly suburbs that one frequently finds in the neighbourhood of a good Negro school. Here, at any rate, it seemed to me, a certain number of coloured people had found themselves, had made a permanent settlement on the soil and were at home.

The history of Wilberforce goes back to a time before the War. In its origin, this is representative of a number of other Negro communities that were established in different parts of Ohio during that period. Most of these communities have disappeared and been forgotten, but there are many coloured people in all parts of the Northern states who trace their history back to one or another of these little Negro settlements that were started partly by fugitive slaves and partly by free coloured people, who left the South in order to find a home in the free soil of the Northwest Territory.

The thing that gives a peculiar and interesting character to many of these ante-bellum Negro settlements is that they were made by Southern slave-holders who desired to free their slaves and were not able to do so under the restrictions that were imposed upon emancipation in the Southern States. Many of the coloured people in these settlements were the natural children of their master. For example, John M. Langston, the first coloured man to represent Virginia in the Congress of the United States, was freed by the terms of his father's will, in 1834. In his autobiography, he has given a vivid description of the manner in which he, in company with the other slaves who had been freed at his father's death, made a long journey across the mountains from Louisa County, Virginia, to Chillicothe, Ohio. Before his election to Congress from Virginia, Mr. Langston graduated in 1849 from Oberlin University, had been admitted to the bar of Ohio in 1854, and elected clerk of several Ohio townships. He was the first coloured man in Ohio, it is said, to be elected to any sort of office by popular vote.

When John Randolph, of Roanoke, Virginia, died, he gave freedom to all his slaves and provided that they should be transported to some other part of the country, "where not less than two thousand and not more than four thousand acres of land should be purchased for them." The Randolph Freedmen went to Ohio with the purpose of settling in Mercer County, but they were not allowed to enter upon the land which had been purchased for them, because the German settlers in that part of the country did not want them there. The community was soon after scattered, but descendants of the Randolph slaves are still living in the neighbourhood of Piqua and Troy, in Miami County, Ohio. The most noted of them, as I have learned, is Goodrich Giles, whose father was a member of the original immigrants. Mr. Giles now owns four hundred and twenty-five acres of land just out of Piqua. He is said to be worth something over $50,000. Two years ago, a sort of family reunion of the descendants of the Randolph slaves was held in Ohio, and, as a result of the gathering, an organisation was formed among a few of the descendants for the purpose of investigating their claims to the land in Mercer County which was purchased for them under the terms of John Randolph's will, but of which they never secured possession.

The little community at Wilberforce grew out of a similar effort of a number of Southern planters to secure a foothold in a free state for their former slaves. In 1856 there was already a considerable number of the free Negroes settled at what was then known as Tawawa Springs. In that year it was decided to establish at this place a school for these coloured immigrants and refugees. At the time of the breaking out of the War this school had nearly one hundred pupils. Many of them were the coloured children of the white planters

who had been sent North to be educated. With
the breaking out of the Civil War, however, the
support this school received from its Southern
patrons ceased. The institution soon fell into
decay and, in March, 1863, it was sold for a debt
of ten thousand dollars to the African Methodist
Episcopal Church. This was the origin of
Wilberforce.

Of the little colony of Negro refugees who settled
in this neighbourhood before 1861, there still remain
a few families. The memories of others are preserved in the names of some of their descendants
who occupy farms in the neighbourhood. But
the community has continued to grow. A few
farmers, attracted by the advantages of the University, have purchased farms in the neighbourhood;
a few former students, who have made a success
elsewhere, have gone back there to make their
home. The rest of the community is made up
of the officers of the school and their families,
together with some four hundred students.

One thing that has given character to this little
town, and made it attractive as a residence for
Negroes, is the number of distinguished men of
the Negro race who have lived and worked there.
Among others whose memories are still preserved
there is Bishop Daniel A. Payne, who was, more
than any one else, responsible for the existence of
the colony. He lived there for many years until

he died in 1892. Bishop Benjamin W. Arnett, who was a real force in Ohio affairs during his connection with Wilberforce, lived in this community for thirty-five years. It is said that he was the first coloured man in the United States to represent a constituency where the majority were white, and the first to be foreman of a jury where all the other members were white. As member from Green County to the Ohio Legislature in 1886 and 1887, he was largely responsible for the repeal of the remnant of what were known as the "Black Laws."

Much was said during the anti-slavery agitation of the efforts of the Southern Church to justify African slavery. There was, in fact, a very serious attempt to find justification in the Bible for slavery, but any one who will study the history of Christianity in the South and its influence upon slavery cannot fail to see that, in spite of all that was said by individual preachers and in spite of all that was done by church organisations, there was always a large number of white slave-holders in the South who felt deep down in their hearts that slavery was wrong. In his will, written in 1819, John Randolph says: "I give my slaves their freedom, to which my conscience tells me they are justly entitled. It has long been a matter of deepest regret to me that the circumstances under which I inherited them and the obstacles thrown in the way by the laws of the land have prevented me in emancipating them in my lifetime, which it is my full intention to do in case I can accomplish it."

These words pretty well express the deepest sentiment of a great many people who held slaves before the Civil War, but owing to the obstacles thrown in the way of emancipation, did not go so far as John Randolph and actually free their slaves. I have often thought that the peculiar interest which former slave-holders have manifested in their former slaves was due to this feeling that they had a special responsibility toward these people whom they had held at one time under conditions which their consciences could not entirely justify.

As a matter of fact, the whole character of the anti-slavery campaign in Ohio differed from the anti-slavery movements in New York and in New England from the fact that so large a number of the people who were engaged in the movement in Ohio were either themselves men who had moved into a free territory in order to free their slaves, or they were the descendants of people who had been slave-holders.

Benjamin Lundy, the man who first interested William Lloyd Garrison in the subject of abolition, was a Southerner who had emigrated from Virginia to Ohio, and started his first paper, *The Genius of Universal Emancipation*, at Mount Pleasant,

Ohio, a little Quaker settlement. James G. Birney, who, while he lived at Huntsville, Alabama, was a member of the American Colonisation Society, finally freed his slaves and moved with them to Cincinnati, where he became the leader in the anti-slavery movement of Ohio. Dr. John Rankin, the famous pastor of Ripley, Ohio, whose house, standing on a hill, and visible from the Kentucky shores, was descended from the Southern abolitionists of East Tennessee. Among the fugitives who took refuge in Dr. Rankin's house was the original of Eliza Harris, the character in "Uncle Tom's Cabin," who crossed the Ohio River on the drifting ice with her child, and was sheltered for several days at this house on the hill.

Another Southerner who became a prominent abolitionist was the famous Levi Coffin, the Quaker, representative of a large number of Quakers who left North Carolina at various times before the Civil War because they had grown to feel that slavery was wrong. Levi Coffin was the man who bore the title of President of the Underground Railroad, and in his reminiscences he has told stories of hundreds of fugitives, whom he aided to escape from bondage. It is said that he aided no less than two thousand fugitives to make their way through Ohio to Canada. Quakers coming from North Carolina settled in an early day near Steubenville, and in a little town called Smithfield there still live descendants of the Negro colonists from North Carolina settled there by Quaker masters.

Not only in Ohio, but in Indiana and in Michigan there were scattered settlements of free Negroes, many of whom had been sent thither by the Quakers of North Carolina. In Hamilton County, Indiana, a family named Roberts settled on about a thousand acres of land in Jackson Township. These were joined, afterward, by other families, until there was a considerable settlement there, which finally gained the name of Robert's Settlement. There was another settlement very much like this, in Randolph, and still another in Wayne County.

A recent investigator says:

It is not generally known that in the North there are thousands of acres of land to which no individual white man has ever held title; the only title under the Government of the United States has been in the name of Negroes. But this is a fact and a large part of these lands exist in Indiana. In Jackson Township, Hamilton County, the Roberts family entered 960 acres of land between 1835 and 1838, and during the lifetime of its original holders, added several hundred acres more to it, all of which was unimproved. In 1907, about 700 acres of the original 960 acres were owned by Negroes and 627 acres besides, making a total of 1,327, the larger part of which is now under cultivation. In Randolph County 2,000 were entered between 1822 and 1845 by a dozen different Negro immigrants, chiefly from North Carolina. In Grant County was what is known as the Weaver Settlement. In Vigo County, before 1840, the holdings of Negroes amounted to 4,000, in this settlement, one man, Dixon Stewart, having acquired more than 600 acres.*

* *Southern Workman*, March, 1908; " Rural Communities in Indiana," Richard R. Wright, Jr., pp. 165, 166.

The interesting thing about these settlements scattered throughout the Northwest Territory is, as I have suggested, that they represented to a very large extent the efforts of the Southern people to bring about the emancipation of their own slaves. This is particularly true in the case of the Quakers. Early in the eighteenth century the Quakers began to consider the question of sinfulness of holding other members of the human race in the condition of servitude. As early as 1688, a small body of German Quakers of Germantown, Pennsylvania, presented a protest to the Yearly Meeting against the "buying, selling, and holding of men in slavery," and in 1696, the Yearly Meeting, although not yet prepared to take action, sent out the advice that "the members should discourage the introduction of slaves and be careful of the moral and intellectual training of such as they held in servitude." From 1746 to 1767 the Quaker, John Woolman, of New Jersey, travelled through the Middle and Southern states teaching that "the practice of continuing slavery is not right." And that "liberty is the natural light of all men equally." *

The minutes of the various Yearly Meetings of the Quaker societies show a steady progress in respect to the sentiment in regard to slave-holding, and in 1776 the Eastern Quarterly Meeting of the

* "Rise and Fall of the Slave Power in America," Henry Wilson, vol. i, pp. 8-10.

North Carolina Yearly Meeting advised Friends to manumit their slaves. Friends were prohibited from importing, buying, or selling slaves, and in 1780 they were prohibited by the Yearly Meeting from hiring them. In 1818, it is recorded regarding slaves that "none held them."

But under the laws as they then existed, it was not without considerable difficulty that Friends, who desired to emancipate their slaves, were permitted to do so. In order to evade this law it became the custom of Friends to confer upon their slaves practical emancipation, allowing them to hire themselves out and use for themselves the money they earned, although their masters still exercised a nominal control over them. In 1817, a case came before the court in which William Dickinson conveyed a slave to the trustees of the Quaker Society of Contentnea to be held in a kind of guardianship until he could be manumitted under the laws of the state. When this case came before the Supreme Court of North Carolina, Chief Justice Taylor declared that this practice of the Quakers was emancipation in everything but name, and therefore contrary to the law. A few years later another case occurred in which Collier Hill left his slaves to four trustees, one of whom was "Richard Graves of the Methodist Church," with the injunction to keep the slaves for such purposes as "they, the trustees, could judge most for the glory of God, and the good of the said slaves." The court held that, as it did not appear that "any personal benefit to the legatees," was intended, the will "was held to constitute them trustees for the purpose of emancipation and that such a purpose was illegal."

It was the difficulties which Southern slave-holders who wanted to ameliorate the condition of their slaves encountered when they undertook to assist their servants to freedom that led the Quakers and so many other Southern people, to found the settlements I have referred to in Ohio and elsewhere in the Northwest Territory.

In the early years of the Colonisation Movement the Quakers, with other Southern abolitionists, had supported the Colonisation Society, believing that that was one method of solving the problem. But, as experience proved that that was a wholly in-adequate remedy, and as many of the coloured people did not desire to leave the country in which they had been born and bred, people who desired to free their slaves were more and more induced to send them to the Northwest Territory.

In 1835, the Pennsylvania Young Men's Society, a Quaker organisation, interested themselves in promoting the emigration of free coloured people to Africa. They looked at the matter in a very practical way and sent out twenty-six Negro col-onists, all of whom were proficient in the trades.

The emigrants were blacksmiths, carpenters, potters, brickmakers, shoemakers, and tailors. Altogether one hundred and twenty-six emigrants were sent out in this way, and these established themselves at Port Cresson, on the coast of what is now Liberia. These Negro colonists were, however, to such an extent under the influence of the Quaker doctrine that, when they were attacked by the native chiefs, the head of the colony refused to resort to arms. The result was that eighteen of the colonists were killed, the houses were all destroyed and those who were not killed were obliged to flee for their lives.*

Some time in the early part of the last century a number of Quakers, who were dissatisfied with conditions in the Southern states, moved from North Carolina to Cass County, Michigan. They brought with them a number of their former slaves. And these made the nucleus for a settlement of free Negroes which was constantly recruited by fugitives from the other side of the Ohio River. In 1847, this Quaker settlement had become so notorious as a refuge for fugitive slaves that a determined effort was made on the part of some of the slave-holders to recapture their runaways. A number of slave-holders, or their representatives, mounted and well-armed, crossed the Ohio River in that year and, riding across the intervening states, made

* "Liberia," Sir Harry Johnston, Vol. I, p. 155.

a bold and determined effort to regain possession of their property. The effort to recapture the fugitives was successfully resisted by the Quakers, coloured people, and the other residents of the community, and the only result was to advertise Cass County, Michigan, as a place where Negroes might live with a reasonable freedom from capture by their former masters. After the raid a still larger number of fugitives poured into the county, the majority of them settling in Calvin Township.

In 1847, the same year in which the Negro communities in Cass County were raided, a large slave holder by the name of Saunders, who lived in Cabell County, Virginia — now part of West Virginia — died, and when his will was opened it was found that he had not only freed all his slaves but had made a generous provision for the purchase of a tract of land in some free State to be divided among these people. The Saunders ex-slaves, forty-one in number, started northward in 1849 and, after a long journey, attended by many hardships, they finally reached Calvin Township, Cass County, Michigan, a few days before Christmas.

Sometime in the latter part of 1902, or the early part of 1903, I visited Cass County and had an opportunity to study, at first hand, the success which the descendants of these Saunders ex-slaves and the other fugitives had made in that county.   At this time, I found that Calvin Township contained a population of 759 Negroes and 512 whites.   In addition to these a large Negro population had overflowed into the adjoining county of Porter, and to some extent all but two of the towns in the county· Among the men I met there at that time was a farmer by the name of Samuel Hawkes, who, I was informed, on good authority, was worth something like $50,000.   Another farmer whose name I recall was William Allen.   He was born in Logan County, Ohio, but his parents were among that numerous class of free coloured people who moved from North Carolina to the free soil, in order to preserve their freedom.   When I visited his farm, I found he had fifty head of cattle, ten horses, three hundred sheep, and twenty-five hogs.   He had paid taxes during the previous year to the amount of $191.00, on property in the two townships of Porter and Calvin.   He had been a justice of the peace for eighteen years, but resigned that office, because, as he said, "it took too much time away from the farm."

One of the supervisors of Calvin Township was a farmer by the name of Cornelius Lawson.   Of the eight schools in Calvin, four of them were taught by coloured teachers.   As we drove through the township, I discovered, posted up beside the road, a notice of the annual school meeting.   It was signed by C. F. Northrup, director.   Mr. Northrup, as I was informed, is a Negro.

Among other things which attracted my attention during my visit was the existence in Calvin of the Grand Army Post, named after Matthew Artis, who was one of the large number of coloured soldiers who enlisted from this township during the War. The commander of the Post at the time of my visit was Bishop Curtis, who was a member of the 54th Massachusetts Regiment, took part in the attack on Fort Wagner and, it is said, was shot with a fragment of the same shell which killed his commander, Robert Gould Shaw.

At the present time, Negroes hold the offices of supervisor, clerk, road commissioner, and school director in the township of Calvin. There are two highway commissioners, two justices of the peace, two constables, two members of the Board of Review, who are Negroes. None of these men, I may add, are professional politicians, and none of them were elected because of their colour. In fact, as near as I could learn, there is no question of colour, but merely of fitness for the duties of offices in the politics of Cass County.

In a recent study of this township, under the title of "Negro Governments in the North," Richard R. Wright, Jr., says:

The Negroes, who make up the township, are, as a rule, land-owners. There are one hundred and sixty-three Negroes on the tax books; they own 8,853.73 acres of land, assessed at $224,062, and with a market value possibly of $400,000. Some of these were included among the land-owners mentioned having property in other townships and counties also; and some own city property. The wealthiest of them owns about 800 acres in all, several pieces of city property, and has personal property amounting to more than $18,000. Several families are reported to be worth from $50,000 to $100,000 and one to be worth more than $150,000.

I have stated the facts in regard to this Negro colony in Cass County at some length because they illustrate what has gone on in a number of other similar colonies in Ohio and neighbouring states. They show, at any rate, the efforts of those Southern people, who sought to give to their slaves the advantage of freedom, were not entirely in vain.

The history of these efforts of Southern white people and the Southern Negroes to lessen, to some extent, the evils of slavery by emigration to the free soil of the Northwest Territory, seems to me one of the most important chapters in the Story of the Negro. It should not be forgotten in this connection that Abraham Lincoln was himself born in the South and that many, if not most of the leaders of the abolition movement in Ohio and Indiana, were in full sympathy with that portion of the Southern people who wanted to do away with slavery. They represented the heart and conscience of thousands of others whose voices were drowned in the factional political strife which grew up as a result of the anti-slavery agitation.

I feel a peculiar interest in the work of those men because I believe that the men in the South, who quietly, earnestly, and unostentatiously are seeking to better conditions in the South to-day, are, in a certain sense, the direct descendants of those Southern anti-slavery people of Ohio and the Middle West. At any rate, they are following in the traditions and working in the spirit of these earlier men.

CHAPTER XIII

THE NEGRO PREACHER AND THE NEGRO CHURCH

O NE of the interesting documents relating to the early history of the Negro in the United States is a paper, written in the quaint, old-fashioned style of a hundred years ago, and entitled: "Narrative of the Proceedings of the Coloured People During the Awful Calamity in Philadelphia, in the Year 1793; and a Refutation of Some of the Censures Thrown Upon Them in Some Publications."

In the year 1792 and 1793, Philadelphia was stricken with a sort of plague. Hundreds of people died and hundreds more left the city, frequently leaving the dead unburied in the houses. It was believed at this time that Negroes were exempt from this epidemic and a call was made upon them to act as nurses and to assist in burying the dead. After the epidemic was over the terror-stricken inhabitants returned again to the city and the charge was made that the coloured people, who had acted as nurses, had demanded exorbitant prices for their services. The narrative to which I have referred is an answer to that charge. In this account of the epidemic, the authors tell how they were induced to take up this work, not because of any reward for themselves, but in answer to an appeal to the coloured people to come forward and assist "the distressed, perishing, and neglected sick."

The narrative goes on to describe the distress which the plague brought on the city; it relates in detail a number of instances of the heroism of Negro nurses during the period when the city was in a condition of panic fear; and concludes with a full account of the way in which the monies, which came into their hands, were expended. From this report it appears that one hundred and seventy-seven pounds, of the four hundred and eleven expended, was contributed from their own pockets, not counting, as the report adds, "the cost of hearses, and maintenance of our families for seventy days, and the support of five hired men during the respective times of their being employed; which expenses, together with sundry gifts we occasionally made to poor families, might reasonably and properly be introduced to show our actual situation in regard to profit."

This narrative of the plague in Philadelphia and of the services of the coloured people to the citizens during this trying period is the more interesting because one of the authors of this account, Richard Allen, was the founder and first Bishop of the African Methodist Church and the other, Absalom Jones, established the First African Church of St. Thomas, which is sometimes called the first Negro church in

America, although it is probable that there were several churches in some of the Southern states which were earlier in origin.

Both Allen and Jones, who were the leaders of the coloured people of Philadelphia at that time, had been slaves and both had purchased their freedom. Richard Allen was born February 14, 1760, a slave to Benjamin Chew, of Philadelphia. He was afterward sold with his father and mother, and his three brothers and sisters, to a man by the name of Stokeley, in Delaware. Of his master Richard Allen says, in his autobiography, "He was more like a father to his slaves than anything else."

After he purchased his freedom, Allen became an itinerant preacher, working, meanwhile, as a common labourer at whatever he could get to do. During the Revolution he was employed as a teamster hauling salt. He had his regular places of stopping along the road, where he would preach to whoever were willing to come together to listen to him. In 1784, he attended the General Conference, at Baltimore, Maryland, which was the first General Conference of the Methodist Church in America, and in 1786 he came to Philadelphia, Pennsylvania. About this time, because of the influx from the country, the coloured population of Philadelphia was increasing rapidly and the white congregation of St. George's Church, where they attended, determined to force them into the galleries. Allen had already made a move in the direction of a separate church, so that the coloured people were already prepared, to some extent, for secession.   The crisis was reached one Sunday morning when the attempt was made to move Jones and Allen from their accustomed places in the body of the church into the gallery, whereupon they and their followers rebelled and walked out.   On April 17, 1787, the coloured portion of this congregation formed, under the leadership of Allen and Jones, what was known as the Free African Society.   The preamble of the articles of association, upon which this society was founded, is interesting as showing the thoughts which were stirring in the minds of the leaders of the coloured people at that time.   The preamble is as follows:

Whereas, Absalom Jones and Richard Allen, two men of the African Race who, for their religious life and conversation, have obtained a good report among men, these persons from a love of the people of their own complexion whom they beheld with sorrow, because of their irreligious and uncivilised state, often communed together upon this painful and important subject in order to form some kind of religious body; but there being too few to be found under the like concern, and those who were, differed in their religious sentiments; with these circumstances they laboured for some time, till it was proposed after a serious communication of sentiments that a society should be formed without regard to religious tenets, provided the persons live an orderly and sober life, in order to support one another in sickness, and for the benefit of their widows and fatherless children.

The Free African Society prepared the way for the African Methodist Episcopal Church, which may be said to have come into existence four years later, in 1790, when Allen and a few followers withdrew from the Free African Society and started an Independent Methodist Church. Allen's congregation worshipped at first in a blacksmith shop on Sixth, near Lombard Street. The other members of the society then became members of the Episcopal Church under the leadership of Jones and, in 1794, built St. Thomas Church, at the corner of Fifth and Philadelphia streets.

The little society maintained by Allen in the blacksmith shop grew rapidly in membership. Some time in 1794, also, Bethel Church was erected by Allen and his followers. About this same time the coloured people withdrew from the white congregations in Baltimore and New York, and in 1816 a conference was held at the Bethel Church in Philadelphia, which resulted in the establishment of the African Methodist Episcopal Church, with Richard Allen as first Bishop.

Six years after Allen withdrew from the Free African Society in Philadelphia, coloured members of the Methodist Episcopal Church in New York decided to hold separate meetings, in which they "might have an opportunity to exercise their spiritual gifts among themselves, and thereby be more useful to one another." They erected a church, which was dedicated in 1800, and to which they gave the name, African Methodist

Episcopal Zion. This congregation formed the
nucleus of what is now known as the "Zion"
Methodist connection. From 1801 to 1820 this
organisation was under the pastoral supervision of
the Methodist Episcopal Church, but during that
time it had its own preachers. In 1820 this arrangement was terminated and a union of coloured Methodist congregations in New York, New Haven,
Long Island, and Philadelphia was formed. These
churches together became the African Methodist
Episcopal Zion Connection.

Directly after the War the two coloured branches
of the Methodist Church invaded the Southern
states. At that time, there were 207,742 coloured
members of the Methodist Church, South. Within
a few years, much the larger proportion of the
coloured members of the Southern Methodist Church
joined either one or the other of the African Methodist
connections so that in 1866 the Methodist Church,
South, had only 78,742 coloured members. In that
year, the Church authorised these coloured members,
with their preachers, to organise separate congregations, and in 1870 two Bishops were appointed
to organise the coloured conferences into a separate and independent church. This new connection
took the name of the Coloured Methodist Episcopal
Church.

In 1908, representatives of the three coloured
Methodist connections met in the First Council of the

United Board of Bishops. This council met in Washington, D. C. Its purpose was to bring the three more important organisations among the coloured Methodists into closer working relations with each other, in the hope that eventually a compact organisation might be formed which would unite in one body more than 13,000 churches and over 1,500,000 communicants.

The Negro seems, from the beginning, to have been very closely associated with the Methodist Church in the United States. When the Reverend Thomas Coke was ordained by John Wesley as Superintendent or Bishop of the American Society in 1784, he was accompanied on most of his travels throughout the United States by Harry Hosier, a coloured minister who was at the same time the Bishop's servant and an evangelist of the Church. Harry Hosier, who was the first American Negro preacher of the Methodist Church in the United States, was one of the notable characters of his day. He could not read or write, but he was pronounced by Dr. Benjamin Rush the greatest orator in America. He travelled extensively through the New England and Southern states and shared the pulpits of the white ministers whom he accompanied. But he seems to have excelled them all in popularity as a preacher.

It is said that on one occasion, in Wilmington, Delaware, where Methodism early became popular, a number of citizens, who did not ordinarily attend the Methodist Church, came together to hear Bishop Asbury. The church was so crowded that they were not able to get in, so they stood outside and listened, as they supposed, to the Bishop, but in reality they heard Harry Hosier. They were greatly impressed, and before leaving, one of them was heard to remark that "if all Methodist preachers could preach like the Bishop, more of us would like to hear him." Some one replied that "that was not the Bishop, but his servant." This served to raise the Bishop still higher in their estimation, for they concluded, if the servant was so eloquent what must the master be.* Harry Hosier remained popular as a preacher to the last. Francis Asbury, Associate-bishop, stated that the best way to get a large congregation was to announce that Harry was going to preach. He died in Philadelphia in 1810.

From the first the Methodist Church was strongly anti-slavery although the sentiment against slavery was always stronger in the North than in the South. The struggle which led to the separation of the Southern and Northern churches, in 1844, was brought about because of the censure voted against Bishop Andrew for having married in Georgia a woman who owned slaves. But even after the separation, the Southern organisation maintained, at least formally,

* Stevens's "History of the M. E. Church," pp. 174, 175. Quoted in Williams's "History of the Negro Race in America," p. 467, vol. ii.

its protest against slavery. The first edition of its discipline, in 1846, declared:

That we are as much as ever convinced of the great evil of slavery. Therefore, no slave-holder shall be eligible to any official position in our Church hereafter, where the laws of the state in which he lives will admit of emancipation and permit the liberated slaves to enjoy freedom. When any travelling preacher becomes an owner of a slave or slaves, by any means, he shall forfeit his ministerial character in our Church, unless he executes, if it be practicable, a legal emancipation of such slaves, conformable to the laws of the state in which he lives.*

Methodism had started in England among the poor and the outcast; it was natural, therefore, that when its missionaries came to America they should seek to bring into the Church the outcast and neglected people, and especially the slaves. In some parts of the South the Methodist meeting-houses were referred to by the more aristocratic denominations as "the Negro churches." This was due to the fact that the Methodists often began their work in a community with an appeal to the slaves.

Methodism began in the early part of the nineteenth century in Wilmington, North Carolina, in this way. A Methodist preacher by the name of William Meredith began his work among the slaves. Through the penny collections which he took from the black people and the scanty contributions of the poor whites, he purchased a lot and completed a building. Bishop Francis Asbury visited the church

* " Slavery in the State of North Carolina." Johns Hopkins University Studies, John Spencer Bassett, p. 55.

in 1807, and John Charles, a coloured preacher, delivered a sermon in the same church at sunrise the same day.*

The Methodist Church in Fayetteville, North Carolina, was started earlier than that at Wilmington, but in much the same way. The story of the founding of that church is told in some detail in Bassett's History of Slavery in North Carolina. The author says:

Late in the eighteenth century, Fayetteville had but one church organisation, the Presbyterian, and that had no building. One day there arrived in town Henry Evans, a full-blooded free Negro from Virginia, who was moving to Charleston, South Carolina, where he proposed to follow the trade of shoemaking. He was, perhaps, free-born; he was a Methodist and a licensed local preacher. In Fayetteville, he observed that the coloured people "were wholly given to profanity and lewdness, never hearing preaching of any denomination." He felt it his duty to stop and work among them. He worked at his trade during the week and preached on Sunday. The whites became alarmed and the Town Council ordered him to stop preaching. He then met his flock in the "sand hills," desolate places out of the jurisdiction of the Town Council. Fearing violence, he made his meetings secret and changed the place of meeting from Sunday to Sunday. He was particular to violate no law, and to all the whites he showed the respect which their sense of cast superiority demanded. Public opinion began to change, especially when it was noticed that slaves who had come under his influence were more docile for it. Some prominent whites, most of whom were women, became interested in his cause. They attended his meetings and through their influence opinion was reversed. Then a rude frame building was erected within the town limits and a number of seats were reserved

* "Early Methodism in Wilmington," Dr. A. M. Chreitzberg, in the annual publication of the Historical Society of the North Carolina Conference, 1897, quoted in "Slavery in North Carolina," p. 57.

for the whites, some of whom became regular attendants at his services. The preacher's reputation spread. The white portion of the congregation increased till the Negroes were crowded out of their seats. Then the boards were knocked from the sides of the house and sheds were built on either hand and in these the blacks were seated. By this time the congregation, which had been unconnectional at first, had been taken into the regular Methodist connection and a regular white preacher had been sent to it. But the heroic founder was not displaced. A room was built for him in the rear of the pulpit, and there he lived till his death in 1810. . . . His last speech to his people is noteworthy. Directly after the morning sermon for the whites it was customary to have a sermon for the blacks. On the Sunday before Evans's death, as the latter meeting was being held, the door of his little shed room opened and he tottered forward. Leaning on the altar rail he said: "I have come to say my last word to you. It is this: None but Christ. Three times I have had my life in jeopardy for preaching the gospel to you. Three times I have broken the ice on the edge of the water and swam across the Cape Fear to preach the gospel to you, and if in my last hour I could trust to that, or anything but Christ crucified, for my salvation, all should be lost and my soul perish forever." Of these words Bishop Capers justly says that they were worthy of St. Paul.*

During the Colonial times the Baptists, to which denomination at the present time the majority of the Negroes in the United States belong, were a persecuted people, not only in New England but in Virginia. At that time this sect drew its followers very largely from the poorer people who did not own slaves, and it was therefore natural that its members should be opposed to slavery. The Baptist Church, however, did not, as did the Methodists, make an effort to draw the Negroes into the churches, but

* "Slavery in the State of North Carolina," pp. 57–59.

took care to bring under religious influence the slaves of their own members, and paid particular attention to the relations of the master and slave. In 1778, it was decided that a marriage between slaves ought to be respected, even though it was against the law of the land. In 1783 the Sandy Creek Association of North Carolina declared that a master should give his servants the liberty to attend family prayers in his house, that he should exhort· them to attend, but not use force. Among the older coloured bishops and ministers, in both the Methodist and Baptist churches, there are a number who attribute their religious life to the influence and teachings which they received through this personal contact with their masters and masters' families.

John Jasper, the famous pastor of the Sixth Mount Zion Baptist Church, Richmond, Virginia, always spoke with the greatest reverence of his former master. The Reverend John Jasper was known as a preacher for sixty years in and about Richmond, twenty-five of which he was a slave. He became a national figure as a result of his efforts to prove by the Bible, that " the sun," as he put it, " do move." Recently, William E. Hatcher, a Southern white man, who knew Jasper for many years, admired him for his sincerity and valued him for the influence that he exercised over his people, has written the story of John Jasper's life. One of the interesting incidents related in this book is that of Jasper's conversion. At the time this took place he was a slave of Mr. Samuel Hargrove, and was employed as a tobacco stemmer in a tobacco factory in Richmond. One day he fell to shouting, while he was at work, and nearly started a revival in the tobacco factory. His master, hearing the uproar, called him into the office. Jasper explained what had come over him and that he really did not mean to make any noise. His own account of what then happened, which Mr. Hatcher has given in his own words, is as follows:

Mars' Sam was settin' wid his eyes a little down to de flo' an' wid a pritty quiv'r in his voice he say very slo': "John, I b'lieve dat way myself. I luv de Saviour dat you have jes' foun', now as you did." Den Mars' Sam did er thing dat nearly made me drop to de flo'. He git out of his chair, an' walk over to me an' giv' me his han', and he say: "John, I wish you mighty well. Your Saviour is mine, an' we are bruthers in de Lord." When he say dat, I turn 'round an' put my arm agin de wall, an' held my mouf to keep from shoutin'. Mars' Sam well know de good he du me.

Art'r awhile he say: "John, did you tell eny of 'em in thar 'bout your conversion?" And I say: 'Yes, Mars' Sam, I tell 'em fore I kno'd it, an' I feel like tellin' everybody in de worl' about it." Den he say: "John, you may tell it. Go back in dar an' go up-stars an' tell 'em all 'bout it, an' den downstars an' tell de hogshed men an' de drivers an' eberybody what de Lord has dun for you."

By dis time Mars' Sam's face was rainin' tears, an' he say: "John, you needn' work no mo' to-day. I giv' you holiday. Art'r you git thru tellin' it here at de factory, go up to de house an' tell your folks; go 'round to your neighbours an' tell dem; go enywhere, you wan' to an' tell de good news. It'll do you good, do dem good, an' help to hon'r your Lord an' Saviour."

John Jasper always contended that his master made a preacher of him. "Oft'n as I preach," he said in one of his sermons, "I feel that I'm doin' what my ol' marster tol' me to do. If he was here now, I think he would fil' up dem kin' black eyes of his, an' say: 'Dat's right, John; still tellin' it; fly like de angel, an' wherever you go carry de Gospel to de people.'" *

John Jasper was born in 1812, and did not secure his freedom until 1864. He preached, as slave and freeman, for something over sixty years. When he died, in 1899, the Richmond *Dispatch* said of him:

He was a national character, and he and his philosophy were known from one end of the land to the other. Some people have the impression that John Jasper was famous simply because he flew in the face of the scientists and declared that the sun moved. In one sense, that is true, but it is also true that his fame was due, in great measure, to a strong personality, to a deep, earnest conviction, as well as to a devout Christian character. Some preachers might have made this assertion about the sun's motion without having attracted any special attention. The people would have laughed over it, and the incident would have passed by as a summer breeze. But John Jasper made an impression upon his generation, because he was sincerely and deeply in earnest in all that he said. No man could talk with him in private, or listen to him from the pulpit, without being thoroughly convinced of that fact. His implicit trust in the Bible and everything in it, was beautiful and impressive. He had no other lamp by which his feet were guided. He had no other science, no other philosophy. He took the Bible in its literal significance; he accepted it as the inspired word of God; he trusted it with all his heart and soul and mind;

* "John Jasper," by W. E. Hatcher, pp. 26–29.

he believed nothing that was in conflict with the teachings of the Bible — scientists and philosophers and theologians to the contrary notwithstanding.

John Jasper was a survival of the ante-bellum days. He was representative of the "old-time" Negro preacher, of the men who were the natural leaders of the slaves on the plantation. He lived in a period, however, when, in many respects, the ante-bellum preacher was on the decline. In the early days, before the severe restrictions were put upon the education of the slaves, many of these men were educated and some of them preached in the white churches.

Among the most noted of the early Negro preachers was George Lisle, who began preaching to the slaves at Savannah, Georgia, during the War of the Revolution. After the evacuation of the country by the British in 1782 and 1783 he went with his master to Jamaica. The existence of the Baptist Church among the Negroes in Jamaica is due to this man. Before his departure for Jamaica he baptised a slave of Mr. Jonathan Bryan, by the name of Andrew.

Andrew Bryan became in after years a great preacher. At the present time there are two churches in Savannah, one of them the Bryan Baptist in the Yamacraw District and the other the First African, both of which claim descent from the little congregation of slaves which Andrew Bryan drew around him in the years after his baptism and previous to 1788, when he was solemnly ordained to the ministry and his congregation formally constituted a church.

The story of the struggle of this little congregation to maintain its existence against the prejudice that existed at that time is interesting because it shows the quality of some of these early slave preachers. In his volume, "The Gospel Among the Slaves," the Reverend W. T. Harrison, of the Methodist Church, South, says of the origin of the First Baptist Church in Savannah:

Their evening assemblies were broken up and those found present were punished with stripes. Andrew Bryan and Samson, his brother,converted about a year after him,were twice imprisoned, and they with about fifty others were whipped. When publicly whipped, and bleeding under his wounds, Andrew declared that he rejoiced not only to be whipped, but would freely suffer death for the cause of Jesus Christ; and that while he had life and opportunity he would continue to preach Christ. He was faithful to his vow, and by patient continuance in well-doing he put to silence and shame his adversaries, and influential advocates and patrons were raised up for him. Liberty was given Andrew by the civil authority to continue his religious meetings under certain regulations. His master gave him the use of his barn at Brampton, three miles from Savannah, where he preached for two years with little interruption.

Toward the close of the year 1792, the Church which Andrew Bryan had founded began to build a place of worship. The city gave the lot for the purpose and the building, which still stands on the old site, though it is not the original structure erected in 1972, has become one of the historic landmarks of the city.

Among the other famous ante-bellum Negro preachers was a man known as Jack of Virginia, of whom Dr. William S. White, of the Southern Presbyterian Church, has written a biography. "Uncle Jack," as he was popularly known, was an African preacher of Nottoway County, Virginia. He had been captured from his parents in Africa and brought over in one of the last cargoes of slaves admitted to Virginia. He was sold to a remote and obscure plantation in Nottoway County which, at that time, was in the backwoods where there was almost no opportunity for religious life and instruction. In some way or other, however, he came under the influence of the Reverend Dr. John Blair Smith, President of Hampden-Sydney College, and of Dr. William Hill, and Dr. Archibald Alexander, of Princeton, both of whom were at that time young theological students. He learned to read from his master's children and became, as Professor Ballagh says in his work on Slavery in Virginia, "so full of the spirit and knowledge of the Bible that he was recognised among the whites as a powerful expounder of Christian doctrine, was licensed to preach by the Baptist Church, and preached from plantation to plantation within a radius of thirty miles, as he was invited by overseers or masters."

His freedom was purchased by a subscription of white people, and he was given a home and a patch of land for his support. It is said that he exercised such remarkable control over the members of his flock that masters, instead of punishing their slaves, often referred them to the discipline of their pastor, of which they stood in greater dread. Professor Ballagh says that the most refined and aristocratic people paid tribute to him, and he was instrumental in the conversion of many whites. He preached for forty years among blacks and whites alike, but voluntarily gave up his preaching in obedience to the law of 1832, which was passed as a result of the Nat Turner Insurrection. Dr. William S. White, his biographer, speaking of Jack of Virginia's relations with the white people in his neighbourhood, says:

He was invited into their houses, sat with their families, took part in their social worship, sometimes leading the prayer at the family altar. Many of the most intelligent people attended upon his ministry and listened to his sermons with great delight. Indeed, previous to the year 1825, he was considered by the best judges to be the best preacher in that county. His opinions were respected, his advice followed, and yet he never betrayed the least symptoms of arrogance or self-conceit. His dwelling was a rude log cabin, his apparel of the plainest and coarsest materials. This was because he wished to be fully identified with his class. He refused gifts of better clothing, saying, "These clothes are a great deal better than are generally worn by people of my colour, and, besides, if I wear them, I find I shall be obliged to think about them even at meeting."*

Another noted Negro preacher was Ralph Freeman, who was a slave in Anson County, North

---

* "The African preacher," quoted by Ballagh in "Slavery in Virginia," pp. 110-112.

Carolina, in the neighbourhood of the Rock River. He was ordained a regular minister and travelled about, preaching at various places in his own and adjoining counties. It is said that the Rev. Joseph Magee, a white Baptist minister, became much attached to Ralph. They used to travel and preach together and it was agreed between them that the survivor should preach the funeral of the one who died first.

It so happened that the Rev. Joseph Magee died first and the task of preaching his funeral sermon fell to Ralph. In the meantime, however, his friend had moved to the West, and the coloured preacher was sent for all the way from North Carolina to come and fulfil the promise he had made in earlier years. Ralph Freeman continued to preach for a number of years. At last his lips were closed also, much to his sorrow, by the law which forbade Negroes to preach to white congregations.

Although Negro Baptists did not succeed in organising an independent National Church until after the War, coloured Baptists were the first among the Negroes to set up separate churches for themselves. In 1836, coloured Baptists in the North began to draw together. The Providence Baptist Association was organised in that year in Ohio. Two years later the Wood River Baptist Association was organised in Illinois. These local or district

organisations, as they were afterward called, grew
rapidly after the Civil War. About 1876 the New
England states formed an organisation which aimed
to be national in its character. In 1880 the
Negro Baptists of the Southern states met at Montgomery, Alabama, to form a Foreign Mission
Convention. Six years later the Southern states
formed the American National Convention, and
in 1894, at Montgomery, Alabama, measures were
taken to bring together into one organisation all
the coloured Baptist organisations in the United
States, seeking to be national in character. By
1897 this national Baptist organisation had been
completed.

According to statistics furnished by the eighty-
nine state organisations and six hundred district
associations there were, in 1908, 18,307 organised
Negro Baptist churches, and 17,088 ordained
preachers in the United States. According to these
same statistics the total membership of these churches
is 2,330,535. The total expenditures of the
coloured Baptist Church for church, Sunday-school
and educational work in 1907 is reported to have been
$2,525,025.66.

The two great independent Negro denominations,
the Methodist and the Baptist, were the first to
break away from the older church organisations of
the white people. These two organisations contain
by far the larger number of the Negroes of the

United States. Perhaps this is the reason that they were the first to seek to establish independent Negro churches. In all the other religious denominations, with the exception of the Roman Catholics, Negroes have separate churches, which stand in a relation of greater or less dependence upon the denominations to which they belong.

The Catholics were the first to send missionaries to Africa. Therefore the Catholic Church is the First Christian Church into which Negroes were received as members. As far back as 1490, two years before the discovery of America, Catholic missionaries visited the mouth of the Kongo River. For several centuries after this a Negro Catholic kingdom existed in that part of Africa. It was eventually overthrown, as a result of wars with neighbouring peoples. Saint Benedict, the Moor, who died in Palermo, Sicily, in 1589, and was afterward canonised by the Catholic Church, was the son of a Negro slave woman. Some of the first Negroes to reach America were Catholics. They came over with the early Spanish discoverers.

Negro Catholics have never been numerous in the United States, except in Maryland, which was a Catholic colony, and in Louisiana. In 1829, a number of Catholic refugees came to Baltimore from Santo Domingo, and at this time there was founded, in connection with the Oblate Sisters of Providence Convent, the St. Francis Academy for Girls. The

Sisters of Providence, who founded the convent and seminary, were coloured women who first came to Baltimore with the Santo Domingo refugees. A few years later, in 1842, an order known as the Sisters of the Holy Family was founded among the free coloured women of New Orleans. The sisters of this order now have charge of three asylums, one of which is the Lafon Boys' Asylum, donated by Mr. Thomy Lafon, the Negro philanthropist, in 1893. The same order carries on schools at Baton Rouge, Mandeville, Madisonville and Lafayette, Louisiana; at Galveston and Houston, Texas; and Pine Bluff, Arkansas. The same Sisterhood has a government school at Stann Creek, British Honduras.

Outside the Catholic Church the first religious denomination in the United States to receive Negroes was the Protestant Episcopal Church. In 1624, only five years after slavery was introduced into Virginia, a Negro child named William was baptised and from that time the names of Negroes can be found upon the register of most of the older churches in Virginia. The first eminent coloured minister in the Episcopal Church in the United States was Alexander Crummell, who was born in New York City in 1818, but his father was a native of the Gold Coast, Africa. After his graduation at Cambridge University, England, Mr. Crummel went to Africa as a missionary. He was for a time a professor in the

Liberian College, in Liberia. Later he returned to the United States and was, for twenty-two years, rector of the St. Luke's Church, Washington, D. C. He is the author of several books upon Africa, and upon the Negro in the United States. In 1897 he established the American Negro Academy, which was designed to bring learned men of the Negro race together and to publish the results of their investigations, particularly upon subjects of interest to the Negro race.

Something like one hundred and fifty Negroes have been ordained as ministers in the Episcopal Church since Alexander Crummell entered that ministry in 1839. In 1874, James Theodore Holly was consecrated Bishop of Haiti and eleven years later Samuel David Ferguson was made Missionary Bishop of Cape Palmas, and adjacent regions in West Africa. There are several Negro archdeacons of the Episcopal Church in the Southern states. One of them is James S. Russell, who was a student at Hampton Institute, at the time I was there, and is now principal of the flourishing Episcopal school for Negroes at Lawrenceville, Virginia.

For some reason or other, probably because its teachings did not address themselves to the comprehension of the slaves, or did not appeal to their emotions, the Presbyterian Church was never as popular among the coloured people as the Methodist and Baptist churches were. Notwithstanding this fact, there were numerous coloured people who were members of the Presbyterian Church in the Southern states before the War. Among them was one free Negro by the name of John Chavis, who became famous. He was a full-blooded Negro and was born in Granville County, North Carolina, about 1763. He early in life attracted the attention of the white people and was sent to Princeton College as an experiment, to see if a Negro could take a collegiate education. The experiment succeeded and Chavis became so thoroughly educated that he afterward became a minister and preached with considerable success until 1831, when he was silenced by the law forbidding Negroes to preach.

After that he set himself up as a school-teacher, teaching in Granville, Wake and Chatham counties in North Carolina. Among his patrons were the best people in the neighbourhood. Willie P. Mangum, afterward United States Senator, and Priestley Mangum, his brother, Archibald and John Henderson, sons of Chief-Justice Henderson, Charles Manly, afterward Governor of the state, Dr. James L. Wortham, of Oxford, North Carolina, and many other men who did not become prominent, were his pupils. Reverend James H. Horner, who is said to have been one of the best teachers in North Carolina, said of John Chavis: "My father not only went to school to him, but boarded in his family. The school was the best at that time to be found in the state."

In his study of Slavery in the State of North Carolina, John Spencer Bassett says:

From a source of the greatest respectability I learned that this Negro was received as an equal socially and asked to table by the most respectable of the neighbourhood. Such was the position of the best specimen of the Negro race in North Carolina in the days before race prejudices were aroused.*

After the Civil War large numbers, as many as seventy per cent., it is said, of the coloured members of the Presbyterian Church went into the African Methodist and into the Baptist churches. Others joined the Northern Presbyterian church, which had begun to establish schools and missions in the South among the Negroes directly after the War. In 1902, the Presbyterian Church, North, had eleven Presbyteries in the Southern states with two hundred and nine ministers, only seven of whom were white.

In spite of the large secession from the Presbyterian Church, South, a considerable number of coloured people still clung to the Southern branch of that Church. In the latter part of the Nineties, however, these coloured churches, at their own request, were set apart from the white churches and organised under the title of the Afro-American Presbyterian Church.

* "Slavery in the State of North Carolina," Johns Hopkins University Studies, p. 75.

The Congregational Church, through the medium of the American Missionary Association, began, directly after the War, to raise large sums of money and establish schools for the Freedmen. A number of these schools, like the one at Hampton, have now become independent of the organisation which started them. But a large number of schools are still being supported in different parts of the South by funds of the American Board. Around these schools there has usually grown up a coloured Congregational church. At first, these churches were located, for the most part, in the cities, but in recent years as the schools in the country districts have increased, the number of churches outside the city has multiplied. In 1902, the number of coloured Congregational churches was 230; the number of ministers and missionaries, 139, and the number of church members, 12,155.*

In 1890, the United States Census Bureau undertook a complete census of the religious denominations. Since that time no complete and systematic study of all the denominations has been made. The following table, however, prepared by Dr. H. K. Carroll, who had charge of the preparation of the church statistics of the Eleventh Census, although it does not agree entirely with the statistics furnished by the religious societies, probably shows

* "The Negro Church, a Social Study," p. 151.

pretty accurately the growth and relative percentage of strength of the different denominations:

Denomination	Ministers	Churches	Communicants
Regular Baptist	13,751	19,030	1,864,877
Church of God (Baptist) . . .	71	93	8,500
Christian	88	34	956
Union American Methodist Episcopal	138	255	18,500
African Methodist Episcopal . .	6,170	6,920	858,323
African American Methodist Protestant	200	125	4,000
African Methodist Episcopal Zion .	3,986	3,280	583,106
Congregational Methodist . . .	5	5	319
Zion Union Apostolic (Methodist) .	30	32	2,346
Coloured Methodist Episcopal .	2,727	2,758	224,700
Evangelical Missionary (Methodist)	92	47	5,014
Cumberland Presbyterian . .	80	150	13,020
Total	27,338	32,729	3,583,661
Coloured members in Methodist Episcopal Churches	2,161	3,611	299,985
Coloured members in other bodies (est'd)	900	1,400	150,000
Grand total . . .	30,399	37,740	4,033,646
Grand total in 1890 . .		23,770	2,674,177
Gains in eighteen years .		13,970	1,359,469

These figures show that nearly half of the Negro population of the United States are members of one or the other of the great religious denominations. This means that, among the Negro population, the church plays a much more important part than it does among the white population, since considerably more than two-thirds of the white population are not enrolled in any church organisation. The influence of the Negro Church is particularly strong in the Southern states. In fact there is hardly a community or a plantation in the South so remote, or so obscure, that it does not possess some sort of place where the coloured people meet and worship.

These churches are not always what they should be. The coloured preacher is often ignorant and sometimes even immoral, but in spite of this fact the Church remains the centre for all those influences that are making for the welfare and the upbuilding of the communities in which they are situated. All these churches are connected more or less directly with the larger denominational organisations and thus serve, to some extent, to connect the people in them with the life and progress of the outside world.

I shall have something to say in a subsequent chapter in regard to the social work of the Negro Church. I wish to emphasise at this point, however, that the Negro Church represents the masses of the Negro people. It was the first institution to develop out of the life of the Negro masses and it still retains the strongest hold upon them. As the Negro Church grows stronger materially and spiritually so do the masses of the Negro people advance. There is no better indication of the progress of the masses of the people than the growth and development of these great Negro organisations.

CHAPTER XIV

A GOOD many stories have been told about John Randolph of Roanoke, and his peculiar opinions in regard to slavery. One of these concerns his reply to a man who asked him who, in his opinion, was the greatest orator he had ever heard. John Randolph was a great orator himself, and he had known Patrick Henry, but, in reply to this question, he said: "The greatest orator I ever heard was a woman. She was a slave. She was a mother, and her rostrum was the auction block." With that he arose and imitated the thrilling tones with which this slave woman had appealed to the sympathy and to the justice of the bystanders, concluding with an indignant denunciation of them and of the traffic in which they were engaged.

"There," said Mr. Randolph, in conclusion, "was eloquence. I have heard no man speak like that."

This story will serve to illustrate what was, from the beginning, the strongest force in the abolition of slavery in the South. I mean the appeal which the slaves made, themselves, not merely in words but in actions, to the sympathy of their masters. It was the faithful servants of the Southern masters who were the first Negro abolitionists.

This appeal which the Negro made for freedom merely through his humanity made its deepest impression, apparently, upon those people who had come to this country to obtain liberty for themselves. One of the very earliest of the anti-slavery men in the country was Anthony Benezet, the son of Huguenot parents who escaped from France on account of the revocation of the Edict of Nantes. He established and taught an evening school in Philadelphia for the instruction of Negroes and, as early as 1780, he made an effort to induce the Legislature of Pennsylvania to begin the work of emancipation. Anthony Benezet, after coming to America, joined the order of Friends, or Quakers as they were called. The people of this sect, who were more persecuted than any of the other English denominations that came to America to obtain religious freedom, were the first to give and to demand for the Negro emancipation.

Another thing that early aroused sympathy for the Negro slave was the sufferings of Americans who had been carried by the Barbary pirates into slavery in Africa. This was particularly true in Massachusetts and in New England, where a large proportion of the people were engaged in

shipping, and consequently suffered more heavily
from these piratical attacks. Among other Americans carried into African slavery was one of the
first graduates of Harvard University, and in 1793,
no less than one hundred and fifteen Americans
were held in slavery in Algiers. The fact of the
sufferings of the white slaves taken to Africa is
frequently mentioned by the early abolitionists in
Massachusetts as a reason for freeing the black
slaves in America. One of the earliest books
written in this country, which obtained any reputation abroad, was the story of the " Algerine Captive,"
which describes the hardships of these white slaves
in Africa, and seeks to turn the sentiment aroused
by this foreign white slavery against the black
slavery at home.*

As a rule the Negro was not an anti-slavery
agitator. In the South the free Negroes were
frequently themselves slave-holders. Nevertheless,
free Negroes were known to be in sympathy with
the desire of the slaves to be free. That was one
reason why they were regarded by slave-holders

* In an elaborate State paper John Jay, while Secretary for Foreign Affairs, in
referring to the connection between white slavery in Africa and black slavery in
America said: "If a war should take place between France and Algiers and in the
course of it France should invite the American slaves there to run away from their
masters, and actually receive and protect them in their camp, what would Congress,
and indeed the world, think and say of France, if, on making peace with Algiers,
she should give up those American slaves to their former Algerine masters? Is
there any other difference between the two cases than this, namely, that the American slaves at Algiers are white people, whereas the African slaves at New York were
black people?" Quoted in a lecture, "White Slavery in the Barbary States,"
before the Boston Mercantile Library Association, 1847. "The Works of Charles
Sumner," vol. i, p. 449.

with so much distrust. In the North free Negroes were very largely engaged in the work of the Underground Railroad. In his history of that institution, Professor Wilbur H. Siebert has preserved the names of more than one hundred and forty coloured people, who maintained Underground Railroad stations in different parts of the United States. In Massachusetts there were Henry Box Brown and William Wells Brown, both of them fugitive slaves. Henry Box Brown was so named from the manner in which he escaped from slavery. William Wells Brown was born in Lexington, Kentucky, in 1816. He was taken as a boy to St. Louis, Missouri, and was employed by Elijah P. Lovejoy, the anti-slavery agitator, who was at that time editor of the St. Louis *Times*. It was here that be got his first education. After a year in Mr. Lovejoy's printing-office, young Brown was hired out to a captain of one of the river steamboats. In 1834 he escaped from the boat and came North. He obtained a position as a steward on one of the steamers on Lake Erie, where he was of great service to fugitive slaves, making their way to Canada. It was said that in a single year he gave free passage across the lake to sixty-five fugitives.

A little later, when he was living in Buffalo, he organised a "vigilance committee" to protect and aid fugitive slaves. During all this time he employed his evenings in study and, in 1843, he was engaged as a lecturer by the Anti-slavery Society, continuing in that position until 1849, when he went abroad.

Another agent of the Underground Railroad in Massachusetts was Charles Lenox Remond, who was born and brought up in Salem, Massachusetts, and as a consequence had the advantage of excellent school training. He became an anti-slavery lecturer in 1838, and went to England in 1846, as a delegate to the World's Anti-slavery Convention. In New York the principal agents of the Underground Railroad were Dr. James McCune Smith, David Ruggles, Bishop J. W. Loguen, the Rev. James W. C. Pennington, and Frederick Douglass. David Ruggles was one of the very early members of the Underground Railroad, and is said to have been connected with the work almost from the beginning. He edited for a number of years a quarterly magazine called the *Mirror of Liberty* and died in 1849.

Dr. James McCune Smith was born in New York, but received his medical education in Scotland. After his return to America he became an active writer for the newspapers and magazines and contributed a number of papers upon the history and progress of the Negro race. James W. C. Pennington was born a slave in 1809, on the plantation of Colonel Gordon, in Maryland, where he learned the trade of blacksmith. He joined the Presbyterian Church, studied in Germany, where he received the degree of Doctor of Divinity from the University of Heidelberg, and, upon his return to America, became the pastor of the Shiloh Church in New York City. He died in 1871.

In Pennsylvania, Robert Purvis, the only coloured man to sign the Declarations of the First American Anti-slavery Convention in Philadelphia in 1833, was the most prominent anti-slavery man of the coloured race. In 1850, he became chairman of the General Vigilance Committee, of which William Still was secretary.* During this time William Whipper, who afterward took a prominent part in the anti-slavery agitation, was a lumber merchant in the little town of Columbia, in the county of Lancaster, in the southeastern corner of Pennsylvania. At this time, this county was one of the principal avenues of escape for fugitive slaves and the coloured lumber merchants, Smith and Whipper,

---

* In an article published in *The Atlantic Monthly*, describing this first anti-slavery convention, John G. Whittier, the Quaker poet, mentions Robert Purvis and other coloured members of that convention. He says: "The president, after calling James McCrummell, one of the two or three coloured members of the convention, to the chair, made some eloquent remarks upon those editors who had ventured to advocate emancipation. At the close of his speech a young man rose to speak, whose appearance at once arrested my attention. I think I have never seen a finer face and figure, and his manner, words, and bearing were in keeping. 'Who is he?' I asked one of the Pennsylvania delegates. 'Robert Purvis, of this city, a coloured man,' was the answer. He began by uttering his heartfelt thanks to the delegates who had convened for the deliverance of his people. He spoke of Garrison in terms of warmest eulogy, as one who had stirred the heart of the nation, broken the tomb-like slumber of the church, and compelled it to listen to the story of the slave's wrongs. He closed by declaring that the friends of coloured Americans would not be forgotten. 'Their memories,' he said, 'will be cherished when pyramids and monuments have crumbled in dust. The flood of time is sweeping away the refuge of lies; is bearing on the advocates of our cause to a glorious immortality.'" *The Atlantic Monthly*, vol. xxxiii, pp. 168, 169.

were known to be active agents of the Underground Railroad. From 1847 to 1860, according to a letter written to William Still, the author of the Underground Railroad, Mr. Whipper expended as much as a thousand dollars a year in assisting fugitive slaves. After the passage of the Fugitive Slave Law in 1850, the coloured population at Columbia decreased from 943 to 487 by emigration and in 1861, when the War broke out, Mr. Whipper was preparing to go to Canada himself.

The number of coloured people engaged in the Underground Railroad was, as I have already said, much larger in Ohio than in any other of the Northern states. At Oberlin, Portsmouth, and Cincinnati, Ohio, and Detroit, Michigan, there were a number of Negroes who worked with the white abolitionists of these cities, in assisting fugitives on their way to Canada. In the neighborhood of Portsmouth, Ohio, slaves were assisted across the river by a barber of the town of Jackson, whose name was Poindexter. At Louisville, Kentucky, there was a coloured man by the name of Wash Spradley, who helped many slaves to escape into the free states across the river. Professor Siebert gives the names of more than one hundred coloured men who were known to be actively engaged in assisting in the escape of fugitive slaves in the State of Ohio. He says:

George W. S. Lucas, a coloured man of Salem, Columbiana County, Ohio, made frequent trips with the closed carriage of

Phillip Evans between Barnesville, New Philadelphia, and Cadiz, and two stations, Ashtabula and Painesville, on the shore of Lake Erie. Occasionally Mr. Lucas conducted parties to Cleveland and Sandusky and Toledo, but in such cases he went on foot or by stage. His trips were sometimes a hundred miles or more in length. George L. Burroughes, a coloured man of Cairo, Illinois, became an agent for the Underground Road in 1857 while acting as porter of a sleeping-car running on the Illinois Central Railroad between Cairo and Chicago. At Albany, New York, Stephens, a Negro, was an agent for the Underground Road for a wide extent of territory. At Detroit there were several agents, among them George De Baptiste and George Dolarson.*

There were fewer stations of the Underground Railroad maintained in Illinois by coloured people than in most of the other Western states. Chicago, however, was the centre of anti-slavery sentiment and there early sprang up in that city a small colony of free Negroes who sometimes assisted fugitive slaves from Missouri to escape. Among the early coloured settlers of Chicago was John G. Jones, who for many years had a tailor shop on Dearborn Street near Madison and was, at the time of his death, in 1879, one of the wealthiest Negroes in Illinois. A few years ago, when Mrs. Jones was visiting her niece, who is the wife of Lloyd G. Wheeler, formerly Business Agent of Tuskegee Institute, I learned that her husband had been for many years a friend of John Brown and when, in the winter of 1858 and 1859, he made his sensational "rescue" of the Missouri slaves,

* "The Underground Railroad," Wilbur H. Siebert, p. 70.

Brown stopped at Mr. Jones's house on his way to Canada.

In addition to those I have already mentioned, there is evidence that there was a pretty well-organised body of coloured people engaged in the Underground Railroad extending the whole length of the Great Lakes from Detroit, Michigan, to Buffalo, New York. This organisation was known as the "Liberty League." John Brown was well acquainted with the members of this organisation and, when he held his famous "convention" at Chatham, Canada, shortly before the raid on Harper's Ferry, it was from the ranks of this organisation that he drew, in all probability, the largest number of his members. Among these were Dr., afterward Major, Martin R. Delany. Dr. Delany, who was chairman of the Chatham Convention, was not merely a physician but a traveller, soldier, lecturer, and editor. He was for a time editor of the anti-slavery paper published at Pittsburgh, Pennsylvania, called the *Mystery*. After the passage of the Fugitive Slave Law he decided to go to Canada. In association with Professor Campbell he was a member of the Niger Valley Exploring Expedition, and afterward lectured upon Africa in various parts of England. During the Civil War he served as a soldier and was a member of General Saxton's staff while the latter was in command at Port Royal, South Carolina. Dr.

Delany died January 24, 1885, at the age of seventy.

Among the early Negro abolitionists were Richard Allen and Absalom Jones, the founders of "The Free African Society," of Philadelphia. This society opened a communication with the Negroes in Boston, Newport, Rhode Island and other places and coöperated with the abolition societies in 1790, in studying the conditions of the free blacks. In 1799 and 1800, Absalom Jones led the Negroes of Philadelphia to draw up a petition to the Legislature, praying for the immediate abolition of slavery, and to send another petition to Congress against the Fugitive Slave Law, and in favour of prospective emancipation for all Negroes.

These two men, Richard Allen and Absalom Jones, were, a little later, supported in their efforts for abolition by James Forten, a sail-maker by trade; a man of education, and of considerable means. James Forten received his education in the school of the Quaker abolitionist, Anthony Benezet, and is described as "a gentleman by nature, easy in manner and easy in intercourse." In 1814, Mr. Forten, with the assistance of Jones and Allen, assisted in raising 2,500 coloured volunteers for the protection of the city of Philadelphia, which was then threatened by the English warships. A battalion was also formed for service in the field, but, before it reached the front, the war with Great Britain had come to an end.

In 1817, James Forten was chairman of the first convention of free Negroes held in Philadelphia. It is said that he drew up the first resolutions of protest against the work of the Colonisation Society, which declared "that we never will separate ourselves voluntarily from the slave population in this country. They are our brethren by the ties of blood, of suffering and of wrong, and we feel that there is more virtue in suffering privations with them than in gaining fancied advantages for a season." Mr. Forten was a firm friend and supporter of William Lloyd Garrison, who refers to him as "the greatly esteemed and venerated sail-maker of Philadelphia." In the early days of the anti-slavery agitation, when Garrison found so little support for his paper that he believed he would have to give it up, James Forten several times came to his rescue, at one time sending him fifty-four dollars for twenty-seven subscribers to the *Liberator*, and at another time assuming a considerable part of the indebtedness which that paper had incurred.

James Forten was born in 1766, in Philadelphia; he died in 1842. He was a friend of Whittier, the Quaker poet, among whose uncollected poems are some verses, written in 1833, but first published in the New York *Independent*, November, 1906,

entitled, "To the Daughters of James Forten."
Two grandchildren of James Forten are now
living in Washington, D. C. One of these is the
wife of Dr. Charles B. Purvis, son of Robert Purvis,
and formerly surgeon-in-chief of the Freedman's
hospital; the other is Mrs. Charlotte Forten Grimke,
the wife of the well-known Presbyterian minister,
Rev. Francis J. Grimke.

One of the interesting results of the anti-slavery
agitation was the opening of Oberlin College to
Negroes. This grew out of the anti-slavery discussions which took place among the students of
Lane Seminary, at Cincinnati, Ohio. Out of one
hundred or more students in attendance in 1833,
more than half were Southerners. In 1834, there
was a debate in the Chapel on the subject of
slavery which lasted for eighteen consecutive nights.
During that debate James Bradley, a former slave,
who had purchased his freedom, was allowed to
give his testimony. He made a speech lasting two
hours, speaking in favour of the abolition of slavery
and of the measures of the Colonisation Society.
Bradley was born in Africa, but stolen from that
country when he was a child. His master, who
lived in Arkansas, died when he was eighteen
years old. For some years afterward he acted
as manager of the plantation for his mistress,
and finally purchased his time by the year.
After five years he paid $655 for his freedom

and emigrated to free territory with $200 in his possession.

As a result of that debate, two Southern students became abolitionists, and afterward the students generally began to start Sunday and day schools for Negro children in Cincinnati. A report of the debate, which was written by one of these Southern students and published in pamphlet, says of Bradley: "He is now a beloved and respected member of this institution."

When in August, 1834, the trustees of the school voted that thenceforth there should be no discussion of slavery in any public room of the Seminary, fifty-one of the students left the school in a body. Just about this time, December, 1833, the Oberlin Collegiate Institution had been established, and the seceding students were invited to come there. The result was that Oberlin was open to students, "irrespective of colour." Since that time it is probable that nearly as many coloured students have been graduated from Oberlin as have been graduated from all other colleges in the North put together, outside of a few schools exclusively for Negroes. It is interesting to note that this result was brought about, to some extent, at least, by the eloquence of an untutored Negro orator.

Negro anti-slavery agitators, largely because of their lack of education, were almost always more influential as speakers than they were as writers.

Nevertheless, the Negro people were not wholly without anti-slavery writers during the period of the struggle for freedom. The first Negro paper published in the United States was an anti-slavery sheet called *Freedom's Journal."* This was published by John B. Russwurm, a graduate of Bowdoin College. The circumstances under which it was established were these: There was published in New York City a paper which was violent in its attacks upon coloured Americans. Some of the prominent coloured men, among them the Rev. Samuel Cornish, met at the home of Boston Crummell and determined to establish a paper through which they could answer these attacks. As a result of this conference the *Freedom's Journal* was launched. Among the contributors was David Walker, the author of "Walker's Appeal," a little pamphlet printed in 1829.* The "Appeal" was, so far as I am able to learn, the first attack upon slavery made by a Negro through the medium of the press. Another contributor to this paper was Stephen Smith, who, as a lumber merchant at Columbia, Pennsylvania, amassed a considerable fortune, with which he afterward endowed a home for aged and

---

* David Walker was born at Wilmington, North Carolina, in 1785, of a free mother by a slave father. He early went to Massachusetts to live and in 1827, having obtained a little education, he began business in Brattle Street, Boston. In 1829, he published his "Appeal," which was widely circulated, and stirred the South as no other anti-slave pamphlet up to that time had done. This pamphlet was the subject of a message of Governor Giles to the Legislature of Virginia in which he referred to the "Appeal" as a seditious pamphlet sent from Boston. "History of the Negro Race in America," Williams, vol. ii, appendix, p. 553.

infirm Negroes in Philadelphia, giving the institution $50,000 during his lifetime and $50,000 more at his death. This paper seems to have been favourable to the work of the Colonisation Society. Its first two numbers contain among other things an article entitled, "The Memoirs of Paul Cuffe," who some years before had taken a ship-load of free coloured people to Sierra Leone.

John Brown Russwurm was born in 1799, at Port Antonio, Jamaica. He was taken to Quebec by his father, who was a white man, and there put to school. Shortly after, his father came to Maine and married. After his father died, Mrs. Russwurm, who had become deeply interested in her stepson, gave him a college education. After leaving college, he was for a time the teacher of the coloured public school in Boston. In 1829, he went to Africa and became superintendent of the public schools of Liberia. At the same time he edited the *Liberia Herald*. In 1836, he was appointed Governor of Maryland, at Cape Palmas, and continued in that position until his death in 1851.

Another paper of some influence, known as the *Coloured American*, was started in 1837, by Philip A. Bell. The editor of this paper, which was published at 9 Spruce Street, New York City, was Charles B. Ray. Between the date of the publication of the *Coloured American* and Frederick Douglass's *North Star*, which was started ten years later, in

1847, several other papers were launched by coloured men. One of these was the *National Watchman*, edited by William G. Allen. He was assisted for a time by Henry Highland Garnet. Mr. Garnet had a remarkable career. He was born in slavery in Kent County, Maryland, December 23, 1815. His grandfather had been an African chief but was captured and sold to the slave-traders, and afterward became the property of Colonel William Spencer. His father escaped from slavery and sought protection with Thomas Garrett a Quaker and noted anti-slavery man. In 1825, he went to New York, where Henry Highland Garnet, his son, entered the African Free School on Mulberry Street. Among the students at the African Free School at this time were Charles L. Reason, afterward head of the coloured high school in Philadelphia, George T. Downing, at one time a noted caterer in Washington, D. C., and Ira Aldridge, the coloured actor.

Young Garnet subsequently attended the high school established for coloured people on Canal Street, and when this was closed he went to the famous school at Canaan, New Hampshire, and finally was graduated at the Oneida Institute at Whitesboro, New York. In 1850 he visited Great Britain, from there he went as a delegate to the Peace Conference, at Frankfort-on-the-Main; was a missionary for some time to Jamaica; chaplain of a coloured regiment during the War; president of Avery Institute at Pittsburgh, Pennsylvania; the first coloured man to hold religious services in Representatives' Chamber of Congress at Washington, D. C. He finally died as Minister Resident in Liberia, February 14, 1882.

After Frederick Douglass entered the anti-slavery field most of the efforts of the coloured people to secure their freedom centered about him. He was an orator of unusual gifts and devoted himself with such singleness of purpose to the task of securing freedom and recognition for his people that he soon became the recognised leader of the coloured people.

Among those who were associated with Frederick Douglass at this time were Samuel R. Ward, H. Ford Douglass, John M. Langston, William Howard Day, and Mifflin W. Gibbs. William C. Nell, the author of a book on "The Coloured Patriots of the Revolution," assisted him for some time in the publication of the *North Star*. Mr. Nell was a friend of Garrison and other anti-slavery men, and when he died in Boston, May 25, 1874, William Lloyd Garrison was one of the speakers at his funeral.

Contemporaneous with Frederick Douglass's paper, *The North Star*, which was published at Rochester, was the *Ram's Horn*, published by W. A. Hodges at 141 Fulton Street, New York City, and *The Alienated American*, published by William

Howard Day, at Cleveland, Ohio. A little later, in 1855, *The Mirror of the Times*, published by Mifflin W. Gibbs, was started at San Francisco, California.

The anti-slavery people to whom I have thus far referred were for the most part fugitive slaves or coloured men who were under the influence of the Northern abolitionists. But there were other Negroes in the Southern states who, by their lives and actions, exercised a very positive influence upon anti-slavery sentiment in the South. In a "History of the Anti-slavery Leaders of North Carolina," Professor John Spencer Bassett, of Trinity College, has given a sketch of one of these men, Lunsford Lane, whom he reckons among the four prominent abolitionists of North Carolina.

Lunsford Lane was a slave of Mr. Sherwood Haywood, a prominent citizen of Raleigh, North Carolina. His parents, of pure African descent, were employed as house-servants in the city of Raleigh. In this way, Lunsford had an opportunity to hear the speeches of many prominent men of the day, among others John C. Calhoun. He waited on Lafayette, when he passed through Raleigh in 1824, and was greatly impressed by what he heard this great man say in regard to his hope of ultimate freedom for the slave. Once he heard a Presbyterian minister, Dr. McPheeters, say: "It is impossible to enslave an intelligent people." The words made a great impression upon him. As a matter of fact, he had early learned to read and write, for at that time this privilege was not yet denied slaves in North Carolina.

It was a custom among the coloured boys of the town, to assemble every Sunday afternoon at a mineral spring in the outskirts of Raleigh in order to discuss, in imitation of the white people, the public questions of the day. At these meetings the slaves, who had had the advantages of hearing these questions discussed, would repeat with great exactness the speeches that they had heard during the week. Frequently the white people attended these meetings and a master who owned a particularly bright slave would take great pride in any exhibition of unusual intelligence his slave showed at these meetings, and would encourage him to improve still further. After the Northampton Insurrection, when it was believed that these meetings had the effect of turning the minds of slaves toward freedom, they were very strictly prohibited. Lunsford Lane grew up, however, where he had the benefit of these opportunities.

Lane early began to save with the purpose of purchasing his freedom, the money which was given him from time to time. He was given considerable liberty by his master and was able to employ his leisure time in occupations that increased the sum of his savings. Young Lane's father had, in some way or other, come into possession of a secret method of making a superior kind of smoking tobacco, and, as he grew older, father and son now began to manufacture this kind of tobacco on their own account. In order to have opportunity to carry on this trade Lane hired his time, paying for it from $100 to $120 a year. The demand for his tobacco grew rapidly; he enlarged his plant and made arrangements by which he was able to sell the product in the neighbouring towns of Fayetteville, Salisbury, and Chapel Hill. At the end of eight years he had saved a thousand dollars. With this sum he went to Mr. Benjamin R. Smith, who was the owner of his wife, and, putting his money in his hands, engaged him to negotiate with his mistress for his freedom.

As soon as he had secured his freedom, Lane was able to extend his business. He added to the manufacture of tobacco the making of pipes. He also opened a wood-yard and bought horses and wagons for use in connection with it. In 1839, he bought a house and lot, for which he paid $500. As soon as he had secured his own freedom he made it the one object of his life to buy his wife, and children, of whom there were now six. Mr. Smith offered to sell them for $3,000, but as his wife and her children had been purchased eight years earlier for $560 it seemed that $3,000, an advance of $2,340, was too much to pay. Mr. Smith, after some negotiation, reduced the price to $2,500 and Lunsford Lane gave five notes for $500 each and received in return the latter's obligation to sign a bill of sale for the whole family when the notes were paid.

"His achievement," says Professor Bassett, "had been wonderful, and is an indication of what a policy of gradual emancipation might have done in developing his race, could circumstances have been so shaped that it might have been entered upon. He had paid $1,000 for his freedom, he had paid $1,000 in yearly wages while he was hiring his time; had supported himself and helped support his family in the meantime; and paid $500 for his home, and had a good business in his own name." *

Although he dressed poorly, fared as simply as if he were a slave, and had been careful, as he said, to seem, if possible, to be less intelligent than he actually was, his prosperity had already begun to attract the notice of a certain class of whites and, as several other Negroes in Raleigh were beginning to make progress in the same way, some of the white people thought it was likely to have a bad effect on the slaves. For that reason they determined to run him out of the community.

The circumstances under which he had obtained his freedom enabled them to do this without much

* "Anti-slavery Leaders of North Carolina," John Spencer Bassett, Johns Hopkins Studies, p. 65.

difficulty. Since, under the laws of North Carolina, he was not able to buy his own freedom, he had gone to New York State to have the articles of emancipation executed. As he had, however, returned to North Carolina, he came under the provisions of the law which forbade free Negroes from other states from coming into North Carolina to live. Free Negroes who violated this act and did not remove out of the state within twenty days after notice had been served on them, were liable to a fine of $500, in default of which they could be sold for ten years. About the first of November, 1840, Lane received notification from two justices of the peace that, unless he left the state within the twenty days prescribed by the law, he would be prosecuted under the statute.

At this time Lane was a private messenger and janitor in the office of the Governor of the state. He at once appealed to Mr. C. C. Battle, private secretary to Governor Dudley, who took up the matter with the prosecuting attorney and secured from him a promise that the prosecution would be suspended until January 1. The purpose of this delay was to get a private law through the Legislature allowing him to remain in the state until he had finished paying for his family. Other free Negroes in the town who were buying their families had received similar notices and they, too, petitioned the Legislature. The petitions were referred to a committee which brought in a favourable report. The bill dragged along, Lane and the other free Negroes following its course, as well as they were able, from information they were able to obtain outside the building, since at the time no Negro was allowed to enter the Chamber of either of the Houses when in session. Finally, a member came out and said: "Well, Lunsford, the Negro bill is killed."

This announcement was a great blow to Lane and his companions, but they bowed to the inevitable and made no open complaint against the decision. Nothing was now left for Lane and his companions but to emigrate to the North, leaving their families behind them. Lane had already paid Mr. Smith $620 on his indebtedness, of which amount $250 was in payment for one child, whom he took North with him and left with friends. Mr. Smith now agreed to accept the house and lot in Raleigh for $500, provided the balance of $1,380 should be paid in cash. These arrangements having been completed, he started for the North.

Lane had made some friends in New York during his previous visit there to secure his own freedom. These friends now assisted him to raise the necessary money to secure the freedom of the remaining members of his family. Most of this money he secured by going about the country as a lecturer, telling in simple and straightforward fashion the circumstances under which he had been compelled to leave his home. Early in 1842 he wrote to his friend, Mr. Smith, in Raleigh asking him to obtain from the Government a written permission to return and get his family. The Governor replied that he had no authority to grant such a privilege but thought it would be perfectly safe for him to come to Raleigh, provided he stayed no longer than twenty days. So it was that on Saturday, April 23, 1842, the ex-slave was again in the city of his birth. He remained with his family during Sunday morning and on Monday morning went to the store of Mr. Smith to have a settlement. Before he could transact his business, however, he was arrested and taken before the Mayor on a charge of " delivering abolition lectures in Massachusetts."

In reply to this charge Lunsford Lane made a statement before the Mayor's court which, because it was the only abolition speech, so far as I know, ever made by a coloured man before a Southern audience, I am disposed to quote at some length.

Lunsford Lane's report of the proceedings was as follows:

He asked me whether I was guilty or not guilty. Retaining my self-possession, I replied that I did not know whether I had given abolition lectures or not; but if it pleased the Court, I would relate the course I had pursued during my absence from Raleigh. He then said I was at liberty to speak for myself.   "The circumstances under which I left Raleigh," I said, "are perfectly familiar to you all. It is well known that I had no desire to remove from this city, but resorted to every lawful means to remain, while in pursuit of an honest calling. Finding that I could not be permitted to stay, I went away, leaving behind everything I held dear, with the exception of one child whom I took with me, after paying two hundred and fifty dollars for her. You are well aware that previous to this I was a slave, the property of Mr. Sherwood Haywood, and after many years of faithful labour purchased my freedom by paying the sum of one thousand dollars. It is also known to you, and to many other persons here present, that I had engaged to purchase my wife and children of their master, Mr. Smith, for the sum of twenty-five hundred dollars, and that I had paid of this sum, including my house and lot, eleven hundred and twenty dollars, leaving a balance to be made up of thirteen hundred and eighty dollars. I could have made up this amount had I been permitted to remain here. But, being driven away for no crime of which I am conscious, no longer permitted to raise the balance due for the liberation of my family, my last resort was to call upon the friends of humanity in other places to assist me. I went to the city of Boston, and there I related the story of my persecutions here, in the same manner that I now state them to you. The people gave a patient hearing to my statements, and one of them, the Reverend Dr. Neale, wrote to Raleigh, unknown to me, to Mr. Smith, inquiring of him whether the statements made by me were correct. After Dr. Neale received Mr. Smith's reply, he sent for me, informed me of his having written and read to me this reply. The letter fully satisfied Dr. Neale and his friends. He placed it in my hands, remarking that it would in a great measure do away with the necessity of using the other documents in my possession. I then, with that letter in my hands, went from house to house, calling upon persons at their places of business, going from church to church, relating, whenever I could gain an ear, the same sad story of my wrongs to which I am now referring you. In pursuing that course, the kind people generously came forward and contributed, the poor as well as the rich, until I had succeeded in raising the whole amount, namely, thirteen hundred and eighty dollars. I may have had contributions from abolitionists; but I did not stop to ask those who assisted me whether they were anti-slavery or pro-slavery. I was too thankful to get the money, and it was immaterial whence it came if it would only accomplish the object I had in view. These are the simple facts as to the manner of my proceeding in the Northern states; and now, sir, I humbly ask whether such a course can be construed into the charge made against me — that I have been giving abolition lectures."

After Lane had made this statement Mr. Loring, the Mayor, held a whispered consultation with some of the leading men of the city who were present, and then remarked that he saw nothing criminal in what had been done. He called upon any one present to make a statement, but no one had anything to say, and Lunsford Lane was therefore discharged.

As Lane was leaving the Mayor's office, however, he was warned that a crowd was waiting outside the building for him and that he had better go directly to the train. He made arrangements with the Mayor to take his money and settle with Mr. Smith and send on the liberated wife and children to Philadelphia. After this was done he started for the train and succeeded in reaching the station as the train was about to leave. The crowd had, however, followed him and refused to allow the train to depart until they had him in their hands. The Mayor was present and appealed in vain to the mob to allow Lane to go. Members of the crowd demanded the Negro's trunk to be searched for abolition literature. While their attention was directed to this task the fugitive was hurried to the jail for protection.

"Looking out from my prison window," said Lane in his account of the affair, "I could see my trunk in the hands of officers Scott and Johnston, and others who were taking it to the city hall for examination. I learned afterward that they broke open my trunk and as the lid flew up, the mob cried out, 'A paper, a paper!' A number seized it at once and set up a yell of wild delight. Among the crowd was a young man of profligate character, a son of one of the most respectable families in the place. When the paper was discovered, he glanced upward toward my prison window and by signs and words expressed his satisfaction.

"The paper proved to be entirely inoffensive, and as nothing further was found in the carpet bag which they searched, the crowd was quiet for a time."

At night, acting upon the advice of his friends, Lane was released from the prison and started for the home of Mr. William Boylan, who was so highly esteemed in Raleigh at that time that it was believed his house would be a safe asylum for the fugitive. It was nine o'clock at night when he left the jail. He had only gone a few yards, however, when he was seized and drawn away to "an old pine field," where a gallows stood. At first he thought they intended to hang him, but finally a bucket of tar and a feather pillow were brought, and then he understood that they intended nothing worse than

a coat of tar and feathers.   After he had been daubed
with tar, and the feathers had been poured over
him, his watch and clothes were handed him and
he was allowed to go home.   Some of the crowd,
however, continued to follow him and, as they
laughingly watched him remove the tar and feathers,
said he might now remain in town as long as he
chose.

By this time his friends had become alarmed
and appealed to the Governor for protection.   He
had gone to the home of his friend, Mr. Smith, to
pass the night and a detail of soldiers was furnished
by the Governor as his guard there.   In the morning
he settled his business matters and made ready to
start with his family for Philadelphia.   He went
to say farewell to his former mistress, who was
then a very old lady.   In describing the scene at
the home of his former mistress, Lane says:

My old mistress was affected to tears, as her mind reverted to
the past — my faithfulness to her and to her children, my struggles
and persecutions.   In late years she had been kind to me, and,
as I learned, she and her daughter, Mrs. Hogg, then present at her
house, had sent a note to the court before which I was tried,
representing that, in consequence of my good conduct from my
youth up, they could not believe me to be guilty of any offence.
And now, with an attachment for me they could not repress, and
with tears — the offspring, as I believe, of genuine sympathy —
they gave me their parting blessing.   My mother was now called
in that I might bid her a final farewell.   I was her only child, and
I had no hope of seeing her again in this world.   Our old mistress
could not witness this scene of our parting unmoved.   Unable to

repress her feelings longer, she decided, to my infinite joy, that my mother should go with me. "Take her, Lunsford, and care for her as I know you will as a dutiful son. Should you ever become able to pay me two hundred dollars, you may; otherwise it shall be my loss."

The story of the treatment which Lane had received had caused the greatest excitement in the city and many of the best citizens in the town now came to his assistance. They gave him food enough to last on his journey; sent a carriage to take him and his family to the station and arranged with the conductor to stop on the edge of the town to take him on, his family having previously been placed on the train at the station. This was accomplished in safety and the whole party started North. A member of the previous day's mob who happened to be on the train made an effort to excite bystanders at the stations at which they stopped to board the train and to drag out the escaping abolitionist, but was unsuccessful.

Lunsford Lane went to live first in Boston, Massachusetts, and after then in Oberlin, Ohio. Two of his children having died there, however, he returned to Boston. He was employed for a time as a lecturer by the Anti-slavery Society but he seems to have had none of the vehemence of the average abolitionist and was never entirely contented with his life in the Northern country. During the War he acted as a hospital nurse, and when the question arose as to what would become of the freedman, he made several public addresses, in which he showed great practical sense and understanding. He emphasised particularly the need of better education and better agriculture in the South. Among other things he said:

The wishes of the coloured people are much misunderstood by their friends, North and South. We desire, in the first place, freedom in its truest and best sense — not a mere license to do as we please. Having secured this, we wish to be situated so as to be profitably employed, so as to benefit the State as well as ourselves. We have no desire to remain in the Northern states, except as a temporary place of refuge from slavery. This is not our native climate. We love warmer suns and a more productive soil. Here our offspring wither and die. They revive and flourish under the warmer skies of the South. As soon as peace is concluded, and security for life and limb is guaranteed, we would return to a clime so well suiting our constitutions. In North Carolina alone there are thousands of acres of unoccupied lands which might be made to flourish under the diligent culture of the black man. We could occupy these lands as tenants or as owners, adding largely to the annual productions of cotton, rice, wheat, and vegetables. . . . We want more freedom for Northern teachers and religious instructors to visit the South, that they may spread before us the life-giving passages of God's Word. Heretofore, ignorance, and prejudice have almost banished these devoted men from the holy labours to which they were willing to devote their lives. We have no desire to leave the United States for a residence in the British Provinces, under a government with which we are not acquainted; nor to emigrate to Liberia, nor to the West Indies. The South is our home; and we feel that there we can be happy and contribute by our industry to the prosperity of our race, and leave the generation that succeeds us wiser and better. No greater mistake can, therefore, be made than to suppose we desire to come North. We only desire a secure freedom in the South. We hope not only to support ourselves, but to add greatly to the wealth of the country, in the way of exports of surplus corn, and cotton, rice and sugar. . . . There is no branch of business or of commerce which would not be benefited by our elevation and industry Millions of acres, now worthless, would be made to bud and blossom as the rose.*

Lunsford Lane remained, to the end, a true son of the South. In spite of the fact that he had been driven out of his native land, he seems to have cherished no bitterness against the people of his native state and city. If he had some enemies there, he had had many friends, the memory of whose kindness he never forgot. Perhaps I can not do better, in concluding what I have to say about this man, than to quote the words of Professor Bassett in regard to him:

The little glimpse that we have of his real self shows what a promise of hope he was for the race he represented. We know enough to be certain that it was a most short-sighted policy in his state that drove him and a number of others out of the community, and made impossible the development of other Negroes like unto him. Since the war we have sadly missed such strong characters in our Negro population. Twenty-five years before the war there were more industrious, ambitious and capable Negroes in the South than there were in 1865. Had the severe laws against emancipation and free Negroes not been passed, the coming of freedom would have found the coloured race with a number of superior individuals who in every locality would have been a core of conservatism for the benefit of both races. Under such conditions Lane would have been of great beneficent influence.†

---

* " Lunsford Lane," Reverend William S. Hawkins, pp. 204-206.

† "Anti-slavery Leaders of North Carolina," Johns Hopkins University Studies, John Spencer Bassett, p. 74.

CHAPTER XV

NEGRO soldiers have fought in every war, I suspect, that has ever been waged on the American continent. Negroes fought at Bunker Hill and all through the Revolutionary War. Before that time, Negroes are known to have been engaged, in one way or another, in most of the Indian wars. They were conspicuous in the battles of New Orleans and of Lake Erie, in the War of 1812. They fought on both sides in the Civil War, and from that time on they have been an important part of the standing army of the United States. In most of these wars, I may add, the Negro has fought not merely in the interest of the country and of the civilisation with which he has become identified, but also, as in the Revolutionary and Civil wars, to secure and maintain his own freedom.

It is impossible to tell just how many Negro soldiers were engaged in the Revolutionary War. In August, 1778, two months after the battle of Monmouth, the official returns of Washington's army showed that there were 755 Negroes scattered among the different regiments. But this did not include the Connecticut, New York, and New Hampshire troops, in which large numbers of Negroes, who had been slaves, had been allowed to take their masters' places in the ranks. It did not include, either, the regiment of Freedmen, raised in Rhode Island, which fought so courageously at the battle of Rhode Island, in August, 1778.* Three years later, in May, 1781, when Colonel Green, of this regiment, was surprised at Point Bridge, New York, his black soldiers, a detachment of whom accompanied him, defended their leader until every one of them was dead.

As a rule, the Negro soldiers were not organised in the Patriot Army into separate organisations, but were scattered through the different regiments. A Hessian officer, writing under the date of October 23, 1777, in reference to his march through Massachusetts, says: "The Negro can take the field instead of his master; and therefore no regiment is to be seen in which there are not Negroes in abundance; and among them are able-bodied, strong, brave fellows. Here, too," he adds, "there are many families of free Negroes who live in good

---

* At a meeting of the Congregational and Presbyterian Anti-slavery Society, at Francestown, New Hampshire, Reverend Dr. Harris, a Revolutionary soldier who had fought in the battle of Rhode Island, said of the service of the Negro regiment in that battle: "Had they been unfaithful, or given way before the enemy, all would have been lost. Three times in succession were they attacked, with most desperate valour and fury, by well-disciplined and veteran troops, and three times did they successfully repel the assault, and thus preserved our army from capture." Quoted from "The History of the Negro Race in America," vol. i, p. 369.

houses, have property and live just like the rest of the inhabitants." *

This statement is further confirmed by the official roll of Massachusetts soldiers, which shows that there were Negroes in the regiments of that state from almost every Massachusetts town. Although no Negro regiment was raised in Connecticut, still in Meigs's, afterward Butler's regiment, there was a company made up entirely of coloured men. George W. Williams, in his "History of the Negro Troops in the War of the Rebellion," after a careful study of the rolls of the Continental Army, reached the conclusion that there were no less than 3,000 Negro soldiers in the Continental army during the Revolutionary War.†

Fewer Negroes were allowed to enter the Patriot Army in the Southern colonies, although a strenuous effort was made by Colonel John Laurens, of South Carolina, and other patriots, to carry out the provisions that the Continental Congress had made for raising a Negro regiment. Free Negroes enlisted in considerable numbers in the Virginia regiments, although there was no law by which their service could be accepted. In 1783, however, the General Assembly passed a law directing the emancipation of a certain number

---

* Quoted from "Schloezer's Briefwechsel," vol. iv, p. 365, in Williams's "History of the Negro Race in America," vol. i, p. 343.

† George W. Williams, "History of the Negro Troops in the War of the Rebellion," p. 35.

of slaves who had served as soldiers in that state, and particularly "of the slave Aberdeen," who had worked for a long time in the state lead mines.

The Revolutionary War contributed, in several ways, toward the emancipation of the slaves. In the struggle of the colonies to secure liberty for themselves the sentiments expressed by Thomas Jefferson in the Declaration of Independence led many people to feel that Negro slavery was wrong. It was partly this sentiment and partly the needs of the Continental Army that led several of the states to pass laws which provided that slaves might serve in the Patriot Army and that, at the end of their service, they should go free. This was the case in New York where, on March 20, 1781, a law providing for two regiments of Negro slaves specified that, after three years of service, these slaves should be free. The Rhode Island law, which provided for a regiment of black men, specified, also, that those who took part in the struggle for freedom of the colonies should have their own freedom. It was, no doubt, largely as a result of the services of the Negro troops during the war that, on February 23, 1784, the General Assembly of Rhode Island passed a law making free all Negroes and mulattoes born in that state after March 1 of that same year.

Negroes not only served in the War of the Revolution, but individual coloured men are still remembered, in the tradition of that time, for the daring exploits in which they engaged. In Trumbull's celebrated historic painting of the battle of Bunker Hill, one of the conspicuous figures is a Negro by the name of Peter Salem, who is said to have been responsible for the death of Major Pitcairn, of the British Marines, who fell just as he mounted the Patriots' redoubt, shouting, "The day is ours!"

Peter Salem was a private in Colonel Nixon's regiment. He was born in Framingham, and was held as a slave until the time he joined the army. Colonel Trumbull, who, at the time of the battle, was stationed with his regiment in Roxbury, and saw the action from that point, has introduced the figures of several other coloured men into his canvas.*

Another coloured man whose name has been preserved in the records of the Revolutionary War was Salem Poor, of Colonel Frye's regiment, Captain Ames's company. He took part in the Battle of Bunker Hill and so distinguished himself that a petition, signed by some of the principal officers who took part in that battle, was drawn up and sent to the General Court of Massachusetts Bay

* A letter written to George Livermore from Aaron White of Thompson, Connecticut, in regard to the death of Major Pitcairn, says: "About the year 1807 I heard a soldier of the Revolution, who was present at the Bunker Hill Battle, relate to my father the story of the death of Major Pitcairn. He said the Major had passed the storm of our fire without, and had mounted the redoubt, when, waving his sword, he commanded, in a loud voice, the rebels to surrender. His sudden appearance and his commanding air at first startled the men immediately before him. They neither answered nor fired, probably not being exactly certain what was next to be done. At this critical moment a Negro soldier stepped forward, and, aiming his musket directly at the Major's bosom, blew him through."

in order to secure recognition for his services. This was less than six months after the battle in which he had taken part had been fought.

Another incident, which illustrates a trait often referred to, namely, the fidelity of Negro soldiers to their officers, has been noticed in the memoir of Major Samuel Lawrence, who took part in the Battle of Bunker Hill. At one time, it is related, Major Lawrence commanded a company, "whose rank and file were all Negroes, of whose courage, military discipline, and fidelity he always spoke with respect." On one occasion, while he and his company were somewhat in advance of the other troops, Major Lawrence was surrounded and on the point of being made prisoner by the enemy. His men, discovering his peril, hurried to his rescue "and fought with the most determined bravery till that rescue was effectually secured." His biographer says that Major Lawrence never forgot that circumstance, and ever after took special pains to show kindness and hospitality to every individual coloured man who came his way. This interest and friendship in the coloured man, which began with Major Lawrence in the way described, was continued to his distinguished grandson, Amos A. Lawrence, who took a prominent part in the struggle for freedom in Kansas, being a member of the Emigrant Aid Society which did so much to make Kansas free.

Negroes played a less conspicuous part in the war in North and South Carolina and Georgia than they did elsewhere. But in White's "Historical Collections of Georgia," there is an account given of a Negro soldier by the name of Austin Dabney, which is so interesting that I am tempted to relate the story here at some length.

Austin Dabney had been born, from all that I can learn, of free parents, but in some way or other, he had fallen into the hands of a man by the name of Aycock, who lived in Wilkes County, Georgia. This man was unable to serve in the Patriot Army himself, and for that reason offered this slave boy as a substitute and, after the circumstances of his birth were explained, he was accepted. Dabney proved himself a good soldier and took part in many a skirmish with British and Tories, in which he acted a conspicuous part. He was with Colonel Elijah Clark at the Battle of Kettle Creek, February 14, 1779, where he was wounded and made a cripple for life. He was unable to do further military duty and was without means to obtain proper medical attention. In this critical condition he was taken into the house of a white man by the name of Harris, where he was kindly cared for until he recovered. So grateful was he to this man, Mr. Harris, for taking him into his home at a time when he was without friends and unable to assist himself, that he afterward devoted a large part of his life to working for and taking care of Mr. Harris and his family.

After the close of the war, Austin Dabney acquired property and became prosperous. He removed to Madison County, carrying with him his benefactor, Mr. Harris, and family. Here he became noted for his great fondness for horses and the turf. He attended all the races in the neighbourhood, and, in the words of Mr. White's chronicle, "his courteous behaviour and good temper always secured him gentleman backers."

Dabney had been freed for his services in the Revolutionary War. He was in receipt of a pension from the Federal Government and in the distribution of public lands by lottery among the people of Georgia, the Legislature gave him a considerable amount of land in the county of Walton. The Representative from Oglethorpe, the Hon. Mr. Upson, was the member who moved this passage of the law.

The granting of this land to a coloured man was strenuously opposed by a number of people and, at the election of members of the Legislature of Madison County, the people were divided into an Austin Dabney and an anti-Austen Dabney party. It was perhaps because he did not enjoy the results of this controversy that Dabney soon after removed to the land given him by the state in Walton County, taking with him the Harris family, for whom he continued to labour. Upon his death he left them all his property. The eldest son of his benefactor Harris sent to Franklin College and afterward supported him while he studied law with Mr. Upson in Lexington. In the account given in White's "Historical Collections," it is stated that Dabney was "one of the best chroniclers of events of the Revolutionary War in Georgia."

As illustrating the character of Austin Dabney and the good repute which he maintained among his neighbours the following anecdote is related in White's "Collections."

He drew his pension at Savannah, where he went once a year for this purpose. On one occasion he went to Savannah in company with his neighbour, Colonel Wyley Pope. They travelled together on the most familiar terms, until they arrived in the streets of the town. Then the Colonel observed to Austin that he was a man of sense, and knew that it was not suitable for him to be seen riding side by side with a coloured man through the streets of Savannah; to which Austin replied that he understood the matter very well. Accordingly, when they came to the principal street, Austin checked his horse and fell behind. They had not gone very far before Colonel Pope passed by the house of General James Jackson, who was then Governor of the state. Upon looking back he saw the Governor run out of the house, seize Austin's hand, shake it as if he had been his long absent brother, draw him off his horse, and carry him into his house, where he stayed whilst in town. Colonel Pope used to tell this anecdote with much glee, adding that he felt chagrined when he ascertained that whilst he passed his time at the tavern, unknown and uncared for, Austin was the honoured guest of the Governor.

It should not be understood from what has been said here that Negroes were admitted at once and without opposition into the Patriot Army. There was at first considerable opposition to them, particularly from the officers in the army. One incident that hastened their entrance into the army was the proclamation by Lord Dunmore, the Royal Governor of Virginia, in November, 1775, offering freedom to all such Negroes and indentured white servants as might enlist for the purpose "of reducing the colony to the proper sense of its duty." Other proclamations inviting the Negroes to join the King's armies and fight against their masters were issued later by Sir Henry Clinton and Lord Cornwallis. As a matter of fact a great many slaves were carried off by the British troops during the war. It is estimated that no less than thirty thousand of them were taken from the plantations and employed by the British troops in pioneer work and in building fortifications, but the greater part of these slaves died from fever and small-pox in the British camps. The remainder were sent to the West Indies, others to Nova Scotia, and still others to the colony of Sierra Leone. Referring to this matter in a speech in the United States House of Representatives, December 12, 1820, the Hon. Charles Pinckney of South Carolina says:

It is a most remarkable fact that, notwithstanding, in the course of the Revolution, the Southern states were continually overrun by the British, and that every Negro in them had an opportunity of leaving their owners, few did; proving thereby not only a most remarkable attachment to their owners, but the mildness of the treatment, from whence their affection sprang. They then were, as they still are, as valuable a part of our population to the Union as any other equal number of inhabitants. They were in numerous instances the pioneers, and, in all, the labourers, of your armies. To their hands were owing the erection of the greatest part of the fortifications raised for the protection of our country; some of which, particularly Fort Moultrie, gave, at that early period of the inexperience and untried valour of our citizens, immortality to American arms; and, in the Northern states, numerous bodies of them were enrolled into, and fought, by the sides of the whites, the battles of the Revolution.*

Although Negro soldiers had fought in the Revolutionary War and in the War of 1812, it was some time before the Federal Government was prepared to enlist Negro soldiers to fight in the Civil War against the people who were still holding black men as slaves. As a matter of fact, it was in the Confederate armies that the first Negro soldiers were enlisted. During the latter part of April, 1861, a Negro company at Nashville, Tennessee, made up of "free people of colour," offered its services to the Confederate Government. Shortly after, a recruiting office was opened for free Negroes at Memphis, Tennessee. On November 23, 1861, there was a grand review of the Confederate troops at New Orleans, Louisiana, one of the features of which was a regiment of fourteen hundred free coloured men. Some of these coloured troops remained in the service of the Confederacy

* George Livermore: "An Historical Research Respecting the Opinions of the Founders of the Republic on Negroes as Slaves, as Citizens, and as Soldiers," p. 155.

until the close of the war, but in few cases did they have an opportunity to participate in any of the important battles.

In the summer of 1862, General Butler organised a regiment of free coloured people in the city of New Orleans, under the title of the "First Louisiana Native Guard." This was the first coloured regiment to be mustered into the Federal Army. General Butler has related in his autobiography, the circumstances under which this regiment was formed. It seems that two regiments of free Negroes called "Native Guards, Coloured," had been organised in New Orleans, while General Butler was at Ship Island. After the fall of New Orleans, many of these coloured soldiers left the city, but some remained. General Butler learned the names and residences of some twenty of the coloured officers of these regiments and sent for them to call upon him at headquarters. In talking the situation over with them, he called their attention to the fact that if the Federal armies were successful Negro slavery would be abolished, and then asked them if they would be willing to organise two regiments of free coloured people to fight for the freedom of their race. After some further consultation, they readily agreed to do this, and fourteen days later, on August 22, 1862, when General Butler went down to the place where he had ordered the recruits to gather, he says he saw such a sight as he had never seen before: "Two thousand men ready to enlist as recruits and not a man of them who had not a white 'biled shirt' on."

Thus the first regiment of coloured troops was mustered into the service of the United States. A short time after this, three regiments of infantry and two batteries of artillery were equipped and ready for service. General Butler says of these soldiers, "They were intelligent, obedient, highly appreciated their position, and fully maintained its dignity."

Previous to this time, General Hunter, who was located at Beaufort, and the Sea Islands, off the coast of South Carolina, had formed a regiment from the slaves which he had found on the abandoned plantations in that district. When this regiment was first organised the Federal Government was not prepared to accept the Freedmen in the positions of soldiers, so that it was not until January 25, 1863, that the "First South Carolina" regiment was actually mustered into service, though it had been in existence as an organisation for some time before this.

Although these were the first Negro regiments organised by the Federal Government, they were not the first coloured soldiers to engage in battle on the side of the Federal Government. In August, 1862, a coloured regiment, composed partly of fugitive slaves from Missouri, was recruited in

Kansas. Although this regiment was not mustered into the service of the United States until January, 1863, a detachment of it was attacked by Confederate soldiers at Island Mound, Missouri, October, 28, 1862, but after considerable fighting the coloured troops succeeded in beating off their opponents. This was the first action in which Negro troops were engaged in the Civil War.

After the emancipation proclamation was issued on January 1, 1863, the work of enlisting coloured soldiers was taken in hand in more serious fashion. Early in the year 1863, Governor John A. Andrews secured permission to organise a regiment of coloured troops. On April 12, of that year, the Fifty-fourth Massachusetts Volunteer Infantry, composed of "persons of African descent," had completed its quota, and shortly after this two other coloured regiments were organised. These were the first soldiers recruited from among the free coloured people of the North. To complete these regiments, coloured people were summoned from all of the Northern states. Governor Andrews was greatly assisted in the work of recruiting the coloured people to fill these regiments by Frederick Douglass and the coloured abolitionists, William Wells Brown and Charles Lenox Remond. Among the coloured soldiers who sailed for South Carolina with the Massachusetts regiments were two sons of Frederick Douglass, Lewis H. and Charles R. Douglass.

Among the coloured people who enlisted in the Federal army at this time there was a large number who afterward distinguished themselves in some way in public life. Among others I recall two bishops of the African Methodist Episcopal Church and several men who afterward became prominent in politics, among them P. B. S. Pinchback, who was in the First Volunteer Louisiana Infantry, and afterward became Lieutenant, and for a time, Acting Governor of Louisiana during the stormiest days of the Republican rule in that state. Charles E. Nash, who was afterward Representative from Louisiana in the Forty-fourth Congress, enlisted as a private in the United States Chasseurs d' Afrique, and afterward rose to the position of Acting Sergeant-major of his regiment.

Bishop Henry M. Turner is said to have been the first coloured chaplain to receive a commission from the Federal army. Bishop Turner was living at this time, in 1863, in Washington, District of Columbia, where he was serving as pastor of Israel Church. Bishop William B. Derrick, the other A. M. E. bishop who served in the war, was born in the Island of Antigua, British West Indies, July 27, 1843, a decade after England had granted freedom to the slaves in the West Indian colonies. He was educated in a Moravian school at Graceland. It was intended that he should be a blacksmith, but he took to the life of the sea, and became a sailor

on vessels travelling between the West Indies and
New York. This led him to enlist in the war
for the freedom of the coloured people in the United
States. He served on the flagship of the North
Atlantic Squadron, the *Minnesota,* and at the close
of the war became a citizen in the United States.

Among the other coloured men who enlisted
in the Civil War was George Washington Williams,
who afterward served as an officer of artillery
in the Mexican army. Mr. Williams was born in
Bedford Springs, Pennsylvania, October 16, 1849.
After the Civil War was over he studied law for a
time in the office of Judge Alphonso Taft, father
of President Taft, and in the Cincinnati Law
School. In 1879 and 1881, he was a member of
the Ohio Legislature. From 1885 to 1886, he was
Minister to Haiti, and in 1888, was a delegate to
the World's Conference of Foreign Missions at
London. He was a writer and a newspaper man
of some note and is the author of a "History of
the Negro Race in America," to which I have
frequently had occasion to refer, in the preparation
of this book.

Joseph H. Rainey, who was a member of the
Forty-second, Forty-third, the Forty-fourth, and the
Forty-fifth Congress, as Representative from South
Carolina, served for a time in the Confederate
Army. Joseph Rainey was born in Georgetown,
South Carolina, June 21, 1832. His father and

mother had been slaves, but had purchased their freedom. When the war broke out Mr. Rainey was working at his father's trade of barber. Being a free man he was drafted into the service of the Confederate Army and compelled to work upon the fortifications, until he succeeded in escaping to the West Indies, where he remained till the close of the war.

A small number of coloured men, probably as many as seventy-five, were granted commissions as officers in the latter part of the war. Major Martin R. Delany, and Captain O. S. B. Wall, both of whom were detailed in the Quartermaster's Department, attained the highest rank of any of the coloured officers in the Army. Dr. A. T. Augusta, who afterward became one of the leading coloured physicians of Washington, District of Columbia, and Dr. Charles B. Purvis, a son of Robert Purvis, the coloured abolitionist of Philadelphia, were the best known of the coloured army surgeons during the Civil War. Dr. Purvis has been for many years a teacher and officer in the School of Medicine at Howard University.

From first to last no less than 178,975 Negro soldiers were mustered into the United States Volunteer Army during the course of the Civil War. Of this number, 36,847 were reported killed, wounded, or missing. The coloured troops did not have an opportunity to participate in many of the great battles of the war. They did, however, serve in nearly every military department in the United States and took part in four hundred and forty-nine battles. In addition to the large military force mentioned there were at least 150,000 Negro labourers employed in the Quartermasters' and Engineering Department. They were employed as teamsters and as cooks or in the building of fortifications.

The first general engagement in which coloured soldiers took part was the assault upon Port Hudson, Louisiana, made by the troops under General Banks, May 27, 1863. There were eight regiments of coloured troops among the forces that took part in this assault, and among them was the first Louisiana Native Guard, organised by General Butler. This regiment is said to have suffered heavier losses than any other regiment engaged in the assault, losing in all one hundred and twenty-nine officers and men.

The soldiers in this same Department did some desperate fighting a few days after, June 6 and 7, 1863, at Milliken's Bend. This post was defended by about fourteen hundred men, all of them newly organised and undisciplined black soldiers, with the exception of one hundred and sixty men of an Iowa regiment which chanced to be there. The battle lasted for eight hours, during which the soldiers came to close quarters and fought hand to hand with bayonets and clubbed muskets. Although the attacking force was said to have been considerably superior to that of the black troops, the latter succeeded in repelling the attack and in driving off the enemy.

Two of the most desperate battles of the war in which coloured troops were engaged were the assault of Fort Wagner, July 18, 1863, in which the Fifty-fourth Massachusetts, the first regiment of coloured soldiers to be recruited in the North, was engaged, and the battle of Honey Hill, South Carolina, November 30, 1864, in which the Fifty-fifth Massachusetts, the second coloured regiment raised in the North, was engaged. It was in the assault of Fort Wagner that the gallant Colonel Robert G. Shaw fell dead at the head of his Negro regiment and mingled some of the best blood of New England with that of these black men whom he had volunteered to lead in the fight for the freedom of their race. It was in this same battle that Sergeant William H. Carney of the Fifty-fourth Massachusetts, though wounded in the head and in the shoulder and in both legs, carried the National flag of his regiment across the open field which separated him from safety, where he handed it over with the words which made him famous: "Dey got me boys, but de old flag neber touched de groun!"

After the war, Sergeant Carney returned to

Massachusetts, and for a number of years, up to the time of his death, in the early part of December, 1908, was employed at the Massachusetts State House in Boston, where the torn flag that he had kept flying upon the battlefield at Fort Wagner is still preserved among the other colours of the Massachusetts regiments.

Following the death of Sergeant Carney, in Boston, Mr. N. P. Hallowell wrote a communication to the Boston *Transcript* in which he gave so accurate and concise a description of this battle and the part that Sergeant Carney had in it that I have ventured to reproduce it here. Mr. Hallowell wrote:

Sergeant William H. Carney was one of the colour-bearers of the Fifty-fourth Regiment, Massachusetts Volunteers, when the famous assault upon Fort Wagner, South Carolina, was made at twilight on the evening of July 18, 1863. In that assault Colonel Robert Gould Shaw fell dead upon the parapet. Captains Russell and Simpkins and other brave men fell while keeping the embrasures free from the enemy's gunners and sweeping the crest of the parapet with their fire. Lieutenant-colonel Edward H. Hallowell reached the parapet. Desperately wounded, he rolled into the ditch, was again hit, and with great difficulty managed to crawl to our lines. An unknown number of enlisted men were killed within the fort. Forty enlisted men, including twenty wounded, were captured within the fort. The State flag, tied, unfortunately, to the staff with ribbons, was lost. The staff itself was brought off. The national colours planted upon the parapet were upheld and eventually borne off by Sergeant William H. Carney, whose wounds in both legs, in the breast and right arm attest his devotion to his trust. His words, "The old flag never touched the ground, boys!" are immortalised in the pages of history and the verses of poetry. The regiment went into action with twenty-two officers and six hundred and fifty enlisted men. Fourteen officers were killed or wounded. Two hundred and fifty-five enlisted men were killed or wounded. Prisoners, not wounded, twenty. Total casualties, officers and men, two hundred and sixty-nine, or 40 per cent. The character of the wounds attests the nature of the contest. There were wounds from bayonet thrusts, sword cuts, pike thrusts and hand grenades; and there were heads and arms broken and smashed by the butt-ends of muskets.

It is fit that the last act, the act which cost his life, should be one of courtesy. In stepping aside to make room for another his leg was caught and crushed. Sergeant William H. Carney was a gentleman. Peace to him.

Coloured troops took part February 20, 1864, in the disastrous battle of Olustee, Florida, in which the losses were quite as severe, it is said, as in any other battle of the Civil War. Speaking of this battle, Colonel J. R. Hawley, who commanded the First Brigade in this engagement, says: "Old troops finding themselves so overmatched would have run a little and reformed with or without order. The black men stood to be killed or wounded, losing more than three hundred out of five hundred and fifty." In the battle of Nashville, the coloured troops were under a life-long Democrat, General James B. Steedman, who was one of the delegates in 1860 to the Charleston Convention which nominated Breckenridge for president. It is related that as he rode over the field immediately after the battle, he said with a grim smile: "I wonder what my Democratic friends over there would think if they knew I were fighting them with 'nigger troops.'"

Coloured troops took part in the campaign which resulted in the fall of Richmond. June 15, 1864, they captured seven guns in front of Petersburg and, on July 30, they took part in the disastrous attack at the "crater" in which 4,000 men were lost, wounded or captured in a fruitless and hopeless assault.

Finally, when General Weitzel took possession of Richmond on April 3, 1865, he was in command of a corps made up entirely of Negro soldiers. It was a Negro soldier who hauled down the Confederate flag and it was Negro soldiers who assisted in quenching the fires which had been started, when the Confederate soldiers evacuated the city, thus saving the helpless citizens who were left behind much loss and suffering. It illustrates to what extent the Negro soldiers had won the favour of the Federal officers who commanded them that black troops were called upon to maintain order in the confusion and anarchy which reigned at this time in the abandoned capital of the Confederacy. Two years before, the same General Weitzel, who was in command of the Negro troops, who at this time took possession of Richmond, had written to General Butler to be relieved of his command in Louisiana because, as he said, he "could not command Negro regiments." At that time he believed that to employ Negroes in the army was to bring about a servile insurrection for which he did not care to be responsible.

The services which the Negro troops performed in the Civil War in fighting for the freedom of their race not only convinced the officers who commanded them and the white soldiers who fought by their side that the Negro race deserved to be free, but it served to convince the great mass of the people in the North that the Negroes were fit for freedom. It did, perhaps, more than any other one thing to gain for them, as a result of the war, the passage of those amendments to the Constitution which secured to the Negro race the same rights in the United States that are granted to white men.

THE STORY OF THE NEGRO

VOLUME II

Part III

THE NEGRO AS A FREEMAN

The Story of the Negro

CHAPTER I

THE EARLY DAYS OF FREEDOM

THE Negro slaves always believed that some day they would be free. From the Bible — the only book the masses of the people knew anything about — they learned the story of the children of Israel, of the house of bondage, and of forty years of wandering in the wilderness, and they easily learned to apply this story to their own case. There was always a feeling among them that some day, from somewhere or other, a prophet would arise who would lead them out of slavery. This faith was the source of the old "freedom songs," which always had for the slaves a double meaning. Interwoven with the religious sentiment and meanings there was always the expression of a desire and a hope, not alone for freedom in the world to come, but of freedom in this world as well.

In their religious meetings, through the medium not only of these songs, but of their prayers as well,

the coloured people expressed their longing for freedom and even prayed for deliverance from slavery,
without apparently arousing the suspicion that they
were thinking of freedom in anything but a spiritual
sense.   The following chorus of the plantation song
will illustrate what I mean:

> Children, we all shall be free,
> Children, we all shall be free,
> Children, we all shall be free,
> When the Lord shall appear.

One of the indications that the slaves on the
plantation believed, near the close of the war, that
freedom was at hand, was the way in which they
began singing, with new fervour and energy, those
freedom songs to which I have referred.

There was one of them which ran this way:

> We'll soon be free,
> We'll soon be free,
> When de Lord will call us home.

The Negroes, in certain parts of South Carolina, sang this song with so much fervour at the
beginning of the Civil War that the authorities
put them in jail, in order to stop it, fearing it might
have the effect of arousing the slaves to insurrection.

Another indication that the masses of the slaves
felt during the war that freedom was at hand was
the interest in which they took, particularly after
the emancipation proclamation had been issued,
in "Massa Linkum," as they called the President of

the United States, and in the movements of the
Union armies. In one way and another many of
the slaves of the plantations managed to keep
pretty good track of the movements of the different
armies and, after a while, it began to be whispered
that soon all the slaves were going to be free. It was
at this time that the slaves out in the cabins on the
plantations began to pray for the success of "Massa
Linkum's soldiers." I remember well a time when
I was awakened one morning, before the break of
day, by my mother bending over me, where I lay
on a bundle of rags in the corner of my master's
kitchen, and hearing her pray that Abraham Lincoln
and his soldiers might be successful and that she and
I might some day be free.

The plantation upon which my mother lived was
in a remote corner of Virginia, where we saw almost
nothing of the war, except when some of those who
had gone away as soldiers were brought home dead,
and it was not until the very close of the war that a
party of Union soldiers came through our part of
the country and carried off with them a few of the
slaves from our community. In other parts of
the country, however, freedom came much earlier.
Wherever the Union armies succeeded in penetrating
the South, work on the plantation ceased, and large
numbers of the slaves wandered off on the trail of
the army to find their freedom. I have frequently
heard older people of my race tell the story of how

freedom came to them, and of the sufferings which so many of them endured, during this time.

One of the curious things about the Emancipation Proclamation of January 1, 1863, was that it probably did not immediately confer freedom on a single slave. This was because it was limited in its application to those territories over which the Federal armies had no control. In the Border states and wherever the Union armies were established the institution of slavery remained, nominally at least, as it had been.

On the other hand, wherever the Federal armies entered upon slave territories, no matter what theory the Government held to, it was found impossible in practice to maintain the slave system. The first proclamation of emancipation was, as a matter of fact, General Butler's ingenious phrase which termed the Negro fugitives who came into the Union lines "contraband of war." Theoretically, these fugitives were still merely property of the enemy which had fallen into the hands of the Federal army, but actually to be "contraband" meant to be free, and from that time on Federal officers were everywhere at liberty to receive and protect fugitive slaves who came into their hands.

The result of this was that wherever the Federal armies went slavery ceased. As a consequence thousands of these homeless and helpless people fell into the hands of the Federal commanders. When General Grant entered Northern Mississippi the refugees became so numerous that he detailed Chaplain John Eaton, of the Twenty-seventh Ohio Infantry, afterward colonel of a Negro regiment, to organise them and set them to work picking the cotton which was then ripe in the fields.

In a somewhat similar manner at Fortress Monroe, Virginia, Washington, District of Columbia, Beaufort and Port Royal, South Carolina, Columbus, Kentucky, and Cairo, Illinois, large numbers of the Freedmen had been collected into camps and the problem of dealing with the Negro in freedom was brought, in this way, for the first time definitely before the Northern people for solution. Freedmen were to be governed, to be educated and, in general, to be started in the new life of freedom which was now open to them. The difficulties that presented themselves were appalling, and immediately aroused the deepest sympathy and concern among the people in the Northern states.

As an indication of some of the unusual problems that presented themselves to the Union officers, who were in command at the points I have named, I may refer to an incident which occurred in New Orleans. A free Negro, by the name of John Montamal, had married a woman who was a slave. From the savings of a small business he had purchased his wife for six hundred dollars, so that he stood to her in the relation of owner as well as husband. As a consequence his children were his slaves. At the time

the Union soldiers arrived in the city his only surviving child was a bright little girl of eleven years of
age, who had had the advantages of a school training
and had become a member of the Catholic Church.
Owing to the troublous character of the times the
father had fallen into debt and, in an evil hour, had
mortgaged his daughter to his creditors, believing
that he would be able to redeem her in time to prevent her being sold. The war prevented his carrying out this plan, and, as a result, the mortgage was
foreclosed and the child sold at auction by the sheriff.
Under these circumstances the man came before
the Provost Court, which had been established by
General Butler, and sought the restoration of his
daughter. Under the laws of Louisiana, which were
nominally, at least, in force at that time, the girl
would have been doomed to slavery, but the Provost
Judge, Colonel Kinsman, promptly decided that
the law was no longer in force and that when
Louisiana went out of the Union she took her "black
laws" with her.

Another anecdote, which illustrates the way in
which Union generals ruthlessly disposed of the old
slave laws, is related by James Parton in his history, "General Butler in New Orleans." When
the Union soldiers arrived in New Orleans they
found, in the State Prison at Baton Rouge, children
who had been born in the prison of female coloured
convicts. By the laws of Louisiana these children

were the property of the State, and if General Butler
had carried out the law he would have sold them as
slaves. When the superintendent applied for orders
with regard to these children, General Butler
promptly decided that they should be taken care of
in the same way as other destitute children, saying
that "possibly the master might have some claim
upon them, but he did not see how the State could
ha e any."

Thus it was that the work of what was afterward
called "reconstruction" began in the South wherever
the Union forces obtained possession of the country.
In the Department of General Banks, Louisiana, there
were 90,000 coloured people; 50,000 were employed
as labourers under the direction of the officers of the
army. Under Colonel Eaton seven thousand acres
of cotton land in Tennessee and Arkansas were
leased and cultivated in order to furnish food for
the 10,000 people who were not able to take care
of themselves. In South Carolina General Rufus
Saxton organised Negro regiments, sold confiscated
estates, leased abandoned plantations and assisted
in the building up of the Negro schools that had been
started under Edward L. Pierce.

March 3, 1865, what was known as the Freedmen's Bureau was organised under General Oliver
O. Howard, to carry on the work that had been begun
under the Federal generals at the different refugee
camps. For the next four years this Freedmen's

Bureau, so far as concerned the Freedman and his relation to his former master, was in itself a pretty complete sort of government. In 1868 there were 900 bureau officials scattered throughout the South, ruling directly and indirectly several millions of men and women. During that time 30,000 black men were sent back from the refuge and relief stations to the farms and plantations. In a single state 50,000 contracts for labour were signed under the direction of the agents of the Bureau. The total revenue of $400,000 was derived from the coloured tenants who had leased lands under the control of the Bureau.

It was under this Bureau that the Negro schools were started in every part of the South. Fisk, Atlanta and Howard universities were established during this time and nearly $6,000,000 was expended for educational work, $750,000 of which came from the Freedmen themselves. Before all its departments were finally closed something like $20,000,000 was expended by the Bureau in the different branches of its service.

One of the results of the organisation of the Freedmen's Bureau was to give employment to a large number of ambitious coloured men, and many representatives of the Negro race, who afterward became prominent in politics, gained their first training in this direction as agents of the Freedmen's Bureau. Among others who went into politics through this door were Hiram R. Revels, the first coloured man to enter the United States Senate, and Robert C. DeLarge, who was a member of the Forty-second Congress from South Carolina.

Hiram R. Revels was born at Fayetteville, North Carolina, September 1, 1822. His parents seem to have been free Negroes. At any rate they had been permitted to give him some education while he was a boy. After he became of age he went North, entered the Quaker Seminary in Union County, Indiana, and finally, about the year 1847, graduated from Knox College, at Galesburg, Illinois. He became a preacher and lecturer throughout Indiana, Illinois, Ohio, and Missouri and, at the breaking out of the war, he was serving as pastor of the Methodist Church in Baltimore. He assisted in raising the first coloured regiment that was organised in the State of Maryland, and afterward organised a second coloured regiment in Missouri. In 1864 he was at Vicksburg, where he assisted the Provost Marshal in managing the Freedmen's affairs. He spent the next two years in Kansas and Missouri, preaching and lecturing, and finally settled at Natchez, Mississippi, where General Adelbert Ames, the Military Governor, appointed him an alderman of the city. In January, 1870, he was chosen United States Senator and on February 25th, took his seat in Congress.

The announcement that a coloured man had been

elected to the Senate of the United States created a great deal of surprise and comment, and the appearance of the new Senator from Mississippi, who was to take the place that had been occupied by Jefferson Davis, President of the Southern Confederacy, was waited with great interest.   Strenuous efforts were made to resist, on the ground that it was unconstitutional and unprecedented, the determination of the Senate to allow him to take his seat.   Charles Sumner made a speech in favour of the admission of the coloured Senator in which he said: "The vote on this question will be an historical event, marking the triumph of the great cause."   Senator Henry Wilson, the second Senator from Massachusetts, accompanied Mr. Revels to the Vice-president's chair where he took the oath.   The chamber and galleries were crowded with spectators eager to witness the event, which was to give formal notice to the world that the revolution, which changed the Negro from a slave into a free man, had been completed.   In the same year two other Negroes, Joseph H. Rainey from South Carolina and Jefferson Long from Georgia, were admitted to Congress.   During the next few years coloured men were representing, either in the Senate or in the House of Representatives, every one of the seceding states with the exception of Texas and Tennessee.

The Freedmen's Bureau went out of existence in 1869 with the proposal by Congress of the Fifteenth

Amendment.* When the bill bringing the Bureau
into existence was under discussion, in 1865, Senator
Davis, of Kentucky had described it as a measure
"to promote strife and conflict between the white
and black races . . . by a grant of unconstitutional power." This puts in a sentence the objec-
tions that were made to the organisation of the
Bureau in the first instance and the criticisms that
have been passed upon it since. It was unfortunate
that the Freedmen's Bureau did not succeed in gaining the sympathy and support of the Southern people.
This was the more unfortunate because, during the
four years of its existence, the Freedmen had learned
to look to this Bureau and its representatives for
leading, support and protection. The whole South
has suffered from the fact that the former slaves were
first introduced into political life as the opponents,
instead of the political supporters, of their former
masters. No part of the South has suffered more
on this account, however, than the Negroes themselves. I do not mean to say that this rupture could
have been avoided. It was one of the unfortunate
consequences of the manner in which slavery was
brought to an end in the Southern states.

In the early days of their freedom, in spite of the
rather harsh legislation of certain of the Southern

* The Freedmen's Bureau went out of existence January 1, 1869, with the exception of its educational work, which was continued to 1872. The Fifteenth Amendment was proposed by Congress February 27, 1869. It was ratified by twenty-nine
states, March 30, 1870. . . . See "The Freedmen's Bureau," W. E. Burghardt Du Bois, *Atlantic Monthly*, March, 1901.

legislatures, the temper of the Southern Freedmen was conciliatory. The first move to obtain some part in the government was made by the Free Negroes of New Orleans. On November 5, 1863, the free coloured people of New Orleans held a meeting and drew up an address to Brigadier-general Shepley in which they refer to the fact that there are among them "many of the descendants of those men whom the illustrious Jackson styled 'his fellow-citizens,' when he called upon them to take up arms to repel the enemies of the country," adding that they were at that time paying taxes on property of which the assessed value was more than nine million dollars. In consideration of these fact and others they ventured to ask that they be permitted to assist in establishing, in the new convention, a civil government for the state.

The next year in that corner of the State of South Carolina occupied by the Federal troops, of which Beaufort is the centre, a mass State Convention was held to which the people of the state were invited, "without distinction of colour," to elect delegates to the Baltimore Presidential Convention. These delegates were not, however, allowed to take part in the proceedings of the Convention. From this time on, numerous meetings of the coloured people were held in different parts of the South and of the North. In 1865, a state convention of coloured people was held in South Carolina "to confer together and to deliberate on our intellectual, moral, industrial, and political condition, particularly as affected by the great changes in the state and country." This convention issued an address to the white people of the state in which they declared, among other things, that "notwithstanding we have been born and reared in your midst and were faithful while your greatest trials were upon you, and have done nothing since which could justly merit your disapprobation," that they had been denied the rights of citizenship which are freely accorded to strangers. The address concludes with the moderate request that the provisions of the "black code," which have denied them the opportunities of education, equal rights before the court, and imposed burdensome regulations upon their personal liberty may be repealed.

There were some such slight evidences in other parts of the country of a disposition on the part of an element of the coloured people and of the Southern white people, to come to terms with each other in order to establish a form of government which would be fairly satisfactory to both races. For instance, the coloured citizens of Tennessee were invited, in 1867, to take part in the political meetings of both parties, and a convention of Coloured Conservatives which met at Nashville, April 5, 1867, adopted among others the following resolutions:

Resolved, That we do not desire to be an element of discord in the community in which we live; that to seek to unite the coloured race against the white, or the poor against the rich, would only bring trouble; that we believe the common good of both depends on the spirit of harmony and justice of each toward the other.

Resolved, That, believing the spirit and tendencies of radicalism are unfavourable to these aims, we take our stand with the true Union Conservatives of Tennessee and invite our race throughout the state to do the same.

Resolved, That our right to vote involves the right to hold office, that its denial is unjust, and that our interests and rights as free men require also that we should have the right to sit upon juries.

The year before, October 1, 1866, Governor Worth, of North Carolina, had spoken in a conciliatory manner to a convention of coloured people assembled at Raleigh. He declared that he was ready to protect them in all their rights and urged them to be industrious, to educate their children, and to keep out of politics, seeing, as he said, "the strife and struggle in which party politics have involved the whites." He added that the general feeling of the men who had been their masters was kindly toward them, and added that "the whites feel that they owe you a debt of gratitude for your quiet and orderly conduct during the war, and you should endeavour to so act as to keep up this kindly feeling between the two races."

Bishop James W. Hood of the A. M. E. Zion Church, who had recently come to the South, was chairman of this convention. Bishop Hood was born in Chester County, Pennsylvania, May 30, 1831. He entered the ministry in 1860, and is said to have been the first regularly appointed missionary of the

Negro race sent to the Freedmen in the South where, it is stated, he founded in North and South Carolina and Virginia more than six hundred church organisations.

Among the Negroes of the Northern states who had gotten their political education under the influence of the Northern abolitionists, the trend of sentiment was naturally much more radical than in the Southern states.

June 15, 1863, a convention of coloured people was held at Poughkeepsie, New York, at which J. W. C. Pennington, a Presbyterian minister, presided. At this convention resolutions were passed, pledging the support of coloured soldiers to the Union cause and expressing the confidence that the Negro soldiers would receive the "protection and treatment due to civilised men."*

On October 3, 1864, a national convention of coloured people was held at Syracuse, New York, to take into consideration the future of the coloured race in America. This convention was the successor of other national conventions of the coloured people which had been held in different parts of America since the first National convention held in Philadelphia, June, 1831. The radical temper of this convention is, perhaps, best represented in a letter written by Frederick Douglass in accepting an invitation to be present. In this letter he demanded "perfect

* Appleton's Annual Encyclopedia, 1864, p. 842.

equality for the black man in every state before the law, in the jury-box, at the ballot-box, and on the battlefield"; and that, in the distribution of officers and honours under the Government, "no discrimination shall be made in favour of or against any class of citizens, whether black or white, of native or foreign birth."

On February 7, 1866, a delegation of coloured men, including George T. Downing, Lewis H. Douglass, William E. Matthews, John Jones, John F. Cook, Joseph E. Otis, A. W. Ross, William Whipper, John M. Brown, and Alexander Dunlop, headed by Frederick Douglass, called upon President Johnson to urge upon him the propriety and necessity of granting to coloured people the rights and privileges of citizenship that had hitherto been and was still denied them.

In reply to the President's statement that the policy they proposed would lead to a race war, and that he did not propose to make himself responsible for more bloodshed, the committee drew up an address to the country in which they brought forward the argument that if the hostility of the two races was actually as great as President Johnson had stated the Negro must be given the ballot "as a means of defence." This address gave public expression to the theory upon which Congress acted when in the following year Negroes were permitted to vote for delegates to the constitutional conventions in all the seceding states.

At this time the Fifteenth Amendment had not been proposed to Congress and there were only six Northern states which permitted the Negro to vote. In Ohio, Indiana, and Illinois, many of the provisions of the " black code," were still in force. Only a few weeks before this time on February 25, 1866, Negroes voted for the first time in the District of Columbia.

Meanwhile the progress of events in the South had been hastened by what the newspapers called a "race war," at Memphis in May, and another and still more bloody riot in New Orleans in which thirty-seven Negroes had been killed and one hundred and nineteen wounded. All this helped to bring into power in Congress the radical party in the North, and this party now proceeded to impose its Government upon the South with the aid of Negro votes.

Negroes sent two hundred and seven delegates out of eight hundred and thirty-four to the constitutional conventions which met, in 1867 and 1868, in Virginia, North Carolina, South Carolina, Georgia, Florida, Alabama, Mississippi, and Texas.* Texas was represented by the smallest number of Negroes. The proportion was nine Negroes to eighty-one white delegates. In South Carolina the Negroes were in control, the proportion being seventy-six blacks to forty-eight whites. Among the other members of

---

* Rhodes's " History of the United States," 1850-1877, Vol. VI., p. 88.

the South Carolina State Convention of 1867, was
Robert Smalls, who first became known during the
Civil War as the black pilot of the famous Confederate ship, the *Planter*, which he boldly steered
out of the Charleston harbour and turned over to
the Federal fleet on the morning of May 13, 1862.
Robert Smalls was born a slave at Beaufort, South
Carolina, April 5, 1839.   In 1851 he came to Charleston, where he worked in the ship-yards as a "rigger,"
and thus became familiar with the life of a sailor.

In 1861, he was employed on the Confederate
transport, the *Planter*.   I have more than once
heard Mr. Smalls tell the story of how he succeeded
in taking this ship out of the harbour under the
guns of the fort and at the same time managed to
carry his wife and family to freedom.

Up to this time the *Planter* was being used as the
special dispatch boat of General Ripley, the Confederate Post Commander at Charleston.   On the
night of May 12th, all the officers went ashore and
slept in the city, leaving on board a crew of eight men,
all coloured.

This was the opportunity Smalls had been looking for.   He spoke to the members of the crew and
found them willing to help him.   Wood was taken
aboard, steam was put on, and, with a valuable
cargo of guns and ammunition intended for Fort
Ripley, the *Planter* moved from her dock about two
o'clock in the morning, steamed to the North Atlantic

wharf, where Small's wife and two children, together with four women and one other child and three men, were waiting to go on board. By this time it was nearly 3:30 o'clock in the morning. The ship was started on its voyage, carrying nine men, five women and three children. Two of the men, who had first agreed to go with the ship, at the last moment concluded to remain behind.

The transport blew the usual salute in passing Fort Johnson, and proceeded down the bay. When approaching Fort Sumter, Smalls stood in the pilot house leaning out the window with his arms folded across his breast, and his head covered with a big straw hat which the commander of the ship usually wore. Here again the usual signal was given, and the ship headed toward Morris Island, and passed beyond the range of the guns of Fort Sumter before any one suspected anything was wrong. The *Planter* steered directly toward the Federal fleet, and was nearly fired upon by one of the Federal ships before the flag of truce was noticed.

As soon as the vessels came within hailing distance of each other, Mr. Smalls explained who they were and what was their errand. Captain Nichols, of the ship *Onward*, boarded the vessel, and took possession. Smalls was transferred to another ship; and was employed for some time as a pilot in and about the neighbouring waters, with which he was familiar. Later, in the war, for meritorious conduct, he was promoted to the rank of captain and was given charge of the *Planter*, which he had so successfully carried out of Charleston harbour. In September, 1866, he carried this boat to Baltimore where it was put out of commission and sold.

After the war Mr. Smalls was elected in 1868 to the House of Representatives of the State Legislature. In 1870 he was elected to the Senate of South Carolina, and afterward served three terms in Congress. He was appointed Collector of the Port of Beaufort, by President Harrison, a position which he was still holding in 1908.

One of the surprising results of the Reconstruction Period was that there should spring from among the members of a race that had been held so long in slavery, so large a number of shrewd, resolute, resourceful, and even brilliant men, who became, during this brief period of storm and stress, the political leaders of the newly enfranchised race. Among them were sons of white planters by coloured mothers, like John M. Langston, P. B. S. Pinchback, and Josiah T. Settle, who had given their children the advantages of an education in the Northern states. Mr. Pinchback's father was Major William Pinchback, of Holmes County, Mississippi. His mother, Eliza Stewart, claimed to have Indian blood in her veins. When he was nine years old young Pinchback and his brother Napoleon were sent to Cincinnati by their father to attend Gilmore's High School. After his father died, Mr. Pinchback's mother came to Cincinnati, and it was there he grew to manhood.

Josiah T. Settle's father was one of those men, of whom there were considerable number in the South, who brought their children by slave mothers North in order to free them. In fact, in Mr. Settle's case, his father not only freed him but married his mother. Mr. Settle got his early education in Ohio, and in 1868 entered Oberlin College. The following year he went to Howard University, where he graduated in 1872. Mr. Settle was active in politics in Mississippi during a portion of the Reconstruction Period, being engaged in the practice of law at Sardis, Panola County, Mississippi. In 1885, he went to Memphis; was appointed assistant prosecuting attorney of the criminal court of Shelby County, and is still practising law in that city, where he is one of the directors of the Negro bank at that place, the Solvent Savings Bank.

Blanche K. Bruce, senator from Mississippi from 1875 to 1881, was born a slave in 1841 in Prince Edward County, Virginia. He received his early education along with his master's son. After freedom came he taught school for a time in Missouri, and studied for a short time at Oberlin College. In 1869, he became a planter in Bolivar County, Mississippi, where he held a number of offices, including that of sheriff and superintendent of public schools. In 1881, President Garfield appointed him Registrar of the United States Treasury. His son, Roscoe Conklin Bruce, graduated with honours from Harvard University; was for a time head of the Academic Department of Tuskegee Institute; and afterward had charge of the coloured schools in Washington, District of Columbia.

Perhaps the most brilliant and, I might add, the most unfortunate of these men of the Reconstruction Period was Robert Brown Elliott, who was born in Boston, Massachusetts, August 11, 1842. His parents were from the West Indies and, while he was still a young boy, they returned to their home in Jamaica. There young Elliott had the advantage of a good schooling. He was sent to England, and in 1853 entered High Holborn Academy, London. Three years later he went to Eton, from which he graduated in 1859. He adopted law as his profession and after some years of travel in South America and the West Indies, settled in Charleston, South Carolina, where he became editor of the Charleston *Leader*, afterward known as the *Missionary Record*, owned by Bishop Richard H. Cain. He soon entered politics and was elected to the Lower House of the State Legislature in 1868.

In 1869, Mr. Elliott was appointed Assistant Adjutant-general of the State, which position he held until he was elected to the Forty-second Congress. He was a member of the Forty-third Congress, but resigned that position to accept the office of sheriff.   In 1881, he was appointed special agent of the United States Treasury, with headquarters at Charleston.   He was transferred from there to New Orleans, Louisiana.   But the fall of the Reconstruction governments in the South carried disaster to him, and he died August 9, 1884, in comparative obscurity and poverty.

Frederick Douglass says of Robert Brown Elliott: "I have known but one other black man to be compared with Elliott, and that was Samuel R. Ward, who, like Elliott, died in the midst of his years."   Samuel R. Ward was, in 1848, editor of the *Impartial Citizen*, published in Syracuse, New York.

Altogether, the Negro race has been represented in Congress by two Senators and twenty Representatives.   In addition to those already mentioned, Richard H. Cain served as a Representative of South Carolina in the Forty-third and Forty-fifth Congress; H. P. Cheatham represented North Carolina in the Fifty-second and Fifty-third Congresses.   Jere Haralson represented Alabama in the Forty-fourth Congress.   Jefferson Long was the Representative of Georgia in the Forty-first Congress.   John Hyman was a member of the Forty-fourth Congress for North Carolina, and James E. O'Hara represented the same state in the Forty-eighth and Forty-ninth Congresses.   Thomas H. Miller was a member of the Fifty-first Congress, and George W. Murray of the Fifty-third and Fifty-fourth Congresses. Both these men were elected from South Carolina. James T. Rapier was elected to the Forty-third United States Congress from Alabama. Benjamin S. Turner represented the same state in the Forty-second Congress. Josiah T. Walls was elected to represent Florida in the Forty-second, Forty-third, and Forty-fourth Congresses. The last man to represent the Negro race in Congress was George H. White, of North Carolina.

In a speech on the subject of the Spanish-American War, January 26, 1899, Mr. White made a sort of valedictory address, which is in many respects so interesting, and created so much comment at the time it was delivered, that I am disposed to quote a portion of it here. Referring to Negro Congressmen, Mr. White said:

Our ratio of representation is poor. We are taunted with being uppish; we are told to be still, to keep quiet. How long must we keep quiet? We have kept quiet while numerically and justly we are entitled to fifty-one members of this House; and I am the only one left. We have kept quiet when numerically we are entitled to a member of the Supreme Court. We have never had a member and probably never will; but we have kept quiet. We have kept quiet while numerically and justly, according to our population as compared with all other races of the world, so far as the United States are concerned, we should have the recognition of a place in the President's Cabinet; but we have not had it. Still we have kept quiet, and are making no noise about it.

We are entitled to thirteen United States Senators, according to justice and according to our numerical strength, but we have not one and, though we have had two, possibly never will get another;

and yet we keep quiet. We have kept quiet while hundreds and thousands of our race have been strung up by the neck unjustly by mobs of murderers. If a man commits a crime he will never find an apologist in me because his face is black. He ought to be punished, but he ought to be punished according to the law as administered in a court of justice. But we keep quiet; do not say it, do not talk about it. How long must we keep quiet, constantly sitting down and seeing our rights one by one taken away from us? As slaves it was to be expected, as slaves we were docile and easily managed; but as citizens we want and we have a right to expect all that the law guarantees to us.

Speaking a little later of the progress which the Negro race has made, Mr. White said some things which seem to me to express very accurately the sober second thought of the Negro people upon their condition in this country, and give a just and proper expression to the legitimate aspiration of the American Negro. He said:

We are passing, as we trust, from ignorance to intelligence. The process may be slow; we may be impatient; you may be discouraged; public sentiment may be against us because we have not done better, but we are making progress. Do you recollect in history any race of people placed in like circumstances who have done any better than we have? Give us a chance and we will do more. We plead to all of those who are here legislating for the nation that while your sympathy goes out to Cuba — and we are legislating for Cuba — while your hearts burst forth with great love for humanity abroad, remember those who are at our own door. Remember those who have worked for you; remember those who have loved you, have held up your hands, who have felled your forests, have digged your ditches, who have filled up your valleys and have lowered the mountains, and have helped to make the great Southland what it is to-day. We are entitled to your recognition. We do not ask for domination. We ask and expect a chance in legislation, and we will be content with nothing else.

This speech of Mr. White marks the end of an episode in the history of the American Negro. In considering the relation of the Negro people to this period it should be remembered that, outside of a few leaders, Negroes had very little influence upon the course of events. It was, to a very large extent, a white man's quarrel, and the Negro was the tennis ball which was batted backward and forward by the opposing parties.

Even as a boy I can remember that all through the days of Reconstruction I had a feeling that there was something in the situation, into which the course of events had pushed the Negro people that was unstable and could not last. It did not seem possible that a people who yesterday were slaves could be transformed within a few days into citizens capable of making laws for the government of the State or the government of the Nation.

There were a good many others who felt as I did.

One of the best illustrations that I happen to remember of the sanity of not a few coloured people on the subject of Reconstruction is Lewis Adams, the man who was more largely responsible, perhaps, than any one else for the location at Tuskegee of the Negro school which now bears the name of the Tuskegee Normal and Industrial Institute.

Lewis Adams lived in Macon County, Alabama, during the days of Reconstruction, and there was no coloured man in the state, I dare say, who had more influence over the masses of the coloured people than did he. During this period Mr. Adams could have been elected a member of the Legislature and, I have no doubt, could have been sent to Congress had he made the slightest effort in that direction. He refused, however, to be a candidate for any office, because, as he told me, he saw the futility and the shallowness of it all. He saw there was no logical foundation upon which the political activity of the Negro could rest and, for that reason, he preferred to devote himself to furthering the education of his people and to building up his own interests. The results show that he was right. When he died, on April 28, 1905, he was among the most honoured, respected, and successful coloured men in Macon County. On the other hand, men who had chosen to travel the political road had not only failed to succeed but some of them died unknown, forgotten, after passing their later years in obscurity and poverty.

CHAPTER II

SOME years ago I was asked by the editor of a well-known English magazine to write an article on what he termed the "Racial Feuds" in the southern part of the United States. I was compelled to reply that I could not write such an article as he desired because, so far as I had been able to learn, no such thing as a feud existed between the races in the Southern states. I said to him, as near as I can remember, that I had frequently heard of feuds among certain of the white people living somewhere in the mountains of Tennessee, but so far as I knew there never had been such a thing as a feud between the black and the white people in the South, and that, in fact, the trouble between the races in the South was of quite a different character.

I mention these facts here to emphasise an observation I have frequently made in regard to reports that are printed and spread abroad in regard to the relations between the white man and the black man in the Southern states. As a rule, the world has heard and still hears the worst that happens; it rarely hears of the best. It hears of the riots and the lynchings, but it knows very little of the friendly and helpful relations which exist between individuals of both races in every community in the Southern states.

In the chapter preceding this I have written something about the manner in which, directly after the war, the two races became divided, politically, so that up to the present time there is a white party and a black party in the Southern states. I told something of the manner in which this black party arose and gained power in the South, and referred briefly to some of the riots and disturbances which this division between the races caused. The story of the evils which came upon both races as a result of what is sometimes referred to as "Negro domination" has been frequently told. The animosities that were kindled between the races at that time have not yet died out, and there has been very little disposition on the part of the politicians, black or white, to allow them to die out. But the fact is that the good relations between the Freedmen and their former masters, which existed directly after the war, were never wholly destroyed by the political contentions of the Reconstruction Period, and in consequence of the emphasis that has been placed upon the disasters of that period by the historians and others who have written about it, the existence of the friendly relations to which I have referred has been too frequently overlooked.

As an illustration of what these friendly relations
between the Freedmen and their former masters
sometimes were, I am reminded of an old coloured
man by the name of Matthews, whom I ran across
some years ago, when I was visiting a little town in
western Ohio. When I met this man he was about
sixty years of age, and in early life he had been a
slave in Virginia, where he had learned the trade
of carpentry. It frequently happened in Virginia,
as it did in other parts of the South, that after a
slave had learned a trade he would buy his own time,
so that he might go about the country working for
whom he chose, making his own contracts and keeping for himself the money that he earned. In such
cases the slave would usually plan to save his money
until he could buy his freedom. This was the case
with Matthews.

About 1858, Matthews proposed to his master
that he would pay $1,500 for himself, a certain
amount to be paid in cash and the remainder to be
paid in instalments. Such a bargain as this was
not uncommon in Virginia at that time. Matthews's
master, having learned to have implicit confidence
in his slave, permitted him, after this contract was
made, to seek work wherever he could secure the
best pay. This went on for some time until Matthews secured the contract for the erection of a
building in the State of Ohio. While he was at
work in that state the war broke out, but Matthews

remained, and continued to work at his trade.   In 1863, he was declared a free man by Abraham Lincoln's Proclamation of Emancipation.   At that time he still owed his former master, according to his contract made before the war, $300.   In telling me the story, Matthews said that he was perfectly well aware that, by the Proclamation of Emancipation, he was released from all legal obligations to pay this money to his master.   He knew that, in the eyes of nine-tenths of the world, he would be released from all moral obligations to pay a single cent of the unpaid balance.   But he said he wanted to begin his life of freedom with a clean conscience. In order to do this, he walked from his home in Ohio, a distance of three hundred miles, much of the way over mountains, and placed in his former master's hand every cent of the money that he had promised years before to pay him for his freedom.

The story which I have just related is an instance of a kind of thing that very frequently happened directly after the War.   I could relate hundreds of instances which have come to my knowledge in which former slaves have shown their fidelity to their former masters and have assisted them in their poverty, and sympathised with them in their troubles, long after slavery had been abolished.   In stating these facts I am not seeking to apologise in any way for the institution of slavery, neither do I mean to suggest that the Negro slaves were ever satisfied with their conditions in slavery. I think there is in the mind and heart of every human being an ever-present longing for freedom, no matter how comfortable, in other respects, his condition in servitude may be. I have often heard it said that some coloured people were better off in slavery than in freedom, but, in all the contact I have had with members of my race in every part of the country, I have never found an individual, no matter what his condition, who did not prefer freedom to servitude.

I remember an acquaintance of mine telling me of an old coloured man he had met somewhere in North Carolina, who had spent the greater part of his life in slavery. My friend, who had known the institution of slavery only through the medium of books, was anxious to find out just what the thing seemed like to a man who had lived in slavery most of his life. The old coloured man said that he had had a good master, who was always kind and considerate; that the food he had to eat was always of the best quality and there was enough of it; he had nothing to complain of in regard to the clothing that was provided or the house that he lived in. He said both he and his family always had the best medical attention when they fell ill. To all appearances, as near as any one could judge, the old man must have been a great deal better off in slavery than he was in freedom. Noticing these things, my friend became more inquisitive and wanted to know whether, after all, there was not a feeling deep down in his heart, that he would rather be back in slavery, with all the comforts that he had enjoyed there, than be free. The old man shrugged his shoulders, scratched his head, thought for a second, and then said: "Boss, dere's a kind of looseness about dis y'ere freedom which I kinder enjoys." It seems to me that the old man has expressed the matter about as tersely and as accurately as it is possible to do.

I have referred to the manner in which the Freedmen have stood by their former masters in the troubles that came upon them during the war and afterward. I want to emphasise, just as strongly, that the Southern white men, who owned slaves, have stood by them and helped and protected them in freedom — in like manner and in the same degree.

In the spring of 1909, I made a trip, in company with a number of well-known and successful coloured men, through the State of South Carolina, spending a week in visiting all the principal cities where I was likely to meet the coloured people of the state in the largest numbers. The purpose of this visit was the same as that of similar journeys of observation that I have made at different times in other parts of the country. I wanted to see for myself the conditions of the members of my race, and, if possible, to say a word of counsel and encouragement, which might help them in their struggle for better things. I was surprised to learn that, in spite of all that I had heard and in spite of all that I had read about the bitter experiences South Carolina went through during the Reconstruction Period, the relations between individual coloured men and individual white men throughout that state were friendly and helpful to a degree that few people outside of the State of South Carolina had comprehended.

On the car in which we travelled, for instance, were a number of prominent and successful coloured men of South Carolina and the neighbouring state of North Carolina. During the week that we were together I learned, directly and indirectly, a great deal about the history of these men and the manner in which they had achieved success in the different lines in which they were working. I recall that, in almost every case, each one of these men attributed a large part of their success to the friendship or to the assistance which they had received from some white man. One of the leading men in this party, who was as responsible as any one else for the success of our campaign, was Richard Carroll, the founder of an industrial home for Negro orphans, and one of the organisers of an association that, in 1908, held the first successful Negro state fair in South Carolina. Mr. Carroll told me that one of the men who had been his constant personal friend and assisted him in all that he had attempted to do for the benefit of the Negro race was United States Senator

Benjamin Tillman, who has the reputation of being the most bitter opponent of the Negro, with perhaps one exception, in the Southern states.

Another man who accompanied us upon this trip was John Merrick, of Durham, North Carolina, the founder of a Negro insurance company, The North Carolina Mutual and Provident Association, which has written insurance, since its organisation in 1898, for over 160,000 members, paid $500,000 in benefits and owns real estate in South Carolina and in North Carolina to the value of something like $50,000. This company owns a block of buildings in Durham, where the home office of the company is located, which, I am informed, is assessed at $30,000, and in order to do business in South Carolina, the officers have had to deposit $10,000 cash with the insurance commissioner to protect the company's contracts in that state.

John Merrick was born at Clinton, North Carolina, in 1859. His mother was a house servant for Judge Almon McCord. Merrick was brought up in Raleigh, North Carolina, where he learned the trade of bricklayer. Because this trade left him without work during the winter, he gave it up and became a barber. After that he went from Raleigh to Durham and made his first start in business for himself there with money he borrowed from a white man, Mr. J. S. Carr. While he was in the barber business at Durham, he made the acquaintance of Mr.

J. B. and Mr. Ball Duke, of the Duke Tobacco Company. These men became interested in him and assisted him not only in his personal affairs, but in the work that he tried to do for the members of his own race. They gave him money at different times to help build a church. They gave him money with which to endow twenty-one beds in the Lincoln hospital for coloured people, which is established at Durham, and they afterward gave $5,000 as an endowment for this hospital. It was not, perhaps, entirely a personal interest in Mr. Merrick that led them to give this money through him to these different institutions. The Duke Tobacco Company employs two thousand or more coloured people in its factories at Durham. They wanted to help the coloured people whom they employed, and because they trusted Mr. Merrick and had confidence in him they gave this money to the coloured people largely upon his suggestion and advice.

Among the other people who accompanied us upon this South Carolina trip was Bishop George W. Clinton, of Charlotte, North Carolina, who was one of a group of young coloured men that entered the University of South Carolina, when it was open to coloured students directly after the war. Bishop Clinton, who, as a young man, lived through a large part of the Reconstruction Period in South Carolina, gave me a great deal of interesting information in regard to the happenings of that time. Among other things he told me a story which illustrates the point that I am trying to emphasise, namely, that in spite of the antagonisms of that period, the individual friendly relations between the races, particularly between the Freedman and his former master, remained in many instances firm and unshaken.

One of his first teachers, he said, was Irving Clinton, a white planter and lawyer, and a brother of his father's master. Bishop I. C. Clinton, who, though he has the same name and title, is no relative of Bishop George W. Clinton, was a slave of this man, he said, and before the war had been for many years the foreman of his plantation. Bishop Clinton, he said, had learned to read while he was a slave; he had been taught by his master. After emancipation the relations between the Freedman and his former master remained intimate and friendly. In fact, Bishop I. C. Clinton became, before his death, the spiritual advisor of his former master; was present at the bedside when his old master died; and erected, at his own expense, in the Presbyterian cemetery, at Lancaster, South Carolina, a monument to his former master and lifelong friend. I may add that Bishop I. C. Clinton was a man of very little learning, so far as the books were concerned. He had had one year's training, I believe, at Hampton Institute, but he was a man of great influence and apparently of great common sense. He died in October, in 1904, at the age of seventy-eight.

I have referred to some individual cases of friendship between white men and black men to show what the character of some of these relations is. The best indication that these friendly relations are more frequent than ordinarily supposed, is the fact of the success that the Negro has made in the South in getting property, and in doing away with the burden of illiteracy with which he entered freedom. It would not be possible for Negroes to own as much property as they do in the South at the present time, unless the majority of the white people were disposed to encourage them to get it. It would not have been possible to reduce the illiteracy in the race from 90 to 47 per cent. if the white people in the South had not been willing to support, to some extent, Negro schools.

It is not possible to determine with exactness just how much property Negroes own, in the United States, at the present time. In most parts of the South, no effort is made to separate tax lists of Negroes from those of white people. The State of Georgia is, however, an exception in this respect, and it is possible to study from records of the Comptroller General's office the progress of the race in that state. The figures obtained in Georgia, however, may be used for estimating the progress in the

South, because it has been found that on the whole
the progress of the Negroes in Georgia runs parallel
to the progress of Negroes in the other Southern
states.   I do not mean by this that Negroes in some
states are not gaining property more rapidly than
they are in others; I do mean that, on the whole,
they seem to be gaining in Georgia at about the
same rate they are throughout the South, taking all
the Southern states as a whole.

In 1866, a year after the close of the War, the
Negroes to Georgia owned about ten thousand acres
of land, to the value of $22,500.   In the next ten
years, they increased the amount of land in their
possession more than forty-five times, having, in
1876, 457,635 acres of land, the tax value of which
was $1,234,104.

The rapid increase in land-getting during this
period is easily accounted for.   A good many
Negroes had served in one way or another in the
Civil War, and the Freedmen's Bureau had paid
out something like $7,000,000 in bounties to Negro
soldiers.   During the first ten years after the War
a large part of this money was invested in land in
the Southern states.   During the next ten years,
from 1876 to 1886, Negroes increased their holdings
in farm land by nearly 100 per cent., having at the
close of that period 802,939 acres of land, the assessed
value of which was $2,508,198.   During the next
ten years the holdings of Negro farmers increased

to 1,043,847 acres, with an assessed value of
$4,234,848.

During the next period of ten years, from 1896 to
1906, the increase in the holdings was slower. In
1906 the amount of property owned by coloured
people in Georgia was 1,420,888 acres, but the value
of that property had increased from four to seven
millions. The last available statistics give, in 1907,
the land-holdings of Georgia Negroes as 1,449,624
acres, valued at $7,972,787. These figures do not
include the amount of property owned by Negroes
in the form of city lots; neither do they include the
various forms of personal property on which they
pay taxes.

The increase in the value of this class of property
has gone on at about the same rate as that of the
property in farm lands. For instance, the value
of city property owned by Negroes in 1866 is given
at $70,000, but in 1907, the value of city and town
property owned by Negroes in that state amounted
to $6,710,189, while the total assessed value of all
Negro property in Georgia had increased during
that period from $450,000 to $25,904,822. This does
not include the value of church and school property
which, according to a careful investigation of Professor Monroe N. Work, made while he was connected with the Georgia State Industrial College,
amounts to something like $7,000,000.

Some efforts have been made to study the progress

of the Negro land-owner in Virginia. Negroes have made great progress all over that state in the matter of land-getting but they have done better, perhaps, in Gloucester County than in any other part of the state. According to the census of 1900, the coloured population of Gloucester County was a little less than the white. According to the public records, when an investigation was made a few years ago, the total value of the land owned by coloured people amounted to $87,953.55. The total assessed value of land at that time was $666,132.33. At the same time the coloured people paid taxes upon $79,387 worth of buildings and improvements, while the total assessed valuation of buildings and improvements in the county was $466,127.05. To state it differently: the Negroes of Gloucester County, beginning forty years before in poverty, had in 1905, at the time of this investigation, reached the point where they owned and paid taxes upon one-sixth of the real estate in that county. This property is held very largely in the shape of small farms, varying in size from ten to one hundred and fifty acres. A very large proportion of these farms contain about ten acres.

I have always believed that in proportion as the industrial, not omitting the intellectual, condition of my race was improved, in the same degree would their moral and religious life improve.

Some years ago, before the home life and economic condition of the people had improved, bastardy was common in Gloucester County. In 1903, there were only eight cases of bastardy reported in the whole county, and two of those were among the white population. During the year 1904, there was only one case of bastardy within a radius of ten miles of the courthouse.

Another gratifying evidence of progress appears in the fact that there is very little evidence of immoral relations existing between the races. In the whole county, during the year 1903, about twenty-five years after the work of education had gotten under way, there were only thirty arrests for misdemeanors; of these sixteen were white, fourteen coloured. In 1904, there were fifteen such arrests — fourteen white and one coloured. In 1904, there were but seven arrests for felonies; of these two were white and five were coloured.

I ought, perhaps, to add that the majority of the teachers in this county were trained at Hampton Institute, and have been teaching there for a number of years. For the most part the teachers of Gloucester County are not mentally superior, but what they lack in methods of teaching and intellectual alertness is more than made up for by their moral earnestness and by the example which they set in their own lives for the people whom they teach. Most of these teachers are natives of the county, and what is more important, most of them own property in the county.

Recently a careful study has been made of the progress which Negro farmers have made in Macon County, Alabama, where the Tuskegee Institute is located.   In 1880, a year before the school opened, the census reported 593 farm-owners in the country surrounding Tuskegee Institute.   Of this number not more than 10 per cent. were owned by Negroes. Twenty years later the census showed 517 farm-owners in the county, of whom 30 per cent. were Negroes.   From 1900 to 1908 the amount of property owned by Negroes in Macon County increased more rapidly than at any other period.   The number of Negro farm-owners increased from 167 in 1900 to 421 in 1908.   Negroes paid taxes on 55,976 acres of land assessed at $236,989.   More than one-seventh of the land and more than one-sixth of the land value is held by Negro farmers.   In addition to this there are 288 Negro owners of town property, which is about one-sixth of the value of the town property in the county.   To sum up, then, of the $2,061,108 worth of real property in Macon County $325,474 worth is owned by Negroes.

One explanation of the rapid progress which Negro farmers have made in recent years in Macon County may be found in the efforts that have been made to build up the country schools.   During the years from 1904 to 1908, largely under the stimulus and encouragement of Tuskegee Institute, the Negro farmers in Macon County raised something over $7,000 to build schoolhouses and lengthen the school terms. This was supplementary to the funds that were given to support the schools by the state. During that same period a special effort was made to bring the influence of the Agricultural School at Tuskegee to bear directly upon the work of the farms in the surrounding territory. The result of all this has been to draw into the county a class of farmers who wanted the advantages of good schools for their children, and to largely increase the productiveness of their farms. I think I can safely say, that whatever the opinion of people in other parts of the South may be, the people of Macon County, both black and white, have been convinced by the results obtained that Negro education can be made to pay.

I have referred to the progress which Negroes are making in Georgia and in certain other parts of the South, where the statistics are available. From my own observation I should say that the advance in the places I have mentioned is not as exceptional as it might appear. From all that I can learn Negroes are making quite as much progress in North Carolina and Mississippi, Texas and Oklahoma as they are in Georgia and Alabama. As near as I can estimate, Negro farmers are increasing their acreage in land at the rate of 5 per cent. annually.

On the other hand, the taxable value of Negro property seems to be increasing at the rate of about 11 per cent. per annum.

Using all the statistics at hand, it is safe to say that Negro farmers in 1909 owned, in the Southern states, not less than thirty thousand square miles of land.   This is an amount of territory nearly equal to five New England states, Vermont, New Hampshire, Massachusetts, Connecticut, and Rhode Island.   From the best estimate I have been able to find I should say that Negroes in the United States own at the present time not less than $550,000,000 worth of taxable property.   If it is true, as I have stated in another place, that the free coloured people of this country owned before the War something like $25,000,000 worth of property, it is safe to say that $525,000,000 worth of property has been acquired by the coloured people of the United States since freedom.

It is difficult for one, who has not lived in the South and has not closely studied the life of the Negro on the Southern farms and plantations, to clearly understand the actual progress that the figures I have referred to stand for.   As a matter of fact, they represent the work that the masses of the Negro people have done for their own emancipation.   It is a mistake to assume that the Negro, who had been a slave for two hundred and fifty years, gained his freedom by the signing, on a certain date, of a certain paper by the President of the United States.   It is a mistake to assume that one man can, in any true sense, give freedom to another.

Freedom, in the larger and higher sense, every man must gain for himself. In this larger and higher sense the Negro is, slowly but surely, gaining his freedom in every state, in every city, and in every village and on every plantation in the South. Here and there this progress seems to halt. Sometimes there seems to be a retrograde movement but, on the whole, the work of emancipation goes steadily forward.

One of the most interesting examples in my experience of this kind of emancipation is that of a coloured farmer of my acquaintance in Alabama. When he was "turned loose," as he put it, at the end of the Civil War, he was about sixty years of age, and at that age, he began life, as a great majority of my race began at that time, with nothing. He did not own a house; he had but little clothing, and no food but a bag of meal and a strip of bacon. He had gotten out of slavery, however, a close and intimate acquaintance with the soil, and the habit of work.

After freedom came he left the plantation on which he had been a slave and went to work on an adjoining place as a "renter." He told me that when he was first free he felt that he had to move about a little, just to find out what freedom was like. But he soon found that in most respects there was very little difference between his condition in freedom and his condition in slavery. The man of whom he rented furnished him rations, directed his planting, and kept after him to see that he made his crop. At the end of the year the charges for rent and interest had eaten up all that he had earned, so that from one year to another he was not any better off than he had been the year before. When he did come out with a little money to his credit the storekeeper soon got it all, and, if he fell sick or anything happened to his family, he sometimes found himself in debt at the end of the year, and then he was worse off than if he had nothing.

One of the chief privileges of freedom he found to be the opportunity for getting into debt, but after he had succeeded in getting into debt he learned that he had lost even the privilege which had remained to him of moving from one plantation to another. The reason for this is that, as a rule, the Negro farmer who rents has no security to give for the money he borrows except his own labour. In order to secure this labour for the payment of debts the custom, and frequently the law in the Southern states, prevents a tenant from leaving the plantation until he has "paid out of debt," as the saying is, or until some other planter has bought him out of debt. This condition, which has grown up naturally and, I might almost say, necessarily, out of the relations between the white land-owner and his Negro tenants, represents a kind of serfdom, and it is these same conditions that so frequently bring about the cases of peonage, of which one occasionally hears in the Southern states. This serfdom, however, is merely one of the stages through which a society, in which slavery has existed, has usually worked its way to freedom.

Gradually something of all this that I have described began to dawn upon the mind of the old coloured farmer. He saw that he was making no headway and that his condition might easily become worse. It was about this time that he began coming to our annual Negro Conference at Tuskegee Institute. There he heard the stories of other Negro farmers, some of whom had worked themselves out of this condition of partial slavery that I have described. As he listened to these stories, he began to realise that what had been possible for others was possible for him also. He began to think for the first time in his life of getting a home of his own. A place, as he told me, where if he drove a nail or planted a tree it would stay there and could be handed down to his children. He began thinking about the land on which he was working, and a passionate desire to own and improve it took possession of him. He wanted to be in a position where he could afford to improve his surroundings and preserve for his children the improvements that he made.

In order to get more out of the soil he arose early in the morning before daybreak, and he and his

wife and his children were out in the field all day
and late at night.   In the midst of this work the
rented mule, which he had been using to make his
cotton crop, died.   This was a terrible blow to him,
but it proved his economic salvation, for it determined him to have an ox or mule that he could
call his own next year.

The old farmer talked the matter over with his
wife and between them they agreed upon this plan:
they would do all the work they could during the
day with their hoes, and after dark, by the light of
the moon, the old man would put the harness that
the mule had worn on his own back and, while his
wife held the plow, he pulled it through the furrow
as well as he could.   This method of cultivating the
soil was so unusual that he did not care to attract
the attention of his neighbours by working in this
way during the day.

At the end of the season he found that he had
cleared enough to buy an ox.   I have heard the old
man tell more than once how proud he felt when
he owned an ox that he could call his own, something, at any rate, that was absolutely free of debt
and no man had a claim upon it.   With the aid
of this ox, he and his wife and his children made
the next year a larger crop and, when the cotton
had been picked, he had in his possession more
money than he ever had before in his life.   With
this money he bought a mule.   Working the mule

and the ox together, he made a still larger crop, and the next year purchased another mule.

Without detailing step by step the method by which the old man went forward, I might say that before many years had gone by he had become the owner in fee simple of over two hundred acres of land. He was living in a good house and had surrounded himself with most of the necessities and some of the comforts of life. Not only was this true, but I learned afterward that he had been able to put considerable money in the local bank, of which he eventually became a stockholder. There were few men of either race who had the confidence and respect of the community in a larger degree than did this man, who emancipated himself in the manner in which I have described.

The story which I have just related is typical of hundreds of other coloured farmers, whom I have known personally, and whose stories have been related from year to year at the annual Tuskegee Negro Conference. Some of these farmers, who have told their stories at the Conference, are men who have made an impression upon the communities in which they live by the success which they have achieved. One of these men, whose name, I remember, is Alfred Smith, known as "the cotton king," of Oklahoma. He was born a slave on a Georgia plantation, but went out to Kansas directly after the War, and eventually moved into Oklahoma.

He is known all over that state for the success he has made in cotton raising. He has a number of times taken the first prize for cotton raised in Oklahoma. He has taken the prize for his cotton in Liverpool, and, in 1900, gained the first prize at the World's Exhibition in Paris, France.

One of the best-known farmers in Georgia is Deal Jackson, of Albany, who owns and works two thousand acres of land upon which he employs forty-six families. For a number of years past he has gained a reputation throughout Georgia by bringing the first bale of cotton to market. One of the most successful farmers in the State of Alabama is a coloured man by the name of John J. Benson, who owns something like three thousand acres of land in Elmore County. He is living on the plantation upon which he was born a slave. He is famous throughout the county not only for his success in raising cotton but quite as much for his success in breeding horses and raising cattle. His son, William E. Benson, is the head of a corporation which owns over nine thousand acres of land adjoining John Benson's plantation.

Negro farmers have not only been successful in getting hold of the land but they have been successful, in one or two instances, at any rate, in greatly improving their methods of farming. There is a farmer by the name of Sam McCord, in Wilcox County, Alabama, who has become famous throughout Alabama from the fact that, while he farms only two acres of land, he raises on that two acres every year four bales of cotton, besides considerable corn and fodder. This is the more remarkable when it is remembered that the average yield per acre in Alabama is a little more than one-third of a bale.

Few people, who are not themselves members of the Negro race, realise to what extent the masses of the coloured people feel that they must be led and guided; that they have no power within themselves to accomplish anything, unless they are controlled and directed by some one else. In the early days of freedom the masses of the people felt that it was hardly possible for coloured people to be their own masters. They felt that it was somehow unnatural to find themselves controlled and directed by one of their own race. I never realised to what extent this was true until I attempted to organise the Normal and Industrial Institute at Tuskegee.

After I came to Alabama, in 1881, and before I attempted to take any definite measures toward founding the Tuskegee Institute, I spent several weeks travelling about among the people in the county, explaining to them my plans and seeking to interest them in what I proposed to do. They listened to me patiently and respectfully, but I could see that, deep down in their hearts, they had the feeling that white people might accomplish some such thing as I proposed, or that coloured people, under the direction and guidance of white people, might do so, but that it was hardly possible for Negroes to succeed in any such enterprise. For that reason they halted and hesitated, and doubted my ability and their own, to carry out the plans I proposed to them.

After we had succeeded in erecting our first building at Tuskegee, however, I could see that we had made an impression upon the people. I can remember how they would come in from the surrounding districts, men, women, and children, to look over the school and see what we had done. It was touching to me to observe the manner in which they would enter the different rooms, treading lightly and cautiously, as if they were afraid they would hurt the floors or, perhaps, that the floors would somehow or other harm them. Then they would stop and look about in a kind of bewildered amazement, as if they were not quite sure whether what they saw was real, and as if in order to test it, they would take hold of the door knobs, put their hands on the glass of the window panes, feel of the blackboards, and then stop and gaze wonderingly again at the plastered walls, the desks and the furniture. It was difficult for them to believe that the buildings and the school grounds really belonged, as I tried to explain, to them. It seemed impossible to them that all this could have been brought into existence for the benefit of Negroes. I was compelled to tell them, over and over again, that I wanted them to feel that the school grounds and the school buildings were theirs, and that I wanted them to have a part in the direction and in the upbuilding of everything connected with the school.

It took some years to really convince the masses of the people in our neighbourhood that what I said to them was literally true. But at last the idea that Tuskegee is theirs has entered deep into the minds and hearts of the members of my race, not only in our immediate neighbourhood, but I believe, also, to a large extent throughout the South. At the present time I think that every coloured man and woman in the South not only feels proud of what Tuskegee has accomplished, but that he feels, also, a little more alive, a little more able to go ahead and do something in the world than he did before our institution came into existence.

It is this feeling on the part of the members of my race that has given to me, and to others who are working with me, the desire to go forward and make our institution bigger and better and more useful, in order that it may help complete the work of this larger emancipation, which began before the Civil War destroyed slavery as a political institution, and has been going on steadily everywhere in the Southern states since that time.

CHAPTER III

THE NEGRO LABOURER AND THE MECHANIC IN
SLAVERY AND FREEDOM

ONE of my most vivid boyish recollections
is of the period just previous to the end of
slavery, when my stepfather, who at that
time was, I take it, a man of about fifty years of
age, would return to his family at Christmas time
and tell us stories of his adventures during his long
absence from home. I recall that I would sit for
hours in rapture hearing him tell of the experiences
he had had in a distant part of Virginia, where he
and a large number of other coloured people were
employed in building a railway. Although he was
employed merely as a common labourer he had
learned something as to the plan and purposes for
which this railway was being built and he had some
idea of the great changes that it was intended to
bring about, and he told it all with a great deal of
interesting circumstance.

In my boyish ignorance at that time, I used to
wonder what interest he could have in a railway of
that kind; whether or not he owned any part in it;
and how it was he was so much interested in the

building of a railroad that he could remain away from home for five or six months and sometimes longer at one time. All through the country, in our part of Virginia, Christmas was a season of great rejoicing, on account of the home-coming of a large number of coloured people who had been at work in different industries in different parts of the state. Some of them had been hired out to work on the farms, some were employed on the railroads, and others were mechanics, and when they came home at Christmas time they brought with them stories, anecdotes, and news of what was going on in different parts of the state.

I am reminded of these facts at this time because they gave me the first idea I had of the extent to which the labour of the coloured man, both in the shops and in the fields, has been employed in the building up of the civilisation of the Southern states. The Negro was first employed in the severe pioneer work of clearing the forests, and planting and harvesting the crops. After that he was employed in building railways; in digging the coal and iron from the mines; in laying out the streets, and erecting the buildings in the cities. He is to-day very largely depended upon for labour in the iron, mining and manufacturing districts, like Birmingham, Alabama, as well as on the great cotton plantations in Mississippi, Arkansas, and Texas.

Not only has the Negro performed this labour,

but he has performed it cheerfully, faithfully, and, on the whole, as far as his education and training would permit, he has performed it well.   The white people of the South, who have known the Negro best, know and value the service that the Negro race has performed in the South.   Although they have not always come forward publicly to defend the Negro against the charges that are frequently made against him, they know, deep down in their hearts, that they owe the Negro a debt of gratitude for what he has done, and they have expressed this feeling to individual Negro men and Negro women, not only in words, but in every-day acts of kindness and good will, particularly toward those who at one time belonged to their families or have in some way or other gained their friendship.

It is largely owing to the manner in which the Negro and the white man were brought together in slavery that there is to-day no place in the world where the Negro has made himself a more valuable and efficient labourer than he has in the Southern states.   At the same time there is no place in the world where, in spite of complaints that one sometimes hears, there is a more general desire to retain the Negro as a labourer, and no place where there is more opportunity for Negroes to engage in all kinds of labour, common and skilled, or to enter into business pursuits.

Although the slaves that were first imported from

Africa were, as a rule, rude and unskilled in the industrial arts of the white man, yet the native African was not wholly without skill in the crafts, and it was not very long before some of the dark-skinned strangers had mastered the trades. Among the slaves of Robert Beverly, who was clerk of the House of Burgesses, in Virginia, in 1670, was a carpenter valued at about thirty pounds. About this same time Ralph Wormeley, a man of considerable distinction in his time, who died in 1701, owned a cooper and a carpenter, each valued at thirty-five pounds. Negroes were employed as iron miners and ship-carpenters, wheelwrights, coopers, tanners, shoemakers, millers and bakers before the Revolutionary War. As early as 1708 Negro mechanics had become common enough in Pennsylvania to arouse the opposition of the free white workmen, who at that time petitioned the Legislature against the practice of hiring out slaves to work in certain of the trades.* In the early part of the nineteenth century the number of Negro mechanics in the District of Columbia was considerable, and one of the men who assisted in laying out and surveying the District of Columbia in 1791 was Benjamin Banneker, the Negro astronomer, who is said to have constructed the first clock that was made in America.

Benjamin Banneker was born November 9, 1731, in Baltimore County, Maryland, near the village

---

* "The Negro Artisan," Atlanta Publications, No. 7, p. 15.

of Ellicott's Mill. He is often referred to as a man of pure Negro ancestry, but the facts seem to be that his grandmother, on his mother's side, was a white woman, by the name of Molly Welsh, who was sent out from England in an early day as a Redemptioner, and after she had served her master for seven years, purchased a small farm and two slaves. One of these slaves, whose name was Banneker, she gave his freedom and married.

Benjamin Banneker seems to have been a great favourite with his grandmother, who taught him to read. At this time there was a "pay school" in the neighbourhood, to which a few coloured children were admitted, and Banneker got a part of his education there. He early seems to have shown an inclination for mechanics, and about the year 1754, with the imperfect tools he was able to command, he constructed a clock, which not only told the time but struck the hours. Three years later the Ellicott flour mills were erected on the banks of Patapsco River, near his home. The construction of these mills was a source of great interest and instruction to Banneker and, in this way, he made the acquaintance of Mr. George Ellicott, who opened to him his library and furnished him with astronomical instruments in order that he might pursue further the studies he had already begun in the subject of astronomy.

From this time on Banneker, who still cultivated a little farm inherited from his father, devoted himself entirely to his scientific studies. He made the acquaintance, through correspondence, with scientific men in all parts of the world. It was after his return home after helping to lay out the District of Columbia, in 1791, that he got out his first almanac for the year 1792. Before this almanac was printed he sent a copy of the manuscript to Thomas Jefferson, with a letter of explanation. In reply, Thomas Jefferson said, among other things: "I have taken the liberty of sending your almanac to Monsieur de Condorcet, Secretary of the Academy of Sciences of Paris, and member of the Philosophical Society, because I consider it as a document to which your whole colour had a right, for their justification against the doubts which have been entertained of them."

Although after 1830 a number of restrictions were put upon the Negro mechanics, limiting the extent to which they might be educated, particularly in knowledge of books, still, as a rule, these laws were not strictly enforced and the number of coloured mechanics continued to increase. In Virginia Negroes worked in the tobacco factories, ran the steamboats, and were employed in numerous kinds of skilled labour. In Charleston and some other places Negroes were employed in cotton factories. Frederick Law Olmsted, who made a journey through the Southern states in 1856, says that he was told in Louisiana that master mechanics often bought up slave mechanics and acted as contractors.

In Kentucky, slaves worked in the hemp-bagging factories, in tobacco factories, and in the iron works on the Cumberland River. Ex-Governor Lowry, of Mississippi, says that before the War the Negro mechanics became masters of their respective trades, as a result of long service under the direction of white mechanics. "During the existence of slavery," he adds, "the contract for qualifying a Negro as a mechanic was made between his owner and the master workman."* In Alabama, there was, some time before the War, as I have heard, an enterprising white man who converted his plantation to an industrial school for slaves. In other words, he would buy untrained slave boys and give them instruction in the different trades that were used upon the plantations, then sell them again at a much larger price than he paid for them. It was not unusual, in fact, for a well-trained mechanic to sell for as high as two thousand dollars while an able-bodied field-hand would sell for eight hundred to one thousand dollars. I mention these facts because they show that, even in slavery, the value of education was clearly recognised.

One of the best mechanics I ever knew was Lewis Adams, whose name I have mentioned in the previous chapter. He was a first-class tinner, shoemaker, and harnessmaker, and could do anything

* Quoted in "The Negro Artisan," Atlanta University Publications, from *North American Review*, p. 14.

from repairing a watch to mending an umbrella.
After the Tuskegee Institute was started, he became
the first teacher of the trades.   During the early days
of the school he taught three distinct trades, and was
not only our tinner, shoemaker, and harnessmaker,
but for some time, also, our engineer.   As illustrating the extent to which the slave obtained education in the trades, Mr. Adams once said that
there were in Macon County before the War twenty-
five Negro carpenters, eleven blacksmiths, three
painters, two wheelwrights, three tinsmiths, two
tanners, and fourteen shoemakers.   Of these
mechanics, he said:

As a rule, they lived more comfortably than the other class of
Negroes.   A number of them hired their time and made money;
they wore good clothes and ate better food than the other class of
people.   A very small number of them were allowed to live by
themselves in out-of-the-way houses.   All the master wanted of
them was to stay on his place and pay over their wages.   As a
rule, a white man contracted for the job and overlooked the
work.   These white men often would not know anything about
the trades, but had Negro foremen under them who really carried
on the work.

One of the men who learned his trade in slavery
was J. D. Smith, who, a few years ago, was a stationary engineer in Chicago.   In a study of the
"Negro Artisan," published by Atlanta University,
in 1902, he is quoted as saying:

On every large plantation you could find the Negro carpenter,
blacksmith, brick and stone mason.   These trades included much

more in those days than they do now. What is now done by machinery was wrought then by hand. Most of our wood-work machinery has come into use since the days of slavery. . . . The carpenter's chest of tools in slavery time was a very elaborate and expensive outfit. His "kit" not only included all the tools that the average carpenter carries now, but also the tools for performing all the work done by various kinds of wood-working machines. . . . The carpenter in those days was also the cabinetmaker, the wood-turner, and coffin-maker, and generally the patternmaker, and the maker of most things which were made of wood. The blacksmith was expected to make anything and everything wrought of iron. He was, to all intents and purposes, the machinist, blacksmith, horseshoer, carriage and wagon ironer and trimmer, gunsmith, wheelwright, and frequently whittled and ironed the hames, the plough-stocks, and the single-trees for the farmers. He was an expert, also, at tempering edged tools and many of the slaves had secret processes of their own for tempering tools which they guarded zealously.

Negro machinists had also become numerous before the downfall of slavery. Slave-holders were generally the owners of all the factories, the machine shops, the flour mills, sawmills, gin-houses, and crushing machines; they owned all the railroads and shops connected with them. In all these, the white labourer and mechanic had almost entirely been supplanted by slave mechanics by the time of the breaking out of the Civil War. Many of the railroads in the South had their entire train crews, except conductors, but including engineers and firemen, made up of slaves.*

At the close of the slavery period the Negro artisan, to a very large extent, had a monopoly of the trades in the Southern states. After slavery disappeared the Negro boy and girl no longer had the same opportunity to learn the trades they had had in slavery time. At the same time, as the country developed,

* "The Negro Artisan," Atlanta Publications, No. 7, p. 16.

and as new machinery and new methods of doing things were introduced, there was a greater demand for skilled labour than there had ever been before. Wherever machinery was introduced to perform work which had previously been performed by hand labour, it generally happened that the white man was employed to do that kind of work.

For instance, the building up of the cotton mills in the South and the rapidly increasing demand for labour that it caused, drained large portions of the country districts of their white population to furnish labour for these factories. All this produced great changes in conditions in the Southern states. It has seemed to many persons that the Negro, in losing his monopoly in the trades, was losing also his position in them. After a careful study of the facts, I have come to the conclusion that this is not true. What the facts do seem to show is that there is in process a re-distribution of the coloured population among the different trades and professions. There were fewer negroes engaged in farm labour in 1900 for instance, but there is a larger proportion of the Negro population engaged in the other four general classes of labour than there was in 1890.

When the census was taken in 1900, 62.2 per cent. of all the Negroes in the United States over ten years of age were engaged in gainful occupations, while, at the same time, only 48.6 per cent. of the white population over ten years of age were so engaged. This does not mean that the Negroes, as a race, are more industrious than the white people; it means that a larger number of those who should be in school, preparing themselves to perform more efficient labour, are at work performing unskilled and inefficient labour. The actual number of Negroes engaged in each of the main classes of the occupations, in 1890 and in 1900, was as follows:

	1890	1900
Agricultural pursuits	1,984,310	2,143,176
Professional service	33,994	47,324
Domestic and personal service	956,754	1,324,160
Trade and transportation	145,717	209,154
Manufacturing and mechanical pursuits	208,374	275,149

While these figures show that a larger number of Negroes is employed in all the main classes of occupations, it does not mean that the percentage of the Negro population engaged in these different kinds of labour was larger in 1900, in all classes, than it was in 1890. As a matter of fact, the percentage of Negroes engaged in agricultural pursuits was nearly 6 per cent. less in 1900 than it was in 1890, as the following statement indicates:

	1890	1900
Agricultural pursuits	59.6	53.7
Professional service	1.0	1.2
Domestic and personal service	28.7	33.0
Trade and transportation	4.4	5.2
Manufacturing and mechanical pursuits	6.3	6.9

While it is true that these figures show a decreased percentage of Negroes engaged in agriculture, still a closer study of the figures indicates that the loss has been in the class of agricultural labourers. There are something over 18,000 less Negroes engaged as agricultural labourers in 1900 than in 1890. On the other hand there has been a gain in the number of Negro farmers, both as to number and as to their percentage of the total farmers. There were 590,666 Negro farmers in 1890, and 757,822 in 1900. Negro farmers were 11.1 per cent. of the total number of farmers in 1890, and 13.3 per cent. in 1900.

Of the 3,998,963 Negroes engaged in gainful occupations, considerably more than one-half were engaged in agricultural pursuits in 1900. The next largest class, that of domestic and personal service, employed 1,324,160 persons. Although there were 64,562 more Negro servants and waiters in 1900 than in 1890, the per cent. which they formed of the total number of Negroes engaged in this kind of service decreased from 42 per cent. in 1890 to 35.1 per cent. in 1900. In other words, although there was a considerable gain in the total number and percentage of Negroes engaged in this kind of service, the chief gains were in those of trades like that of barbers and hair-dressers, boarding-house and hotel keepers, janitors, and sextons, launderers and laundresses, nurses and mid-wives, and in the class of unspecified domestic and personal service.

These figures indicate the direction which this re-distribution of Negro labourers among the different trades has taken.

Manufacturing and mechanical pursuits gave employment to 275,149 Negroes. This class included carpenters and joiners, stone and brick masons, painters, glaziers, and varnishers, paper hangers and plasterers, plumbers, gas and steam fitters, roofers and slaters, brick and tile makers, glass workers, marble and stone cutters, potters, fishermen and oystermen, miners and quarry men, butchers, bakers, butter and cheese makers, confectioners, millers, blacksmiths, iron and steel workers, machinists, steam-boiler makers, stove, furnace, and grate makers, tools and cutlery makers, wheelwrights, wire workers, boot and shoemakers and repairers, harness and saddle makers and repairers, leather curriers and tanners, trunk and leather-case makers, bottlers and soda-water makers, brewers and maltsters, distillers, and rectifiers.

Other kinds of manufacturing and mechanical pursuits, in all of which Negroes were found engaged, are cabinet makers, coopers, saw-mill and planing-mill employees, glass workers, clock and watch makers and repairers, gold and silver workers, tin plate and tinware makers, bookbinders and paper-box makers, engravers, printers, lithographers and pressmen, operatives in paper and pulp mills, bleaching and dye works, carpet factories, carpet, cotton, hosiery, and knitting, silk, and woollen mills, dress-makers, hat and cap makers, milliners, seamstresses, tailors, broom and brush makers, charcoal, coke and lime burners. Negroes were also engaged as engin-eers and firemen, glovemakers, model and pattern makers, photographers, rubber factory operatives, tobacco and cigar factory operatives and uphol-sterers. In all these manifold occupations, except fifteen, the number of Negroes employed increased in the period from 1890 to 1900.

Negroes lost numbers in the trades of carpentry, plastering, brick and tile making, marble and stone cutting, blacksmithing, wheelwrighting, bootmaking and shoemaking, harness and saddle making, leather currying and tanning, trunk, valise and leather-case making, engraving, hosiery and knitting and woollen milling. But the same census shows that in more than half of these trades, owing, per-haps, to the larger use of machinery, there has been a decrease in the total number of persons employed, whether white or coloured. This indicates another reason than that of racial competition for the redis-tribution in the trades.

I have referred to the trades in which there appears to be a falling off of Negro employees; let me say a word concerning some of the trades in which the Negro has made exceptional gains. The num-ber of Negro miners in 1890 was 15,809. By 1900 this number had been increased to 36,568, a gain during ten years of 20,759, or 132 per cent. In 1890, the number of Negroes engaged as brick and stone masons was 9,647. In 1900, this number had been increased to 14,387, an increase of 4,740 or 49 per cent. In the meantime, the number of white men reported as engaged in this occupation had decreased 1.8 per cent.

The number of dressmakers in 1890 was 7,479. The number in 1900 was 12,572, an increase during the decade of 65.3 per cent; meanwhile the number of white dressmakers in 1890 was increased to 17.4 per cent., which is between one-third and one-fourth of the increase of the coloured dressmakers. In 1890, the number of Negro iron and steel workers was 5,790. In 1900 the number was 12,327, an increase of 6,537, or 112.7 per cent.; meanwhile the number of white iron and steel workers had increased 100 per cent. The number of Negro stationary engineers and firemen in 1890 was 6,326. In 1900, they had increased to 10,277, or 62.4 per cent. During the same time the increase for the white engineers and firemen was only 60 per cent.

The rapid increase of the Negro labourers in the iron and steel industries was undoubtedly due to the rapid development of that industry in the Southern states. Perhaps this industry, together with the coal and iron mining, has drawn more heavily than other industries upon the labouring population of the country districts. Some

figures and observations, indicating the progress
that the Negro has made in these industries, were
furnished to me by Mr. Belton Gilreath, of the
Gilreath Coal and Iron Company, and the Union
Coal and Coke Company, of Birmingham, Alabama,
who, after a very careful inquiry, has found that
Negroes in the Birmingham region mine about 90
per cent. of the iron ore and about 50 per cent. of
the coal.

"Twenty years ago," he says, "when the mines
were first being opened in this district, the ore-
mining was done by white miners with coloured
labourers, mostly foreigners, who in turn taught some
of the white men here. After a while, the Negro
labourers began to be the miners, and now Negroes
have almost completely monopolised the iron ore-
mining. Negroes perform both the work of labourers and miners until about 90 per cent. of the ore-
miners are coloured."

Mr. Gilreath added that in the coal mining industry Negroes have likewise made progress, but are
not mining as large a proportion of the coal as they
are of the ore. "As near as I can estimate," he said,
" from the best information I am able to secure, one-
half the coal produced is gotten out by coloured
miners."

According to the census for 1900, 209,154 Negroes
were employed in occupations which are classified
under "trade and transportation." This class

includes: agents, bankers, and brokers, bookkeepers and accountants, clerks, and copyists, commercial travellers, draymen, hackmen, teamsters, foremen and overseers, hostlers, hucksters and peddlers, livery-stable keepers, merchants and dealers, messengers, errand and office boys, officials of banks and corporations, packers, and shippers, porters and helpers, salesmen and saleswomen, steam railway employees, stenographers and typewriters, street railway employees, telephone and telegraph linemen, telegraph and telephone operators. In nearly all these occupations Negroes have made considerable gains. Among other facts I note that the number of Negro draymen and hackmen, teamsters, and so forth, increased from 43,963 in 1890 to 67,727 in 1900, an increase of 54 per cent. The increase among the whites for the same period was 45.9 per cent.

In 1900 there were over 200,000 Negroes engaged in occupations requiring skill in some form or other. These were: miners and quarry men, 36,568; sawmill and planing-mill employees, 33,266; dressmakers and seamstresses, 24,110; carpenters and joiners, 21,114; barbers and hair-dressers, 19,948; tobacco and cigar operatives, 15,349; brick and stone masons, 14,387; iron and steel workers, 12,327; engineers and firemen, 10,227; blacksmiths, 10,104; brick and tile makers, 9,970. In addition to these there were 2,585 Negro operatives in factories and mills, 52 architects, designers and draughtsmen, 185 electricians, 120 civil engineers and surveyors, 1,262 machinists, 198 tool and cutlery makers, 342 cabinet makers, 109 clock and watch makers, 66 gold and silver workers, 86 bookbinders, 22 engravers, 1,845 men and women tailors, 15 glove makers, 24 model and pattern makers, 247 photographers, and 1,045 upholsterers.

A thing that should be considered is that Negroes are, more and more every year, becoming themselves the employers of Negro labour. When Negroes go into business they employ other Negroes as clerks, bookkeepers, agents, and salesmen. All these things tend to draw coloured people from the trades and occupations in which they were formerly employed. The Negro barber is a good illustration of what I mean. The census of 1900 shows that there were not only a larger number but a larger percentage of barbers at that time than there were ten years before. During this same period, however, there has been a very large increase in the number of white barbers not only in the North but in the South. In many cases, particularly in the South, white barbers have taken the places of the Negro barbers, who formerly had a monopoly of that trade. In spite of this fact, as I have said, the number of Negro barbers has steadily increased. The explanation is that a much larger number of barbers are now employed by Negroes than there were a few years ago. The whole number of barbers increased from 1890 to 1900 to 54 per cent., while the number of Negro barbers increased during that period only 14 per cent.

A little earlier in this chapter I made the statement that, with the growth of factories and the introduction of machinery into the Southern states, to perform work that had previously been performed by hand, the white man rather than the Negro was used to perform that kind of labour. In recent years, however, there has been a growing disposition to employ Negro labour in the factories. For example, in 1900 a silk mill was established in Fayetteville, North Carolina, by the firm of Ashley and Bailey, who are the owners of a number of silk mills in different parts of the North.

This firm decided, after carefully considering the matter, to try the experiment of using Negro labour in the spinning and weaving of silk. In order to do this they purchased a considerable tract of land just outside of Fayetteville, and started to build up there a Negro colony. They rented to each family they employed a tract of land and a house. They erected a schoolhouse, in which there was a nine months' school, and built a church for the use of the colony. They obtained the services of an energetic Negro minister to bring together a number of Negro families and settle them on the land and in the houses they had erected. After that they invited the children to take employment in the mills. These mills, which employ about five hundred persons, are now conducted under the direction of a white superintendent, who has under him a coloured foreman, who is in charge of the mill which spins the thread.

Under the direction of these two men some five or six hundred children, from twelve to sixteen years of age, have been trained until they have become very satisfactory mill operatives. The superintendent, Mr. G. W. Kort, says it will take a number of years to bring these children up to the point where they will equal the trained and disciplined operatives in the Northern mills. He says, also, that the company has found certain special difficulties in controlling these children, most of whom have come directly from the farm to take up their work in the mills. Most of these difficulties can be traced back to the irregularities in the home life of the parents. Nevertheless, the Fayetteville silk mill has been a success, and is no longer, I understand, to be considered an experiment.

Negro labour has also been tried successfully in a number of hosiery mills. One of these is located in Savannah, Georgia, and another in Durham, North Carolina. In 1897, a group of coloured men in Concord, North Carolina, organised the Coleman Manufacturing Company, and erected a cotton mill,

which employed for a time some two hundred
coloured boys and girls. Just after the mill had been
fairly started, however, Mr. Coleman, the man who
organised the company, died, and the mill was sold
to a company of white men who decided to employ
white labour.

From the ranks of Negro mechanics, there have
come from time to time a number of Negro inventors.
The first of these inventors, to whom the Patent
Office records refer, is Henry Blair, of Maryland,
who was granted a patent for a corn harvester in
1834, and another patent for a similar invention in
1836. This man was probably "a free person of
colour," as slaves were not allowed to take out
patents for inventions in those days. The rule in
regard to the inventions of slaves was laid down, in
1858, by the Commissioner of Patents and confirmed by the Attorney-general of the United States.
The circumstances were these: A Negro slave, living with his master in the state of Mississippi, per-
fected a valuable invention which his master sought
to have patented. His application was refused on
the grounds that he was not the inventor. He
then sought to have the invention patented as
assignee of his slave, but under the law a slave
could not hold property and therefore could not
assign this invention to his master. The case
was appealed to the Attorney-general, and, as
I have said, he confirmed the decision of the

Commissioner of Patents. The result of this law was that neither the slave nor his master could secure the protection of the Government for any invention that a slave succeeded in making.

In 1862 a Negro slave belonging to Jefferson Davis, President of the Southern Confederacy, invented a propeller for vessels, which was finally put into use, it is said, by the Confederate navy. A Negro slave in Kentucky is said to have invented the hemp-brake, a machine in which the hemp fibre is separated from the hemp stalk. Negro mechanics also have been the builders of some of the most important buildings erected in the South before the War. When I was in Vicksburg, Mississippi, a few years ago, my attention was called to the courthouse, that was erected before the War, and is still the most imposing building in the city. I was told that this building was planned and built under the direction of a Negro slave.

A few years ago, in 1899, an attempt was made to find out from the Patent Office at Washington, and through inquiries directed to prominent patent attorneys in different parts of the United States, the number of patents that had been taken out by coloured inventors. Something over three hundred and seventy patents, taken out by two hundred and seven inventors, were found to have been taken out by coloured men. Elijah McCoy, of Detroit,

Michigan, had taken out at that time twenty-eight patents on appliances to be used for lubricating engines and locomotives. This was the largest number of patents taken out by any coloured man. The next largest number of patents was taken out by Granville T. Woods, an electrician. Mr. Woods has patented many valuable improvements in tele-graph and telephone instruments. One of his telephone inventions was sold to the American Bell Telephone Company. Another important series of inventions, covering machinery to be used in soling shoes, was made by J. E. Matzeliger. These included a lasting machine, a nailing machine, a tack-separating mechanism, and a mechanism for distributing tacks.*

One interesting fact in regard to the Negro mechanic in slavery time is that the demand for more efficient and more skilled labour made the slave mechanic a freer and more independent person than the other slaves. In a recent study of the condition of slave labour in the Charleston Dis-trict, Professor Ulrich B. Phillips, of the University of Wisconsin, has pointed out that, all through the South and particularly in the cities where the demand for skilled labour was greatest, there was a con-stant disposition on the part of slave-owners to do away, in one way or another, with the restrictions

* "The Negro as an Inventor," N. E. Baker, and " Twentieth Century Negro Literature," pp. 399-413.

that were imposed upon the intellectual progress and personal freedom of their slave mechanics. Upon this point, Professor Phillips says:

The system had to be made flexible by giving to every trustworthy slave, who was capable of self-direction, a personal incentive to increase his skill and assiduity. Under such conditions the laws which impeded industrial progress were increasingly disregarded and became dead letters. Slaves by hundreds hired their own time; whites and blacks, skilled and unskilled, worked side by side, with little notice of the colour line; trustworthy slaves were practically in a state of industrial freedom; and that *tertium quid*, the free person of colour, always officially unwelcome, was now regarded in private life as a desirable resident of a neighbourhood, provided he were a good workman. The liberalising tendencies were fast relieving the hard-and-fast character of the régime, so far at least as concerned all workmen who were capable of better things than gang and task labour.

The great mass of the common Negroes, it is true, were regarded as suited only for the gangs and unfit for any self-direction in civilised industry; but even in this case a few thinking men saw vaguely from time to time that a less expensive method of control ought to be substituted for chattel slavery, involving as it did the heavy capitalisation of lifetime labor as a commodity.*

Under the influence of the conditions here described a considerable portion of the slaves were gradually making their way out of slavery. Many of them purchased their freedom and moved North; others, though nominally slaves, were practically free. They were allowed to purchase their own time, and in many cases engaged in business for themselves. Such was the case, for instance, of

* *Political Science Quarterly*, September, 1907, vol. xxii., pp. 427–429.

the father of Mr. R. R. Taylor, Director of Mechanical Industries, at Tuskegee Institute. Mr. Taylor's father was the son of a white man who was at the same time his master. Although he was nominally a slave, he was early given liberty to do about as he pleased. While he was still a young man in Wilmington, North Carolina, he made the acquaintance of a white man who owned a sailing vessel, and they entered into a sort of partnership together. The young coloured man collected and bought up naval stores and other merchandise which he turned over to his partner, who carried them off in his ship and sold them. In this way they made a considerable amount of money together so that after all the losses of the war, Mr. Taylor's father was able to send him through one of the best technical training schools in the United States, the Boston Institute of Technology. I could mention a hundred other cases which illustrate the way men and women, though nominally slaves, succeeded in reaching a condition that was very close to that of freedom.

It was not an unusual thing in slavery days for a coloured man and a white man to go into business together. Negro and white artisans worked side by side during slavery, and the freedom to labour and to engage in business, without prejudice, has always existed. In all the ordinary forms of business and of labour there is no prejudice against the Negro. I should rather say that, other things being equal, a Southern white man who has a job of work to do would prefer to have a Negro perform it.

If slavery had continued as it began, merely an industrial system, a method of obtaining and directing labour, it is very likely that the slaves would have succeeded finally in working out their own freedom; but slavery had become, with the course of time, not only an industrial but also a political system and, by the beginning of the nineteenth century, many people in the South had begun to feel that it was absolutely necessary to preserve this system. In order to do this they found it necessary to pass laws which would limit and set bounds to the progress which the slaves were making. It was in the interest of this system that laws were passed to prevent masters emancipating their slaves. It was in the interest of the same system that laws were passed limiting the direction in which slave labour might be employed and the extent to which slaves might be instructed in the trades and in books. For instance, North Carolina allowed slaves to learn mathematical calculation, but not reading and writing. A law was passed in Georgia that no one should permit a Negro "to transact business for him in writing." In 1830, Mississippi passed a law which forbade employment of slaves in printing-offices, and, in 1845, the Legislature of Georgia declared that slaves and free Negroes could not take contracts for building and repairing houses.*

These restrictions bore most heavily upon the class of industrious and ambitious slaves. It was largely from this class that the fugitives, who, at the beginning of the nineteenth century, began to make their way northward, were recruited. It was from the sufferings of these fugitives and the hardships which they endured in order to preserve their liberty, that the Northern people became acquainted with the evils of slavery in the South. Many of the fugitive slaves, like Frederick Douglass, Bishop Loguen, and William Wells Brown, joined in the anti-slavery agitation in the North, and by their eloquence helped prepare the North for the struggle with slavery that was soon to take place. Thus the effect of the laws made in the South, to suppress the efforts of the Negro slaves to be free, produced conditions in the North which finally resulted in the destruction of the slavery system.

Perhaps it is fair to say that the real cause of the downfall of slavery was not so much the hardships that it imposed upon the masses of both races, black and white, but the fact that it attempted to build up a dam that would hold back and restrain the forces that were making for progress inside the system itself. No page of history, I venture to say, better illustrates the fact that it is not possible to pass a

---

* "The Negro Artisan," Atlanta University Publications, No. 7, p. 15.

law to permanently stop the progress of civilisation. The hardest and most ungrateful task, that any individual or any race can undertake, is that of holding down and under another individual or another race that is trying to rise.

CHAPTER IV

NEGRO CRIME AND RACIAL SELF-HELP

NEGRO crime in the United States reached its highest point in the years of financial strain, beginning in 1892 and ending in 1896. The United States Census Statistics of Crime show that from 1870 to 1890 there was an enormous increase of Negro criminality, particularly in the Northern states. The total number of Negro criminals enumerated in the Census of 1870 was 8,056; in 1880 this number had increased to 16,748; in 1890 it was 24,277; and in 1904 it was 26,087. This meant that for every one hundred thousand Negroes in the United States there were, in 1870, 162 criminals; in 1880, 248 criminals; in 1890, 325 criminals. Fourteen years later, however, in 1904, the number of Negro criminals to every one hundred thousand of the Negro population had fallen to 282.

Some time between 1890 and 1904 the wave of Negro criminality which, up to that time, had seemed to be steadily increasing, reached its highest point and began to recede. Between these two periods no census figures for the whole country are available, but a special study of the criminal statistics of cities, North and South, shows that about 1894 and 1895 there was a marked decrease in Negro crime.

Statistics for Washington, District of Columbia, from 1881 to 1902, showed that the maximum rate of 184 police arrests per thousand of Negro population was reached in 1893. In Charleston, South Carolina, the rate of arrests reached its maximum of 92 per thousand in 1902. Cincinnati, Ohio, reached its maximum rate of 276 per thousand of the Negro population in 1894. In Savannah, Georgia, the highest rate of 165 was not reached until 1898. In Chicago the rate of arrests of Negroes reached its maximum of 586 per thousand in 1892, the year of the World's Fair. At this time, there was a considerable transient population in Chicago, and, as the rate of Negro criminality per thousand is estimated on the basis of the permanent population, these figures are like to be misleading.

The rate of arrests in St. Louis, Missouri, reached its maximum, when the number of arrests per thousand of the Negro population was 269. Statistics from the cities of New York and Philadelphia, the only cities for which data covering the period prior to 1866 are available, show that the rate of Negro arrests per thousand of the Negro population was about as great prior to 1866 as it was in 1902. The maximum rate for New York was reached in 1899 when the number of arrests per thousand of the Negro population was 111. The rate of arrests per thousand of the Negro population in Philadelphia has, at no time previous to 1902, been greater than it was in 1864, when there were 150 arrests per thousand of the Negro population.

The thing that makes these figures the more significant is the fact that it is, as a rule, in the large cities that much the larger proportion of crimes is committed. At any rate, it is in the cities that the larger proportion of crimes committed gets into court and is recorded. Furthermore, it is in the cities that the larger proportion of the increase of recorded crime has taken place during the period that I have mentioned. This is, no doubt, the reason why statistics show that there are more Negro criminals in the North than in the South. Seven-tenths of the Negroes in the Northern states live in the cities having at least more than 2,500 inhabitants, and more than one-third of the Negroes in the Northern states live in cities having more than one hundred thousand inhabitants.

A comparison of the criminal statistics of the Northern and Southern states will illustrate what I mean:

Negro Prisoners in Northern States:

1870	1880	1890	1904
2,025	3,774	5,635	7,527

Negro Prisoners per 100,000 of Negro Pop. in Northern States:

1870	1880	1890	1904
372	515	773	765

Negro Prisoners in Southern States:

1870	1880	1890	1904
6,031	12,973	19,244	18,550

Prisoners per 100,000 of Negro Pop. in Southern States:

1870	1880	1890	1904
136	221	284	220

The increase in the amount of Negro crime in the United States during the period of 1870 to 1890 was so rapid and so marked that it made a great impression on the public, North and South. A thing that helped to emphasise these facts and make them seem more serious than they actually were, particularly in the Southern states, was the outbreak, at this time, of mob-violence so savage and so terrible in its manifestations, as to attract, for a time, the attention of the whole civilised world. From 1882 to 1892 the number of persons lynched in the United States increased from 114 to 235 per annum. From that time on to 1903 the number decreased to 104 per annum. The total number of Negroes lynched during this period of twenty-two years was 2,060; the total number of whites lynched during the same period was 1,169. In the case of the Negroes there was an average of 93 and 7-11 per year; in the case of the whites the average was 53 and 3-22 per year.

Of the 2,060 put to death in this way during this period, 1,985, or more than 96 per cent., were lynched in the Southern states. The offences for which these people suffered death from the wild vengeance of the mob were not, as has been supposed, in the majority of cases assaults upon women. A little more than one-third of the lynchings were due to assaults, attempted assaults, upon women or insults to them. The larger number were occasioned by the crime of murder.

The minor offences for which Negroes were lynched were such things as robbery, slander, wife-beating, cutting levees, kidnapping, voodooism, poisoning horses, writing insulting letters, incendiary language, swindling, jilting a girl, colonising Negroes, political troubles, gambling, quarrelling, poisoning wells, throwing stones, unpopularity, making threats, circulating scandal, being troublesome, bad reputation, drunkenness, rioting, fraud, enticing a servant away, writing letters to white women, asking a white woman in marriage, conspiracy, introducing small-pox, giving information, conjuring, concealing a criminal, slapping a child, passing counterfeit money, elopement with a white girl, disobeying ferry regulations, running quarantine, violation of contract, paying attention to a white girl, resisting assault, inflammatory language, forcing white boys to commit crime, lawlessness.*

These cases of mob-violence and the crime which occasioned them, were, as I have said, widely advertised by the press through the North and through the South. And they helped to give the impression that the Negroes in the South were much more

---

* "Lynch Law," Cutler, p. 167.

lawless than they were in other parts of the country, much more lawless than other races in the same stage of civilisation as the Negro. As a matter of fact, as may be seen from the statistics I have given, the Negro criminals in the North were always much more numerous, in proportion to the Negro population, than they were in the South. Furthermore, as I hope to show later in this chapter, the amount of crime committed by other peoples who have come here from Europe, and particularly from the South of Europe, where the social conditions are in some sense comparable to the social conditions of the Negro in the South, is considerably larger in proportion to the number of population they represent, than is true in the case of the Negro.

The single fact to which attention was directed, as a consequence of this outbreak of mob-violence, was that the number of Negro criminals, in proportion to the Negro population, was three times as great as that of the white criminals in proportion to the white population, and that Negro crime was increasing with much greater rapidity than was the crime committed by whites.

One of the wholesome results of these outbreaks of mob-violence and of the discussion that they aroused, has been to direct the attention of earnest men and women of the Negro race to a study of the actual facts and their causes, in the hope of improving conditions by getting at the sources of Negro crime. The attention of Negro teachers and students was first called to these facts by the Hampton Negro Conferences, and studies were begun under the direction of these Conferences as early as 1898. Some years later, in 1903 and 1904, a study of Negro crime was made under the direction of W. E. Burghardt Du Bois, Professor of Sociology at Atlanta University. This study of Negro crime, which was published in 1904, is all the more interesting because it was made under the direction of a Negro and represents, in so very large a degree, the results of the studies and observations of Negro students and teachers upon the sources of crime among the people of their own race.

Referring to the work that Negro schools are doing in the way of studying the social conditions of the Negro people, I am reminded of something said to me a few years ago by a gentleman who had been devoting some months to travel through the Southern states, in order to gather material for a book upon the subject of the Negro and his relations to the white man in the South. He told me, among other things, that he had been greatly surprised to observe to what extent educated coloured men, in all parts of the country, had taken up in a serious and systematic way the study of the social conditions of their own people. He said that he had been informed in the North that educated Negroes had little or no interest in studying the conditions of their own people, but were interested rather in getting as far away as they were able from the masses of the Negro race. On the other hand, he had been told in the South that Negroes were so wholly ignorant and unreliable that if he wanted to really get at the truth about the Negro he must get his information from a white man.

When he came to meet the educated Negroes in the Southern states, however, he had learned that they were not only well-informed in regard to the conditions of their own people but that they frequently seemed to have gained a deeper insight into the actual conditions of the Negro people, and to have a more accurate knowledge of the situation, as it looked to a man from the outside, than many white men he had met. He added that, considering the persons he referred to were in many instances the sons and daughters of slave parents, and that few of them had had opportunities for study that men and women of the white race have had, this seemed to him an evidence of very genuine progress on the part of the Negro race.

The study of Negro crime to which I have referred is interesting, however, not merely as an indication of the serious interest that educated Negroes have begun to take in the condition of the Negro race, but it is interesting also for the new facts which were first brought to light in this study, and have since been confirmed by a census of crime published by the United States Census Bureau in 1907.

One of the facts brought out by this census concerns the method of enumeration used by the Census Office. For instance, up to 1904 it had been the practice, in taking the census of crime, to count all persons who were in jails or prisons on a certain day. The result was supposed to give the relative number of criminals in different parts of the country and so indicate the comparative amount of crime committed in these different places.

A closer study of the statistics shows, however, that it has been customary to sentence prisoners for longer terms in some parts of the country than in others, even though the crime committed was of the same character or class. This is true, for instance, of the Southern states as compared with the Northern states. The result has been that an undue amount of crime has been credited, by this method of enumeration, to the Southern states.

I can, perhaps, make this point clear by an illustration. Consider the case of a man who is engaged in raising chickens, and who, for some reason or other, desires to confine a certain number of his chickens, while the others are allowed to run loose. He has, let us suppose, two breeds, and he puts five chickens of each breed into the hen-yard every day, with, however, this difference, that the chickens of one breed are confined in the hen-yard one week, while the chickens of the other breed are confined two weeks. Now it is evident that if you put five chickens of each breed in the hen-yard every day, you will have, at the end of the first week, an equal number of each breed, namely, thirty-five. From that time on, however, the number of chickens in the hen-yard which are confined two weeks will be larger than that of the breed confined one week. So that at the end of the second week there will be still only thirty-five chickens of the first breed, while there will be seventy of the second. In other words, there will be twice as many of the second in confinement as of the first breed.

The result is the same whether we are counting chickens in a hen-yard or prisoners in a penitentiary. This illustrates, in a simple way, how it is that in the Southern states, where the sentences imposed upon criminals are heavier than they are in the Northern states, the number of criminals enumerated at any one time will be disproportionately large.

In order to correct this error it was determined, in the Census of 1904, not merely to enumerate the persons found in confinement at any particular date, but to obtain figures as to the number of commitments, that is to say, to find out the number of persons who had been sent to jail during the period of a year. By this means, the Census of 1904 took account not merely of those who happened to be in the jails or the prisons at a given period, but also of those who had come in during the year, and, either because they had been able to pay their fines or because they served their sentences, had been released.

The results showed at once some striking changes in the statistics of crime, and materially corrected some wrong impressions as to the relative amount of crime committed in the different sections. For example, the number of prisoners enumerated according to the earlier method gave the North Atlantic states in 1904, 27,389 prisoners. The number of commitments for that same year was 76,235. In other words, according to the second method of enumeration, there was 48,846 more crimes committed in the Northern states than there appeared to be by the first method of counting. This was an increase of nearly 200 per cent.

On the other hand, in the South Atlantic states there were 11,150 prisoners enumerated, but only 10,643 had been committed to prison during the year. By this method of reckoning it appeared that there were 507 criminals less than were shown by the earlier method of enumeration. The same differences appear when the South Central states are compared with the North Central states and the Western states. By the census enumeration, it appeared that there were 14,614 prisoners in the penitentiaries and jails in the South Central states while only 10,206 had been committed to prison during the year. This was a decrease of 4,408. In the North Central states, reckoning by the methods of enumeration, there were 21,000 prisoners, but by the method of commitment there were 38,603. In other words, there appeared to be 17,603 more criminals by this latter method of enumeration than by the former. In the Western states there were 7,619 prisoners enumerated, but there were 14,004 commitments during the year.

One explanation of these differences is, as I have said, that in the Southern states the sentences are longer than they are in the Northern states. I do not know exactly why the Southern courts impose heavier sentences upon prisoners than the Northern courts. Perhaps it is because the crimes committed in the South are more serious than those committed in the North and deserve heavier punishment. But that, of course, is no reason why we should count those crimes twice in making up our estimates of the criminal population, as I fear has, in effect, sometimes been done in comparing the amount of crime committed in the South with the amount of crime committed in the North.

The method of computing crime which has made so large a difference in the apparent amount of crime committed in the South, as compared with the North, has been responsible for crediting a disproportionate amount of crime to the Negro. For instance, in the South Atlantic states, 8,281 criminals were enumerated as in jails and prisons in 1904. In the same year, however, only 6,847 prisoners had been committed to prison. In the South Central states, 10,269 prisoners were enumerated in the prisons and jails during the year 1904. At the same time it was found that only 6,066 prisoners had been committed during that year. In other words, if we were to estimate the amount of Negro crime in the South by the number of persons found in the prisons and jails, there would be 5,643 more criminals found for the year 1904 than if we had counted the actual number of Negroes arrested, convicted and committed to prison. The reason here again is that Negroes in the South are given longer sentences than white men. For example, 50 per cent. of the Negroes convicted of crime in the South Atlantic states were sentenced to terms of one year or more, while only 38 per cent. of the white men so convicted were sentenced to terms of a year or more.

No doubt, also, there is a difference in the crimes committed by the white and black population. It is said that, in the South, stealing and all crimes against property are punished relatively with more severe sentences than crimes of violence, or crimes against the person, as they are termed. An illustration of this is given in an article upon the "Negro in Crime," in the *Independent* for May 18, 1899, where the following items clipped from the Atlanta *Constitution*, of January 27, are quoted. The items are:

Egbert Jackson (coloured), aged thirteen, was given a sentence of $50, or ten months in the chain gang, for larceny from the house·

The most affecting scene of all was the sentencing of Joe Redding, a white man, for the killing of his brother, John Redding. . . .

Judge ——— is a most tender-hearted man, and heard the prayers and saw the tears, and tempered justice with moderation, and gave the modern Cain two years in the penitentiary.

The two cases I have just cited are, perhaps, exceptional, but they illustrate the kind of crime upon which the Southern courts are disposed to put the emphasis. At the time the crimes referred to in these clippings were committed, there were, so far as I know, no juvenile courts in any of the Southern states, and with the exception of the Virginia Manual Labour School, started in 1897, no reformatories to which Negro children could be sent. Where the principle of the juvenile court has been established, an offence committed by a child, such as the one referred to in the foregoing quotation, is not considered a crime in the same sense in which an offence committed by an adult person is so considered. The imposition of heavier sentences for minor offences and especially the disposition of Southern courts to impose relatively heavier penalties on children, has had the effect of largely increasing the number of Negroes in the jail and prison population.

It should be remembered, in this respect, also, that among the members of the Negro race, owing, no doubt, to the condition of the home surroundings, to poverty, and, perhaps, also, to the fact that mothers are so frequently employed away from home, a much larger proportion of Negro criminals are children than is true with the white race. This makes the system which prevailed a few years ago, and still continues in a less degree, of sending children, particularly Negro children, to the penitentiaries and the chain-gang, bear so heavily upon the members of my race. When children are sent to prison, they are not only subjected, during the period when they are most impressionable, to the influences of evil companions, but they sometimes get to thinking of the prison as a place to which they naturally belong, and where they expect to spend the larger part of their lives. It is a very serious matter when a race or a class of people reaches the point where it begins to feel that it is looked upon by those to whom it has been taught to look for guidance and control, as a criminal people.

A few years ago, when I was in Kentucky, I remember hearing a story which struck me as peculiarly pathetic. One morning the officers of the State Prison found, in counting over their prisoners, that they had one too many. Upon investigation, they discovered a young coloured boy, who had been discharged from prison a few days before, had actually broken into the prison during the night, apparently in order to find a place to sleep. As I remember the story, the boy said, when questioned, that after leaving the prison he had wandered about till he was very hungry, and as he had no place to stay he finally decided to come back and crawl into the stockade, where there were at least people who knew him, and where he could find a place to sleep. From all that I could learn, this boy had lived so long in prison that he had come to feel more at home there than he did outside.

Another reason why prison sentences are longer in the South than they are in the North is because, under the convict-lease system, crime has been or has seemed to be immensely profitable, not only to the states but to individuals. For instance, in 1900, the state of Georgia received $61,826.32 from the earnings of prisoners. From 1901 to 1903, the net income was $81,000 a year. In 1904, new contracts were made for a period of five years beginning April 1, 1904, which netted the state on an average of $225,000 per annum.

It is only slowly that the public has begun to realise that the new form of slavery, represented by the convict-lease system, has made the condition of the convict-slave infinitely worse than was possible under a system of slavery in which the slave belonged to his master for life. Gradually, however, the evils of a system which made crime profitable have been coming to light. In 1908, Georgia, seeing the horrible conditions that existed in the convict camps, abandoned its old methods of disposing of convict labor and has since that time employed convicts in building the public roads. The conditions that formerly existed in Georgia still exist, however, in several of the other Southern states.

In most cases where an effort has been made to determine the relative criminality of the Negro it has been customary to compare the Negro with the white man. Because the white man stood higher in the scale of civilisation, was better educated, had a better home and was more respected, this comparison has been to the disadvantage of the Negro.

The criminal statistics of 1890 showed, for example, that there were 104 white and 325 Negro criminals in the United States for every one hundred thousand of the respective races. In other words, the crimes of Negroes were more than three times those of the whites. In the Northern states, the ratio was even greater, the crimes of Negroes being more than five times those of the whites.

In 1904, however, when the races were compared upon the basis of the actual number of persons committed to prison during the year, it was found that the commitments per hundred thousand were 187 for the whites and 268 for the Negroes. That is to say, the two races stood to each other, in respect to the amount of crime committed by each, in about the ratio of one to one and one-half. In the Northern states, Negro crime, instead of being five times, was a little more than four times that of the whites.

By the census of 1890 it appeared that the Negro

offenders in Southern states compared with the white offender in those states, were in the ratio of 2 to 9. That is to say, in those states, comparing the races by the methods I have described, there were four and one-half times as much crime committed by Negroes as by whites. In 1904, however, considering the actual number of both races committed to prison, it appears that the Negro crime, compared with the white, was in the ratio of less than three and one-half to one — a decrease of 21 per cent.

In looking further into the statistics of crime with special reference to the nationality of the criminals, I have found that among the foreign-born people in the United States, the different nationalities range themselves, at very diverse distances, on two sides of the general average of crime committed by the foreign population as a whole. On the one side, there are nationalities which fall far below the average. On the other hand, there are others which rise far above that average.

In comparing the Negro with the immigrants now coming into the United States in such large numbers from the South of Europe, we are comparing him with races which in Europe have been, and still in America are, living in the conditions that are in many respects comparable to those in which the masses of the Negro people now live. The people to whom I refer are, in many instances, less advanced in education in books than the majority of the coloured people in the Southern states, though they are, no doubt, far ahead of them in some of the more fundamental things.

For instance, among the Italian people, as a whole, more than 38 per cent. of the population can neither read nor write. Of the people who come into the United States, particularly from Sicily and Southern Italy, no doubt a much larger per cent. are illiterate. In Russia, more than 70 per cent. of the population are without education. In other parts of Southern Europe, like Roumania, 89 per cent. of the people are wholly illiterate.

A good many of these people are now coming into certain parts of the South. The following comparison, therefore, of the relative criminality of these different races as compared to the Negro is peculiarly interesting:

Nationality	Number in U. S. according to census 1900	Prison commitments in 1904	Commitments per 1,000 of each nationality
Mexicans . . .	103,410	484	4.7
Italians . . .	484,207	2,143	4.4
Austrians . . .	276,249	1,006	3.6
French . . .	104,341	358	3.4
Canadians . .	1,181,255	3,557	3.0
Russians . . .	424,096	1,222	2.8
Poles	383,510	1,038	2.7
Negroes . . .	8,840,789	23,698	2.7

There is another class of crimes with which the Negro has been more associated in the public mind than any other. I refer to the assaults upon women, to which attention has so often been directed because they have so frequently been made the occasion of, or excuse for, outbreaks of mob-violence, not only in the Southern states but in the Northern states as well. The total commitments for rape, in 1904, were 620; of this number 450 were by white persons, 170 by coloured, and 111 by persons of foreign birth.

The number of cases of rape committed by coloured people, including all the races in the United States classed under that title, was 1.8 per hundred thousand of the total coloured population. The total number of commitments for the white population was 0.6 per hundred thousand of the white population. The number of commitments for this crime per hundred thousand of the foreign population was 1. In other words, the number of commitments for rape was proportionately three times as great for the coloured population as it was for the whites. It was nearly twice as great, proportionately, as that for the foreign population.*

A comparison of the coloured committed for this crime with that portion of the foreign-born population which is nearest to the coloured in respect to education and social condition shows, however, that the Negro is by no means the worst offender in respect to this crime. The following table shows the number of commitments per hundred thousand for

---

* The census for 1904 does not separate the Negro from the other coloured populations in respect to the crime of rape.

this crime of the foreign-born people to whom I
have referred:

Italians 5.3	Hungarians . . 2.0
Mexicans . . . 4.8	French 1.9
Austrians . . . 3.2	Russians . . . 1.9

For other portions of the foreign-born population
the percentage is less. For example, among the
Canadian-born population statistics indicate for
every one hundred thousand of the population that
1.2 are guilty of assaults on women. For other
foreign-born portions of the population the figures
are Polanders 1.0, Germans 0.4, Irish 0.3.

While it is true that the Negro furnishes a proportionately large number of the crimes of assault
upon women, I do not think it is true, if we are to go
by the statistics, that there is any more disposition on
the part of men of the Negro race to commit this
crime than on the part of men of other races.
While no statistics can possibly determine this fact,
I have taken the trouble to find out what per cent. of
the major offenders, that is to say, of the men who
committed the worst crimes, were sent to prison for
the crime of rape during the year 1904. From these
figures it appears that only 1.9 per cent. of the coloured
offenders committed for major offences were committed for the crime of rape. On the other hand,
2.3 per cent. of the white and 2.6 per cent. of the
foreign major offenders were committed in 1904
for that crime. The following table will show the

per cent. of major offenders of the races to whom
I have already made reference, who were committed
for this offence:

Hungarians . . . 4.7	Canadians . . . 3.0
Italians 4.4	Mexicans . . . 2.7
Austrians . . . 4.2	Poles 2.1
French 3.1	Germans . . . 1.8
Russians . . . 3.0	Irish 1.3
Coloured . . 1.9	

As a further confirmation of the facts which these
statistics show, I might mention that in the South
Atlantic states, where 35.7 per cent. of the total population are Negroes, the rate of commitments per
100,000 of the population for assault on women is
0.5. On the other hand, in the Western Division,
where only 0.7 per cent. of the total population are
Negroes, the commitments for rape amount to 1.4
for each 100,000 of the population. In the North
Atlantic states, where Negroes represent 1.8 per cent.
of the population, the number of commitments for
this crime per hundred thousand is 0.9. In the South
Central states, where 29.8 per cent. of the population
are Negroes, the number of commitments for rape
per hundred thousand is 0.7.

It may be said that the reason the commitments
for assaults upon women are lower in those regions
where the Negro population is proportionately larger,
is due to the fact that the men who commit these
crimes are summarily executed by lynch law. The

fact is, however, that were the total number of Negroes lynched for rape in the United States in 1904 added to those arrested and committed to prison, it would not change these percentages more than a quarter of one per cent.

Before concluding what I have to say on the subject of Negro crime I want to add a word in regard to the work that Negroes, sometimes in association with their white neighbours and sometimes independently, have done and are doing to get at and destroy the sources of crime among members of their race.

Immediately after the Atlanta Riot, September 22, 1906, during which ten white people and sixty coloured people were wounded, and two white and ten coloured people were killed, there came forward two men, among others, with definite measures of "re-construction." These men were ex-Governor W. J. Northen and Charles T. Hopkins.

Ex-Governor Northen set on foot what was at first known as the "Christian League," an organisation composed of leading coloured men and leading white men, formed for the purpose of putting down mob-violence. Charles T. Hopkins, a prominent young lawyer of Atlanta, organised, in association with Reverend H. H. Proctor, pastor of the First Coloured Congregational Church, and some others, what was known as the Civic League, the purpose of which was to bring leading coloured men and leading white men of the city together in order to cooperate in doing away with the conditions which had brought about the Atlanta Riot.

One of the first things that this dual organisation did was to defend in the courts a Negro named Joe Glenn, who had been charged with an assault upon a woman. In fact, he had been identified by the woman upon whom the assault was committed, and the members of this organisation, both white and coloured, believed that Joe Glenn was guilty. Their purpose was merely to secure for him a fair and speedy trial. Upon examination into the evidence, however, they came to the conclusion that the man was not guilty, and succeeded not only in proving his innocence before the trial was ended, but in finding the man who was guilty, and thus, undoubtedly, saved the life of an innocent man.

The Civic League confined its operations to the city of Atlanta, but ex-Governor Northen sought to extend the influence of his organisation throughout the state of Georgia and into adjoining states. Up to 1909, he had organised eighty-three of what came to be known as the Christian Civic leagues. These organisations were located mainly in counties containing the larger Negro populations, and were composed of the very best people in the state, white and black.

One of the indirect results of this " re-construction " movement was the erection, under the direction of Reverend H. H. Proctor, and at a cost of $50,000, of

a handsome institutional Negro church. This
church was dedicated in February, 1909. It was
intended to do a work among the coloured people that
would attack the causes of racial friction and make
mobs like that of 1906 impossible.

Before this time, however, Negro people themselves,
with very little assistance from their white neighbours, had undertaken a kind of work intended to
remedy the evils in their present condition. All
over the South, and in many parts of the North,
wherever the Negroes live in large numbers, coloured
orphan asylums have been established to care for the
neglected children from among whom Negro criminals are so frequently recruited. As near as I have
been able to learn, there are not less than fifty or
sixty of such asylums already in existence in different
parts of the United States. A number of these, like
the Carrie Steele Orphanage, of Atlanta, have been
started upon the small savings and pious faith of
some good coloured woman.

Carrie Steele, the founder of the orphanage at
Atlanta, which bears her name, was born a slave in
Georgia. For many years she was employed at
the Atlanta Union Depot. Here she had an opportunity to see something of the dangers to which
homeless and neglected coloured children were subjected. In order to raise money to carry out the
plan she then formed of establishing an orphans'
home, she wrote a little book, which was the story

of her life. This book found a ready sale among the charitably disposed people, and with the proceeds a home was organised in 1890. This institution began with five orphans. In 1906, it was caring for ninety-seven children, and had an income of $2,000 a year, a portion of which is paid by the coloured people and the remainder by the city.

In 1897, a Negro reformatory association was organised in Virginia by John H. Smythe, former minister to Liberia. It had a Negro board of directors, and an advisory board of seven white people, and its purpose, as stated, was to "rescue juvenile offenders." The association purchased a large tract of land, amounting to four hundred and twenty-three acres, which had been part of the "Broadneck" estate in Hanover County, Virginia. For a number of years this reformatory was supported by private philanthropy, but eventually it became a state institution.

In conclusion, I want to say a word here about a work that the Negroes of Birmingham, Alabama, have undertaken, at the suggestion and under the direction of Judge N. B. Feagin, of the Municipal Court.

Judge Feagin is not only a lawyer, but a student of sociology. Some years ago, when he first became judge of the Municipal Court, there was no way of disposing of children convicted in the City Courts except to send them to the chain-gang. In 1898, however, there was established at East Lake, about twenty miles from Birmingham, a reformatory for white boys.

The large number of juvenile offenders who found their way into courts were, however, Negro children. Nothing had been done, up to this time, to keep them out of prisons and chain-gangs. Every year large numbers graduated from the prisons into the ranks of professional criminals. In 1903, an attempt was made to remedy this by passing a juvenile court law, but it failed. March 12, 1907, however, a law was passed making it a misdeameanor to send any child under fourteen years of age to jail or prison. If there had been practical means for executing this law, it would have effected a revolution in the treatment of criminal children in Alabama. But, as in the case of the Negro children, no such means existed; the law was repealed the following August.

Meanwhile, Judge Feagin determined to establish, upon his own responsibility, a modern system of dealing with criminal children in Birmingham. He found that there are thirty Negro churches in Birmingham. He determined to call the preachers of these churches together and explain his purpose to them. He then asked them if they could not induce the women of their congregation to raise two dollars per month to support a coloured probation officer. He said if they would do that, instead of sending the coloured children, who were brought into his court, to the chain-gang, he would send them back to their homes or to the homes of relatives and friends, on probation.

A coloured probation officer was appointed and the city divided into thirty districts, in which three women from each of the thirty Negro congregations in the city were appointed to coöperate with the probation officer in looking after the children on probation. In order to arouse interest in this plan, an association was formed of the coloured women of the thirty different churches, and Judge Feagin went around to the different Negro churches to speak to the people in order to assist the association, in this way, in raising money to support the voluntary probation officer he had appointed.

So far as the plan outlined was carried out, it concerned only those children who were brought into the court for the first time. It was necessary to devise some means for taking care of those who were guilty of a second offence. Judge Feagin decided that the way to dispose of them was to send them to the country districts. He then announced this plan in the papers and declared that wherever he could find a coloured farmer of good character, who would take these children and put them to work, he would turn them over to him, under certain conditions, which were named.

About twelve miles from Tuscaloosa, the former capital of Alabama, there is a Negro farmer by the name of Sam Dailey, who owns five hundred and thirty-five acres of land. This man, reading of Judge Feagin's proposal, came to see him and made a proposition to set aside one hundred and twenty-five acres of his farm, on which he would employ the children whom Judge Feagin sent him. Sam Dailey has been receiving these boys since 1903. With the aid of funds which he has been able to collect and from the profits of the farm he has established a school, which is conducted by a coloured preacher employed for that purpose. During this time, and up to 1909, he had had on his farm over one hundred Negro boys. Some few of them have run away. Several have been sent back to their relatives in the city. Others have become permanently settled in the farming districts and are making good citizens.

As a result of the interest aroused in this work, two other reformatories for juvenile offenders of the Negro race have been started. One of these is on the outskirts of Birmingham, and the other is at Mount Meigs, a few miles from Montgomery. At the time this is written, the probation officer, Reverend J. D. James, is supported not merely by the contributions he receives from the coloured churches, but also from two of the coloured secret orders in Birmingham. It is the hope of Judge Feagin and those who are associated with him that the work which is being done will eventually receive the sanction and support of the state, and that the juvenile court law, which was passed and repealed, will then be reënacted.

CHAPTER V

IN THE spring of 1907, Colonel Henry Watterson, of Louisville, Kentucky, the noted Democratic editor and statesman, made an address at a great meeting in Carnegie Hall, New York City, in the interest of Negro education in the South. Speaking of the work that has been accomplished in this direction since the War, he said: "The world has never yet witnessed such progress from darkness into light as the American Negro has made in the period of forty years."

When the Negro was made free and became an American citizen, it is safe to say that not more than 5 or, at most, 10 per cent. of the race could read and write. In 1900, at the end of less than forty years of freedom, 55½ per cent. could both read and write. If Negro education has made as much progress in the last ten years, as it did from 1890 to 1900, it is safe to say, at the present time, that not more than 32 per cent. of the Negro population is without some education in books. As Mr. Watterson said, no race in history can show a similar record.

What was it that so aroused a whole race, a nation within a nation, numbering at the present time ten millions of people, to make such strides in education? How has this work been done?

Perhaps the best answer I can make to this question is to relate my own experience. When I was a boy in Virginia, I used sometimes to accompany the white children of the plantation to the schoolhouse, in our neighbourhood. I went with them to carry their books, to carry their wraps, or their lunches, but I was never permitted to go farther than the schoolroom door. In my childish ignorance, I did not understand this. During the hours when the white children were not in school, we played and chatted together about the house or in the fields. We rode together our wooden horses; we fished together in the nearby streams; we played marbles, town-ball, "tag," and wrestled together on the parlour floor. And yet, for some reason I did not understand, I was debarred from entering the little schoolhouse with the children of my master.

The thing made such an impression upon my mind, that I finally asked my mother about it. She explained the matter to me as best she could, and from her I heard for the first time that learning from books in a schoolroom was something that, as a rule, was forbidden to a Negro child in the South. The idea that books contained something which was forbidden aroused my curiosity and excited in me a desire to find out for myself what it was in these books that made them forbidden fruit to me and my race.

From the moment that it was made clear to me that I was not to go to school, that it was dangerous for me to learn to read, from that moment I resolved that I should never be satisfied until I learned what this dangerous practice was like. What was true in my case has been true in the case of thousands of others. If no restriction had been put upon Negro education, I doubt whether such tremendous progress in education would have been made.

When I became free all the legal restrictions against my getting education were removed. Nevertheless I heard it stated in public speeches that the Negro was so constituted that he could not learn from books, and that time, effort and money would be thrown away in trying to teach him to master the studies of the ordinary school curriculum. When I heard this, I resolved again that, at the price of any sacrifice, I would do my part in order to prove to the world that the Negro possessed the ability to get an education, and to use it. If I had heard no such prediction regarding the ability of the Negro to get education, I question whether I would have been any more interested in mastering my school studies and text-books than the ordinary white boy.

Directly after the War the whole race was conscious that a large part of the American people doubted the ability of the Negro to compete with other races in the field of learning. But when the Negro heard people freely discussing his abilities and making predictions about his future he determined to see to it that these predictions should not be fulfilled.

My experience is that it is very unsafe to make predictions either in regard to races or in regard to individuals. Sometimes the mere statement of a prophecy tends to bring about its own fulfillment. In this case, if the predictions made are evil, the prophets become, to a certain extent, responsible for their consequences. At other times predictions stimulate the people, in regard to whom they are made, to do something entirely different than the thing predicted. But in that case, of course, the predictions do not become true. In either case prophecy is likely to be unprofitable.

In order to gain a just idea of the distance the Negro has travelled during the years since freedom came we should compare his progress with that of the people of some of the countries of Europe that have been free for centuries. For example, in Italy, 38.30 per cent. of the population can neither read nor write. In Spain the percentage of illiteracy is 68.1 per cent.; in Russia, 77 per cent.; in Portugal, 79 per cent.; in Brazil, 80 per cent.; in Venezuela,

75 per cent.; and in Cuba 56.6 per cent. By comparison, the progress of the American Negro represents a remarkable achievement.

In the early days, when slavery was still merely an economic and not yet a political institution, there seems to have been no special restrictions put either upon the education of slaves or of free Negroes. If Negroes did not obtain an education it was because there were few opportunities in the Southern colonies for any one to receive an education. In fact, before the Revolution, there was no such thing as a public school system in any colony south of Connecticut. The colonies were opposed in principle to public schools. It was considered an interference on the part of the state to undertake the education of the younger children, who were supposed to be taught at home.

People in England who sent out the first colonies were interested, however, in the religious education of the Indians and as the number of slaves increased they became interested in the education of the Negroes, who, at that time, were also a "heathen" people. In fact, the first public school in Virginia, which was started about 1620, was erected for the benefit of these native Americans. The Indian War of 1622 destroyed this school, however, and thus little or nothing was done to educate either the Indian or the Negro in the English colonies until the year 1701, when a society was organised in England to carry the gospel and its teachings to the Indians and Negroes in America. In June, 1702, Reverend Samuel Thomas, the first missionary of this society, in reporting upon his work in South Carolina, said that he "had taken much pains, also, in instructing the Negroes, and learned twenty of them to read."

In 1704, Elias Neau, a French Protestant, established a catechising school for the Indian and Negro slaves in New York. His work continued successfully until 1712, when a conspiracy of the Negro slaves was discovered in New York, which was said to have had its origin in Mr. Neau's school. Upon the trial, however, it appeared that the guilty Negroes were "such as never came to Mr. Neau's school. And what is very observable," the chronicle adds, "the persons whose Negroes were found most guilty were such as were declared opposers to making them Christians." In 1738, the Moravian or United Brethren first attempted to establish missions exclusively for Negroes. In the Moravian settlement at Bethlehem, Pennsylvania, a painting is preserved of eighteen of the first converts made by these missionaries in America prior to 1747. Among the number are Johannes, a Negro of South Carolina, and Jupiter, a Negro from New York.

The religious instruction of Negroes was begun by the Presbyterians in Virginia in 1747. In a letter written in that year, Reverend Samuel Davis refers to "the poor, neglected Negroes who are so far from having money to purchase books that they themselves are the property of others." A little further on in this same letter, speaking of the eagerness of the Negro slave to hear the gospel and to learn to read, he says:

There are multitudes of them in different places who are willing and eagerly desirous to be instructed and to embrace every opportunity of acquainting themselves with the doctrines of the gospel; and though they have generally very little help to learn to read, yet to my agreeable surprise many of them, by dint of application in their leisure hours, have made such progress that they can intelligently read a plain author, and especially their Bibles, and pity it is that any of them should be without them.*

Two years earlier than the date of this letter, in 1745, the Society for Propagating the Gospel in Foreign Parts established a school in Charleston, South Carolina. It had at one time as many as sixty scholars and sent out annually about twenty Negroes, "well instructed in the English language and the Christian faith." This school was established in St. Philip's Church and some of its scholars were living as late as 1822, when the Denmark Vesey Conspiracy resulted in the closing of the schools for free Negroes as well as for slaves.

It seems probable that prior to the Revolution some attempt was made to teach the Negroes, wherever they were brought into touch with the Church. In this way, the Negro Sunday-schools

---

* "The Gospel Among the Slaves," W. P. Harrison, p. 51.

gave the Negroes the first opportunity for education and his first school book was the Bible. In 1747, when slavery was introduced into the colony of Georgia, respresentatives from twenty-three districts met in Savannah and drew up resolutions in regard to the conduct of masters toward their slaves. Among other things they declared in substance "that the owners of slaves should educate the the young and use every possible means of making religious impressions upon the minds of the aged."

In 1750, the Reverend Thomas Bacon, who was himself a slave-holder, established in Talbot County, Maryland, a mission for the poor white and Negro children. The majority of the colonied children who attended this school were slaves.*

In the Methodist Conference of 1790 the question was raised: "What can be done in order to instruct poor children, white and black, to read?" to which the following reply was made:

Let us labour as the heart and soul of one man to establish Sunday-schools in or near the place of worship. Let persons be appointed by the bishops, elders, deacons, or preachers to teach gratis all that will attend and have a capacity to learn, from six in the morning till ten, and from two in the afternoon till six, where it does not interfere with public worship. The Council shall compile a proper school book to teach them learning and piety.

The opposition to the teaching of the slaves seems to have begun in South Carolina. In 1740 that

* "A Pioneer in Negro Education," Bernard C. Steiner, in the *Independent*, August 24, 1899.

state passed a law imposing a fine of one hundred pounds upon any one who should teach any "slave or slaves in writing in any manner whatsoever." In 1770 Georgia passed a similar law punishing with a fine of twenty pounds any person teaching a slave to read and write.

Immediately after the Revolution there was a feeling all over the United States that slavery was soon to pass away. About 1792, however, a Yankee schoolmaster, Eli Whitney, invented the cotton-gin. This invention suddenly made Negro slave labour valuable, particularly in the new states of the Southwest. From this time on, the feeling that slave labour was necessary to the economic life of the Southern states grew to a conviction that slavery was to be a permanent institution in the Southern states.

The change in public opinion is reflected in the laws. In 1819, Virginia passed an act prohibiting all meetings of slaves, free persons, and mulattoes, in the night, or any school or schools for teaching them reading and writing in either day or night. Ten years later, Georgia passed a law forbidding any person of colour from receiving instruction from any source. In 1830, Louisiana forbade free Negroes entering the state and passed a law against the printing and distribution of seditious matter among people of colour and against their being taught. A year later Mississippi passed a law against any coloured person, free or slave, from preaching the gospel. The next year Alabama passed a law against teaching any free person of colour or slave and, in 1835, North Carolina abolished the schools for free persons of colour, which up to that time had been taught for the most part by white teachers. The law passed in North Carolina at this time provided that no descendants of Negro parents, to the fourth generation, should enjoy the benefit of the public school system. Similar laws were passed in Mississippi and Missouri.

In spite of this fact Negroes continued, in one way or another, to keep alive the little tradition of learning they had already possessed. In New Orleans, and in Charleston, South Carolina, there were clandestine schools in which the children of free Negroes had an opportunity to get some sort of an education. In New Orleans it had long been the custom for planters, who had children by slave mothers, to send them abroad to France or to some of the Northern states for their education. One of the most interesting, as well as one of the most pathetic, chapters in American history is that which has to do with this class of white men who felt in honour bound to support, educate and protect their illegitimate offspring. To do this meant in many cases ostracism, loss of property, and reputation.

In 1833, the city of Mobile was authorised by

an act of legislation to grant licence to suitable persons to give instruction to the children of the Creole Negroes in that city. This act applied only to the county of Baldwin and to the city of Mobile. The basis for it was the treaty between France and the United States by which all the rights and privileges of citizens were guaranteed to them. It should be remembered, also, that schools for free coloured people were never abolished in Maryland, Kentucky, Tennessee, Florida and Texas.

The census of 1860 shows that there were 1,355 free coloured children attending school in Maryland. The schools were such as the coloured people could support, from the African Institute on Saratoga Street, Baltimore, with its hundred or more scholars, "to the half-dozen urchins learning their words under the counter of a little tobacco shop in Annapolis." One of these, known as the Wells school, was established in 1835 by Nelson Wells, a coloured man, who applied the income of $7,000 to its support.

The coloured people who got sufficient education during the days of slavery to read their Bible may be divided into four classes: those who were taught by their owners in spite of law; those who had white fathers; those who, in some way or other, obtained their freedom; those who literally stole their education. There were always a few cases in all the states where the master or mistress, or some other member of the family, took sufficient interest in some individual slave to teach him to read. Sometimes this was done out of mere curiosity, just to see if the Negro could learn. I have met dozens of former slaves who told me their owners taught them to read, and described the great precautions sometimes taken to keep the fact that such teaching was going on from other members of the same family and from the neighbours.

The desire to read the Bible was a plea that usually touched the heart of the more kindly disposed master. To this day there is an intense longing among a number of the older people to learn to read the Bible before they die. No matter how the slaves obtained their knowledge of reading and writing, in every case it was like bringing the germs of an infectious disease into the household; it spread. Among the free Negroes of Charleston, the learning that the older people had obtained previous to 1822 was handed down from generation to generation until the War brought freedom to the slave and the free Negro alike.

During his journey through Northern Mississippi, Frederick Law Olmsted one day stopped to talk with a small planter who seemed to have an exceptionally good class of slaves. Mr. Olmsted referred to the fine appearance of his Negro labourers, whereupon the following conversation as reported by Mr. Olmsted ensued:

"Well, I reckon it's my way o' treatin' 'em, much as anything. I never hev no difficulty with 'em. Hen't licked a nigger in five year, 'cept maybe sprouting some of the young ones sometimes. Fact, my niggers never want no lookin' arter; they just tek ker o' themselves. Fact, they do tek a greater interest in the crops than I do myself. There's another thing — I 'spose 'twill surprise you — there ent one of my niggers but what can read; read good, too — better'n I can, at any rate."

"How did they learn?"

"Taught themselves. I b'lieve there was one on 'em that I bought, that could read, and he taught all the rest. But niggers is mighty apt at larnin', a heap more'n white folks is."

I said that this was contrary to the generally received opinion.

"Well, now, let me tell you," he continued; "I had a boy to work, when I was buildin', and my boys jus' teachin' him night times and such, he warn't here more'n three months, and he larned to read as well as any man I ever heerd, and I know he didn't know his letters when he come here. It didn't seem to me any white man could have done that; does it to you, now?"

"How old was he?"

"Warn't more'n seventeen, I reckon."

"How do they get books — do you get them for them?"

"Oh, no; get 'em for themselves."

"How?"

"Buy 'em."

"How do they get the money?"

"Earn it."

"How?"

"By their own work. I tell you my niggers have got more money 'n I hev."

"What kind of books do they get?"

"Religious kind of books ginerally — these stories; and some of them will buy novels, I believe. They won't let on to that, but I expect they do it." *

When slaves living on the distant plantations in the back country of Mississippi succeeded in learning to read it is not difficult to understand that in the cities, where exceptional opportunities were given to the slaves employed in the household services of their masters, a considerable number should in one way or another learn to read and write. Frederick Douglass, in the story of his life, has given a description of the manner in which he learned to read, which is probably typical of other slaves in the same class as himself. He says:

The frequent hearing of my mistress reading the Bible aloud, for she often read aloud when her husband was absent, awakened my curiosity in respect to this mystery of reading, and roused in me the desire to learn. Up to this time I had known nothing whatever of this wonderful art, and my ignorance and inexperience of what it could do for me, as well as my confidence in my mistress, emboldened me to ask her to teach me to read. With an unconsciousness and inexperience equal to my own, she readily consented, and in an incredibly short time, by her kind assistance, I had mastered the alphabet and could spell words of three or four letters. My mistress seemed almost as proud of my progress as if I had been her own child, and supposing that her husband would be as well pleased, she made no secret of what she was doing for me. Indeed, she exultingly told him of the alphabet of her pupil, and of her intention to persevere in teaching me, as she felt her duty to do, at least to read the Bible. Master Hugh was astounded beyond measure, and probably for the first time proceeded to unfold to his wife the true philosophy of the slave system, and the peculiar

---

* Olmsted, "The Cotton Kingdom," vol. ii, pp. 70, 71.

rules necessary in the nature of the case to be observed in the management of human chattels. Of course he forbade her to give me any further instruction.

In learning to read, therefore, I am not sure that I do not owe quite as much to the opposition of my master as to the kindly assistance of my amiable mistress. I acknowledge the benefit rendered me by the one, and by the other, believing that but for my mistress I might have grown up in ignorance.

Filled with the determination to learn to read at any cost, I hit upon many expedients to accomplish that much-desired end. The plan which I mainly adopted, and the one which was the most successful, was that of using my young white playmates, with whom I met on the streets, as teachers. I used to carry almost constantly a copy of Webster's spelling-book in my pocket, and when sent on errands, or when playtime was allowed me, I would step aside with my young friends and take a lesson in spelling.

Fortunately, or unfortunately, I had earned a little money in blacking boots for some gentlemen, with which I purchased of Mr. Knight, on Thames Street, what was then a very popular school book, namely, "The Columbian Orator," for which I paid fifty cents. I was led to buy this book by hearing some little boys say they were going to learn some pieces out of it for the exhibition. This volume was indeed a rich treasure, and every opportunity afforded me, for a time, was spent in diligently perusing it.*

In another portion of his narrative, Mr. Douglass describes how he used to pick pieces of waste paper from the gutters of Baltimore, and try to read them. Sometimes he made use of other devices for getting the knowledge he wanted. For example, he would bet the white boys, with whom he frequently played, a marble or a piece of candy that they could not read an advertisement he found

* " Life and Times of Frederick Douglass," written by himself, pp. 69-75.

on the fences or on the side of a house. This wager would tempt the white boys, of course, to spell out and read these advertisements, and as they did this young Douglass was able to learn from them what the words of the advertisement meant. This same method of learning to read was adopted by more than one ambitious slave boy.

It sounds strange to-day, but it was nevertheless true that up to a few years before the Civil War there was almost as much opposition to Negro education in the North as there was in the South. In 1882, John F. Slater, of Norwich, Connecticut, gave a million dollars to be used in the education of the Negro race. Up to that time this was the largest sum that had ever been given at one time for a like purpose. Yet, fifty years before, in the neighbouring town of Canterbury, Prudence Crandall, a young Quaker schoolmistress, who ventured to open a school for coloured children, was mobbed by some of the inhabitants of that town, and so great was the opposition to the school that a special law was passed, making it a crime to open a school for Negroes in that state.

In 1831, when the first national coloured convention assembled at Philadelphia, it was determined to establish a college for coloured people, and the Reverend Samuel E. Cornish, a coloured Presbyterian clergyman, was appointed agent to secure funds. In the course of the next year, he succeeded in raising $3,000 for establishing "a school on the manual labour plan." Arthur Tappan, the philanthropist, succeeded in buying several acres of land in the southern part of New Haven, Connecticut, and had completed arrangements for erecting a building. As soon as it was discovered, however, that it was proposed to erect a Negro school in New Haven, there was a great outcry and protest from the citizens. At a public meeting, at which the mayor presided, it was resolved by a vote of seven hundred to four, that "the founding of colleges for educating coloured people is an unwarrantable and dangerous undertaking to the internal concerns of other states and ought to be discouraged," and that "the mayor, aldermen, common-council, and freemen will resist the establishment of the proposed college in this state by every lawful means."

About this time, the Noyes Academy, of Canaan, New Hampshire, opened its doors to coloured students. Several young men entered the academy, and for a time the coloured people believed that they had found a school where they might obtain advanced education in the United States. On the 3rd of July, 1835, however, a town meeting was called and a committee was chosen to "remove the academy." A little more than a month later, this committee, aided by some three hundred persons and a hundred yoke of oxen, proceeded to literally carry out the instruction of the town meeting. In

many other of the Northern states, particularly
in Ohio, Indiana and Illinois, even where there
was no law prohibiting the education of Negroes,
no provision was made for educating them in the
public schools.

In spite of the opposition which manifested
itself from time to time against Negro education,
there was a steady increase in the number of
Negro schools in most of the large Northern cities.
I have already referred to the school established by
Anthony Benezet, in 1750.   This first noted teacher
of Negroes, who died May 3, 1784, left in his will
property to put this school on a permanent foundation.   The school was continued in the charge
of a committee of Friends, and received donations
from time to time, one donation of three hundred
pounds coming from a coloured man by the name
of Thomas Shirley.   In 1849, it appeared from a
statistical study of the condition of coloured people
at Philadelphia, made at that time, that there were
among others the following schools for coloured persons: A grammar school with 463 pupils; five other
schools with 911; an infant school in charge of the
abolition society with 70 pupils; a "moral reform"
school with 81 pupils.   In addition to the public
schools there were also about 20 private schools
with 296 pupils, making an aggregate of more than
1,800 pupils receiving an education of one kind or
another.

In 1832, ten thousand dollars was left by the will of Richard Humphreys, an ex-slave-holder, to establish "An Institute for Coloured Youth." The school was accordingly started in 1837. A farm was purchased in Bristol Township, Philadelphia County, in 1839, but later sold, and a school building erected on Lombard Street, Philadelphia. In 1852, the school was opened and conducted for a time by Charles L. Reason, of New York. Ebenezer D. Bassett, afterward for nearly eight years Minister and United States Consul-general at Porte au Prince, Haiti, was for many years the principal of this school. A few years ago, sufficient funds were raised to enable the school to carry out the original purpose of its founder and it was removed to Cheyney, Pennsylvania, and transformed into an industrial school for the special purpose of training teachers.

The circumstance that a number of free persons of colour were frequently kidnapped in New York City resulted in the formation in an early day of "The New York Society for Promoting the Manumission of Slaves and for Protecting Such of Them as Have Been or May Be Liberated." The same gentlemen who organised this society became the Board of Trustees of what was known as the New York African Free School, which was, or afterward became, the first public school in New York City. This school was located on Cliff Street, between

Beekman and Ferry streets, and was opened in 1786 with forty pupils. In 1824, when General Lafayette was in this country, he visited this school, and a little coloured boy, who afterward became Dr. James McCune Smith, was delegated to make an address to him in behalf of the students.

This school and others established by the society continued to flourish until 1832, when they, with their 1,400 students, were formally turned over to the public school society and became part of the public school system of the city. The first normal school for coloured teachers was established in 1853, with John Peterson, a coloured man who had long been a teacher in the coloured schools of New York, principal.

The first coloured school for Negro children in Ohio was established in 1820. Owen T. B. Nickens, a public-spirited and intelligent Negro, was largely responsible for bringing these schools into existence. In 1844, the Reverend Hiram S. Gilmore founded the "Cincinnati High School" for coloured youth, and in 1849, the Legislature passed an act establishing public schools for coloured children. The law provided that the school funds should be divided among the white and coloured children, but for a long time this law was not enforced, until, under the leadership of John I. Gaines, the coloured people took the matter to the court. In 1856, a law was passed giving the coloured people the right by ballot to elect their own trustees, and in 1858, Nicholas Longworth built the first school house for coloured people, giving them a lease for fourteen years, during which time they were to pay the $14,000, which the building cost.

The first separate school for coloured children in Massachusetts was established at the home of Primus Hall, in Boston, in 1798. This school continued to be held in the house of Primus Hall until 1806, when the coloured Baptists erected a church on Belknap Street, and fitted up the lower rooms as a school for coloured children. This school continued until 1835, when a coloured schoolhouse was erected from a fund left for that purpose by Abiel Smith. This became the famous "Smith schoolhouse." This Smith schoolhouse continued in existence until 1855, when a law was passed abolishing separate schools for coloured children.

Although slavery was not abolished in the District of Columbia until April 16, 1862, the free coloured people, who were very numerous in the District, early succeeded in establishing and maintaining schools for their children. The first schoolhouse built for coloured pupils was erected by three coloured men named George Bell, Nicholas Franklin and Moses Liverpool. All these men had been slaves in Virginia, and not one of them knew a single letter of the alphabet. From this time on, the number of schools increased rapidly with the

increase of the free coloured population. One
of the most noted of the early coloured teachers
was John F. Cook. He had been born a slave,
but had been purchased by his aunt, Alethia Tanner,
who at the same time purchased his mother, Laurena
Cook, and four other children. John F. Cook
learned the shoemaker's trade in his boyhood and
worked very hard after the purchase of his freedom
to make some return to his aunt for the money she
had spent in setting him free. He picked up the
rudiments of an education in the Treasury Department, and thereupon began teaching school. During
the Snow Riot of September, 1835, his schoolhouse
was destroyed, and, to escape the mob, he fled to
Pennsylvania. In the next year he returned,
re-opened his school on a more generous plan than
before, and kept it up until his death, March 21,
1855, when the work was taken up by his sons,
John F. and George F. T. Cook.

Among the other noted teachers in Washington
before the War were Louisa Park Costin, the daughter
of William Costin, who was for twenty-four years
the messenger for the bank of Washington, and
who was well known and respected by all the old
residents of Washington, District of Columbia.
Another was Maria Becraft, who was the head of
the first seminary for coloured girls in the District
of Columbia. This seminary was established, in
1827, in Georgetown, under the auspices of Father

Vanlomen, who was the pastor of the Holy Trinity
Catholic Church.   In 1831, Maria Becraft gave
up her school to the care of one of the girls she had
trained.   In October of that year she joined the
convent of the coloured Catholic Sisters at Baltimore, where she was known as Sister Aloyons.

Little struggling schools, that sprang up here
and there in the cities North and South before the
Civil War, served to give the rudiments of an
education to a few coloured people, but it was not
until after 1865, when four millions of Negro slaves
were made free, that the education of the race
really began.   I shall never forget the strange,
pathetic scenes and incidents of that time.   Nothing
like it, I dare say, had ever before been seen.   It
seemed that all at once, as soon as they realised
that they were free, the whole race started to go to
school, but not in the usual orderly fashion.   It
was as if four million people had been shut up
where they could not get food until they had reached
the starving point, and then were suddenly released
to find food for themselves.

The primer, the first reader, and most frequently
of all, the Webster's blue-back speller, suddenly,
as if by a miracle, made their appearance everywhere.   Even before the thousands of Negro
soldiers had been disbanded, they inveigled their
officers into becoming their schoolmasters, and
scores of Negro soldiers in every regiment were

learning to read and to write and to cipher. On every plantation, and in nearly every home, whether in the town or city, the hidden book that had been tucked away under the floor or in an old trunk or had been concealed in a stump, or between mattresses, suddenly came out of its hiding-place and was put into use.

I can recall vividly the picture not only of children, but of men and women, some of whom had reached the age of sixty or seventy, tramping along the country roads with a spelling-book or a Bible in their hands. It did not seem to occur to any one that age was any obstacle to learning in books. With weak and unaccustomed eyes, old men and old women would struggle along month after month in their effort to master the primer in order to get, if possible, a little knowledge of the Bible. Some of them succeeded; many of them failed. To these latter the thought of passing from earth without being able to read the Bible was a source of deep sorrow.

The places for holding school were anywhere and everywhere; the Freedmen could not wait for schoolhouses to be built or for teachers to be provided. They got up before day and studied in their cabins by the light of pine knots. They sat up until late at night, drooping over their books, trying to master the secrets they contained. More than once, I have seen a fire in the woods at night with a dozen or more people of both sexes and of all ages sitting about with book in hands studying their lessons. Sometimes they would fasten their primers between the ploughshares, so that they could read as they ploughed. I have seen Negro coal miners trying to spell out the words of a little reading-book by the dim light of a miner's lamp, hundreds of feet below the earth. In the early days of freedom, public schools were not infrequently organised and taught under a large tree. Some of the early schoolhouses consisted of four pieces of timber driven into the ground and brush spread overhead as a covering to keep out the sun and rain. It was a simple and inexpensive schoolhouse, but I am sure that the students were more earnest than many who have since had much greater advantages.

The night school became popular immediately after freedom. After a hard day's work in the field, in the shop, or in the kitchen, men and women would spend two or three hours at night in school. A great many of the Freedmen got their first lessons in reading and writing in the Sunday-school. In fact, there were frequently more spelling-books in the Sunday-school than Bibles. I, myself, got my first knowledge of the alphabet by perusing a spelling-book in the Sunday-school.

A teacher in the first few years of freedom was likely to be any one who knew something some one else did not know. Sometimes it happened that some would be able to read better than they could write; others would be able to write better than they could read. In that case the former became teachers of reading and the latter became teachers of writing. As may well be understood, there was very little organisation in these first schools; they were just groups of people moved by a common impulse in coming together for study. But almost before the proclamation of freedom had been issued, white teachers of all classes and both sexes began to pour into the South from the Northern states. Along with them came numbers of Negro men and women who had escaped from slavery and, having gained some education in the North, now returned to the South to become the teachers of their race. It should be added, also, that many of these teachers were Southern white people, who, when they found no other occupation directly after the war, were glad to turn to teaching the Freedmen in order to eke out a livelihood.

It was during this same period that the people of the Northern states, through their religious and missionary organisations, began sending not merely teachers, but money, books, and clothing to provide for the schools and for the pupils in the Negro schools that were springing up everywhere. It was during this period that many of the most noted schools in the Southern states were founded. Berea

College had been established since 1856, by the Reverend John G. Fee, a Kentucky minister who had been converted to anti-slavery views by taking a course at Lane Seminary, Cincinnati, Ohio. In 1865, Lincoln Institute, at Jefferson City, Missouri, was founded with the assistance of contributions of the Sixty-second and Sixty-fifth United States coloured regiments, who generously contributed something over $6,000 of the wages they received from the Government to help establish the school. The same year Shaw University was started at Raleigh, North Carolina. In 1866, Hampton Institute was founded by General S. C. Armstrong, and in the same year Fisk University was established at Nashville, Tennessee. The next year Atlanta University was established at Atlanta, Georgia; Biddle University, at Charlotte, North Carolina; and Howard University, named after General O. O. Howard, at Washington, District of Columbia; two years later, in 1869, Straight University, at New Orleans, Louisiana; Tougaloo University, at Tougaloo, Mississippi; Talladega College, at Talladega, Alabama; and Clafin University, at Orangeburg, South Carolina.

In speaking of the contribution which the people of the United States made at this time to the education of the Negro in America, it should not be forgotten that Negro education has contributed something in return to the people of the United States. It was through the Negro that industrial education in this country had its start. Neither in the North nor in the South, before the starting of Hampton Institute in Virginia, was any systematic instruction in the industries given in any kind of educational institution. The success of the Hampton and Tuskegee institutes in giving industrial education to the Negroes led the way to the introduction of industrial education into the Northern schools and white schools in the South, as well as in many other parts of the world.

The desire for education among the Freedmen was a veritable fever for the first ten or twelve years after emancipation. Since that time I do not think the desire for education has diminished among the coloured people, but the methods for obtaining it have become more profitable and less picturesque. This is shown particularly in the effort which the coloured people are making everywhere to add to the meagre funds which are given them by the states in order to prolong their school terms, to secure better teachers, and build comfortable schoolhouses. Negro parents will still make all kinds of sacrifices, frequently depriving themsevles not merely of the comforts, but many times of the necessities of life, in order that they may have the satisfaction of seeing their children able to read and write.

All sorts of devices are now employed in the

coloured communities to eke out the salary of the coloured school-teacher. In some communities teachers will impose an extra tax of ten cents per month for every student who comes to school. In other cases each family will take turns in boarding the teacher for a day or for a week. Sometimes they will donate a pig, a chicken, a dozen eggs, a fish, or a rabbit to help the school-teacher out. A method that is now growing in popularity, for the purpose of meeting the expenses of a first-class school, is what is known as the "school farm." This means that three or four acres of land will be secured near the schoolhouse and on a given day, usually Saturday, parents and children come together to plant, plough, or harvest the cotton which is to be sold to increase the length of the school term.

Some idea of the difficulty under which the coloured schools labour in the South may be gathered from the fact that, while in the Northern and Western states something like five dollars per pupil is spent every year for the education of the children of school age, in several of the Southern states only fifty cents per pupil is expended for coloured children. While a number of office-seekers in the South, complaining about the burden of education under which the South laboured, have been advocating that no money be spent for the education of the Negro, and that everything possible be done to check his advancement in this direction, a few courageous State Superintendents of Public Instruction in the South have begun to point out that, not only is the Negro not a burden upon the South so far as his education is concerned, but in some instances Negro taxpayers are supporting white schools. In a careful study made of the statistics of education some years ago in Florida, the superintendent in that state came to the conclusion that "the schools for Negroes not only were not a burden upon the white people, but four thousand five hundred and twenty-seven dollars contributed for Negro schools from other sources was in some way diverted into the white schools." Speaking of the conditions in middle Florida, where the Negro population is most dense and the educational conditions are at their worst, he said:

The usual plea is that this is due to the intolerable burden of Negro education, and a general discouragement and inactivity were ascribed to this cause. The figures show that the education of the Negro in the middle of Florida does not cost white people of that section one cent. . . . It is the purpose of this paragraph to show that the backwardness of the education of the white people is in no degree due to the presence of the Negro, but that the presence of the Negroes has actually been contributing to the sustenance of white schools.

At a meeting of the Conference for Southern Education, in Atlanta, Georgia, in the spring of 1909, Charles L. Coon, Superintendent of Schools at Wilson, North Carolina, read a paper on " Public

Taxation and Negro Schools," in which he attempted to show, for the whole South, what he had previously shown for North Carolina, that the Negroes were not only not getting their share of the public education fund, which they were entitled to under the law, but their education was not, as has so often been asserted, a piece of philanthropy on the part of whites to the coloured race. He found, by the study of actual statistics, that while Negroes represented 40.1 per cent. of the total population of the eleven Southern states they received only 14.8 per cent. of the money spent for education. In Mississippi, where Negroes represent 58.7 per cent. of the population they received 21.9 per cent. of the school funds. In Louisiana, where they represent 47.2 per cent. of the population, they received 8.6 per cent. of the school funds.

After a careful study of all the available statistics, Mr. Coon reaches the conclusion, to put it in his own words, "that the Negro school of the South is not a serious burden on the white taxpayer. On the contrary, if all the Negro children of the Southern states were white, it would cost to educate them just about five times as much as it does now to give the same number of Negroes such education as they are getting."

Mr. Coon points out, and quotes articles from several Southern papers to support him, that the Negro is not only almost the only dependable

labourer in the Southern states, but even those
people who are most ready to abuse him "as a
burden and a curse" are loud in their complaint
"whenever any one attempts to lure him away."

In 1891, the Negroes of North Carolina listed
$8,018,446 worth of property. In 1898, they listed
$21,716,922, an increase of 171 per cent. in seventeen
years. The property listed by the whites during
that time increased only 89 per cent. In other
words, the taxable value of property of Negroes
increased in seventeen years nearly twice in proportion to that of the white people. In Georgia,
in 1891, Negroes listed $14,196,735 worth of prop-
erty. In 1907, they listed property to the value
of $25,904,822, an increase of 82 per cent.
The taxable property of white people increased
during this same period only 39 per cent. This
again indicates that the ratio of increase of
Negro property in Georgia during the last sixteen
years has been twice that of the property of the
white people.

"Such facts as these," says Mr. Coon, in concluding his report, "give us glimpses of the economic
importance of Negroes, and abundantly justify
us in hoping that the senseless race prejudice which
has for its object the intellectual enslavement of
Negro children will soon pass away. I do not
believe that any superior race can hope for the
blessings of heaven upon its own children while

it begrudges more light and efficiency for those of an inferior race."

In all that has been said, bearing upon what the Negro has done to help himself in education through the public schools in the South, the fact should not be overlooked that he owes much to the Southern white people. Especially is this true in the large cities and towns of the South, where generous provision has been made for the education of the Negro child in the public schools. While in the country districts, as a rule, the schools are poor, almost beyond description, still in not a few country districts broad-minded and courageous Southern white men have seen to it, and are seeing to it, that the Negro gets a reasonable chance for education in the public schools. It should also be stated that while the Negro at present is paying in a large part for his own education in the public schools, in the years immediately following emancipation he paid very little and during this time the burden of his education fell heavily upon the Southern white people.

It should be remembered also that it is only within the past fifty or sixty years that many of the Northern states have begun to have a system of education which sought to educate all the people irrespective of race or colour. The world is slow to learn that when we attempt to stop the growth of our fellow-man, we are doing the thing that will most surely stop our own growth. How much faster the world would go forward if every one should learn, once for all, that nothing is ever permanently gained by any attempt to retard or stop the progress of any human being!

CHAPTER VI

THE NEGRO SECRET SOCIETIES

THERE are about twenty national Negro secret societies in America. The older and better known of these are the Masons, the Odd Fellows, Knights of Pythias, United Brothers of Friendship, Improved Benevolent and Protective Order of Elks, Knights of Tabor, Benevolent Order of Buffaloes, Ancient Order of Foresters, The Grand United Order of Galilean Fishermen, Good Samaritans, Nazarites, Sons and Daughters of Jacob, The Seven Wise Men, Knights of Honour, Mosaic Templars of America, and the True Reformers.

In addition to these there are a number of smaller organisations, most of them local in character, but quite as interesting in their workings and history as the larger organisations.

The Masonic order, which is the oldest, and so far as its history is concerned, the most interesting of these orders, had its origin in the following manner: During Revolutionary days there lived in Boston a Negro of exceptional ability, named Prince Hall. On March 6, 1775, he and fourteen other Negroes

were initiated into the secrets of Free Masonry by
an army lodge attached to one of the regiments of
British soldiers stationed there.   According to a cus-
tom of the day, these fifteen coloured men were
authorised to assemble as a lodge, to walk on St.
John's Day, and to bury their dead with due form.
They, however, could do no "work" and make no
Masons until they were warranted.

On March 2, 1784, the members of this lodge
applied to the Grand Lodge of England for a warrant.   It was issued to them on September 29, 1784,
as "African Lodge, No. 459," with Prince Hall as
master, but because of various delays it was not
received until April 29, 1787.   The lodge was
formally organised May 6, 1787.

The original warrant establishing Masonry among
the Negroes in America is, considering the time and
the circumstances under which it was issued, a
document of such historical interest that I venture
to reproduce it here in full.   The text is as follows:

To all and every our right worshipful and loving Brethren, we,
Thomas Howard, Earl of Effingham, Lord Howard, etc., etc.,
acting Grand Master under the authority of His Royal Highness,
Henry Frederick, Duke of Cumberland, etc., etc., Grand Master
of the Most Ancient and Honourable Society of Free and Accepted
Masons, send greeting:

Know Ye, that we, at the humble petition of our right trusty and
well-beloved Brethren, Prince Hall, Boston Smith, Thomas Sanderson and several other Brethren residing at Boston, New England,
in North America, do hereby constitute the said Brethren into a
regular Lodge of Free and Accepted Masons under the title or

denomination of the African Lodge, to be opened in Boston aforesaid, and do further, at their said petition, hereby appoint the said Prince Hall to be Master, Boston Smith, Senior Warden, and Thomas Sanderson, Junior Warden, for the opening of the said Lodge and for such further time only as shall be thought proper by the brethren thereof, it being our will that this appointment of the above officers shall in no wise affect any future election of officers of the Lodge, but that such election shall be regulated agreeable to such by-laws of said Lodge as shall be consistent with the general laws of the society, contained in the Book of Constitutions; and we hereby will and require you, the said Prince Hall, to take especial care that all and every one of the said Brethren are, or have been, regularly made Masons, and that they do observe, perform and keep all the rules and orders contained in the Book of Constitutions; and further, that you do, from time to time, cause to be entered in a book kept for the purpose, an account of your proceedings in the Lodge, together with all such rules, orders and regulations as shall be made for the good government of the same; that in no wise you omit once in every year to send us, or our successors, Grand Master, or to Roland Holt, Esq., our Deuputy Grand Master, for the time being, an account in writing of your said proceedings, and copies of all such rules, orders and regulations as shall be made as aforesaid, together with a list of the members of the Lodge, and such a sum of money as may suit the circumstances of the Lodge and reasonably be expected towards the Grand Charity. Moreover, we will require you, the said Prince Hall, as soon as conveniently may be, to send an account in writing of what may be done by virtue of these presents.

Given at London, under our hand and seal of Masonry, this 29th day of September, A. L. 5784, A. D. 1784.

By the Grand Master's Command,

R. HOLT, D. G. M.

Witness: WM. WHITE, G. S.

By the terms of this decree Prince Hall became the first Grand Master of the first Grand Lodge of Negro Masons in the United States, and in 1797 issued a licence to thirteen men of colour who had been made Masons in England and Ireland to assemble and work as a lodge in Philadelphia. At Providence, Rhode Island, under Hall's authority, a lodge was organised for Negro Masons who resided in that vicinity. In 1808, these three lodges joined and formed the African Grand Lodge of Boston, which was afterward called the Prince Hall Lodge of Massachusetts.

The second coloured Grand Lodge was called the "First Independent African Grand Lodge of North America, in and for the commonwealth of Pennsylvania." Some time after this, the Hiram Grand Lodge of Pennsylvania was organised, and in 1847, these three Grand Lodges united in forming a National Grand Lodge. From this time this order has grown steadily among the Negroes of the United States until, in 1904, there were 1,960 Masonic lodges with 45,835 members.

It is an interesting fact in the history of these lodges that Negro Masons formed a part of the funeral procession of the first President of the United States, George Washington.

The Negro Masons, like other secret orders formed in the United States before the Civil War, encountered all the difficulties under which free Negroes laboured at that time. It is said, however, that they often received indirect recognition by white Masons. For example, the first Kentucky lodge of coloured Masons, known as Mount Moriah, No. 1, was organised by residents of Louisville in 1850. It was organised under the jurisdiction of Ohio, and for three years, on account of the "black laws," which forbade the assembling of free people of colour, met in New Albany, Indiana. After that time the lodge removed to Louisville. Shortly after, the rooms of the order were forcibly entered by the police and twenty-one of the members were arrested. On arriving at the prison, however, the jailors, it is said, refused to receive them. The judge of the court, who was consulted, ordered them discharged upon their personal recognisance to appear for trial the next morning. The next morning when they appeared in a body for trial, they found the entrance to the courthouse guarded by police, by whom they were denied admission. They were told to quietly go their way, say nothing, and they would not again be disturbed. The explanation given by the coloured Masons to this extraordinary proceeding is that the jailors and the judge were Master Masons.

The next secret order to be formed in the United States was the Odd Fellows. In 1842, certain members of the Philomathean Institute of New York and of the Library Company and Debating Society of Philadelphia, applied for admission to the International Order of Odd Fellows, but were refused on the ground of their colour. Peter Ogden, however, who had joined the Odd Fellows in England, secured from the English order a charter for the first American Negro lodge of Odd Fellows, which was called the Philomathean, No. 646, of New York. This lodge was organised March 1, 1843. The Negro Odd Fellows in America are still under the jurisdiction of England and regularly represented in the general meetings of the order. In 1904, there were 4,643 lodges in the United States, with 285,931 members.

Two other national secret organisations were organised in the United States before the War. One of these was the Galilean Fishermen. Another was the Nazarites. The United Brothers of Friendship was organised at Louisville, Kentucky, August 1, 1861. It was first a benevolent organisation and later became a secret order. The Knights of Pythias of the World was first organised in Washington, District of Columbia, February 19, 1864.

No other city in the South has been the birth-place of so large a number of coloured secret and beneficial orders as Baltimore, Maryland. There are societies still existing in Maryland that date back as far as 1820. They were formed in order that the members might help one another in sickness, and provide for a decent burial through a system of small but regular payments. Twenty-five of these societies were formed before the war. From 1865 to 1870, seventeen more were added to this number, and since 1870 it is said that at least twenty more have been added to these.

In 1884 a meeting was held of many persons connected with these societies in order to arouse a more general interest in their work. At this meeting forty of these societies claimed an aggregate membership of 2,100. It was stated at this time that nearly fourteen hundred members had been buried by these orders, and more than $45,000 paid out for funeral expenses. Something like $125,000 had been paid as sick dues, and thirty of the societies paid $27,000 to widows. Among the other items of expense were $10,700 for house rent and $11,300 paid for incidental expenses. There had been paid back to members of the societies, from unexpended balances, $40,000, and there remained in the banks and in the hands of the treasurers, $22,800. Five of these societies had considerable sums invested. In one case the amount was nearly $6,000. The total amount of money handled had been nearly $200,000. One of these organisations was the Coloured Barbers' Society. It was over fifty years old, and paid eighty dollars at the death of a member. It is said that one coloured woman organised three of these local societies that at one time were very successful.

It was among these local beneficial and secret orders of Baltimore that four of the national societies had their origin. These are the Samaritans, the Nazarites, the Galilean Fishermen, and the Seven Wise Men. The order of Galilean Fishermen, composed of men and women, was started in Baltimore in 1856, but was not legally incorporated until 1869. It is said to have more than five thousand members in the State of Maryland alone.

It is said that the beneficial and local secret orders of Philadelphia date back to the eighteenth century, and that by 1838 there were as many as one hundred of these small organisations, with 7,448 members, in the city. Ten years later there were 8,000 members, belonging to 106 societies. The plan usually followed by these societies was to collect twenty-five cents per month from each of their members with the understanding that in case of sickness members should be entitled to receive aid to the amount of $1.50 to $3.00 per week. In addition to this, sums varying from ten dollars to twenty dollars were paid upon the death of any member. A good many of these organisations have since gone out of existence, but it is said that at least four thousand Negroes in Philadelphia still belong to secret orders and collect annually something like $25,000, a part of which is paid out in sick and death benefits and a part invested. The real estate and personal property of these local organisations is said to amount to no less than $125,000. One of the oldest of these organisations is known as the Sons of St. Thomas. It was founded in 1823, and was originally confined to the members of the St. Thomas Church.

In recent years there have grown up, to take the place of the older beneficial organisations, local insurance companies. One of these, known as the Crucifixion, is connected with the Church of the Crucifixion. Still another, the Avery, is connected with the Wesley A. M. E. Zion Church. Both of these have large membership, and are said to be well conducted.*

With the organisation of the national benevolent and secret orders, large sums of money have come into the hands of the officers of these societies to be held in trust for the members of the organisations. A considerable part of this sum has found permanent investment, where it frequently yields a good return. The profits of the Masons indicate that this organisation has at least one million dollars invested. Similar reports from other organisations show that the Odd Fellows have $2,500,000 worth of property, the Pythians $500,000, the Brothers of Friendship $500,000, and the True Reformers $800,000. The other secret orders own over one-half a million dollars' worth of property, so that it has been estimated that the Negro secret societies in the United States own between $5,000,000 and $6,000,000 worth of property.

The Odd Fellows have erected in the city of

---

* Du Bois, "The Philadelphia Negro," p. 221 et seq.

Philadelphia a building which is reported to have cost $100,000. The Supreme Lodge of Knights of Pythias has erected in Chicago a building costing about the same amount. The Knights of Pythias in New Orleans also have erected a seven-story business block at a cost of about $100,000.

While on a visit to Pine Bluff, Arkansas, I was very agreeably surprised to find that the finest and most expensive office building in the town had been erected by the Negro Masonic order. The building was erected for the purpose of furnishing offices for Negro business and professional men, but it was so advantageously situated and was so well adapted for business purposes that it was entirely occupied by white tenants.

It often happens in a city, where there are a number of local lodges of the same order, that they coöperate and erect a building for lodge and business purposes. Such a building is the coloured Masonic Temple at Savannah, Georgia, which was erected by the local Masonic lodges of that city. This building was erected through a building and loan association. The income derived from the renting of store and lodge rooms in the building has kept up the running expenses and paid for its erection. The principal reasons why the orders are erecting buildings are to provide themselves with permanent homes and to meet the demand of coloured business and professional men for store and office rooms.

Directly and indirectly the secret societies, in addition to providing for the families of their members after death, are doing a considerable amount of charitable work. For instance, several of the orders have erected homes and orphanages in different parts of the country. The Masons are perhaps leading in this respect at the present time. They established homes for the aged members of their order in Georgia, North Carolina, Illinois, and Tennessee. The Odd Fellows, in addition to the sum paid for sick benefits and in insurance to widows and orphans, contribute annually from ten to fifteen thousand dollars to various kinds of charities. Sometimes the surplus monies of these different organisations are invested in other ways. For instance, in 1905, the Masons of Mississippi purchased a thousand acres of land in that state. In Maryland and in the District of Columbia the same organisation has organised joint stock building associations. In Massachusetts, which is the home of Negro Masonry, a monument costing $500 has been erected to Prince Hall, the first Grand Master of the order. A few years ago, also, the Massachusetts Masons published Upton's "Negro Masonry."

Perhaps the secret order having the most romantic history is the International Order of Twelve of the Knights and Daughters of Tabor, which was founded by Reverend Moses Dickson. Mr. Dickson was born in Cincinnati, Ohio, in 1824. For a number

of years he worked upon different steamboats run-
inng up and down the Ohio and Mississippi rivers
from Cincinnati.   During this time he had an opportunity to see slavery in some of its most disagreeable
aspects, and as a consequence he early determined
to do something positive toward securing the freedom of the slaves.   In 1844, so the story goes, he
and eleven other young men met and formed an
organisation for no less a purpose than the overthrow of slavery in the United States.   After
thinking it over, however, the members decided
to take two years to study over and develope a
plan of action, and agreed to meet in St. Louis,
August 12, 1846.

During the intervening years Mr. Dickson travelled up and down the Mississippi River as far South
as New Orleans, and as far North as Iowa and Wisconsin, seeking to prepare plans for the project
he had in view.   According to agreement, the
twelve young men met and organised what was
known as the Knights of Liberty.   This organisation having been formed, the twelve members
separated with the understanding that they were
to travel through the South, organising local societies
in the different states through which they travelled.
Mr. Dickson, however, remained at the headquarters of the order at St. Louis.

It had been agreed among the twelve that they should
spend ten years, slowly and secretly making their

preparations, and extending the organisation of the society. At the end of this time, however, owing to the change in conditions in the North and the South, it was decided to change the plan of operation. From that time on the Knights of Liberty became actively connected with the Underground Railroad, and it was claimed that they assisted yearly thousands of slaves to escape. The methods by which the Knights of Liberty expected to accomplish their great object have never been definitely known, if, indeed, they were ever definitely formulated. When the Civil War broke out, Mr. Dickson enlisted. At the close of hostilities he settled again in Missouri, and took an active part in establishing the Lincoln Institute at Jefferson City. For a number of years he was trustee and vice-president of the Board of Trustees of that institution.

The emancipation of the slaves ended the work for which the Knights of Liberty had been formed, whereupon Mr. Dickson decided to establish a beneficial order in memory of the twelve orginial organisers of that society. As a result, the first Temple and Tabernacle of the Knights and Daughters of Tabor was established in 1871. The object of the society is to "encourage Christianity, education, morality, and temperance among the coloured people." The order is now reported to have something over fifty thousand members.

Immediately after the War, when the coloured

people were no longer hindered by restrictive legislation, a vast number of societies for mutual protection were organised. The most of these societies
were founded upon the plan of the earlier benevolent
and beneficial societies, with the purpose "of caring
for the sick and burying the dead." At first no
attention was paid to differences of age, and very
little to condition of health of members who were
insured in these organisations. Gradually, as the
societies gained in experience, they learned the
necessity of discriminating in these matters. Eventually there grew out of these mutual benefit organisations something corresponding to the insurance
companies conducted upon the mutual benefit plan
by white organisations. Many of the insurance
societies formed in this way had not the excuse of
ignorance for the bad manner in which they were
managed. Many of them, however, have done good
service and have grown in strength from year to
year. In 1907, no less than sixty-five of these organisations were known to exist in different parts of the
United States.

In the meantime, nearly all the secret orders have
added insurance to the other benefits they offer to
their members. No definite figures are at hand to
show the amount of business done by these different
insurance companies connected with the secret
orders. It is estimated, however, that in seven
years the Masonic Benefit Association of Alabama,

which is the title of the insurance department of the Masons in that state, is reported to have paid over $100,000 to widows and orphans of deceased members. The Texas association reports that in ten years it has paid $150,000 in death claims. The Galilean Fishermen claim to have paid $48,900 in death claims in five years. According to the statement issued by the True Reformers, that society paid $606,000 in death claims and $1,500,000 in sick benefits in twenty years. The total amount paid out since the organisation of the society in sick and death benefits amounted in 1907 to $2,856,989.25.

There has been one secret and benevolent organisation of national repute organised in Arkansas. It was known as the Mosaic Templars of America, and was organised in 1882 by C. W. Keatts and Hon. J. E. Bush. In twenty years this organisation paid $175,000 for the relief of the widows and orphans of deceased members. During this same time it paid $51,000 to its policy holders, and in 1902 reported a property valuation of $225,000. These figures give a pretty good idea of the amount of money that is collected and expended for the purposes of benevolence and insurance among the coloured people in this country.

One of the most original and interesting of the benevolent and secret orders formed in the method I have described is what is known as The Grand

United Order of True Reformers. This organisation is the more interesting because of the singular way in which it has widened and extended its activities, until, while still retaining its fraternal and benevolent features, it has become a great business organisation.

The True Reformers, like most secret and benevolent organisations among Negroes in the Southern states, was started in a very small and obscure way, and has grown, apparently, in response to needs that are peculiar to the coloured people. The order was started in 1881 by Reverend William Washington Browne. Mr. Browne was not an educated man, and he knew very little at the time he started this organisation about the ordinary methods of conducting a business of this or any other character. He was a man of great energy, however, and grew with the organisation, so that at the time of his death he had succeeded in building up one of the strongest business organisations at that time in existence among the Negro people.

This organisation is in many respects so unusual that it was made the subject of an investigation by the United States Department of Labour, from which I am able to give some details in regard to its history. I cannot here describe in detail the different departments of this organisation nor the methods by which they are conducted, but will merely indicate the different activities in which the order is engaged and suggest the necessities out of which its different departments have grown.*

In 1882 the Grand Fountain, which was the central and controlling organisation of the whole order, established a real estate department. This grew out of the need of offices and buildings in which to carry on the business of the order. The Grand Fountain had collected a considerable amount of funds and this offered an opportunity for safe investment, while at the same time it furnished the subordinate organisations with the halls in which to hold their meetings.

The next by-product of the organisation was a depository for the funds of the Grand Fountain. I shall describe in a later chapter the circumstances under which the True Reformers' bank was organised.

Next the order felt the need of a publication by which its members, who were now scattered in different parts of the country, could be kept in touch with each other and the purposes of the organisation advertised to the general public. In 1892, therefore, the publication of *The Reformer* was begun. It was described at the time "as the headlight of the organisation, an industrial, agricultural and financial paper and economic journal of the Negro race." It was first published as a bi-monthly, but after a few months of existence it became a

---

* Bulletin of the United States Department of Labour. No. 41, pp. 807-14.

weekly paper. In 1900, this paper had a circulation of over 8,000. In that year a job printing department, which added considerably to the income of the paper, was established.

The next advance of the True Reformers was along charitable lines. In 1893, the Grand Fountain, through its subordinate lodges, began to collect money for the erection of an Old Folks' Home, "for the benefit of the old people of the entire race, regardless of society or denomination." In 1897, the Grand Fountain advanced sufficient funds to purchase the Westham Farms and the site of the Westham Iron Furnace, six miles from Richmond, in Henrico County. The price paid was $14,400, and the next year, in August, 1898, an association was formed under the title of The Old Folks' Home of the Grand Fountain of the United Order of True Reformers. In the same year a part of the Westham Farm was laid out in town lots and a town was started in the neighbourhood of the Old Folks' Home. By the sale of these lots the purchase money advanced by the Grand Fountain was repaid.

At the annual session of the Grand Fountain in September, 1899, it was decided to apply for a new charter which would cover all the various activities which the order was now carrying on. The importance of this new charter was second only to the charter granted eleven years before to the True Reformers' Bank.

The purposes of the new organisation, known as the "Reformers' Mercantile and Industrial Association," as stated in the charter granted at this time, are as follows:

First, to manufacture, buy, and sell, at wholesale or retail, or both, groceries, goods, wares, implements, supplies, and articles of merchandise of any and every description, manufactured or grown, in this state or any other states or country, on its own account, and also for others on commission or otherwise; and to establish and maintain warehouses and stores at such places as may be agreed upon by the board of directors;

Second, to build and erect a hotel in the city of Richmond, Va., to lease out said hotel so erected or to conduct and carry on the hotel business therein, as shall be determined by the board of directors of said association;

Third, to conduct and carry on newspapers, book and job printing business in all its branches, and do generally all the things that pertain to a printing establishment;

Fourth, to buy and sell and improve land in the State of Virginia or elsewhere, with the right to lay off the same into lots, streets, and alleys, to improve said lands by erecting buildings thereon, maintain any structure and machinery needful for the manufacture of any kind of wood, metals, wool, cotton and other materials.

Fifth, to conduct a building and loan business and loan association.

Under this charter the association in April, 1900, opened a grocery and general merchandise store in Richmond. In March, 1901, a second store was opened in Washington, District of Columbia, and in December, 1901, a third, fourth and fifth store was opened successively in Portsmouth, Manchester, and Roanoke, Virginia. These stores seem to have been conducted on a sound basis; supplies were bought in large quantities for cash and were sold again at retail for cash. The managers of the stores made weekly reports and remittances. It is reported that these stores do an annual business of more than $100,000.

About this time the Hotel Reformer was opened at 900 North Sixth Street, Richmond, Virginia. This hotel has prospered and grown until now it has accommodations for one hundred and fifty guests. Most of the office force of the Grand Fountain make their homes in this hotel. Another enterprise of the organisation is "The Reformers' Building and Loan Association," which was incorporated for the purpose of encouraging industry, frugality, and home building, particularly among the members of the True Reformers' Association.

The headquarters of the Grand Fountain are in a large, four-story brick building, 604-608 North Second Street, Richmond, Virginia. This building contains, in addition to the various offices of the Grand Fountain, a large hall, which is sometimes used as a theatre and for other entertainments. In this same building are the offices of the True Reformers' Bank, the printing-office and the rooms of the real estate department. In 1908, this department had three farms and twenty-seven buildings of a total value of $400,000 under its control. It leases for the benefit of the order twenty-three other buildings.

As the members of the association continued to increase in numbers and the business operations continued to multiply, there was need in 1901 for an amendment to the charter to provide for further expansion of the organisation. One of the changes made in the charter at that time provided that the control of all the affiliated organisations of the order should remain in the Grand Fountain, which is the legislative body of the order, and meets annually. Another provision of the charter increased the amount of real estate that the order might hold from $25,000 to $500,000.

While the True Reformers was the first and, perhaps, the most extraordinary of the benevolent associations which have developed into coöperative business organisations it is still merely one among a number of others that have sprung up within recent years in the Southern states. While it is probably true that these organisations, owing to the inexperience of the men who started them, have not always been formed upon the best business models, it is still true that they have responded to some very definite needs of the Negro people, otherwise they could not have prospered as they have.

In the first place I think it may be safely said that these organisations have collected from the masses of the coloured people large amounts of money that would not otherwise have been saved. In doing this they have created a considerable capital, which has been at the disposal of Negro business men. It has enabled Negroes to erect buildings, invest in lands, and greatly increase property in the hands of members of the race. Indirectly, these organisations have stimulated thrift and industry among the masses of the people.

One thing that has made these organisations especially attractive and valuable to the masses of the coloured people is that they have grown out of a kind of organisation for mutual helpfulness with which coloured people have long been familiar. Furthermore, they seem to be democratic in their organisation, although, as a matter of fact, I think that has seldom been true where the organisations have been successful. At any rate, the members of the fraternal organisation have felt that they were directing and controlling, to some extent, their own investments, and that gave them an interest in the business of the organisation that they would not otherwise have felt.

The chief value of the Negro societies and benevolent organisations has been that they have been the schools in which the masses have been taught the value and the methods of coöperation. In order to succeed these organisations have been compelled to enforce upon the masses of the people habits of

saving and of system which they would not otherwise have been able or disposed to learn. These
societies have contributed in this way, in spite of
their failings, in no small degree to the intellectual
and material development of the Negro race.

CHAPTER XXII

THE NEGRO DOCTOR AND THE NEGRO PROFESSIONAL
MAN

IT WAS not until 1884, as near as I can now remember, that the first coloured physician,
Dr. C. N. Dorsette, set up an office and began
to practise medicine in Montgomery, Alabama.
Previous to that time I do not think there was a Negro
doctor, dentist or pharmacist in the state. At the
present time there are more than one hundred,
and the members of these three professions in
Alabama maintain a flourishing state association,
which in turn is connected with the National
Medical Association, having representatives in ten
Southern and twelve Northern states. I may
add that the first woman physician who was ever
granted a licence to practise medicine in the State
of Alabama was a coloured woman, Dr. Sadie
Dillon, a daughter of Bishop Benjamin Tanner,
and a sister of H. O. Tanner, the distinguished Negro
painter.

It is an indication of the progress of Negro doctors
of Alabama, since Dr. Dorsette first came to the state,
that there are at the present time no less than six

infirmaries or hospitals which have been established since then and are largely maintained under the direction of the Negro physicians of this state. There are, for instance, the Cottage Home Infirmary, conducted by Dr. W. E. Sterrs, at Decatur; the Home Infirmary, conducted by Dr. U. G. Mason and Dr. A. M. Brown; the Selma Infirmary, conducted by Dr. L. L. Burwell, of Selma, Alabama; and the Harris Infirmary, conducted by Dr. T. N. Harris, at Mobile. In addition to these there is the Hale's Infirmary at Montgomery, Alabama, and the Institute Hospital at Tuskegee, conducted by Dr. J. A. Kenney, who is, I may add, Secretary of the National Medical Association.

The Hale's Infirmary was given to the coloured people at Montgomery by James H. Hale and his widow, Ann Hale, at a cost of something like twenty-five thousand dollars. When the building was first opened in 1899, Mrs. Ann Hale conducted it with her own means and what she was able to solicit from other sources. At the present time it is supported in part by money given by the city and by donations from women's clubs, the contributions of churches and lodges of the secret orders of the city.

The rapid advancement of the Negro physician in Alabama is an indication of the progress which is taking place elsewhere throughout the South. A few years ago almost the only Negro doctor one ever heard of in the Southern states was an individual known as "the root doctor," a kind of mendicant medicine-man, who travelled about through the country districts with a little stock of herbs and philters and a large stock of superstition, with which he traded upon the credulity of the country people. The medicines these men used were mostly harmless and the cures they performed consisted largely in convincing the people that they were going to get well, thus putting them in a way to actually recover from their ailments. They were, in fact, a kind of faith-healers, though mostly, I fear, they were merely frauds.

The "root doctor" has not entirely disappeared from the country districts of the South, but more and more the masses of the people are overcoming their instinctive distrust of hospitals and surgeons, and are learning to have faith in scientific medicine. A striking illustration of one of the ways in which this change is coming about was furnished me during a recent journey through South Carolina. At the Voorhees Industrial School, which is situated a few miles from Denmark, in the midst of a rich farming district of Central South Carolina, I observed that a large and commodious hospital had been erected. Although at the time I was there this hospital had not yet been fully equipped and put in working order, yet it suggested to me one of the unexpected ways in which an industrial school like this, situated in the open country as it is, can exercise and is exercising a civilising and uplifting influence upon the masses of the people.

Outside of the larger hospitals, like the Freedmen's Hospital in Washington, District of Columbia, the Provident Hospital in Chicago, Illinois, and the Frederick Douglass Hospital in Philadelphia, there are, in almost every city in the South, these smaller institutions to which I have referred, established by coloured physicians in order to provide for the needs of the coloured population. Although most of these institutions are poorly equipped, they have proved a great blessing to the communities in which they were established. Frequently they have been the only places in which Negroes, suffering from some unusual form of disease, could obtain anything like proper treatment. They have provided the only places in which serious surgical operations would be performed, with the assurance that the patient would be properly cared for after the operation was completed.

At first all the serious surgical operations were performed by white men but, as coloured surgeons in different parts of the country have gained in skill and in reputation, they have been invited to attend the meetings of the different state associations and to hold clinics at the different Negro infirmaries and hospitals. In these clinics the coloured physicians have had an opportunity to see major operations performed by experts and specialists of their own race and thus have gained knowledge and experience in their profession that they could not otherwise obtain. For instance, at a recent meeting of the Alabama State Association at Birmingham there were present, Dr. George C. Hall of Chicago, Dr. A. M. Curtis of Washington, and Drs. Boyd, Stewart and Roman of the Maharry Medical College of Nashville, Tennessee. All of these men have gained a national reputation, either as teachers of medicine or as surgeons.

One of the hospitals to which I have referred, the Taylor-Lane Hospital, at Orangeburg, South Carolina, was started by a coloured woman, Dr. Matilda A. Evans. Dr. Evans, aside from the fact that she was the first woman doctor in Orangeburg, and perhaps also in the State of South Carolina, has an interesting history. Her grandmother, who was Edith Willis, was kidnapped from Chester County, Pennsylvania, when she was a child, and taken to Charleston, South Carolina, where she was sold as a slave. She eventually became a cook on the plantation of Mr. John Brodie, who was a descendant of one of the old families of South Carolina. Dr. Matilda Evans was born on this plantation six years after emancipation. She was educated in the famous Schofield School at Aiken, South Carolina, and eventually studied medicine at the Woman's Medical College in Philadelphia. Before she started North, however, she stopped for a few days with a coloured family at Orangeburg. There she heard for the first time about Dr. B. W. Taylor, "Mars Ben," as the people she lived with called him. These people impressed upon her that if she ever intended to return to Orangeburg, to practise medicine, she must go to see "Mars Ben" because he would help her.

After she had completed her course at the medical college in Philadelphia, the young woman physician wrote to Dr. Taylor, and he encouraged her to return to Orangeburg and take up the profession. From the first, she says, he, as well as the other white physicians in the town, assisted her in every way. She has been unusually successful. About half of her practice in Orangeburg, I have been told, is among the white people. Among her patients are the descendants of the family to which her grandmother and mother had belonged as slaves. At the same time she is on the best of terms with all the doctors in the town, white and black, who have assisted her in establishing and maintaining the Taylor-Lane Hospital, of which she is the founder and has the entire management.

It would be a mistake to assume from what I have said, thus far, that there were no Negro physicians in the United States before the Civil War. The earliest Negro doctor to attain any degree of distinction was James Derham.

James Derham was born a slave in Philadelphia in 1767. His master taught him to read and write, and employed him in compounding medicines. After a time the young slave became so skilful that he was employed as an assistant by a new master to whom he was afterward sold. He succeeded, while he was still a young man, in purchasing his freedom and eventually removed to New Orleans, Louisiana, where he built up a lucrative practice. The celebrated Dr. Rush published an account of him in the American Museum in which he spoke in the highest terms of his character and his skill as a physician.

Another Negro doctor, who gained considerable reputation previous to the Civil War, was Dr. James McCune Smith, who, unable to obtain a technical education in the United States, went to England and eventually graduated at Glasgow. He practised in New York for twenty-five years, where he became one of the most influential men of his race. Dr. Smith was the first coloured man to establish a pharmacy in the United States.

In 1854, Dr. John V. De Grasse was admitted in due form as a member of the Massachusetts Medical Society, probably the first instance of such an honour being conferred upon a Negro in this country. When the professional schools began to receive coloured students after the close of the Civil War, a number of young men eagerly took advantage of the opportunity to equip themselves for professional careers. Howard University in Washington has graduated over a thousand students from the medical department alone and almost half that number from the department of law.

The majority of the Negro doctors, dentists and pharmacists in the South have been educated at Howard University, Washington, District of Columbia, at Meharry Medical College, Nashville, Tennessee, or at the Leonard Medical College at Raleigh, N. C. At the Leonard Medical College from the beginning, a majority of the professors have been Southern white men residing in Raleigh.

In this connection, I may add, that the Negro doctor, as soon as he shows fitness for his profession, is usually treated with every courtesy by white physicians. White doctors have everywhere encouraged the building of hospitals for coloured patients. They have shown themselves, with a few exceptions, willing and even glad to consult with Negro physicians whenever they are called upon to do so. In almost every part of the South which I have visited the Negro physician is treated with great respect by white people as well as coloured, and as a rule, I think it is true that the Negro physicians are entitled to the consideration and respect of the communities in which they live. There are comparatively few of them who have not held their own, from a moral point of view. The number of those who have gone down on account of drink, or other had habits, is comparatively small.

More and more, also, the white people of the South

are beginning to recognise that their own interests, as far as health is concerned, are intimately interwoven with those of the coloured race. Disease draws no colour line. It is not possible that the conditions of life in that part of the city where the coloured people live should be filthy and degrading, such as tend to produce disease and crime, without these conditions sooner or later affecting the lives of those who live in other parts of the city. If the woman who does the household washing lives in a part of the city where there is consumption or smallpox, the seeds of that disease will eventually be carried into the homes of all her employers, no matter how carefully guarded they are in other respects. If the servant who prepares the food or has the care of the children spends a large part of her life among people who are unclean, and in a region that is infected with disease, it is inevitable that sooner or later she will impart that disease to the family under her care.

In the education of the people in the laws of healthful living and in the improvement of conditions among the poorer classes the Negro doctor is able to perform a great service, not only for the people of his own race, but for all the people in the community in which he lives.

One of the agencies that has done most to build up the medical profession among the Negroes is the National Medical Association, which includes among its members some three hundred and fifty Negro physicians, surgeons and pharmacists, and reaches through correspondence some fifteen hundred others. This Association grew out of a congress of Negro physicians and surgeons that was held at the Exposition at Atlanta, in 1895. Dr. I. Garland Penn, the assistant general secretary of the Epworth League of the Methodist Episcopal Church, who was commissioner of Negro exhibits for the Atlanta Exposition, was indirectly responsible for it. He conceived the idea that, in connection with the other features of the Exposition, an attempt should be made to bring together as large a number of Negro physicians and surgeons as possible, because he believed that the meeting would not only be of advantage to the Negro physicians themselves, but also would give the world some idea of the progress Negroes were making in that branch of science.

It was Dr. R. F. Boyd, of Nashville, afterward chosen as the first president of the Association, who was largely responsible for making this congress a permanent institution. During the first years of its existence the Association met irregularly. Since 1900, however, the meetings have been held annually. One of the features of these annual meetings has been the surgical clinics held by Doctors Daniel H. Williams, George C. Hall and A. M. Curtis and others.

Dr. Daniel H. Williams and Dr. George C. Hall, of Chicago, are probably the most noted Negro surgeons in the United States. They have to their credit the performance of some of the most noteworthy operations that have been undertaken by any surgeon of any race.

The influence of the Negro doctor in the elevation of the race has extended further than the mere practice of medicine. In many cases it will be found that he is a successful busines man in the community in which he lives and the owner of valuable property. In Montgomery, Alabama, for instance, the Negro doctors own and operate four drug-stores. The same is true in Birmingham and Mobile. In fact, outside of the real estate business there is probably no kind of enterprise in which Negroes have been so largely successful as in the drug business. There is hardly a city of any importance in the Southern states in which there are not Negro druggists. From such investigations as I have been able to make I have learned that, at the present time, there are no less than one hundred and thirty-six druggists in the Southern states, and, in most cases, these stores have been started, in the first instance, by or under the direction of Negro physicians.

In cases where a Negro physician has started a store in connection with his office, he will often have a wife or brother, or, after a time, a son or daughter, who is a professional pharmacist. He will place his daughter or his wife in charge of the store, while he attends to the duties of his profession. In this way he is able not only to make certain economies in the business, but also to widen the economic opportunity of the other members of the family and of the members of his race.

The progress of the Negro physician and surgeon is but an instance and an indication of the rise of the professional class among the coloured people in America. The first and largest class, since the first and most pressing need of the Negro after emancipation was education, is that of teachers. According to the census of 1900 there were 21,268 Negro teachers in schools and colleges. This was an increase of 6,168 from 1890 to 1900, or 40.8 per cent., which was more than twice as rapid as the increase of the Negro population. The increase of the white teachers for the same period was 27.7 per cent.

It is probable that in the ten years the increase has been proportionately less among the teachers than among the other professions, the professions of medicine, dentistry and pharmacy having become especially popular in recent years. Next to the teachers the ministers make up the largest group among Negroes in the professions. In 1900, the number of Negro ministers was 15,530, an increase of 3,371 from 1890 to 1900, or 27.7 per cent. During the same decade white ministers increased less rapidly, or 26.4 per cent.

In the other groups of the professional class of Negroes there were 1,734 physicians and surgeons,

212 dentists, 728 lawyers, 99 literary and scientific persons and 210 journalists.   In each of these groups there have arisen, within the short period of forty years, several men and women who, by reason of their mental and moral qualities, were an honour to their profession and an inspiration to the members of their own race, who have seen in their success a concrete example of what Negroes can do to raise themselves and make themselves of service to the world.

In the profession of teaching the work of coloured women has been, to a marked degree, one in which heroism has played a part worthy of record and remembrance.   Were I asked to select an example of the best type of the Negro woman's work for the uplift of her race since freedom began, without a moment's hesitancy my choice would be the coloured woman teacher, especially the one who has borne the burden of teaching in the rural districts of the South, where she has had to labor, for the most part, without the hope of material reward or the praise of men.

I know the names of hundreds of these devoted women, who have gone out into the country districts of the South and given their lives in a self-sacrificing and often apparently hopeless effort to lift up the masses of their own people.   Perhaps the most remarkable example of what these women have accomplished is the work of Elizabeth E. Wright, the founder of Voorhees Industrial School, at

Denmark, South Carolina.   She came to us at Tuskegee, a frail young woman without means and, as it often seemed, without the physical strength to carry her through the struggle necessary to complete her course.   She was compelled to give up for a time and go home until she could obtain means and strength to go on.

After being graduated at Tuskegee, she became a teacher in the little town of Denmark, South Carolina, and, at that place, before she died, succeeded in building up a school of her own, modelled on that of Tuskegee Institute.   This school stands to-day. as a monument to this young woman's faith and persistence.   It is one of the largest and best equipped of the industrial schools for Negroes in the Southern states, and has gained a recognition and support, not only of the coloured but of the white people in the community in which it is situated.   Having established the school, Elizabeth Wright literally gave her life in the effort to support and maintain it, and she lies buried on the grounds of the school which she erected with her own life.

The profession of law has enlisted from an early date a considerable number of talented coloured men and a few women.   The first coloured woman lawyer was Charlotte Ray, a daughter of Charles Ray, who was at one time pastor of the famous Shiloh Presbyterian Church.   She graduated from Howard University about 1872, and was still living in 1908,

I understand, though she was then something over sixty years of age.

Macon B. Allen was the first coloured attorney regularly admitted to practice in the United States. He was admitted to the bar in Maine in 1844. Robert Morris was admitted to the Boston bar in 1850, on motion of Charles Sumner, where he practised with marked success until his death in 1882. He was associated with Mr. Sumner in 1849, in the famous case before the Supreme Court of Massachusetts, to test the constitutionality of separate coloured schools in Massachusetts. John M. Langston was admitted to the Ohio bar in 1854. The first coloured man admitted to practice before the Supreme Court of the United States, was John S. Reck, of Boston, Massachusetts. He was admitted Feb. 1, 1865, on motion of Mr. Sumner.

A few of the coloured men who became Members of Congress from the Southern states had a legal training, as well as two or three who have been in the diplomatic and consular service of the United States. Among the coloured department clerks in Washington a surprising number have taken the law course at Howard University in that city. In the effort of the American Negro to widen his economic life, the lawyers of the race are finding a field for their talents which they have not hitherto had an opportunity to enter. For instance, in the building and loan associations; in the mercantile, real estate, coöperative companies and savings banks of various kinds that are now everywhere springing up, the coloured lawyer is finding a clientele far different from the young coloured men who began the study of law in the early years following the Civil War, and looked forward then to a public career, either in State or national politics as the goal of their ambition.

I have always believed that the stronger the economic and industrial foundation of the masses of the race and the more numerous those engaged in gainful occupations became, the more successful and prosperous would the professional class among the race become.

Some mention should be made of the fact that several Negro lawyers have obtained, either by election or appointment, a number of minor judicial positions in which they discharged their duties in an eminently satisfactory manner. Mifflin W. Gibbs, for instance, city judge in Little Rock, Arkansas, in 1873, was the first coloured man to be elected to such a position in the United States. George L. Ruffin was appointed a judge of a district municipal court in Massachusetts in 1883. James C. Matthews was elected a few years ago to a city judgeship, as a Democrat in the city of Albany, New York. E. M. Hewlett and R. H. Terrell were appointed by President Roosevelt as city magistrates in the District of Columbia; the latter holds his position at the present writing and is regarded as a very capable and

efficient official.   A few assistants to district attorneys, municipal and Federal, have been given
appointments.   In none of these cases have I heard
of a failure.

Another profession in which Negroes have been
making progress in recent years is that of journalism.
The Negro journals were, in certain respects, at
their best before the Civil War, during the period of
the anti-slavery struggle.   At that time, when Frederick Douglass was editor of *The North Star*, and all
the anti-slavery leaders among the Negro race contributed more or less to the racial papers, Negro
journals were, for the most part, inspired by high
aims and were a source of inspiration to the masses
of the coloured people in their struggle for freedom.
After emancipation came, the number of these newspapers increased, but, too frequently, they became
the mere organs of a party or a clique, with no higher
reason for their existence than the temporary success
of some political partisan or the petty spoils that fall
to the lot of the Negro politician.

In recent years, however, the Negro journals,
following the lead of the white journals, have become
less party organs and more newspapers, seeking to
report events and reflect the life and progress of the
whole race.   There are at present no less than two
hundred Negro newspapers published in the United
States.   Many of them are ably edited.

One hears a great deal in both the Northern and

Southern states of the Negro politician and, incidentally, of the Negro lawyer and journalist. One hears, however, very little of the Negro physician and surgeon. Nevertheless, of all the professions in which the Negro is engaged, that of medicine is probably the one in which he has attained the highest degree of technical skill and the greatest usefulness to the community in which he lives. In no other direction, I dare say, has the Negro travelled so far from the primitive condition and civilisation of his savage ancestors in Africa.

I was reminded of this fact the more forcibly, a few years ago, by an incident related to me by Dr. George C. Hall, of Chicago. In 1905, Dr. Hall was engaged in holding a surgical clinic before the Alabama Medical, Dental and Pharmaceutical Society, at Mobile. While there he visited the African colony to which I have already referred, situated a few miles out from Mobile in what is known as the African village. He had just come from his lectures and demonstrations in the city of Mobile, where he had been the guest of an organisation composed of men who were engaged in applying the latest results of modern science to the solution of one of the most complicated of human problems, namely, the cure of disease. In a half-hour's ride on the street cars he found himself in the midst of a settlement of native Africans, who for fifty years had held themselves and their descendants apart from the Negroes of Mobile, and had had as little as possible to do with the white people about them. Although they were employed as labourers in the saw-mills nearby, and cultivated the little patches of ground which they owned, they had remained, in most other respects, practically untouched by the civilisation about them.

"I could not help thinking," said Dr. Hall, in speaking of the incident, "that less than half a century ago the men with whom I had been conferring, or their ancestors and ours, were as undeveloped as these primitive people of the African village. I never realised before the wonderful opportunities which our race has had in being thrown into contact with the science and civilisation of this modern world. Here we can see our people, practically under our own eyes, making their way, in a few years, or, at most, a few generations, from the age of stone to the age of electricity."

Few people, black or white, realise that in the Negro race, as it exists to-day in America, we have representatives of nearly every stage of civilisation, from that of the primitive African to the highest modern life and science have achieved. This fact is at once a result and an indication of the rapidity with which he has risen.

CHAPTER VIII

THE NEGRO DISFRANCHISEMENT AND THE NEGRO IN
BUSINESS

WHEN I began my work in Tuskegee in 1881 the coloured people of Alabama had just been deprived — in a way that is now familiar — of many of their political rights. There were some voting but few Negroes held office anywhere in Alabama at that time. The Negroes set great store by the political privileges that had been granted them during the Reconstruction Period, and they thought that when they lost these they had lost all.

Soon after I went into Alabama a new President, James A. Garfield, was inaugurated at Washington. A little community of coloured people not very far from Tuskegee were so impressed with the idea that the new Administration would do something to better their condition, especially in the way of strengthening their political rights, that, out of their poverty, they raised enough money to pay the expenses of one of their number to Washington, in order that he might get direct information and return and report to them what the outlook was. This incident struck me as the more pathetic because I happened to know the man who went on this errand. He was a good, honest, well-meaning fellow, but entirely lacking in knowledge of the world outside his own community. I doubt that he ever got near enough, even to the inauguration ceremonies, to see the President, and I am sure he never got inside the door of the White House. He returned to his people, at any rate, with a very gloomy report and, although it was never quite clear whom he had seen or what he had done, the people understood what it meant.

The people did not say much about their loss. They preserved outwardly, as a rule, the same good nature and cheerfulness which had always characterised them, but deep down in their hearts they had begun to feel that there was no hope for them.

This feeling of apathy and despair continued for a long time among these people in the country districts. A good many of them who owned land in the county at this time gave it up or lost it for some reason or other. Others moved away from the county and there were a great many abandoned farms. Gradually, however, the temper of the people changed. They began to see that harvests were just as good and just as bad as they had been before the changes which deprived them of their political privileges. They began to see, in short, that there was still hope for them in economic, if not in political directions.

The man who went to Washington to call on the President is still living. He is a different person now, a new man, in fact. Since that time he has purchased a farm; has built a decent, comfortable house; is educating his children, and I note that never a session of the monthly Farmer's Institute assembles at Tuskegee that this man does not come and bring some of the products from his farm to exhibit to his fellow-farmers. He is not only successful, but he is one of the happiest and most useful individuals in our county. He has learned that he can do for himself what the authorities at Washington could not do for him, and that is, make his life a success.

A large part of the work which Tuskegee Institute did in those early years, and has continued to do down to the present time, has been to show the masses of our people that in agriculture, in the industries, in commerce, and in the struggle toward economic success, there were compensations for the losses they had suffered in other directions. In doing this we did not seek to give the people the idea that political rights were not valuable or necessary, but rather to impress upon them that economic efficiency was the foundation for every kind of success.

I am pointing out these facts here in order to show how closely industrial education has been connected with the great economic advance among the masses of the Negro people during the last twenty-five years. If the effect of disfranchisment of the

Negro was to discourage and in many instances to embitter him, industrial education has done much to turn his attention to opportunities that lay open to him in other directions than in politics. It has had the effect of turning attention to the vast quantities of idle lands in many parts of the South and the West, and in many instances, has helped him take up these lands and make himself an independent farmer. It has turned attention to the opportunities in business and led him to perceive that in the South, particularly, there are opportunities for better service to his own race, which he can perform and more profitably than any one else.

The fact is, that the coloured people who went into politics directly after the war were, in most cases, what may be called the aristocracy of the race. Many of them had been practically, if not always legally, free, made so by their masters, who were at the same time their fathers, by whom they had been educated and from whom they frequently inherited considerable property. They had formed their lives and characters on the models of the aristocratic Southern people, among whom they were raised, and they believed that politics was the only sort of activity that was fit for a gentleman to engage in. The conditions which existed directly after the war offered these men the opportunity to step in and make themselves the political leaders of the masses of the people.

In the meantime, however, between the close of the war and the period to which I have just referred, there had grown up a middle class among the coloured people. This class is composed, for the most part, of men who had been slaves before the War. Some of them had been house servants and had the advantage of intimate contact with their master's family; many of them had been slaves of that class of planters sometimes referred to in the South as the "yeomanry"; others had been field hands on the big plantations. The majority had had very few opportunities before the War, except such as they obtained in practising the different trades, which were carried on about the plantations. It is from this class that the greater portion of the Negro landowners have sprung; from this class that the greater number of mechanics formerly belonged, and it was from this class that the majority of the business men of the Negro race have arisen.

A farmer, who became the owner of a large plantation of a thousand acres or more, necessarily became something of a business man. Very likely he opened a store on his plantation in order to supply the tenants on his land. That was the case, for instance, with the Reid brothers, Frank and Dow, who live in Macon County, Alabama, about twelve miles from Tuskegee at a little place called Dawkins. The father of these young men had for a long time leased and worked a large plantation of some 1,100 acres. He was enabled to send his sons to school at Tuskegee and, after their return from school, they leased 480 acres more and subsequently added to that by purchase 605 acres, making a total of 2,185 acres of land under their control. A larger portion of this land they sublet to tenants and, as the necessities of the community they had established manifested themselves, they established successfully a store, a cotton-gin, a blacksmith shop, and a grist-mill.

Frequently, in the early days some young coloured man who had worked in a restaurant or as a waiter in a hotel, after saving a little money, would start a business for himself in a small way. Gradually he would accumulate more capital and enlarge his business. That was the case of my friend, John S. Trower, of Germantown, Philadelphia, who is now one of the leading caterers in the city of Philadelphia, and, also, with William E. Gross, proprietor of the Gross Catering Company, of 219 W. 134th Street, New York. In Philadelphia, New York, Baltimore, and Washington, there are a number of noted Negro caterers who began life in the small way I have described.

Among the earlier caterers of New York was Peter Van Dyke, who owned a place at 130 Wooster Street. He became wealthy and left his children and grandchildren in good circumstances. Another of these early caterers was Boston Crummell, father of the late Alexander Crummell, one of the first Africans to be ordained as a priest by the Episcopal Church. Boston Crummell was born in West Africa and brought to America when he was a child. It is an interesting fact that his son, Alexander Crummell, after having studied in Queen's College, Cambridge, England, went to Africa, as one of the first coloured missionaries sent out from this country to Liberia.

Thomas Downing, who kept the once famous "Downing Oyster House," was one of the early Negro caterers of New York. His son, George T. Downing, built the Sea-Girt House at Newport, Rhode Island, and was afterward a caterer in Washington, where he became a friend of Charles Sumner, Wendell Phillips, Henry Wilson, John Andrews, and others of the anti-slavery party of that time.

Charles H. Smiley, who was born at St. Catherine's, Canada, and was at one time one of the leading caterers of Chicago, began his life in Chicago as a janitor, but was employed during his spare time as a waiter at dinners and parties. Francis J. Moultry, who in 1909 was still conducting a large catering establishment at Yonkers, New York, got his training and accumulated his capital for his business career as a waiter in New York City. Mr. Moultry was at that time one of the large taxpayers of his city. He owned stock in several of the Yonkers banks and is proprietor of what is or was a few years ago the largest apartment house in Yonkers. Mr. Moultry owned valuable reality in various portions of the city and has more than once been on the bond of more than one of the county officers.

The training which many of the coloured servants received, both before and after emancipation, gave them a certain capital in the way of experience with which to go into business on their own account. Perhaps the most successful coloured hotel-keeper in the United States has been E. C. Berry of Athens, Ohio. "Hotel Berry," as I learned when I visited Ohio, has had an almost national reputation. Mr. Berry was one of the most respected citizens of the town in which he lives and so successful has he been in conducting his hotel that it is regarded by the citizens as one of the institutions of the town.

Mr. Berry was born in Oberlin, Ohio, in 1854. When he was two years old he was taken by his parents to the little town of Albany, which is about seven miles below Athens. At that time, there were a number of lines of the Underground Railway, which, starting at different points on the Ohio River, passed through Albany and Athens. At Albany there was early established what was known as the Enterprise Academy for coloured children, and it was at this Academy that Mr. Berry obtained his schooling. He first came to Athens when he was sixteen years old, and went to work in a brick-yard at the small sum of fifty cents per day, which was soon increased to one dollar and twenty-five cents. With the money that he earned in this way he helped to support the members of his family, who were still living in Albany. Eventually he secured employment in Athens in a restaurant, and it was the training he received there that enabled him later on to start a little place of his own.

Mr. Berry was successful in business from the first, and, finally, after giving the matter due consideration and talking it over with friends in the city, he made up his mind to open a hotel. It was an entirely new thing at that time to see a coloured man in the hotel business in that part of the country, and Mr. Berry knew that he was going to meet with opposition on account of his race. He determined to overcome this prejudice by making his hotel more comfortable than any other in the city, and by giving his guests more for their money than they were able to get anywhere else, not only in the city but in the state. One thing I remember which impressed me as indicating the care and thoughtful atttention which Mr. Berry gave to his guests was the fact that at night, after his guests had fallen asleep, he made it a practice to go to their rooms and gather up their clothes and take them to his wife, who would repair rents, add buttons where they were lacking, and press the garments, after which Mr. Berry would replace them. Mr. Berry's hotel, I may add, is said by Mr. Elbert Hubbard, the lecturer, who has had an opportunity to test the quality of a large number

of hotels in different parts of this country, to be one
of the best in the United States.

There are a number of other successful hotel men
among the members of my race of whom I have made
the acquaintance in different parts of the country.
Joseph W. Lee, who, until he died a few years ago,
kept the very popular and successful hotel at Squantum, a summer resort just outside of Boston, was one
of these.

Negroes both before the War and after, entered
very easily into the barber business, and there is no
business, I may add, in which the Negro has met
more competition from foreign immigrants. In
many cities, both North and South, the Negro barber's trade is almost wholly confined, at the present
time, to members of his own race. It is interesting
to observe however, that this has in no way lessened
the number of Negro barber shops, and the fact is an
indication of the increasing economic welfare of the
masses of the Negro people. In spite of the competition which I have mentioned, some of the largest
and best conducted barber shops in the United States
are carried on by Negroes.

As an illustration, I might mention the shop of
George A. Myers, of Cleveland, Ohio, whose place of
business is fitted up, not only with all conveniences
that you will find in other first-class shops, but also
with some that you will not find there. For instance,
when I was last in his shop, he had devised an

arrangement by which a customer could be connected at once by telephone with any one he wished to speak to, and that without leaving his chair. He has also provided a young woman stenographer, to whom patrons can dictate business letters if they desire, without interrupting the work of the barber.

Another business in which the Negro early found an opportunity to be of service to his people is that of undertaking. As far as they were able, the Negro people have always tried to surround the great mystery of death with appropriate and impressive ceremonies. One of the principal features of the Negro secret organisations has been the care for the sick and the burial of the dead. The demand that these organisations sought to meet has created a business opportunity, and Negro business men have largely taken advantage of it.

One of the first men to perceive the opportunity for coloured business men in this direction was Elijah Cook, a Negro undertaker of Montgomery, formerly a member of the State Legislature of Alabama. Mr. Cook was born a slave in Alabama. He was several times sold on the auction block during slavery, and at one of these sales he was separated from his brother, of whom he has never since heard. He was taught the carpenter's trade, however, and, after he had served his apprenticeship, was permitted to hire his time for $25 per month. When the Civil War broke out, Mr. Cook still paid his master's wife the stipulated sum per month and continued to do so faithfully until he was emancipated. He was a leader in founding the first coloured school in Montgomery, which was held in a basement, under a dilapidated church. He himself was one of the first scholars and, after working hard all day, was a faithful attendant of the night school.

Right after the War there was no coloured undertaker in Montgomery and frequently the corpses of the coloured people were hauled to the cemetery in rough wagons. Mr. Cook seeing this, bought a hearse and went into the undertaking business for himself. He accumulated a small fortune during the twenty years or more that he was in business, and became one of the respected citizens of Montgomery.

James C. Thomas, who, at the time I write, is said to be the richest man of African descent in New York, made a large part of his fortune in the undertaking business. Mr. Thomas came originally from Harrisburg, Texas, where he was born in 1864. In 1881, while he was employed by a steamer plying between New Orleans, Mexico, and Cuba, yellow fever broke out in New Orleans. The boat he was on came to New York to escape the quarantine. It was thus, quite by accident, that Mr. Thomas became a New Yorker.

There have been Negro undertakers in New York, I have been informed, for over 150 years. There were several Negro undertakers in New York and Brooklyn, at the time Mr. Thomas went into business, but the larger part of the trade, which should have come to the coloured undertakers, went to white men. In 1909, Mr. Thomas had one of the largest businesses of any undertaker, white or black, in the city of New York. He was, in addition, the owner of a number of valuable properties in New York City and owned stock in the Chelsea National Bank of New York.

I shall have occasion to make mention, in another connection, of the success the Negro has had as a banker, real estate dealer, and as a druggist, and in some other forms of business. As illustrating, however, the variety of enterprises into which the Negro had entered, I might mention the fact that one of the best conducted grocery stores in the city of Montgomery is run by Victor H. Tulane, who started in business in 1893 in a little building, twelve by twenty in size, with no experience and a capital of $90. Mr. Tulane, in 1909, was doing a business of forty thousand dollars a year. He has been for a number of years one of the trustees of the Tuskegee Normal and Industrial Institute.

During my visit of observation and study in the State of Mississippi in the fall of 1908, I found that the largest book-store and, I was told, the only one at that time in the city of Greenville, Mississippi, was conducted by a coloured man, Granville Carter.

Mr. Carter told me that at one time there had been as many as five book-stores in the town but he had succeeded, by close attention to business and offering his books at prices more favourable than his rivals, in outliving them all, until at the time I was there, his was the only book-store in the town. He told me that he handled the entire book business of the county and that he sold books in several of the adjoining counties. He regularly employs four helpers to assist him in the business and at Christmas time he has been compelled to increase this number to ten.

In Jackson, Mississippi, H. K. Rischer had had for nearly twenty years, at the time of my visit, a practical monopoly of the bakery business. Mr. Rischer's bakery was one of the first concerns of its kind to be established in Jackson. His business, which amounts to about $30,000 a year, gives employment to twelve persons and was first established in 1881.

While it is true, as I have already pointed out, that the disposition of the Negro people to turn their attention more and more to practical matters and to business manifested itself at about the same time that I came to Alabama and has grown with the increasing interest in industrial education, it is likewise true that only since 1897 or 1898 has there been any marked and rapid increase in the amount of business conducted by coloured people.

When the National Negro Business League met in Boston, 1900, there were but two Negro banks in the United States; at the present time there are nearly, if not quite, fifty such institutions.

In order to illustrate the improvement of the general mass of the coloured people in the South during the ten years since 1899, I shall take as an example the city of Jackson, Mississippi, where in the summer of 1898, a special study was made of the economic condition of the people. Up to 1896, Negroes who represented at that time more than half of the population, were not reckoned in the business life of the town. Few of them owned property of any kind. At the present time, the Negro population is less than half of the total population of the town, and the 8,000 Negroes who make their homes there, own, it is estimated, one-third of the area of the town, although this area represents but one-eleventh of the value of the city property. Negroes own, for instance, according to the tax records of the city, $581,580 worth of property. Over one-third of the 566 Negroes on the tax books were assessed for more than $1,000 and six of them for more than $5,000. The largest single assessment amounted to $23,800.

A careful investigation brought to light the fact that about one-half the Negro families of that town own their own homes, while more than two-thirds of the houses in which the Negroes live are in the possession of their own race. Next to the possession of property, the amount of money deposited in banks by Negroes is an evidence of their economic condition. In speaking of this matter during the summer of 1908, the president of one of the prominent white banks said that Negroes had just begun to save their money during the last ten or twelve years. He was in a position to know, for Negroes had deposited in his bank more than $25,000. Altogether Negro savings in Jackson banks amounted, at the time, to something over $200,000, more than one-third of which was in the hands of the Negro banks.

Perhaps the most successful Negro business man in Jackson, at that time, was Dr. S. D. Redmond. Dr. Redmond received his medical training at the Illinois Medical College and the Harvard Medical College. When he settled in Jackson ten years ago he had practically nothing. At the time this is written he is president of the American Trust and Savings bank, the oldest of the Negro banks in Jackson and a stockholder in three banks controlled by the white people, as well as in the electric power and light company which lights the city streets. He owns two drug-stores, one of which is situated on the chief business street of the town. He receives rent from more than one hundred houses.

There were in 1908 more than one hundred business enterprises conducted by Negroes in Jackson. Among them were the two banks already mentioned, four drug-stores, two undertaking companies, two real estate companies, Mr. Rischer's bakery, four shoemaking and repair shops, one of these doing the largest business of its kind in the town. One millinery shop, besides numerous stores, barber shops, and other smaller business concerns of various kinds. Forty-five of these, including five contracting firms, did something like $380,000 worth of business during the year 1907-1908, and gave employment to two hundred and thirty persons.

It used to be said, before much was known about Africa, that the condition of the African people had remained the same in all parts of Africa through thousands of years and nothing furnished so convincing a proof of the inability of the African to improve as the fact that during all this time he has not changed. I have already suggested, in what I have written, that an enormous change has taken place in the condition, in the feeling and in the ambitions of the coloured people in this country, since they obtained their freedom a comparatively few years ago.

The Negro came out of slavery with a feeling that work was the symbol of degradation. In nearly all the schools conducted by Negroes in the South at the present time, Negro children are learning to work. The Negro came out of slavery with almost no capital except the hard discipline and training he had received as a slave. In the years since that time, he has not only become a large land-owner, and, to a large extent, the owner of his own home, but he has become a banker and a business man. He came out of slavery with the idea that somehow or other the Government, which freed him, was going to support and protect him, and that the great hope of his race was in politics and in the ballot. In the last decade the Negro has settled down to the task of building his own fortune and of gaining through thrift, through industry, and through business success that which he has been denied in other directions.

Many of the men to whom I have referred in this chapter, if I had time to relate their histories, would illustrate in their own lives the changes to which I refer. For instance, L. K. Attwood, the president of the Southern Bank, the second Negro bank in Jackson, Mississippi, was born a slave in Wilcox County, Alabama, about 150 miles from Tuskegee, in 1851. He was sold on the block when he was eighteen months old. His mother bought him for $300 and moved with him to Ohio. In 1874, he graduated from Lincoln University, Pennsylvania. Two years later he was admitted to the bar in Mississippi. He served two terms as a member of the Mississippi Legislature from Hinds County, and has held the positions of United States Commissioner and United States Deputy Revenue Collector for the Louisiana and Mississippi districts. He is one of a group of professional coloured men who have found that business pays better than politics. In addition to his connection with the bank, Mr. Attwood has been actively identified with a number of other Negro enterprises in the town. He has amassed considerable property and is generally respected as a shrewd and aggressive business man among the people of his community.

While I am on this subject, I should, perhaps, mention one other notable example of the business men who have found a larger opportunity in business than they did in politics. C. F. Johnson, of Mobile, Alabama, Secretary and General Manager of the Union Mutual Aid Association, was for many years Secretary of the Republican State Executive Committee of Alabama. He was for a time, also, secretary to the Collector of Customs at the port of Mobile, but when Mr. Cleveland was elected President he gave up that position and took the position as elevator man instead. One day after he had been there for some time the new collector, who had been appointed by Mr. Cleveland, noticed him there and, thinking the time had come to complete his political house-cleaning, dismissed him from that position. Because the new man whom the Collector had to take his place did not do the work satisfactorily, he asked Mr. Johnson to return. Johnson said he would come back if he could have the appointment for four years, but the Collector would not agree to that, so Johnson went permanently out of office and into business. He was largely responsible for the organisation of the company of which he has been general manager and is now one of the wealthiest coloured men in the State of Alabama.

So far as I have been able to learn, no coloured man has ever been classed among the millionaires, though several men have had the reputation of being in that class.

A few years ago there was a coloured man by the name of Wiley Jones in Pine Bluff, Arkansas, who owned a street railway, a stable of trotting horses, and private trotting park. When he died it was learned for the first time that he had investments in real estate in a number of large Western cities, but his estate did not reach, as I remember, more than one hundred thousand dollars. John McKee, of Philadelphia, was reputed to be a millionaire, but his estate in Philadelphia, when he died, amounted to but $342,832. In addition to this he owned land in Atlantic County, New Jersey, which was assessed at $20,650. He also owned a tract of coal and mineral land in Kentucky, which was assessed at $70,000, which he hoped would eventually be of great value. Colonel McKee gave directions in his will that the rents and incomes of his estate should accumulate until the death of all his children and grandchildren. It was to be used to establish a college for the education of fatherless boys, white and coloured.

Perhaps the nearest approach to a coloured millionaire was Thomy Lafon, of New Orleans, who died

December 23, 1893, leaving an estate appraised at $413,000, the bulk of which was divided among the various charities of the city of New Orleans. I understand, however, that Mr. Lafon had disposed of a considerable portion of his estate in order to found various charities before his death.

Mr. Lafon was born in New Orleans, December 28, 1810, of free Negro parents. He began life as a school-teacher; then he ran for a time a small dry-goods store on Orleans Street. As he accumulated a little money he began loaning it out at advantageous rates of interest, and went from that into land speculations, which made him very wealthy. Before he died he became much attached to the late Archbishop Janssens and, under his direction, as I understand, began disposing of his fortune for philanthropic purposes. Before his death he had established an asylum for orphan boys called Lafon Asylum, and after his death he bequeathed the sum of $2,000 in cash and the revenue amounting to $275 per month of a large property at the corner of Royal and Iberville streets.

Other legacies were in favor of the Lafon Old Folks' Home, previously established, the Charity Hospital, of New Orleans, the several universities for coloured children in New Orleans and a number of charities in charge of the Catholic Church.

In this benevolent way the two largest fortunes which members of my race have yet accumulated were dispersed.

CHAPTER IX

THE NEGRO BANK AND THE MORAL UPLIFT

IN the year 1888, the statement was made upon the floor of the United States Senate that, with all the progress it had made in other directions, the Negro race had not a single bank to its credit. At the time this statement was made it was intimated that the Negro race never would support a bank; that, in short, the bank was the limit of the progress of the Negro in the direction of business.

Twenty years later, in 1908, no less than fifty-five Negro banks, large and small, had been started in the United States, and of these forty-seven were then in operation. There were eleven in Mississippi, ten in Virginia, five in Oklahoma, four in Georgia, four in Tennessee, four in North Carolina, four in Texas, two in Alabama, one in Arkansas, one in Pennsylvania, and one in Illinois.

These facts illustrate how difficult it is, in the case of a race which is coming for the first time into contact with new conditions or new opportunities, to predict from what it has done in the past what it is likely to do in the future.

In the course of my travels about the country, for

example, I am constantly meeting men who are introduced to me as "the first Negro who ever did" this thing or that thing. Sometimes the claims made for these men are more modest. In such cases I am likely to hear not that such a man is the first and only Negro who ever achieved the particular distinction mentioned, but that he is the first Negro in that particular state or community who has done so. As I have said, I meet hundreds of these men every year, and the number of them indicates to my mind that the Negro in America is making great progress. I mean that, as a race, and with reference to what they have done in the past, Negroes are probably doing more new things every year than can be said of any other race with the exception of the Japanese.

Negro banks are of various kinds and descriptions. Some of them, like the Bank of Mound Bayou, started by Charles Banks, March 8, 1904, are doing a regular commercial business. This bank is the centre of the cotton-raising community, and, during the cotton season, its clearings, through its correspondents and through other banks, have amounted to something over $200,000 per month. It had, in 1908, a paid in capital of $25,000 and resources amounting to $100,000. Other institutions, like the One Cent Savings Bank of Nashville, Tennessee, started in 1903 by J. C. Napier, are savings banks, pure and simple. Mr. Napier is one of the substantial business men of Nashville, Tennessee. He has been four times elected a member of the City Council, and is the owner of a handsome three-story brick building located on one of the best streets of that city, containing the offices of the bank, a spacious hall, and a number of other offices. This building is known as the Napier Court.

Quite as interesting as these banks, which have been started on the models of similar institutions conducted by white men, are some of the smaller and more obscure savings and loan associations, which have been started, frequently by untrained men, in order to meet the necessities of peculiar and local conditions. I have in mind such a mutual banking association as was started by fifteen Negro farmers in the neighbourhood of Courtland, Virginia, the home of Nat Turner, and the scene of the Northampton insurrection of 1831. This association was started under the leadership of Reverend O. C. Jenkins, and was formed primarily to enable the coloured farmers in that part of the country to assist each other in buying land and in carrying on their farming operations. I mention this organisation not because of its success but because it illustrates the sort of experiments that men, untrained in business, are making in all parts of the South in order to improve their condition and lift themselves up to a higher plane of living.

Before there were any banks owned by Negroes

there was the Freedmen's Bank, an institution for Negroes, established in Washington, District of Columbia, under the auspices of the Freedmen's Bureau. No work was ever undertaken for the benefit of the Freedmen more laudable in its purpose or more designed to assist a people who had just come out of slavery to get on their feet. From 1866, when this bank was started, to 1874, when it failed, the total amount of deposits had increased from $305,167 to $55,000,000, and when the bank closed its doors there was due to depositors $3,013,670. The number of depositors to whom this money was due was 61,131. Up to March, 1896, $1,722,548 had been re-paid to these depositors. There still remains in the hands of the Government $30,476.*

This bank had agents all over the South, and coloured people were induced to deposit their earnings with it in the belief that the institution was under the care and protection of the United States Government. When they found that they had lost, or been swindled out of all their little savings, they lost faith in savings banks, and it was a long time after this before it was possible to mention a savings bank for Negroes without some reference being made to the disaster of the Freedman's Bank. The effect of this disaster was the more far-reach-

---

* "Economic Coöperation among Negro Americans." Atlanta University Publication, No. 12, p. 135.

ing because of the wide extent of territory which
the Freedmen's Bank covered through its agencies.

In March, 1888, the Legislature of Virginia
granted a charter for a savings bank to the Grand
Fountain of the United Order of the True Reformers.
This bank was opened for business April 3, 1889,
and received deposits to the amount of $1,268.69
the first day. This was the origin of the oldest
and best established Negro bank in the United
States. It is said that when application was made
to the Virginia Legislature for a charter for this
institution the matter was not treated seriously.
Members of the Legislature looked upon a Negro
bank as a joke, and granted the charter in a spirit
of fun, never expecting to see a real Negro savings
institution in operation in Virginia.

Some years ago W. P. Burrell, secretary of the
True Reformers, in a report made at the Hampton
Negro Conference, related an interesting anecdote
in regard to the circumstances under which this
bank was started. "It might be interesting to
know," said Mr. Burrell, "that this bank, founded
by William W. Browne, had its origin in a lynching which occurred in Charlotte County, at a point
called Drake's Branch. A branch of the organisation of True Reformers had been founded at Mossing-
ford and the fees of the members, amounting to
nearly $100, had been deposited in the safe of a white
man, who had thus an opportunity to see that the

Negroes of the county had some money, and that they were organising for some purpose. He decided that this was an unwise thing, and so determined to break up the organisation. This fact was reported to Mr. Browne. By a personal visit to the place, he succeeded in saving the organisation and, at the same time, had his attention called to the need of a coloured bank, where coloured people could carry on their own business. The idea of a bank was first advanced by a countryman named W. E. Grant, and immediately adopted by Mr. Browne. Thus it came to pass that, because of an unpleasant race feeling in Charlotte County, Virginia, the oldest incorporated Negro bank came into existence."

In the report to which I have referred, Mr. Burrell calls attention to the fact that, with the exception of the True Reformers' and the Nickel Savings Bank, which was started in Richmond, Virginia, in 1896, all the banks then existing in Virginia had been started since the passage of the new suffrage laws requiring Negro voters in Virginia to be property owners, or to be educated, or to be war veterans.

In the early history of the coloured banks of Virginia it has been told me that considerable difficulty was experienced because these institutions were not connected directly with the Clearing House. The result was, it is said, that the "coloured" depositors were unwilling to open accounts in "coloured" banks, since no means existed by which an exchange of checks among the "coloured" and "white" banks could take place, and the "white" banks refused to accept these checks because they could not "clear" them in the ordinary way. This policy was broken up, however, when the white merchants, who had accepted checks upon the Negro banks, threatened to withdraw their deposits unless the "white" banks made some arrangements by which checks on the "coloured" banks could be cashed. This led, finally, to the voluntary offer of one of the National Banks to act as clearing-house agents. At the present time all the "coloured" banks clear through some member of the Clearing House, for which privilege they pay a small annual tax.

Since it was started, the capital of the True Reformers' Bank has been increased from $4,000 to $100,000, all of which has been paid in. In addition to this, the bank had, on February 5, 1909, a surplus of $35,000, and undivided profits to the amount of $30,220. Since it was organised in 1881 it has held on deposit more than ten million of dollars, for the most part money collected by the True Reformers' Association from its members, and has handled a sum amounting to over eighteen million dollars, derived largely from the same sources.

After emancipation the masses of the Freedmen did not turn immediately to the getting of property and land. The first property acquired by the former slaves was their churches. Of the twenty-six thousand churches and the forty million dollars' worth of property, which these churches represent, the larger part was contributed by men and women who had little or no property of their own. It was the women who toiled over the wash-tub, and the men who worked by the day, from whose earnings for the most part this property was accumulated.

In conversation, some time ago, with a Southern white man, who is a trustee of Tuskegee Institute, he told me that a woman who had worked for a number of years in his house as a servant, contrib-uted, year after year, half of her earnings to the support of the church to which she belonged. This man had reason to know the facts, since he was frequently called on to assist in the support of the same church, and in this way had come to know something definite about its financial affairs.

After the church, the thing that has appealed most directly to the masses of the people, has been the need of making provision for sickness, death and burial. This is the origin of the Negro benevolent and fraternal societies, of which there is a large number at the present time in the United States. It was out of these benevolent societies that the first Negro banks sprang. The names of a number of these banks indicate their origin: for instance, the

True Reformers' Bank, of Richmond, Virginia; the St. Luke's Penny Savings Bank, of the same city; the Bank of the Grand United Order of the Galilean Fishermen, of Hampton, Virginia; the Knights of Honour Savings Bank, of Greenville, Mississippi; and the Bank of the Sons and Daughters of Peace, of Newport News, Virginia. All of these banks and a number of others first came into existence as the repositories for funds of fraternal organisations.

The histories of some of these banks illustrate the manner in which the Negro has succeeded in getting hold of corporate methods of doing business and applying them to his needs. Some time in the neighbourhood of 1894 a young man by the name of L. S. Reed came to Savannah, Georgia, from Atlanta, as the agent of an industrial insurance company, conducted by white men, with an office in New York City. He was more than usually successful in selling this insurance and, because of his ability in dealing in a business way with the coloured people, he was sometimes employed by the Germania Bank to make collections. At the same time, he was engaged in selling real estate, in which he had considerable success. About 1903, taking advantage of the experience he had had as an agent for industrial insurance, he organised a company of his own, called the Union Benefit Association. Like the other associations this one was intended to afford protection to its members in case of accident, sickness, or death. In one respect it differed from the older type of benefit associations: it did not confine its membership to a single locality, but extended its work, through the medium of agents, all over the state of Georgia and into adjoining states. At the same time the monthly dues were not the same for every individual, as they had been in earlier forms of mutual aid associations. Thus the monthly dues ranged from twenty cents to two dollars, and the sick benefits from $1.25 to $8 per week.

The result of this more elaborate form of insurance was the accumulation of a considerable amount of capital, the total income for a single year amounting to as much as $25,000. Having this amount of funds in hand, it seemed necessary to re-invest them in some way. For this purpose, in 1905, a bank known as the Union Savings and Loan Company was organised. This bank became the depository for the funds of the benefit association. The character of this bank is indicated by the fact that it had, at the beginning, 450 stockholders, and a large part of its loans were made to its own stockholders.

A few years later the same people, under the leadership of Mr. Reed, organised the Savannah Mutual & Fire Insurance Co. This Company was organised at the suggestion of Professor

D. C. Suggs, of the Georgia State Industrial College. Professor Suggs is a large property owner in Greensboro, North Carolina. He has, I understand, a street named after him in that city upon which he owns most of the houses. He had become familiar, while in Greensboro, with the fire and insurance business, and saw an opportunity for coloured people succeeding in that line in Savannah.

There is, or was in 1908, another small bank in Savannah which has an interesting history. It is known as the Afro-American Union Savings, Loan & Trust Co. This company was organised by Reverend William Gray and has received most of its support from the members of his own congregation. Reverend William Gray was a coachman who turned preacher. He started a little church in a shanty on Hartridge, between Broad and Price streets, with only eleven members. He has now one of the largest congregations in the city, and his church, a brick and frame structure, cost between fifteen and twenty thousand dollars.

After he became a preacher, Mr. Gray found out that he needed education. After thinking the matter over he stated the facts to his congregation, and told them that he had decided to attend the Georgia State Industrial College at Thunderbolt, just outside Savannah. His congregation were very proud of their minister, and very proud that he had determined to go to college, so proud, in fact,

that they not only gave their support to his reso-
ultion, but decided to pay his expenses while he was
there.   Mr. Gray was already a mature man when
he started to get his education, but he was a man of
sound understanding, of great industry, and with
considerable administrative ability.   He managed,
in some way, to keep up his church work and stick
to his studies until he finally graduated.   It is said
of him in Savannah that he has always dealt fairly
and squarely with his people, both in his church
and in business, and, as the man who explained the
circumstances of his success to me said: "He owes
this reputation to the fact that he made the welfare
of his people his burden."

The first and most successful Negro bank in
Savannah in 1908 was the Wage Earners' Loan &
Investment Co.   This company was started in
1900.   It has an authorised capital of $50,000, of
which, however, only $12,663.40 was paid in up to
1908.   This company was started by a number of
well-to-do business men and some others, successful
in other ways, in Savannah.   The president, L. E.
Williams, was formerly a railway mail-clerk.   The
vice-president, W. R. Fields, was an undertaker.
The secretary-treasurer, Walter Scott, who graduated from Tuskegee Institute in 1905, was a dry goods
merchant.   One of the directors of the company, John
H. Deveaux, was collector of customs for the port of
Savannah.   Another, Sol. C. Johnson, was editor

of the Savannah *Tribune*. Among the other directors were L. M. Pollard, a mail-clerk, R. B. Brooks, a dealer in antique furniture, and J. H. Bugg, a physician.

In the statement issued by this company October 5, 1908, it is said that the bank began business in 1900 with $102. Its combined assets, which included $47,836.36 in deposits, a reserve fund, and undivided profits in the sum of $8,014.22, amounted in 1908 to $70,553.58. It is also stated that the paid up stock has earned 12 per cent. dividends for six consecutive years.

A large part of the business of this bank, like that of most other of the Negro banks, has been to assist coloured people in buying homes. In order to encourage the accumulation of money to buy property, the bank agreed to accept its own stock as cash in payment for real estate. In this way, it was constantly selling and buying its own stock, in order to encourage the investment of money in homes.

While, perhaps, the majority of the banks in the Southern states are doing business largely upon capital which has been accumulated by the fraternal societies and insurance companies, a bank was established in Chicago, Illinois, in 1908, which has grown out of a real estate business conducted very largely among coloured people. The *Commerical Chronicle* of November, 1908, records the completion of the handsome new office building by Jesse

Binga, 3633 State Street, "where he will conduct his real estate and loan business, and in addition he will shortly open a bank at the same place." This is known as the Jesse Binga Bank, and purports to do a commercial and savings banking business. Mr. Binga is one of the nine or ten coloured real estate dealers in Chicago, and one of the four or five who have been doing, during the past ten years, an extensive business among the increasing Negro population in Chicago.

A careful study of the property owned by Negroes in Chicago, in the period previous to 1902, has shown that at that date Negroes owned, according to its assessed valuation, property to the amount of $1,960,105. More than five-sixths of this property was in the hands of 604 individuals, of whom three owned real estate valued at more than $50,000 each.* A more recent investigation made by Mr. R. R. Wright, Jr., indicates that, during the past decade, Negroes have been purchasing property in Chicago at a more rapid rate than at any previous time. He estimates the present value of the real estate held by coloured people in Chicago to be $4,000,000.

The Negro bank with the most interesting history of any of these yet established is that known as the Alabama Penny Savings & Loan Co., which first opened its doors on October 15, 1890, and

---

* "Study of Negro Property Owners in Chicago," Monroe N. Work, p. 19.

received on that day $555. This sum, added to the $3,000 already paid in from the sale of stock, constituted the capital upon which this important and helpful institution began business.

In February, 1909, this bank had a paid-in capital of $25,000, with a surplus of $6,000, and deposits to the amount of $193,000. It is the owner of a handsome three-story brick building, valued at $25,000, and of real estate to the amount of $52,000.

This bank is important not merely from the success it has made, but because of the motives that inspired its organisation. Its workings clearly illustrate the deep and far-reaching influence that these savings institutions exercise upon the social conditions and the moral life of the Negro people.

Birmingham is the centre of a large labouring population. Negroes are employed very largely in the extended mining region, of which Birmingham is the centre, and in the rolling-mills by which it is surrounded. These men earn good wages, but the temptations of the city are very great. It is therefore extremely important that something should be done there to encourage them in the practice of habits of thrift and industry. The first man to clearly perceive this was Reverend W. R. Pettiford, who came to Birmingham in 1883, as pastor of the Sixteenth Street Coloured Baptist Church. It was the perception of this need that suggested to him the importance of establishing at Birmingham a Negro bank. In 1900, at the first meeting of the National Negro Business League in Boston, Mr. Pettiford told the story of this bank:

"I was riding on the electric railway in a suburb of Birmingham," he said, "where a large number of coloured people were employed. There were a number of these people on the car who had just been paid their weekly wage. I had not gone far when I was shocked by seeing a woman among the crowd on the car drinking whiskey. I spoke to her but, though I was a minister and she knew me, I found I had no influence over her. It was at that time that the thought came to me that there should be some sort of business which would take care of the money of that class of people, and that such an institution would enable me, as a minister, to instruct them in ways in which they might better dispose of their earnings. It was in the early part of the year 1890 that the first notion of establishing a bank came into my mind."

Shortly after this occurrence, Mr. W. W. Browne, who was at that time president of the True Reformers' Bank at Richmond, Virginia, visited Birmingham. Mr. Browne was an old acquaintance of Mr. Pettiford, and they discussed the project of forming a bank in Birmingham, similar to the one in Richmond. It was Mr. Browne's idea that the coloured people in Birmingham should form a branch bank of the one in Richmond, but, after talking it over, it was decided to start in Birmingham an independent institution. At the time the movement to start this bank was begun, the True Reformers' Bank, although historically not the first bank in the United States, was the only one then in existence. It seemed doubtful whether a Negro bank could be started and maintained without the advantage of a large fund collected by a fraternal organisation, and without the confidence of a large number of people to back it, such as it would have if started by a fraternal organisation instead of by individuals. But Mr. Pettiford and his associates in Birmingham decided to try the experiment.

It took about three months' agitation to get enough sentiment back of the project to give any assurance of success. After the projectors had succeeded in getting a small capital of $3,000 together it was necessary for the president and cashier to study bookkeeping under a special teacher in order to prepare themselves for the novel business experiment which they proposed to undertake. After they had collected all their resources in cash and had taken an inventory of their combined business knowledge the sum did not amount to very much. Mr. Pettiford, who was a minister, had had some business experience as Financial Agent of Selma University, of Selma, Alabama. The man who was to act as cashier, a graduate of Talladega College, had been the first coloured school-teacher of Birmingham, and was at this time a successful grocer. The vice-president had been a bartender, but he was a man who had a reputation for honesty and had the confidence of the coloured population generally.

The necessities of the business, however, were soon to increase the business knowledge of the directors of the new bank, and that in directions in which very little was to be learned from books. They found that, in starting a Negro bank on a purely business basis, they had a task before them quite different from that which confronts the average white banker. They had to make known to the coloured people what the value and use of a bank was; they had to instruct them in saving, and show them, later on, how to make investments with the money they had saved. In order to accomplish this the officers of the bank began a campaign of education. It was here that the advantage of having a preacher attached to a Negro business organisation became apparent. In order to instruct the coloured people as to the importance of saving their money and depositing it in a bank, it was necessary to preach to them the necessity of securing homes of their own, and of providing for the education of their children. In the course of their campaign, Mr. Pettiford and his associates distributed a vast number of circulars intended to educate the masses of the people on the subject of banking. They made repeated addresses in all the coloured churches in the city and in the suburbs, and they were successful in arousing interest.

After the meeting of the Business League in Boston, in 1900, Mr. Pettiford made it a custom to repeat the story of his bank to members of the League every year. I am convinced that the story of that one bank has done more than any other one thing to call into existence the fifty and more banks started since 1900.

In spite of the fact that Mr. Pettiford told his story so frequently, it was always interesting because he invariably suceeded in bringing out in his account some new fact or point of view. For instance, at the meeting of the Business League in New York, in 1905, he emphasised the fact that one of the considerations which led him and his associates to establish this bank was that it might serve to prevent the squandering not merely of wages but the little accumulation of property that the people in the Birmingham district had succeeded in making.

"During my pastorate in Birmingham," he said, "there was a family who had two children. Both of the parents died and the property left to the children was squandered. The estate was estimated at $10,000. The administrator sold to the boy, the elder of the two children, who inherited the property, old horses and carriages for his interest in the estate. To make a bond of $20,000, as was necessary in this case, was impossible for any coloured man at that time. When I perceived our helplessness to aid orphan children in saving the property earned by their parents, I saw that if we had a strong financial institution which could make bonds and save the property for the benefit of the heirs to whom it was left, it would greatly help the race."

As an indication of the progress which the bank had made, Mr. Pettiford said:

The next day after the opening I took my seat as president, and made the first loan in the history of our bank. This loan was for $10 for thirty days; the interest was fifty cents. The last loan I made in the fifteenth year of the bank's business was just before visiting the National Business League in New York City in 1905, for $14,000; time ten years. The borrower was the Knights of Pythias of Alabama, and the money was for the erection of their magnificent three-story brick building.

One of the things which has helped to make the Alabama Penny Savings and Loan Co. and the other Negro banks succeed, under conditions and difficulties which banks of white people would not survive, is the advantage that Negro bankers have in dealing direct with Negro people.

"As a rule," said Mr. Pettiford, in one of his addresses before the Business League, "the officers of banks conducted by persons of the other race, are not well acquainted with coloured persons who apply for a loan, and, therefore, are unable, in most cases, to accommodate them. The coloured banker, however, knows his own people, and is thus enabled to extend them credit with discrimination."

"By careful and safe methods of extending credit," continued Pettiford, "our bank has assisted many persons in the establishment of small business concerns, and such persons after getting on their feet, have proved to be valuable customers. The management of our bank has all along recognised the fact that, in order to strengthen the bank, the constituency must be strengthened. For this reason, as well as to do good generally, it has been its constant aim to lose no opportunity to assist in the general uplift of the people with whom the bank has had to deal. In this effort not only has the Negro benefited, but the general welfare of the community has been subserved."

I have repeated here, in some detail, the story of the founding and working of this bank, because it illustrates better than any incident I have been able to lay my hands on, how closely the moral interests of the people are interwoven with their material and economic welfare. The savings bank teaches to save, to plan, to look ahead, to build for the future. It is, in fact, one of the most effective means of developing those latent forces in the masses of the people from which the fabric of civilisation is woven. As I have said at another time in another place: "There is no wealth in the mines or in the seas

equal to that which is created by the growth and
establishment in a people of habits of thrift and
intelligent forethought." The importance of Mr.
Pettiford's work in connection with this bank is that
he, and those associated with him, have been far-
seeing enough to perceive this fact and act upon it.

It happened a few years ago that an afternoon
paper in Birmingham published a report to the
effect that there was a run on the Alabama Penny
Savings Bank, and that it was in a shaky condition.
This report grew out of the fact that it was Christmas week and an unusually large number of coloured
people were crowding into the bank to draw money
to be used during the holidays. This report spread,
and caused the officials of the bank, as well as its
friends, much uneasiness, and it was, for a time,
very uncertain as to what effect it was likely to have.
In the meantime, a white business man, a large coal
operator in the Birmingham district, heard of the
report, and at once telephoned to the Negro bank
that if, on account of the report which had been
spread, they needed any money with which to pay
depositors the next day, he would be glad to let
them have all the cash that was needed. It turned
out, however, that the good offices of the white
friend were not needed, as there was no run on
the bank.

In recent years I have had the privilege of visiting nearly every one of the communities where

Negro banks are located, and I can state without exaggeration that I have not found a single one of them that did not have the good-will and support of the white business men of the communities in which they are located. In fact, in a number of cases, the white bankers have stated that the starting of a Negro bank has increased the number of Negro depositors in the white banks, because of the general moral uplift which the influence of the coloured bank had brought about.

CHAPTER X

IN THE year 1821, one of the best known among the coloured people of Richmond, Virginia, was a Baptist preacher by the name of Lott Cary. This man had an extraordinary history. He was born a slave, about the year 1780, on a plantation thirty miles below the city of Richmond. In 1804, when he was twenty-four years of age, he was taken to the city of Richmond and employed as a common labourer in the Shockoe Tobacco Warehouse.

At this time he could neither read nor write, but one Sunday, listening to the minister in the white church which he attended read the words of Christ to Nicodemus, he was seized with the desire to learn to read. In some way or other he succeeded in carrying out the purpose he then formed. He read the Bible first but, as his mind was opened to new thoughts and ideas, he began reading every book he could lay his hands upon. His reading extended, finally, to the subject of political economy, for it is related that he was discovered one day reading Adam Smith's "Wealth of Nations." In the mean-

time, he made himself so valuable in the tobacco warehouse in which he was employed that he was given
considerable sums at different times and for different
purposes as a reward for his services. By the year
1813 he had acquired money sufficient to buy his
own liberty and that of his two children. The sum
paid was $850.

Shortly after this time the subject of colonisation
had become a subject of earnest discussion among
the coloured people, particularly of Maryland and
Virginia. Lott Cary and a brother preacher by the
name of Collin Teage, who was a saddler and
harness-maker by trade, conceived the idea of going
to Liberia to assist in founding the proposed colony
there. Although Cary was at that time in the possession of a snug little farm in the vicinity of Richmond and was earning a handsome salary of $800 a
year, he decided to give them up and go to Africa as
a missionary.

He sailed in company with Teage in January, 1821.
When the first settlement was made, the following
year, at Cape Mesurado, Lott Cary became one of
the most active agents in establishing what was,
in fact, though not in name, the first colony of the
United States. During all the difficulties and dis-
couragements of the first years of that colony he was,
next to Jehudi Ashmun, the leading spirit of the
colony. In 1826, Cary was elected to the position of
vice-agent and, after the departure of Ashmun,

continued until the time of his death the virtual head of the colony.

Cary, when asked by a brother-minister how he could think of quitting a position of so much comfort and usefulness as he at that time occupied among the coloured people of Richmond, replied: "I am an African; and in this country, however meritorious my conduct, and respectable my character, I cannot receive the credit due to either. I wish to go to a country where I shall be estimated by my merit — not by my complexion; and I feel bound to labour for my suffering race."

An interesting thing about these efforts at colonisation of Africa by American Negroes is that when the colonists reached Africa they found that they were Africans only on the outside. They were Africans in colour but not, so far as they could see, in any other respect. Two hundred and fifty years of slavery in America had converted them into Americans, at least in all their feelings and in all their traditions, just as completely as any other race which has settled on this continent. Thus Liberia has become in its laws, in its customs, and in its aspirations an American colony controlled by American Negroes.

After the settlement of Liberia and while the desire for colonisation was still strong among the free coloured people, Benjamin Lundy, the Quaker abolitionist, established a colony for Freedmen on the

Samana Peninsula on the island of Haiti in the district of what is now Santo Domingo. Among the Freedmen sent out had been slaves of David Patterson, of Grange County, North Carolina. Mr. Patterson had been converted to emancipation by Lundy's preaching and desired to emancipate his slaves, but was not able to do so until he had provided for their removal from the state.

In March, 1825, Lundy opened at Baltimore an Haitian office of emigration. He was assisted in this work by Richard Allen, the founder of the African Methodist Episcopal Church. Among the shipments from Lundy's office at that time was a colony of eighty-eight slaves, valued at $30,000, who had been emancipated by their owner, David Minge, of Charles City, Virginia. These slaves were sent to Haiti, under an arrangement with the Philanthropic Society of Haiti, which agreed to advance money for the expense of their passage with the understanding, however, that each Freedman was to repay the Society by working on its plantation for a certain length of time after his arrival. After the expiration of his apprenticeship, every Negro man, who had a family, was to receive fifteen acres of land.

Lundy continued to send colonists to Haiti under the arrangements with the Philanthropic Society for some years. In 1825, within a few weeks after his return from Haiti, he sent out a hundred and sixteen emancipated slaves and in 1829 he found it necessary to visit Haiti a second time. He took with him a small colony of Freedmen, and upon his return, announced that he had made arrangements whereby Negroes who wished to go to Haiti could obtain leases of plantations with buildings on them for seven years, the first two years free of charge, and the remaining five at a moderate rent.

In his newspaper, *The Genius of Universal Emancipation*, for November 13, 1829, there appeared an advertisement addressed "to humane and conscientious slave-holders," asking for from twenty to sixty slaves "to remove to and settle in the Republic of Haiti, where they will be forthwith invested with the rights of free men and receive constant employment and liberal wages in a healthy and pleasant section of the country." The advertisement is signed, LUNDY & GARRISON. The outbreak at Northampton shortly after this seems to have put an end to this emigration, but remnants of these colonies speaking an English dialect may be still found living on the Samana Peninsula.

Benjamin Lundy did not at this time cease his efforts to find a place of refuge for the Freedmen. He travelled through Mexico and he visited Canada, in the interest of this purpose. It was in Canada that the next settlements of Negro colonies of any size took place. Slavery had been introduced there under the French. At the request of the inhabitants a royal mandate was issued as early as 1689, permitting the holding of Indians as slaves. When Canada came under the possession of England in 1760 this form of slavery was continued and Negroes were introduced from the West Indies. But in February, 1800, the slave Robin, belonging to James Frazier, was discharged from servitude upon a writ of habeas corpus. In this case the court followed the ruling of Lord Mansfield, in the famous Somerset case, which put an end to slavery in England. The result of the case of Robin was to put an end to legalised slavery in Canada in the same way that it had been done away with in England and in Massachusetts.

Although slavery was not formally abolished by law until the act of 1833, and slaves were held to some extent in Lower Canada until that time, fugitive slaves had already begun to turn their steps in the direction of Canada in the early part of the century. A good many of these slaves found refuge among the Indians. The famous Mohawk Chief, Captain Brandt, was a holder of Negro slaves. He had large estates on Burlington Bay and Grand River. Many runaway Negroes took refuge there, were treated hospitably, and began working and living with the Indians, often adopting their customs and mode of life.

After the War of 1812, the soldiers who had served in that war brought back the news that there was a country to the north of the United States where coloured men and women were free and there was no danger of their being captured and taken back into slavery. From that time on the North Star came to have a special and peculiar interest for the discontented slaves, and many of them turned their feet northward with no other guide than its light to direct them.

In 1850, it is said that there were thirty thousand fugitives from slavery in Canada. After the passage of the Fugitive Slave Law, this number was greatly increased. In 1860, the number of coloured people in Canada was variously estimated at from 60,000 to 75,000, of which it is said 15,000 were free-born.

As a result of this influx of refugees, there grew up on the outskirts of the cities numerous communities of coloured people. In 1855, Benjamin Drew, who had visited these communities in the interest of the anti-slavery societies, published an account of the condition of the fugitives of fourteen different settlements. These were located at St. Catherine's, Toronto, Hamilton, Galt, London, Queens-Bush, Chatham, Buxton, Dawn, Windsor, Sandwich, Amherstburg, Colchester, and Gosfield, all in the province of Ontario. The most important and interesting of these colonies were the Dawn Settlement, at Dresden, the Elgin Settlement at Buxton, and the Refugees' Home near Windsor.

In 1849, the Reverend William King, a Presbyterian clergyman from Louisiana, emancipated his slaves and settled them on the tract which afterward became known as the "Elgin Settlement." His company of fifteen Freedmen formed the nucleus of the community which was called Buxton, in honour of the noted philanthropist, Thomas Fowell Buxton. This community grew rapidly and in 1850 it was incorporated as the Elgin Association. Under the direction of Mr. King, the plan was carried out which provided for the parcelling of the land into farms of fifty acres each, which were to be sold to the colonists at the government price of $2.50 per acre. A court of arbitration was established for the adjudication of disputes, and a day and Sunday school, supported by a missionary society of the Presbyterian Church of Canada, were started, in order to give the colonists the instruction they needed. Twelve years later, in 1862, when Dr. Samuel G. Howe visited this community, he found a settlement of about one thousand men, women, and children, who owned two thousand acres of land, one-third of which had been paid for, including the principal and interest.

"Buxton," said Dr. Howe, in his report, "is certainly a very interesting place. Sixteen years ago, it was a wilderness. Now good highways are laid out in all directions through the forest; and by their side, standing back thirty-three feet from the road, are about two hundred cottages, all built after the same pattern, all looking neat and comfortable. Around each one is a cleared space, of several acres, which is well cultivated. The fences are in good order, the barns seem well filled, and cattle and horses and pigs and poultry abound. There are signs of industry and thrift and comfort everywhere; signs of intemperance, idleness, of want, nowhere. There is no tavern and no groggery; but there is a chapel and a schoolhouse."

Reverend Mr. King said: "I consider this settlement has done as well as a white settlement would have done under the same circumstances."

The colony known as Refugees' Home, which was located at Windsor, Ontario, directly opposite Detroit, was started by Henry Bibb, himself a fugitive slave. Soon after the passage of the Fugitive Slave Law of 1850 he suggested the formation of "a society which should aim to purchase 30,000 acres of Government land . . . for the homeless refugees from American slavery to settle upon."

In the first year of the association's existence forty lots of twenty-five acres each were disposed of, and arrangements were made for a school and a church. Mrs. Laura S. Haviland, who opened a day school and a Sunday school there in the fall of 1852, says: "They had erected a frame house for school and meeting purposes. The settlers had built for themselves small log houses, and cleared from one to five acres each on their heavily timbered land, and raised corn and potatoes and other garden vegetables. A few put in several hundred acres of wheat and were doing well for the first year."

The oldest of these communities in Canada, and in many respects the most interesting, was the Dawn Settlement at Dresden. It was at this settlement that Josiah Henson, the original "Uncle Tom" in Harriet Beecher Stowe's story, lived and worked for many years. In the year 1842 a convention of coloured people was called to decide upon the expenditure of some $1,500 which had been collected in England by James C. Fuller, a Quaker. Reverend Hiram Wilson, a missionary, and Josiah Henson were on the committee to decide in what way this money should be expended. It was determined, upon the suggestion of Mr. Henson, to start a "manual labour school, where the children could be taught those elements of knowledge which are usually the occupations of a grammar-school; and where the boy could be taught, in addition, the practice of some mechanic art, and the girl could be instructed in those domestic arts which are the proper occupation and ornament of her sex."*

In 1852 there were, according to the first annual report of the Anti-slavery Society of Canada, sixty pupils attending this school, and settlers on the land of the institute had increased to five hundred.

---

* "Father Henson's Story of His Own Life," p. 169. Quoted in Siebert's "Underground Railroad," p. 206.

In the neighbourhood of the school there was a coloured population of between three and four thousand.

Josiah Henson, who was so long connected with this colony, was born a slave at Fort Tobacco, Maryland, and escaped to Canada in 1828. He became a Methodist minister and an anti-slavery lecturer of considerable influence. He made three trips to England and, on his final visit to that country, in 1876, he was entertained by Queen Victoria.

After the Civil War the interests which had brought these colonies into existence had disappeared. Many of the coloured people, particularly those who had gone out to Canada since 1850, moved back to the United States. The communities gradually dwindled away or were absorbed into neighbouring cities, on whose outskirts they had grown up. In the winter of 1895 and 1896, when I made a visit to several cities in Canada, I had an opportunity to get information from some of these fugitives. In Toronto, there was living at the time I visited the city, Dr. A. R. Abbott, who had graduated from the Toronto Medical University before or shortly after the breaking out of the Civil War in the United States. He enlisted in one of the coloured regiments and was among the first coloured men to be admitted to the Army Medical Service. After the war he returned to Toronto, where he practised his profession for many years.

It is not often one meets a coloured man acting in the capacity of mayor of a city of 200,000 inhabitants, but I met on this visit to Toronto a Negro who had occupied that position during the previous summer, while the regular mayor was absent in Europe. This man was the Honourable William P. Hubbard, president of the Toronto Board of Control, a body which, in the government of Toronto, occupies the position of the mayor's cabinet. Mr. Hubbard was born in Toronto in 1848. His parents, who were of African, Anglo-Saxon and Indian origin, came to Canada from Richmond, Virginia, in 1844. They had been, like the parents of Dr. Abbott, "free people of colour." His father, having been employed for several years as a carver in a Richmond hotel, had accumulated something like $800 before he left the South. The family settled on a little piece of land on the outskirts of the city, where his mother kept for many years a market garden, while his father worked in the city. After getting a pretty good education in the Toronto schools, young Hubbard went to work as an apprentice in a bakery shop, where he later served eight years as foreman. After that he went into the livery business with his brother, Alexander. In this business he prospered, and putting his savings into real estate, soon accumulated a small fortune. I was told at the time of my visit that Mr. Hubbard paid taxes on $36,000 worth of property. In 1894, he was elected to the position of alderman from the Tenth Ward. He held that position until he was elected, in 1899, to the position he held at the time of my visit. At this time Mr. J. C. Hamilton, who has made a study of the Negro in Canada, said: "Hubbard has about the best record of any alderman we have. I should not wonder if he would be mayor of Toronto some day."

I learned also that Mr. Hubbard had a reputation outside of Toronto and throughout the Province of Ontario, for he has been elected, during previous years, president of the Ontario Municipal Association.

I referred, in an earlier chapter, to the town and colony of Mound Bayou, which is situated in the centre of the Yazoo Mississippi Delta, about midway between Vicksburg and Memphis. This colony which, as I have said, was founded by Isaiah T. Montgomery, who had been a slave of Joseph Davis, the brother of the president of the Confederacy, was started about 1890. I frequently have heard Mr. Montgomery tell the story of the way in which he succeeded in arousing the interest of the first settlers in this project. When he first went there the country was a perfect wilderness; it was not believed that white men could live in that region, and that was one reason that it was decided to try the experiment of settling a colony of coloured people there. Mr. Montgomery finally succeeded in inducing a party of coloured men to come down and look over the country. A South-bound train dropped them off at a saw-mill in the midst of the woods one morning, and they walked several miles up the railroad track to the site that Mr. Montgomery had selected for the town.

"We had been pretty silent on the way up the track," said Mr. Montgomery, "for we were in the midst of a perfect wilderness. After we reached the point where I desired to locate, I turned and pointed in the direction of the woods and said to the men: 'You see what this country is, but you should remember this whole state was once like this. Your fathers cleared it, cultivated it, and made it what it now is. They did this for the white man. Now, the question is, can we do the same thing for ourselves?'

"Well," continued Mr. Montgomery, "some of them saw the point, and with these men we started in and began cutting down the timber, and making it into railway ties. Then we built the saw-mill and, by that time, the town was fairly started."

I visited the town of Mound Bayou in the fall of 1908. I found a little village, with between five hundred and a thousand inhabitants, which was the centre of a community of perhaps four or five thousand people, among whom there was not a single white man. There were twenty or thirty little country stores, three cotton gins, a bank, which at the time had resources amounting to $100,000, and I was told had paid 10 per cent. dividend on its stock of $25,000. The town looked raw, but it looked like the real thing. I learned that it had been growing slowly but steadily. During the whole period of its existence an earnest effort was being made to build up the schools, and to adapt the teaching in them to the actual needs of the people.

During my visit I made an address to the people of that colony. As there was no hall sufficiently large enough to accommodate the crowds that had assembled, I spoke from a platform erected upon the foundation of a new cotton-seed oil mill which was being erected at the cost of $40,000, a sum collected among the coloured people in different parts of the State of Mississippi. The interesting thing to me was that I found there a sober, earnest, orderly community of coloured people, who had the respect of all their neighbours, including the sheriff of the county, and were going forward in the solution of their problem, along the lines of orderly industrial progress.

Mound Bayou is, so far as I know, the oldest exclusively Negro community established since the War. There is, however, a flourishing little town in Oklahoma called Boley, which was started in 1903. There is a story told in regard to Boley, which, even if it is not true in all its details, illustrates the temper of the coloured people and their relations to the white people in that region. Early in the spring of 1903, so the story goes, a number of gentle-men were discussing, at the neighbouring city of Weleetka, the inevitable race question. The point at issue was the capability of the Negro for self-government. One of the gentlemen, who hap-pened to be connected with the Fort Smith Railway, maintained that the Negro had never been given a fair chance; that if Negroes had been given a white man's chance they would have proved themselves as capable of self-government as any other people of the same degree of culture and education. The other gentlemen naturally asserted the contrary, and the result of this argument was, to state it briefly, Boley.

Just at this time a number of town sites were being laid out along the railway which connects Guthrie, Oklahoma, with Fort Smith, Arkansas. In order to put the capability of the Negro for self-government to test, there was established in August, 1903, seventy-two miles east of Guthrie, the site of a Negro town. It was called Boley after the man who built that sec-tion of the railway, and it was widely advertised as a town which was to be exclusively under the control of Negroes.

One thing that, perhaps, made this town attractive to coloured people was the fact that there are a number of communities in Oklahoma which rigidly exclude Negroes from settlement. On the other hand, there has grown up in other parts of Okla-homa, communities, like the little town of Taft, which, although not settled exclusively by Negroes, are sometimes referred to as "Negro towns," because of the large proportion of the Negroes in the population.

A large proportion of the settlers of Boley were farmers from Texas, Arkansas and Mississippi. The proprietor of the largest cotton-gin was, in 1907, C. W. Perry, who came from Marshall, Texas. Perry had worked in the railway machine shops for a number of years and had gained enough of the trade of a machinist to be able to set up his own cotton-gin and the machinery connected with it. E. L. Lugrande, one of the principal stockholders in the second bank in Boley, came to this new country, like many others, to get land. He had owned 418 acres of land in Denton County, which he had purchased some years before at a price of four and five dollars an acre. In recent years land has gone up in price and Mr. Lugrande was able to sell his property for something like fifty dollars an acre. He came to Boley and purchased a large tract of land just outside the town. Now a large part of this acreage is in the centre of the town. Mr. Lugrande is representative of the better class of Negro farmers who, for several years past, have been steadily moving into the new lands in the West.

I might add, in conclusion, that from all I have been able to learn Boley, which, like Mound Bayou, is entirely controlled by Negroes, is one of the most peaceful towns in that part of Oklahoma. When I was at Topeka, Kansas, in 1907, I was told that not a single citizen of Boley had been arrested for two years.

I have spoken of the settlements of Negroes in Liberia, in Canada, and in the different parts of the United States in the same connection, because they seem to me to represent the same wholesome desire of members of my race to do something for which they will be respected, not merely as individuals but as a race; to achieve something in their own way and in their own right, which would be a worthy contribution to American civilisation.

The story told by one of the most successful citizens of Boley, for example, illustrates the motives which have inspired the building of this bustling and progressive little Negro city. This man had been a railway brakeman, was well respected by his employers, owned a little home of his own, and had a bank account. When it was learned that he was selling his property in Texas in order to emigrate to Oklahoma a number of the prominent white citizens of the community called upon him and asked him why he was going to leave. "We know you," they said, "and you know us. We are behind you and will protect you."

"Well," he replied, "I have always had an ambition to do something for myself. I do not always want to be led; I want to do a little leading."

Whatever one may be disposed to think of this segregation of the white and black races which one sees going on, to a greater or lesser extent, in every section of the country, it is certain that there is a temporary advantage to the Negro race in the building up of these "race towns." They enable the masses of the people to find a freer expression to their native energies and ambitions than they are able to find elsewhere, and, at the same time, give them an opportunity to gain that experience in coöperation, self-direction, and self-control, which it is hard for them to get in the same degree elsewhere.

In the year 1905 I had occasion to visit Winston-Salem, in North Carolina, to speak in a public meeting in the interest of the Slater industrial and State Normal School, at that place. This school had been established some years before by Mr. S. G. Atkins, who is now Secretary of Education in the A. M. E. Zion Church. He had been a teacher in the public schools in Winston. In 1892 he moved to some high ground outside the city and built himself a home. A few years later he started a little Industrial School at this place. As time went on the school increased in size and importance and a little community grew up around it.

After the school had been established, Mr. R. J. Reynolds, of the Reynolds Tobacco Company, gave Mr. Atkins $4,500 to assist him in building out there a hospital for coloured people. Mr.

Reynolds was a large employer of coloured labour in the tobacco factory, and he assisted in establishing this hospital in order to made some adequate provision for his own employees in case of sickness. The thing that impressed me at the time about this little community was the fine location chosen for it and the number of thrifty little cottages which I saw growing up, nearly all of which, I learned, had been paid for by the people who lived in them.

This was the first time, I think, that my attention had been specially drawn to a number of quiet, clean, thrifty little Negro communities that are growing up everywhere in the South at the present day, frequently in the neighbourhood of some school. Particularly has this been true in the last ten years, since Negro banks and building and loan associations have sprung up to encourage the people in all parts of the South, as well as in some of the Northern cities, to purchase their own homes. Since my visit to Winston-Salem in 1905 the coloured people in that city have, I understand, prospered greatly. This is due, to some extent, to the fact that since the organisation of the Tobacco Trust they have had steady employment in the tobacco factories, but it is also due in a large part to the assistance and encouragement the coloured people have received from the white people of that city, particularly from the descendants of the Moravians of Salem.

In May, 1907, the Forsythe Savings and Trust Co.

was organised at Winston-Salem.   This bank, which
was organised largely for the purpose of assisting
coloured people in securing homes, reported in
December, 1908, that it had transacted a volume of
business from the time it was organised which
amounted to $302,738.86.   In close connection with
this bank there was organised the Twin City Reality
Company, of which Mr. S. G. Atkins was president,
and Andrew Jackson Brown vice-president.

Mr. Brown is an interesting character.   He came
from Lynchburg to Winston to work in the tobacco
factory.   After he was forty years old, his home having been broken up by the death of his wife, he
decided to go to school.   He made his home in the
little community, Columbia Heights, which had
sprung up around Mr. Atkins's school.   He had been
the chief agent of the True Reformers' Association
in the region before this time, and he supported himself mainly in this way while he was in school.   He
was a man of simple manners and sturdy honesty,
and has become, I have been told, a very positive
constructive force in his community.

What I have described as taking place in Winston-
Salem has been going on, in much the same way, in
every other part of the country where any considerable
portion of the population belongs to the Negro race.
In some places, like Baltimore, Philadelphia, and
New York, whole avenues for considerable distances
have been taken up by coloured people who have

moved out of the slums, in which the masses of the Negro people are usually to be found during the first years of their life in the cities. In these new districts they have been building comfortable and frequently handsome houses.

Perhaps I cannot better describe the change that has taken place, in this and other parts of the South, than in the words of a Southern white man who has watched the changes I have referred to, and has been able to appreciate their significance. Writing in the *Century* Magazine for June, 1906, Harry Stillwell Edwards, speaking of this matter, says:

Thirty years ago, when I was a boy in Georgia's central city, one part of the suburbs given over to Negroes contained an aggregation of unfurnished, ill-kept, rented cabins, the occupants untidy and, for the most part, shiftless. Such a thing as virtue among the female members was in but few instances conceded. Girls from this section roamed the streets at night, and vice was met with on every corner. Recently, in company with a friend, who was interested in a family residing in the same community, I visited it. I found many families occupying their own homes, flowers growing in the yards and on the porches, curtains at the windows, and an air of homelike serenity overflowing the entire district. In the house we entered, the floors were carpeted, the white walls were hung with pictures, the mantels and the tables held bric-à-brac. In one room was a parlour organ, in another a sewing-machine, and in another a piano, where a girl sat at practice.

In conversation with the people of the house and neighbourhood we heard good ideas expressed in excellent language and discovered that every one with whom we came in contact was possessed of sufficient education to read and write, while many were much further advanced.

Just one generation lies between the two conditions set forth, and the change may be said to indicate the urban Negro's mental and material progress throughout the whole South. Of those of us who see only gloom ahead for the Negro, the question may fairly be asked: Where else in the world is there a people developing so rapidly?

In the course of my journeys about the country I have had an opportunity to go into many Negro homes in all parts of the United States, where I have found, not merely the comforts, but some of the elegancies of life. Books, pictures, fine table-linen, furniture, carpets, and not infrequently mementoes of travel in many parts of this country and of Europe. What interests me more than anything else, however, is to see the number of them who are collecting books, histories, pictures, and all kinds of material concerning their own race or of work by members of their own race, showing evidences of its progress.

Aside from Chicago, Philadelphia is the only city, so far as I know, in which a systematic and careful study has been made of the condition of the Negro population. In 1897, Professor W. E. B. Du Bois estimated that Negroes owned $5,000,000 in that city. A more recent investigation made by Richard R. Wright, Jr., indicates that the number of home owners has increased 71 per cent. since 1900. In 1907 he stated that within twenty months seven real estate companies had been organised among Negroes in Philadelphia. One of these had succeeded in providing homes for twenty-five Negroes within a year.

Probably the most important influence in assisting coloured people to obtain homes in Philadelphia has been the Berean Building and Loan Association, established in connection with the Berean Presbyterian Church, which is one of the three coloured Presbyterian churches in Philadelphia. According to a report published in 1906, this association has purchased one hundred and forty-five homes for its members, valued at $304,500 and has paid back matured stock to the value of more than $80,000. The Berean is the largest and the oldest of seven building and loan associations of Philadelphia.

So far as I know there is no city in the United States where the coloured people own so many comfortable and attractive homes in proportion to the population, as in the city of Baltimore. In what is known as the Druid Hill district of the city, there are, perhaps, fifteen thousand coloured people. For fifteen blocks along Druid Hill Avenue nearly every house is occupied or owned by coloured people. In the latter part of the ninties Dr. R. M. Hall, who is one of the oldest coloured physicians and one of the wealthiest coloured men in Baltimore, moved into 1019 Druid Hill Avenue. He was almost the first coloured man to make his home upon that street. Since that time the white people who lived there have moved out into the suburbs and the coloured people have moved in to take their places. I have been told that fully 50 per cent. of the coloured people on Druid Hill Avenue own their homes, though, so far as I know, no systematic investigation has been made of the facts. This part of the city has had for a number of years its own coloured representative, Harry S. Cummings, in the city council. This district which Mr. Cummings represented in the city council in 1908 was that, I have been told, in which, forty-five years before, his parents had been held as slaves.

CHAPTER XI

THERE is an African folk-tale which tells of a mighty hunter who one day went into the forest in search of big game. He was unsuccessful in his quest, and sat down to rest. Meanwhile he heard some strange and pleasing noises, coming from a dense thicket. As he sat spellbound, a party of forest spirits came dancing into view, and the hunter discovered it was they who were making the sounds he had heard. The spirits disappeared, and the hunter returned to his home, when, after considerable effort, he found that he was able to imitate the sounds which he had heard. In this way, it is said, the black man gained the gift of song.

The Bantus of South Africa say that African music at the present time is not what it used to be in the old days. There was a time, they say, before the coming of the white man, when musicians had power to charm the beasts from the forest and the birds from the trees. Be this as it may, we find at the present day that singing is a universal practice among the Africans in every part of the Dark

Continent.   The porters, carrying their loads along
the narrow forest paths, sing of the loved ones in
their far-away homes.   In the evening the people
of the villages gather around the fire and sing for
hours.   These songs refer to war, to hunting, and
to the spirits that dwell in the deep woods.   In
them all the wild and primitive life of the people is
reflected and interpreted.

When the Negro slaves were carried from Africa
to America they brought with them this gift of song.
Nothing else which the native African possessed,
not even his sunny disposition, his ready sympathy
or his ability to adapt himself to new and strange
conditions, has been more useful to him in his life
in America than this.   When all other avenues of
expression were closed to him, and when, sometimes,
his burden seemed too great for him to bear, the
African found a comfort and a solace in these simple
and beautiful songs, which are the spontaneous
utterance of his heart.

Nothing tells more truly what the Negro's life
in slavery was, than the songs in which he succeeded,
sometimes, in expressing his deepest thoughts and
feelings.   What, for example, could express more
eloquently the feelings of despair which sometimes
overtook the slave than these simple and expressive
words:

> O Lord, O my Lord! O my good Lord!
> Keep me from sinking down.

The songs which the Negro sang in slavery, however, were by no means always sad. There were many joyous occasions upon which the natural happy and cheerful nature of the Negro found expression in songs of a light and cheerful character. There is a difference, however, between the music of Africa and that of her transplanted children. There is a new note in the music which had its origin on the Southern plantations, and in this new note the sorrow and the suffering which came from serving in a strange land finds expression.

The new songs are those in which the slave speaks, not merely the sorrow that he feels, but also the new hope which the Christian religion has lighted in his bosom. The African slave accepted the teachings of the Christian religion more eagerly than he did anything else his master had to teach him. He seemed to feel instinctively that there was something in the teachings of the Bible which he needed. He accepted the story that the Bible told him literally, and, in the songs he composed under its influence, he has given some wonderfully graphic and vivid pictures of the persons and places of which the Bible speaks, as he understood them. Grotesque as some of these pictures may seem, they are merely the vivid and literal interpretation of what he heard, and all of them are conceived in the spirit of the deepest reverence.

Neither the words nor the melodies of these songs

originated after the manner in which music is ordinarily composed nowadays. In fact, these songs are not the music of any one individual. They were composed under the excitement of a religious meeting. Some black bard, under the inspiration of the moment, flung out a musical theme which was taken up by the whole company, and words and music were thus spontaneously composed upon the spot. These songs, still sung with the old-time fervour in the little country churches throughout the South, were created in the same way in which the students of literature and language tell us that the early Scotch and English ballads were composed, by crowds of men and women singing together.

Thomas Wentworth Higginson was, I believe, one of the first, if not the first man to make a study of this music of the slaves. While he was in charge of a black regiment at Port Royal, South Carolina, he had abundant opportunity to hear these songs, as they were sung by the Negroes, who had been freshly recruited from the plantations in that region. In his interesting book, "Army Life in a Black Regiment," he has given a very vivid and a very accurate description of this music. Among other things he says:

I had been a faithful student of the Scottish ballads, and had always envied Sir Walter Scott the delight of tracing them out among their own heather, and of writing them down piecemeal from the lips of ancient crones. It was a strange enjoyment, therefore, to be suddenly brought into the midst of a kindred world of

unwritten songs, as simple and indigenous as the Border Min-
strelsy, more uniformly plaintive, almost always more quaint,
and often as essentially poetic. . . . Almost all their songs
were thoroughly religious in their tones, however quaint their
expression, and were in a minor key, both as to words and music.
The attitude is always the same, and as a commentary on the life
of the race, is infinitely pathetic. Nothing but patience for this
life — nothing but triumph in the next.

One of the songs which Mr. Higginson quotes,
and which he regards as one of the most expressive
songs that he heard while he was in the South, is
the following:

> I know moon rise, I know star rise,
>   Lay dis body down,
> I'll walk in de graveyard,
>   To lay dis body down.
>
> I'll lie in de grave and stretch out my arms,
>   Lay dis body down,
> I'll go to de Judgment in de evenin' of de day,
>   When I lay dis body down.
> And my soul and your soul will meet in de day,
>   When I lay dis body down.

"Never, it seems to me," says Mr. Higginson,
"since man first lived and suffered, was his infinite
longing for peace uttered more plaintively than in
that line, 'I'll lie in de grave and stretch out my
arms.'"

Another and more familiar one of the plantation
hymns which Mr. Higginson quotes is the following:

> O wrestlin' Jacob! Jacob!
> Day's a-breakin';
>   I will not let you go!

O wrestlin Jacob! Jacob!
Day's a-breakin'
    He will not let me go!
O! I hold my brudder
Wid a tremblin' han'!
    I would not let him go!
I hold my sister
Wid a tremblin' han'!
    I would not let her go!

There is something in this slave music that touches the common heart of man.   Everywhere that it has been heard this music has awakened a responsive chord in the minds and hearts of those who heard it. Antonin Dvorak, the eminent Bohemian composer, who lived for several years in this country, in his admirable symphony, "Out of the New World," used several themes taken from these Negro folk songs. S. Coleridge Taylor, the well-known coloured English composer, has used this music for many of his best known piano compositions. Edward Everett Hale once said it was the only American music.

Not only is the music of these songs strangely touching and beautiful, but the songs themselves contain many striking and significant expressions, as Mr. Higginson has pointed out, which indicate a native talent in the masses of the people for poetic expression. For example, one of these songs in referring to the Judgment Day, describes it as the time "when the stars begin to fall."   Another of these songs suggests the terrors of the last Judgment, in the refrain, "O Rocks, fall on me."

There was a time, directly after the War, when the coloured people, particularly those who had a little education, tried to get away from and forget these old slave songs. If they sang them still, it was about the home and not in public. It was not until after years, when other people began to learn and take an interest in these songs, that these people began to understand the inspiration and the quality that was in them. It is an indication of the change that has gone on among the Negro people in recent years that more and more they are beginning to take pride in these folk-songs of the race, and are seeking to preserve them and the memories that they evoke.

As an illustration of what I have said, I cannot do better than quote the lines of James W. Johnson, a Negro poet and writer of popular songs, which suggest, better than anything I have heard or read, what seems to me the true significance of this music. In the *Century* Magazine for November, 1908, the following poem was published, addressed to the unknown singers who first sang these heart songs of my race:

O BLACK AND UNKNOWN BARDS!

O black and unknown bards of long ago,
　How came your lips to touch the sacred fire?
How, in your darkness, did you come to know
　The power and beauty of the minstrel's lyre?

Who first from midst his bonds lifted his eyes?
  Who first from out the still watch, lone and long,
Feeling the ancient faith of prophets rise
  Within his dark-kept soul, burst into song?

There is a wide, wide wonder in it all,
  That from degraded rest and servile toil,
The fiery spirit of the seer should call
  These simple children of the sun and soil.
O black singers, gone, forgot, unfamed,
  You — you alone, of all the long, long line
Of those who've sung untaught, unknown, unnamed,
  Have stretched out upward, seeking the divine.

You sang not deeds of heroes or of kings:
  No chant of bloody war, nor exulting pæan
Of arms-won triumphs; but your humble strings
  You touched in chords with music empyrean.
You sang far better than you knew, the songs
  That for your listeners' hungry hearts sufficed
Still live — but more than this to you belongs:
  You sang a race from wood and stone to Christ.

I have already referred to the fact that Thomas
Wentworth Higginson was the first, so far as I know,
to take note of this slave music and make a serious
study of it. The first man who seems to have realised that this music would touch the popular heart,
if it could be made known, was George L. White,
the man who was responsible for the success of the
Jubilee Singers of Fisk University, Nashville, Tennessee. It was the Fisk Jubilee Singers who first
made the Negro folk-music popular in America
and in Europe. They not only made this music
popular, but upon their return from their second

concert tour, in 1874, they brought back ninety thousand dollars as their contribution to Fisk University.

Perhaps one thing that made the singing of these songs more effective was that the singers themselves had, in many cases, been slaves, or were directly descended from slave parents, and they felt the music they sang more deeply than others who have tried to sing it since. One of the most interesting of these singers was Ella Sheppard, who was born in Nashville, in 1851. Ella Sheppard's father ran a livery stable in Nashville before the War. He had succeeded in purchasing his own freedom for $1,800, and was hoping to be able to purchase that of his wife and family, when suddenly he was separated from them by the fact that his wife's master removed from Nashville to Mississippi. Mr. Sheppard heard very little from his wife and child after this until one day a white man, who had been in Mississippi on business, returned and told him that his little girl was dying from neglect. He added that, as the child was sickly, possibly her father would be able to purchase her for a small sum. Mr. Sheppard started to Mississippi, purchased his child for $350, and brought her back to Nashville. Shortly after this he attempted to purchase his wife, but for some reason or other, after the sale had nearly been completed, her master refused to sell her and she did not succeed in gaining her freedom until the Civil War finally emancipated her.

Before freedom came, Mr. Sheppard failed in business and was compelled to move secretly to Cincinnati to prevent his creditors seizing his children for debt. There Ella Sheppard gained a little education in what was known as the Seventh Street Coloured School. When she was thirteen years old she commenced taking lessons in music from a German music teacher. About this time her father died and she was compelled, as she says, to go to work, for herself "in right good earnest." Fortunately, she made the acquaintance of Mr. J. P. Ball, of Cincinnati, who adopted her and gave her a thorough musical education, with the understanding that she was to repay him at some future time.

"I took twelve lessons," she says, "in vocal music of Madame Rivi. I was the only coloured pupil, and was not allowed to tell who my teacher was. More than that, I went up the back way to reach my teacher and received my lesson in the back room upstairs from nine to a quarter of ten at night."

After teaching school for a time, Ella Sheppard entered Fisk University, where, by teaching music and sewing at odd moments, or when she was confined to her bed, as she frequently was by illness, she managed to make her way through the University until she joined the first campaign of the Jubilee Singers through the Northern states. Ella Sheppard is still living in Nashville. She is now the wife of Reverend George W. Moore, who is the field superintendent of the church work of the American Missionary Association, and one of the most distinguished men of his race. Mr. Moore was, for a number of years, pastor of the Lincoln Memorial Church in Washington, District of Columbia. In all the work which this church attempted to do for the masses of the coloured people in Washington, Mr. Moore was greatly assisted by the labours and counsel of his wife.

Another distinguished member of the Jubilee Singers' Band, as it was called, was Jennie Jackson, who afterward became the wife of Professor DeHart, until recently teacher in the public schools of Cincinnati. Jennie Jackson was born free, but her grandfather was a slave and body-servant of General Andrew Jackson. During the War and afterward her mother supported the family by washing and ironing. It was by assisting her mother in this work that Jennie Jackson earned enough money to make her way through school, until, her voice having attracted the attention of her teachers, she became a member of the Jubilee Singers, whose fortunes she shared until the end of their campaign.

Maggie Porter was another of the singers who distinguished herself. She was born in 1853, at Lebanon, Tennessee. Her master was Henry

Frazier, and the owner of some two hundred slaves. Her mother was a house servant, and Maggie was brought up in the household of her master. In January, 1866, when the Fisk School was first opened, Maggie Porter was one of the three hundred pupils who gathered, during the first week, in the old hospital barracks. She was one of the first of the pupils at the Fisk School to enlist as a teacher in the country districts. She taught in different parts of Tennessee until Mr. White, who knew of her natural musical talent, sent for her to take the part of Queen Esther in the cantata that the students of Fisk University were preparing to give. She was so successful in this part that she became a member of the first band of Jubilee Singers that went out from Fisk in the following fall of 1871. After the disbandment of the Jubilee Singers Maggie Porter travelled for a number of years as a concert singer in various parts of the United States. Her name at present is Maggie Porter Cole. She is living with her husband in Detroit, where she has a beautiful home, and is making her life of great service to her people.

Of the other singers of whom I have been able to get some recent record, I recall the name of Thomas Rutling, who is now a teacher of English language and literature in a school at Geneva, Switzerland. He was the son of a runaway slave, and was born while his mother was hiding out in the woods in Wilson County, Tennessee.

There was, as I have said, a peculiar pathos about the old slave songs that invariably touched the hearts of those who heard them. Through these songs the slaves found a means of telling what was in their hearts when almost every other means of expressing their thoughts and feelings was denied them. For this reason, if for no other, they will always remain a sacred heritage of the Negro race.

The creation of music so original, by a people so wholly lacking in musical education, indicates a natural taste and talent for music in the Negro race which, perhaps, has not been equalled by any other primitive people. This native talent has manifested itself not only in the songs, spontaneously produced by the slaves on the plantation, but by the ease with which Negro musicians have been able to execute and interpret the music of all other peoples.

The most noted example of this native talent for music in a member of the Negro race is Thomas Greene Bethune, who was better known under the name of "Blind Tom." Blind Tom was born near Columbus, Georgia, May 25, 1849, and died July 3, 1908. He was blind from birth, and while deficient in some other directions, he manifested from infancy an extraordinary fondness for musical sounds. He is

said to have exhibited his musical talent before he
was two years old.

It is said that he showed, from the first, great
interest in every kind of musical sound, "from the
soft breathing of the flute to the harsh gratings
of the corn-sheller." He also showed a remarkable
power for judging the lapse of time. There was a
clock in his master's house that struck the hour.
Every hour in the day, just before this clock made
the sharp click preparatory to striking, Tom would
be there and remain until the hour was struck, and
it was evident that he took the greatest delight in
the musical tones which the clock gave forth. Frequently in the evening the young ladies of his master's family would sit on the steps and sing. At
such times Tom would invariably, if he were allowed
to do so, come to the house and sing with them. One
evening one of the young ladies said to her father:
"Pa, Tom sings beautifully, and he don't have to
learn any tune, for as soon as we sing he sings right
along with us." Then she added: "He sings
fine seconds to anything we sing."

When Tom was about four years of age his master
purchased a piano and brought it to the house. The
first note from this new instrument brought Tom
into the house. He was permitted to indulge his
curiosity by running his fingers over the keys. As
long as anyone would play on this piano Tom was
content to stay out in the yard, where he would

dance and caper to the music, but as soon as the
music ceased he would try to get to the instrument
in order to continue the sweet sounds in which he
took such delight.

One night when the parlour door had been left open,
Tom escaped from his mother and crept into the
parlour.   Early in the morning the young ladies of
the household were awakened by hearing some one
playing upon the piano.   The music continued to
reach their ears from time to time, until at the usual
hour they arose and went into the parlour where,
to their astonishment, they saw Tom playing the
piano in what seemed to them a remarkable way.
Notwithstanding this was his first attempt to play
this instrument, they noted that he played with
both hands, and used black as well as white keys.

After a time Tom was allowed free access to the
piano and commenced to play everything he heard.
After he had mastered all the music that he heard
any one play, he commenced composing for himself.
He would sit at the piano for hours playing over
pieces he had heard, then he would go out, run and
jump about the yard for a little while and, after
returning, play something of his own.   If any one
asked him what he was playing, he replied that it
was something that the wind said to him, or "what
the birds said to me," "what the trees said to me,"
or what something else said to him.   Speaking of
the natural sense for music which this strangely

gifted Negro boy displayed, the biographer of Blind Tom says:

There was but one thing that seemed to give Tom as much pleasure as the sound of the piano. Between a wing and the body of the dwelling there is a hall, on the roof of which the rain falls from the roof to the dwelling, and runs thence down a gutter. There was in this water something so enchanting to Tom, that from his early childhood to the time he left home, whenever it rained, whether by night or day, he would go into the passage and remain as long as the rain continued. When he was less than five years of age, having been there during a severe thunderstorm, he went to the piano and played what is now known as his "Rain Storm" and said it was what the rain, the wind, and the thunder said to him.*

When Tom was eight years of age he was permitted to appear in a regular concert in the city of Columbus, at which a German, the leading musician of the town, was present. The next day this man was asked to undertake Tom's musical education. He replied: "No, sir, I can't teach him anything; he knows more of music than any of us know or can learn. All that can be done for him is to let him hear fine playing. He will work it all out by himself after a while, but he will do it sooner by hearing fine music."

This man was correct. Tom did work it all out by himself after a while, and became one of the most noted musicians in the world. He gave concerts in every important city of the United States, and in all the principal cities of Europe. It was said of him,

* J. M. Trotter. "Music and Some Highly Musical People," p. 146.

as showing the remarkable power which he possessed, that he could stand with his back to a piano and let any number of chords be struck simultaneously, thereupon he would instantly be able to tell every note sounded, showing that his memory retained all the notes distinctly, and in such a manner that he was able to discriminate between every sound made.

In 1867 Blind Tom gave a concert in Glasgow, Scotland. The following morning the Glasgow *Herald*, in its account of his performance, made the following interesting statement, which gives a very accurate estimate of Tom's musical talent at this time:

Mozart, when a mere child, was noted for the delicacy of his ear and for his ability to produce music on a first hearing; but Burney, in his History of Music, records no instance at all coming up to this Negro boy for attainments in phonetics, and his power of retention and reproduction of sound. He plays first a number of difficult passages from the best composers; and then any one is invited to come forward and perform any piece he likes, the more difficult the more acceptable, and if original the more preferable. Tom immediately sits down at the piano, and produces verbatim et literatim the whole of what he has just heard. To show that it is not at all necessary that he should be acquainted with any piece beforehand to produce it, he invited any one to strike any number of notes simultaneously with the hand or with both hands; and immediately, as we heard him do yesterday, he repeats at length, and without the slightest hesitation, the whole of the letters with all their inflections representing the notes. Nor are his wondrous powers confined to the piano, on which he can produce imitations of various instruments and play two different tunes — one in

common time and a second in triple — while he sings a third, but
he can, with the voice, produce with the utmost accuracy any note
which his audience may suggest.

Some of the most interesting music, produced
by the Negro slaves, was handed down from the
days when the French and Spanish had possession
of Louisiana. All these songs, many of which
have been preserved through the writings of George
W. Cable, were composed in the Creole dialect of
Louisiana.

From the free Negroes of Louisiana there sprang
up, during slavery days, a number of musicians and
artists who distinguished themselves in foreign
countries to which they removed, because of the prejudice which existed against coloured people. Among
them was Eugène Warburg, who went to Italy and
distinguished himself as a sculptor. Another was
Victor Séjour, who went to Paris and gained distinction as a poet and composer of tragedy. Another
by the name of Dubuclet was a physician and musician of Bordeaux, France. The Lambert family,
consisting of seven persons, were noted as musicians. Richard Lambert, the father, was a teacher
of music, Lucien Lambert, a son, after much hard
study, became a composer of music. He left New
Orleans, however, and went to France, where he
continued his studies. Later he went to Brazil,
where he engaged in the manufacture of pianos.
Among his compositions are: "La Juive," "Le

Départ du Conscript," "Les Ombres Aimées," "Le Niagara."

Another brother, Sidney Lambert, stimulated by the example and fame of his father and brother, made himself a name as a pianist and a composer of music. He wrote a method for the piano of such merit that he received a decoration in recognition of his work from the King of Portugal. At last accounts he was a professor of music in Paris. Edmund Dèdè, who was born in New Orleans, in 1829, learned while a youth to play a number of instruments. He was a cigar maker by trade and, being of good habits and thrifty, accumulated enough money to pay his passage to France. Here he took up a special study of music and finally became director of the Orchestra of L'Alcazar, in Bordeaux, France.

The late J. M. Trotter, of Boston, himself a Negro of unusual intelligence, has written a history of the Negroes who distinguished themselves in music in the period from 1850 to 1880. In this history he mentions more than fifty Negroes who achieved distinction in some form of music, either as singers, performers on musical instruments, or composers. One of the most famous of these was Elizabeth Taylor Greenfield, who was known as the "Black Swan." She was born in Natchez, Mississippi, in 1809. When about a year old she was brought to Philadelphia by an exemplary

Quaker lady, Mrs. Greenfield, by whom she was carefully reared. One evening, while visiting at the house of a neighbour, the daughter of the house, who knew something of her ability, invited her to sing. Every one present was astonished at the power and richness of her voice, and it was thereupon agreed that she should receive music lessons.

These lessons were carried on at first without the knowledge of Mrs. Greenfield, because, according to the discipline of the Friends, music, like every other art, was a forbidden occupation. When the good lady learned that Elizabeth was taking music lessons, she summoned her to her presence. Elizabeth came, trembling, and prepared for a severe reprimand.

"Elizabeth," said she, "is it true thee is learning music and can play upon the guitar?"

"It is true," Elizabeth reluctantly confessed.

"Go and get thy guitar and let me hear thee sing."

The girl obeyed, and when she had finished was astonished to hear her kind friend say: "Elizabeth, whatever thee wants thee shall have."

From that time on Mrs. Greenfield assisted her in every way to make herself proficient in the profession of music, which she had chosen to follow.

When her benefactress died, the young coloured girl was thrown upon her own resources. Remembering some friends in Western New York, who had been very kind to her, she resolved to visit them.

Her chance singing upon a boat, which was crossing Lake Seneca, gained her new friends and opened a way for her to come prominently before the public.

In 1851 she gained a reputation by her singing before the Buffalo Musical Society. From that time on she was known as the "Black Swan," and invitations to sing in concerts came to her from cities in all parts of the North. In 1853 she gave a concert in Exeter Hall, London, England, where she made a great success.

Among other distinguished singers of this period were the Luca family, father and three sons, of Cleveland, Ohio. The father was born in Milford, Connecticut, in 1805. He was a shoemaker by trade. He became a chorister in one of the Congregational churches of New Haven, and his choir was considered one of the best in the city. The children inherited their father's talent, and in the fifties travelled about the Northern states, giving musical entertainments.

Among the more recent singers, perhaps the most distinguished is Madame Sissieretta Jones. She was born in Portsmouth, Virginia, in 1870. Her father was pastor of the local Methodist Church. When still a young woman her parents moved to Providence, Rhode Island, where her voice soon attracted public attention. After making a number of public appearances in Providence, she was invited to go to New York and sing at Wallack's Theatre. Her success was so great that she was immediately engaged to tour South America and the West Indies. In 1886 she sang with great success in Madison Square Garden. She has sung with success in all the principal cities of Europe, and during recent years has had her own company, known as the Black Patti Troubadours, at the head of which she has appeared in every important city in the United States.

Except as a singer in concerts or as a musician, almost the only opportunity that the Negro has had until recently to appear upon the stage has been as a minstrel. The first Negro minstrels were white men, and they sang songs and cracked jokes that were invented by white men in imitation of the songs and jokes of the Negroes, with which the Southern people had become familiar during slavery days. Immediately after the War, however, there was a company of coloured minstrels organised, known as the "Georgia Minstrels." These minstrels became famous and were succeeded by others. Out of these minstrels there grew later a kind of Negro comedy, in which there was some attempt to depict the characters and tell the story of Negro life. The man who made this transition from the old Negro minstrels to the more modern Negro comedy was Ernest Hogan, who died in the spring of 1909, in New York, and was buried from the church of St. Benedict the Moor, an honoured and respected member of his profession.

The success of Ernest Hogan has made it possible for other Negro comedians to gain a foothold in the better class of the theatres, and create a more worthy kind of Negro comedy. Among the more talented of these players are Bert Williams, George Walker, and his wife, Aida Overton Walker, Bob Cole, and J. Rosamond Johnson.

Year by year the character of the pieces produced by these men has improved in quality, both as to the music and as to the manner and style of presentation. At the present time I have heard it said that there are few musical comedies on the American stage that equal those that are produced by some of the players to whom I have referred.

Little by little these players, and the men who have written their songs and music, have managed to bring into connection with the rather rough humour of these comedies, music and songs of a much higher order than are usually heard in this kind of entertainment. Among the men who write the music and these songs are some men like James W. Johnson, whose poetry I have already quoted, and Harry T. Burleigh, a concert singer of more than ordinary cultivation and refinement. The songs which these young men have written are not only among the most popular songs of the day, but some of them must be counted among the very few which have real and permanent value. There is a note in the best of them which is entirely distinctive.

The most noted figure among Negroes who have appeared upon the stage was Ira Aldridge. He was born near Baltimore in 1804. In 1826 he met Edmund Kean, with whom he travelled for several years. He accompanied Keene to Europe, and when, finally, he expressed to him a desire to become an actor himself, the distinguished tragedian encouraged him in that ambition. Ira Aldridge made his first appearance as Othello at Covent Garden, London, April 10, 1839. Keene took the part of Iago, and from that time on the success of the coloured actor was assured.

In 1852 Ira Aldridge appeared in Germany, where his success was so great that the King of Prussia conferred a decoration upon him and sent him an autograph letter, expressing his appreciation of his performance. The coloured actor afterward received the Cross of Leopold from the Emperor of Russia. He played in all parts of Europe, and finally died at Lodz, Poland, just as he was preparing to come to America to fulfil an engagement.

In recent years the number of coloured performers upon the stage has multiplied rapidly. At the present time one of the regular features of the coloured newspaper is a theatrical column, which is devoted entirely to chronicling the doings of the

coloured theatrical performers. So successful have
these performers been that, in a number of cities,
theatres owned and conducted by coloured people
have been started expressly for the use of coloured
companies.   Theatres were owned and operated
by coloured people in 1909 in Chicago, Illinois; New
Orleans, Louisiana; Jackson, Mississippi; Memphis,
Tennessee; Atlanta, Georgia; Columbus, Ohio;
Jacksonville, Florida; Yazoo City, Mississippi; Baton
Rouge and Plaquemine, Louisiana.

The ability which the Negro has shown to express
his feelings in the form of music is also shown, in a
lesser degree, in expressing himself in poetry and
in other forms of art. The natural disposition
of the native African to express himself poetically
has been frequently noted by students of African
life. The traveller Schweinfurth noted among the
peoples of Central Africa a number of striking
expressions. For example, one tribe referred to
a leaf as "an ear of the tree," and in speaking of
a man's chest, called it "the capital of the veins."
In many parts of the black man's Africa there are
professional singers who practise the art of impro-
vising songs upon almost any topic that may be
assigned to them.

I have myself frequently noticed the striking
expressions that are sometimes used by the people
in the country districts, when they wish to make
any particular impressive statement. For instance,

in talking with an old farmer in the vicinity of my
home at Tuskegee, I happened to give expression
to some opinion or idea that struck him with peculiar force when he exclaimed: "Mr. Washington,
you said a thousand words in one." At another
time there was a coloured preacher who had a church
which was near a plantation school and settlement
that had been started by some of the teachers at
Tuskegee. Some one asked this preacher if the
school had made any change in conditions in that
neighbourhood since it had been established. He
raised his hands and exclaimed: "I'll tell you in a
word. When this school started it was midnight;
now it is dawn." Upon another occasion, when one
of these men was describing his religious experience,
how he "came through," as the expression is, he
used these words: "All of a sudden a star busted in
my breast and I was mighty happy in the Lord."

This same natural gift of expression, which is
frequently possessed by some of the rude and unlettered people of my race, has been frequently noted
by other persons. A typical example of this is
Harriet Tubman's description of the Battle of Gettysburg, which Professor Albert Bushnell Hart has
noted in his "History of Slavery and Abolition." He
heard this description from Harriet Tubman's own
lips as she was describing some of her experiences
during the Civil War. One sentence from that
description was as follows: "And then we saw

the lightning, and that was the guns; and then we heard the rainfall, and that was the drops of blood falling; and when we came to get in the crops, it was dead men that we reaped."

It is this same natural ability for picturesque expression which makes the Negro a natural orator. Even the disposition of the Negro to pick up and repeat high-sounding words and expressions is but another indication of his sense for impressive language.

I have noted, also, that where Negro college students do not excel their fellows of the white race in other branches of study, they frequently come off first in oratorical contests. For example, in 1907, a Zulu, who some years before came from Africa to America to get an education, carried off the oratorical honours at Columbia University. The name of this orator was Pixley Isaka Seme. When I last heard from Mr. Seme he was a student at Jesus College, Oxford, where he, with a number of other African students, was studying preparatory to going back to South Africa to enter the colonial civil service.

One of the most striking illustrations of the natural poetic talent in a member of the Negro race is in the verses of Phillis Wheatley. It requires a considerable amount of natural talent for any person to master a strange language and to learn to express himself poetically in it. It would seem that this must be particularly difficult for one coming from a condition and a life as remote and as different from that of a civilised European people as that of the primitive African. Nevertheless, the Negro has shown his ability to accomplish this feat.

One day in the year 1761, Mrs. John Wheatley, of Boston, went into the city slave market to purchase a Negro servant girl. She selected as suitable for her purpose a child between seven and eight years of age who had but recently come from Africa, and was hardly able to speak a word of English. The little girl was taken home and soon showed such marked intelligence that her mistress's daughter determined to teach her to read. Within sixteen months she had so far mastered the English language that she could read with ease and apparent understanding the most difficult passages of the Scriptures. She acquired the art of writing, it is said, almost wholly by her own exertion and industry. The great interest that she showed in learning to read and write, and the eagerness with which she read the books that were supplied to her, were so unusual at that time that it attracted general attention.

After a time she began to write verses. She was about fourteen years old when she wrote the first verses that attracted any particular attention. From this time until she was nineteen years of age

she seems to have written all the poems which she
gave to the world.   They were published in London, in 1773, and dedicated to the Countess of
Huntingdon, who had been her friend and patron.
A letter of recommendation, signed by the Governor,
Lieutenant-governor and several other respectable
persons of Boston, was printed by the publishers as
a sort of introduction to this little volume.   This
letter of recommendation was as follows:

To the Public:

As it has been repeatedly suggested to the publisher, by persons
who have seen the manuscript, that numbers would be ready to
suspect they were not really the writings of Phillis, he has procured
the following attestation from the most respectable characters in
Boston that none might have the least ground for disputing the
original:

"We whose names are underwritten, do assure the world, that
the poems specified in the following pages were (as we verily
believe) written by Phillis, a young Negro girl, who was but a
few years since brought, an uncultivated barbarian, from Africa,
and has ever since been, and now is, under the disadvantage of
serving as a slave in a family in this town.   She has been examined
by some of the best judges and is thought qualified to write them."

Phillis Wheatley addressed a poem to General
Washington, which seemed to have pleased him very
much.   In a letter to Joseph Reed, dated February
10, 1776, from Cambridge, General Washington
made the following reference to this poem:

I recollect nothing else worth giving you the trouble of, unless
you can be amused by reading a letter and poem addressed to me
by Miss Phillis Wheatley.   In searching over a parcel of papers

the other day, in order to destroy such as were useless, I brought
it to light again. At first, with a view of doing justice to her poetical
genius, I had a great mind to publish the poem; but not knowing
whether it might not be considered rather as a mark of my own
vanity, than as a compliment to her, I laid it aside, till I came
across it again in the manner just mentioned.

This kindly reference of George Washington
to the Negro slave girl poet and the uniform kindness and courtesy with which he is known to have
treated black men and women in every station
in life has gone far to endear the memory of the
Father of our Country to the coloured people of
the United States.

Phillis Wheatley died December 5, 1784, when she
was thirty-four years of age. She was one of the first
women, white or black, to attain literary distinction
in this country. I have frequently noticed, in
travelling in different sections of the country, that
many of the literary organisations and women's clubs
among the members of my race bear the name of
Phillis Wheatley, showing how well her name is still
remembered among the masses of the Negro people.

Another slave poet whose name is remembered,
but whose history is shrouded in mystery, is George
M. Horton, of Chatham County, North Carolina.
Horton could not write, but his poems were taken
down by some white man and were regarded as of
such importance that they were printed in a small
volume in 1829.

Frequently I have run across the names of Negroes

from the West Indies or elsewhere who have written poetry in the Spanish or French languages. Now and then I have received a volume of poems in some language that I was not able to read, which were written by some Negro poet in some part of the world. The great national poet of Russia, Alexander Sergeievich Pushkin, although of noble family, inherited African blood from his mother.

The history of Alexander Dumas, who was born of a Negro mother in one of the West Indian islands belonging to France, is familiar.

One of the most charming writers of verse in America at the present day, William Stanley Braithwaite, of Boston, is a young coloured man who was born in the West Indies. He is the author of several books of verse, one of them entitled "Lyrics of Love and Life," published in 1904. He is a frequent contributor to the magazines.

I should mention here, also, the name of Charles W. Chesnutt, the novelist, who makes his home in Cleveland, Ohio. Mr. Chesnutt, although he was born in the North, is descended from free coloured people of North Carolina. Shortly after the War his parents returned to the South, where Mr. Chesnutt was for some time a school-teacher. It was while thus occupied that he obtained that acquaintance with the South upon which his stories are founded. Among them are: "The Conjure Woman," "The House Behind the Cedars," "The

Wife of His Youth," and "The Marrow of Tradition." This latter is said to be the best description of the Wilmington riot and the events that led up to and produced it that has yet been written. Mr. Chesnutt's last story of Southern life is called "The Colonel's Dream," and describes the efforts of a Southerner who had gone North and become wealthy to return to his native village and build up its resources and make it prosperous.

But the poetry to which I have referred was written for the most part at a time when the masses of the Negro people could not read. It was the work of men who were, to a large extent, out of touch with the masses of the Negro people. The poems they wrote were not in the language which the masses of the people spoke, sometimes not even in a language which they could understand, and did not in any sense express or interpret the life of the Negro people.

Almost the first representative poet of my race was Paul Laurence Dunbar. Of Dunbar, William Dean Howells, to whom he owed to some extent his success, said that Dunbar was the only man of pure African blood and of American civilisation "to feel the Negro esthetically and express it lyrically." And that the Negro race "had attained civilisation in him." Mr. Howells believed that Dunbar more than any other Negro had gained for the Negro a permanent position in English literature.

Paul Laurence Dunbar was born in Dayton, Ohio, in 1872. His parents had been slaves. He received a high school education, but before his education was completed, while he was still working as an elevator boy, he began to write verses. He succeeded after a hard struggle in gaining recognition for his poetry, and became a frequent contributor to the leading magazines of the country. He was, likewise, a successful reader of his own verse. He published a number of volumes of poetry and of prose. To the time of his death, February 9, 1906, he seemed to be gaining in intellectual power and in popularity.

Shortly before he died, when it had become clear, even to his naturally hopeful mind, that he had not long to live, he wrote the following verses which are so full of pathos and express so clearly at once the strength and the weakness, as he felt them, not only of himself, but perhaps also of his race, that I quote them here:

> Because I had loved so deeply,
>   Because I had loved so long,
> God in His great compassion
>   Gave me the gift of song.
>
> Because I have loved so vainly,
>   And sung with such faltering breath.
> The Master in infinite mercy
>   Offers the boon of Death.

It has always seemed strange to me that Dunbar, who was born in a Northern state, and knew so little from actual experience of the life of the Negro in the South, could have been able to interpret that life so sincerely, so sympathetically, and so beautifully. No doubt the most that he knew about the life of the Negro before and after the War he gathered from the lips of his devoted mother, who had been a slave and had known and felt it all. There were no bitterness and no harsh notes in Dunbar's music. Perhaps this also is due to the fact that he saw the condition of his race sympathetically, through his mother's eyes. His songs have been of great service not only to his own race, but to the rest of the world. He was in a sense a direct descendant of the old slave singers. He expressed intelligently and poetically the deeper feelings and thoughts of the masses of the Negro people, so that the world could understand them. He was, in fact, the poet laureate of the Negro race.

From among the Negroes in the United States there have come from time to time not merely singers, but artists. One of the most noted of these, and the earliest to gain reputation, was Edmonia Lewis, who was born of Negro and Indian parentage in the State of New York, in 1845. During a visit to Boston she chanced to see a statue of Benjamin Franklin. She stood transfixed before it. Perhaps it was the latent genius within her which was stirred, for after looking at it with deep emotion she said: "I, too, can make a stone man."

It was William Lloyd Garrison to whom she turned for advice, who gave her encouragement to study sculpture. She first attracted attention by exhibiting in Boston, in 1865, a bust of Colonel Robert Gould Shaw. The same year she went to Rome to study and has resided there permanently since 1867. She has created a number of works of merit, the most noted of which are, "The Death of Cleopatra," which was exhibited at the Centennial Exhibition at Philadelphia, in 1876; "Asleep," "Marriage of Hiawatha," "Madonna with the Infant Christ," and the "Freedwoman." She has made a number of portrait busts in terra cotta, among which are those of Longfellow, Charles Sumner, John Brown, and Abraham Lincoln. The bust of Abraham Lincoln is in the public library at San José, California.

A younger sculptress, who has recently attracted attention, is Meta Vaux Warrick. She was born in Philadelphia, and gained her first lesson in modelling clay flowers in the public kindergarten. Afterward she secured a free scholarship in the Pennsylvania School of Industrial Art. Her first piece of original work in clay was the head of Medusa. In 1899 Miss Warrick went to study in Paris. She finally succeeded in attracting the attention of the famous French sculptor, Rodin, who is said to have given her his approval in these words: "My child, you are a sculptress. You have the sense of form." One of her best pieces of work was made for the Jamestown Tercentennial, and represented the advancement of the Negro since he landed at Jamestown, in 1619.

The Negro artist who has gained greatest fame, however, is Henry O. Tanner, son of Bishop Benjamin T. Tanner, of the A. M. E. Church. After studying for a time in the Pennsylvania Academy of Fine Arts, he opened a photograph gallery in Atlanta, Georgia. This venture was unsuccessful, however, and the next year he taught freehand drawing in Clark University, in the same city. His ambition, however, was to go to Paris and study under one of the living masters of art. By the assistance of friends he was finally able to gratify this desire. His first picture to receive official recognition was entitled, "Daniel in the Lions' Den," which received honourable mention in the Paris Salon of 1896. The next year his "Lazarus Rising from the Dead," received the third medal, and was purchased by the French Government for its collection of modern art in the Luxembourg gallery.

From that time until this Mr. Tanner has produced something every year, and every year the painting which he exhibited has been better than that of the previous year. In December, 1908, a comprehensive exhibition of his paintings was made in New York City. At the time the art critic of the New York *Herald* said of Mr. Tanner and his art:

Works of Mr. Henry Tanner, a distinguished American artist, long resident in Paris, who has been honoured abroad, are shown in a comprehensive exhibition for the first time at the American Art Galleries. All are religious paintings and reveal, as in flights of poetic fancy, the story of the "Prince of Peace." The thirty-three canvases form a veritable epic, and unfold the life of Christ from the Nativity to Golgotha, and then picture events that followed the Resurrection.

Mr. Tanner is a son of a bishop, and from his earliest years the inspiring traditions of the Old Testament and the New have been to him realities. With the development of his genius came the wish to show his conception of the ideals which to him had been realities from a child. Yet his point of view is not that of a religionist, but that of the true artist. He has sensed events, removed by the lapse of nineteen centuries, and has depicted them with such sincerity and feeling that the personages seem to live and breathe. Such qualities as these enabled him to make a deep impression in Paris, and two of his canvasses were purchased by the French Government for the Luxembourg.

The largest painting in the present exhibition was received with the warmest praise and occupied a prominent place in the last Paris Salon. It is entitled "Behold, the Bridegroom Cometh," and its theme is the familiar parable of the wise and foolish virgins. The painting, with its numerous figures of life size, occupies an entire panel of one of the lower galleries. The Master of Ceremonies is in the act of giving his summons and the maidens are forming themselves into the procession which is to go forth and meet their Lord. The masterly composition, the Oriental richness yet softness of the colouring, the instinctive command of detail have drawn the various elements together into a convincing picture.

Among notable canvases are several which, on account of the ideality of their conception and beauty of their tone, will at once draw to them the notice of the observer. They are, "Christ at the Home of Mary and Martha," "Christ and Nicodemus," "The Return of the Holy Women," "On the Road to Emmaus" and "He Vanished Out of Their Sight."

What impresses me most about Mr. Tanner's paintings is the vividness, the sincerity and, I may say, literalness with which he has depicted the incidents of the Bible story. He paints all these things, it seems to me, with something of the spirit in which these same incidents are pictured in the old plantation hymns, vividly, as I have said, literally, and with a deep religious feeling for the significance of the things that he paints.

CHAPTER XII

NEGRO WOMEN AND THEIR WORK

DURING his travels in Africa Mungo Park, the famous African explorer, came one day to Sego, the capitol of the Kingdom of Bambara, which is situated on the Niger River. Information was carried to the king of that country that a white man wished to see him. The king in reply sent one of his men to inform the explorer that he could not be received until his business was known. He was advised to find lodgings for the night in a neighbouring village. To his great surprise, Park found no one would admit him. After searching for a long time he finally sat down, worn out, under the shade of a tree, where he remained for a whole day without food.

As night came on the wind arose and a heavy storm threatened. To the other dangers of the situation was added the fear that he might be devoured by the numerous wild beasts that roamed about in that region. Just as he was preparing to climb into a tree, however, a woman passed by and perceiving his weary and dejected appearance, spoke to him and inquired why he was there. On receiving his explanation she told him to follow her to her house. Here he was given food and a mat was spread on which he lay down to sleep. The women of the house were meanwhile employed in spinning cotton and, as they worked, they lightened and enlivened their labour by songs. One of these songs was extemporised in honour of their guest. Park described this music, in the story of his travels, as sweet and plaintive. The words were:

> The wind roared and the rain fell.
> The poor white man, faint and weary,
> Came and sat under our tree;
> He has no mother to bring him milk,
> No wife to grind his corn.
>
> Let us pity the white man,
> No mother has he to bring him milk,
> No wife to grind his corn.

This incident has been often quoted. Sometimes it has been referred to as an illustration of the easy and spontaneous way in which the African people are accustomed to express their thoughts and feelings in song. To my mind, however, it seems rather an illustration of that natural human sympathy which is characteristic of the women of most races, but particularly so of Negro women, whether in Africa or elsewhere.

Whatever may be said about the thoughts and the failings of Negro women, no one, so far as I know, has ever denied to them this gift of sympathy. Most people have recognised this quality but nowhere is the kindness and helpfulness of Negro women better known and appreciated than among the white people of the Southern states. The simple-hearted devotion of the Negro slave women to their masters and their masters' families was one of the redeeming features of Negro slavery in the South.

The devotion the slaves sometimes showed to their masters did not fail to inspire a corresponding affection in the members of the master's family. I know of scarcely anything more beautiful than the tributes I have heard Southern white men and women pay to those old coloured mammies, who nursed them as children, shared their childish joys and sorrows and clung to them through life with an affection that no change of time or of circumstance could diminish.

Southern literature is full of stories which illustrate the strength of this mutual affection, which bound the young master or the young mistress to his or her faithful Negro servant. When all other ties which bound the races together in the South have snapped assunder, this tie of affection has held fast.

I remember reading a few years ago, shortly after the Altanta riots, a story written by a young Southern white man entitled, "Ma'm Linda." The central theme of this story was the affection of a young white woman for her coloured "mammy." This affection was strong enough to resist and finally overcome attachments that divided the community in which these two persons are supposed to have lived. It put an end to an exciting episode which would otherwise have terminated in a most hideous mob murder.

As an illustration of this devotion of some of the slave women to their masters and masters' families, the following incident, which took place in Washington, District of Columbia, in 1833, is in many ways typical. A Southern gentleman and his family were stopping at a Washington hotel when he began a conversation with some persons who were opposed to slavery. After they had discussed the question at some length the slave-holder said to them: "Here is our servant; she is a slave, and you are at liberty to persuade her to remain here if you can." The anti-slavery people sought out the young woman and informed her that having been brought by her master into the free states she was, by the law of the land, a free woman.

The young woman promptly replied that this could not be so. They talked the matter over thoroughly and made every effort to show her that she was free under the existing laws, but she shook her head, saying that a legal decision did not touch her case, "for you see," she said, "I promised my mistress that I would go back with the children."

An attempt was then made to induce her to break her promise. It was pointed out that a promise made while she was not free could not be binding, but the young slave woman refused to look upon it in that light.

At length one of the abolitionists said: "Is it possible that you do not wish to be free?"

"Was there ever a slave that did not wish to be free?" the girl replied. "I long for liberty. I will get out of slavery, if I can, the day after I return, but I must go back because I have promised."

Among those slaves who became free, either through the kindness of their owners or as a result of their own individual efforts, the number of Negro women is large. Olmsted, in his "Cotton Kingdom," records an instance of a woman who had obtained her freedom in Virginia, but, being in fear that she might be reënslaved, fled to Philadelphia. Here for a time she almost starved. One day a little girl, who saw her begging on the streets, told her that her mother wanted some one to do her washing. When the poor woman applied for this work she was at first refused, because her prospective employer was afraid to trust valuable clothing to so unfortunate appearing a creature. The coloured woman begged earnestly for the chance to do this work and finally suggested, if there was any fear she would not return the clothes, that she should be locked in a room until the work was completed. She pleaded so earnestly that she was allowed to do this work, and in this way began her life in Philadelphia.

Ten years afterward a white man from her old home in Virginia happened to be in the city. The coloured woman recognised him and was over-joyed to see some one from her old home. She invited him to come to her house. He did so and found it a handsomely furnished three-story building. From the window she pointed out three other houses in the vicinity which she owned and rented. In order that her children might be educated she had employed for them a private instructor. This story illustrates the manner in which many other Negro women set to work, after emancipation, to build homes for themselves and their children.

To the twenty-five million dollars, which it is estimated the free Negroes accumulated before the Civil War, the thrift and industry of Negro women contributed no small amount. Likewise, in the remarkable amount of property accumulated and in the home-building which has gone forward for the last forty years, the women of the Negro race have ever been foremost.

I have seldom found an instance where a man of my race has accumulated property, that his wife has not only urged that a home be bought but has like-wise aided, by extra work, in buying it. In the struggle for homes and for a substantial family life the women of no race have shown a greater devotion and more constant self-denial than have the Negro women since the masses of the race have become free. They have engaged in all forms of personal and domestic service, to supplement the small wages of their husbands, in order that their children might be fed, clothed, kept in a school and something laid aside to pay on a home that more than likely is being purchased through some building and loan association. These women have frequently had almost no learning in books and but little idea of the settled and traditional regard of mankind for the sacredness of the home and family ties. When they began to lay the foundation of the Negro family life they were simply following the dictates of their own hearts, and the natural instincts which their ancestors had brought from Africa. For, contrary to the general notion, it will be found that family life, where native institutions have not been broken down through contact with the white race, is highly developed among the native Africans.

Some idea of the part that the Negro women are taking in the economic development of the race may be gained by considering how large a place they hold in the field of industry. The statistics show that coloured women, as wage-earners, do more than their full share of the work of the race. According to the census of 1900, for every thousand coloured women or girls, ten years of age and over, four hundred and seven were reported as bread-winners. In the case of white women, on the contrary, the corresponding number was one hundred and fifty. This means that about two coloured women out of five and one white woman out of six work for wages. Of the total number of Negroes engaged in gainful occupations in 1900, nearly one-third were women. The proportion of coloured women to the whole number of Negroes employed in various groups of occupations was as follows: in agriculture 27.1 per cent., in the professions 32.9 per cent., in domestic and personal service 51.5 per cent., in trade and transportation 1.9 per cent., and in manufacturing and mechanical pursuits 12 per cent.

In the professional class there were 262 women who followed the stage as a career; 164 were ministers, 7 dentists, 11 journalists, 10 lawyers, 25 were engaged in literary and scientific work, 86 were artists and teachers of art, 160 physicians, 1,185 musicians and teachers of music, and 13,525 were school-teachers. In the 140 groups of occupations, concerning which statistics are given in the census, coloured women are represented in 133. The remaining groups were of such a character that men alone could be employed in them.

It is, perhaps, in the matter of educating their children that Negro women have made their greatest sacrifices. I have referred to the freed woman in Philadelphia, who employed private teachers for her children. Thousands of Negro women at the present day are working in the kitchen, over the washtub, or in the field in order that their children may have the advantages of an education.

A considerable number of Negro women have distinguished themselves as teachers of their people. The fourth school established in the District of Columbia for coloured children was started by Mrs. Anne Maria Hall. This school was opened in 1810. The Costin sisters, Louisa and Martha, from 1823 to 1839, did much to improve the character of the education of coloured children in the District of Columbia. Fannie Jackson Coppin, wife of Bishop Levi J. Coppin, of the African Methodist Episcopal Church, was one of the best known of the women coloured teachers in the United States. She was born a slave in Washington, District of Columbia, in 1837, and was purchased by her aunt. She graduated with honours from Oberlin College and began to teach in 1865. From 1869 to 1899 she was principal of the Institute for Coloured Youth in Philadelphia. The present principal of that school, Hugh M. Browne, was her pupil.

The first coloured school-teacher in the public schools of Philadelphia was Cordelia A. Jennings, who for a number of years maintained a private institution for coloured children in the city. In 1864, her school having reached an enrollment of one hundred and fifty, Miss Jennings decided to apply for recognition and support as a public school. Under the regulations that prevailed at that time she was entitled to do this. The request aroused considerable discussion, but was finally granted, and Miss Jennings's school became part of the public school system, with its former teacher as principal.

After forty-five years, this school is still in existence. During this time it has had but two principals; the present incumbent being Miss Caroline R. Le Count, who has under her as teachers a number of those who had previously been her pupils. It is now well known under the name of the Catto school, named after Octavius V. Catto, a coloured schoolmaster, who was killed in the election riot in October, 1871.

Miss Jennings was born in Poughkeepsie, New York, in 1843. She graduated from the Institution of Coloured Youth in Philadelphia. After leaving Philadelphia, she helped to establish at Louisville, Kentucky, in 1886, the first coloured high school in that state. While there she became the wife of Reverend Joseph S. Attwell. Mr. Attwell, who was born in Barbadoes, British West Indies, in 1831, had come to America about 1864, to collect funds to assist a number of his countrymen to emigrate to Liberia. He succeeded in collecting about twenty thousand dollars, and thus became instrumental in founding the settlement known as Crozerville, on the Liberian coast.

After the close of the War, Mr. Attwell went South as agent of the Episcopal Church. He established mission churches in several cities in Kentucky, founded a mission church in Petersburg,

Virginia, and was for several years rector of St. Stephen's Church, Savannah, Georgia. He finally became rector of St. Philip's Church, where he died in 1881. St. Philip's Church, New York, is said to be the richest coloured church in the United States. It bears, in this respect, somewhat the same relationship to the other coloured churches that Trinity Church, New York — from which, in fact, it is an offshoot — does to the white churches of the city.

During all this time Mrs. Attwell was active as a teacher or as a worker in other directions, for the benefit of her race. She was principal of the parochial school, at Petersburg, and principal of the West Broad Street School, at Savannah, and after her husband's death, in 1881, she worked as a professional trained nurse. Mrs. Attwell was, for a time, matron of the Home for Aged and Infirm Coloured Persons in Philadelphia, and was afterward in charge of the Industrial Home for Working Women, at Germantown, Pennsylvania. At present, 1909, she is living with her son, Ernest T. Attwell, who is Business Agent of the Tuskegee Institute.

Mrs. Attwell's mother, Mrs. Mary McFarland Jennings, was herself a school-teacher. When, in the summer of 1909, I made an extended trip of observation through the Southern part of Virginia, I passed through Kenbridge, Lunenburg County, where Mrs. Jennings was born, and where, after the War, she conducted a school for many years for Freedmen. For four years after the close of the War, Mrs. Jennings carried on this school at her own expense and without salary. In 1869, however, through the intervention of her son-in-law, Mr. Joseph S. Attwell, the support of the school was taken over by the Domestic Missionary Society of the Protestant Episcopal Church. The school was closed in 1894, but at the time of my visit to Kenbridge, citizens of the county and former pupils of the school had purchased land and were preparing to erect a building for a memorial school to be established there in memory of Mrs. Jennings and her work.

Lucy C. Laney, a graduate of Atlanta University, has done an interesting and important work in education in Georgia. She was for a time principal of a public school in Savannah. In 1886, however, she resigned this position and went to Augusta, Georgia, in order to establish in that city an industrial school. Although she started this school almost unaided, making herself responsible for the support of the teachers and the expense of the institution, somehow or other the school has grown steadily from the time it was started. It has since then received a liberal support from the Presbyterian Church and is now the chief school supported by this denomination south of North Carolina.

In this connection I want to mention the noble work for the care and education of orphans and neglected children, which has been carried on for many years by Dinah Pace at Covington, Georgia. This is known as the Reed Home and School. After years of struggle Miss Pace has been able to build up at Covington, largely through the assistance of her own pupils and teachers, an industrial school and orphans' home which is valued at the present time at about ten thousand dollars. Another of the early schools established in the way I have described is the Industrial School at Manassas, Virginia, which was started by a coloured woman by the name of Jennie Dean, and is now in charge of Mr. Leslie P. Hill and his wife, both of whom were formerly teachers in the institute.

I feel certain that, if I had space to do so, I could name hundreds of other women who are doing, in different parts of the South, a work similar to that I have already mentioned. The names of these women are frequently scarcely known outside of the communities in which they live and labour, but the value of the service they have rendered is greater than can ever be fully measured or known.

In speaking of the coloured women who have distinguished themselves as teachers, I should not fail to mention the name of Maria L. Baldwin, a coloured woman who is principal of one of the best graded schools of Cambridge, Massachusetts, in which she has under her care not less than 600 white children. Miss Baldwin is one of the best known women of her race in New England and is frequently called upon to address teachers' associations in different parts of New England. At Hampton Institute, Hampton, Virginia, and at the Institute for Coloured Youth at Cheyney, Pa., her summer-school classes have had a large and enthusiastic attendance.

Negro women have not only been, to a very large extent, the teachers of their race, both before and since the War, but several of them played important parts in the antebellum struggle for freedom. I have already referred, in another part of this volume, to the story of Harriet Tubman. Another woman, who did much to change sentiment in the United States in regard to slavery, was Sojourner Truth, one of the most original and best known of anti-slavery characters.

Sojourner Truth was born about 1775. She was brought as a child with her parents from Africa and sold as a slave in the State of New York. She has described this incident in her own picturesque language.

"Ye see," she once said, "we was all brought over from Africa, father an' mother an' I with a lot more of us. We was sold up an' down, an' hither an' yon; an' I can 'member, when I was a little thing, not bigger than this," pointing to her grandson, "how my ole mammy would sit out o' doors in the evenin', an' look up at the stars an' groan. She'd groan an' groan, an' says I to her: 'Mammy, what makes you groan so?' An' she'd say, 'Matter enough, chile! I'm groanin' to think o' my poor children: they don't know where I be, an' I don't know where they be; they looks up at the stars an' I looks up at the stars, but I can't tell where they be.'"

Sojourner Truth was called Isabella by her parents. Her parents' names were James and Betsy. They were owned by Colonel Ardinburgh, who lived in Hurley, Ulster County, New York. At nine years of age Isabella was sold to John Nealy, of the same county, for $100. She thought that her sale in some way was connected with a flock of sheep. At any rate, it was the beginning of her trials, for her former master belonged to the class of people called Low Dutch, and she had not learned the English language and no one in the family except Mr. Nealy, her new master, understood the Dutch language. This led to frequent misunderstandings and punishments for Isabella. Her mother had said to her when she was very small, that when she should grow up and be sold away from all of her old friends and had great troubles, that she was to go to God and he would help her.

"An' says I to her, 'Who is God, anyhow, mammy?' An' says she, 'Why chile, you jes look up dar! its him dat made all dem.'"

At the Nealys' she had many occasions to remember the words of her mother. Once she was ordered to go to the barn, where she found her master with a bundle of rods waiting for her. She was stripped to her waist and given the most cruel beating she ever received, and she never knew why she was so cruelly whipped. Often afterward she would say: "When I hear 'em tell of whippin' women on the bare flesh it makes my flesh crawl an' my very hair rise on my head. Oh, my God, what a way is this of treatin' human bein's!" And then she said, "I thought about what my old mammy had told me about God, an' I thought I had gone into trouble sure enough, an' I wanted to find God, an' I heerd somebody tell a story about a man that met God on the threshing floor, an' I thought, good an' well, I will have a threshing floor.

"So I went down in the lot an' I thresh down a place real hard, an' I used to go down there every day an' pray an' cry with all my might, a-praying to the Lord to make my massa an' missus better."

The Lord, however, did not answer her prayer and so she said, "Why, God, maybe you can't." She then proposed to the Lord that if He would help her to get away she would be good. "But if You don't help me I really don't think I can be."

Then she said the Lord told her to get up about three o'clock in the morning and travel. In the course of the day she came to the house of some

Quakers, who treated her very kindly, and after supper they took her into a room in which there was a bed and told her to sleep there. But instead of sleeping in the bed she slept under it, and in the morning, when they came to ask her if she hadn't been asleep, she said, "Yes, I never slep' better."

"Why, you haven't been in the bed at all," they exclaimed.

"Laws, you didn' think of sech a thing as my sleepin' in dat ar bed, did you?" she replied. "I never heerd o' sech a thing in my life."

The immediate cause of Sojourner's running away from her master was that, by an act of the New York Legislature, passed in 1817, all slaves forty years of age were to be liberated at once, children on reaching their majority, and the others, in 1827. Sojourner would have been free on July 4, 1827, but her master, in consideration of her long years of faithful service, had promised to give her free papers a year in advance of the time which the law had set. He backed out of this agreement, however, on the plea that during the year her hand had been disabled; and, therefore, she had not performed as much work as he had expected.

The next year, after the law had made her free, Sojourner's former master came to her and invited her to come back and see his family. When she reached her master's house, she found, to her great sorrow, that her son, who was a small boy, although free according to law, had been carried off by the daughter of her former mistress to Alabama. Sojourner vowed that she would have the child back. She was told to present her case to the Grand Jury. She had never heard this word, Grand Jury, before, and thought it meant some sort of a very important individual. She went to town, therefore, when the court was in session.

"An' I stood 'round the court-house," she said, "an' when dey was comin' out I walked right up to de grandest one I could see and I says to him, 'Sir, be you a Grand Jury?'"

The Grand Jury took up her case, and, in the course of time, her child was restored to her. Then an incident took place which illustrates how easily a Negro woman forgives and forgets, as soon as her sympathies are touched.

When she found that her child had been unlawfully taken to Alabama, Sojourner prayed, in the bitterness of her despair, that the Lord would render unto her mistress double for all the trouble and sorrow she had been instrumental in bringing upon her former slave. Shortly after this Sojourner happened to be at the home of her former master when a letter was received, saying that the daughter in Alabama had been murdered by her husband, while he was in a drunken frenzy. Sojourner, feeling that her prayer had been answered, now repented having called upon the Lord to revenge her injury. Her account of what then took place has been reported as follows:

Then says I, "O Lord, I didn' mean all that. You took me up too quick." Well, I went in an' tended that poor critter all night. She was out of her mind cryin' an' callin' for her daughter an' I held her poor ol' head on my arm an' I watched her as if she had been my baby, an' I watched by her an' took care of her an' she died in my arms, poor thing.

A few years after this Sojourner felt called of God to labour for the salvation of souls, and the good of her own people. It was at this time she decided to change her name. She has described how this was done:

My name was Isabella; but when I lef' the house of bondage I lef' everythin' behind. Wan't goin' to keep nothin' of Egypt on me. An' so I went to the Lord an' asked him to give me a new name. An the Lord gave me Sojourner, because I was to travel up an' down the land, showin' the people their sins an' bein' a sign unto 'em. Afterward I told the Lord I wanted 'nother name, cause everybody else had two names, an' the Lord gave me Truth, because I was to declare the truth to the people.

Sojourner could neither read nor write, but she soon became widely known in the North, and was a prominent figure at anti-slavery meetings. One day she was speaking at one of these meetings when a man interrupted her and said: "Old woman, do you think that your talk about slavery does any good? Do you suppose that people care about what you say? Why, I don't care any more for your talk than I do for the bite of a flea."

"Perhaps not," she answered, "but, the Lord willin', an' I will keep you scratchin'."

About this time an insect known as the weevil appeared in different parts of the country and destroyed a large part of the wheat crop. Sojourner, taking this for her text, made the following point on the Constitution:

Children, I talks to God, an' God talks to me. Dis mornin' I was walkin' out, an' I got ober de fence into de field. I saw de wheat a-holdin' up its head, lookin' very big. I goes up an' takes hold ob it. You believe it, dare was no wheat dare? I says, 'God (speaking the name reverently), 'what is de matter wid dis wheat?' an he says to me, 'Sojourner, dare is a little weasel in it.' Now I hears talkin' about de Constitution, an' de rights ob man. I comes up an' I takes hole ob dis Constitution. It looks mighty big, an' I feels for my rights, but dar ain't any dar. Den I says, 'God, what ails dis Constitution?' He says to me, 'Sojourner, dar is a little weasel in it.'

On another occasion Parker Pillsbury, in speaking at an abolition meeting one Sunday afternoon, criticised the attitude of churches in regard to slavery. Just then a furious thunderstorm came up, and a young Methodist minister arose and interrupted the speaker, saying, among other things, that he was fearful God's judgment was about to fall on him for daring to sit and hear such blasphemy; he said it almost made his hair rise in terror.

"Chile," said Sojourner in a voice that was heard above the rain and thunder, "don't be skeered; you're not goin' to be hurt. I don' spect God ever hearn tell on you."

On another occasion Sojourner Truth was at a woman's rights convention, in which the ministers of the town turned out and took issue against the ladies. Public sentiment was turned against them, and for a time the women sat in despair. Suddenly Sojourner voluntarily stepped to the front and made a speech which won a complete victory for the women. This speech contains so much unlettered eloquence that it seems to me worth repeating here. As reported, this is what she said:

"Well, chil'en, what's all dis here talkin' about? Dat man ober dar say dat womens needs to be helped into carriages, and lifted ober ditches, an' to have de bes' place everywhar. Nobody eber helped me into carriages, or ober mud puddles, or gives me any bes' place (and raising herself to her full height and her voice to a pitch like rolling thunder, she asked), an' ar'n't I a woman? Look at me! Look at my arm!" And she bared her right arm to the shoulder, showing her tremendous muscular power. "I have plowed, an' planted, an' gathered into barns, an' no man could head me — an' ar'n't I a woman? I could work as much an' eat as much as a man, when I could git it, an' bear de lash as well — an' ar'n't I a woman? I have borne thirteen children, an' seen 'em mos' all sold off into slavery, an' when I cried out with a mother's grief, none but Jesus heard, an' ar'n't I a woman? Den dey talks 'bout dis ting in de head; what dis dey call it?" ("Intellect," whispered some one near.) "Dat's it, honey. What's dat got to do with woman's rights or niggers' rights? If my cup won't hold but a pint an' yourn holds a quart would n't ye be mean not to let me have my little half-measure full?" Thereupon she pointed her finger and directed a keen glance at the minister who had made the argument.

"Den dat little man in black dar, he say woman can't have as much rights as man, cause Christ wa'n' a woman. Whar did your Christ come from? From God and a woman. Man had nothing to do with him. If de fust woman God ever made could turn the world upside down, all 'lone, dese togedder ought to be able to turn it back an' git it right side up agin, an' now dey is askin' to do it, de men better let 'em."

Wendell Phillips said that he never knew but one human being who had the power to bear down a whole audience by a few simple words, and that person was Sojourner Truth. As a case in point, he relates how once, at a public meeting in Boston, Frederick Douglass was one of the chief speakers. Douglass described the wrongs of the Negro, and, as he proceeded, grew more and more excited until he ended by saying that there was no hope of justice from the whites, no possible hope except in their own right arms. It must come to blood. They must fight for themselves or it would never be done.

Sitting on the very front seat, facing the platform, was Sojourner Truth and, in the hush of deep feeling, as Douglass sat down, she rose and uttered these words:

"Frederick, is God dead?"

The effect was electrical, and thrilled through the house, changing, as by a flash, the whole feeling of the audience.

Mr. Story, the sculptor, has attempted to preserve the spirit of Sojourner Truth and the impression she made upon him, in his statue called the Lybian Sybil. After a sojourn of more than one hundred years on this earth, during which she always proclaimed the truth, Sojourner Truth passed to her reward November 26, 1883.

I have ventured to describe the doings and sayings of this remarkable woman at some length, because the pithy sayings she uttered, and the sympathy with suffering that she showed, are typical of a large class of Negro slave women.

Another woman, of a very different type, who distinguished herself during slavery days, was Frances Ellen Watkins. Born in Baltimore, Maryland, in 1825, she went to school to her uncle, Reverend William Watkins, who taught a school in Baltimore for freed coloured children. About 1851 she moved to Ohio and began teaching. A little later she taught at Little York, Pennsylvania. It was here that she became acquainted with the workings of the Underground Railway.

A law had been enacted in Maryland preventing free people of colour from entering that state, on pain of being imprisoned and sold into slavery. A free coloured man, however, who had unwittingly violated this statute, had been sold into Georgia, but had escaped by secreting himself behind a wheel-house of a northbound steamship. Before he reached freedom, however, he was discovered and sent back to slavery. This incident, which came directly under her notice, made a great impression upon the young coloured school-teacher, and it was this that finally determined her to devote her life to the cause of anti-slavery.

After she came to Philadelphia, Miss Watkins made her home at the station of the Underground Railway. Here she had abundant opportunity to see the passengers and hear their tales of hardship and suffering. She began her career as a public lecturer in 1854, and, for a year and a half, spoke in the Eastern states. In 1856 she visited Canada and lectured in Toronto. From 1856 to 1859 her work was mainly in Pennsylvania, New Jersey, New York and Ohio.

Not only did she give of her time, but of her limited means to the cause of freedom. William Still, in his Underground Railway, gives a number of instances where she gave him financial aid. In one case she wrote: "Yesterday I sent you thirty dollars; my offering is not very large, but if you need more send me word."

In the fall of 1860 she was married in the city of Cincinnati to Fenton Harper. She gave up her public work until the death of her husband, May 23, 1864. She had by this time become known as an anti-slavery writer in both prose and poetry. After the close of the War she came South, and began to work for the uplifting of her people in the states of South Carolina, Georgia, Alabama and Mississippi.

To the present generation of coloured people

Mrs. Harper is known principally as a writer. She has published a number of books of poetry. Her best known prose work is "Iola Leroy, or the Shadows Uplifted." On returning from her work in the South she became a lecturer and writer on temperance, and for some time had charge of the W. C. T. U. among the coloured people. She now makes her home in Philadelphia.

Another somewhat remarkable character is Amanda Smith, the evangelist. She was born a slave at Long Green, Maryland, January 23, 1837. Her father wanted to free himself and his family, so he worked at night, making brooms and husk mats, and burning lime. During harvest time he would work in the grain fields until one and two o'clock in the morning. In this way he first purchased himself and then set himself to the task of buying his wife and five children. After he had succeeded in this, he moved his family to Pennsylvania.

Amanda taught herself to read by cutting out large letters from the newspapers, laying them on the window sill, and getting her mother to make them into words. When she was eight years old, she attended a private school for six weeks. Five miles from her home there was a white school, to which the few coloured children in the neighbourhood were allowed to go. They were, however, placed at a disadvantage, for all the white children had their full lessons first and then, if any time was left, the coloured children had a chance. It often happened, therefore, that after Amanda had walked the five miles through the deep snow she would get but one lesson, and that would be while the white children were taking down their dinner pails and putting on their wraps. In this way she received three months' schooling, and this was the end of her education in the schoolroom.

Amanda joined the Methodist Episcopal Church, and it was in the great camp-meetings of this church in the seventies, that her power as an evangelist was first manifested. In a little book, "Amanda Smith's Own Story," an extended sketch of her evangelistic labours are given. In this work she laboured not only in this country, but also in India, in Africa, in England and Scotland. Bishop J. M. Thoburn, of the Methodist Episcopal Church, gives the following concerning her:

During the summer of 1876, while attending a camp-meeting at Epworth Heights, near Cincinnati, my attention was drawn to a coloured lady dressed in a very plain garb (which reminded me somewhat of that worn by the Friends in former days), who was engaged in expounding a Bible lesson to a small audience.

I was told that the speaker was Mrs. Amanda Smith, and that she was a woman of remarkable gifts, who had been greatly blessed in various parts of the country.

The meetings of the day had not been very successful, and a spirit of depression rested upon many of the leaders. A heavy rain had fallen and we were kneeling somewhat uncomfortably in the straw which surrounded the preacher's stand. A number had prayed and I myself was sharing the general feeling of depression, when I was suddenly startled by the voice of song. I lifted my head, and at a short distance, probably not more than two yards from me, I saw the coloured sister of the morning kneeling in an upright position, with her hands spread out and her face aglow.

She had suddenly broken out with a triumphant song, and while I was startled by the change in the order of the meeting, I was at once absorbed with interest in the song and the singer. Something like a hallowed glow seemed to rest upon the dark face before me, and I felt in a second that she was possessed of a rare degree of spiritual power.

That invisible something that we are accustomed to call power, and which is not possessed by any Christian believer except as one of the fruits of the indwelling spirit of God, was hers in a marked degree. From that time onward I regarded her as a gifted worker in the Lord's vineyard, but I had still to learn that the endowment of the spirit had given her more than the one gift of spiritual power.

A few years after my return to India, in 1876, I was delighted to hear that this chosen and approved worker of the Master had decided to visit this country. She arrived in 1879, and after a short stay in Bombay, came over to the eastern side of the empire, and assisted us for some time in Calcutta. She also returned two years later, and again rendered us valuable assistance. The novelty of a coloured woman from America, who had in her childhood been a slave, appearing before an audience in Calcutta, was sufficient to attract attention, but this alone would not account for the popularity which she enjoyed throughout her whole stay in our city.

She was fiercely attacked by the narrow-minded persons in our daily papers and elsewhere, but opposition only seemed to add to her power. During the seventeen years that I have lived in Calcutta, I have known many famous strangers to visit the city, some of whom attracted large audiences, but I have never known anyone who could draw and hold so large an audience as Mrs. Smith.

She assisted me both in the church and in open-air meetings, and never failed to display the peculiar tact for which she is remarkable. I shall never forget one meeting which we were holding in the open square, in the very heart of the city. It was at a time of no little excitement, and some Christian preachers had been roughly handled in the same square a few evenings before. I had just spoken myself when I noticed a great crowd of men and boys, who had succeeded in breaking up a missionary's audience on the other side of the square, rushing toward us with loud cries and threatening gestures.

If left to myself I should have tried to gain the box on which the speakers stood, in order to command the crowd, but at the critical moment our good Sister Smith knelt on the grass and began to pray. As the crowd rushed up to the spot, and saw her with her beaming face upturned to the evening sky, pouring out her soul in prayer, they became perfectly still, and stood as if transfixed to the spot! Not even a whisper disturbed the solemn silence and, when she had finished, we had as orderly a meeting as if we had been within the four walls of a church.

During Mrs. Smith's stay in Calcutta, she had opportunities for seeing a good deal of the native community. Here, again, I was struck with her extraordinary power of discernment. We have in Calcutta a class of reformed Hindoos called Brahmos. They are, as a class, a very worthy body of men, and at that time were led by the distinguished Keshub Chunder Sen.

Every distinguished visitor who comes to Calcutta is sure to seek the acquaintance of some of these Brahmos, and to study, more or less, the reformed system which they profess and teach. I have often wondered that so few, even of our ablest visitors, seem able to comprehend the real character either of the men or of their new system. Mrs. Smith very quickly found access to some of them, and beyond any other stranger whom I have ever known to visit Calcutta, she formed a wonderfully accurate estimate of the character, both of the men and their religious teaching.

She saw almost at a glance all that was strange and all that was weak in the men and their system. This penetrating power of discernment which she possesses in so large a degree impressed me more and more the longer I knew her. Profound scholars and religious teachers of philosophical bent seemed positively inferior to her in the task of discovering the practical value of men and systems which had attracted the attention of the world!

I have already spoken of her clearness of perception and power of stating the undimmed truth of the Gospel of Christ. Through association with her, I learned many valuable lessons from her lips, and once before an American audience, when Dr. W. F. Warren was exhorting young preachers to be willing to learn from their own hearers, even though many of the hearers might be comparatively illiterate, I ventured to second this exhortation by telling the audience that I had learned more that had been of actual value to me as a preacher of Christian truth from Amanda Smith than from any other one person I had ever met.

Amanda Smith has now largely given up her evangelistic labours and conducts the Amanda Smith Orphans' Home for Coloured Children, at Harvey, a suburb of Chicago, Illinois.

One of the ablest and best known women lecturers before the public at the present time is Mary Church Terrell. Her opportunities and training have been exceptional. She was born in Tennessee, a daughter of well-to-do parents, graduated with honours from Oberlin College in 1884, and finally spent two years in European study and travel. She was for a time a teacher of ancient and modern languages at Wilberforce University, and later, in the high school for coloured children in Washington, District of Columbia. At the International Congress of Women in Berlin, Germany, in 1904, it is said that Mrs. Terrell had the unique distinction of delivering one speech in excellent German and another in equally good French. Mrs. Terrell has been prominent in the work of the National Association of Coloured Women, of which she several times has been president.

Another woman who has gained some public distinction is Mrs. Lucy Thurman, of Jackson, Michigan, who succeeded Mrs. Francis E. W. Harper in charge of the work of the W. C. T. U. among the coloured people.

The most important work done by coloured women for coloured women has been through the coloured women's club movement. As early as 1890 there were coloured women's clubs in nearly every large city where there was any considerable coloured population. The best known of these are, perhaps, the Phillis Wheatley Club, of New Orleans, of which Mrs. Sylvania Williams is the head, and the Woman's Era Club, of Boston, which was founded by Mrs. Josephine St. Pierre Ruffin. In addition to these clubs there were in existence at the date of which I have mentioned, the Ellen Watkins Harper Club, of Jefferson City, Missouri; the Loyal Union Club, of Brooklyn, New York; the Ida B. Wells Club, of Chicago, Illinois; the Sojourner Truth Club, of Providence, Rhode Island; and, quite as influential as any other, the Woman's League, of Washington, District of Columbia.

The first National Conference of Coloured Women was held in Boston in the latter part of July, in 1895. The person more responsible than any one else for the first national meeting of coloured women was Mrs. Josephine St. Pierre Ruffin, the founder and first president of the Woman's Era Club, of Boston.

Mrs. Ruffin was born in Boston, in 1844. Her father, John St. Pierre, had the blood of three races in his veins — namely, French, Indian, and African. Her mother was an English woman, a native of Cornwall, England. As a girl Mrs. Ruffin attended the public schools of Salem, Massachusetts, and later studied at a private school in New York. While still a girl in school she married George Ruffin, of Richmond, Virginia. I have already referred, in an earlier chapter, to the position which Mr. Ruffin made for himself in Massachusetts.

Mrs. Ruffin early became interested in the advancement and welfare of coloured women. During the period of the "Kansas Exodus," in 1879, she called together the women of her neighbourhood, in the West End of Boston, and organised the Kansas Relief Association. In the work that this association undertook Mrs. Ruffin was greatly aided by the counsel of William Lloyd Garrison, and other prominent anti-slavery people. A large amount of clothing, old and new, and a considerable sum of money were collected and forwarded to the Kansas refugees.

The success of this work of philanthropy lead to Mrs. Ruffin's connection with the Associated Charities which, at that time, was just being organised in Boston. For the next eleven years she acted as a local visitor for this organisation. She also became a member of the Country Week Society, devoting herself to the difficult task of finding places in the country for coloured children.

The work that Mrs. Ruffin did in this, and other directions, brought her in contact with many of the best and most cultivated women of New England. She became a member of the Massachusetts Moral Education Association, and of the School Suffrage Association, of Massachusetts; was for a number of years one of the members of the executive board of both these organisations. Later she became prominent in the Woman's Educational and Industrial Union, of Boston.

The work Mrs. Ruffin did in these various organisations did not cause her to lose interest in the work she had begun to do for the members of her own race. On the contrary, the experience she obtained served to make her more useful in all that coloured women were at this time attempting to do for themselves.

The Woman's Era Club, of which, as I have said, Mrs. Ruffin was founder, became one of the most influential of coloured women's clubs in America. In the interest of this organisation a paper, *The Woman's Era*, was started, and Mrs. Ruffin was for years its editor. It was as editor of this paper that she first gained a national reputation. It was through this paper that, in 1894, she advocated the holding of a National Conference of Women's Clubs.

The immediate cause of holding this conference,

however, was the publication, by an editor in Missouri, of an open letter to Mrs. Florence Belgarnie, of England, who had manifested interest in the American Negro. In this letter the editor declared that the coloured women of America had no sense of virtue and were altogether without character. As a result of the agitation begun at this time, about one hundred women representing about twenty-five clubs, from ten different states, gathered in Boston, July 29, 1895. As a result of this meeting it was determined to establish a permanent organisation. The first officers of the association were: Mrs. Booker T. Washington, of Tuskegee, Alabama; Mrs. U. A. Ridley, of Brookline, Massachusetts; secretary, Mrs. Libbie C. Anthony, of Jefferson City, Missouri; treasurer, and Mrs. Victoria E. Matthews, of New York, chairman of the executive committee.

For the organisation of the National Federation of Coloured Women's Clubs, Mrs. Ruffin was largely responsible. Through the paper, of which she was editor, she has exercised influence on the coloured women throughout the United States. Under her influence the Woman's Era Club had a large part in enlarging what is known as Mrs. Sharpe's Home School in Liberia, Africa. When the American Mt. Coffee School Association was formed in January, 1903, to aid this work, Edward Everett Hale was elected president and Mrs. Ruffin vice-president. She is still active in all good work for the coloured women of her race, not only in New England but throughout the United States.

Since the organisation of the National Feder-ation of Coloured Clubs the number of these clubs has greatly multiplied. In many cases they have been organised into State Federations.

As an illustration of the sort of work that these women's clubs do in some of the Southern states, I may cite the case of the Alabama Federation, of which I happen to know more than of some of the other organisations. A few years ago this Alabama Federation of Coloured Women's Clubs established a reformatory for boys which is located at Mt. Meigs, Alabama. During the year 1908, over forty boys were received at this reformatory from the police court of Montgomery and Birmingham. During that year the clubs raised something like $2,283.73, a large part of which was expended in paying for and maintaining the reformatory at Mt. Meigs, to which I have referred.

The work of the women's club at Tuskegee is typical of what many of the other clubs are doing. The work of this club is carried on through the following departments: current literature, music, prison work, open-air meetings, settlement work, and temperance work. At the present time this club is carrying on a Sunday-school in a neglected part of the Tuskegee town. Sunday meetings are held in the town jail, more than twenty mothers' meetings have been organised among the farmers' wives in the country districts surrounding the town. These mothers' meetings are maintained under the supervision of the club. A woman's rest room, for the benefit of farmers' wives, who usually come into town on Saturday in large numbers, is maintained in town. The club has recently taken care of the family of a man who has been sent to prison for life. It is paying for the education of a boy and girl of whom it has had charge since they were small children. The Tuskegee Town Reading Room, Library, and Night School, which are now carried on by the Tuskegee Institute, were first established by the Tuskegee Woman's Club.

These facts show, it seems to me, that Negro women, in spite of criticism, are going forward quietly and unostentatiously doing those things which develop that character and moral sense in the members of the race in which it is sometimes said that Negro women are lacking.

CHAPTER XIII

THE SOCIAL AND MISSION WORK OF THE NEGRO
CHURCH

THE first mission of the Negro Church was started in 1824, in the Black Republic of Haiti. This was only eight years after the first general conference of the African Methodist Church was held at Philadelphia. Bishop Allen, the first bishop of the African Methodist Church, was associated about this time with Benjamin Lundy, the Quaker abolitionist, in the effort to colonise free coloured people on free soil, outside the limits of the United States, in Mexico, Canada, and Haiti. The Black Republic, where a few years before Negroes had established an independent government, seemed a proper place to establish a branch of the Independent African Church. Thus it came about that in close connection with the colony started by Benjamin Lundy, the mission work of the African Methodist Church was begun.

This Church has, in the meantime, extended its influence over several of the other West India Islands, chiefly in those regions which have not yet been reached to any extent by missions of the other

Protestant churches. The society reports fifteen missionaries in the Windward Islands, three in Cuba, and twenty stations in British Guiana, with five thousand adherents.

About the same time that the African Methodist Church was seeking to extend its work and influence to the Republic of Haiti, Lott Cary, the noted slave preacher of Richmond, Virginia, was the head of a little local missionary association, started by the Negro Baptists of Richmond, Virginia.

The Negro churches of Richmond seem to have been stirred at that time by the general excitement aroused by the colonisation movement, and this mission society was founded by the Negro Baptists at this time in the hope of sending out a missionary from its own number to Africa.

As a matter of fact, Lott Cary, who went out to Liberia in 1821 with the second shipload of colonists from America, became the first Negro missionary to that country. The mission work of the Baptist Church owing to its congregational organisation, has never been so systematic or so vigorously carried on as that of the African Methodist Society, which has maintained a strong central organisation. It is, nevertheless, worth noting that the first Negro missionary to Africa was of that denomination and the name and memory of Lott Cary are still preserved to-day among the Negro Baptists in this country, through the work of the Lott Cary Missionary Society.

At the present time, the African Methodist Church has mission stations in Sierra Leone, Lagos, and Liberia on the west coast of Africa. It also has churches scattered all over South Africa, as far north as Rhodesia. It supports at the present time more than three hundred preachers and has 11,000 members among the native Africans.

The rapid growth in numbers and influence, during recent years, of the African Methodist Church in South Africa has been due to the withdrawal, in 1894 and 1895, of a number of the native members of the Wesleyan Methodist Church in the Transvaal, in order to form an independent Ethiopian Church. The seceders afterward united with, and became a part of, the African Methodist Episcopal Church of the United States.

Whatever may have been the occasion for this independent movement, the real causes for it seem to be similar to those which have gradually brought about a separation of the races, in their church life, in this country. While there are some disadvantages in this arrangement, and these disadvantages may be greater in South Africa than they have been in the United States, there are reasons, more potent than those which appear on the surface, that have brought this separation about and made it perhaps inevitable. It seems rather curious to Americans that the secession of a few of the native churches should have caused so much alarm in

South Africa. In this country, whenever the Negro takes it into his head to go off by himself, the white people usually give him every encouragement. It is a little hard to understand why a similar movement in South Africa should make a commotion. Perhaps, as has been asserted, the time was not ripe for such a separation. I am inclined to believe, however, that if it is wisely dealt with, the so-called Ethiopian Movement, which has been the source of so much apprehension to the British Government in South Africa, should work to the advantage of both races in Africa, just as the separate church movement has done, on the whole, it seems to me, in the United States.

In my opinion, there is no other place in which the Negro race can to better advantage begin to learn the lessons of self-direction and self-control than in the Negro Church. I say this for the reason that, in spite of the fact that other interests have from time to time found shelter there, the chief aim of the Negro Church, as of other branches of the Christian Church, has been to teach its members the funamental things of life and create in them a desire and enthusiasm for a higher and better existence here and hereafter.

More than that, the struggle of the masses of the people to support these churches and to purify their own social life, making it clean and wholesome, is itself a kind of moral discipline and one that Negroes need

quite as much as other people. In fact, I doubt if
there is any other way in which the lessons that
Christianity is seeking everywhere to enforce, could
be brought home to the masses of the Negro people
in so thorough-going a way as through their own
societies, controlled and directed by the members
of their own race.

Aside from those missionaries sent out to Africa
by the African Methodist Episcopal Church, some
of the most enterprising and successful missionaries
sent out to Africa by the white churches have been
Negroes. Some of the most distinguished of these
men, also, have been native Africans. There was,
for instance, Samuel Crowther, who was rescued
when a boy from a slave-ship; taken to Sierra Leone,
where he was educated in Fourath Bay College, and
in 1864, consecrated in Canterbury Cathedral, England, the first native Bishop of Africa. In the
same year he received the title of Doctor of Divinity
from the University of Oxford, and afterward became
a member of the Royal Geographical Society, because
of the contributions he made to the knowledge of
the geography of Africa. He helped to translate
the Bible into the Yoruba language, and his studies
in the Nupe and Ibo languages are said to have
shown unusual ability.

The story of Daniel Flickinger Wilberforce,
another and a later of these African missionaries,
reads like a romance. Daniel Flickinger was a

companion of George Thompson in Africa. He aided in establishing the United Brethren Mission on the west coast of Africa, and made six voyages through that continent. During his first visit to Africa, in 1855, while at Good Hope Station, Mendi Mission, on the eastern banks of Sherboro Island, he employed a native to watch him at night. While this native was so employed, his wife gave birth to a child, which he named Wilberforce, and then, in honour of the visiting missionary, he added the name Daniel Flickinger.

Sixteen years later, in 1871, while his boxes were being loaded and unloaded at the American mission rooms in New York, Dr. Flickinger noticed a young Negro employed about the offices of the Missionary Association, who seemed to take an unusual interest in the names upon the boxes which he was assisting to load and unload. It turned out that the name of this boy was Daniel Flickinger Wilberforce, and the reason he was so interested in the boxes was that he had been able to decipher a portion of his own name upon them. It appeared that the boy had been sent over from Africa as a servant to one of the missionaries who was returning home ill. Dr. Flickinger became so interested in the young man that he determined to give him an education. He was sent to Dr. Flickinger's office in Dayton, Ohio, with an express-tag around his neck. Seven years later he returned to Africa as a preacher, teacher and physician. He had succeeded in completing his education in the primary school in four years, from there he went into the Dayton High School, where he graduated at the head of his class, having completed the course in three years. In the meantime he had been given instruction in medicine and in theology, so that he went out to Africa a fully equipped missionary.

While young Wilberforce was studying in the high school, Paul Laurence Dunbar, who was born in Dayton, Ohio, was a boy playing about the streets. Daniel Flickinger Wilberforce left Dayton in 1878, and returned as a missionary to his own people, where he has since lived and worked.

One of the most successful of the missionaries of Africa to-day is W. H. Sheppard, who was a student in my day at Hampton Institute, and later at the Stillman Institute at Tuscaloosa, Alabama. He went out to the Kongo in 1896 with Reverend Samuel N. Lapsley, of Alabama, as a missionary of the Southern Presbyterian Church. Mr. Lapsley chose a station to establish his mission at Luebo, far in the interior of Africa, and Mr. Sheppard remained and worked with him there until Mr. Lapsley's death. After this the work of the mission was continued, with great success by Mr. Sheppard, in association with Mr. William Morrison. Mr. Sheppard has returned to America several times since then, and spoken throughout the South in the interest of his work in Africa.   Everywhere I hear him referred to with the greatest respect, and even affection.

I have spoken thus far of the work that the Negro churches are doing for missions in Africa and elsewhere.   The amount of money raised for this purpose is small compared to that which is contributed every year by the Negro churches for the purpose of education.   Unfortunately, no detailed study has ever been made, so far as I know, which gives any adequate notion of the money that is actually contributed by Negroes through all the religious organisations to which they belong, to their own education.

The Negro Baptists, for example, have never published a complete list of the schools conducted by their different churches and church organisations. In the Year Book for 1907, one hundred and ten schools were reported as owned by Negro Baptists. There were 16 in Louisiana, 13 in North Carolina, 11 in Mississippi, 9 in Kentucky, 8 in Arkansas, 6 in Texas, 5 in Virginia, 5 in South Carolina, 5 in Florida, 4 in Georgia, 3 in Tennessee, 3 in West Virginia, 2 in Illinois, 2 in Oklahoma, 1 in Kansas, 1 in Missouri, 1 in Ohio, 1 in Maryland, 1 in Indiana, and 5 in Africa.   Besides those mentioned in the Year Book there are, I have been told, several others in Louisiana, Virginia, and North Carolina, so that all together there are no less than 120 schools owned entirely by Negro Baptists.

During the year 1907, these schools employed 613 teachers, and gave instruction to 18,644 students. During this year also the Baptist churches reported collections for educational purposes amounting to $97,032.75. This did not include the amounts raised in Maryland, Tennessee, Texas, and Virginia, churches in those states for some reason or other making no report.

Educational work of the Negro Baptist churches was at first largely carried on under the control of the American Baptist Home Mission Society, which is managed by white people. In recent years, however, there has been a movement among Negro Baptists to do their educational work independently.

One of the first things that was done after the Negro Baptists had decided to carry on their Sunday-school and educational work independently of the white Baptist churches, was to establish a printing plant in order to publish books and pamphlets needed in Sunday-school and church work. In 1896, Reverend R. H. Boyd established the National Baptist Publishing Company. Mr. Boyd had been a preacher in Texas, and his only experience as a publisher was a brief one, in association with a white man, from which he emerged, as he says, with much valuable experience, but with a financial loss of five hundred dollars.

The new publishing business was started with almost no capital, and under the most discouraging circumstances. Nevertheless, the enterprise has prospered steadily until, at the present time, the value of the stock equipment and property of the concern is worth, according to an inventory made by Bradstreet's Agency, not less than $350,000.

The building in which the company is located occupies half a block in the business portion of Nashville, Tennessee. According to a statement made at the National Negro Business League at Louisville, Kentucky, in 1909, the Company circulated, during the previous year, not less than 12,000,000 issues of the different periodicals that it published. During the same year the Company paid its employees $165,000 for labour.

Notwithstanding that many Negro Baptists have become independent, the Baptist Home Mission Society (white) is every year receiving an increasingly large number of contributions for the schools they maintain from the Negro themselves. Of the twenty-three schools under the direction of this society, for instance, fourteen are owned by Negroes themselves. The report of the educational work of the society for the year 1907-08 shows that the receipts for that year from all sources, including the fees paid by students, were $269,795.78. Of this amount $10,782.36 was contributed by white churches and individuals, while $27,724.42 was contributed by Negro churches and individuals.

The educational work of the African Methodist

Episcopal Church began in 1844, with the purchase of 120 acres of land in Ohio for the Union Seminary, which was opened in 1847. In 1856, the A. M. E. Church united with the Methodist Episcopal Church (North) in establishing Wilberforce University. In 1863, this University became the sole property of the A. M. E. Church. At the present time this denomination maintains twenty schools and colleges, one or more in each of the Southern states, two in Africa, and one in the West Indies. These schools and colleges employ 202 teachers and have something like 5,700 pupils.

The third Sunday in September is set aside in all of the A. M. E. churches as Educational Day. On this day a general collection is taken in all the churches for educational purposes. The amount collected in 1907 was $51,000. In addition to this, every member of the church is taxed eight cents per year for the general educational fund. I have not been able to learn the amount of money collected in this way, but the quadrennial reports show that these schools collect from all sources, including the fees paid by students, something like $150,000 a year.

The A. M. E. Zion Church carries on educational work in twelve institutions, four of which are colleges, one a theological seminary and seven secondary schools. These schools have 150 teachers and more than 3,000 pupils. During the year 1907, these schools raised from all sources something over $100,000.

In 1906 I had an opportunity to be present and take part in the twenty-fifth anniversary exercises of Livingstone College at Salisbury, North Carolina. This college was established and has been maintained by the A. M. E. Zion Church. The leading spirits in establishing it were the present Senior Bishop, Right Reverend J. W. Hood, and the late Dr. Joseph C. Price, who was its first president, and did the most to put the college on its feet and make it known to the world.

Joseph Price was a remarkable man. He was, in the first place, like Lott Cary, Alexander Crummell, and Henry Highland Garnet, a man of unmixed African blood. He was a remarkable orator, and when only twenty-seven years of age, he was sent as a delegate of the A. M. E. Zion Church to the Ecumenical Council in London. While he was there, through the eloquence with which he described the condition of education in the South, he succeeded in raising ten thousand dollars, which was used in purchasing the grounds upon which Livingstone College now stands, and in erecting some of the buildings.

During the days that the anniversary celebration lasted, something like $8,000 in cash and pledges was secured for the benefit of the college. I was interested to see the way in which this money was secured. When the hour for taking the subscriptions arrived, you would see, perhaps, a coloured bishop rise and announce his subscription for something like fifty dollars. Then a coloured woman would stand up and announce that she would give ten dollars. Then others would announce more modest sums. Altogether the amounts of the different contributions ranged, as I remember, from twenty-five cents to a thousand dollars. The man who gave a thousand dollars would not permit his name to be known, but it is now an open secret that this generous gift was contributed by Dr. W. H. Goler, the Negro president of the college.

The Coloured Methodist Church, which was organised among the coloured people who, after the Civil War, still clung to the Southern branch of the Methodist Church (South), has done, according to the number of its members, quite as much as any other coloured religious organisation for the education of the Negro race. This denomination controls six educational institutions, among them Lane College, at Jackson, Tennessee, founded by Bishop Isaac Lane, and the Mississippi Theological and Industrial College, founded by Bishop Elias Cottrell, of Holly Springs, Mississippi.

The interesting thing about Bishop Cottrell's school is that it was started as a result of the veto by Governor Vardaman of the appropriation for the State Normal School, which was formerly located at Holly Springs. When that school went out of existence, as a result of this action of the Governor, the Negroes of Mississippi, under Bishop Cottrell's leadership, determined that they would build a school of their own to replace it. They succeeded in raising in the short period of three years something like $65,000, and erected two handsome modern buildings. At the last meeting of the National Negro Business League in Louisville, Kentucky, Bishop Cottrell said that within the last eight years, the Coloured Methodist Church had raised, within the State of Mississippi alone, over $100,000, of which all but $35,000 had been collected in small contributions from the Negro people themselves.

The African Union Methodist Protestant Church, which has less than 6,000 members, has been able, in spite of its small membership, to support three schools — one at Baltimore, Maryland, one at Franklin, Pennsylvania, and a third at Holland, Virginia.

Besides the contribution of Negroes to Negro education, made through their own Negro organisations, the coloured people have contributed largely to education through the Freedmen's Aid Society of the Methodist Episcopal Church (North); the Freedmen's Board of the American Missionary Association, the Church Institute for Negroes of the Episcopal Church, and through the Catholic Church.

No record has been published of the amount of money contributed by Negroes to the support of schools conducted by the Catholic Church, but the total amount must have been considerable. For instance, in 1829, when the St. Francis Academy was founded in Baltimore by Negro sisters of the Catholic Church in the West Indies, these sisters gave all that they had in the way of furniture and real estate to this institution. Nancy Addison left this institution $15,000 and a Haitian, by the name of Louis Bode, left the institution $30,000. The contributions of Colonel John McKee, of Philadelphia, and Mr. Thomy Lafon, of New Orleans, made to the Catholic schools and benevolent institutions, amounted, at a low estimate, to something like a million dollars.

The contributions, made through the churches, do not include those that are constantly made by coloured people to local and independent institutions, which are not connected with any church organisation. For example, Tuskegee Institute receives annually a number of small contributions from the coloured people of the country, and from its former students. The largest sum received in this way was the legacy of Mrs. Mary E. Shaw, a coloured woman of New York City, which amounted to $38,000.

Among the other notable contributions which have been made from time to time to Negro educa-

tion by Negro philanthropists, I might mention
that of a coloured man by the name of George
Washington, a former slave, of Jerseyville, Illinois,
who is said to have left $15,000 to Negro education.
Mr. Thomy Lafon gave Straight University, of
New Orleans, $6,000.   It is known that Bishop D.
A. Payne, the founder of Wilberforce, gave at different times and in different amounts, several thousand
dollars to that institution.   Mr. Wheeling Gant
gave $5,000 to Wilberforce.   Bishop J. B. Camp-
bell gave $1,000, Bishop and Mrs. J. A. Shorter
gave $2,000, and Henry and Sarah Gordon gave
$2,100 toward the endowment of this same school.

Recently Mr. French Gray gave land, said to be
valued at $2,000, to the Dooley Normal and Indus-
trial School in Alabama.   Bishop Isaac Lane has
given at various times considerable more than a
thousand dollars to the college bearing his name
at Jackson, Tennessee.   Fisk University received
from Mrs. Lucinda Bedford, of Nashville, Tennessee, $1,000, and John and James Barrows, of the
same city, gave $500 to the same institution.   Joshua
Park gave $6,000 to the State College of Delaware,
George, Agnes and Molly Walker gave $1,000 to
Straight University, New Orleans.

After the Kentucky Legislature, in 1904, passed
a law which made it illegal for white and black
students to attend the same school, Berea College,
which had been conducted as a mixed school for

both races since 1865, was closed to Negroes. After the case had been finally settled in the highest courts, a campaign of education was started under the direction of Reverend James Bond, the coloured trustee of the college, to raise money to found a school for coloured students to take its place. In about twelve months, $50,000 was raised in the state of Kentucky. Of this sum, $20,000 was pledged by the coloured people of Kentucky.

Considering the small amount of money that Negroes have thus far accumulated, and the hard struggle that they have had to get it, the facts that I have mentioned indicate that Negroes appreciate the value of education for their race and are willing to contribute generously to its support.*

While the chief work of the Negro church has been and still is among the people of the small towns and the country districts, where the bulk of the Negro population is located, in recent years a serious effort has been made by some of the larger city churches to deal with some of the comparatively new problems of the city Negro. I have already mentioned the work of the First Congregational Church, under H. H. Proctor, in Atlanta, and of the Berean Presbyterian Church, of Philadelphia. In addition to the Berean Building and Loan Asso-

---

* "Self-Help in Negro Education," Publications of Committee of Twelve, R. R. Wright, Jr.

ciation, to which I have referred, the Church started, in 1884, a free kindergarten, which it still maintains. Then in 1889 the Berean Manual Training and Industrial School was started, which gives instruction in carpentry, upholstering, millinery, practical electricity, plain sewing and dressmaking, stenography, cooking, waiting and tailoring. Two years before this, in 1897, a bureau of mutual help was established in order to find employment, particularly in domestic service, for the large numbers of coloured people who are constantly coming to Philadelphia from the South.

Another organisation, the Berean Trades Association, seeks to aid Negro tradesmen and other skilled workmen to find employment in the trades. In addition to these the church has charge of the Berean Seaside Home, a seaside resort for respectable coloured persons, near Asbury Park, New Jersey. In 1900 the Berean Educational Conference was started, and in 1904 there was added to this the Berean Seaside Conference. All of these institutions, though started and maintained by this Church, are each independent of the other, and are patronised by thousands of persons who are neither members of the congregation of the Berean Church, nor of the Presbyterian denomination.

In addition to these institutional churches there have grown up in connection with the large city churches, literary societies and organisations for mutual improvement, which meet Sunday afternoon to read papers or discuss general topics. These societies help to furnish wholesome recreation for young men and women, and sometimes they do something more than this. For example, there was organised in Savannah, Georgia, in 1905, what was known as the Men's Sunday Club. At that time there was very little effort made to close the saloons in Savannah on Sunday; a law against minors entering these places was not enforced, at least with respect to the coloured youths. Thousands of coloured people spent their Sundays at a park in the suburbs of the city, which had been erected for the special use of the coloured people, and which was infested by a number of disreputable characters who made it a dangerous place for young men and girls to go.

The Young Men's Sunday Club, which was composed of some of the better educated and more serious young men of the city, determined to do something to counteract the evil influences of this resort. By means of this club hundreds of young men and women were kept off the streets, and were induced to come to the meetings of this society, where they heard interesting discussions, not merely of literary subjects, but topics of vital interest to the coloured people of the city. One of the things that the club attempted to do was to inculcate a respect for law and order, and make the coloured people realise the fact that it was especially impor-

tant for them, who so frequently needed the protection of the law, to see to it that they themselves
obeyed it.

One of the chief temptations to the coloured
young men and women of Savannah were dance halls,
run in connection with saloons in those sections of
the city in which the majority of the coloured people
lived. The Men's Club was instrumental in having these dance halls abolished by law. After the
law had been passed a committee of the club was
appointed to see that it was enforced.

After a time there was organised, in connection
with the Men's Club, a woman's auxiliary, which,
in turn, organised a number of mothers' clubs in
various sections of the city.

In these mothers' meetings an effort was made
not only to interest mothers in keeping their children
off the streets, and away from the association of
criminals, but also to teach the proper care of children and inculcate some of the simple rules of the
hygiene of the home.

Another organisation which is now doing an
important and valuable work for Negroes is the
coloured Y. M. C. A. Under another name the
work of this organisation has been carried on since
before the Civil War, although no definite organisation was formed until 1879, when the first international secretary to take charge of the work among
the coloured people was appointed.

From 1879 to 1890 this work was carried on under the direction of Henry E. Brown. In 1890, the first coloured international secretary, Mr. W. A. Hunton, was appointed to do this work. In 1898 another secretary, Dr. J. E. Moorland, was appointed to assist Mr. Hunton.

These two men now have under their supervision one hundred and ten associations. Seventy-three of these are student associations, and thirty-seven of them are city associations. Sixteen of these associations employ general secretaries and twelve of them conduct night schools. The total membership in these associations now exceeds 9,000 men. Twelve associations own real estate to the value of $80,000.

One of the most interesting of these associations is that which was formed at Buxton, Iowa. This town is made up almost wholly of Negro miners. Of the population of five thousand, 93 per cent. are black and 7 per cent. white. It has no regular city government, since all the property in the town belongs to the Consolidated Coal Company, in which these men are employed.

This mining company is therefore enabled to exercise a benevolent despotism, so far as maintaining order in the community is concerned, and no disreputable characters are allowed to remain there. In the company's plan of government the Y. M. C. A., which was conducted for some time, and very successfully, under the direction of Lewis E. Johnson, a young coloured man, who is now secretary of the Y. M. C. A. in Washington, District of Columbia, has played an important part.

The mining company at Buxton erected a $20,000 Y. M. C. A. building, which was provided with a library, and served as a social centre for the 1,500 coloured employees of the company, which make up the bulk of the population. By furnishing innocent recreation for the miners during the time that they were idle, by encouraging them to read, save their money, and by giving them religious instruction, it was found possible to maintain something approaching perfect order in this little town, without the necessity of banishing any large number of the employees of the company for misbehaviour.

Perhaps the greatest achievement, in a material way, of the coloured Y. M. C. A., has been the undertaking to erect a $100,000 building in Washington, District of Columbia. Washington has the largest coloured population of any city in the United States, and in this city the problems of city life present themselves in a most difficult form. It is, therefore, peculiarly appropriate that in the nation's capital, where so large a number of coloured people live, the work of the Y. M. C. A. should be conducted on a scale adequate to the need.

In the fall of 1906 Mr. John D. Rockefeller offered to give $25,000 toward the erection of a permanent home for the coloured Y. M. C. A. in Washington, provided a similar sum could be collected from among the coloured people of the city. From April 7 to May 7, 1908, a campaign was carried on among the coloured residents of Washington, and $30,535 in subscriptions was secured. Since that time this amount has considerably increased, and it is hoped eventually to raise enough money to insure the erection of a $100,000 building, for which plans have already been drawn.

Aside from the direct influence which the coloured Young Men's Christian Association has been able to exert upon its members, these local organisations have frequently exercised an important indirect influence for good in the community. For example, I learned, during the meeting of the National Negro Business League, in Louisville, in August, 1909, that the Young Men's Christian Association had been largely instrumental in securing, for the coloured people of Louisville, the magnificent library they now possess, erected in 1908 by the generosity of Mr. Andrew Carnegie. This library, which is a regular branch of the Louisville Public Library, is probably the most complete and best equipped library for coloured people in the South. The total cost, including the books, was something like $42,000. Thomas F. Blue, who was formerly Secretary of the Coloured Young Men's Christian Association, is the librarian in charge.

The work of the coloured Y. M. C. A. began in the colleges. It is gradually reaching out, however, to the larger cities and, to some extent, into the smaller towns. As this work extends steadily it is getting a larger hold upon the masses of the coloured people, and is forming a nucleus for work of social service in the cities, the places where that work is most needed. In this way the Y. M. C. A. is supplementing the mission and social work of the Negro Church.

CHAPTER XIV

NOT infrequently I hear it said that, since the overthrow of the Reconstruction governments, and particularly since the passage of the disenfranchisement laws, the Negro has lost his place in Southern politics. This depends, to some extent, on what one means by politics. Negroes still vote in all the Southern states, though the number of Negro voters has been very greatly curtailed in some states, and particularly in those which suffered most from the vices and mismanagement of the Reconstruction governments. Negroes still hold offices under the Federal Government, and the proportion of Negroes in the civil service of the United States is constantly increasing.

Aside from the number of votes cast, however, and the number of offices which these votes controlled, Negroes probably exercise a greater influence on public order and public policy in the Southern states to-day than they ever did before. Directly and indirectly, through their churches and through their schools; through their doctors of medicine, lawyers, and business men; through their lodges,

banks, corporations, clubs, law and order leagues,
etc., Negroes are exercising a very large and a very
positive influence upon the lives of the communities
in which they live. As an illustration of what I
mean I want to relate, as briefly as I am able, the
story of the coloured Law and Order League, of
Baltimore, Maryland.

In the city of Baltimore there is one of the largest
and most populous coloured neighbourhoods in any
city in the world. I have already referred to this
neighbourhood as one which possibly contains more
homes and better homes, owned and occupied by
coloured people, than any other similar district in
any of the large cities of the country.

This district extends along Druid Hill Avenue
from Utah Street to North Avenue, and with the
adjacent streets covers an area a mile and a half
long, by from one-sixteenth to one-half a mile wide.
The upper part of this district is given up to the
better class of residences, usually three-story brick
buildings, fronting directly on the street, and is
comparatively free from saloons or other nuisances.
A few years ago this region was inhabited by some
of the best white families in the city, but as the
city has grown these people have moved out into
the suburbs, and the coloured people have come
in to take their places.

The lower end of Druid Hill Avenue is a district
of quite a different character. In a section seven

blocks long and two blocks wide there were, a few years ago, before the coloured Law and Order League began its work, no less than forty-two saloons. What made this situation the more disagreeable, and even dangerous, was the fact that these saloons were located in close proximity to most of the Negro churches and Negro schools in that district. For example, there were, all in close proximity to the saloons I have mentioned, fifteen churches, twelve schools, one home for old people, one home for friendless children, the Coloured Young Men's Christian Association, and the Coloured Young Women's Christian Association. In addition to the forty-two saloons there were, in this same region, numerous dance-houses, billiard-halls, and club-rooms, where gambling was openly carried on, which frequently became places of assignation for girls and young women.

The better class of coloured people on Druid Hill Avenue had long looked with concern on the condition of things that existed in the lower part of the district. But it is not an easy thing for Negroes to take the initiative in matters of this kind. For one thing, Southern white people, as a rule, do not expect it of them, and it is true of the race as it is of an individual, that you rarely get from them anything more or better than you expect. Another thing that, perhaps, made the coloured people hesitate was the fact that a large proportion of the saloons in the district, more than half, although they were supported by Negroes, were kept by white people. Besides that, these places seemed to have had a sort of police protection, which, because it was long established, would be hard to break up. It was, perhaps, true also, that in Baltimore, as in some other cities, saloons and dens of vice which were not allowed to exist in other parts of the city, were permitted to take refuge in the districts where the masses of the coloured people lived. For this reason many people have been led to assume that respectable and industrious Negroes do not have the same objection to the presence of vice among them that other people have.

It was the Atlanta riot, I have been told, that set the better class of coloured people to thinking, and led them finally to the conviction that this reform movement must be undertaken by themselves. In October, 1906, a meeting was called by Reverend John Hurst, one of the most progressive of Baltimore's coloured ministers. At this meeting there were present W. Ashbie Hawkins, one of the leading coloured lawyers of the city; Dr. Howard E. Young, a druggist; Dr. Whitfield Winsey, a physician who had practised for thirty years among the coloured people; Dr. Thomas S. Hawkins, one of the younger coloured physicians of the city; Heber E. Wharton, vice-principal of one of the coloured public schools; Harry T. Pratt, a grade supervisor in the public schools; Dr. J. H. N. Waring, principal of the Coloured High School; Reverend E. F. Eggleston, pastor of the Grace Presbyterian Church, and Reverend J. Albert Johnson, who shortly afterward became a bishop of the A. M. E. Church.

At this first meeting it was decided to make a careful study of the actual conditions among the coloured people in the city. The committee divided themselves into sub-committees. One of these made a study of the sanitary conditions; another investigated the moral influence surrounding the schools.

One of the facts which the committee learned from a study of a map furnished by the health office, was that a narrow street, called Biddle Alley, running off from Druid Hill Avenue, was the "tuberculosis centre" of the state. This meant that in that particular region there were more deaths from tuberculosis than at any other point in the whole State of Maryland. One line from the report of the Association for the Improvement of the Condition of the Poor, indicates at least one cause for this condition. The report stated that of the two hundred and fifteen houses in Biddle Alley seventy-one had leaky roofs.

In these narrow alleys, however, tons of washing were gathered every week from the best homes in the city, to be laundered by the Negro washerwomen who lived in this district. This condition

is, of course, not different from what may be found
in almost any other Southern city, but it makes
clear the danger that threatens the more well-to-do
portion of the population, when the people, who
work for them and are dependent upon them,
are thus neglected and allowed to live in filthy,
unwholesome, and immoral surroundings.

As the committee progressed in its investigation
and sought to lay its plans to improve the conditions that they had discovered, they were made
to feel their dependence upon the white people of
the city and their inability to accomplish anything
unless they secured their support. Liquor boards
had been accustomed to ignore the protests of the
coloured churches. Police boards were not inclined
to consider their complaints. There seems to have
been a general feeling that coloured people were
either themselves so criminal, or so disposed to shield
and protect criminals of their own race, that their
protests against lawlessness and law-breaking were
not to be taken seriously. It became absolutely necessary, therefore, that the committee should secure the
support of the influential white people of the city, if
they hoped to be successful in the campaign they had
planned.

The next move, therefore, was to appoint a sub-
committee to secure the active interest of leading
white men. This committee visited the late Daniel
C. Gilman, ex-president of Johns Hopkins University;

Mr. Douglas H. Wylie, at that time president of the Chamber of Commerce; Mr. Eugene Levering, president of the Commercial National Bank; Bishop Paret, head of the Episcopal Church in the Baltimore Diocese; Mr. Joseph Packard, at that time president of the Board of School Commissioners; Mr. Robert H. Smith, a leading lawyer; Mr. John C. Rose, United States District Attorney, who subsequently acted as legal advisor for the committee; Mr. Isaac Cate, a retired capitalist; Mr. John M. Glenn, secretary of the Sage Foundation; Judge Alfred S. Niles, of the Supreme Court of Maryland, and Mr. W. Hall Harris, city postmaster.

All of these men, as soon as the matter was fairly presented to them, showed the heartiest interest in the plans and purposes of the committee. The members of the committee found, however, that there were certain questions, which continually occurred, to which they felt compelled to find a definite answer. For instance, one of the questions that was frequently asked was whether or not the saloons and dives, which they wanted suppressed, and the conditions of immorality surrounding them, were not due for the most part to the idleness and laziness of the coloured people. A study of the statistics compiled by the U. S. Census Bureau showed, however, that a larger percentage not only of the coloured women, but of the coloured men of Maryland, were at work than is true of the whites.

The committee were frequently asked in regard to the home life of the coloured people. In reply to this inquiry the committee pointed out that, while the conditions in Negro homes are, in many cases, not what they should be, nevertheless the rapid increase in the ownership of homes, particularly in the Druid Hill District, indicated that there was an upward movement in this direction, and this is true not only in the cities, but in the country districts as well. The statistics of the United States Census Bureau show, for instance, that the coloured farmers of the State own 57 per cent. of the farm lands they till.

Another question frequently asked of members of the committee concerned the effect of education upon the Negro. One of the men, I was informed, who was most helpful to the committee in its work, did not believe that the education paid the state what it cost, or was of any particular value to the Negro himself. In reply to this question the committee was able to show that the Coloured High School, which has been in existence more than twenty-five years, in all its history had furnished but one inmate for a jail or penitentiary. The committee was able to show, not only that this school had not made criminals of its students, but that, on the contrary, its former students and graduates were nearly all of them engaged in occupations in which they were more useful to the community than they otherwise could have been.

In order to illustrate the value of the education of the Negro to the community at large the committee cited the history of a Negro criminal, Ike Winder by name, who had murdered a toll-gate keeper in Baltimore County. To arrest, try, imprison and execute Ike Winder cost the state $2,000 more than it cost to educate one of the graduates of the Coloured High School. Assuming that Ike Winder, if he had been graduated from the high school, would have done as well as the other graduates, the state lost, not only the money expended in convicting and executing him, but it lost the economic value of an educated citizen. The committee estimated that the average earnings of an ignorant Negro in the state of Maryland were not much more than fifteen dollars a month, while the average earnings of an educated Negro averaged about seventy-five dollars a month.

The full and frank discussion of these questions between the members of the committee and representative white citizens whom they visited showed that there was a basis for coöperation between the best whites and the best blacks of the city. The result was the formation of a joint plan of action in which both races might unite their efforts. It was decided, among other things, to appoint an advisory committee of the whites to act in conjunction with a similar committee of the coloured people.

The first thing attempted was the organisation of a larger and more representative body of coloured men to be known as the Law and Order League. The purpose of this Law and Order League was, first of all, to create a public spirit among the masses of the coloured people which could be positively opposed to all forms of vice, immorality and crime, such as is fostered by the low saloon and dive. Petitions were drawn up and sent to the Liquor Board and the Police Board for the purpose of securing a better enforcement of the law and, if possible, a suppression of some of the more notorious saloons in the district. A series of meetings were held at Grace Presbyterian Church, at which the coloured ministers, doctors, lawyers, and business men all took part. In this way a campaign was begun to give Baltimore's coloured children a real chance in life.

A law and order league was formed and a petition to the Liquor Licence Board was drawn up. A bill was drawn up for presentation to the Legislature to prevent the sale of liquor in certain sections of Baltimore.

Finally, it was decided, in order to arouse sentiment in favour of the work of the League among the white people, to take measures to present their case to the ministers of both races. Members of the committee appeared before the Association of Presbyterian, Congregational, and Reformed Church ministers, before the Ministerial Union, the Methodist Ministers' Association, before the African Methodist Episcopal Ministers' Association and the Coloured Ministerial Union. One of the ministers, who was most helpful to the committee, I was informed, was an ex-Confederate chaplain, and three or four of the other white men who took an active interest in the work were Confederate soldiers.

After the petition, drawn up by the Law and Order League, had been approved by the Advisory Committee of white men, it was presented to the Board of Liquor Licence Commissioners. Perhaps because of the source from which the petition came, it created considerable comment in the newspapers. The Baltimore *Sun*, in commenting upon it, said:

The Liquor Licence Board's action upon the petition of many good citizens for a reduction of the number of licences for saloons at certain points in northwest Baltimore is awaited with much interest by that portion of the public which is concerned in the good order of that section of the city. It is a section which has not in the past had the best reputation for freedom from acts of violence and disorder on the part of Negro roughs and bad characters, and this is believed to be connected with the fact that in a comparatively small area there are as many as forty-five saloons, of which eight are conducted by Negroes. As a considerable portion of the Negro population of the city has its habitat there, it is interesting to note that the most urgent advocates of a reduction of the number of the saloons are the Coloured Law and Order League, with many coloured ministers, teachers and lawyers. . . . The white element of the northwestern section is also concerned to have eliminated, as far as possible, the danger to peace and order created by the objectionable places in its neighbourhood. It is clearly up to the Liquor Licence Board to exercise, in the public interest, the wide discretion it possesses. When saloons are excessively numerous and a menace to good people, licences may and should be withdrawn till the quota for each neighbourhood is within reasonable limits.

An interesting feature of the struggle was the petition sent in by property-holders on McCulloh Street. McCulloh Street immediately adjoins Druid Hill on the north, and marks the boundary between the white and the coloured districts. The people in this street bitterly resented the "invasion" of Druid Hill Avenue by the blacks. Their action in coming to the support of the Law and Order League was consequently a great and welcome surprise.

One of the points brought out in the discussion before the Board of Liquor Licence Commissioners was that the presence of so large a number of saloons in this neighbourhood had depreciated the value of the property in some cases as much as 100 per cent. There was a disposition at first to charge this depreciation in value to the presence of coloured people. It was asserted that coloured people always lowered the value of property. This charge was easily disproved by showing that on the upper end of Druid Hill Avenue, in the neighbourhood into which the better class of coloured people were moving, property was actually selling at higher prices than it had reached when it was inhabited wholly by whites. One of the first coloured men to buy property in the upper Druid Hill District bought a house in a row in which prices have advanced over 60 per cent. It is said that houses in this neighbourhood rent and sell for from 20 to 50 per cent. higher than prevailed when the neighbourhood was white.

The testimony offered by the coloured people, by the men who owned the saloons and by the police, was so conflicting that the Liquor Licence Commissioners determined to make a personal inspection. They found eleven saloons openly violating the law, and determined that these eleven should not be re-licensed. The next day the Baltimore *News* gave the following account of the results of the inspection made by the Licence Commission:

The Board of Liquor Licence Commissioners deserve, and will receive, public commendation for their refusal yesterday to grant eleven saloon licences which the Law and Order League protested against. The saloons are situated on Druid Hill Avenue, Pennsylvania Avenue and adjacent streets, and have been the subject of grave complaint. President Howard and his associates could not signalise the close of their term of office better than by setting such an example to the incoming Liquor Licence Commissioners.

There is one development in connection with the hearings in these cases which calls for more than passing notice, and that is the testimony of the police as to the character of the saloons. It is a remarkable thing that with so many respectable people in a neighbourhood complaining about these saloons, the police — who should be most familiar with conditions — could find nothing wrong about them. Worse than this, in the case of saloons so plainly objectionable that the Liquor Licence Commissioners, on personal inspection, discover reason enough for refusing licences, policemen are found blandly swearing that they are decent, orderly places.

The report of the Liquor Licence Commissioners is a serious

indictment of the credibility of policemen as witnesses in hearings of this character, and suggests the need of a searching investigation to ascertain why the police are ignorant of conditions in the neighbourhood in question, which are shown to be shockingly bad.

The rejection of the application of the eleven saloons for renewal of their liquor licences was immediately followed by renewed applications under other names. But the Law and Order League had the support of all the best white and coloured people in the city, and the licences were not renewed.

I have described the work of the Baltimore Law and Order League* at some length because it illustrates the way in which the better element in both races are quietly getting together, in many parts of the South, in order to bring about an improvement in conditions which are dangerous to both races. Similar efforts in other directions and on a smaller scale are being made in many of the smaller cities in the Southern states. Even where these movements have not been wholly successful, the effort of the two races to get together in the way I have described seems to me a hopeful sign, and one on which we cannot place too much emphasis.

In regard to the political influence of the Negro, I might say, also, that close observation in every state in the South convinces me that while the Negro does not go through the form of casting the ballot

---

* A more complete account of the " Work of the Coloured Law and Order League," will be found in the publication of the Committee of Twelve, by James H. N. Waring, under that title.

in order to express his political influence to the extent that the white man does, in every Southern community there is a group of property-holding men, and often women, of high character, who do always exert political influence in the matters that concern the protection and progress of their race. Sometimes this influence is exerted individually, sometimes in groups, but it is felt nevertheless. I know any number of Negroes in the South whose influence is so strong because of their character that their wish or word expressed to a local or state official will go almost as far as the word of any white man will go. There is a kind of influence that the man exerts who is prosperous, intelligent and possesses high character, a kind of influence that is intangible and hard to define, but which no law can deprive him of.

I do not mean to suggest that the sort of personal influence I have described is in any way a substitute for the ballot, or can be expected to take its place. It ought to be clearly recognised that, in a republican form of government, if any group of people is left permanently without the franchise it is placed at a serious disadvantage. I do not object to restrictions being placed upon the use of the ballot, but if any portion of the population is prevented from taking part in the government by reason of these restrictions, they should have held out before them the incentive of securing the ballot in proportion as they grow in property-holding, intelligence, and character.

I have already referred, in another part of this book, to the town of Mound Bayou, Mississippi. This town, with the colony of which it is the centre, is one of the few places in this country in which the government is carried on entirely by Negroes. A few years ago I made a special study of this town, and I was very much impressed with a statement which I heard frequently repeated that Mound Bayou was one of the most orderly communities in the Yazoo Delta.

The records of the mayor's court show that, as Delta towns go, Mound Bayou is a remarkably quiet and sober place. There have been but two homicides in twenty years. Both of these were committed by strangers — men who drifted into the community in the early days before the local self-government and the traditions of the town had been established. One of the men killed was Benjamin T. Green, who was the partner of Isaiah T. Montgomery in the early days of the town. The man who committed this crime was afterward identified as a fugitive from justice, who was wanted for some desperate crime committed in the vicinity of Mobile. The murder was the result of a trivial altercation in regard to a box of tacks.

During the whole twenty years of the town's existence, only three persons have been sent to the Circuit Court for trial. Two of these were men convicted of theft. Since the town obtained its charter in 1898, there have been, up to February, 1907, but 163 criminal cases tried in the town. Of these, fifty were committed by strangers or by men who had come into town from the surrounding community. Twenty-eight cases were either never tried or were of so trivial a nature that no fine was imposed. Sixty-four were cases of disturbing the peace.

It is interesting to read the records of the mayor's court. They are an index to the life of the village, and reflect the changing current of public opinion in regard to the moral discipline and order of the town.

In July, 1902, the records show that fourteen persons were arrested and fined for failure to pay the street tax. Every citizen of the town is required to do three dollars' worth of work on the streets every year. Some had neglected to pay this labour tax, and allowed the streets to fall into a condition of neglect. As a result of a discussion of the matter in the town council, a number of the delinquents were arrested and compelled to pay fines amounting to $3.30, and costs amounting to $1.40 each.

Again, in 1904, a man was arrested for gambling. He had established what is known in sporting parlance as a "crap" game, and on Saturday nights a number of young men of the village were accustomed to gather at his place to gamble. He was repeatedly warned, and finally the town marshal and some of the more substantial citizens made a raid upon the place and arrested fifteen persons. The cases were dismissed after each man had paid a fine of two dollars. A year later, another man was arrested for running a "blind tiger," selling liquor without a licence. He formerly owned a store in the town, but began selling liquor, then commenced to drink, and was rapidly going to the dogs. After his place had been closed, he went out into the country and took up farming again. It is reported that he is doing well there.

During the year 1905, there were several disturbances in the town which were traced directly to the illicit liquor sellers. Men would come into town on Saturdays to do their marketing, fall to drinking, and end in a fight. Things became so bad at last that a public meeting was held in regard to the matter. As a result of this meeting, the town marshal, the mayor, and the treasurer were appointed to get evidence and secure the conviction of those who were guilty. Six persons were convicted and fined at that time. One of these, a woman, left town. Another is still under suspicion, and the rest, now on their farms, have become respectable citizens.

To my mind, the interesting fact in regard to these prosecutions is that they served not merely to correct a public abuse, but to reform the men who were prosecuted. In most cases, these men went back to the farms and became useful members of the community.

It seems to be pretty well agreed that the moral
conditions of the Mound Bayou colony are better
than those in other Negro settlements in the Delta.
Some years ago, when the question was an "issue"
in the community, a committee was appointed from
each of the churches to make a house to house can-
vass of the colony in order to determine to what
extent loose family relations existed. The report
of this committee showed that there were forty families in the colony where men and women were living together without the formality of a marriage
ceremony. As a result of this report, the people
of the town gave notice that these forty couples
would have to marry within a certain length of time
or they would have to be prosecuted. Nearly all
of them acted upon this suggestion; the others moved
away.

"Since then," said Mr. Montgomery, the founder
of the colony, in speaking about the matter, "we
have had no trouble of this kind. Upon occasions,
the women who are conspicuous in towns and cities,
and who travel in the Delta, making the various
camps on pay-days, and who more or less infest
the larger plantations, have tried to get a footing
here, but have never succeeded. They can get no
place to stay and have to leave on the next train.
This is now generally known and we have no trouble
on that score."

When I asked Mr. Montgomery how he explained

the fact that they had been able to obtain such good results in the way of order and morality among the people of the colony, he said: "I attribute it to the force of public opinion. The regulations that we enforce have public sentiment behind them. The people recognise that the laws, when they are enforced, represent the sentiment of the community and are imposed for their own good. It is not so easy for them to realise that where the government is entirely in the hands of white men."

One thing that has helped to maintain order in the colony is the fact that Bolivar County prohibits the sale of liquor. More than once the liquor men have attempted to pass a law that would license the selling of liquor in the county. Some years ago a determined effort was made to repeal the prohibition law. In order to secure the vote of Mound Bayou, which seems to have the balance of power in the county on this question, a "still hunt" was made among the voters in the community. A plan was arranged by which a saloon was to be established in the town and one of the citizens made proprietor.

"This scheme came very near going through," said Mr. Montgomery. "The plan was all arranged before we heard of it. Then we called a meeting and I simply said to the people that experience in our own town had taught us that a saloon was a bad thing to have in the community. I said that if the law was passed, a coloured man might run the saloon here, but in the rest of the county they would be in the hands of white men. We would pay for maintaining them, however, and we would be the ones to suffer. We voted the law down and there has been no serious attempt to open the county to the liquor traffic since."

In a certain sense, it may be said that the Mound Bayou town and colony have been a school in self-government for its colonists. They have had an opportunity there, such as Negro people have rarely had elsewhere, to learn the real meaning of political institutions and to prepare themselves for the duties and responsibilities of citizenship.

It is interesting to note, in this connection, that this is one of the few instances in which Negroes have ever organised and maintained in any Southern state a government which has gained the entire respect of the Southern people. A writer in a recent number of the *Planter's Journal*, published in Memphis, says:

Will the Negro as a race work out his own salvation along Mound Bayou lines? Quien sabe? These have worked out for themselves a better local government than any superior people has ever done for them in freedom. But it is a generally accepted principle in political economy that any homogeneous people will in time do this. These people have their local government, but it is in consonance with the county, state, and national governments and international conventions, all in the hands of another race. Could they conduct as successfully a county government in addition to their local government and still under the state and national governments of another race? Enough Negroes of the Mound Bayou type, and guided as they were in the beginning, will be able to do so.

In view of the oft-repeated statement that Negroes have made a failure of government wherever they have tried it, either in Africa or America, how can we account, we may ask, for the success of the Mound Bayou colony?

In the first place, I should say it was due in part to the fact that the colony is small. I think it will be found that in most cases where a people have learned to govern themselves they have taken their first lessons in small communities. In fact, government in the United States has grown gradually out of the Town Meeting, where the interests of all individuals were so closely knit together that each member was able to feel and understand his responsibility to every other as he could not so readily have done elsewhere.

Another reason why this town has succeeded thus far is, I believe, because it is a pioneer work of Negroes themselves. The men who came and settled in this town have had an opportunity to grow up with it and the growth of the town has been an education to them. Besides, in this town Negroes are not merely inhabitants, but they are owners, and they feel the responsibility of ownership. They possess the land, they own the stores, the cotton-gins, the bank, and the cotton-seed oil mill.

More than any other one thing, however, the Mound Bayou colony owes its success, I suspect, to the vision, the enterprise, and the public spirit of the men who have been its leaders: Isaiah T. Montgomery, the founder, and Charles Banks. These have clearly seen that their own permanent success is identified with the success of the people by whom they were surrounded, and that their greatest opportunities are in helping to build up the members of their own race.

I have spoken, in what preceded, of what Negoes are doing in the way of self-government in towns like Mound Bayou, and of what Negroes are doing through the Law and Order Leagues, as in Baltimore, to secure the enforcement of the law in the communities in which they live. I should like to say a word, in conclusion, of another organisation, which although it has not sought to exercise any direct influence in securing good government and the proper enforcement of the law, has done much to bring about better conditions, in this and other directions, among the people where it exists. I refer to what is known as the Farmers' Improvement Society, of Texas, one of the most interesting of the many organisations of coloured people which have sprung up since emancipation, and one that has exercised an inspiring and helpful influence upon the people it has reached.

This society, which had a membership, in 1908, of

9,256 among the Negro farmers of Texas, was organised, in 1895, under the leadership of R. L. Smith, of Paris, Texas. It was the outgrowth of a village improvement society which Mr. Smith organised in Freedmantown, which was the name given to the coloured quarter of Oakland, Texas, where he was teaching at the time. It is an interesting fact in this connection that Mr. Smith received the suggestion for the organisation of this society from reading an article in the *Youths' Companion*, describing the work of the Village Improvement Society in Litchfield, Connecticut. This circumstance suggests one of the benefits which the art of reading conferred upon the coloured people of which we do not usually take an account.

While the first purpose of this society was to save money for its members by purchasing provisions in common, and in large quantities, it eventually sought to improve its members in every direction. In order to do this, Mr. Smith decided to adopt the forms of fraternal organisations and confer degrees, first, upon those who succeeded in getting out of the chronic condition of debt in which they lived; and, second, upon those who, in the comprehensive language of Mr. Smith, "made the most progress in civilisation."

The degrees were twelve in number. The first degree was conferred upon the member who succeeded in "running" himself three months,

without opening an account; the second, upon the
member running himself six months; the third,
nine months, and the fourth twelve months; the
fifth was conferred upon the members who maintained themselves the entire year, and had a surplus of twenty-five dollars; the sixth, the same, with
a surplus of one hundred dollars; the seventh the
same, with a surplus of one hundred and fifty dollars; and the eighth, with a surplus of two hundred
dollars; and so on, up to the twelfth degree, which
was called the Grand Patriarch degree, and entitled
its possessor to membership in the annual convoca-
tion without election, "thereby creating," as Mr.
Smith explains, "a permanent delegateship of successful members, who had worked out their salvation and were actually fitted for leadership by growth
in the essentials of civilisation."

In 1907 members of the organisation owned
71,439 acres of land, which were worth considerably over one million dollars. The estimated value
of their live-stock was $275,000.

In 1906 the Farmers' Improvement Association,
having raised among its members something over
twelve hundred dollars, purchased land and started
an Agricultural College. The purpose of the
society was to provide a school in which their sons
and daughters could have the sort of training that
would prepare them to stay on the farm, and not
leave it for the doubtful advantages of the city.

R. L. Smith is one of the younger generation of coloured men. Born in Charleston, South Carolina, in 1861, he was a student for a while during Reconstruction days at the University of South Carolina, but was eventually starved out when the law passed which cut off the funds for the scholarships of Negro students. He afterward was graduated at Atlanta University, returned to Charleston and ran a Republican paper. That enterprise naturally failed with the downfall of the Reconstruction government in the South, and Mr. Smith decided to go to Texas and begin life anew as a teacher.

Although he had intended to keep out of politics after leaving South Carolina, he found himself, in 1895, running for the Legislature of Texas. Much to his surprise he was elected, a majority of white voters having given him their support. "Since the white people," said Mr. Smith, in relating this experience, "were kind enough to say that a man who felt so much interest in the upbuilding of his own race should be endorsed in some way by the whites, I thought that the race problem was solved sure enough."

Mr. Smith has continued in the work which he began, and, although he had had one or two offices under the Federal Government since that time, he has never permitted that to turn him aside from the important original work which he has undertaken for the improvement of the Negro farmers in Texas.

In spite of Mr. Smith's election to the Legislature, the race problem is not yet solved in Texas. Nevertheless, at our annual Negro Conference at Tuskegee, Mr. Smith has never failed to be present and to report progress.

CHAPTER XV

ONE of the most striking and interesting things about the American Negro, and one which has impressed itself upon my mind more and more in the course of the preparation of this book, is the extent to which the black man has intertwined his life with that of the people of the white race about him. While it is true that hardly any other race of people, that has come to this country, has remained, in certain respects, so separate and distinct a part of the population as the Negro, it is also true that no race, which has come to this country, has so woven its life into the life of the people about it. No race has shared to a greater extent in the work and activities of the original settlers of the country, or has been more closely related to them in interest, in sympathy and in sentiment, than the Negro race.

In fact, there is scarcely any enterprise, of any moment, that has been undertaken by a member of the white race, in which the Negro has not had some part. In all the great pioneer work of clearing forests, and preparing the way for civilisation, the Negro, as I have tried to point out, has had his part. In all the difficult and dangerous work of exploration of the country the Negro has invariably been the faithful companion and helper of the white man.

Negroes seem to have accompanied nearly all the early Spanish explorers. Indeed, it has even been conjectured that Negroes came to America before Columbus, carried hither by trade winds and ocean currents, coming from the west coast of Africa. At any rate, one of the early historians, Peter Martyr, who was an acquaintance of Columbus, mentions "a region in the Darian District of South America where Balboa, the illustrious discoverer of the Pacific Ocean, found a race of black men who were conjectured to have come from Africa and to have been shipwrecked on this coast."

It is said that the first ship built along the Atlantic Coast was constructed by the slaves of Vasquez de Ayllon, who, one hundred years before the English landed there, attempted to found a Spanish settlement on the site of what was later Jamestown, Virginia. There were thirty Negroes with the Spanish discoverer, Balboa, and they assisted him in building the first ship that was constructed on the Pacific Coast of America. Cortez, the Conquerer of Mexico, had three hundred Negro slaves with him in 1522, the year in which he was chosen Captain-general of New Spain, as Mexico was then called, and it is asserted that the town of Santiago del Principe was founded by Negro slaves who had risen in insurrection against their Spanish masters.

In the chronicles of the ill-starred Coronado expedition of 1540, which made its way from Mexico as far north as Kansas and Nebraska, it is mentioned that a Negro slave of Hernando de Alarcon was the only member of the party who would undertake to carry a message from the Rio Grande across the country to the Zunis in New Mexico, where Alarcon hoped to find Coronado and open communication with him.

I have already referred to the story of Estevan, "little Steve," a companion of Pamfilo Narvaez, in his exploration of Florida in 1527, who afterward went in search of the seven fabulous cities which were supposed to be located somewhere in the present state of Arizona, and discovered the Zuni Indians.*

Negroes accompanied De Soto on his march through Alabama, in 1540. One of these Negroes seems to have liked the country, for he remained and settled among the Indians not far from Tuskegee, and became in this way the first settler of Alabama. Coming down to a later date, a Negro servant accompanied William Clark, of the Lewis and Clark Expedition, which, in 1804, explored the sources of the Missouri River, and gained for the United States

---

* R. R. Wright, "American Anthropologist," vol. xiv, 1902.

the Oregon country.   Negroes were among the first adventurers who went to look for gold in California; and when John C. Fremont, in 1848, made his desperate and disastrous attempt to find a pathway across the Rockies, he was accompanied by a Negro servant named Saunders.

Recently in looking over the pages of the *National Geographical Magazine*, I ran across an article giving an account of Peary's trip farthest north. Among the pictures illustrating that article I noticed the laughing face of a black man.   The picture was the more striking because the figure of this black man was totally encased in the snow-white fur of a polar bear.   I learned that this was the picture of Matt Henson, the companion of Peary in his most famous expedition to reach the pole.   Just now, as I am writing this, I learn from the newspapers that Peary claims he has reached the North Pole and that Matt Henson was his companion on this last and most famous journey.

One reason why the Negro is found so closely associated with the white man in all his labours and adventures is that, with all his faults, the Negro seldom betrays a specific trust.   Even the individual who does not always clearly distinguish between his own property and that of his neighbour, when a definite thing of value is entrusted to him, in nine cases out of ten, will not betray that trust. This is a trait that characterises the Negro wherever he is found. I have heard Sir Harry H. Johnston, the African explorer, use almost exactly the same words, for example, in describing the characteristics of the native African.

Some years ago I was travelling through Central Alabama, and I chanced to stop at a crossroads country store. While I was talking with the store-keeper a coloured man, who lived some distance away, chanced to pass by. It happened that the merchant had a considerable sum of money which he wanted to send to some of his friends some miles distant. He called the coloured man into the store and put the money into his hands with the request that he deliver it to his friend as he passed by the house on his road home. My attention was attracted by this trans-action, and I asked the white merchant how it was that he was willing to entrust so large a sum of money to this particular coloured man. My question brought out the fact that the merchant did not even know the name of the man to whom he had entrusted this money. He was familiar with his face, knew that he had lived in the neighbourhood for a number of years, and felt quite secure in putting the money in his hands to carry to its destination.

In explanation the merchant told me that, in all his experience in dealing with coloured people in that neighbourhood, he had never been deceived when he asked one of them to perform some specific act which involved direct, personal responsibility. He went on to say that while the man to whom he had given this money, if the opportunity offered itself, might yield to the temptation of pilfering, he still felt perfectly sure that the money he had entrusted to him would be delivered in exactly the shape in which it had been turned over.

It is a common thing in the South for the heads of the household to leave home and be away for weeks and even months, without a single thing of value in the house being left under lock and key. In such cases Southern white people are willing to entrust, apparently, all their property to the care of Negro servants. In spite of this fact, I have rarely heard of a case of this kind in which the Negro servants have proved dishonest. I very seldom go into any Southern city that some banker, or retail or wholesale merchant does not introduce me to some individual Negro, to whom he has entrusted all that is valuable in connection with his banking or mercantile business.

I have already referred to the part that the Negro took in the wars which were fought to establish, defend and maintain the United States. One of the soldiers of the Revolutionary War who afterward distinguished himself in a remarkable way was Reverend Lemuel Haynes, and as I have not mentioned him elsewhere, I will do so here. Lemuel Haynes was born in West Hartford, Connecticut, in 1753. In 1775 he joined the Colonial Army as a Minute-man, at Roxbury, Massachusetts, having volunteered for the Ticonderoga Expedition. At the close of the War he settled in Granville, New York, where he worked on a farm, meanwhile studying for the ministry. By some means or other he succeeded in securing an exceptionally good education. In 1785 he succeeded in securing a position as a minister to a white congregation in Torrington, Connecticut. As there was objection from some members of the congregation on account of his colour, he removed to Rutland, Vermont, where he served as a minister from 1787 to 1817. In 1818 he went to Manchester, New Hampshire. It was while there that he made himself famous by opposing the execution of the Boone brothers, who had been condemned to death for murdering an insane man. He visited the brothers in the prison, and having listened to their story became convinced of their innocence, whereupon he took up their defence in the face of violent opposition. In spite of his efforts they were convicted, but a few days before their execution the man they were supposed to have killed, Louis Calvin, returned alive to his home. At that time people generally believed it was the coloured minister's prayers that brought him back.

In 1822 Mr. Haynes returned to his former home, at Granville, where he continued to preach until his death. He is most widely known for his "sermon against universalism," which he preached in opposition to Hosea Ballou. This sermon, which was preached impromptu and without notes, created a great impression. It was afterward published and circulated widely all over the United States and in some parts of Europe. Lemuel Haynes died in Granville, in 1832. He was, so far as I know, the first coloured Congregational minister.

During the Civil War there were several Negro officers appointed to take charge of the Negro troops, and immediately after the War several Negroes were admitted to West Point. Three of these have graduated. The only one of these now in the service is First Lieutenant Charles Young, who was Major of the Ninth Ohio Battalion United States Volunteers in the Spanish-American War.

Negro soldiers took a more prominent part in the Spanish-American War than in any previous war of the United States. In the first battle in Cuba the Tenth Cavalry played an important part in coming to the support, at a critical moment, of the Rough Riders under Colonel Theodore Roosevelt, at the Battle of Las Guasimas.

The Twenty-Fifth Infantry took a prominent part in the Battle of El Caney. It is claimed by Lieutenant-colonel A. D. Daggett that the Twenty-fifth Regiment caused the surrender of the stone fort at El Caney, which was the key to all the other positions in that battle for the possession of San

Juan. Eight men of this regiment were given certificates of gallantry for their part in the battle of San Juan Hill. The other Negro regiments which took part in these battles was the Ninth Cavalry and the Twenty-fourth Infantry, both of whom did heroic service in the famous battle for the crest of San Juan hill.

What impresses me still more, however, is the part which these black soldiers played after the battle was over, when they were called to remain and nurse the sick and wounded in the malarial-haunted camp at Siboney, at a time when the yellow fever had broken out in the army.

To engage in this service required another and a higher kind of courage, and I can perhaps give no better idea of the way in which this service was performed by these black soldiers than to repeat here the account given by Stephen Bonsal in his story of the fight for the possession of Santiago. He says:

The Twenty-fourth Infantry was ordered down to Siboney to do guard duty. When the regiment reached the yellow fever hospital it was found to be in a deplorable condition. Men were dying there every hour for lack of proper nursing. Major Markley, who had commanded the regiment since July 1st, drew his regiment up in line and Dr. LaGarde, in charge of the hospital, explained the needs of the suffering, at the same time clearly setting forth the danger for men who were not immune of nursing and attending yellow fever patients. Major Markley then said that any man who wished to volunteer to nurse in the yellow fever hospital could step forward. The whole regiment stepped forward. Sixty men were selected from the volunteers to nurse, and within forty-eight hours forty-two of these brave fellows were down, seriously ill with yellow or pernicious malaria fever.

Again the regiment was drawn up in line, and again Major Markley said that nurses were needed and that any man who wished to do so could volunteer. After the object lesson which the men had received in the last few days of the danger from contagion to which they would be exposed, it was now necessary for Dr. LaGarde to again warn the brave blacks of the terrible contagion. When the request for volunteers to replace those who had already fallen in the performance of their dangerous and perfectly optional duty was made again, the regiment stepped forward as one man.

When sent down from the trenches the regiment consisted of eight companies averaging about forty men each. Of those who remained on duty the forty days spent in Siboney, only twenty-four escaped without serious illness, and of this handful not a few succumbed to fever on the voyage home and after their arrival at Montauk. As a result thirty-six died and about forty were discharged from the regiment, owing to disabilities resulting from sickness which began in the yellow fever hospital.

I have described the manner in which the Negro has adapted his own life to that of the people around him, uniting his interests and his sympathies with those of the dominant white race. Perhaps I should say a word here of the way in which he has managed to keep his life separate and to prevent friction in his dealings with the other portions of the community. Few white people, I dare say, realise what the Negro has to do, to what extent he has been compelled to go out of his way, to avoid causing trouble and prevent friction.

For example, in one large city I know of a business place in which there is a cigar stand, a bootblacking stand, a place for cleaning hats and a barber shop, all in one large room. Any Negro can, without question, have his hat cleaned, his boots blacked, or buy a cigar in this place, but he cannot take a seat in the barber's chair. The minute he should do this he would be asked to go somewhere else.

The Negro must, at all hazard and in all times and places, avoid crossing the colour line. It is a little difficult, however, sometimes to determine upon what principle this line is drawn. For instance, customs differ in different parts of the same town, as well as in different parts of the country at large. In one part of a town a Negro may be able to get a meal at a public lunch counter, but in another part of the same town he cannot do so. Conditions differ widely in the different states. In Virginia a Negro is expected to ride in a separate railway coach, in West Virginia he can ride in the same coach with the white people. In one Southern city Negroes can enter the depot, as they usually do, by the main entrance; in another Southern city there is a separate entrance for coloured people. While in one Southern city the Negro is allowed to take his seat in the main waiting-room he will be compelled at another depot, in the same city, to go into a separate waiting-room. In some cities Negroes are allowed to go without question into the theatre; in other cities he either cannot enter the theatre at all, or he has a separate place assigned to him.

In all these different situations, somehow or other, the Negro manages to comport himself so as to rarely excite comment or cause trouble.

He often hears the opinion expressed that the Negro should keep his place or that he is "all right in his place." People who make use of these expressions seldom understand how difficult it is, considering the different customs in different parts of the country, to find out just what his place is. I might give further illustrations of this fact. In the Southern states the Negro is rarely allowed to enter a public library. In certain parts of the United States the Negro is allowed to enter the public high school, but he is forbidden to enter the grammar school, where white children are taught. In one city the Negro may sit anywhere he pleases in the street car; in another city, perhaps not more than twenty miles away, he is assigned to special and separate seats. In one part of the country the Negro may vote freely, in another part of the country, perhaps across the border of another state, he is not expected to vote at all.

As illustrating the ability of the Negro to avoid the rocks and shoals, which he is likely to meet in travelling about the country, and still manage to get what he wants, I recall an experience of a coloured man with whom I was travelling through South Carolina some time ago. This man was very anxious to reach the railway train and had only a

few minutes in which to do so. He hailed, naturally
enough, the first hackman he saw, who happened
to be a white man. The white man told him that
it was not his custom to carry Negroes in his carriage. The coloured man, not in the least disturbed,
at once replied: "That's all right, we will fix that;
you get in the carriage and I'll take the front seat
and drive you." This was done, and in a few minutes they reached the depot in time to catch the train.
The coloured man handed the white man twenty-
five cents and departed. Both were satisfied and
the colour line was preserved.

The facts I have detailed serve to illustrate some of
the difficulties that the coloured man has in the North,
as well as in the South, with the present unsettled
conditions as to his position in the community. The
Negro suffers some other disadvantages living in the
midst of a people from whom he is so different, with
whom he is so intimately associated, and from whom
he is, at the same time, so distinctly separate.

In living in the midst of seventy millions of the
most highly civilised people of the world, the Negro
has the opportunity to learn much that he could not
learn in a community where the people were less
enlightened and less progressive. On the other
hand, it is a disadvantage to him that his progress
is constantly compared to the progress of a people
who have the advantage of many centuries of civilisation, while the Negro has only a little more than

forty years been a free man.   If the American Negro, with his present degree of advancement, were living in the midst of a civilisation such as exists to-day in Asia or in the south of Europe, the gap between him and the people by whom he is surrounded would not then be so wide, and he would receive credit for the progress that he has already made.

In speaking of the progress of the Negro in America, I want to refer to a letter, published in Virginia in 1801, and addressed to a member of the General Assembly of Virginia.   This letter, which in many respects is a remarkable document, is supposed to have been written by the Honourable Judge Tucker, and was occasioned by a slave conspiracy which greatly disturbed the people of Virginia about that time.   This letter is, in part, as follows:

There is often a progress in human affairs which may indeed be retarded, but which nothing can arrest. Moving with slow and silent steps, it is marked only by comparing distant periods. The causes which produce it are either so minute as to be invisible, or, if perceived, are too numerous and complicated to be subject to human control. Of such a sort is the advancement of knowledge among the Negroes of this country. It is so striking as to be obvious to a man of most ordinary observation. Every year adds to the number of those who can read and write; and he who has made any proficiency in letters becomes a little centre of instruction to others.

This increase of knowledge is the principle agency in evolving the spirit we have to fear.

. . . .

In our infant country, where population and wealth increase with unexampled rapidity, the progress of liberal knowledge is proportionately great. In this vast march of the mind, the blacks, who are far behind us, may be supposed to advance at a pace equal to our own; but, sir, the fact is they are likely to advance faster, the growth and multiplication of our towns tend in a thousand ways to enlighten and inform them. The very nature of our government, which leads us to recur perpetually to the discussion of natural rights, favours speculation and inquiry. By way of marking the prodigious change which a few years has made among this class of men, compare the late conspiracy with the revolt under Lord Dunmore. In the one case, a few solitary individuals flocked to that standard, under which they were sure to find protection; in the other, they, in a body, of their own accord, combine a plan for asserting their claims and rest their safety on success alone. The difference is, then, they sought freedom merely as a good; now they also claim it as a right. This comparison speaks better than volumes for the change I insist on.

But, sir, this change is progressive. A little while ago their minds were enveloped in darkest ignorance; now the dawn of knowledge is faintly perceived and warns us of approaching day. Of the multitude of causes which tend to enlighten the blacks I know not one whose operation we can materially check. Here, then, is the true picture of our situation. Nor can we make it less hideous by shutting our eyes to it. These, our hewers of wood and drawers of water, possess the physical power to do us mischief, and are invited to do it by motives which self-love dictates and reason justifies. Our sole security consists, then, in their ignorance of this power and of their means of using it — a security which we have lately found was not to be relied upon, and which, small as it now is, every day diminishes.

I have quoted this letter at some length because it seems to me to describe, in a very remarkable way, the process and the method by which the Negro masses have advanced slowly but steadily before emancipation, more rapidly but not less steadily since.

The story of the American Negro has been one of

progress from the first. While there have been times when it seemed the race was going backward, this backward movement has been temporal, local or merely apparent. On the whole, the Negro has been and is moving forward everywhere and in every direction.

In speaking of his experiences in the South Mr. Ray Stannard Baker, whose articles on Southern conditions are in many respects the best and most informing that have been written since Olmsted's famous "Journey through the Seaboard Slave States," said that before he came into the South he had been told that in many sections of the country the Negro was relapsing into barbarism. He, of course, was very anxious to find these places and see for himself to what extent the Negro had actually gone backward. Before leaving New York he was told that he would find the best example of this condition in the lowlands and rice-fields of South Carolina and Georgia. He visited this section of South Carolina and Georgia, but he did not find any traces of the barbarism that he expected to see. He did find, however, that coloured people in that part of the country were, on the whole, making progress. This progress was slow, but it was in a direction away from and not toward barbarism.

In South Carolina he was told that while the people in that part of the country had not gone back into barbarism, if he would go to the sugar cane regions of Louisiana he would find the conditions among the Negroes as bad as in any other part of the United States. He went to Louisiana, and again he found not barbarism but progress. There he was told that he would find what he was looking for in the Yazoo Delta of the Mississippi. In Mississippi he was told that if he went into Arkansas he would not be disappointed; he went to Arkansas, but there, also, he found the coloured people engaged in buying land, building churches and schools, and trying to improve themselves. After that he came to the conclusion that the Negro was not relapsing into barbarism.

The Negro is making progress at the present time as he made progress in slavery times. There is, however, this difference: In slavery the progress of the Negro was a menace to the white man. The security of the white master depended upon the ignorance of the black slave. In freedom the security and happiness of each race depends, to a very large extent, on the education and the progress of the other. The problem of slavery was to keep the Negro down; the problem of freedom is to raise him up.

The story of the Negro, in the last analysis, is simply the story of the man who is farthest down; as he raises himself he raises every other man who is above him.

In concluding this narrative I ought to say, perhaps,

that if, in what I have written, I seem to have emphasised the successes of the Negro rather than his
failures, and to have said more about his achievements than about his hardships, it is because I
am convinced that these things are more interesting
and more important. To me the history of the
Negro people in America seems like the story of a
great adventure, in which, for my own part, I am
glad to have had a share. So far from being a misfortune it seems to me that it is a rare privilege to
have part in the struggles, the plans, and the ambitions of ten millions of people who are making their
way from slavery to freedom.

At the present time the Negro race is, so to speak,
engaged in hewing its path through the wilderness.
In spite of its difficulties there is a novelty and a zest
as well as an inspiration in this task that few who
have not shared it can appreciate. In America the
Negro race, for the first time, is face to face with the
problem of learning to till the land intelligently; of
planning and building permanent and beautiful
homes; of erecting schoolhouses and extending school
terms; of experimenting with methods of instruction and adapting them to the needs of the Negro
people; of organising churches, building houses
of worship, and preparing ministers. In short,
the Negro in America to-day is face to face with
all the fundamental problems of modern civilisation,
and for each of these problems he has, to some extent,

to find a solution of his own. The fact that in his case this is peculiarly difficult only serves to make the problem peculiarly interesting.

We have hard problems, it is true, but instead of despairing in the face of the difficulties we should, as a race, thank God that we have a problem. As an individual I would rather belong to a race that has a great and difficult task to perform, than be a part of a race whose pathway is strewn with flowers. It is only by meeting and manfully facing hard, stubborn and difficult problems that races, like individuals, are, in the highest degree, made strong.

THE END

INDEX

Abbott, Dr. A. R., coloured graduate Canadian University, II, 244.

Abolition, of slavery, in Canada, II, 239; in New York, 313; effect of, on free coloured people, I, 200.

Acadians, in Louisiana, I, 122.

Adams, first slave on Calhoun plantation, I, 150.

Adams, Lewis, responsible for location of Tuskegee Institute, II, 28, 29; on extent to which slaves were educated in the trades, 63, 64.

Addison, Nancy, endows St. Francis Academy, Baltimore, II, 346.

Africa, Coloured Baptist Mission in, II, 333; Ethiopian movement in, 334, 335; mission of A. M. E. Church in, 334; native method of smelting ores in, I, 32; slave trade in, 95; intermingling of races in, 22.

African Colony, Mobile, Ala., I, 103; visited by members of Alabama Coloured Medical Society, II, 138.

African, folk-tale of the origin of music, II, 259.

African Free Schools, New York, II, 132.

African Law, I, 70-72.

African Literature, I, 72, 73.

African Kings, artistic sceptres, I, 47.

African Medicine, I, 67, 68.

African Methodist Episcopal Church, founded 1790, I, 255; first general conference of, Philadelphia, 1816, 255.

African Methodist Episcopal Zion Church, started New York, 1800, I, 255, 256; founded 1820, 256; missionary of, to freedmen, II, 16, 17.

African Natives, at Tuskegee, I, 39.

African Native Markets, I, 49, 50.

African Natives, skill in hand-crafts of, I, 46-49.

African Religion, I, 65.

African Story Tellers, I, 72.

African Students, at Oxford, Eng., II, 285.

African Union Methodist Protestant Church, II, 345.

African Women, distrust white man's civilisation, I, 61.

Afro-American Presbyterian Church, see Presbyterian Church.

Agriculture, need of better in South emphasised by former slave, I, 308.

Agriculture, number of Negroes engaged in, II, 67, 68.

Aimes, H. H. S., slavery in Cuba, I, 120.

Alabama, Negro first settler in, II, 385; number of Negro banks in, 211; State Association of Coloured Physicians of, 175.

Albany, O., Station of Underground Railway in, II, 197.

Alarcon, Hernando de, Negro slave of, in 1540 carries message from Rio Grande to New Mexico, II, 385.

Aldridge, Ira, famous coloured actor, I, 294; II, 282.

Allen, Bishop Richard, founder of Free African Society, I, 253-255; founder and first bishop of the A. M. E. Church, 252-255; Abolitionist, 288; Associated with Lundy in Haitian colonisation movement, II, 237, 332.

Allen, Macon B., first coloured attorney in the United States, II, 185.

Allen, William G., editor National Watchman, coloured anti-slavery newspaper, I, 294.

Alexander, Archibald, influence of, on Jack of Virginia, I, 267.

Alienated American, The, ante-bellum coloured newspaper, I, 295.

Aloyons, Sister, convent name of Maria Becraft, II, 136.

American Board, see American Missionary Association.

American Missionary Association, work among Negroes, I, 276; Freedmen's Board of, II, 345.

American Mount Coffee School Association, II, 329.

American Music, slave songs, the only, II, 264.

American Negro, interest in Africa, I, 34; influence of, on African people, I, 35; so-called savage instincts of, I, 180.

Ames, General Adelbert, appoints Negro alderman, Natchez, Miss., 1866, II, 11.

Anderson, Charles W., United States Internal Revenue Collector, I, 93.

Anderson, Osborne, Negro companion of John Brown at Harper's Ferry, I, 175, 177.

Andrew, Bishop James Osgood, M. E. Church South, referred to, I, 258.

Andrews, Gov. John A., of Massachusetts, organises regiments of coloured troops, I, 323; friend of George T. Downing, II, 196.

Anthony, Mrs. Libbie C., officer National Federation of Coloured Women's Clubs, II, 329.

Anti-slavery Convention, first American, only coloured man to sign declarations of, I, 284.

Anti-slavery Convention, World's, in England, 1846, attended by Negroes, I, 283.

Anti-slavery, in Ohio and New England compared, I, 239.

Anti-slavery Society, coloured lecturer of, I, 307; fugitive slave shipped to, 217, 218; of Canada, report on refugee slaves, II, 243, 244; rooms of in Philadelphia, I, 215.

Arab Merchants, at Kano, I, 22.

Arkansas, number of Negro banks in, II, 211.

Armstrong, Samuel Chapman, experiment with Indian boys, I, 125.

Arnett, Bishop Benjamin W., first coloured man to represent a white constituency in the Legislature, I, 238.

Artis, Matthew, Grand Army Post named in honour of, I, 248.

Asbury, Bishop Francis, estimate of Harry Hosier, I, 258.

Ashanti people, skilled in hand-crafts, I, 46.

Ashmun, Jehudi, leading spirit in foundation of Liberia, II, 235.

Askia, Mohammed, African ruler, I, 55, 56.

Assaults on women, see Rape.

Athens, O., station of Underground Railway, II, 197.

Atkins, S. G., founds coloured normal school at Winston-Salem, II, 252; president of a realty company, 254.

Atlanta Exposition, first meeting of coloured doctors at, 1895, II, 180.

Atlanta Riot, some results of, II, 107.

Atlanta University, founded Atlanta, 1867, II, 140.

Attucks, Crispus, in Boston Massacre, I, 132.

Attwell, Mrs. Cordelia A. Jennings, first coloured public school-teacher in Philadelphia, II, 305–308.

Attwell, Ernest T., son of Rev. Joseph S., Business Agent, Tuskegee Institute, II, 307.

Attwell, Rev. Joseph S., coloured Episcopal minister, II, 306, 307.

Attwood, L. K., coloured banker, Jackson, Miss., II, 207, 208.

Augusta, Dr. Alexander T., coloured army surgeon, I, 326.

Augusta, Ga., Lucy C. Laney, school in, II, 308.

Avery Institute, ante-bellum coloured school at Pittsburg, Pa., I, 295.

Avery, Negro insurance company, Philadelphia, II, 156.

Avery, Elroy McKendree, on government expenditures for Indians, I, 137.

Avis, Captain John, jailer of John Brown, I, 175.

Ayllon, Vasquez de, Spanish explorer, Negro accompanies, I, 88, 89; constructs first ship on Atlantic Coast of North America with Negro labour, II, 384.

Bacon, Rev. Thomas, establishes 1750 mission for poor white and Negro children, II, 121.

Baganda, casuistic Christians, I, 28; of Uganda, 28.

Bahima, related to ancient Egyptians, I, 28.

Baker, Ray Stannard, statement of, in regard to Negro progress, II, 398.

Balboa, Vasco, Nunez de, Negro companions of, I, 87; finds race of black men in Darian Districts, South America, II, 384.

Baldwin, Maria L., coloured principal of white school, Cambridge, Mass., II, 309, 310.

Ball, J. P., adopts Ella Sheppard, gives her musical education, II, 268.

Ballagh, James, on white servitude in Virginia, I, 110, 111; quoted on rights of Negroes and Indians to hold white servants, 115; on Jack of Virginia, 267, 268.

Ballot, coloured delegation calls on President Andrew Johnson in regard to, II, 18; right of Negroes to, in Ohio, 134; restrictions upon, 370.

Ballot, see Politics.

Ballou, Hosea, coloured minister preaches famous sermon in opposition to Universalist teachings of, II, 390.

Baltimore, coloured secret orders of, II, 153, 154; homes of Negroes in, 254, 257; coloured high school of, 363; coloured ministers' association of, 366; coloured Law and Order League of, 358, 368, 369.

Baltimore Sun, comment on the work of Coloured Law and Order League, II, 364–368.

Bancroft, George, Historian, on religious and race prejudice in the colonies,

I, 90; on population of Negroes at time of New York "Negro Plot," 94; on white servitude, 108–110.

Banks, Charles, Negro banker, Mound Bayou, Miss., I, 24; referred to, II, 373.

Banks, deposits of Negroes in, Jackson, Miss., II, 205.

Banks, General Nathaniel P., commands coloured troops, I, 327; reconstruction work in department of, II, 9.

Banneker, Benjamin, assists in laying out District of Columbia, II, 60; achievements of, 60–62; tribute of Thomas Jefferson, to 62.

Bantus, of South Africa, legion of, II, 259.

Baptist Church, in relation to slaves, I, 261, 262.

Baptist Home Mission Society, educational work of, supported by Negroes, II, 341.

Baptists, coloured, start school in Boston, 1806, II, 134; schools supported by, 339; established publishing house in Nashville, 1896, 340.

Barbary pirates, sufferings of white slaves among, arouses sympathy for Negro slaves, I, 280, 281.

Barbers, society of coloured in Baltimore, II, 154.

Barrows, John, of Nashville, Tenn., referred to, II, 347.

Barth, Henry, travels of in North Central Africa, I, 22; descriptions of Kano, 53–56.

Bassett, Ebenezer D., principal of Institute of Coloured Youth, Philadelphia, II, 132.

Bassett, John Spencer, on displacement of white servitude by Negro slavery, I, 113; on right to enslave Negroes, 114, 115; on relations of master and slave, 148, 149; on free Negro in North Carolina, 201–203; on foundation of First Methodist Church in Fayetteville, N. C., 260; on social equality, 275; sketches life of Lunsford Lane, free Negro of North Carolina, 296–309.

Battle, C. C., aids Lunsford Lane to avoid disabilities of free Negroes, I, 300, 301.

Beaufort, Negro regiment organised in, I, 322; state convention in, "without distinction of colour," II, 14.

Becraft, Maria, principal first seminary for coloured girls in Washington, D. C., II, 135, 136.

Bedford, Mrs. Lucinda, of Nashville, Tenn., referred to, II, 347.

Belgarnie, Mrs. Florence, letter to, concerning Negro women causes organisation of National Federation of Coloured Women's Clubs, II, 329.

Bell, George, one of three coloured men to build first schoolhouse for coloured pupils in District of Columbia, II, 134.

Bell, Philip A., early Negro editor, I, 293.

Benedict, The Moor, Saint, son of a slave woman, I, 271.

Benezet, Anthony, abolitionist, starts evening school for Negroes, Philadelphia, 1750, II, 131; teacher of James Forten, I, 288.

Benford, Charles, held in trust as a slave by a free Negro, I, 206.

Benin, bronze castings, of I, 47.

Benson, John J., successful Negro farmer, II, 53.

Benson, William E., son of John J., II, 53.

Berea College, founded 1856, II, 140; exclusion of Negroes from, 347, 348.

Berean Building and Loan Association, II, 257.

Berean Educational Conference, II, 349.

Berean Presbyterian Church, Philadelphia, social work of, II, 349.

Berean Seaside Conference, II, 349.

Berean Seaside Home, Asbury Park, II, 349.

Berean Trades' Association of Philadelphia, II, 349.

Bermudas, Indians sold as slaves to, I, 130.

Berry, E. C., successful coloured hotel keeper, II, 197, 198.

Bethune, Thomas Greene, blind Tom, musical prodigy, sketch of, II, 271-276.

Beverly, Robert, slave of a corporation, II, 60.

Bibb, Henry, fugitive slave, forms organisation to purchase home for fugitive slaves in Canada, II, 242.

Bible, one book slaves knew, II, 3; desire to read, among Negroes, 125; Negro slaves interpretation of, 261.

Biddle Alley, coloured quarter, Baltimore, Md., II, 360.

Biddle University, Charleston, N. C., 1867, II, 140.

"Big House," the centre of slaves' world, I, 8.

Binga, Jesse, coloured banker in Chicago, II, 223.

Birmingham, Ala., Negroes employed in and near, II, 225.

Birney, James G., takes slaves North to freedom, I, 146, 240.

Black Code, in Ohio, Illinois and Indiana, II, 19.

Black Patti, see Madam Sissieretta Jones.

Black Swan, see Elizabeth Taylor Greenfield.

Blair, Henry, first Negro inventor, II, 77.

"Blind Tom," story of, II, 271-276.

Blue, Thomas F., librarian coloured library, Louisville, Ky., II, 354.

Boaz, Dr. Franz, art of smelting ores by Africans, I, 32; on race prejudice, 42, 43; on artistic industries of Africa, 47; on agriculture of Africans, 50; on native African culture, 58, 59; on African law, 71; on character of African states, 74, 75.

Bode, Louis, endows St. Francis Academy, Baltimore, II, 346.

Boley, Negro town in Oklahoma, II, 248-251.

Bond, Rev. James, coloured trustee of Berea College, II, 348.

Bond Servants, first sent out by London Company, I, 110; number imported to Virginia, 112.

Bonsal, Stephen, account of Twenty-fourth Regiment coloured regulars at Siboney, Cuba, II, 391.

Boston, Mass., separate schools for Negroes in, II, 134.

Boston Slave Market, Phillis Wheatley, purchased in, II, 286.

Boyd, Rev. R. H., founder National Baptist Publishing Co., II, 340.

Boyd, Robert Fulton, coloured physician and surgeon, II, 175; aids in establishing coloured National Medical Association, II, 180.

Bower, Charity, fortunes and vicissitudes of slave life illustrated by, I, 167-169.

Bowler, Jack, leader of slave insurrection, Virginia, 1800, I, 172, 173.

Boylan, William, friend of Lunsford Lane, I, 305.

Bradley, James, former slave testifies in Lane Seminary debate on slavery, I, 290.

Bragg, Fellow, free Negro, North Carolina, I, 202.

Braithwaite, William Stanley, coloured poet, II, 289.

Brandt, Captain, Indian, holder of Negro slaves, II, 239.

"Brierfield," plantation of Jefferson Davis, I, 153, 156.

Bristol, Eng., former stronghold of white slave trade, I, 111.

Brodie, John, referred to, II, 175.

Brooks, R. B., director of coloured bank, II, 223.

Brothers of Friendship, Negro secret order, property owned by, II, 156.

Brown, Andrew Jackson, vice-president coloured bank, II, 254.

Brown, Dr. Arthur M., conductor of coloured infirmary, II, 172.

"Brown Fellowship Society," organisation of Free Negroes of Charleston, S. C., I, 210, 211.

Brown, Henry Box, remarkable escape from slavery, I, 217, 218, 282.

Brown, Henry E., first coloured Y. M. C. A. secretary, II, 352.

Brown, John, Negroes with at Harper's Ferry, I, 175; rescue of Missouri

.slaves, 286; bust of, by coloured sculptress, II, 293.

Brown, J. C., free Negro, organises a society for colonisation in Canada, I, 226.

Brown, John M., one of delegation to President Johnson in interests of Negro citizenship, II, 18.

Brown, William Wells, agent Underground Railway, I, 282; sketch of 282, 283; assists in raising coloured troops, 323; Negro anti-slavery agitator, II, 83.

Browne, Hugh M., principal Institute for Coloured Youth, Cheney, Pa., II, 305.

Browne, Rev. William Washington, founder True Reformers, I, 24, II, 163; organises True Reformers' Bank, 216; referred to, 226.

Bruce, Blanche K., political leader of Reconstruction period, II, 23; sketch of, 23, 24.

Bruce, Roscoe Conklin, son of Blanche K., II, 24.

Bryan, Andrew, founder of Negro Baptist church, Savannah, I, 265, 266.

Buffaloes, Benevolent Order of, coloured, II, 148.

Bugg, Dr. J. H., director coloured bank, Savannah, II, 223.

Bukerè, Doalu, inventor of Vei alphabet, I, 72, and footnote.

Bunker Hill, Negroes in battle of, I, 310, 314; in Trumbull's painting, 314.

Burleigh, Harry T., coloured concert singer, II, 281.

Burrell, W. P., account of founding of True Reformers' Bank, II, 215, 216.

Burroughs, George L., agent Underground Railway, I, 286.

Burwell, Dr. L. L., conductor of coloured infirmary, II, 172.

Bush, John E., founder with Chester W. Keats, of the Mosaic Templars of America, II, 162.

Bushman, a student at Tuskegee, I, 25; colour of, 23, 24.

Bushmen, not black, I, 18; low estimate of by other African peoples, 19; not Negroes; 25, 26.

Business League, National Negro, meetings of in Boston and in New York, II, 229.

Butler, Gen. Benjamin Franklin, organises first coloured regiment, New Orleans, I, 321, 322; receives General Weitzel's letter objecting to Negro troops, 331; issues first proclamation of emancipation, II, 6; in New Orleans, 8, 9.

Buxton, Ia., work of coloured Y. M. C. A. in, II, 352.

Buxton, Ontario, Canada, settled by freedmen from Louisiana, II, 241, 242.

Buxton, Thomas Foxwell, refugee colony in Canada named after, II, 241.

Cable, George W., account of white woman sold as slave from Louisiana, I, 122; on Creole slave songs, II, 276.

Cain, Bishop Richard H., runs Reconstruction newspaper, II, 24; coloured congressman, 25.

Calhoun, Patrick, father of John C., becomes a slave-owner, I, 149, 150.

Calhoun, John C., early life on plantation, I, 149-152; impression of speeches on Lunsford Lane, I, 296.

Calvin, Louis, coloured minister saves white men from execution for death of, II, 389.

Calvin Township, Cass County, Mich., settled by Saunders' Freedmen, I, 246; condition of coloured settlers of, 246-249.

Cambridge, Mass., coloured woman principal of school in, II, 309.

Campbell, Bishop Jabez B., referred to, II, 347.

Canaan, New Hampshire, seat of Noyes Academy for Negroes, II, 130.

Canada, settlements of fugitive slaves in, I, 227; refuge for freedmen in, II, 238; becomes known as free soil to slaves, 239, 240.

Cape Palmas, referred to, I, 273.

Cape to Cairo Railway, constructed by native African labour, I, 30.

Carib Indians, enslavement of, I, 129.

Cary, Lott, extraordinary history of, II, 234-236; first Negro missionary to Liberia, 333; referred to, 343.

Carney, Sergt. William H., sketch of, I, 328-330.

Carr, J. S., referred to, II, 37.

Carroll, Henry King, church statistics of, I, 276, 277.

Carroll, Richard, on personal relations of whites and Negroes, II, 36, 37.

Carter, Granville, successful coloured book dealer, Greenville, Miss., II, 202, 203.

Carter, John, provides for emancipated slaves, I, 197.

Cass County, Mich., settled by freedmen and fugitive slaves, I, 245.

Caste System, growth of in United States, I, 199.

Cate, Isaac, retired capitalist, Baltimore, supports work of Coloured Law and Order League, II, 362.

Catholic, classed with Indians and Negroes, I, 91.

Catholic Church, schools conducted by, I, 271, 272; II, 346.

Catto, Octavius V., coloured schoolmaster killed in Philadelphia riot, II, 306.

Century Magazine, article of, on Negro homes, quoted, II, 255; poem by James W. Johnson, quoted from, 265.

Chain-gang, Negro children in, II, 110.

Chambersburg, Frederick Douglass's last interview with John Brown at, I, 176.

Charles, John, early Negro preacher in North Carolina, I, 260.

Charleston, Indian slaves bought and sold in, I, 129; colony of "free persons of colour in," 205; Negro population of in 1860, 206; Negro crime in, II, 86; clandestine schools in, 123.

Chatham Convention, I, 287.

Chatelain, Heli, African folk tales collected by, I, 73.

INDEX

Chavis, John, first Negro educated at Princeton, I, 274; school for whites of, in North Carolina, 274, 275.

Cheatham, H. P., coloured congressman, II, 25.

Cherokees, Indian slave-owners of Georgia, I, 133.

Chesnutt, Charles W., coloured novelist, I, 203; descended from free Negroes of North Carolina, II, 289, 290.

Chew, Benjamin, master of Richard Allen, I, 253.

Cheyney, Pa., industrial school for Negroes in, II, 132.

Chicago, Negro crime in, II, 86; Provident Hospital, coloured, in, II, 174.

Chickasaws, conspiracy of with slaves of New Orleans, I, 133.

Chretien, Paul, wealthy Creole Negro, I, 208.

Christianity, relation of to slavery, I, 115, 116, 238.

Christian League, organisation of by ex-Gov. Northen, II, 107, 108.

Christmas in Virginia, II, 57.

Church, Negro, the richest, in United States, 307.

Church Institute, for Negroes, of Protestant Episcopal Church, II, 345.

Churches, Negro, amounts collected annually by, for education, 342, 343.

Churchill, Winston, the Kingdom of Uganda, described by, I, 76, 77.

Cincinnati, Negro refugees in, I, 227; Negro crime in, II, 86; High School for Negroes in, 133.

Civic League, organisation of in Altanta II, 107, 108.

Claflin University, Orangeburg, S. C., II, 140.

Clark, Col. Elijah, referred to, I, 316.

Clark, William, accompanied by Negro servant in exploration of Oregon Country, II, 385.

Clay, Cassius M., publishes anti-slavery paper in Kentucky, I, 193.

Cleopatra, death of, represented by coloured sculptress, II, 293.

Cleveland, President Grover, effect of appointment on a Negro politician, II, 208.

Clinton, Bishop George W., reminiscences of Reconstruction, II, 38, 39.

Clinton, Bishop I. C., spiritual adviser of former masses, II, 39.

Clinton, Sir Henry, invites Negro to enlist in King's Army, I, 319.

Coffin, Levi, Quaker, abolitionist, President Underground Railway, I, 240.

Coke, Bishop Thomas, Negro companion of, I, 257.

Cole, Bob, Negro comedian, II, 281.

Coleman, organiser of coloured cottonmill company, II, 76, 77.

Coleridge-Taylor, S., Negro composer, I, 13.

Colleges, for Negroes, II, 140.

Collins, Captain Jack, free Negro, I, 209.

Collins, Winfield N., on domestic slave trade, I, 96, 98; on kidnapping free Negroes, I, 196, 197.

Colonisation, African, interest of Virginia Negroes in, II, 235.

Colonisation, see Liberia.

Colour line, difficulty of defining, I, 21; II, 393, 394.

Coloured American, Ante-bellum coloured newspaper, I, 293.

Coloured Citizen, Ante-bellum newspaper, I, 204.

Coloured Conservators, meets at Nashville, Tenn., adopts resolutions, II, 15, 16.

Coloured High School, record of the Baltimore, II, 363.

Coloured Library, of Louisville, Ky., promoted by coloured Y. M. C. A., II, 354.

Coloured Methodist Church organised, 1866, I, 256; schools supported by, II, 344.

Coloured Methodists, of Mississippi, money raised by, for support of schools, II, 345.

Coloured Patriots of the Revolution, the, I, 310.

Coloured Women's Clubs, national conference of in Boston, 1895, II, 329; names of, 326; first officers of, 329; work of the state federations of, 330.

Coloured Women, see Women, Negro.

Colquhoun, Archibald, desire of Africans for education, referred to, I, 80, 81.

Columbia Heights, coloured suburb of Winston-Salem, N. C., II, 254.

Columbia University, New York, Zulu takes oratorical honors at, II, 285.

Columbian Orator, The, Frederick Douglass, gets first notion of freedom from, I, 184.

Concklin, Seth, loses life in attempt to rescue slave family, I, 221.

Congregational Churches, coloured, in South, I, 276; First, of Atlanta, II, 107.

Connecticut, rights of Free Negroes in, I, 199.

Continental Army, number of Negroes on rolls of, I, 312.

"Contraband of War," effect of phrase on condition of slaves, II, 6.

Convention, Coloured, South Carolina, 1865, II, 14, 15; national, at Syracuse, 1864, 17; at Poughkeepsie, N.Y., 1863, 17; at Philadelphia, 1831, 17; constitutional of 1867, 18.

Convict Lease System, effect of, in Georgia, II, 100, 101.

Cook, Elijah, successful undertaker, coloured, II, 200.

Cook, George F. T., takes up work of father, John F., II, 135.

Cook, John F., coloured teacher in District of Columbia, II, 135; member of delegation which urged President Johnson to grant Negroes citizenship, II, 18.

Coon, Charles L., superintendent of schools, Wilson, N. C., on the cost of public schools in the South for Negroes, II, 143-146.

Copeland, John A., Negro companion of John Brown at Harper's Ferry, I, 175, 176.

Coppin, Mrs. Fanny Jackson, coloured teacher, II, 305.

Coppin, Bishop Levi J., referred to II, 305.

Corn Shucking Bees, I, 159, 160.

Cornish, Rev. Samuel, helps starts first Negro newspaper, I, 292; financial agent for coloured industrial school, 1831, II, 129, 130.

Cornwallis, Lord Charles, invites Negroes to join King's army, I, 319.

Coronado, Francisco Vasquez de, Spanish explorer, Negroes accompany, I, 88.

Cortez, Fernando, Negro slaves accompany to Mexico, II, 384.

Costin, Louisa Park, coloured teacher, Washington, D. C., II, 135, 305.

Costin, Martha, Educational worker in Washington, D. C., II, 305.

Costin, William, Washington, D. C., II, 135.

Cottin gin, effect of invention of, on slave labour, II, 122.

Cotton growing, in Africa, Tuskegee students as teachers of, I, 37, 38.

Cottrell, Bishop Elias, founder of Mississippi Theological and Industrial College, II, 344, 345.

Country Week Society, Boston, Mass., coloured woman a member of, II, 327.

Covent Garden, London, Eng., first appearance of Negro actor in, II, 282.

Covington, Ga., Dinah Pace's school in, II, 309.

Craft, Ellen, remarkable escape of from slavery, I, 227-229.

Craft, Henry K., grandson of William and Ellen, I, 231.

Craft, William, remarkable escape from slavery of, I, 227-229; attempt to kidnap, 230; later history of, 231.

Crandall, Prudence, prosecution for conducting Negro school, Canterbury, Conn., I, 200, II, 129.

Creole slave songs, described by George W. Cable, II, 276.

Creeks, Indian slave owners of Alabama, I, 133.

Crime, Negro statistics of, II, 85; maximum rate of, 87; in Northern and

Southern states, 87, 88; method of enumeration, 93–95; striking changes in statistics of, 95; in South Atlantic and Western states, 95; in Northern and Southern states, 96, 97; length of sentence in Northern and Southern states, 96; profits of, under convict lease system, 100; per cent. of, compared with seven nationalities in United States, 103; effect of education on, 363, 364; in Mound Bayou, 372, 373.

Criminal, juvenile Negro, II, 99; care of, in Birmingham, Ala., 110–113.

Cross of Leopold, conferred upon Negro actor, II, 282.

Crowther, Samuel, native African missionary, II, 336.

Crucifixion, Negro insurance company, Philadelphia, II, 156.

Crum, William D., former collector of customs, Charleston, S. C., I, 230, 231.

Crummell, Alexander, coloured episcopal minister, I, 272, 273; referred to, II, 195, 196.

Crummell, Boston, assists in starting first Negro newspaper in New York, I, 292; referred to, II, 195.

Cuffe, Paul, Negro colonisationist, I, 132.

Cummings, Harry S., member of Baltimore city council, II, 258.

Curry, Rev. A. B., on character of Negro, I, 164, 165.

Curtis, Bishop, coloured commander Grand Army Post, I, 248.

Curtis, Dr. Austin Maurice, coloured physician and surgeon, II, 175, 180.

Cutler, James Elbert, on lynching of Negro, II, 89.

Dabney, Austin, coloured soldier of Revolutionary war, I, 316–318.

Daggett, A. D. Lieut. Col., 25th Regiment, statement of in regard to 25th Regiment, coloured regulars at El Caney, Cuba, II, 390.

Daggett, David, decision of in Prudence Crandall case, I, 199, 200.

Dailey, Sam, sets aside part of farm for Negro reform school, II, 113.

Dahomey, slaves from uplands of, I, 103, 104.

Dance Hall, work of coloured men's club in abolishing in Savannah, II, 351.

Darian District of South America, race of black men of, II, 384.

Davis, E. M. aids in escape of Henry Box Brown, I, 218.

Davis, Jefferson, slave of, invents a ship propeller, II, 78; relations of master and slave on plantation of, I, 153–157; seat of United States Senate occupied by Negro, II, 12.

Davis, Joseph, brother of Jefferson, I, 155, 156; former owner of Isaiah T. Montgomery, II, 246.

Davis, Mrs. Jefferson, reference to Benjamin Montgomery in memoirs of, I, 155.

Davis, Rev. Samuel, letter of, 1747, on "the poor neglected Negroes," II, 119, 120.

Davis, Senator Garrett, opposes Fredmen's Bureau, II, 13.

Dawn, settlement of fugitive slaves, Dresden, Ontario, Canada, II, 240, 243.

Day, William Howard, coloured anti-slavery agitator, I, 295.

Dayton, Ohio, Daniel Flickinger, Wilberforce educated in, II, 337; Paul Laurence Dunbar born in, II, 338.

Dean, Jennie, founder of industrial school, II, 309.

De Baptiste, George, agent Underground Railway, I, 286.

Dédé, Edward, coloured musical director in Bordeaux, France, II, 177.

De Grasse, Dr. John V., first Negro member of Massachusetts Medical society, II, 277.

Delany, Martin R., coloured officer Federal Army, I, 326; anti-slavery agitator, 287, 288.

DeLarge, Robert C., coloured congressman, II, 11.

Delaware, rights of Free Negroes in, I, 199.

Denmark, South Carolina, seat of Voorhees Industrial School, II, 183, 184.

Derham, James, first Negro physician, II, 176, 177.

Derrick, Bishop William B., sailor in Civil War, I, 324.

De Soto, Fernando, Negroes accompany, I, 88.

Deveaux, John H., collector of customs, Port of Savannah, II, 222.

Dickinson, William, conveys a slave in trust to Quaker society, I, 243.

Dickson, Moses, founder of Knights and Daughters of Tabor, II, 158-160.

Dillon, Dr. Sadie, first woman granted license to practice medicine in Alabama, II, 171.

Dismal Swamp, scene of Nat Turner's insurrection, I, 174.

District of Columbia, Negro crime in, II, 86.

Dober, Leonard, Moravian missionary sells self into bondage, I, 119.

Dolarson, George, agent Underground Railway, I, 286.

Dooley, Normal and Industrial Institute, Alabama, gift to, II, 347.

Dossen, J. J., vice-president Liberia, I, 144, 145.

Dorsette, Dr. Cornelius Nathaniel, first Negro physician in Montgomery, Ala., II, 171.

Douglass, Frederick, fugitive slave, I, 8; Indian ancestry of, 132; interview with John Brown at Chambersburg, 176; first notions of freedom of, 184; opposed to emmigration of Negroes from the South, 186; member of Free Negro society, Baltimore, 212; escape from slavery, 223; Underground Station Agent, 223, 283; editor, North Star, 293; leader of Negro anti-slavery agitation, 295; assists in raising coloured troops 323; sons enlist as soldiers, 323; letter of, demanding political and military equality for Negro, II, 18; member of coloured delegation to President Johnson urging grant of Negro citizenship, 18; estimate of Robert Brown Elliott, 25; anti-slavery agitator, 83; describes how he learned to read, 127-129.

Douglass, H. Ford, coloured anti-slavery agitator, I, 295.

Dowd, Jerome, sociological studies of Africa quoted, I, 28; on instability of West African Kingdom, 75.

Downing, George T., noted Negro caterer, I, 294; member of coloured delegation to President Johnson, urging grant of citizenship to Negro, II, 18; friend of prominent abolitionists, 196.

Downing, Thomas, early coloured caterer, New York, II, 196.

Druid Hill, coloured district of Baltimore, Md., II, 257; invasion of by Negroes, 367.

Drummond, Henry, on native labour, Central Africa, I, 30.

DuBois, W. E. Burghardt, on slave trade, I, 95; on Freedmen's Bureau, II, 13; on Negro property owning, 256.

Dubuclet, coloured physician and musician in France, II, 276.

Duke, Ball, assists Negro hospital, Durham, N. C., II, 38.

Duke, James B., referred to, II, 38.

Dumas, Alexander, Negro blood of, II, 289.

Dunbar, Paul Laurence, poet, I, 25; interpretation of Negro life, II, 290-292; referred to, 338.

Dunlop, Alexander, member of coloured delegation urging President Johnson to grant Negro citizenship, II, 18.

Dunmore, Lord, Governor of Virginia, offers freedom to Negroes joining King's army, I, 319.

Dunn, J. P., Jr., statement concerning Indian cannibalism, I, 136.

East Baltimore Mental Improvement Society, society of Free Negroes, I, 212.

Ecumenical Council, London, Joseph C. Price delegate to, II, 343.

Education, conference for Southern, cost of Negro education discussed there, II, 143.

Education, Negro, Colonel Henry Waterson speaks in interests of, II, 114; work of Methodist Church for, 121; restrictions upon, 122, 123; special privileges granted Negroes, 124; opposition to in the North, 129; in Ohio, 133; in Massachusetts, 134; Northern aid to, 139; sacrifices of Negroes for, 141; relative cost of, and of white, 142; women work for, 305; amount collected for, by the A. M. E. Church, 342; amount collected for, in 1907 by A. M. E. Zion Church 342; economic effect on Negro, 363 364.

Education, Negro, see Schools.

Education of emancipated slaves, II, 136-140.

Education of native Africans in cotton growing, I, 37-39.

Education, restrictions on, during slavery, II, 118.

Educational day of A. M. E. Church, II, 343.

Edwards, Henry Stillwell, on progress of the Negro, II, 255.

Eggleston, Rev. E. F., pastor Grace Presbyterian Union Church, Baltimore, Md., II, 360.

Elgin Settlement, of fugitive slaves at Buxton, Ontario, Canada, II, 241.

Elks, Improved Benevolent and Protective Order of, coloured, II, 148.

Ellicott, George, friend and benefactor of Benjamin Banneker, II, 61.

Elliott, Robert Brown, coloured congressman, II, 24, 25.

Emancipation, agitation begun for in Pennsylvania, I, 280; of slaves in Rhode Island, 1788, I, 313.

Emancipation Proclamation, limited in its application, II, 6.

Emigrant Aid Society, Amos A. Lawrence member of, I, 315.

Emigration office, Haitian, at Baltimore, II, 237.

Enterprise Academy, ante-bellum coloured school at Albany, O., II, 197.

Estevan, Negro explorer, discovers the Zuni Indians, II, 385.

Ethiopian Church, II, 334, 335.

Ethiopian Movement, II, 334, 335.

Evans, Henry, founder of Methodist Church in Fayetteville, N. C., I, 260, 261.

Evans, Phillip, agent Underground Railway, I, 286.

Evans, Dr. Matilda A., founder of coloured hospital, Orangeburg, S. C., II, 175.

Exodus, Negro, to Kansas, I, 186.

Fairbank, Calvin, slave abductor, I, 221, foot-note.

Fanti People, customary law of, I, 7c.

Farmers' Improvement Association, of Texas, II, 378-380.

Farmers' Institute, at Tuskegee, Ala., II, 192.

Fayetteville, N. C., founding of Methodist Church in, I, 260, 261.

Fee, Rev. John G., establishes Berea College, II, 140.

Feagin, Judge N. B., establishes voluntary probation system for coloured juvenile offenders, II, 110-113.

Fellani, ruling class at Kano, I, 22.

Fellani, see Fuhlas.

Ferdinand and Isabella, Letter of, to Juan de Valladolid, coloured, I, 86, 87.

Ferguson, Samuel David, Bishop of Cape Palmas, I, 273.

Fetishism, a system of thought, I, 66, 67.

Fields, W. R., vice-president Coloured Bank, II, 222.

Fifty-fourth Massachusetts, First Regiment of Coloured Troops raised in the North, I, 328, 329.

Fisk University, founded at Nashville, Tenn., 1866, II, 140; gifts to by Negroes, II, 347.

Flickinger, Daniel, missionary to West Coast, Africa, II, 337.

Florida, cost of Negro education in, II, 143; Everglades of, home of Afro-Indians, I, 133; slave raiders visit coast of, 129.

Folk tales of Angola, I, 73.

Foresters, ancient order of, II, 148.

Fort Wagner, Negroes' part in battle of, I, 328.

Forten, James, Negro abolitionist, I, 288, 289; sketch of, 290.

Fortune, T. Thomas, Seminole ancestors, I, 132.

Franklin, Benjamin, statue of, inspires Edmonia Lewis, II, 292.

Franklin College, free Negro sends a white boy through, I, 318.

Franklin, Nicholas, one of three Negroes to build first coloured schoolhouse in District of Columbia, II, 134.

Frazier, Henry, former master of Maggie Porter, II, 270.

Frazier, James, slave of, freed in Canada on writ of habeas corpus, II, 239.

Freeman, Ralph, anti-bellum Negro preacher, I, 268, 269.

Free African Society, founded in Philadelphia, 1787, I, 254.

Free Coloured Women, sisters of the Holy Family, founded among, I, 272.

Free Negroes, increase of from 1790 to 1860, I, 195; number of, in Maryland, 196; re-enslaved, 196, 197; rights of, in English colonies, 198, 199; restrictions upon, 200; of North Carolina, 201; property owned by, in Charleston, S. C., 205; societies formed among, 210; mutual benefit associations among, permitted in Maryland, 213; arrested for assembling in Washington, D. C., 213; number engaged in work of Underground Railway, 282; first convention of in 1817, 289; of Raleigh, N. C., 299; regiment in Confederate army, 320; regiment of, organised by General Butler, 321; in Massachusetts in 1777, 311; enlist in Virginia regiments in Revolutionary War, 312; of New Orleans, seek to obtain part in the Government, II, 14; rights of, in Northern states in 1866, 19; restrictions upon, 83; number of, attending school in

Maryland in 1860, 124; educational advantages of Creole, 123, 124; methods of obtaining education, 124, 125; business enterprises of, in the North, 195, 196; total value of property owned by, 209; help to found Liberia, 235; of North Carolina, Charles W. Chesnutt descended from, 289.

Freedman, relations with former master, II, 39.

Freedmantown, coloured quarter of Oakland, Texas, II, 379.

Freedmen, colony, in Haiti, II, 237, 238; difficulties in dealing with, II, 7; education of, 136-140; from Louisiana, settled at Buxton, Ontario, Canada, 241.

Freedmen's Aid Society, Negroes contribute to education through, II, 345.

Freedmen's Bank, history of, II, 214; effect of failure of, on freedmen, 215.

Freedmen's Bureau, organisation of, II, 9-13; coloured men employed by, 10; bounties paid to Negro soldiers by, 41.

Freedom's Journal, first coloured newspaper, I, 292.

Freedmen's Hospital, Washington, D. C., II, 174; Dr. Charles B. Purvis, surgeon-in-chief of, I, 290.

Friends, of North Carolina, slavery among, I, 240; German, protest against slavery in 1696, 242; progress of anti-slavery sentiment among, 242, 243; efforts of, to free their slaves, 243, 244; settlement of, in Cass County, Mich., refuge for runaway slaves, 245, 246; first schools for Negroes, established by, 280; aid to Elizabeth Taylor Greenfield, by member of, II, 277, 278.

Fugitive Slaves, shipped as express package, I, 218.

Fugitive Slaves, in Ohio, I, 240; names of distinguished, II, 83; settlements of in Canada, 240; names of, 240.

Fugitive Slave Law, effect of, in Ohio, I, 226, 227; increases number of fugitives in Canada, II, 240.

Fulah, compared with Hausas, I, 54.

Fuller, James C., collects funds in England for refugees in Canada, II, 243.

Gabriel, leader of slave insurrection, 1800, I, 172, 173.

Gaines, John I., leads coloured people, Cincinnati, in struggle for equitable division of school funds, II, 133.

Galilean Fisherman, Grand United Order of, II, 148; amount in death claims by, 162; Bank of Grand United Order of, Hampton, Virginia, 219.

Gambia, price of slaves in, I, 60.

Gant, Wheeling, referred to, II, 347.

Garfield, President James A., appoints Blanche K. Bruce Registrar of the Treasury, II, 23, 24; effect of election of, upon coloured people of Alabama, II, 190.

Garnet, Henry Highland, career of, I, 294, 295.

Garrett, noted anti-slavery Quaker, I, 294; becomes an abolitionist, I, 192.

Garrison, William Lloyd, meeting of with Benjamin Lundy, I, 192, reference of, to James Fort, 289; speaks at funeral of William C. Nell, 295; encourages Edmonia Lewis to become a sculptress, II, 293; referred to, 327.

Gayarré, Charles Étienne, author, on emigrants replaced by Negro slaves in Louisiana, I, 121.

Genius of Universal Emancipation, The, Benjamin Lundy's anti-slavery newspaper, II, 238.

Georgia, rights of free Negroes in, I, 199; Historical Collections of, 316; story of Austin Dabney, 316; introduction of slaves into, II, 121; property of Negroes in, 145; number of Negro banks in, 211.

German Labour, in Brazil, I, 121.

Germans, in Louisiana, replaced by Negroes, I, 121; found Bombardopolis, 122; in New Orleans, 122.

Gibbs, Mifflin W., coloured anti-slavery agitator, I, 295, 296; first coloured judge of a city court, II, 186.

Gibson, G. W., ex-president of Liberia, I, 68, 69; purchased by father and sent to Liberia, 195.

Giles, Goodrich, wealthy Negro farmer of Ohio, I, 236.

Gilman, Daniel, C., ex-President Johns Hopkins' University, supports Coloured Law and Order League, Baltimore, Md., II, 361, 362.

Gilmore, Rev. Hiram S., founder Cincinnati High School, II, 133.

Gilreath, Belton, on progress of Negroes in coal and iron mining, II, 72.

Glenn, Joe, defended on charge of rape, by Atlanta Civic League, II, 108.

Glenn, John M., Secretary Sage Foundation, supports Coloured Law and Order League, II, 362.

God, slave's idea of colour of, I, 23.

Gold Coast, inhabitants of, I, 70.

Goler, Dr. W. H., President Livingstone College, II, 344.

Good, John, supports master's children, I, 202.

Good Samaritans, Negro secret order, II, 148.

Gorden, Henry, referred to, II, 347.

Graceland, Moravian coloured school, Antigua, West Indies, I, 324.

Grace Presbyterian Church, Baltimore, meeting-place of coloured law and Order League, II, 365.

Grant, General Ulysses S., care of refugees slaves, II, 6, 7.

Grant, W. E., first suggests organisation True Reformers' Bank, II, 216.

Graves, Richard, trustee for purpose of emancipating slaves, I, 243, 244.

Gray, French, referred to, II, 347.

Gray, Rev. William, minister and founder of bank, II, 221, 222.

Green, Benjamin T. with Isaiah T. Montgomery, founder of Mound Bayou Miss., II, 371.

Green, Beriah, founder Oneida Institute for Negroes, I, 225.

Green, John P., Negro lawyer, Justice of the Peace, I, 203.

Green, John Y., free Negro carpenter and contractor in North Carolina, I, 202.

Green, Shields, Negro companion of John Brown at Harper's Ferry, I, 175-177.

Greene, Colonel Christopher, defended by Negro troops, I, 311.

Greene, John Richard, on white slavery in England, I, 111.

Greenfield, Elizabeth Taylor, coloured singer, II, 277-279.

Grimke, Mrs. Charlotte Forten, granddaughter James Forten, I, 290.

Grimke, Francis J., coloured Presbyterian minister, I, 290.

Gross, William E., caterer New York City, II, 195.

Guiana, Dutch and British, maroons of, I, 131.

Haiti, revolt of slaves in, I, 172; Benjamin Lundy settles colony of Freedmen in, 192; Bishop of, 273; U. S. Consul-general, II, 132; Philanthropic Society of, 237; A. M. E. Church in, 332.

Hale, Mrs. Ann, first conductor Hale Infirmary, II, 172.

Hale, James H., founder of Hale Infirmary, II, 172.

Hall, Mrs. Anne Maria, opens first school for coloured children, District of Columbia, II, 305.

Hall, Dr. George C., coloured physician, Chicago, Ill., II, 175, 180; visits African colony, Mobile, Ala., 188, 189.

Hall, Dr. R. M., wealthy coloured physician, Baltimore, Md., II, 257.

Hall, Primus, first separate coloured school in house of, Boston, Mass., II, 134.

Hall, Prince, founder coloured Masonic order, U. S., II, 148-151.

Hallowell, N. P., on Sergeant Carney in assault on Fort Wagner, I, 329.

Hallowell, Lieutenant-colonel, Edward H., referred to, I, 329.

Hamilton County, Ind., ante-bellum coloured settlement in, I, 241.

Hamilton, J. C., on Negro in Canada, II, 246.

Hampton Institute, becomes independent of A. M. A., I, 276; teachers of, in Gloucester Co., Va., II, 44; founded, Hampton, Va., 1866, 140; industrial teaching at, 141; summer school for teachers at, 310.

Hampton Negro Conference, studies of Negro crime, II, 91; story of True Reformers' Bank told at, 216.

Handlemann, Heinrich, on Negro in Brazil, I, 120.

Haralson, Jere, coloured congressman, II, 25.

Hargrove, Samuel, John Jasper's master, I, 263, 264.

Harper, Fenton, referred to, II, 320.

Harper's Ferry, John Brown's raid on, I, 175; pamphlet on, Osborne Anderson, referred to, 177.

Harris, Eliza, fugitive slave, original of Uncle Tom's Cabin, I, 240.

Harris, Joel Chandler, inventor of "Uncle Remus," I, 162.

Harris, Thomas N., conductor of coloured infirmary, Mobile, II, 172.

Harris, W. Hall, referred to, II, 362.

Harrison, W. P., gospel among the slaves, II, 119, 120; on origin of First Baptist Church, Savannah, I, 266.

Hart, Albert Bushnell, on slave insurrections, I, 171; on fugitive slaves in Ohio, 226; on Harriet Tubman, II, 284.

Hatcher, William E., life of John Jasper quoted, I, 262-264.

Hausa, colour of, I, 23; and Fulahs compared, 54.

Hausa, merchant, at Kano, I, 22.

Hawkes, Samuel, wealthy Negro of Cass County, Mich, I, 247.

Hawkins, Dr. Thomas S., coloured physician, Baltimore, Md., II, 359.

Hawkins, Rev. William S., life of Lunsford Lane quoted, I, 309.

Hawkins, W. Ashbie, referred to, II, 359.

Hawley, Colonel Joseph Roswell, on conduct, coloured troops, in assault of Fort Wagner, I, 330.

Haviland, Mrs. Laura S., opens school for refugees in Canada, II, 242, 243.

Haynes, Rev. Lemuel, Revolutionary soldier, first coloured Congregational minister, II, 388–390.

Haywood, Sherwood, owner of Lunsford Lane, I, 296.

Hazel, Richard, Free Negro, blacksmith, North Carolina, I, 202.

Heidelberg, University of, confers degree upon Negro, I, 284.

Henderson, John, pupil of coloured school-teacher, John Travis, I, 274.

Henson, Josiah, fugitive slave, original "Uncle Tom," II, 243; assists in establishing manual labour school in Canada, 243.

Henson, Matt, companion of Peary in discovery of North Pole, II, 386.

Hewlett, E. M., coloured city magistrate, Albany, N. Y, II, 186.

Higginson, Thomas Wentworth, on plantation melodies, II, 262–265.

Hill, Collier, leaves slaves to trustee, I, 243, 244.

Hill, Leslie P., principal Manassas Industrial School, Manassas, Va., II, 309.

Hill, William, influence of, on Jack of Virginia, I, 267.

Hodges, Willis A., coloured anti-slavery editor, I, 295.

Hodgson, W. B., account of slaves' translation of Gospel of John, I, 53.

Hogan, Ernest, coloured comedian, II, 280, 281.

Holloway, Richard, Free Negro of Charleston, I, 206.

Holly, James Theodore, Bishop of Haiti, I, 273.

Holly Springs, Miss., progress of Negroes in, I, 187.

Holt, Roland, helps establish Negro Masonry in America, II, 149, 150.

Honey Hill, Negroes part in battle of, I, 328.

Hood, Bishop James W., chairman first coloured convention, North Carolina, II, 16; first missionary in the coloured church to the Southern states, 17; leading spirit in founding Livingstone College, 343.

Hopkins, Charles T., organises Civic League, Atlanta, II, 107.

Horner, Rev. James H., referred to, I, 274.

Horton, George, M., slave poet, II, 288.

Hosier, Harry, first Negro preacher in Methodist Church, I, 257, 258.

Hospitals, for Negroes, the larger named, II, 174.

Howard, General Oliver Otis, organises Freedmen's Bureau, II, 9; Howard University named after, 140.

Howard, Thomas, Earl of Effingham, assists in establishing Negro Masonry in United States, II, 149, 150.

Howard University, founded at Washington, D. C., 1867, II, 140; medical school of, 178; graduates first woman lawyer, 184.

Howe, Dr. Samuel G., on Canadian refugee colonies, II, 241, 242.

Howells, William Dean, estimate of Paul Laurence Dunbar, II, 290.

Hubbard, Elbert, commends Hotel Berry, Athens, O., II, 198, 199.

Hubbard, William P., acting mayor of Toronto, II, 245, 246.

Humphreys, Richard, ex-slave-holder, establishes Negro school, II, 132.

Humphreys, Solomon, Negro slave purchases freedom and becomes business man, I, 200.

Hunter, General David, enlists regiment of former slaves, I, 322.

Huntingdon, Countess of, friend and patron of Phyllis Wheatley, II, 287.

Hunton, William A., secretary coloured Y. M. C. A., II, 352.

Huntsville, Ala., homes of James G. Birney, former slave-owner and abolitionist, I, 240.

"Hurricane," plantation of Joseph Davis, I, 153, 156.

Hurst, Rev. John, coloured minister of Baltimore, II, 359.

Hyman, John, coloured congressman, II, 25.

Ibo, Negro translates Bible into language of, II, 336.

Illinois, rights of free Negroes in, I, 199; coloured settlements in, 226; black code in, II, 19; number of Negro banks in, 211.

Impartial Citizen, anti-slavery coloured newspaper, II, 25.

India, Negro woman evangelist in, II, 322.

Indian, The, recedes before white man, I, 77; compared with Negro as a labourer, 120; compared with Negro, 125; and Negro at Hampton, 125; feeling of superiority of, 126; intimate association of, with Negro in America, 128; Negro white man and, 128, 136; as a labourer, 141, 142; mother of P. B. S. Pinchback on, II, 22.

Indians, intermarriage with whites prohibited, I, 130; intermixture with Negroes, 131; remnants of in West Indies, 132; Chickasaws conspire with slaves of New Orleans, 133; bounty on scalps of, 135; cannibals in United States, 136, note; cost of, to govern of United States, 137; numbers of compared with Negroes, 137; and Negroes at Hampton Institute, 138, 139; of Charleston, S. C., 206; first public school in Virginia for benefit of, II, 118; and Negroes, religious education of, 118, 119; fugitive slaves found refuge among, 239.

Indian Slaves, absorbed by Negroes, I, 131; price of, in Massachusetts, 129; sold to West Indies, 129.

Indian Slave-holders, in Georgia and Alabama, I, 133; in Western states, 141.

Indian Territory, Negroes slaves in, I, 134.

Independent, article on Negro crime quoted, II, 97.

Industrial Education, connection with economic advance in Southern states, II, 192.

Institute for Coloured Youth, started 1837, Philadelphia, II, 132; summer school for teachers at, 310.

Iowa, rights of free Negroes in, I, 199.

Insurance, Negro, II, 37; local companies in Philadelphia, 155; number of companies in United States, 1907, 161.

International Congress of Women, Berlin, Germany, Negro women represented at, II, 325.

Insurrection, slave, of Nat Turner, I, 173; of Denmark Vesey, 173; of Gabriel and Jack Bowler, 173; not inspired by revenge, 181.

Island Mound, Mo., first battle of coloured troops near, I, 323.

Italians, given privileges in United States not enjoyed by Negroes, I, 118.

Jack of Virginia, ante-bellum Negro preacher, I, 267, 268.

Jackson, Andrew, reference to proclamation of, to Free Negroes of New Orleans, II, 14.

Jackson, Deal, Negro farmer of Georgia, II, 53.

Jackson, Egbert, Negro youth receives severe sentence, II, 97.

Jackson, Gov. James, invites Austin Dabney to home, I, 318.

Jackson, Jennie, of original Fisk Jubilee Singers, II, 269.

Jackson, Miss., special study of economic condition of Negroes in, II, 204–206.

Jamaica, Henry Highland Garnet, missionary to, I, 294; maroons of, 171.

James, Rev. J. D., coloured probation officer, Birmingham, II, 113.

Jamestown, Va., first slave landed at, I, 85.

Jasper, ante-bellum Negro preacher, I, 262–265.

Jay, John, on white slavery in Africa, I, 281.

Jefferson, Thomas, sentiments on Negro slavery, I, 313; correspondence with Benjamin Banneker, II, 62.

Jenkins, Rev. O. C., founds Negro Farmers' Banking Association, Northampton, Va., II, 213.

INDEX

Jennings, Mrs. Mary McFarland, mother of Mrs. Cordelia A. Attwell, II, 307.

"Jerry Rescue," I, 225.

Johannes, among first converts of Moravian missionaries, II, 119.

John, emancipated slave appointed guardian his former master's ward, I, 197.

Johnson, Anthony, Negro slave and land owner in colony of Virginia, I, 198.

Johnson, Bishop J. Albert, A. M. E. Church, member of Baltimore Law and Order League, II, 360.

Johnson, C., Ferst, quits politics for business, II, 208.

Johnson, James W., coloured poet, poem on "Black and Unknown Bards," II, 265, 266; musical composer, 281.

Johnson, J. Rosamond, Negro comedian, II, 281.

Johnson, Lewis E., secretary coloured Y. M. C. A., Washington, D. C., II, 353.

Johnson, President Andrew, coloured delegation visits to urge Negro citizenship, II, 18.

Johnson, Richard, obtains patent to land in Colony of Virginia, I, 198.

Johnson, Sol. C., editor Savannah *Tribune*, coloured, II, 222.

Johnson, William H., Henry Box Brown shipped from Virginia to, I, 218.

Johnston, Sir Harry H., on diversity of native types in Africa, I, 28; on Negro slaves in India, 75; on character of emigrants to Liberia, 244, 245; on character of native African, II, 387.

Johnston, John, Negro owner of estate in Colony of Virginia, I, 198.

Jones, Absolom, joint author of account of plague in Philadelphia, I, 251, 252; establishes first Negro Episcopal Church in America, 252, 255; joint founder of "Free African Society," 253-255; petitions Legislature of Pennsylvania and Congress against first Fugitive Slave Law, 288.

Jones, John, visits President Johnson in interest of Negro citizenship, II, 18.

Jones, John G., wealthy Negro, Chicago, Ill., agent Underground Railway, I, 286.

Jones, Madam Sissieretta, coloured singer, II, 279, 280.

Jones, Wiley, owner street railway, Pine Bluff, Ark., II, 209.

Journalism, Negro, II, 187, 188.

Journalism, Negro, see Ante-bellum newspaper.

Jubilee Singers, Story of, II, 266-271.

Jupiter, Negro converted by early Moravian missionary, II, 119.

Juvenile Court, coloured, in Alabama, II, 111.

Kaffirs, drive Bushmen out of South Africa, I, 135.

Kano, Negro city, Western Soudan, I, 22; market of, described, 50; first visit of white man to, 53; compared with Chicago, 54, 55.

Kansas Relief Association, organised in Boston by Mrs. St. Pierre Ruffin, II, 327.

Kean, Edmund, plays Iago to Negro actor's Othello, II, 282.

Keatts, Chester W., joint founder of Mosaic Templars of America, II, 162.

Keebe, Ossie, native African of African Colony, Mobile, Ala., I, 104.

Kenbridge, Va., seat of school for freedmen, II, 307, 308.

Kenny, John A., coloured physician, Tuskegee Institute, Ala., II, 172.

Kentucky, rights of Free Negroes in, I, 199.

Kettle Creek, Battle of Negro soldier in, I, 316.

King, Rev. William, emancipates slaves and settles them, Elgin, Canada, II, 240, 241.

King of Prussia, confers distinction on Negro actor, II, 282.

Kingsley, Mary H., on importance of native labour in West Africa, I, 29, 30; estimate of the Negro, 43, 44,

46; native women's distrust of white civilisation, 61; Africans' point of view, 66; African religion, 67, 68; African slave trade, 101, 102.

Knights and Daughters of Tabor, International Order of Twelve, story of, II, 158-160.

Knights of Honour Savings Bank, Greenville, Miss., II, 219.

Knights of Honour, coloured secret order, II, 148.

Knights of Liberty, Negro anti-slavery secret order, II, 159.

Knights of Pythias, coloured, when organised, II, 153; property owned by, 156, 157.

Kongo people, basketry of, I, 47.

Koran, slave who could read, I, 53.

Kru people, farms and gardens of, I, 46.

Labour, of Negro in Southern states, I, 117.

Lafayette, Marquis de, Lunsford Lane meets, I, 296; visits Negro school, II, 133.

Lafon, Thomy, Negro philanthropist, I, 272; reputed millionaire, II, 209, 210; referred to, 346, 347.

Lake Erie, Negroes in the battle of, I, 310.

Lambert, Lucien, coloured musical composer, II, 276.

Lambert, Richard, father of Lucien, II, 276.

Lambert, Sidney, coloured pianist and composer, II, 277.

Land Owners, in Farmers' Improvement Association, Texas, II, 380.

Land Owners, see Farmers.

Lane, Bishop Isaac, founder Lane College, Jackson, Tenn., II, 344; referred to, 347.

Lane, Lunsford, free Negro of Raleigh North Carolina, I, 296-309; makes abolition speech to Southern audience, I, 302.

Lane College, Jackson, Tenn., II, 344; gifts to, by Bishop Lane, 347.

Lane Seminary, Cincinnati, O., growth of anti-slavery agitation at, I, 290;

Rev. John G. Fee, converted to abolitionism at, II, 140.

Laney, Lucy C., founder industrial school, Augusta, Ga., II, 308

Langston, John M., Negro congressman from Virginia, I, 235; terms by which, obtained freedom, 235; anti-slavery agitator, 295; Reconstruction makes political leader of, II, 22; date of admission to bar of, 185.

Lapsley, Rev. Samuel N., Southern white missionary to Africa, II, 338.

Las Casas, Bartolomé de, Negro bodyguards, I, 88.

Las Guasimas, Negro soldier's part in battle of, II, 390.

Laurens, Colonel John, on enlistment of Negro soldiers in Revolutionary War, I, 312.

Law, John, imports Negro slaves into Louisiana, I, 121.

Law and Order League, of Baltimore, II, 365.

Lawrence, last slave ship, I, 104.

Lawrence, Amos, member of the Emigrant Aid Society, in Kansas struggle, I, 315.

Lawrence, Major Samuel rescued by Negro troop, I, 315.

Lawrenceville, Va., Negro industrial school in, I, 273.

Lawson, Cornelius, coloured supervisor Cass County, Mich., I, 247.

Lawyer, first coloured in United States, II, 185.

Leader, coloured newspaper referred to, II, 24.

Leary, John S., first Negro admitted to bar in North Carolina, I, 204.

Leary, Lewis, Negro companion of John Brown at Harper's Ferry, I, 175.

Leary, Mathew, Free Negro, North Carolina, land and slave-owner, I, 203, 204.

Leary, Mathew, Jr., Reconstruction politician, North Carolina, I, 204.

LeCount, Caroline R., principal coloured school, Philadelphia, Pa., II, 306.

Lee, Joseph W., coloured hotel keeper, Squantum, Mass., II, 199.

Leonard Medical College, coloured, work of, II, 178.

Leupoldt, Tobias, Moravian missionary, sells self into bondage, West Indies, I, 119.

Levering, Eugene, President Commercial National Bank, Baltimore, Md., supports work of coloured Law and Order League, II, 362.

Lewis, Edmonia, Negro sculptress, II, 292, 293.

Liberator, Garrison's, assisted by James Forten, I, 289.

Liberia, struggle with native slave-traders, I, 145; settlement of Port Cresson, by Quaker Negroes, 245; American Negro in, II, 236; Mrs. Sharpe's Home School in, 329.

Liberia *Herald*, I, 293.

Liberian, see Colonisation.

Liberian College, Alexander Crummell, teacher in, I, 273.

Liberty League, coloured anti-slavery organisation, I, 287.

Lincoln, Abraham, Southern birth of, I, 249; Emancipation Proclamation of, referred to, II, 33; head of, by coloured sculptress, 293.

Lincoln Institute, founded 1865, Jefferson City, Mo., II, 140.

Lisle, George, early Negro preacher, Savannah, Ga., I, 265.

Livermore, George, views of the Nation's Founders concerning Negro, I, 319-320.

Liverpool, Moses, one of three coloured men to build first coloured school-house District of Columbia, II, 134.

Livingstone College, anniversary celebration of, II, 343, 344.

Loguen, Bishop Jarmain W., conductor Underground Railway, I, 224; sketch of, 224, 225; referred to, 283; anti-slavery agitator, II, 83.

Long, Jefferson, coloured congressman, II, 12, 25.

Longfellow, Henry W., bust of by coloured sculptor, II, 293.

Longworth, Nicholas, builds first coloured school in Cincinnati, II, 134.

Louisiana, Strange, True Stories of, by George W. Cable, referred to, I, 122.

Louisville, Ky., coloured Y. M. C. A. in, II, 354; meeting of National Negro Business League in, 341.

Lovejoy, Elijah, William Wells Brown associated with, I, 282.

L'Overture, Toussaint, leader slave insurrection Santo Domingo, I, 172.

Lunda, African Empire of, I, 74, 75.

Luca, Alexander C., Sr., father of family of distinguished coloured singers, II, 279.

Lucas, George W. S., agent Underground Railway, I, 285, 286.

Lugrande, E. L., coloured business man, Boley, Okla., II, 250.

Lundy, Benjamin, editor first abolition paper in United States, I, 192; interests Garrison in abolition, 239; starts abolition paper, Mount Pleasant, O., 239; meets prosperous free coloured man in Texas, 200, 201; establishes colony of Negro freedmen in Haiti, 192; II, 237, 238.

Lynchings, statistics of, II, 88; by what offences occasioned, 89.

McCarty, Owen, runaway white servant, I, 107.

McCord, Sam, successful Negro farmer II, 53, 54.

McCoy, Elijah, Negro holder of 28 patents, II, 78, 79.

McKee, Colonel John, of Philadelphia, coloured philanthropist, II, 346.

McKim, J. Miller, secretary Pennsylvania Anti-slavery Society, I, 217.

McKissack, E. H., treasurer Mississippi Odd Fellows, I, 188.

Magee, Rev. Joseph, friendship of, for a coloured preacher, I, 269.

"Ma'm Linda," story of Southern life, referred to, II, 299.

Manassas, Va., Industrial school at, started by Jennie Dean, II, 309.

Mangum, Priestly, pupil of John Chavis, coloured teacher, I, 274.

Mangum, Willie P., United States Senator, pupil of John Chavis, I, 274.

Manly, Charles, Governor of North Carolina, pupil of John Chavis, I, 274.

Maroons, of Dutch and British Guiana, I, 131; of Jamaica, 171.

Martyr, Peter, Spanish historian, belief of, that Negroes reached America before Columbus, II, 384.

Maryland Journal advertising runaway Irish servant, I, 107.

Maryland, rights of Free Negroes in, I, 199.

Masai, of Uganda, I, 28.

Mason, Dr. Ulysses G., conductor of coloured infirmary, Birmingham, Ala., II, 172.

Masonic Benefit Association, business of Alabama branch of, II, 161, 162.

Masons, Negro, first lodge of, in America, II, 149, 150; at funeral of George Washington, 151; number of lodges in United States, 1904, 151; second lodge in United States of, 151, in Louisville, 152; property owned by, 156–158; charities of, 158.

Massachusetts, Negro population of, in 1741, I, 94.

Matthew, freedman, completes payment to his master for his freedom after emancipation, II, 32, 33.

Matthews, James C., city judge, Albany, N. Y., II, 186.

Matthews, Mrs. Victoria E., officer National Federation Coloured Women's Clubs, II, 329.

Matthews, William E., member of coloured delegation urging President Johnson to grant Negro citizenship, II, 18.

Matzeliger, J. E., Negro inventor of machinery for soleing shoes, II, 79.

May, Samuel J., abolitionist, aids in the "Jerry Rescue," I, 225.

Meharry Medical College, coloured, Nashville, Tenn., work of, II, 178.

Memphis, race war in, 1866, II, 19.

Menendez, Pedro, settles Negroes, St. Augustine, Fla., I, 89.

Meredith, William, builds first Methodist Church, Wilmington, N. C., with aid of donations of slaves, I, 259.

Merrick, John, founder North Carolina Mutual and Provident Association, II, 37; account of, 38.

Methodist Church, coloured, see Coloured Methodist Church.

Methodist Church, Negroes attend first general conference of, 1784, I, 253; establishes Sunday schools for slaves, 1790, II, 121.

Methodist Discipline, in regard to slavery, I, 259.

Methodism, beginning of in North Carolina, I, 259, 260.

Methodists, Negro, first general conference of leading denominations, Washington, D. C., 1908, I, 257.

Mexico, Benjamin Lundy seeks a refuge for freedmen, II, 238; Negroes with Cortez in, 384.

"Middle Passage," slave memories of, I, 6; described by Mungo Park, I, 101; losses of slave during, 102.

Miller, Thomas H., coloured congressman, II, 25.

Milliken's Bend, Negroes part in battle of, I, 327.

Ministerial Union, coloured, Baltimore, II, 366.

Ministers, Negro, number of in United States, II, 182.

Minstrels, Negro, the first, II, 280.

Mirror of the Times, Ante-bellum coloured newspaper, I, 296.

Missions, coloured Baptist Church, II, 333; of the A. M. E. Church, 332, 333.

Mississippi, number of Negro banks in, II, 211.

Mississippi Theological and Industrial College, Holly Springs, Miss., II, 344.

Mob Violence, see Lynchings.

Mobile, Ala., colony of Africans near, I, 103; Creole Negroes of, 208, 209; grants license for education of Creole Negro, II, 124.

Mobile Bay, favourite haunt of slave smugglers, I, 103.

Mohammedan Fanatics, among Negroes of Uganda, I, 28; Negro, 54.

Mon Louis Island, Creole settlement on, I, 209.

Montamal, John, incident of Reconstruction in New Orleans, II, 7, 8.

Montgomery, Benjamin, manager of Davis plantation, I, 154-156.

Montgomery, Thornton, former slave of Joseph Davis, I, 155, 156; letter to Mrs. Jefferson Davis, 157.

Montgomery, Isaiah T., referred to, I, 24; former slave of Joseph Davis, 155; founder of Mound Bayou, II, 246, 247, 371; opinions of, in regard to moral and political conditions in Mound Bayou, 374-376.

Moore, Rev. George W., coloured field superintendent, A. M. Association, II, 269.

Moore, George Henry, on law of slavery in Massachusetts, I, 130.

Moorland, Dr. J. E., secretary coloured Y. M. C. A., II, 352.

Moravians, Negro, II, 119; established missions for Negroes, 119; of Salem, N. C., II, 253.

Moral Education Association of Boston, coloured woman a member of, II, 328.

Morris, Albert, Free Negro in North Carolina, I, 202.

Morris, Freeman, Free Negro in North Carolina, I, 202.

Morris, Robert, coloured attorney admitted to bar on motion Charles Sumner, II, 185.

Mosaic Templars of America, founded 1882, business of, II, 162.

Moten, Major Robert R., commandant Hampton Institute, I, 25; great-grandfather of, kidnapped from Africa, 102, 103.

Mott, James and Lucretia, aid in escape of Henry Box Brown, I, 218.

Moultry, Francis, J, coloured caterer, II, 196.

Mound Bayou, Miss., Negro colony in Yazoo Delta, I, 156, II, 246-248; self government in, 371; moral conditions in, 374.

Mount Meigs, Reformatory for coloured children at, II, 113.

Murray, George W., coloured congressman, II, 25, 26.

Music, of native Africans, II, 260.

Myers, George A, successful barber, II, 199, 200.

Mystery, Ante-bellum coloured newspaper, I, 287.

Napier, James C., founder One Cent Savings Bank, Nashville, Tenn., II 212.

Narvaez, Panfilo de, Spanish explorer, Negroes accompany, I, 88; accompanied by Negro Estevan, II, 385.

Nash, Charles E., Negro soldier and congressman, I, 324.

Nassau, Rev. R. H., on African religion, I, 65.

Natchez Indians, sold as slave to Santo Domingo, I, 130.

National Bank, Chelsea, N. Y., stock owned in, by Negro, II, 202.

National Baptist Publishing Company, II, 340, 341.

National Medical Association, coloured, sketch of, II, 179-181.

Nazarites, coloured secret order, II, 148.

Neau, Elias, establishes, 1704, school for Indian and Negro slaves in New York, II, 119.

Negro, The, in Africa, as represented in school books, I, 8; American, natives of Africa, 10, 18; colour, basis of solidarity of, 33, 34; the true, better than the Asiatic, 43; in the country districts of the South, 62, 63; power of adaptation of, 77; compared with the Indians, 125-143 part of, in slavery, 144; as an individual and as a race, in the South, 179; the educated, II, 91, 92; literacy of, compared with European nations, 117, 118; colonies, value of, 252; gift of poetic expression of, 284; mission for, in Maryland, 121; natural eloquence of, 318; relation to white man in slavery and freedom, 399.

Negro Abolitionists, I, 288; speech of at Raleigh, N. C., 1842, 302.

Negro Arch-deacons, in Episcopal Church, I, 273.

"Negro Artisan," Atlanta University Studies, II, 64, 65.

Negro Baker, large business of, in Jackson, Miss, II, 203.

Negro Banks, names of, II, 204, 207, 219–224, 250, 253, 254; number of, 211; types of, 212, 213; Alabama Savings and Loan, of Birmingham, 225, 226; moral and material interests interwoven in the work of, 231.

Negro Baptists, statistics of, I, 270.

Negro Barbers, increase of, II, 74; trade of frequently confined to Negroes, 199.

Negro Blacksmith, his place in social life of Africa, I, 47, 48.

Negro Booksellers, successful at Greenville, Miss, II, 202, 203.

Negro Business Enterprises, number of in Jackson, Miss, II, 205, 206.

Negro Business League, National, II, 204, 341.

Negro Business Men, origin of, II, 194, 195.

Negro Caterers, names of ante-bellum, II, 195, 196.

Negro Catholics, in Maryland and Louisiana, I, 271, 272.

Negro Church, work of in Africa, I, 34; Berean Presbyterian, social work of, II, 257.

Negro Churches, support voluntary probation officers, Birmingham, Ala., II, 111.

Negro Churches, see Churches, Negro.

Negro College, plan for, at New Haven, Conn., 1832, II, 129, 130.

Negro Conference, annual at Tuskegee, II, 50.

Negro Congressmen, names of, I, 324; II, 12, 25, 26.

Negro Craftsmen in Virginia, II, 60.

Negro Crime, case of Ike Winder, II, 364.

Negro Crime, see Crime, Negro.

Negro Domination, evils of so-called, II, 31.

Negro Education, see Education, Negro.

Negro Education, made to pay in Macon County, Ala., II, 46.

Negro Explorers, II, 384.

Negro Farmer, amount of land owned by, in United States, II, 47; conducts reformatory at Tuscaloosa, Ala., II, 112; of Maryland, 363.

Negro Farmers, names of successful, II, 52–54, 250.

Negro Farmers, see Landowners.

Negro Folk Songs, II, 4.

Negro Governor, elected in Connecticut, I, 87, foot-note.

Negro Grocer, II, 202.

Negro Hotel Keeper, most successful, II, 197.

Negro in Africa, diversity of stocks of, I, 20; as a labourer, 29, 30; inventor of art of smelting ore, 32; compared with American Negro, 33, 34, indefinable bond connecting with America, 34; affection for mother of, 44; stability of economic conditions of, 50.

Negro in Brazil, I, 129.

Negro in Business during slavery, II, 81; in Jackson, Miss., 205.

Negro in Canada, study of by J. C. Hamilton, II, 246.

Negro in Cuba, I, 120.

Negro Inventors, II, 77–79.

Negro Labour, in America compared with, in Africa, I, 31; Lower South, 117; in West Indies, 118; compared with Indian, 120; compared with white, 121; compared with that of other primitive people, 138, 141; most efficient in United States, II, 59; in hemp-bagging factories, 63; re-distribution of, 66; statistics of, in factories, 75; in Maryland, 362; used to build the first ship on Pacific Coast of North America, 384.

Negro Labourer, compared with white in South, I, 142; in cotton factories, II, 62; losing monopoly of trades in the South, 66.

Negro Landowners, in Virginia in the seventeenth century, I, 198; in Georgia, II, 41, 42, in Gloucester

County, Va., 43; in Macon County, Ala., 45; rate of increase, 46; compared with white in North Carolina and Georgia, 145; origin of, 194; in Chicago, 224.

Negro Mechanics, before the Revolution, II, 60; restriction upon, after 1830, 62; slave educated as, 63; number of, in slavery, 64, 65.

Negro Millionaire, reputed, II, 209.

Negro Missionaries in Africa, II, 336–338.

Negro Musicians of Louisiana, II, 276.

Negro Philanthropists, II, 209, 210, 346.

Negro Physician, drug stores owned by, II, 181.

Negro Plot, of 1741, I, 91–94.

Negro Poets, names of several, II, 288, 289.

Negro Politicians, names of, II, 22; character of those of Reconstruction period, 193; history of two former, 207, 208.

Negro Preachers, names of, ante-bellum, I, 257, 260, 262–265, 267, 269.

Negro Princes, in India, I, 75.

Negro Problem, courage quoted as solution of, I, 191.

Negro Progress, referred to, in speech of Congressman White, II, 27; in Georgia, 41, 42; in Macon County, Ala., 45, 46; since emancipation, 114; nature of, in United States, 206, 207; during slavery, 396.

Negro Schoolmaster, conducts white school in Granville County, N. C., I, 274.

Negro Self-government, test of, at Boley, Okla., II, 249; example of, at Mound Bayou, 371–378.

Negro Self-help, II, 158.

Negro Senator, first, II, 12.

Negro Slave, condition of, in seventeenth century, I, 112; appointed guardian of white girl in Virginia, 197.

Negro Slaves, in Greece and Rome, I, 85; fresh levies necessary, 118; in Indian Territory, 134.

Negro Slaves, see Slaves.

Negro Soldiers, contribute to the founding of Lincoln Institute, Jefferson City, Mo., II, 140.

Negro State, in Brazil, I, 75.

Negro Surgeons, the most noted named, II, 180.

Negro Surveyor, laid out District of Columbia, II, 60.

Negro Teacher, anecdote of an early, I, 42.

Negro Undertakers, II, 200–202.

Negroes, number of Louisiana in 1728, I, 121; intermixture with Indians, 131; Creole, 158, 207; home for aged and infirm, Philadelphia, 292, 293; industrial home for, in South Carolina, II, 36; employed in Durham, N. C., tobacco factories, 38; as employers of labour, 74; support voluntary probation officer in Birmingham, Ala., 112; special privileges of Creole, 124; in the professions, statistics of, 182; effect upon, of laws of political rights, 190–193; religious instruction of, by Presbyterians, 119; wealth of, in Louisiana, I, 207–208.

Nell, William C., coloured anti-slavery editor, I, 295.

Newby, Dangerfield, Negro companion of John Brown at Harper's Ferry, I, 175.

New Jersey, rights of free Negroes in, I, 199.

New Mexico, Negro explorer in, II, 385.

New Orleans, Negroes in battle of, I, 310; riot in 1866, II, 19; clandestine schools in, 123; reputed Negro millionaire of, 210.

Newport, R. I., headquarters of slave trade, I, 145.

Newspapers, ante-bellum coloured, I, 287, 293, 294.

Newspapers, coloured, I, 204; number of, in the United States, II, 187.

New York African Society, coloured ante-bellum mutual relief society, I, 212, 213.

New York City, Negro population of, in 1741, I, 94; headquarters of slave smugglers, 145; rights of free Negroes in, 199; Negro crime in, II, 86; coloured schools of, 132, 133; Negro caterers in, 195, 196; homes of Negroes in, 254.

New York *Herald*, criticism of Henry O. Tanner's painting quoted, II, 295.

Nickens, Owen T. B., aids in establishing first coloured schools in Cincinnati, O., II, 133.

Niles, Judge Alfred S., supports work of coloured Law and Order League, Baltimore, Md., II, 362.

North Carolina, life of free Negroes in, I, 199; mutual and provident associations, account of, II, 37; property of Negroes in, 145; number of Negro banks in, 211.

Northen, William J., organises league of white and Coloured men, II, 107, 108.

North Pole, Negro accompanies Peary to, II, 386.

Northrup, C. F., referred to, I, 248.

North Star, Frederick Douglass's paper, I, 295.

Noyes Academy, Canaan, N. H., open to Negroes, II, 130.

Nupe, Negro translates Bible into language of, II, 336.

Oberlin Collegiate Institute, founded 1833, I, 291.

Odd Fellows, coloured, of Mississippi, I, 188; first lodge of, II 152; under jurisdiction of England, 153; property owned by, 156,157; charities of, 158.

Ogden, Peter, secures charter from England for Negro Odd Fellows, II, 153.

Oglethorpe, James Edward, reports slave conspiracy in New York, I, 92; opposes slavery in Georgia, 116.

O'Hara, James E., coloured congressman, II, 25.

Ohio, rights of free Negroes in, I, 199; coloured settlements in, 226; black code in, 238; II, 19; first coloured school in, 133.

Oil mill, cotton-seed, erected at Mound Bayou, II, 248.

Oklahoma, number of Negro banks in, II, 211; Negro towns in, 250.

Old Folks Home, founded by True Reformers, Henrico County, Va., II, 165.

Olmstead, Frederick Law, on free Negroes of Louisiana, I, 207, 208; on arrest of free Negroes, District of Columbia, 213; on Negro mechanics, II, 62, 63; on literacy of Negroes in the back country of Mississippi, 125–127; on success of free coloured women, 301, 302.

Olustee, battle of, I, 330.

Oneida Institute, school for Negroes, Whitesboro, N. Y., I, 225, 294.

Ontario, Canada, Negro President Municipal Association, II, 246.

Oregon, Negro accompanies first explorer of, II, 386.

Orphanage for Negroes, founded by coloured woman at Atlanta, II, 109, 110.

Orphans' Home, for coloured children at Harvey, Ill., founded by Amanda Smith, II, 325.

Osceola, Negro wife of, I, 133.

Otis, Joseph E., visits President Johnson in interest of Negro citizenship, II, 18.

Oviedo y Valdes, Gonzalo Fernandez de, Negroes in Spanish settlement of North Carolina with, I, 83.

Oxford University, African students at, II, 285; Negro receives degree from, 336.

Pace, Dinah, founds industrial school and orphans' home, II, 309.

Packard, Joseph, President Board of School Commissioners, Baltimore, Md., supports work of Law and Order League, II, 362.

Page, Thomas Nelson, Negro characters of, referred to, I, 162–164.

Palmares, Negro state in South America, I, 75.

Panama, inhabitants of, mixed Spanish, Indian and Negro blood, I, 131.

Paret, Rt. Rev. William, Baltimore, Md., supports work of Coloured Law and Order League, II, 362.

Paris Exposition, Negro gains prize at, for cotton, II, 53.

Park, Joshua, referred to, II, 347.

Park, Mungo, travels of, in Soudan, I, 53; on African slave trade, 95–101; befriended by African woman, II, 297, 298.

Parton, James, history of General Butler in New Orleans, II, 8.

Patterson, David, sends slaves to Haiti, II, 237.

Payne, Bishop Daniel A., befriended by free Coloured Society, Charleston, S. C., I, 211; founder of Wilberforce University, 237, 238; referred to, II, 347.

Peary, Robert E, Negro accompanies, to North Pole, II, 386.

Pemberton, James, manager Jefferson Davis plantation, I, 156.

Penn, I. Garland, brings about the first national meeting of Negro physicians, Atlanta Exposition, 1895, II, 179, 180.

Pennington, Rev. James W. C., agent Underground Railway, I, 283, 284; presides at coloured political convention, Syracuse, 1863, II, 17.

Pennsylvania, Negro population of, 1754, I, 94; rights of free Negroes in, 199; number of Negro banks in, II, 211.

Pennsylvania Young Men's Society, promotes Negro emigration to Africa, I, 244.

Perry, C. W., of Boley, Okla., II, 250.

Peterson, John, coloured principal first normal school for coloured teachers, New York, II, 133.

Pettiford, Rev. W. R., establishes Negro bank in Birmingham, II, 225–233.

Pharmacist, first Negro in the United States, II, 177.

Philadelphia, influx of coloured population to, I, 253; Negro crime in, II, 86, 87; coloured secret orders of, II, 155, 156; Frederick Douglass

Hospital in, 174; Negro caterers in, 195; homes of coloured people in, 254, 257; social work of Presbyterian Church in, 349.

Phillips, Ulrich B. on progress of slave mechanics in Charleston, II, 79, 80.

Phillips, Wendell, referred to, II, 196; on Sojourner Truth's oratorical powers, II, 318.

Physicians and Surgeons, number of, II, 182.

Pierce, Edward L., starts Negro school at Beaufort, S. C., II, 9.

Pillsbury, Parker, Sojourner Truth replies to a young minister at meeting of, II, 316.

Pinchback, Pickney, B. S., soldier of Civil War, I, 324; lieutenant and acting Governor, 324; Reconstruction political leader, II, 22, 23.

Pinchback, Major William, father of P. B. S., II, 22.

Pinckney, Charles, on fidelity of slaves during Revolutionary War, I, 319.

Pine Bluff, Ark., coloured Masonic temple at, II, 157; street railway owned by Negro in, 209.

Pizarro, Francisco, Negro bodyguard of, I, 87, 88.

Plantation hymns, I, 13, 165; II, 263, 264.

Planter, The, Confederate transport stolen by Negro crew, II, 20–22.

Planters' Journal, comment of, on Mound Bayou, II, 376.

Poindexter, coloured Underground Railway agent, I, 285.

Politics, Negro in, II, 193, 356.

Politics, see Ballot.

Political Rights, effect of loss of, on Negroes of Alabama, II, 190.

Pollard, L. M., director coloured bank, Savannah, Ga., II, 223.

Poor, Salem, in battle of Bunker Hill, I, 314.

Pope, Colonel Wyley, referred to, I, 318.

Port Cresson, Liberia, settled by Negro colonists, I, 245.

Port Hudson, Negroes' part in battle of, I, 327.

Porter, Maggie (Mrs. Cole), early Fisk Jubilee singer, II, 269, 270.

Pratt, Harry T., supervisor Baltimore, Md., Public Schools, II, 359.

Presbyterian Church, among Negroes, I, 273; Afro-American, 275; North, number of ministers and presbyterys in Southern states, 275; of Canada, schools for fugitive slaves, started by, II, 241; Southern African missions of, 338, 339.

Price, Dr. Joseph C., I, 24; first President Livingstone College, II, 343.

Proctor, Rev. Henry Hugh, coloured member Atlantic Civic League, II, 107; establishes institutional church, 108, 109; referred to, 348.

Progress, of Negro, observations of Dr. George C. Hall, in Mobile, Ala., II, 189; signs of, 212.

Property, of Negroes, value of, II 47; of secret orders, 156; in Jackson, Miss., 204; of individuals, 209, 210; in Chicago, 224.

Protestant Episcopal Church, first coloured minister in, I, 272; first Negro baptised in, 1624, I, 272; number of Negroes ordained in 273; work of Domestic Missionary Society of, II, 308.

Provident Hospital, coloured, Chicago, II, 174.

Purvis, Dr. Charles B., army surgeon, I, 326; professor Howard University, 326.

Purvis, Mrs. Charles B., granddaughter of James Forten, I, 290.

Purvis, Robert, chairman Philadelphia Vigilance Committee, I, 215; signs declaration First American Antislavery Convention, 284; John G. Whittier describes, 284, foot-note.

Pushkin, Alexander Sergeievich, national poet of Russia, African origin of, II, 289.

Pygmies, of Elgon and Semliki forests, I, 28.

Race Distinctions, made first on ground of religion, I, 114.

Race Prejudice in the South, I, 142.

Race War, in Memphis, Tenn., 1866; II, 19; in New Orleans, La., 19.

Racial Identity, Negroes sometimes ashamed of, I, 12, 16.

Racial Intermingling, in the South and West Indies, I, 131; some products of, 132; Indian Territory, 134; Negroes and Indians, 142.

Rainey, Joseph H., Negro congressman, I, 325, II, 12.

Ram's Horn, anti-bellum coloured newspaper, I, 295.

Randolph Freedmen, attempt to settle in Mercer County, O., I, 235.

Randolph, John A., of Roanoke, Va., on fear of Negro insurrection, I, 178; frees slaves, 194; provides for slaves in will, 235, 236; describes eloquence of slave woman, 279.

Rankin, John, abolitionist of Ripley, O., I, 240.

Rape, Negro and white commitments for, compared, II, 104; disposition of Negro to commit, II, 105, 106; Negro acquitted of, in Atlanta, Ga., 108.

Rapier, James T., coloured Congressman, II, 26.

Ray, Charles B., early editor Negro newspaper, I, 293.

Ray, Charlotte, first coloured woman lawyer, II, 184, 185.

Reason, Charles L., Negro educator, I, 294; in Philadelphia, Pa., II, 132.

Reck, John S., first coloured man admitted to United States Supreme Court, II, 185.

Reclus, Jean Jacques Elisée, on German labour in Brazil, South America, I, 121, 122.

Reconstruction, in Southern states, II, 19, 20; opinion of coloured man upon, 29; results of so-called, in Atlanta, Ga., 108, 109.

Redding, Joe, white man receives light sentence for murder, II, 98.

Redmond, S. D., coloured physician and business man in Jackson, Miss., II, 205.

Reed, Joseph, letter to, from George Washington, concerning Phyllis Wheatley, II, 287, 288.

Reed, Lindsay S., establishes insurance company in Savannah, Ga., II, 219, 220.

Reed Home and School, conducted by Dinah Pace, at Covington, Ga., II, 309.

Reformatory, for Negro children, Hanover Co., Va., II, 110; at Mt. Meigs, Ala., 113, 330.

Refugees' Home, for fugitive slaves, Windsor, Ont., Canada, II, 240.

Reid, Dow, Negro farmer, Macon Co., Ala., II, 194.

Reid, Frank, Negro farmer, Macon Co., Ala., II, 194.

Reilly, Barnard, advertises for runaway bond-servant, I, 107.

Relations of whites and blacks, peculiar in the South, I, 11.

Remond, Charles Lenox, agent Underground Railway and anti-slavery lecturer, I, 283; assists in raising coloured troops, 323.

Revels, Hiram R., first coloured U. S. Senator, II, 11.

Reynolds, R. J., tobacco manufacturer of Winston-Salem, assists in building coloured hospital, II, 252, 253.

Rhode Island, coloured regiment in battle of, I, 311.

Rhodes, James Ford, on slave labour, I, 152; on Negro delegates to Southern constitutional conventions, II, 19.

Rice culture, Negro labour necessary in, I, 117.

Richmond, Va., part of Negro troops in the fall of, I, 331; Negro banks of, II, 219.

Ridley, Mrs. U. A., officer National Federation of Coloured Women's Clubs, II, 329.

Riot, the Atlanta, effect upon coloured people of, II, 359.

Riot, see Race war.

Rischer, H. K., successful baker, Jackson, Miss., II, 203.

Roberts Family, Free Negro settlement of, in Ohio, I, 241.

Robin, discharged from servitude in Canada on writ of habeas corpus, II, 239.

Robinson, John, Tuskegee graduate in West Africa, I, 37.

Rockefeller, John D., contributed to coloured Y. M. C. A. Bldg., Washington, D. C., II, 353.

Rodin, Auguste, coloured sculptress's work attracts attention of, II, 293.

Root Doctor, The, in the country districts, II, 173.

Rose, John C., U. S. District Attorney, Baltimore, Md., legal adviser Coloured Law and Order League, II, 362.

Ross, Alexander, goes from Canada to Southern states to rescue slaves, I, 221, foot-note.

Ross, A. W., calls on President Johnson in interest of Negro citizenship, II, 18.

Rough Riders, Negro soldiers go to support of at Las Guasimas, II, 390.

Roman, Dr. C. B., coloured oculist, Nashville, Tenn., II, 175.

Royal Geographical Society, Negro made member of, II, 336.

Ruffin, Chief Justice, North Carolina, defines relation of master and slave, I, 148.

Ruffin, George, L., Judge of municipal court, Charlestown, Mass, II, 186.

Ruffin, Mrs. Josephine St. Pierre, coloured club, woman, II, 326–330.

Ruggles, David, agent Underground Railway, I, 283; editor *Mirror of Liberty*, 283.

Rush, Dr. Benjamin, opinion of, concerning Harry Hosier, I, 257.

Russell, James S., archdeacon and principal of Episcopal school at Lawrenceville, Va., I, 273.

Russwurm, John B., edits first Negro newspaper in United States, I, 292, 293.

Rutling, Thomas, of original Fisk Jubilee singers, II, 270; teacher of English in Switzerland, II, 270, 271.

Salem, Peter, slayer of Mayor Pitcairn, I, 314.

Salzburgers, see Moravians.

Sampson, Benjamin, teacher at Wilberforce, I, 204.

Sampson, James D., Free Negro in North Carolina, I, 204.

Sampson, John P., editor *Coloured Citizen*, I, 204.

Sampson, George M., teacher, Florida State Normal School, I, 205.

San Juan Hill, Negro soldiers in battle of, II, 391.

Sanderson, Thomas, one of founders Negro Masonry in America, II, 149.

Sandys, George, sells bond-servant for debt, I, 110, 111.

Sanifer, J. M., Negro farmer of Pickens County, Ala., I, 63, 64.

Santo Domingo, slaves introduced into, 1505, I, 87; Indians sold as slaves to, 130; revolt of slaves in, 172; refugees from, found St. Francis' Academy, Baltimore, 271, 272.

Sarbah, John Mensah, native African, author Fanti Customary Law, I, 70, 71.

Saunders, Negro servant of John C. Fremont, II, 386.

Savannah, Ga., Negro crime in, II, 86; example of Negro business in, 219, 220; Negro banks of, 219, 222; seat of Georgia State Industrial College, 221; Negro business concerns of, 219-223; mission work of Young Men's Sunday Club in, 350.

Savings and Loan Association, examples of, among Negro, II, 213.

Saxton, General Rufus, at Beaufort, S. C., II, 9.

Schofield School for Negroes, Aiken, S. C., II, 175.

School Farm, for support of rural Negro schools, II, 142.

School Law, separate, in Massachusetts, tested by coloured lawyer, II, 185.

School Suffrage Association, of Boston, coloured woman member of, II, 328.

Schools, ante-bellum, for Negro, I, 200, 212, 225, 236, 271, 280, 294; II, 123, 129-132, 134-136, 197, 308-310, 319.

Schools, Negro, II, 175, 221, 227, 252, 307, 344, 346, 349, 363, 380.

Schools, Negro, gifts to, by Negroes, II, 346-348; supported by Negro Baptists, 339-341; supported by Negro Methodists, 341-345.

Schweinfurth, George August, quoted on Africa, II, 283.

Scipio, North Carolina slave, blacksmith, owner of livery stable, I, 202.

Scott, Walter S., secretary and treasurer, coloured bank, Savannah, Ga., II, 222.

Seaboard Slave States, Olmstead's journey through, referred to, II, 398.

Sego, Capital of Bambara, West Africa, Mungo Park visits, II, 297.

Séjour, Victor, coloured musician, gains distinction in Paris, II, 276.

Selma University, of Selma, Ala., II, 227.

Seme, Pixley Isaka, African student, gains oratorical honours at Columbia University, II, 285.

Seminoles, of Florida, intermingle with runaway slaves from Georgia, I, 133.

Serfdom, effort to re-establish, in Georgia, I, 116.

Servants, white, condition of, like Negro slaves in the colonies, I, 113.

Servitude, white in North Carolina, I, 113; in the colonies, 107-116.

Settle, Josiah T., political leader, Reconstruction Period, II, 22, 23.

Seven Wise Men, The, coloured secret order, II, 148.

Shaker Abolitionist, Seth Concklin, I, 221.

Shaler, Nathaniel Southgate, on Negro as labourer, I, 139-142.

Shaw, Mrs. Mary E., coloured benefactress of Tuskegee Institute, II, 346.

Shaw, Robert Gould, white commander Negro regiment, Civil War, I, 248, 328; killed in assault on Fort Wagner, 328; bust of, by coloured sculptress, II, 293.

Shaw University, Raleigh, N. C., 1865, II, 140.

Shepley, General George F., in New Orleans, II, 14.

Sheppard, William H., coloured missionary in Africa, II, 338.

Sheppard, Ella, of original Fisk Jubilee Singers, II, 267; wife of Rev. George W. Moore, 269.

Shiloh Church, Ante-bellum Negro, New York City, I, 284.

Shirley, Thomas, endows Negro school, Philadelphia, II, 131.

Shorter, Bishop James A., referred to, II, 347.

Siboney, Cuba, Negro soldiers at, II, 391, 392.

Siebert, Wilbur H., on Underground Railway, I, 282, 285, 286.

Silk Mill, Fayetteville, N. C., Negro labour in, II, 75, 76.

Slater Industrial and State Normal School, Winston-Salem, N. C., II, 252.

Slater, John F., makes first large gift for Negro education in the South, II, 129.

Slave Caravan, Mungo Park's description of, I, 97-101.

Slave Code, see Slave Laws.

Slave-consuming countries, I, 105.

Slave Girl Poet, Washington's kindness to, II, 288.

Slave-holders, efforts of Southern, to lessen evils of slavery, I, 249.

Slave in Business, with white man, II, 81.

Slave Insurrection, effect of Northampton, on condition of slaves, I, 297; fear of, during Civil War, II, 4.

Slave Laws, distinguishing between Christians and heathen, I, 114–116; show slavery on its harsher side, 147; made emancipation difficult, 178; of North Carolina, restricting emancipation, 243, 244, 300, 301; referred to, II, 62, 82, 83, 118, 122-124.

Slave Mechanics, price of, II, 63; treatment of, 64; independent position of, 79; restrictions on intellectual powers of, 80.

Slave-raiders, visit of, to coast of Florida, I, 129.

Slavery, in Africa and America and America compared, I, 96-100; advantages derived from by Negro, 135; judgment of Supreme Court, of North Carolina, on, 147, 148; the idea at bottom of, 149; on the small plantations, 149-151; on the large plantations, 152, 153; in Virginia, 165; white, in Africa, 280, 281; an industrial and political system, II, 82; real cause of downfall of, 83, introduction of, into Georgia, 121; in Canada, 239; in New York, Sojourner Truth's account of, 311-315; progress of Negro under, 396, 397.

Slaves, African, proportion of in population of America, I, 95.

Slaves, Fugitive, from industrious and ambitious class, II, 83.

Slaves, Negro, in the West Indies, 1501, I, 87; number of, in America, in 1800, 95; price of, 1820-1830, 96; number of, brought to America, 105, 106; light colour of, in Louisiana, 123; runaway, intermingle with Seminoles of Florida, 133; treatment of, on plantation, 146; plan of Mississippi planter for freeing, 194; public discussions of, 297; freedom given those taking part in Revolutionary War, 313; invited to join King's Army in Revolutionary War, 319; some practically free, II, 80, 81; conspiracy of, in New York, 119; school for Indian and Negro, in New York, 119; education among, in Back Country, 137; New York Society for promoting manumission of, 132.

Slaves, proportion of, to free men in Africa, I, 95; twenty landed at Jamestown in 1619, 85.

Slave Ship, the last, I, 104.

Slave Songs, I, 100, 160; compared with African music, II, 261; study of, by Thomas Wentworth Higginson, 262-264; origin of, 262; poetic language of, 264, 265; Creole, 276.

Slave Trade, extent of, from West Coast of Africa, I, 57; corrupts native customs, 58, 59; in seventeenth century, 60; begun, 1442, by merchants of Seville, Spain, 86; transition of domestic into foreign, in Africa, 95; domestic, in United States, 98, note; foreign, made a crime in 1808, 101; loss of life from, 102, note; survivors of last slave ship, 103; white, 111.

Smalls, Robert, carries off Confederate transport *Planter*, II, 20, 22; congressman, 22; collector of customs at Beaufort, 22.

Smiley, Charles H., coloured caterer, Chicago, Ill., II, 196.

Smith, Abiel, founder of "Smith School," Boston, Mass., II, 134.

Smith, Adam, Lott Cary reads "Wealth of Nations," of, II, 234.

Smith, Alfred, Negro "Cotton King," Oklahoma, II, 52, 53.

Smith, Amanda, coloured evangelist, II, 321-325.

Smith, Benjamin R., aids Lunsford Lane to purchase freedom, I, 298.

Smith, Boston, one of founders of American Negro Masonry, II, 149.

Smith, Gerrit, abolitionist, aids in the "Jerry Rescue," I, 225.

Smith, Dr. James McCune, agent Underground Railway, I, 283; speech of welcome to Lafayette, II, 133; gains distinction as a physician, 177.

Smith, James A., aids in the escape of fugitive slaves from Richmond, Va., I, 217.

Smith, Dr. John Blair, of Hampton-Sydney College, Va., influence of, on Jack of Virginia, I, 267.

Smith, John D., statement concerning slave mechanics, II, 64, 65.

Smith, Robert H., attorney, supports work of Coloured Law and Order League of Baltimore, II, 362.

Smith, Robert L., founder of Farmers' Improvement Association, of Texas, II, 378-382.

Smith, Stephen, wealthy Negro endows Old Folks Home, Philadelphia, I, 292.

Smithfield, O., ante-bellum coloured settlement in, I, 240, 241.

Smythe, John H., former minister to Liberia, founds reformatory for coloured children in Virginia, II, 110.

Snow Riot, Washington, D. C., 1835, II, 135.

Soldiers, Negro, number of, in Revolutionary War, I, 310; numbers of, in Confederate Army, 320; numbers of, in Federal Army, 326; first fight of, 322, 323; names of, 324-326; in Spanish-American War, II, 390, 392.

Sons and Daughters of Jacob, coloured secret order, II, 148.

Sons and Daughters of Peace, bank of, Newport News, Va., II, 219.

Sons of Saint Thomas, founded 1823, II, 155.

South Africa, African student's description of people of, I, 78, 79; desire of natives for education in, 80.

South America, slave-raiders visit, I, 129.

South Carolina, Negro population of, 1740, I, 94; rights of free Negroes in, 199.

Southampton County, Va., insurrection of slaves in, I, 173.

Southern States, Negroes' place in literature of, I, 7.

Solvent Savings Bank, of Memphis, Tenn., II, 23.

Spradley, Wash., agent Underground Railway, I, 285.

Squantum, Mass., hotel conducted by Negro at, II, 199.

St. Francis Academy, Baltimore, Md., founded by Negroes, I, 271, II, 346.

St. Louis, Mo., Negro crime in, II, 86.

St. Luke's Church, Washington, D. C., Alexander Crummell, pastor of, I, 273.

St. Luke's Penny Saving Bank, Richmond, Va., II, 219.

St. Philip's Church, slaves held by, Charleston, S. C., I, 207.

St. Philip's Church, Episcopal, in New York City, II, 307.

St. Pierre, John, father of Mrs. Josephine St. Pierre Ruffin, II, 327.

St. Thomas Church, Philadelphia, 1794, I, 255.

Stanley, John C., Free Negro in North Carolina, I, 201, 202.

Stark, Colonel W. Pinkney, on slavery in South Carolina, I, 150–152.

Statistics of Churches, I, 276, 277.

Steedman, General James B., commands Negro troops, battle of Nashville, Tenn., I, 330, 331.

Steele, Carrie, founder of coloured orphanage, Atlanta, Ga., II, 109, 110.

Steiner, Bernard C., on missionary school, Maryland, 1750, for poor white and Negro children, II, 121.

Sterrs, Dr. W. E., conductor of Cottage Home Infirmary, II, 172.

Stevens, Rev. William B., on the importation of white bondsmen into Georgia, I, 116, 119.

Stewart, Dr. F. A., coloured physical, Nashville, Tenn., II, 175.

Stewart, Eliza, mother of P. B. S. Pinchback, II, 22.

Still, Peter, finds his brother William in Philadelphia, Pa., I, 219–221; efforts of, to rescue family, 221.

Still, William, secretary Philadelphia Vigilance Committee, I, 215, 216; author of "The Underground Railroad," I, 216–221; chairman General Vigilance Committee, 284, 285.

Story, William Wetmore, statue of Sojourner Truth by, II, 318, 319.

Stow, George W., author of "Native Races of South Africa," quoted, I, 19.

Stowe, Harriet Beecher, original of her "Uncle Tom" a refugee in Canada, II, 243.

Straight University, New Orleans, La., 1869, II, 140; gift to, by Thomy Lafon, 347.

Suggs, Daniel C., referred to, II, 221.

Sumner, Charles, on white slavery in Africa, I, 281; speech in favour of seating Negro senator, II, 12; aids

coloured attorney to win admission to bar, 185; aids first coloured man to gain admission to U. S. Supreme Court, 185; referred to, 196; bust of, by coloured sculptress, 293.

Sunday School, Negro, started by Southern theological students, Lane Seminary, Cincinnati, O., I, 291.

Sunday Schools, gave Negroes first opportunity for education, II, 121.

Surgeons, coloured, progress of, II, 174, 175.

Swaney, Negro playmate of John C. Calhoun, I, 150.

Syracuse, N. Y., station of Underground Railway, I, 224.

Talladega College, Talladega, Ala., 1869, II, 140, 227.

Taney, Chief Justice Roger B., frees slaves, I, 194.

Tanner, Bishop Benjamin T., referred to, II, 171; father of Henry O. Tanner, 294.

Tanner, Henry O., referred to, II, 171; coloured painter, II, 294–296.

Tappen, Arthur, buys land in New Haven for Negro industrial school, II, 130.

Taxation and Negro schools, paper on, by Charles L. Coon, superintendent of schools, Wilson, N. C., II, 143.

Taylor, Dr. W. Benjamin, befriends a coloured woman doctor, II, 176.

Taylor, John Louis, Chief Justice Supreme Court, North Carolina, decision in case of Quakers prosecuted for freeing slaves, I, 243.

Taylor, Robert R., referred to, II, 81.

Taylor-Lane Hospital, coloured, Orangeburg, S. C., II, 175, 176.

Teachers, Negro, number of, II, 182.

Teage, Collin, companion of Lott Cary in Liberia, II, 235.

Tennessee, number of Negro banks in, II, 211.

Tenth Cavalry, coloured, at Las Guasimas, Cuba, II, 390.

Terrell, Mrs. Mary Church, coloured woman lecturer, II, 325.

Terrell, Robert H., coloured city magistrate, Washington, D. C., II, 186.

Texas, number of Negro banks in, II, 211.

The Genius of Universal Emancipation, Benjamin Lundy's anti-slavery paper, Mount Pleasant, O., I, 239.

The North Star, Frederick Douglass's paper, Rochester, N. Y., II, 187.

The True Reformer, organ of the True Reformers, Richmond, Va., II, 164.

Theatre, coloured cities where located, II, 283.

Thoburn, Bishop James Miles, life of Amanda Smith sketched by, II, 322-325.

Thomas, James C., coloured undertaker, New York City, II, 201, 202.

Thomas, Rev. Samuel, first missionary to Indians and Negroes in America, II, 119.

Thompson, George, African missionary referred to, II, 337.

Thurman, Mrs. Lucy, in charge of coloured W. C. T. U. work, II, 326.

Tillman, Benjamin R., kindly personal relation sof, with Negroes, I, 179; II, 36, 37.

Togoland, West Africa, Tuskegee students in, I, 37.

Toronto, Canada, Negro acting Mayor of, II, 245.

Torrey, Rev. Charles T., goes South to rescue slaves, I, 221, foot-note.

Tougaloo University, Tougaloo, Miss., 1869, II, 140.

Trades Education, opportunities of Negroes for, II, 65.

Tribune, Savannah, coloured newspaper, II, 223.

Trotter, James M., history coloured musicians, quoted, II, 274-277.

Trower, John S., coloured caterer, Philadelphia, Pa., II, 195.

True Reformers, referred to, II, 148; property owned by, 156; history of, 163-168; report of U. S. department of labour on, 163; bank of, 215-217.

Trumball, John, Negro portrait in picture of Bunker Hill by, I, 314.

Truth, Sojourner, sketch of, II, 310-319.

"Tuberculosis Centre," of Maryland, II, 360.

Tubman, Harriet, Underground Railway operator, I, 222, 223; graphic description of battle of Gettysburg by, II, 284, 285.

Tucker, Nathaniel Beverly, jurist, letter on Negro progress in Virginia, in 1801, II, 396, 397.

Tulane, Victor H., coloured grocer, Montgomery, Ala., II, 202.

Turkana, of Uganda, I, 28.

Turner, Benjamin S., coloured congressman, II, 26.

Turner, Bishop Henry M., first coloured chaplain in Federal Army, I, 324.

Turner, Nat, slave insurrection of, Northampton County, Va., 1831, I, 172-175; sketch of, 182, 183; causes Jack of Virginia to stop preaching, 268; Negro banks started in home of, II, 213.

Tuscaroras, not wanted as slaves in Northern states, I, 130.

Tuskegee Institute, founding of, II, 54, 55; work of, 56; in the early days, II, 192; support of, by former students of, 346; gift to, by coloured woman, 346.

Tuskegee Night School, started by Women's Club, II, 331.

Tuskegee Woman's Club, work of, II, 330.

Twenty-fifth Infantry, coloured, II, 390.

Twin City Realty Company, of Winston-Salem, II, 254.

Uganda, people of, I, 28; Winston Churchill on, 76, 77.

"Uncle Remus," prototype of, in Africa, I, 72; referred to, 162.

Underground Railway, records of, by William Still, I, 216; number of agents of, in the South, 232; part of Knights of Liberty in, II, 160; station at Albany, O., 197; station in Philadelphia, 320.

United Brothers of Friendship, coloured secret order, II, 148; organised 1861, 153.

United States Supreme Court, first Negro admitted to practice before, II, 185.

"Up from Slavery," I, 3.

Valladolid, Juan de, mayor of the Negroes of Seville, I, 86, 87.

Van Dyke, Peter, coloured caterer, New York, II, 195.

Vanlomen, Father, establishes seminary for coloured girls in Washington, D. C., II, 136.

Vardaman, James K., referred to, I, 179; vetoes appropriation for State Normal School at Holly Springs, II, 345.

Vei people, inventors of an alphabet, I, 72.

Verner, Samuel P., African missionary, I, 48, 49.

Vesey, Denmark, leader of slave insurrection, Charleston, S. C., 1822, I, 172, 173; sketch of, 181, 182; conspiracy of, results in restrictions on the liberty of free Negroes, 211.

Vigilance Committee, in Philadelphia, I, 215.

Virginia Manual Labour School, reformatory for Negro children, 1897, II, 98.

Virginia, rights of Free Negroes in, I, 199; number of Negro banks in, II, 211.

Voorhees Industrial School, Denmark, S. C., hospital of, II, 173; founder of, 183, 184.

Walker, Agnes, referred to, II, 347.

Walker, Aida Overton, coloured comedienne, II, 281.

Walker, David, first Negro to attack slavery through the press, I, 292.

Walker, George, coloured comedian, II, 281; referred to, 347.

Walker, Molly, referred to, II, 347.

"Walker's Appeal," first anti-slavery tract issued by Negro, I, 292.

Wall, Captain O. S. B., Federal officer, Civil War, I, 326.

Walls, Josiah T., coloured congressman, II, 26.

Wanderer, carries 510 slaves to Georgia 1858, I, 104.

Warburg, Eugène, coloured sculptor, II, 276.

Ward, Samuel R., coloured anti-slavery agitator, I, 295; anti-slavery editor, II, 25.

Waring, Dr. J. H. N., principal, Baltimore, Md., Coloured High School, II, 360.

Warrick, Meta Vaux, coloured sculptress, II, 293, 294.

Washington, D. C., freedmen's hospital in, II, 174; coloured Y. M. C. A., in 353, 354.

Washington, George, will of, frees slaves, I, 193, 194; Negro Masons attend funeral of, II, 151; letter of concerning Phyllis Wheatley, 287.

Washington, George, former slave, leaves $15,000 to Negro education, II, 347.

Washington, Mrs. Booker T., first president of National Federation of Coloured Women's Clubs, II, 329.

Washington, settlement of Free Negroes in Louisiana, I, 207.

Watkins, Frances Ellen, coloured anti-slavery lecturer and writer, II, 319–321.

Watkins, Rev. William, uncle of Ella Watkins Harper, II, 319.

Watterson, Colonel Henry, on Negro progress, II, 114.

W. C. T. U., work of, among the coloured people, II, 326.

Weitzel, General Godfrey, commander corps Negro soldiers, I, 331; letter to General Butler, objecting to Negro troop, I, 331.

Wells, Nelson, ante-bellum coloured schoolmaster, II, 124.

Wells School, Baltimore, Md., established by coloured men, II, 124.

West Hartford, Conn., birthplace of Lemuel Haynes, first coloured Congregational minister, II, 388.

West Indies, Negro labour in, I, 118; slave insurrections in, 171; A. M. E. Church in, II, 332.

West Point, Negro students in, II, 390.

Westons, wealthy family free coloured people, Charleston, S. C., I, 206, 207.

Wharton, Heber E., vice-principal coloured school, Baltimore, Md., II, 359.

Wheatley, Mrs. John, purchases Negro girl, Phyllis Wheatley, II, 286.

Wheatley, Phyllis, Negro poetess, II, 285-288.

Wheeler, Lloyd G., former business agent, Tuskegee Institute, I, 286.

Whipper, William, coloured lumber merchant, Columbia, Pa., agent Underground Railway, I, 284, 285; referred to, II, 18.

White, George H., coloured congressman, II, 26; valedictory speech of, 26-28.

White, George L., teacher of Fisk Jubilee Singers, II, 266.

White, William S., biographer of Jack of Virginia, I, 267, 268.

Whitehead, Thomas, emancipates slave, John, I, 197.

Whitney, Eli, inventor of cotton gin, II, 122.

Whittier, John G., member anti-slavery convention, 1833, I, 215; description of Robert Purvis, 284; poem on the daughters of James Forten, 289, 290.

Wilberforce, O., Negro college town, I, 233; early settlement of, 234, 236; colony of free Negroes at, 236.

Wilberforce, Daniel Flickinger, native African missionary, educated, Dayton, O., II, 336-338.

Wilberforce University, Mary Church Terrell teacher at, II, 325; origin of, 342; gifts to, by Negro, 347.

William, first Negro received into Presbyterian Church, I, 272.

Williams, Bert, Negro comedian, II, 281.

Williams, Dr. Daniel H., Negro surgeon, II, 180.

Williams, George W., on religious and race prejudice in the colonies, I, 91; account of slave conspiracy in New York, 93; on first Negro Methodist preacher, 258; on Negro soldiers in Revolutionary War, 312; soldier in Civil War, 325.

Williams, Lucius E., president coloured bank, Savannah, Ga., II, 222.

Williams, Mrs. Sylvania, president coloured women's club, New Orleans, La., II, 326.

Willis, Edith, kidnapped and sold into slavery, II, 175.

Wilson, Henry, on Quaker abolitionists, I, 242; escorts first coloured U. S. Senator to take oath of office, II, 12, referred to, 196.

Wilson, Rev. Hiram, aids in establishing manual labour school for Negro refugees in Canada, II, 243.

Wilson, Rev. Leighton, African Missionary of the Southern Presbyterian Church, I, 44, 45.

Winder, Ike, Negro criminal, cost of, to State of Maryland, Md., II, 364.

Winsey, Dr. Whitfield, coloured physician, Baltimore, Md., II, 359.

Winston-Salem, visit to, in 1905, II, 252.

Witch Doctors, I, 68-70.

Woods, Granville T., Negro inventor of electrical appliances, II, 79.

Woolman, John, early Quaker abolitionist, I, 242.

Woman's Era Club, coloured, Boston, Mass., II, 328.

Women, coloured, work for education of, II, 183; in poetry and arts, 286, 292, 293; power of sympathy of, 298; status of, in industries, 304; part in anti-slavery struggle, 310; represented at International Congress of Women, Berlin, Germany, 325.

Women's Medical College, Philadelphia, Pa., coloured woman graduate of, II, 175.

Work, Henry, buys freedom of framily, I, 195.

Work, Monroe N., referred to, I, 195; on Negro property holding, II, 42 224.

Wormeley, Ralph, slaves of, skilled tradesmen, II, 60.

Worth, Governor Jonathan, before North Carolina coloured political convention, 1866, II, 16.

Wortham, Dr. James L., of North Carolina, pupil of John Chavis, I, 274.

Wright, Elizabeth E. founder of, Voorhees Industrial Institute, Denmark, S. C., II, 183, 184.

Wright, Elizur, member anti-slavery convention of 1833, I, 215.

Wright, Richard R., on Negro explorers, II, 385.

Wright, Richard R., Jr., on land ownership in Indiana, I, 241; in Cass County, Mich., 248; on Negro property owning, Chicago, Ill., II, 224; on Negro property owning, Philadelphia, Pa., 256.

Wylie, Douglas H., former President Chamber of Commerce Baltimore, Md., supports work Coloured Law and Order League, II, 362.

Yazoo-Mississippi Delta, Negro labourer in I, 118; Negro settlement in, II, 246; Negro town in, 371.

Y. M. C. A., story of, II, 351-355; work of, in Louisville, Ky., 354; of Baltimore, referred to, 358.

Yorubas, Negro translates Bible into language of, II, 336.

Young, Dr. Howard E., coloured druggist, Baltimore, Md., II, 359.

Young, First Lieutenant Charles, Negro graduate of West Point, II, 390.

Zulu, takes oratorial honours at Columbia University, II, 285.

Zuni, Indians, preserve legend of Negro explorer, Estevan, II, 385.